Fodo

Great Britain

FODOR'S TRAVEL PUBLICATIONS, INC.
New York & London

ISBN 0–679–01640–6

Fodor's Great Britain

Editors: Richard Moore, Thomas Cussans
Assistant Editor: Caz Philcox
Contributors: Robert Brown, Kathy Ewald, Leslie Gardiner, Mark Lewes, Nicholas Stevenson
Drawings: Beryl Sanders
Maps: C. W. Bacon, Swanson Graphics
Photographs: Peter Baker, British Tourist Authority
Cover Photograph: Charles C. Place/Image Bank

Cover Design: Vignelli Associates

MANUFACTURED IN THE UNITED STATES OF AMERICA
10 9 8 7 6 5 4 3 2 1

CONTENTS

FOREWORD

For all her tendency to urban shabbiness, her strikes, her unpredictable weather, her high hotel and restaurant costs, Britain is still a desirable destination to the visitor with a sense of tradition and a love of those things that matter in life. For beneath all her problems, Britain still breathes an air of history; her gardens are among the most lovely and luxuriant in the world; her countryside has that indefinable look of being manicured and wild at the same time; her art galleries are bursting with the world's treasures—many of them looted when Britain still rode high among the nations; her artistic life is rich and varied; her monarchy the cynosure of those who have to make do with episodic presidencies; in short, Britain still has that to offer which can make a vacation a voyage of discovery.

We very much hope that this edition of our guide to Great Britain will help you on that voyage. With a country so steeped in history—and so currently alive—it would take a shelf of books to do justice to the subject. We have attempted to provide as much background and practical information as we can in the following pages, and we hope that you will find the information you need to make your visit an exciting one.

While every care has been taken to assure the accuracy of the information in this guide, the passage of time will always bring change, and consequently the publisher cannot accept responsibility for errors that may occur.

All prices and opening times quoted in this guide are based on information available to us at press time. Hours and admission fees may change, however, and the prudent traveler will avoid inconvenience by calling ahead.

Fodor's wants to hear about your travel experiences, both pleasant and unpleasant. When a hotel or restaurant fails to live up to its billing, let us know and we will investigate the complaint and revise our entries where the facts warrant it.

Send your letters to the editors of Fodor's Travel Publications, 201 East 50th Street, New York, NY 10022. European readers may prefer to write to Fodor's Travel Publications, 30–32 Bedford Square, London WC1B 3SG, England.

FACTS AT YOUR FINGERTIPS

Planning Your Trip

EXCHANGE RATES. All prices mentioned in this book are indicative of costs at the time of going to press (mid 1988), at which time the rate of exchange was about £1 = $1.72. We suggest that you keep a weather eye open for fluctuations in exchange rates, both while planning your trip—and while on it. It's a simple precaution, but it can pay handsome dividends, both in peace of mind and hard cash.

WHAT IT WILL COST. This is about the hardest travel question to answer in advance. A trip to Britain (or to Europe) can cost as little (above a basic minimum) or as much (with virtually no limit) as you choose. Budgeting is much simplified if you take a prepackaged trip. As an indication: a five-day stay in London, including hotel, meals except lunches, but with lunch included on two full-day sightseeing trips, visits in London and to Windsor and Hampton Court and theater, costs anything between £150 and £450, depending upon the hotel category required. A good-quality package 6-day coach tour of Britain can be had for about £200-£400 (depending on the quality of hotel used). This should be regarded as a good and relatively inexpensive way to see Britain.

Sample Costs. For hotel and restaurant rates see the relevant sections later in *Facts At Your Fingertips*.

A man's haircut will cost from £4 (around £8 in a central London barbers); a woman's anywhere from £10 to £20. It costs about £1.50 to have a shirt laundered, from £3 to dry-clean a dress or £3.50 a man's suit. A local paper will cost you about 25p and a national daily 30p. A pint of beer is £1.20 and a small gin and tonic £1. Your evening out means spending £4.50 to £15 for a theater seat (Covent Garden very much higher), £2 to £6 at the cinema, and about all you have at a nightclub—exact figures vary greatly, since you have to pay a membership fee to "join" a nightclub the first time you go, and the fee is highly elastic.

MONEY. You may take into the United Kingdom any amount of currency of any kind in the form of travelers' checks, letters of credit and so forth and any amount of notes in any currency. You are entitled to take out of the country foreign currencies in the amount you brought in, or any amount in sterling.

When you change dollars or travelers' checks, unfortunately, you will probably lose a few cents on the dollar, from 1c or 2c at banks, to 4c at hotels and shops, as the former convert at "bank rates" and the latter at any rate they feel like. The small *bureaux de change* that are springing up throughout central London usually have a minimum charge of at least 50p, and frequently very much more.

1

British Currency. The decimal currency is based on the pound sterling, and is divided into 100 pence. Bank notes are in values of £50, £20, £10 and £5. The decimal coins are: £1, 50p and 20p (both seven-sided), 10p (the old 2 shilling piece, still legal, has the same value), 5p (equivalent to the old 1 shilling piece, also still legal), all cupro-nickel (silver); 2p and 1p bronze.

CREDIT CARDS are now an integral part of the western financial way of life, and, in theory at least, are accepted all over Europe. But, while the use of credit cards can smooth the traveler's path considerably, they should not be thought of as a universal answer to every problem.

Firstly, there has been a growing resistance in Europe to the use of credit cards. A great many restaurants, for example, object to paying the percentage which the parent organizations demand. If they are able to get American Express, etc., to lower their rates, then the situation may well change, but at the moment you would be well advised to find out if the restaurant of your choice does take credit cards. Otherwise you may find yourself in an embarrassing situation.

Another point that should be watched with those useful pieces of plastic is the problem of the rate at which your purchase may be converted into your home currency. We have ourselves had two purchases, made on the same day in the same place, charged ultimately at two totally different rates of exchange. If you want to be certain of the rate at which you will pay, insist on the establishment entering the current rate onto your credit card charge at the time you sign it—this will prevent the management from holding your charge until a more favorable rate (to them) comes along, something which could cost you more dollars than you counted on. (On the other hand, should the dollar or pound be revalued upward before your charge is entered, you could gain a little.)

We would advise you, also, to check your monthly statement very carefully indeed against the counterfoils you got at the time of your purchase. It has become increasingly common for shops, hotels or restaurants to change the amounts on the original you signed, if they find they have made an error in the original bill. Sometimes, also, unscrupulous employees make this kind of change to their own advantage. The onus is on you to report the change to the credit card firm and insist on sorting the problem out.

CLIMATE. The regular tourist season in Britain runs from mid-April to mid-October. The spring is the time to see the countryside at its fresh greenest, while in September and October the northern moorlands and Scottish highlands are at their most colorful. June is a good month to visit Wales, the Lake District and Ireland. July and August are the months when most of the British take their vacations and that is when accommodation in some popular resorts is at a premium. The winter season in London is brilliant with the Covent Garden Opera, Royal Ballet and theater among the main attractions. In the main, the climate is mild, though the weather is very changeable and unpredictable. London has summer temperatures in the 80s at times, and can be humid. A good guide is the early morning radio forecast.

Average afternoon temperatures in Fahrenheit and Centigrade

	Jan.	Feb.	Mar.	Apr.	May	Jun.	Jul.	Aug.	Sep.	Oct.	Nov.	Dec.
London												
F°	43	45	49	55	62	68	71	70	65	56	49	45
C°	6	7	9	13	17	20	22	21	18	13	9	7
Edinburgh												
F°	43	43	47	50	55	62	65	64	60	53	47	44
C°	6	6	8	10	13	17	18	18	16	12	8	7

WHAT TO TAKE. The first principle is to travel light. The restrictions, either by size or weight, that are imposed on air travelers, act as added incentives to keep baggage within bounds of commonsense. Don't forget, too, that you may have to carry your cases yourself. Porters are scarce.

Britain is sometimes cool even in midsummer. You will want sweaters and you will *certainly* need rainwear. The kind of raincoat which has a detachable warm lining might have been invented with the British winter in mind. In keeping with the climate, ordinary everyday dress, especially for traveling, runs very much to the casual and to sportswear; tweeds and non-matching jackets for men, mix-and-match separates for women. If you are going to be doing a lot of walking, even if it is the indoor variety in museums, then be sure that you are well equipped with comfortable, supportive shoes. Dressing in the evening during summer is not practiced widely in England these days, but if you want to go to the very best places (top night clubs or the opera at Glyndebourne, for example) better bring a black tuxedo.

If you wear glasses or contact lenses, take along the prescription or, even better since opticians charge the earth in Britain, take along a spare pair.

Baggage. The transatlantic airline baggage allowance to most countries is based on size rather than weight. First-class passengers are allowed two pieces of baggage, the sum of the height, width and the length of each piece not to exceed 106 inches. Economy-class passengers are allowed two pieces, neither piece to exceed 62 inches and the two together not to exceed 124 inches. Under-seat baggage allowance is the same for both classes, a volume of no more than $9 \times 14 \times 22$ inches. The charges for excess are high: New York to western Europe $54 per piece. If, after breaking your journey, you are going on to the Continent or beyond you will, however, not be able to take more than one piece, the total dimensions of which must not exceed 62 inches. This applies to both first class and economy. Moreover, there are some domestic flights in Europe that allow only 15 kg or pay extra. The only exception to the rule is passengers who are in transit after a transatlantic flight.

TRAVEL DOCUMENTS. Apply several months in advance of your expected departure date. **U.S. residents** must apply in person to the U.S. Passport Agency in Boston, Chicago, Honolulu, Houston, Los Angeles, Miami, New Orleans, New York, Philadelphia, San Francisco, Seattle, Stamford (Conn.), or Washington DC, or to their local County Courthouse. In some areas selected post offices are equipped to handle passport applications. If you still have your latest passport issued within the past 12 years you may use this to apply by mail. You will need (1) Proof of citizenship, such as a birth certificate, (2) two identical photographs, two inches square, in either black and white or color, on non-glossy paper and taken within the past six months; (3) $35 for the passport itself plus a $7 processing fee if you are applying in person (no processing fee when applying by mail) for those 18 years and older, or if you are under 18, $20 for the passport plus a $7 processing fee if you are applying in person (again, no extra fee when applying by mail); (4) proof of identity such as a driver's license, previous passport, any governmental ID card, that includes a photo and signature. Adult passports are valid for 10 years, others for five years. When you receive your passport, write down its number, date and place of issue separately; if it is later lost or stolen, notify either the nearest American Consul or the Passport Office, Department of State, Washington D.C. 20524, as well as the local police.

If you are a resident alien you must file a Treasury sailing permit, Form 1040C—if a non-resident alien file Form 1040NR certifying that all Federal taxes have been paid; apply to your District Director of Internal Revenue for this. You will have to present various documents: (1) blue or green registration card; (2) passport; (3) travel tickets; (4) most recently filed Form 1040; (5) W-2 forms for the most recent full year; (6) most recent/current payroll stubs or letter; (7) check to be sure this is all! To reenter the United States, resident aliens with green cards staying abroad more than one year file Form I-131 45 days before departure. If abroad less, your Alien Registration Card will get you in on return. Apply for the Reentry Permit in person at the nearest office of the Immigration and Naturalization Service, or by mail to the Immigration and Naturalization Service, Washington D.C. (Naturalized American citizens may now stay abroad an unlimited length of time, even in the country of their origin.)

Canadian citizens entering the United Kingdom must have a valid passport. In Canada, apply in person to regional passport offices in: Edmonton, Halifax, Montreal, Toronto, Downsville (Ontario), Vancouver or Winnipeg. Or, write to: Bureau of Passports, Complexe Guy Favreau, 200 Dorchester West, Montreal, P.O. Canada H2Z 1X4. A $25 fee, evidence of citizenship, a guarantor, and two photos are required. Passports are valid for five years. Canadian citizens living in the US need special forms from their nearest Canadian Consulate.

Visas. Not required for entry into Britain by American citizens, nationals of the British Commonwealth and most European and South American countries. Citizens of EEC countries do not need passports but must be able to prove their nationality.

TRAVEL AGENTS. Once you decide where you want to go, your next step is to consult a good agent. If you haven't one, the American Society of Travel Agents, 1101 King St., Alexandria, VA 22314; or the Association of British Travel Agents, 55 Newman St, London W1P 4AH, can help. Whether you select *Maupintour, Diners Club-Fugazy, American Express, Cook's,* or a smaller firm is a matter of preference. All of the major operators have branch offices or correspondents in the larger European cities. The *American Automobile Association,* 8111 Gatehouse Rd., Falls Church, VA 22047, can also help you plan your trip.

A good travel agent can help you avoid costly mistakes due to inexperience. He can help you take advantage of special reduction in rail fares and the like that you would not otherwise know about. Most important, he can save you *time* by making it unnecessary for you to waste precious days abroad trying to get tickets and reservations. Thanks to his work, you are able to see and do more.

North American Agencies Specializing in British Tours

American Express, 822 Lexington Ave., New York, N.Y. 10021 (800–241–1700).

Barclay Travel Ltd, 767 Third Ave., New York, N.Y. 10017 (212–872–8357), specializes in individual, small-group, out-of-the-way and special-interest (e.g. mansions, gardens, antiques) tours of Britain.

Caravan, 401 North Michigan Ave., Chicago, Ill. 60611 (312–321–9800).

Cartan, 12755 Highway 55, Minneapolis, MN 55441 (800–422–7826).

C.I.E., 122 E. 42nd St., New York, N.Y. 10168 (212–972–5600).

Cosmos/Globus-Gateway, 95–25 Queens Blvd., Rego Park, N.Y. 11374 (718–268–1700).

Esplanade Tours, 581 Boylston St., Boston, Mass. 02116 (617–266–7465).

Lynott Tours, 350 Fifth Ave., Suite 2619, New York, N.Y. 10118 (212–760–0101).

Maupintour, 1515 St. Andrews Dr., Lawrence, Kansas 66044 (800–255–4266).

Trafalgar Tours, 21 East 26th St., New York, N.Y. 10010 (212–689–8977).

SOURCES OF INFORMATION. A large selection of brochures, booklets and general information may be had from *B.T.A. (British Tourist Authority),* the national tourist organization, which has over 20 overseas offices.

In the US: 40 West 57th St., New York, N.Y. 10019 (212–581–4700). 875 North Michigan Ave., Chicago, IL 60611 (312–787–0490).

World Trade Center, 350 South Figueroa St., Los Angeles, CA 90071 (213–628–3525).

Cedar Maple Plaza, 2305 Cedar Springs, Dallas, TX 75201 (214–720–4040).

In Canada: 94 Cumberland St., Suite 600, Toronto, Ont. M5R 3N3 (416–925–6326).

In Britain: The principal administrative tourist office in the U.K. is the British Tourist Authority, Thames Tower, Blacks Rd., London W6. Note that they will deal with written enquiries only. But in addition, every sizeable town and city of tourist interest within each region has its own information centers from which local information may be obtained. These display a sign outside with a distinctive "i" and are usually open throughout the year during normal office hours (Monday-to-Friday, 09.00 to 17.00). Some centers are open only during the summer months. Others, especially in the big seaside resorts, are also open on Saturday during the summer. Information centers are usually situated at the town hall, council offices or central library. The English Tourist Board publishes a booklet containing a complete list of local information center addresses throughout England, but the main Regional Tourist Boards are as follows (the numbers in brackets are dialing codes from London).

England

British Travel Center, 12 Regent St., London SW1. Tel. 01–730 3400. For information on all parts of Britain.

National Tourist Information Center, Victoria Station Forecourt, London SW1. Tel. 01–730 3488; for information on London and the English regions.

The London Tourist Board, 26 Grosvenor Gardens, London SW1, handles written enquiries on London.

East Anglia Tourist Board, Toppesfield Hall, Hadleigh, Suffolk 1P7 5DN. Tel. (0473) 822922.

East Midlands Tourist Board, Exchequergate, Lincoln LN2 1PZ. Tel. (0522) 531621. Written and telephone enquiries only.

Cumbria Tourist Board, Ashleigh, Holly Rd., Windermere, Cumbria LA23 2AQ. Tel. (096 62) 4444. Written and telephone enquiries only.

Northumbria Tourist Board, Aykley Heads, Durham DH1 5UX. Tel. (091) 384 6905.

South-East England Tourist Board, 1 Warwick Park, Tunbridge Wells, Kent TN2 5TA. Tel. (0892) 40766.

Southern Tourist Board, Town Hall Center, Leigh Rd., Eastleigh, Hants. S05 4DE. Tel. (0703) 616027.

Thames and Chilterns Tourist Board, 8, The Market Place, Abingdon, Oxon OX14 3UD. Tel. (0235) 22711.

Northwest Tourist Board, Last Drop Village, Bromley Cross, Bolton, Lancs BL7 9PZ. Tel. (0204) 591511. Written and telephone enquiries only.

West Country Tourist Board, Trinity Court, 37 Southernhay East, Exeter, Devon EX1 1QS. Tel. (0392) 76351.

Heart of England Tourist Board, Box 15, Worcester WR1 2JT. Tel. (0905) 613132. Written and telephone enquiries only.

Yorkshire and Humberside Tourist Board, 312 Tadcaster Road, York YO2 2HF. Tel. (0904) 707961.

Scotland

Scottish Tourist Board, 23 Ravelston Terr., Edinburgh EH4 3EU. Tel. 031–332 2433. Also at 19 Cockspur St., London SW1Y 5BL. Tel. 01–930 8661.

In association with the STB, Scotland has 32 local tourist boards administering the following areas: Angus; Aviemore and Spey Valley; Ayrshire and Burns Country; Ayrshire Valleys; Banff and Buchan; Caithness; City of Aberdeen; City of Dundee; Clyde Valley; Dumfries and Galloway; Dunoon and Cowal; East Lothian; Forth Valley; Fort William and Lochaber; Gordon District; Greater Glasgow; Inverness, Loch Ness and Nairn; Isle of Arran; Isle of Skye and Wester Ross; Kincardine and Deeside; Loch Lomond, Stirling and Trossachs; Mid-Argyll, Kintyre and Islay; Oban and Mull; Orkney; Outer Hebrides; Perthshire; Ross and Cromarty; Rothesay and Bute; Scottish Borders; Shetland; St Andrews and North East Fife; Sutherland.

Wales

Wales Tourist Board, P.O. Box 1, Cardiff CF1 2XZ. Tel. (0222) 27281.

Wales Tourist Board, 34 Piccadilly, London W1. Tel. 01–409 0969.

Mid Wales Tourism Council, Owain Glyndwr Center, Maengwyn Street, Machynlleth, Powys. Tel. (0654) 2401.

North Wales Tourism Council, 77 Conway Road, Colwyn Bay, Clwyd. Tel. (0492) 531731.

South Wales Tourism Council, Ty Croeso, Gloucester Place, Swansea S4 1TY. Tel. (0792) 465204.

Channel Islands

The States of Guernsey Tourist Board, Box 23, White Rock, Guernsey, Channel Islands. Tel. (0481) 23552.

Jersey Tourism, Weighbridge, St. Helier, Jersey, Channel Islands. Tel. (0534) 78000.

Isle of Man

Isle of Man Tourist Board, 13 Victoria St., Douglas, Isle of Man. Tel. Douglas (0624) 74323.

Isle of Wight

Isle of Wight Tourist Office, Quay Store, Town Quay, Newport, Isle of Wight, PO30 2EF. Tel. (0983) 524343.

SPECIAL EVENTS. Below are some of the special attractions that might influence you in selecting the date for your vacation in Britain.

January. Burns Night celebrations on the 25th at Ayr and elsewhere; Up Helly Aa at Lerwick in the Shetland Islands at the end of the month. During the winter in London you can enjoy the attractions this great and ancient city offers—opera at Covent Garden and the Coliseum (English National Opera), the art exhibitions at the Royal Academy, the Royal Ballet, symphony concerts, variety shows, and, above all, the one place in Europe where you can have your fill of plays in English! The International Boat Show is held during the first two weeks of the month at Earl's Court, London.

February is the month of Cruft's Dog Show in London. The end of February usually heralds the start of the skiing season in the Scottish Highlands at Aviemore. Chinese New Year celebrations in London, around Gerrard St.

March has among its famous events the Grand National Steeplechase at Liverpool and the Ideal Home Exhibition, Earl's Court, in London. The Oxford v. Cambridge boat race on the Thames takes place just before Easter. Chelsea Spring Antiques Fair, London. The Queen distributes Maundy Money in March, on Maundy Thursday; there is an Easter Parade in London's Battersea Park. This month also sees the beginning of the Shakespeare Season at the Royal Shakespeare Theater, Stratford-upon-Avon, and the Edinburgh Folk Festival.

April is the month of the Badminton Horse Trials. Shakespeare's Birthday Celebrations on the 23rd at Stratford-upon-Avon (which is also the feast day of England's patron saint, St. George); the English Bach Festival at London, then Oxford; the Spring Flower Festival at Southend-on-Sea and the London Marathon, the largest marathon in the world. At the end of the month the Pitlochry Music and Drama festival opens in Perthshire (until end of Sept.).

May sees the Royal Windsor Horse Show; the International Trophy Race (automobiles) at Silverstone; the Chelsea Flower Show in London; the beginning of the Chichester Festival Theater Season (until Sept.) and the Glyndebourne Festival Opera Season (until August); the Bath Festival, the Perth Festival and the Malvern Festival. Skye Week on the island of that name, Scotland; and it's a good month to go out to Kew Gardens for the spring display. May also sees a crowd of 80,000 at Wembley Stadium, London, for the F.A. Cup Final (soccer) although tickets are rarely obtainable: if you like soccer—and this is the best—find a television set!

In **June,** there's the Derby at Epsom, the world's most famous horse race; the international motorcycle races on the Isle of Man; Trooping the Color for the Queen's birthday; the Fine Art and Antiques Fair at Olympia; racing at Royal Ascot; the Aldeburgh Festival, in Suffolk; the lawn tennis championships at Wimbledon; the Royal Horse Show at Richmond (Surrey); the Royal Highland Agricultural Show, Edinburgh; and the yachting fortnight on the estuary of the Clyde.

July. In July there's the Royal Regatta at Henley-on-Thames, where American crews, among others, compete with the British; the British Open, often in the home of golf, Scotland. On the Isle of Man in the first week of July, you can see the Tynwald Ceremony and the Peel Viking Festival; there's an 18th-century costume fair at Alnwick, Northumberland; in the middle of July, the British Grand Prix (cars) takes place at Silverstone; and at Builth Wells, the Royal Welsh Show (third week in July). In London you might wish to take in the Royal International Horse Show at White City or the Royal Tournament at Earl's Court; and the Festival of the City of London. Also the Riding of the Marches in Annan and several other towns in Scotland. In Wales, the International Musical Eisteddfod at Llangollen. The Henry Wood Promenade Concerts—or "Proms"— start in the middle of the month and last till Sept.

In early **August,** Cowes Week, the big event for yachtsmen; the 12th sees the opening of the grouse shooting season; in Wales there's a coracle regatta at Cilgerran; the Royal National Eisteddfod at Newport (Gwent); and the International Sheep Dog Trials are staged in each country in turn. On the first Thursday of the month, the Isle of Jersey in the Channel Islands celebrates the Battle of Flowers. The International Festival of Music and Drama opens in Edinburgh where a spectacular Military Tattoo also takes place; regattas take place at Torquay in Devon, and at many other south coast resorts. Around the 1st of the month, watch the Doggett Coat and Badge Race from London Bridge. Grasmere has its Old English Games, while Scotland is the site for Highland Games at Edinburgh and Crieff, and Highland Gatherings at Dunoon, Oban, Aboyne and Perth among others (all from the middle of the month).

In **September,** the partridge shooting season starts. The Royal Autumn Show is held in Edinburgh, and Royal Highland Gatherings at Braemar and Pitlochry. The St. Leger is run at Doncaster races. The International Farnborough Air Show. The Burghley Horse Trials in Lincolnshire; while in Staffordshire, you can watch the Abbots Bromley Horn Dancers, the St. Giles Fair at Oxford or the Cricket Festival at Scarborough. Mid-month sees the 2nd of the biannual Chelsea Antiques Fairs.

In **October,** a third bird joins the list of permissible game, the pheasant. Birdies, not birds, at the Ryder Cup golf matches (alternate years in U.S.A.). And the International Motor Show comes off. The Horse of the Year Show at Wembley, London, is held at the beginning of the month, while Nottingham holds its Goose Fair (a huge fun fair).

November is the month for fairs, with Mop Fairs (originally where labor was hired) at Stratford-upon-Avon and Warwick. On the 5th, in Leamington Spa, boys kick a burning football around the streets. You can watch the children burn the guys on Guy Fawkes Day (Nov. 5), and on November 11 see the Lord Mayor's Show pass through the City of London (that is, the part of the capital around the Bank of England and St. Paul's). You can also observe the Queen on her way to the State Opening of Parliament during the first week or, from a vantage point such as Westminster Bridge, the veteran car run to Brighton.

In **December,** there are many events connected with the Christmas season, such as: the Festival of Carols in Ely Cathedral, King's College, Cambridge (always broadcast), and most country churches (often the best for visitors who want to meet local people); mumming plays at Andover and Marshfield; and carol services everywhere. On New Year's Eve, the Hogmanay Celebrations in Edinburgh and the mild revelry in Trafalgar Square, London, climax the evening, although the parading with blazing tar barrels on the head in Allendale (Northumberland) is hard to top! Details of any of these events are available at National or Regional Tourist Offices, addresses on pages 5 and 6.

HISTORIC BUILDINGS AND GARDENS. Opening days and admission charges for houses, etc., are liable to change from season to season, especially as many are still privately owned and occupied. We therefore list only approximate days and times throughout this book.

In our regional chapters we are able to list only some of the outstanding stately homes, castles, and other properties that may be visited. Two extremely useful publications, giving opening times and admission fees of hundreds of houses and gardens open to the public, also museums and galleries, both covering Great Britain and Ireland are: *Stately Homes, Museums, Castles and Gardens* (£3.50) and *Museums and Galleries* (£2.95). They are available from all good bookshops or from International Services Ltd., Windsor Court, East Grinstead House, East Grinstead, East Sussex, England (tel. 0342–26972). The entrance fee to most houses varies from about 75p to £3.50.

Many historic houses, gardens and monuments throughout Britain give free entry to holders of an *Open to View* ticket. Specially designed for overseas visitors, it can be purchased from British Rail offices or travel agents in your country, or from the British Travel Center, 12 Regent Street, London S.W.1 on production of a non-British passport.

Other schemes are also worth considering. Membership of English Heritage for around £10, for example, gives admission to over 350 castles and historic places in England; it is worthwhile if you intend to visit more than five or six of the monuments in the scheme (which includes, for example, the Tower of London). Details from: *English Heritage,* Fortress House, 23 Savile Row, London W1X 2HE. A similar scheme is operated in Wales by *Cadw: Welsh Historic Monuments,* Brunel House, Cardiff CF2 1UY.

Many houses belong to the National Trust, a privately funded organization, founded to help preserve the national heritage. An annual membership (£16, or £25.50 for two people) entitles you to visit free some 250 historic properties; for information write *The National Trust,* 42 Queen Anne's Gate, London SW1. Or, for Scotland only, *The National Trust for Scotland,* 5 Charlotte Sq., Edinburgh 2. Further information about gardens can be obtained from: *National Gardens Scheme,* 57 Lower Belgrave St., London SW1, and *Scotland's Gardens Scheme,* 26 Castle Terr., Edinburgh 1. The National Gardens Scheme publish a valuable guide, the *Yellow Book* (£2.25, including postage and packing), to over 2,000 visitable gardens.

In the *Practical Information* sections at the end of each chapter you will find lists of historic houses and museums, with those belonging to the National Trust marked (NT). These lists are, of course, not exhaustive, but do give the main buildings to be seen in each area. Since staff (guides and so forth) are frequently volunteers from the locality, the opening times tend to be flexible. We suggest that you always try to check before visiting, to be sure that the property will be open. You should also note that most houses close their doors around half-an-hour before the announced time in order to allow the last party to circumnavigate the place.

Getting to Britain

FROM NORTH AMERICA BY AIR. London's Heathrow and Gatwick airports are the gateways to both Britain and the Continent. As air fare wars are waged (and when are they not?), the battles frequently zero in on the trans-Atlantic routes which land travelers at these very airports. Thus, the flights to Britain are generally among the lowest priced of all those going to Europe. Not only that, but flights from London to the Continent—especially charter or package deals—tend to be cheaper, more abundant, and more readily available than from the U.S. Regardless of the type of fare, from Concorde super luxury to spur-of-the-moment standby, service to either or both of London's airway ports of entry is frequent.

Direct flights leave from most major cities in the U.S. and Canada, and through-flights with one stop-over can be arranged from many other points. Although there are some daytime flights, most services tend to depart from east coast cities during evening hours in order to arrive early the next morning (U.K. time, that is); flights from more westerly points are timed accordingly. The one major drawback to this arrangement is that some hotels may not allow you to check in before noon or even 1 P.M., and that can leave you feeling exhausted with no place to nap or unwind for several hours. In-flight travel time from the east coast is usually between five and six and a half hours.

Fares. Air fares from the U.S. to Britain are in a constant state of flux, and there are a bewildering array of special fares ranging in price from the relatively inexpensive to the astronomically costly. Our best advice is to consult a travel agent and let him or her make your reservations for you. Agents are familiar with the latest changes in fare structures, as well as with the rules governing various discount plans.

Generally, on regularly scheduled flights, the basic breakdown is as follows: Concorde and First Class fares run at the very top of the cost scale. The substantial extra money involved—often well over twice that of other fares (at presstime, a one-way ticket on British Airways Concorde from New York was $3,210!)—will buy all on-board amenities at no extra cost, a shortened flight time (about 3½ hours on Concorde flights), and a more comfortable seating arrangement. No restrictions are put on these tickets, i.e. you may book, travel, and change flight dates at any time, and have stopovers when required.

Economy fares are less pricey than the above, but can still be expensive. As with First Class tickets, there are no restrictions, though there may be an additional charge for stopovers.

APEX (Advance Booking Excursion) or Super Saver fares are just about the best bargains available. These fares offer enormous reductions on the price of a First Class or Economy ticket. But in exchange for the lower cost, a number of restrictions are imposed. The basic requirements are a 21-day advance booking and payment, plus a minimum stay of seven days. APEX tickets are only available on round-trips, and once booked, flight dates may not be changed.

Standby fares are no less expensive than full economy but are useful if you make your decision at the last minute.

Virgin Atlantic still offers some of the lowest fares, flying from Newark to London (Gatwick).

Charter service has decreased in recent years, but some charters are still available. Again, an agent will be able to recommend which ones are reliable. Sometimes it is also worth investigating package tours even if you do not wish to use the other services (hotels, meals, etc.). Because the packager can block book seats, the price of a package vacation is often less than the cost of an air fare booked independently.

FROM NORTH AMERICA BY SEA. *Cunard,* 555 Fifth Avenue, New York, N.Y. 10017 (212–661–7777 or 800–221–4770), has had ships on the North Atlantic route since 1839. The company's flagship, the *QE2,* now maintains the only regular trans-Atlantic service. It runs from April to October between New York, Cherbourg (France) and Southampton (England). Fares are high, albeit for a duly luxurious mode of travel. Off-season is relatively less expensive. Cunard will also arrange special air-sea combination tickets.

Freighter travel was for years the most popular way to cross the Atlantic inexpensively. Shipping companies now realise money can be made from carrying passengers on their modern container ships. More berths are becoming available, not only direct to the U.K., but also to ports including Rotterdam, which have good connections to Britain. Consult *Air Marine Travel Service,* 501 Madison Ave., New York, N.Y. 10022 (212–371–1300), publisher of the *Trip Log Quick Reference Freighter Guide* for details on freighter passage.

FROM THE CONTINENT AND IRELAND BY AIR. Between the services of the main U.K. airlines and those of Continental carriers, London and over a dozen provincial cities have links with some 65 European destinations, either by non-stop or through-plane flights. For example, every European capital—with the exception of Tirana (Albania)—has a direct flight to London; from France there are flights from no fewer than 14 cities plus Paris. With a very few exceptions, all of these operate throughout the year, mostly on a daily basis but on the busier routes anything from three to a dozen flights daily.

Besides London (Heathrow and Gatwick) the following U.K. cities have direct flights to continental destinations—Birmingham, Manchester,

Newcastle, Glasgow, Edinburgh, Cardiff, Bristol, Leeds, Norwich, South-ampton, Aberdeen, Belfast, Exeter and Plymouth. From Ireland there are flights into London, Liverpool, Manchester, Glasgow and a number of other cities—mostly from Dublin and less so Cork and Shannon.

The variety of fares offered is very wide indeed. Consult with your travel agent and airlines. Remember, too, that if you have a full-fare ticket from the U.S.A./Canada to a European destination it can often allow you a stopover in the U.K.

FROM THE CONTINENT AND IRELAND BY SEA. Although the talk of a Channel Tunnel linking England with France still goes on, the reality remains somewhere in the future. However, there are over 70 drive-on, drive-off car ferries operating to no fewer than 13 ports in England.

Here are the main routes on the drive-on, drive-off services, all of which carry foot passengers. They are ordered from the northernmost one, round the coast of Europe to Spain—

Bergen (Norway) to Newcastle-upon-Tyne
Stavanger (Norway) to Newcastle-upon-Tyne
Kristiansand (Norway) to Harwich
Oslo (Norway) to Harwich
Gothenburg (Sweden) to Newcastle-upon-Tyne, Harwich
Hirstals (Denmark) to Harwich
Esbjerg (Denmark) to Newcastle-upon-Tyne, Harwich
Helsinki (Finland) to Purfleet (near London)
Hamburg (West Germany) to Harwich
Rotterdam (Holland) to Hull
Hoek van Holland (Holland) to Harwich
Zeebrugge (Belgium) to Hull, Felixstowe, Dover
Vlissingen (Holland) to Sheerness
Oostende (Belgium) to Dover
Dunkerque (France) to Ramsgate
Calais (France) to Dover
Boulogne (France) to Dover, Folkestone
Dieppe (France) to Newhaven
Le Havre (France) to Portsmouth
Caen (France) to Portsmouth
Cherbourg (France) to Weymouth, Poole, Portsmouth
St. Malo (France) to Portsmouth
Roscoff (France) to Plymouth
Santander (Spain) to Plymouth

In addition to these there are Hovercraft services operated by *Hover-speed* from Calais and Boulogne to Dover. And the newest of the "surface skimmers" the *Jetfoil* operates from Oostende to Dover. The latter carries passengers only.

Between Ireland and the U.K. the following services operate—
Belfast to **Liverpool**
Cork to **Swansea**
Larne to **Stranraer, Cairnryan** (both in southwest Scotland)
Dublin to **Liverpool**
Dun Laoghaire (near Dublin) to **Holyhead**
Rosslare to **Fishguard**
All are drive-on, drive-off ferry services.

CUSTOMS. There are two levels of duty free allowance for people entering the U.K.; one, for goods bought outside the EEC or for goods bought in a duty free shop within the EEC; two, for goods bought in an EEC country but not in a duty free shop.

In the first category you may import duty free: 200 cigarettes or 100 cigarillos or 50 cigars or 250 grams of tobacco (*Note* if you live outside Europe, these allowances are doubled); plus one liter of alcoholic drinks over 22% volume (38.8% proof) or two liters of alcoholic drinks not over 22% volume or fortified, still or sparkling wine; plus two liters of still table wine; plus 50 grams of perfume; plus nine fluid ounces of toilet water; plus other goods to the value of £32.

In the second category you may import duty free: 300 cigarettes or 150 cigarillos or 75 cigars or 400 grams of tobacco; plus 1½ liters of alcoholic drinks over 22% volume (38.8% proof) or three liters of alcoholic drinks not over 22% volume or fortified, still or sparkling wine; plus five liters of still table wine; plus 75 grams of perfume; plus 13 fluid ounces of toilet water; plus other goods to the value of £250 (*Note* though it is not classified as an alcoholic drink by EEC countries for Customs' purposes and is thus considered part of the "other goods" allowance, you may not import more than 50 liters of beer).

In addition, no animals or pets of any kind may be brought into the U.K. The penalties for doing so are severe and are strictly enforced; there are *no* exceptions. Similarly, fresh meats, plants and vegetables, controlled drugs and firearms and ammunition may not be brought into the U.K. There are no restrictions on the import or export of British and foreign currencies.

Entering Scotland from any other part of the U.K., you will face no customs formalities. But anyone coming from Northern Ireland may face a security check.

Anyone planning to stay in the U.K. for more than six months should contact H.M. Customs and Excise, Kent House, Upper Ground, London S.E.1 (tel. 01–928 0533) for further information.

Staying in Britain

HOTELS. Booking: Always try and make your reservations in advance for hotels and other forms of accommodation; it is far better to be safe than sorry, particularly during the summer months. When you book, remember to stipulate: numbers of double, single, twins or suites required, and number of persons; date of arrival and approximate time; number of nights and date of departure. In smaller country hotels it's wise also to request those meals that you will require. Remember also that breakfast is often *not* included in hotel rates, so bear this in mind when comparing prices.

Confirm rates before making that final booking, and don't be afraid to request hotel brochures to assist your decision. Many hotels have "good" and "bad" sides; when apparently similar accommodation bears different rates, it is therefore worth inquiring why. You can easily be kept awake by passing traffic or moaning plumbing for the sake of a small saving, and you may decide that it is better to pay slightly more, particularly in older hotels where these problems usually occur, and in Britain an "older" hotel might have been around for 400 years!

Many U.K. hotel groups do have American offices, which we list below, so you can often book before leaving home and be sure of a room. Do read the small print on your booking confirmation though, especially with regard to time of arrival; some hotels will not honor your reservation after a certain time. And if you have to cancel, do so as far in advance as possible. Remember that it is increasingly common for hotels to demand payment if rooms cannot be re-let.

Hotel Prices

Prices for two people in a double room

	London	Country
Super-Deluxe	£150 and up	—
Luxury (L)	£130–£150	over £100
Expensive (E)	£100–£130	£75–£100
Moderate (M)	£60–£100	£40–£75
Inexpensive (I)	under £60	under £40

Hotel Gradings. Most British hotels and motels have most rooms with private bathrooms. So do many inns, pensions, guest houses, and stately homes. But, on the other hand, there is still a fair proportion of establishments, especially in the country areas, that have only a few private bathrooms. There is no official system of hotel classification in U.K., but an unofficial word-of-mouth system usually ensures that price/facility relationships are well observed. Our policy is to grade solely according to price in a simple Expensive (E), Moderate (M) and Inexpensive (I) system. There is also a Luxury (L) grade for London and some places in the country.

Reservations Before You Leave. A travel agent will be best equipped to help with advance planning and contacting local booking offices. He can also telex for reservations directly. Among the larger hotel groups with representatives in the U.S.

Intercontinental Hotels, 1120 Ave. of the Americas, New York, N.Y. 10036 (tel. 800–327–0200).

Rank Hotels Ltd., 6 E. 43rd St., New York, N.Y. 10017 (tel. 800–223–5560 or 212–972–5175).

Trusthouse Forte Hotels Inc., 1800 Northern Blvd., Roslyn, N.Y. 11576 (tel. 800–223–5672).

Others include *Embassy, Ladbroke, Crest, British Transport, Best Western* and*Consort.* The British Tourist Authority offices in New York, Chicago, Dallas and Los Angeles can provide addresses and phone numbers for U.S. booking offices, but also urges using a travel agent.

Hotel Groups and Consortia. You will probably be faced at some time during your holiday, either in the planning stages or while on the trip, with the choice of booking your accommodation through a hotel group or using independent hotels. Hotel groups have several advantages. They maintain a fairly even standard of comfort and cuisine throughout their chains; as they have establishments in many places, they can *book ahead* for you; they may well have extra facilities that individually-run hotels cannot afford to provide. But they also tend to iron away those individual traits that make travel interesting. And, to be quite frank, some of the chains treat their clients in an assembly line way that is practical from their point of view, but soulless from the travelers'.

Undoubtedly the needs and pressures of your trip will determine whether you choose between one of the groups' facilities or those of individually-run hotels. If you have the time to plan it out, get the best of both worlds. Certainly, not to stay in one of the better owner-managed hotels, where excellent cooking and attentive service are the order of the day, would be to miss one of the delights that is still possible when traveling.

Tourist Accommodation Services. If you are having problems finding overnight accommodation in a particular town or country area during your visit, you could try the *Tourist Accommodation Service,* operated by the Tourist Boards at many of their local Tourist Information Centers. The service is available to personal callers only, and a complete list of centers throughout Great Britain is available from the National Tourist Information Center, Victoria Station Forecourt, London SW1. In addition, they also operate a hotel reservation service, as does their office at Heathrow Airport (actually at Heathrow Central underground station). A small, non-returnable fee is charged. At the time of reservation, you must pay a small deposit which is deducted from your final bill.

Hotel Bargains. Time was when guests would beat a path to even the remotest reception desk. Today hoteliers have learnt that marketing pays, and everybody loves a bargain. Over 600 hotels (complete list from the English Tourist Board, Thames Tower, Blacks Rd., London W6 (01–846–9000)) offer special weekend and low season bargain holiday packages between October and April. You should ask for details from the groups and consortia, as well as when writing to individual hotels. Ask, too, about an English Tourist Board/National Holidays scheme called "Great English City Breaks," where 13 cities offer bargain-priced short stays at good quality hotels. Book through travel agents in Britain.

Bed and Breakfast. The French call it a "Pension" and such romantic tones tend to uplift the simple English "Guest House." By either name, these are budget accommodation houses, generally small, and almost always family-run. They are often without private bathrooms and dining facilities, other than for breakfast. Certain guest houses are known as bed and breakfast establishments—tending toward fewer facilities and lower prices. If you are after a budget holiday, we can heartily recommend that you try a bed-and-breakfast place, they are almost always friendly and excellent value. You will find, too, the added advantage of getting to know local people much more than you would in a hotel.

Farmhouses. There has been a tremendous increase in farmhouse accommodation. Prices are very reasonable, but don't expect hotel-style standards. But that is its appeal—you're a guest of the family and will also get an insight into rural life. Ask at local tourist offices for details.

Plush Surroundings. It is possible to stay as a paying guest in certain famous British stately homes. Arrangements generally include breakfast, dinner and accommodation; prior booking is obligatory and the cost is usually just as stately as the house. Further information from the B.T.A., Thames Tower, Blacks Rd., London W6.

As you read our hotel listings, you will quickly note that many British hotels are converted houses or castles whose architectural merits range from Jacobean manor houses to Regency elegance. As a way of soaking in atmosphere they are to be recommended.

Holiday Cottages. The largest selection of furnished property available for holiday letting is published by *Taylings Holiday Cottages,* 14 High St., Godalming, Surrey, tel. (04868) 28522. Their brochure lists over 1000 properties, most of which sleep a minimum of 4 persons, while many accommodate numbers up to 12 or 14. A vast selection includes Georgian mansions, 13th-century thatched cottages, a converted Methodist Chapel, castles and farms. Taylings act as agents and standards vary, but their descriptions are by no means always rhapsodic, and they state frankly where amenities are less than perfect. They also provide useful advice concerning specific suitability for children. Any price guide is misleading in view of the variety, but £250 per week to sleep 5 in summer, and about two-thirds that out of season, gives some idea.

A well-researched, 250-page book the *Good Holiday Cottage Guide,* is available from bookshops at £1.95, or from Swallow Press, P.O. Box 21, Hertford, Herts. SG14 2BH. From abroad add £1 for postage.

Also to be recommended is an organization based in Norfolk, but with West Country and Welsh properties as well as many in East Anglia: *English Country Cottages,* Claypit Lane, Fakenham, Norfolk NR21 8AS, tel. (0328) 51155. They have a huge number of properties in every price range and of every kind.

The Landmark Trust, Old Garden Cottage, Shottesbrook Park, Whitewaltham, Maidenhead, Berks. (tel. 062882–5925), specializes in refurbishing and renting landmarks which would otherwise slowly disintegrate. This charity publishes a fascinating booklet ($2 postage voucher) detailing these properties and rentals. You may stay in the medieval Bath Tower at Caernarfon, or Purton Green Farm, a 13th-century timber-framed house, where a car cannot get closer than 400 yards. Many of their beautifully preserved properties include mills and other industrial relics still in working order. Demand is naturally high, so book early, particularly in the season. The cost is around £250 per week to sleep 6 in the summer.

Universities. Certain university Halls of Residence in holiday areas have accommodation to let during the vacations. These offer compact single sleeping units, arranged normally in groups of four, with kitchen-diner, bathroom and lavatory. They can be rented on a nightly or longer basis, but British students are unaccountably expected to be celibate, so remember that single accommodation *only* is available. In certain instances, breakfast is provided, but selfcatering is normal with rooms averaging £10 per night per head. Further information from: British Universities Accommodation Consortium, University Park, Nottingham.

Youth Hostels. Your Youth Hostel membership card is accepted at all British hostels, and anyone can join the association overseas or in UK, of course. Hostels are closed during the day and available for stays of up to 3 nights. Everyone lends a hand with simple domestic chores—one reason why charges are so low, ranging from £1.50 to £3.00 per night, dependent upon age and hostel standard. Further information, including details on their special adventure holiday series from *YHA,* Trevelyan House, 8 St. Stephen's Hill, St. Albans, Herts. In North America, for membership and information, write to *American Youth Hostels, Inc.,* PO Box 37613,

Washington, DC 20013; or *Canadian Youth Hostels Association,* Tower A, 333 River Rd., 3rd Floor, Ottawa, Ontario U1L 8H9.

RESTAURANTS. Prices vary widely according to region, but in a very modest restaurant in London or an average place in the provinces you will pay from £5 up for lunch and from £8 up for dinner—more if you dine à la carte. Popular chain cafés provide a reasonable 3-course lunch for about £5 and up and at a snack bar or self-service restaurant you might pay less.

In a restaurant a bottle of house wine will cost from £5 and a half-pint of beer around 90p. A glass of wine in a wine bar costs about £1.30, whisky or gin £1 depending on the bar you are in; coffee is 50p a cup. Water has to be asked for and it's not likely to be iced.

Restaurant Prices

Prices are for two people and include wine

Luxury (for London only) £90 and way, way up

	London	Country
Expensive (E)	£60–£90	£50–£80
Moderate (M)	£30–£60	£25–£50
Inexpensive (I)	under £30	under £25

TIPPING. Many large hotels and most of those belonging to chains automatically add a 10% to 15% service charge on your final bill. In this case you are *not* expected to tip, and any staff member who attempts to insinuate otherwise should be ignored, if not reported to the management. If you have received exceptional service from any member of staff, then you may of course tip accordingly. If, of course, you are *dissatisfied* with the service, then say why and do not pay the service charge. You will be legally in the right.

If there is no service charge, then you may divide a sum equivalent to 10% of your total bill between those personnel who have been of service during your stay. These will generally include the chambermaid, porter and restaurant staff. In restaurants, tip 10–15% of the check but *be sure* it has not already been added in. Bellhops and porters about £1.

Taxi drivers get about 10% of the fare. Beware however of those London Airport sob stories that frequently greet the traveler and concern waiting time! They are usually calculated to produce a bigger tip! You should pay about £18 to central London from Heathrow Airport.

You do not tip while drinking at the bar in a pub, but you can offer the barman a drink if you are a habitué of the place. Do not tip cinema or theater ushers, nor elevator operators. Hairdressers and barbers are tipped 20%.

HINTS FOR DISABLED TRAVELERS. One of the newest, and largest, groups to enter the travel scene is the handicapped. There are millions of people who are physically able to travel and who do so enthusiastically when they know they will be able to move about with safety and comfort. A growing number of travel agencies specialize in this market. Generally their tours parallel those of the non-handicapped traveler, but at a more leisurely pace, with everything checked out in advance to eliminate all inconvenience, whether the traveler happens to be deaf, blind or in a wheelchair. For a complete list of tour operators who arrange such travel, write to the *Society for the Advancement of Travel for the Handicapped,* 26 Court St., Brooklyn, New York, 11242, tel. 718–858–5483. An excellent source of information in this field is the book *Access to the World: A Travel Guide for the Handicapped,* by Louise Weiss, available from Facts on File, 460 Park Ave. South, New York, N.Y. 10016 (212–683–2244).

Another major source of help is the *Travel Information Center,* Moss Rehabilitation Hospital, 12th St. and Tabor Rd., Philadelphia, Penn. 19141, tel. 215–329–5715. Also helpful is the *Information Center for Individuals with Disabilities,* 20 Park Plaza, Rm 330, Boston, MA 02116 (617–727–5540).

Awareness of the special needs of the handicapped traveler is growing in Britain, enormously aided by the Year of the Disabled in 1981. Public transport is becoming easier; British Rail is the only railway system in Europe which allows wheelchair passengers to travel in the van. The National Bus Company has also made considerable efforts to improve facilities for disabled passengers, and produces a leaflet on the subject. Many hotels are trying to provide accommodation for the disabled, and there are more efforts being made in theaters, museums, historic houses etc., to ease visits by disabled people.

The *Royal Association for Disability and Rehabilitation (RADAR),* 25 Mortimer St., London W1N 8AB, in addition to publishing its excellent handbooks *Holidays for Disabled People* and *Motoring and Mobility,* also acts as an information service. A booklet entitled *Britain for the Disabled* is available from the British Tourist Authority, 40 West 57th St., New York, N.Y. 10019. The *Access Guide to London* can be bought by mail from Access, 39 Bradley Gardens, West Ealing, London W.13 (tel.01–828 4661), price £3 for U.K. residents, £5 (at current exchange rate) for U.S. residents.

CLOSING TIMES. Legal holidays (Bank Holidays is the English term) are not uniform throughout Great Britain. In England and Wales, the holidays are New Year's Day, Good Friday, Easter Monday, May Day, Spring Holiday (late May), August Bank Holiday (late August), Christmas Day, and Boxing Day (Dec. 26). Northern Ireland adds St. Patrick's Day, March 17, to this list. Scotland does not universally observe Easter Monday or Boxing Day, but celebrates New Year's Day, (plus at least one day), and in Edinburgh and Glasgow the spring and autumn holidays are observed. The Channel Islands add Liberation Day, May 9.

Usual shopping and business hours are 9 to 5 or 5.30 P.M. Banks open at 9.30 or 10 A.M., and close at 3.30 P.M. Mon.-Fri., closed Sat., though some banks are open on a Sat. morning once again. Outside the main centers, most shops will close for half-a-day a week, usually either on Wed., Thurs., or Sat.; check locally. Big West End of London stores stay open until 7 or 8 P.M. one day a week, generally Wednesday or Thursday.

Drinking Hours. Pubs in Great Britain are allowed to open between 11 A.M. and 11 P.M. Monday to Saturday, and from 12–3 and 7–10:30 or 11 on Sundays, though the landlord may choose not to be open all the time during these hours. Young people of 14 and under are not generally allowed in pubs in England and Wales. Under 18s cannot purchase or consume alcohol. In Scotland, young people under 18 are not allowed in licensed bars and rooms—even for a soft drink—and in some remote communities women are unwelcome in pubs!

SHOPPING—VALUE ADDED TAX. To the eternal fury of Britain's shopkeepers, who struggle under cataracts of paperwork, Britain is afflicted with a 15% Value Added Tax. Foreign visitors, however, need not pay V.A.T. if they take advantage of the Personal Export Scheme.

Of the various ways to get a VAT refund, the most common are *Over the Counter* and *Direct Export.* Note that though practically all larger stores operate these schemes, information about them is not always readily forthcoming, so it is important to ask. Once you have gotten onto the right track, you'll find that almost all of the larger stores have export departments that will be able to give you all the help you need.

The easiest, and most usual way of getting your refund is the *Over the Counter* method. There is normally a minimum value for goods you purchase of £75, below which VAT cannot be refunded. You must also be able to supply proof of your identity—your passport is best. The sales clerk will then fill out the necessary paperwork, Form VAT 407. Keep the form and give it to Customs when you leave the country. Lines at major airports are usually long, so leave plenty of time. The form will then be returned to the store and the refund forwarded to you, minus a small service charge, usually around $3. You can specify how you want the refund. Generally, the easiest way is to have it credited to your charge card. Alternatively, you can have it in the form of a sterling check, but your bank will charge a fee to convert it. Note also that it can take up to eight weeks to receive the refund.

The *Direct Export* method—whereby you have the store send the goods to your home—is more cumbersome. You must have the VAT Form 407 certified by Customs, police or a notary public when you get home and then send it back to the store. They in turn will refund your money.

If you are traveling to any other EEC country from Britain, the same rules apply, except in France. Here you can claim your refund as you leave the country.

ELECTRICITY. If you're bringing electric shavers, irons, hair driers, etc., with you, it's best to check that they can be safely used on British voltages. The most general are 200 to 250 volts, AC., 50 cycles. Since most American appliances are designed to operate on 120 volts, 60 cycles, visitors from the United States will need transformers. Most hotels have special razor sockets which will take both voltages.

MAIL. The postage rates: *Inland:* letters and postcards up to 60g, 14p (slow), 19p (fast). *To Europe:* letters up to 20g, 23p, cards the same (19p if they are going to an EEC country). Letters and cards go by air at these rates if this makes for earlier delivery, so there is no need to use airmail stickers, though lightweight paper will make for minimum postal rate. *To the U.S. and Canada:* letters and cards up to 10g, 32p, postcards 27p; airmail stickers should be used. **Note:** these rates may be increased during 1989.

Telegrams. Inland telegrams for Britain were done away with in October 1982, to be replaced by Telemessages. But it is still possible to send an overseas telegram by dialing 190. You may send telegrams from a phone or over the counter, but if sending from a public phone booth, have the correct amount ready for insertion when the operator has counted the words. Telegrams can be sent by telephone any hour of the day or night.

TELEPHONE. Overseas rates can be had on application at a post office or from any operator. Telephone kiosks are plentiful in the streets (most are still painted red, but British Telecom is in the process of repainting them all yellow) and in post offices. The working of coin-operated telephones varies but instructions are affixed to the kiosk. Most have STD (timed) calling and you'll need a supply of 10p coins for the old style telephones; the new ones take 10p, 20p, 50p and £1 coins.

Dialing codes in the Greater London area: for general information 191; for directory inquiries 192; for inland long-distance calls 100; for overseas calls 155; cables 190 (international).

In making overseas calls remember the difference in time zones. Thus, 12 noon in London is 7 A.M. in New York, 6 A.M. in Chicago, etc.

For *emergency calls* (fire, police, ambulance) throughout the country dial 999.

All-figure telephone numbers have now been introduced throughout Britain. Each large city or region has its own prefix (London's is 01–, Birmingham's 021–) which is used when dialing from outside the city; when already in the city, the prefix is dropped and the seven-figure number should be used.

Throughout this guide the national dialing code number is given (in brackets) for the establishments listed. When calling from the town concerned this number should be omitted. When calling from nearby, the code may be different. The local dialling code will be listed in the local directory or can be obtained from Directory Inquiries (192). The exchange name will be that of the town under which the listing is made, unless otherwise stated.

Warning. You are warned *not* to make long-distance phone calls from your hotel room without checking very carefully what the cost will be. Hotels frequently add *several hundred percent* to such calls. This is an international practice, not one confined to Britain. It is worthwhile utilizing your telephone credit card for these calls to avoid the massive hotel surcharge and certain U.S. cards are valid in Europe for this purpose.

Traveling in Britain

GETTING AROUND BRITAIN BY CAR. Any visitor who is a member of a recognized automobile club in his own country can, when bringing a car to Britain, have the assistance of the *AA* on a reciprocal basis. If not, the *Automobile Association,* Fanum House, Basingstoke, Hants (tel. 0256–20123) offer Associate Membership £22.50. The *Royal Automobile Club,* 49 Pall Mall, London SW1 (tel. 01–839 7050) also offers Associate Membership. AA Associate Membership gives normal roadside assistance in case of breakdown, but special recovery services such as Relay, which gets you and your car to your destination, are extra.

Both the AA and the RAC have their highly organized touring departments represented at all the principal ports and in a number of provincial towns. It is, however, a good idea before leaving home to get advice from your own automobile club concerning procedure and documentation. Providing that you have with you your car registration papers, a nationality plaque and a current driving license, visitors are free to drive their own cars in Britain. If they have no registration papers or plaque, they will be issued with temporary papers and what are called "Q" plates, i.e. special registration plates for visitors. These cost £10.50. (*Note*: legislation may change all this—check with your auto club.)

Rules of the Road. In Britain one drives on the left-hand side of the road and tries to sort out the various speed limits. In the center of cities and most built-up areas, it is 30 mph; on some suburban roads it is 40; on divided highways and motorways 70; and on all other roads 60 mph. The beginning and end of all limited sections are marked with round warning signs, except the 60s. When a suburban road is limited to 40 mph, or is de-restricted, it carries small applicable signs on the lamp posts. Hardly any foreigners can make head or tail of all this, and nor can many British drivers. The AA and RAC maintain highway services to help in emergencies such as a flat tire or no-go engine, but they no longer patrol the roads. Instead they are equipped with walkie-talkie and can be summoned by telephone.

Maps. To get about Britain with any degree of success it is essential to have maps. Simple maps giving sightseeing information are available, mostly free, from the British Tourist Authority. Good overall planning maps come inexpensively from the AA, while the RAC covers the whole country in 11 excellent sectional maps at 3 miles to the inch, from which it will be seen that England now has motorways running almost the length of the country in both west and east, with three links connecting them in the south, midlands and north. The network is excellent for covering, toll free, long distances but you see almost nothing of the countryside.

However, if you wish to see the "real" Britain, the best maps to buy are the Ordnance Survey 1:50,000 series. They show all the roads, tracks and footpaths. They will allow you to discover the many treasures of the countryside, as well as taking you off the heavily-used main roads. The Ordnance Survey also produce maps which are especially aimed at the tourist, covering areas such as the Lake District, the New Forest, Dartmoor and Exmoor.

When planning a holiday in Britain it is necessary to realize that once you get off the motorways travel is slow. To keep up an overall average of 35 mph is not easy. In Wales it is more difficult than in England; in some parts of Scotland it is impossible. Similarly it should be noted that motor travel in Scotland and the North might be impossible from January to March because of sudden bad weather laid on top of difficult roads.

Gas. As we go to press—mid-1988—the price of gasoline (petrol in Britain, though everyone understands "gas") is approximately £1.80 per gallon. Lubricating oils average around £1.20 a liter. Remember that the British imperial gallon is substantially larger than the American, four of the former equal five of the latter. But you may find, anyway, that metrication has changed all that.

Car Hire. Prices vary according to the size of the car and length of hire. With unlimited mileage, you can hire a Ford (automatic) for £450 per week. All firms require a deposit, normally £80–100, plus the estimated cost of hire, unless you use a recognized credit card, when all charges can be paid later. Some winter rates are lower. Rates for chauffeur-driven cars: expect to pay around £120 per day plus a mileage charge, inclusive. It is possible to arrange for a self-drive car to be waiting for you at your port of arrival, or any railway station.

Don't forget when planning your trip that at the end of your tour there are great advantages in leaving your car at a different city from that in which you picked it up.

Avis Rent-a-Car, International Reservations, Trident House, Station Rd., Hayes, Middlesex (tel. 01–848 8733).

4 Saunders Rd, Station Approach, Cardiff, Wales (tel. 0222–42111).

100 Dalry Rd, Edinburgh, Scotland (tel. 031–337 6363).

Gateway Garage, Piccadilly Station Approach, Manchester (tel. 061–236 6716).

Godfrey Davis Europcar, Bushey House, High St., Bushey, Watford (tel. 01–950 5050).

Monaco House, Bristol St, Birmingham (tel. 021–622 5311).

5/11 Byron St (off City Rd), Cardiff, Wales (tel. 0222–498978).

24 East London St., Edinburgh, Scotland (tel. 031–661 1252).

Hertz Europe, Rental Centre, 44 The Broadway, London S.W.19 (tel. 01–542 6688).

Terminal Building, Edinburgh Airport, Scotland (tel. 031–333 1019).

47 Corporation St, Manchester (tel. 061–834 4806).

Kenning Car Hire, Manor House, Old Rd., Chesterfield, Derbys. (tel. 0246–77241).

40/44 Duff St, Edinburgh, Scotland (tel. 031–343 3377).

210 Cheetham Hill Rd, Manchester (tel. 061–834 8151).

Swan National, 305 Chiswick High Rd, London W.4 (tel. 01–995 4665).

2 City Rd., Cardiff, Wales (tel. 0222–496256).

Bomac Self Service, 19–21 Glasgow Rd., Corstorphine, Edinburgh, Scotland (tel. 031–334 9245).

3 Ringway Trading Estate, Shadowmoss Rd., Wythenshawe, Manchester (tel. 061–436 3290).

Motorail. The development of the motorway network and the increasing comfort of motor cars over the last decade have greatly reduced both the need for (and attractiveness of) Motorail services. There are currently six routes in total: Four from London Euston—one to Inverness*, another serves both Edinburgh and Aberdeen*, one to Carlisle which is ideal for the Lake District and the Borders, and a summer only service to Stirling. From London Paddington there's year-round service to Penzance in the extreme southwest of England and, finally, a year-round link from Bristol* to Edinburgh. *The services marked with an asterisk run daily.*

To give an idea of the cost, the roundtrip fare for a car plus driver and one passenger on the London (Euston)–Inverness overnight run, using second class sleeper accommodations, ranged from £301 off peak to £403 peak season in 1988. The cost may appear high but there are nonetheless considerable advantages in traveling overnight—savings on overnight hotel accommodations, no heavy driving, reduced petrol costs, and, most importantly, a gain in valuable vacation time!

Auto Tape Tours. Tourists who expect to take an automobile trip during their stay in Great Britain may be interested in travel cassettes produced by Auto Tape Tours. These cassettes are presented as "play as you drive" tours of the area. They are timed for local speed limits. Contact CCInc. Auto Tape Tours, Box 385, Scarsdale, NY 10583 (914–472–5133).

GETTING AROUND BRITAIN BY TRAIN. In spite of the severe financial restrictions put on British Railways (a state-owned but independently operated organization) by various governments, the U.K. has one of the best railway networks in the world—though you will hear many criticisms from the British, especially the commuters. Today, however, for speed, safety, comfort, but not necessarily time keeping, British Rail (or B.R. as it is usually known) is second to none.

Pride of place must go to the InterCity network which links London with every main city and many of these with each other. Fast diesel or electric trains provide a high-density service, all trains carrying both first- and standard-class carriages.

Of these, the new high speed electric trains which are being introduced on the east coast main service to Leeds and Newcastle (and will run to Edinburgh in the near future) are the most modern. These impressive trains are fully airconditioned, spaciously comfortable (in standard as well as 1st), carry full restaurant and/or buffet facilities, and are marketed under the banner of InterCity 125s. Unlike many European railways, British Rail does not charge extra for travel on their premier express trains.

These high speed trains are used on quite a large number of routes—even on some where their speed cannot be fully realized. They now run from London (Paddington) to Bristol, South Wales, Devon and Cornwall; from London (St. Pancras) to Leicester, Derby, Nottingham and Sheffield; from London (Kings Cross) to York, Hull, Middlesbrough, Edinburgh, Dundee, Aberdeen, and Inverness. Most recently they have been brought into use on the cross-country route from Newcastle and Leeds in the northeast to Bristol and Cardiff in the southwest, with some trains running through to Exeter and beyond.

To give an idea of the capabilities of the 125s, the *Flying Scotsman*—not unfortunately the famous steam train of the same name—leaves Kings Cross at 10.30 and arrives in Edinburgh some 4½ hours and 393 miles later.

On those other InterCity routes, where 125s are not used, services are nonetheless still good. On the main lines from London to Birmingham, Liverpool, Manchester and Glasgow electric trains travel at up to 110 m.p.h. Standards have been improved as more modern coaches have been brought into use. But on some shorter distances, comfort and speed vary considerably, and on some occasions leave the modern image of British Rail a bit tarnished. Nevertheless there are some very useful services such as from London (Waterloo) to Bournemouth, and from London (Victoria) to Brighton. The 108 miles to Bournemouth are covered in just over an hour and a half by the hourly fast train.

Local services present a slightly different picture. Some parts of London's vast commuter network are good while others are awful! Many lines are electrified and some have benefitted from the introduction of modern rolling stock. The current pièce de résistance is the electrified Thameslink route from Bedford running via Luton Airport through London to Gatwick Airport which was brought into operation in mid-1987. The majority of London's commuter lines have a service which runs at at least half-hourly intervals. 1986 saw the rebranding of London's main commuter

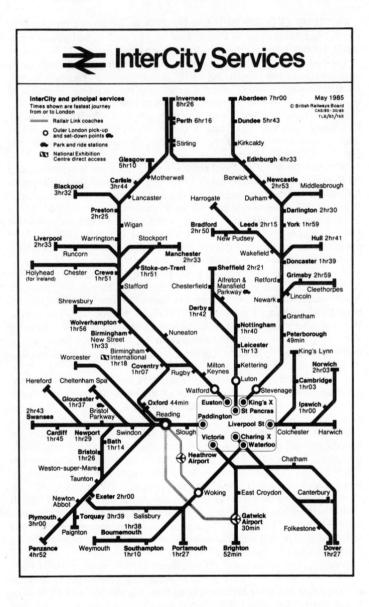

InterCity Services

InterCity and principal services
Times shown are fastest journey
from or to London

=== Railair Link coaches

○ Outer London pick-up
   and set-down points

▲ Park and ride stations

National Exhibition
Centre direct access

May 1985
© British Railways Board
CAS/85 - 30/85
TLB/85/168

Inverness 8hr26
Aberdeen 7hr00
Perth 6hr16
Dundee 5hr43
Stirling
Kirkcaldy
Glasgow 5hr10
Motherwell
Edinburgh 4hr33
Carlisle 3hr44
Berwick
Newcastle 2hr53
Middlesbrough
Blackpool 3hr32
Lancaster
Harrogate
Durham
Darlington 2hr30
Preston 2hr25
Wigan
Bradford 2hr50
Leeds 2hr15
York 1hr59
Liverpool 2hr33
Warrington
Stockport
New Pudsey
Hull 2hr41
Runcorn
Manchester 2hr33
Wakefield
Doncaster 1hr39
Holyhead (for Ireland)
Chester
Crewe 1hr51
Stoke-on-Trent 1hr51
Sheffield 2hr21
Grimsby 2hr59
Stafford
Chesterfield
Alfreton & Mansfield Parkway
Retford
Cleethorpes
Shrewsbury
Lincoln
Newark
Derby 1hr42
Grantham
Wolverhampton 1hr56
Nottingham 1hr40
Birmingham New Street 1hr33
Nuneaton
Peterborough 49min
Worcester
Birmingham International 1hr18
Leicester 1hr13
King's Lynn
Hereford
Cheltenham Spa
Coventry 1hr07
Rugby
Kettering
Norwich 2hr03
Milton Keynes
Luton
Cambridge 1hr03
Gloucester 1hr37
Watford
Stevenage
Ipswich 1hr00
2hr43 Swansea
Bristol Parkway
Oxford 44min
Euston
King's X
Reading
St Pancras
Cardiff 1hr45
Newport 1hr29
Swindon
Slough
Paddington
Liverpool St
Colchester
Harwich
Bath 1hr14
Bristol 1hr26
Victoria
Charing X
Waterloo
Weston-super-Mare
Heathrow Airport
Chatham
Taunton
Newton Abbot
Exeter 2hr00
Woking
East Croydon
Canterbury
Plymouth 3hr00
Torquay 3hr39
Salisbury
Gatwick Airport 30min
Paignton
Bournemouth 1hr38
Folkestone
Penzance 4hr52
Weymouth
Southampton 1hr10
Portsmouth 1hr27
Brighton 52min
Dover 1hr27

services. Network Southeast, with its own distinctive livery, is committed to improving service quality with investment in new trains and refurbished stations.

Other major cities such as Liverpool, Birmingham and Manchester have useful local rail systems well integrated with local bus services. On Tyneside the superb public transport system operated by Tyne and Wear Passenger Transport Executive is a national showpiece, combining rail, bus and Metro. This last is the jewel in the crown, and is an object lesson in the design and operation of a new light rail system.

In Scotland the center of the rail network is Edinburgh, from where services radiate with good connections to all parts of Scotland. However, Glasgow retains the best suburban public transport system in Scotland with its coordinated bus, rail and ferry services. The underground system here has been fully rebuilt and given new trains—and has been dubbed "The Clockwork Orange" due to the livery!

Sleepers. There is a good sleeping-car service, mostly centered on London. Services have been significantly improved, with airconditioning and double glazing the norm, as well as improved toilet facilities. Likewise more luggage space has been provided. First class compartments have a single berth, while standard has two, an upper and a lower. Attendants travel on every train to serve drinks and snacks all night, and complimentary morning tea or coffee with biscuits.

Supplements are charged for sleeping cars. It is best to reserve as far in advance as possible, especially if you are traveling at weekends or during the holiday season.

The principal routes are from London to Glasgow, Edinburgh, Aberdeen and Inverness. There are also services to Plymouth and Penzance in the southwest, Liverpool and Manchester in the northwest, and a cross-country route from Bristol to Scotland.

InterCity Pullman. In coaches designed for maximum comfort, 1st-class travelers can enjoy a varied menu and service of the highest standard. InterCity Pullmans are available on selected trains between London and Liverpool, Manchester, Leeds and Newcastle. Two new Pullman services linking Birmingham and Sheffield with London are scheduled to begin operation from May 1987.

Note: One thing must be stressed about rail travel to and from London. The city has no fewer than 8 InterCity termini. Be *quite certain* which one your train departs from or arrives at. All have Underground stations either on the premises or within a couple of minutes' walk; they are also served by many bus routes.

Fares. Fares on British Rail are high in comparison to many other European countries. At the same time, however, there is a wide (and often bewildering) range of reductions. Unfortunately, ticket clerks cannot always be relied upon to tell you what these are, so always ask at the information office first.

Here is a run-down on the range of reduced rate tickets:

BritRail Pass. The U.K. equivalent of the Eurailpass, the Britrail Pass is the best value, giving unlimited travel over the entire British Rail network. It is available only to overseas visitors. To obtain one, you must get a voucher in your home country at a BritRail Travel Information Office (addresses below) or from a travel agent. This is exchanged for the pass on arrival in Britain. Less expensive versions are the *Youth Pass* for young people between 16 and 26, and the *Senior Citizen Pass* for the over 60's. These passes can be bought for periods of 8, 15, 22 days and one month. The cost for the adult Gold Pass (first class) is $230, $350, $440, and $520 respectively; for the Silver Pass (standard class), $166, $249, $319, and $369. These prices are valid until the end of 1988. Compared with standard rail fares in Britain these tickets are excellent value for money. The *BritRail Pass* can be bought in some 47 countries world-wide.

Railrover. Though expensive (£135 for 7 days in standard, £225 in 1st), it gives unlimited travel over the entire network. There are also a series of regional Railrover tickets. However, only the *Freedom of Scotland* ticket covers a large area. British Rail regions publish leaflets detailing all these tickets.

Two further regional tickets are the *Scottish Highlands and Islands Travel Pass* and the *Pass Cambria.* The latter is valid for mid-Wales (an area bounded by Blaenau Ffestiniog in the north and Brecon in the south). Both give unlimited travel on all public transport, including, in Wales, the Great Little Railways (steam trains).

Cheap Day Returns. These are ideal for round-trip journeys of up to 50 miles each way (longer journeys can be made in the southeast of England), though you must come back the same day. They are valid only on the day of issue. In the London area—and on some other heavily used lines—they are not valid before 9.30 A.M. Mon. to Fri.

Saver Fares. Good for longer trips, of up to a month, or for day trips. They are not valid on some rush-hour trains (especially in the London area). On peak travel days (Fri. and summer Sat.) a higher price applies; even so, Savers are always the cheapest return ticket of their kind.

Other tickets. For some trips, there may be special offers, perhaps to special events. Ordinary 1st and standard class, single and return fares are available on all trains without restrictions.

Reservations. At peak holiday periods and on popular routes seat reservation is strongly recommended, especially for medium- and long-distance travel. On some days, such as Saturdays in mid-summer, seat reservation is obligatory on express trains to Devon and Cornwall. On other specified trains such as *The Flying Scotsman,* seating is restricted and reservations are advisable at all times. The cost of reserving a seat in 1st class is currently £2, and in standard, £1. Small groups of up to four passengers traveling together on standard tickets can reserve up to four seats for just £1.

For the Disabled. An informative booklet (price £2) giving a wide range of information on rail travel for the disabled has been published entitled *British Rail: A Guide for Disabled People.* It is available from The Royal Association for Disability and Rehabilitation (R.A.D.A.R.), 25 Mortimer St., London, W1N 8AD. British Rail offer special fare concessions for the disabled and people accompanying them—ask for the leaflet *British Rail and Disabled Travellers,* available from any British Rail office.

Rail Drive. One of the U.K.'s leading car hire companies, Hertz has self-drive cars available from Inter City stations in most important centers throughout the country. You can make a reservation before boarding the train and a car will be awaiting you on arrival, whatever the time of day or night. At busy periods, however, it is advisable to book further in advance. The vehicle can be hired from one station and returned to any other Hertz rail-drive station.

Rail Holidays. A highly successful part of B.R.'s marketing has been the *Goldstar* scheme. These offer package deals in a score of cities, towns and holiday centers, including Continental resorts (Great Little Escapes), with rail travel as part of the deal. There are many resorts and destinations to choose from. The holidays are for one night upwards, and include rail travel, or can be hotel accommodation only. Prices begin at around £160 for a week. Ask for the fully comprehensive brochure about these at any mainline station or Travel Center.

Another tour offer specifically aimed at visitors based in London who have limited time available is the *Britainshrinker* (one, two, three or six-day tours). These tours combine the best of both worlds for long distance sightseeing from the capital—fast rail travel with the flexibility of a countryside coach tour. How else could you tour Dartmoor and be back in your hotel in a day? Other places you can visit with this scheme are York, Stonehenge, Oxford and Canterbury. Meals are included, as is accommodation on the two- and three-day programs to Scotland. Prices begin at £41, with reductions for BritRail Pass holders.

The new *Great Britain Express* tour gives you six days of fast, comfortable trains for main journeys, and motor coaches for sightseeing. Hotel accommodation and meals are also included in the price. The tour begins in London, and includes trips to Stonehenge, Bath, Stratford-upon-Avon, the Lake District, Edinburgh and many other places. The tour costs £632 per adult, with discounts for BritRail Pass holders.

Further Information. British Rail have established a network of Travel Centers throughout the country based in main railway stations. These act as general information centers as well as booking offices where tickets can be bought and reservations may be made. In London they are to be found at the following termini—Kings Cross, Euston, Liverpool Street, Paddington, Waterloo, Victoria, London Bridge, Charing Cross, Cannon Street and St. Pancras. In addition the British Travel Center at 12 Regent St., S.W. 1, (only two minutes' walk from Piccadilly Circus) and the B.R. Offices at 407 Oxford St., W1; 14 Kingsgate Parade, Victoria St., SW1; 87 King William St., EC4; and at Heathrow and Gatwick Airports, can all supply information.

We strongly recommend that you use these Travel Centers for all rail travel plans. A useful book is the *ABC Rail Guide.* This is published monthly and gives the train times from London to all major centers in an easily readable form. Fares information is included as well! It will pay for itself many times over and can be bought from most bookstalls in London.

Finally, if you are nostalgic for the "Age of Steam" then, in addition to Britain's preserved steam railways (see next section), British Rail are beginning to put some of their old engines back on the track. The British Rail Travel Center at London's Euston Station (tel. 01-388 0519) will have details of the regular steam trips available, and of the excellent range of Intercity luxury land cruises.

North American Addresses. For all information on rail travel in the U.K. contact *BritRail Travel International Office,* 630 Third Ave., New York, N.Y. 10017 (tel. 212-599-5400); Cedar Maple Plaza, 2305 Cedar Springs, Dallas, TX 75201 (214-748-0860); Suite 603, 800 S. Hope St., Los Angeles, CA 90017 (213-624-8787); 94 Cumberland St., Toronto, Ontario M8V 3S4 (416-929-3333).

PRESERVED STEAM RAILWAYS. As befits the country which gave birth to railways, the United Kingdom has more preserved steam-operated railways of one type or another than any other country in the world. These range from custom-built narrow-gauge lines such as the Romney, Hythe and Dymchurch line which runs for 14 miles across the Romney Marsh in Kent, to sections of former branch railway lines now operated only by enthusiasts, such as the Severn Valley Railway which runs for about 16 miles through lovely country from Bridgnorth in Shropshire. These preserved lines exist from the Strathspey Railway at Aviemore in Scotland down to the Torbay Steam Railway in south Devon. All of them are accessible by public transport (train or bus or a combination of the two) and at each there are souvenir shops and cafés. Some operate throughout the year (but with very limited winter service, only at weekends if that) but they are all in full swing during the summer months.

Wales has no fewer than ten of these "Little Railways," some of them traveling through parts of the finest scenery in the principality. The Wales Tourist Board issues a special brochure on these Welsh railways.

The British Tourist Authority issues a colorful map guide covering most of these preserved railways in England and Wales. It also gives details of the various team centers where the engines and rolling stock can be visited. Called *Steam in Britain* the map guide is issued free of charge to all overseas visitors through B.T.A. and other offices.

In addition to these preserved railways British Rail permits a limited number of steam-hauled enthusiast specials to run on designated stretches of their track. There are now several routes "open for steam." British Rail sponsors some steam specials of its own which operate midweek during the summer. These are usually based on "Steamtown" at Carnforth near the Lake District and the National Railway Museum at York where working mainline locomotives are housed. In summer regular trains are steam hauled along the beautiful West Highland Line from Fort William to Mallaig in Scotland.

Other routes see steam hauled specials on occasion. For details of the services which operate on the preserved railways a useful guidebook is *Railways Restored,* published annually by Ian Allan Ltd., Shepperton, Surrey. For the British Rail steam specials advance booking is not essential.

STANDARD GAUGE

Bluebell Railway. Runs from Sheffield Park, Sussex, to Horsted Keynes, a distance of 5 miles. Diverse collection of locomotives and rolling stock and presents the Edwardian branch line scene. Works daily in summer, Wed., Sat., and Sun., in spring and autumn.

Severn Valley Railway. Probably the finest preserved railway, running for 16 miles through delightful countryside between the historic towns of Bridgnorth and Kidderminster, where a connection is now made with British Rail from Birmingham New Street. The route is a "slice of Britain," and if the timetable permits leave the train at one of the immaculately restored intermediate stations and have a look around. There are plenty of welcoming pubs and sylvan riverside walks. The railway has a superb collection of G.W.R., L.M.S. and B.R. locomotives and rolling stock. Operates daily from early June to the beginning of September. Ideal for a day out from London.

Great Central Railway. A 5½-mile stretch of the former Great Central Railway mainline track from Loughborough to Rothley in Leicestershire, and should extend this year to Birstall on the outskirts of Leicester. The line is famed for its *Wine and Dine* specials.

Mid-Hants Railway. "The Watercress Line"—its local name coming from the fact that watercress was one of the main products carried on the trains—runs from the delightful village of New Alresford, near Winchester, (which is well worth exploring) to Alton via Medstead and Four Marks. Connection with British Rail services from London (Waterloo) is made at Alton. This makes it a very easy, as well as different, day out from London. Runs daily from June through September; otherwise weekends only.

Keighley & Worth Valley Railway. With its headquarters at Haworth, this very popular line—used for the filming of *The Railway Children*—runs from the satanic mills of Keighley to the Brontë village of Haworth and its terminus close to the moors at Oxenhope. A trip on the line is an essential part of any visit to this area, with its elegantly restored stations and Victorian impressions. Runs daily through July and August.

STEAM CENTERS

These are depots where collections of the large mainline steam engines are restored and kept between mainline railtours. Those listed are all based in former steam engine sheds or locomotive depots.

Didcot Railway Center operated by the Great Western Society. Here you can see, in the authentic setting of the carefully restored locomotive depot, the finest collection of engines and carriages built by the Great Western Railway. The newest exhibit is the broad gauge railway area complete with one of Brunel's broad gauge trains and a replica of the famous locomotive the "Iron Duke."

Steamtown Carnforth. Situated on the mainline from London to Glasgow the museum is contained in the former British Railways depot. Based here are the engines for working the mainline steam tours mentioned earlier. The collection includes many famous locomotives—the Flying Scotsman, Sir Nigel Gresley and Lord Nelson—as well as several from Europe.

GETTING AROUND BRITAIN BY BUS. American visitors planning to travel round Britain by bus will encounter a problem of terminology between buses and coaches. Buses in Britain (either double or single decker) generally form part of local public tranport systems and are used in towns and cities and in their immediate vicinity; they stop frequently. Coaches, on the other hand, are more like Greyhounds; that is, they are more comfortable than buses and are used on longer trips. They are quite separate from local public transport and often use completely different departure points.

Coach Travel. For the visitor it is best to stick to the coach services operated by National Express. They have by far the largest number of routes of any coach operator in Britain. Fares are considerably cheaper than train travel. For example, National Express charge £24 peak, £20 off peak round-trip for the London–Plymouth trip; British Rail's least expensive Saver fare for the same trip is £32 off peak, £42 peak (1988 figures). At the same time, however, coach travel is significantly slower than train travel, though journey times on the major routes have lately been considerably reduced—but highway congestion is now causing many and often unpredictable delays. Coach travel has also become very much more comfortable in recent years, not leastasit has grown as a real alternative to train travel. On their principal routes, National Express now operate a Rapide service. On Rapide services, coaches have individual seat ventilation, hostesses serve sandwiches and drinks (non-alcoholic), there are toilet facilities (a new and welcome development) and videos showing movies.

For those wishing to see something of the British countryside rather than simply dash from A to B, the less important coach routes are the most interesting. Express Services tend to stick to motorways; fast but boring. So if time is on your side, make use of some of the cross country services which connect the smaller towns. A good number of the runs take you at a sedate pace through some of the most charming countryside in England. Many of these services also connect towns not otherwise served by railways. But seats are limited so booking is essential.

During the summer National Express run daily *Tourist Trail* buses linking 33 tourist destinations. Three interchangeable services allow flexibility with itineraries. While separate fares between each point can be purchased, the best value is a *Tourist Trail* ticket allowing unlimited travel on the three routes for 4, 8, 15 or 30 days; price range £39–£199 with reductions of a third for children up to 16.

Tickets. National Express also issues a discount ticket, the Brit Express Card, for overseas visitors, which covers all the National Express and Scottish City-link services. It is available in the States from *Worldwide Marketing,* 7136 W. Grand Ave., Chicago, IL 60635 (800–621–3405), or *The Kemwell Group,* 106 Calvert St., Harrison, N.Y. 10528 (800–678–0678), or, possibly, your travel agent—cost $10. The card gives a one-third discount on all U.K. bus travel in any one-month period. Tickets can be purchased from many travel agents as well as National Express coach stations. For further information contact the Coach Travel Center, 13 Regent Street, London S.W.1 (tel. 01–730 0202 or 01–925 0188). Brit Express cards are issued free to overseas holders of *Tourist Trail* tickets.

Finally, always call in at local tourist information offices in the town where you are staying and enquire about day or half day excursions by coach to nearby places of interest; stately homes, castles, gardens, etc. There are many small coach operators—too many to list here—who offer excellent days out at low prices. Keep your eyes open!

Bus Travel. Buses are basically divided into two types. First, there are the city and town buses. For details regarding the routes and the frequency of services enquire at the local tourist information office where map and timetables can be purchased. Secondly there are the longer distance bus services, which tend to serve the outer areas of towns and cities beyond the radius of the local bus services. For information on these services it is best to enquire at or write to the local tourist information office in the area concerned.

Many bus companies also run a wide range of organized day excursions from central points as well as offering *Explorer* round trip tickets on ordinary bus services. They also sell local runabout/rover tickets for unlimited day travel. For these it is necessary to enquire at the local bus station.

GETTING AROUND BRITAIN BY INLAND WATERWAY. There are around 3,000 miles of navigable inland waterways in the United Kingdom—rivers, lakes, canals, lochs and loughs—all available for leisure travel. Although there are no scheduled water-borne services there are hundreds of yachts, narrow boats (used on the canals) and motor cruisers available for hire throughout much of the year. A popular area for this type of holiday is the Norfolk Broads in East Anglia, a network of rivers, lakes, canals and lagoons. Also the Rivers Thames, Ouse, Trent and Severn are popular for this type of holiday as are all the canals.

For general information on these get in touch with the *Inland Waterways Association,* 114 Regents Park Rd., London NW1 8UQ (tel. 01–586 2510).

In addition you can now cruise the beautiful sea lochs and canals of Scotland in an original coal-fired Clyde Puffer. Details from: *Vic 32,* Crinan, Lockgilphead, Argyll. Also if you are in Scotland during the summer months, look out for the paddle-steamer *Waverley.* A cruise on her around Bute or Arran is a never-to-be-forgotten experience. Details: Waverley Steam Navigation, Anderston Quay, Glasgow (tel. 041–221–8152).

The British Tourist Authority publish a special brochure called *U.K. Waterway Holidays* on this type of vacation and there are several other guides.

There are numerous companies offering this type of holiday but the two leading ones are *Hoseasons,* Sunway House, Lowestoft, Suffolk NR32 3LT, and *Blakes,* Wroxham, Norwich NR12 8DH. Although they specialize in the Norfolk Broads and adjacent waterways they also act as agents for companies with boats on various rivers and canals all over the country. Another firm with many offers for boating vacations is *Boat Enquiries Ltd.,* 43 Botley Rd., Oxford OX2 0PT. In the U.S. contact *Floating Through Europe,* 271 Madison Ave., New York, N.Y. 10016 (tel. 212–685–5600 or 800–221–3140), for gourmet cruising on luxury hotel barges; cruises vary in length from a few days to two weeks.

GETTING AROUND BRITAIN BY AIR. For a comparatively small country the U.K. does have an extensive network of internal air routes operated by about a dozen airlines with British Airways, maintaining several of the main trunk routes. These include the Shuttle Services between London and Glasgow, Edinburgh, Belfast and Manchester. These are either hourly or every two hours, seven days a week. They are on a no reservations basis. Turn up and walk on with a guaranteed seat and back-up flights. Passengers can book in up to about half-an-hour before flight departure times.

This is a period of great turmoil in the British aviation scene as some of the routes formerly operated by *British Caledonian* have been reallocated so check with your travel agent for up to the minute details of who flies where. *British Midland* go to Teesside, Belfast, Liverpool and the Isle of Man from London (mainly Heathrow), while *Dan Air* fly from Gatwick to Newcastle and Aberdeen, and from Heathrow to Inverness.

Air UK have an extensive system of internal routes having taken over many formerly operated by British Airways. These go to places like Leeds-Bradford, Southampton, Birmingham and Norwich.

In Scotland *Loganair* fly to and within the Hebrides, the Orkney and Shetland islands and seasonal services to a number of other destinations. Likewise *Air Ecosse* operate several routes from Aberdeen.

In the south west of England *Brymon Airways* fly to and from Plymouth and Exeter and to the Scilly Isles, which also has a helicopter service run by British Airways. The Channel Islands and the Isle of Man are served especially in summer by air routes from up to twenty cities and towns on the mainland.

Do not, however, expect the internal air services of Britain to be as commercially competitive as those of the U.S. It is often much cheaper, and not very much more time-consuming, to take a train. Remember that the distances are not very great and if you add the time it will take you to get to and from airports, air travel is only minimally time-effective.

Leaving Britain

CUSTOMS GOING HOME. If you propose to take on your holiday any *foreign-made* articles, such as cameras, binoculars, expensive timepieces and the like, it is wise to put with your travel documents the receipt from the retailer or some other evidence that the item was bought in your home country. If you bought the article on a previous holiday abroad and have already paid duty on it, carry with you the receipt for this. Otherwise, on returning home, you may be charged duty again.

U.S. residents may bring in $400 worth of foreign merchandise as gifts or for personal use without having to pay duty, provided they have been out of the country more than 48 hours and provided they have not claimed a similar exemption within the previous 30 days. Every member of a family is entitled to the same exemption, regardless of age, and the exemptions can be pooled.

The $400 figure is based on the fair retail value of the goods in the country where acquired. Included for travelers over the age of 21 are one liter of alcohol, 100 cigars (non-Cuban) and 200 cigarettes. Any amount in excess of those limits will be taxed at the port of entry, and may additionally be taxed in the traveler's home state. Only one bottle of perfume trademarked in the U.S. may be brought in. However, there is no duty on antiques or art over 100 years old—though you may be called upon to provide verification of the item's age. Write U.S. Customs Service, Washington D.C. 20229 for information regarding importation of automobiles and/or motorcycles. You may not bring home meats, fruits, plants, soil or other agricultural items.

Gifts valued at under $50 may be mailed to friends or relatives at home, but not more than one per day (of receipt) to any one addressee. These gifts must not include perfumes costing more than $5, tobacco or liquor.

If you are traveling with such foreign made articles as cameras, watches or binoculars that were purchased at home, it is best either to carry the receipt for them with you or to register them with U.S. Customs prior to departing. This will save much time (and potentially aggravation) upon your return.

Canada. In addition to personal effects, and over and above the regular $300 per year exemption, the following may be brought into Canada duty free: 40 ounces of alcohol, 50 cigars, 200 cigarettes, and 2 lbs of manufactured tobacco. For personal gifts the rules are the same as for the U.S.—"unsolicited Gift (Nature of Gift), Value Under $40." For details ask for the Canada Customs brochure *I Declare*.

DUTY FREE is not what it once was. You may not be paying tax on your bottle of whiskey or perfume, but you are certainly contributing to somebody's profits. Duty free shops are big business these days and mark ups are often around 100 to 200%. So don't be seduced by the idea that because it's duty free it's a bargain. Very often prices are not much different from your local discount store and in the case of perfume or jewelry, they can be even higher.

As a general rule of thumb, duty free stores on the ground offer better value than buying in the air. Also, if you buy duty free goods on a plane, remember that the range is likely to be limited and that if you are paying in a currency different from that of the airline, their rate of exchange often bears only a passing resemblance to the official one.

THE
BRITISH
SCENE

INTRODUCING BRITAIN

A Free Kind of Place

The British are "different," and proud of it. They still have odd customs, like driving on the left and playing cricket. Only reluctantly have they decimalized, turning their cherished pints into liters and inches into centimeters (but they stick to miles: no kilometers, yet). Until 1971 they still had a bizarre three-tier non-decimal coinage, whereby a meal check might add up, say, to four pounds six shillings and sevenpence halfpenny (today that would translate as £4.33p).

These are all symptoms of the psychological gulf still existing between Britain and the rest of Europe, a gulf that has not been greatly narrowed by her membership of the EEC since 1973. The English Channel, those 22 miles of water between Dover and Calais, has played a crucial role in British history, acting as a kind of moat to protect the "island fortress" from invaders (witness 1940), and also perpetuating a separate mentality. Most Britons want to keep that moat: hence their wariness—more emotional than economic—of plans to build a Channel Tunnel. Even today, few of them really feel "Europeans": that oft-quoted old headline, "Fog in Channel, Continent isolated," still retains some validity. And yet, this proud and insular nation is not unwelcoming to visitors. On its own terms, it is glad to show them the delights and virtues of an unusually free and tolerant society, one of the most genuinely civilized in the world.

There is still some truth in the popular foreign perception that the British are inherently reserved. They are less talkative than Latins, and given to understatement—"It's not bad," is the nearest a Briton may get to showing enthusiasm. The British may look a little solemn and stiff-upper-lipped, for they do not readily exteriorize their joy, as some other peoples do. Yet they are not on the whole unhappy, even in today's anxious times. In fact a recent international Gallup survey, for what it is worth, showed that far more people in Britain than in neighboring countries considered themselves as leading happy lives. The British are easygoing, tolerant of nonconformism and eccentricity, and their strong sense of humor and love of the absurd keeps them from excessive loss of temper. They have a strange habit of poking fun good-humoredly at what they love, without meaning disrespect, not least at royalty and religion. This kind of humor often disconcerts foreigners. It has to be explained that British institutions—such as the monarchy—are so strong and stable that the British can afford to ridicule them in fun without endangering them.

Landscape with Figures

It is a densely populated land. Scotland and Wales have wide open spaces but in England people are crammed 920 to the square mile, more thickly than in any other European country save Holland. Yet it is also a green and fertile land, and just because the countryside is a limited commodity, so the English tend it with a special loving care. Everywhere are trim hedgerows, tidy flower-beds, and lawns mown as smooth as billiard tables—one Oxford don, asked by an American visitor how the college lawn came to be so perfect, said casually, "Oh, it's been mown every Tuesday for the past 500 years." The English love gardens, but are also at ease in wilder nature. They love hiking over moors where the westerly gales blow, or splashing rubber-booted through streams, or birdwatching in some quiet copse. Some people, in their black or scarlet coats and riding-caps, still go fox-hunting with hounds—but others today condemn this blood-sport as cruel ("the unspeakable in full pursuit of the uneatable" as Wilde put it).

This smallish island contains great scenic variety. The Midlands and much of eastern England tend to be flat and dull. But in the watery fenlands, between Cambridge and the sea, the low horizons—broken by rows of poplars or by a distant windmill or tall church spire—have a misty poetic quality, and the sunsets and swirling clouds evoke the subtlety of a Turner skyscape. Kent, southeast of London, with its cherry and apple orchards, is known as "the garden of England"; west of here are the wooded hills of Surrey, and south-west stretches the bold, bare ridge of the South Downs, beloved of Kipling. While the east coast of Britain is mainly smooth, with long sandy beaches and an occasional chalky cliff, the west coast is far more rugged: here the Atlantic gales set the seas lashing against the rocky headlands of Cornwall and South Wales.

The spine of northern England is a line of high hills, the Pennines, where sheep graze on lonely moors, and just to the west is the beautiful mountainous Lake District, where Wordsworth lived. Scotland, to the north, is even more lovely and mountainous. Once beyond the urban belt of the lowlands, around Glasgow and Edinburgh, you enter the romantic realm of the Highlands, a sprawling, thinly-populated region where heather and gorse cover the hillsides above silent fjord-like lochs and verdant glens. Roads here are few, but they all seem to lead westwards to the Isles, blue-grey jewels in a silver Atlantic sea, with their strange Celtic names, Barra, Eigg, Benbecula, Skye . . .

Western Britain is washed by the warm waters of the Gulf Stream, and therefore its climate is mild and damp. Indeed, Britain's weather is something of a stock joke, and some foreigners imagine the whole country permanently shrouded in fog. This is not in fact true, especially as the use of smokeless fuel has now cleared the polluted mists from urban skies. Yet the weather *is* very changeable, by south European standards, with shower and shine often following each other in swift succession. At least it provides the thrill of the unexpected.

Geordies, Cockneys and Celts

The people are as varied as the landscape, coming as they do from a variety of origins, Celtic, Viking, Saxon, Norman, not to mention later immigrations. Modern mobility, and the drift towards the warmer and wealthier South, has tended to mix them up, so that today the London area teems, for instance, with Scots and Tynesiders. Yet regional differences remain distinct, and local loyalties are fierce, even parochial. A London politician newly settled in north Yorkshire was warned by his constituents, "Take no notice o' folk t'oother side o' water!" He feared, as well he might, that this was some anti-EEC or anti-American hostility—but then he found they were referring to the people just ten miles away across the river Tees, in County Durham.

Lancashire and Yorkshire folk retain their old rivalry, if less violently than in the days of the 15th-century Wars of the Roses. Yorkshiremen are sturdy, bluff, self-confident, much devoted to making money ("brass," they call it), and sometimes regarded as a bit *too* brash. Their Lancashire neighbors are a little more reserved and unsure, especially if they are Liverpudlians (locally known as "Scouses"), that is, denizens of the once-rich but now down-at-heel seaport city of Liverpool. To the north-east, the "Geordies" of the Tyneside conurbation, around Newcastle, also retain a curious mixture of inturned local pride and chip-on-the-shoulder bitterness at the decline of their once-mighty industrial homeland: here recession hit deepest in the 1930s (remember the Jarrow hunger march?) and is biting again today. They also retain one of the few surviving genuine British dialects—not simply a marked regional accent but a whole vocabulary. For a Geordie living in the South, returning to Newcastle is really "ganning hyem." Further south are the "Brummies" from the area around Birmingham, known as the Black Country since the early days of the Industrial Revolution. They, too, are proud of their roots: their flat Midlands accent would have been familiar to the young William Shakespeare in Stratford-upon-Avon. Today, a Warwickshire farmer may still call his cattle "beasts" and send them to drink from the "brook."

The western part of the British Isles is the Celtic fringe, whither the Celts withdrew after the Saxon invasions of the Dark Ages. This includes Ireland (not part of this book) and Cornwall, Wales and Scotland. Each region has its own fierce identity. The Cornish are too few in number (380,000) to nourish dreams of secession: but their place-names and surnames, often beginning with "Tre," "Pol" or "Pen," bear witness to their own special origins. They are a tough seafaring people, not unlike their Breton cousins across the Channel.

Wales, though now administratively joined to England, regards itself as a "nation," and in many country areas the Welsh language is still the vehicle of daily speech. The stocky Welsh are true Celts, at once passionate and humorous, devotees of choir-singing and rugby football, their private lives a quaint mélange of low-church piety and Dylan Thomas-style lechery.

Nationalism is still a force in parts of Wales, though on the wane. It remains stronger in Scotland, though here too it is in decline. Yet Scotland is a true nation, with its own Church, its own legal and educational systems. When you cross the border from England, you are at once aware of arriving in another country, and are almost surprised not to have passed through customs or passport controls. The people speak with a delightful lilting accent, and they wear their Scottishness with pride—the biggest insult you can pay a Scot is to speak loosely of "England" or "the English" when you mean Britain and the British.

Economically and socially Scotland did relatively well in the recession years of the early '80s. The reason was not simply the discovery of major oil reserves in the North Sea—although in the '70s this transformed Aberdeen into Britain's leading boom-town, with restaurant prices and property values to match. More fundamentally, the Scots found themselves able to pull together in adversity. While English cities like Birmingham, Liverpool and even Bristol witnessed outbreaks of social unrest, the Scots tried to grapple with high unemployment and innercity decline. The urban renewal projects in Glasgow, Edinburgh and Dundee put most of those south of the border to shame; and, while steel, coal and shipbuilding declined, the Scots busied themselves learning how to serve new masters—micro-electronics, petrochemicals and tourism. It is with considerable pride that they have adopted an American journalist's tag of "Silicon Glen" for the emerging high-technology heartland between Fife and the Clyde estuary.

Culturally too, the last decade has seen the Scots coming to the fore in a number of fields. Scottish actors (mainly through mastery of comedy) have achieved prominence, not just on stages north and south of the border but also on television and in a series of slightly quirky Scottish-produced movies, best typified by Bill Forsyth's *Local Hero*.

England—North and South

In England itself, North and South are two distinct cultures. The North bore the brunt of the early industrial revolution and still wears its scars. Here are grimy, unlovely cities that grew up hurriedly in the 19th century to serve the new industries—the potteries of Staffordshire, the Lancashire mill-towns, the mining and metalwork centers of Yorkshire and the North-East. And today, with these industries in decline, the towns carry the marks of decay.

These have not been merely physical. Talk of a "lost generation" is perhaps too severe: but many young people from the North have learned the hard way that "the mill" and "the pit" no longer offer the economic and social certainties that they offered their parents and grandparents.

Like the Scots, some northerners have displayed their gritty determination in holding communities together while waiting for new industries to arrive and fill the gaps left by the decline of the old. Sheffield has lost most of its steelworks, yet retains a unique sense of identity; Stoke-on-Trent has created a park-like industrial zone from the wasteheaps of its potteries; and Manchester has managed to stage an innercity renaissance by restoring some fine examples of its Victorian architectural heritage. Other towns have been less able to cope: the industrial disruptions have been too great, the shifts of jobs and population too sudden, and the early attempts to stem the decline in the '60s (with ill-sited factories and badly designed housing projects) have simply made matters worse. Nowhere is this cycle of decline more apparent than in the once-great port city of Liverpool.

The contrast with the South of England could not be more striking. Over the past 30 years, the South has been steadily accumulating both capital and labor—the two essentials for rapid economic growth. Towns like Swindon, Guildford and Colchester know little of the unemployment or the social problems of the industrial North. By playing host to a mixture of light (mainly advanced-technology) industry and (mainly financial) services, they offer new, clean, attractive and above all steady jobs at a time when the North and Midlands offer old-fashioned heavy industrial work (to the lucky few)—or the prospect of life on the dole.

Quietly, Britain's productive center of gravity is shifting: away from its traditional Birmingham–Newcastle axis—the cradle of the world's first Industrial Revolution—toward the lusher pastures of the "Western Corridor" between Thames Estuary and the Bristol Channel or the "Solent Cities" of Southampton and Portsmouth. Exports, which once left through the Clyde and the Mersey, bound for North America or the far-flung Empire, today make the short hop from Dover or Harwich to the Continent of Europe.

Southeast of a line from the Severn to the Wash, a new society is emerging. True there are still hearty seafaring Hampshiremen and solid Somerset farmers—but they are getting to be as rare as "authentic Californians" or "indigenous Floridians." The South is Britain's new social melting pot, imprinting its rather bland amalgam of English cultural values on its steadily growing population. The irony in the birth of this new meritocracy is that it is the result of the free-market policies of a Conservative government, rather than the conscious egalitarianism of a Labor administration. To the traditionalist, the snob, or the committed class-warrior, the result is a parvenu, suburban espousal of all that is offensively bourgeois. To Americans and Australians—whose own societies reflect a similar process of assimilation—the result is a healthy breach in the walls of the English class system, a new-found pride in working hard and "getting ahead," and a general breath of fresh air in English society's stuffy conventions.

From either standpoint, there is little doubt that the South is not only very different from the North, but has changed faster and further in a decade than anyone could have predicted. Most people in the South now own their own homes; most have a car (and many have two); their horizons are widening beyond the confines of their own communities. For many ordinary families in the South, the winebar, the video and the annual flight to Marbella are as typical as the working-men's club, the football stadium or the trip to Blackpool are for ordinary families in the North. True, it's not a particularly distinctive "culture" as such: but it does account for England's new-found fascination with good food and wine; it has rekindled popular interest in fashion and interior design; and it has sustained the excellence of English drama and publishing at a level apparently unsustainable in a country facing "terminal decline" (to cite the critics) as recently as 1978. Above all, this model of society appears to be what a majority of England's people wants. In the affluent (many would say complacent) South, the continuing bitterness of the northerners—expressed in their humor, their sport, their poetry and their politics—seems somehow passé, like a distant echo of the Mersey Beat in a bright suburban disco.

The Great Wen

There is one great exception to this general picture of a stark North-South divide. Well to the south of the Gloucester-King's Lynn line lies London. To the casual visitor's eye, the city may appear to typify the new, southern culture. Wine bars and chic restaurants spring up daily; employment (and salaries) in the banks and brokerage houses of the City of London have soared; and (despite the impression created by the popular *EastEnders* television soap-opera) the capital is no longer populated by jovial Cockneys brought up in settled communities for generation upon generation. Nearly everyone is a newcomer. Like the rest of the South, it is a social melting pot, with its own unique lifestyle. But the world's first industrial megalopolis suffers from most of the inner-urban problems known to its sister 19th-century cities in Europe and North America.

Many of London's 6½ million citizens are poor; some shockingly so. Some have no settled homes (you can catch glimpses of them asleep under Hungerford Bridge) or around the South Bank arts complex; some have turned to narcotics for solace; and others have fallen back on petty crime. Unlike in Scotland or the more settled cities of the North (from where many young people still come in search of the bright lights) they are cut off from their roots; they have few solid social or cultural foundations—like the extended family, the church, the union, or the terrace of houses where they live—to fall back on. The capital's underprivileged must rub shoulders with Britain's most affluent élite, day in day out, with little more than an overburdened welfare system and overstretched police force to prevent friction. The fact that the creaking social edifice has held together so well—in spite of the odd flare-up—is more of a tribute to the basic tolerance and "let's get on with it" attitude of the Londoners, both rich and poor, than it is to the massed ranks of bureaucrats, social workers and law enforcers who grapple with the city's problems for a living.

For all this, the capital is a city that works—it is neither an ossified showcase nor a crime-ridden ghetto. You'll still find phones that ring; Underground trains that are safe and comfortable to ride; policemen that still give friendly directions to hapless visitors; and shops that won't attempt to relieve you of your last cent. Above all, if you can find a ticket that hasn't been avidly snapped up by your fellow visitors, London offers the visitor the very best of Britain's theater, art and music.

Meat for the Culture Vultures

Britain today is a land where the arts flourish. It is true that the artist, writer or philosopher is not held in the same public esteem as, say, in France, for the average Briton affects a certain philistinism, and "intellectual" and "arty" can even be terms of reproach. And yet, in practice, sales of books and of theater and concert tickets are amazingly high. Helped along by the world-wide spread of the English language, the British publishing industry produces around 50,000 new titles a year—perhaps *too* many for profitability. A passion for classical music developed during the last war and has continued ever since, so that even the smallest town has its choral society performing Bach or Handel and its season of concerts by visiting artists. The London theater is regarded by many as the best in the world, alike for its standards of production and acting and for its new writing; and this richness is reflected in the provinces where hundreds of theaters, some of them small fringe groups in makeshift premises, attract ready audiences.

The British cinema saw a golden age in the 1950s and '60s, first with the Ealing comedies, then with "new wave" realist dramas of provincial life; after this it declined, as much of the best talent drifted into television, but it has recently made a modest come-back with such films as *Chariots of Fire* and *Gandhi*. Above all, British television is unquestionably the best in the world. The BBC, a peculiarly British institution, is publicly-owned yet autonomous: thus it is neither under direct State pressures, like TV in France, nor under commercial domination like the American networks. This helps it to keep up a high standard of serious and provocative programs—including some satirical ones where even the Royal Family are lampooned.

Culture thrives also in a more classical mold—for example, through the Royal Shakespeare Company with its base in the bard's home town of Stratford-upon-Avon. Shakespeare is just one of many leading British writers and other creative artists who are closely associated with some particular place, in a land where literature and the other arts have always been nourished by strong local roots, by some *genius loci*. A tour round Britain can thus become a series of cultural pilgrimages—to Dorset that inspired the novels of Thomas Hardy, to the wild Yorkshire moors where the Brontë sisters lived and wrote, to Wordsworth's beloved Lake District, to the Scottish Border landscapes that pervade the novels of Walter Scott, to Arnold Bennett's Five (pottery) Towns, to Laugharne on the South Wales coast that Dylan Thomas' *Under Milk Wood* has immortalized, to Dickensian London, to John Betjeman's mid-Surrey with its echoing ping and pang of tennis-balls, and not forgetting the Constable country on the Suffolk/Essex border, or nearby Aldeburgh where composer Benjamin Britten lived.

History in Brick and Stone

These personalities belong to British history—a long history that Britons tend to take for granted, though it lies deep in their psyche.

Its memorials are on every side.

It began in times long before Christ, when the Druids held their rites at Stonehenge on the Wiltshire downs. Then came the Romans, who have left their imprint across the land up to Hadrian's Wall in the far north. Great feudal castles survive as reminders of the dark days when barons and kings were in constant conflict, while stately red-brick Elizabethan manors bear witness to the more settled and civilized age of Good Queen Bess.

Britain is rich in picturesque old towns and villages, dating from medieval or Elizabethan days, or later, and many have streets lined with quaint half-timbered houses, where black beams criss-cross the white plasterwork. In many areas, buildings are in local stone—most strikingly in the mellow golden-brown Cotswold villages—and often a simple cottage is topped with a neat thatched roof. Above all, British architecture is famed for its 50 or so cathedrals, dating mostly from the Middle-Ages—Wells, Ely and Durham among the finest. Local churches, too, are often of great beauty, especially in East Anglia where the wealth of the 15th century wool trade led to the building of majestic churches on the edge of quite modest villages. Today the influence of the Church of England may not be what it was, and only a minority of people attend services on Sundays: yet in many a village the parish church remains a major focus of local life.

Pub Talk and Folk Dancing

Despite the inrush of modernism, the British are keeping up many of their special traditions. On a village green in summer, you may see a cricket match in progress between two white-clad teams—it is a slow and stately game that may seem boring to the uninitiated, yet is full of its own skills and subtleties. In village pubs, people frequently play darts, or maybe backgammon, checkers or chess. The English pub, that venerable institution, is today as popular as ever—especially with younger people—and it comes in many varieties. With some exceptions, pubs in towns tend to be dull, and many have been modernized in dubious taste, with too much chrome, plush and plastic. But the country pub is often a real joy. Maybe it will bear a quaint name such as *The Dog and Whistle,* and very possibly it will have old beams and inglenooks, and a blazing log-fire in winter. If you sit at a table in the corner, you can have privacy, of a sort; but between those who prop up the bar, conversation is general, no introductions are needed, and new acquaintances are quickly made.

The British are as keen as ever on their hobbies, which can take bizarre forms—for indeed the British are a nation of amiable eccentrics. Some people indulge in the more obvious pastimes such as collecting stamps or butterflies, or making model aeroplanes (almost as popular with adults as with children); but others might collect bottletops, or brew their own beer, or spend their time memorizing cricket statistics or other useless information. The British are still great gardeners, and many a small town or village has its annual competition for growing the finest dahlias or the largest leeks or marrows. Hundreds of clubs are devoted to pigeon-fancying or to keeping budgerigars. The annual cat and dog shows in London draw huge crowds, for the British are great lovers of animals—they often prefer them to humans, for they cannot answer back and disturb the British love of privacy and reserve. Finally, like many other Western peoples, the British today are reviving their folk-traditions, in a bid to resist the pressures of commercial pop culture. Here it is the young who are setting the lead. Many of them form clubs for folk-singing or folk-dancing. In village streets you can sometimes see groups of Morris-dancers—men in funny hats with jingling bells on their ankles, waving handkerchiefs and beating sticks together.

Many Strains

Once when I told a Frenchman that Britain today was a cosmopolitan, multi-racial society, he said in some surprise, "Ah, but I thought you were *une race pure!*" Fortunately, we are not. Multi-racialism may bring hazards, yet it has also done much to reinvigorate Britain and make it a more varied and fascinating place. The cosmopolitanism takes many forms—and one is purely touristic. The number of annual visitors to Britain has risen sharply in the past 20 years and today stands at over 13.5 million. A tourist may find some things in Britain that irritate him, such as the absurdly high prices of hotel rooms, and the rip-offs that can trap the unwary in London streets. But foreigners are rarely disappointed by the welcome from individual Britons, who will usually go out of their way to be helpful.

The millions of foreigners who have come to live in Britain have had a generally positive influence. They have widened the horizons of an insular—in every sense of the word—people. They have even helped to civilize the British in such matters as cuisine: whereas until the '50s almost all restaurants served just dull British fare, today even in the smallest provincial town you will find Indians, Chinese, Greeks, Italians, French and others, all serving their national dishes—and very popular they are too.

The same can't always be said of the immigrants themselves, especially those from what is euphemistically dubbed the "New Commonwealth"—meaning the Asians and Afro-Caribbeans brought into Britain in the '50s and '60s to provide essential services and fill a chronic labor shortage. Most middle-class British people will profess themselves broadmindedly multiracial of course, but their day-to-day attitudes still suggest—in strong contrast to post-Civil Rights America—that their commitment to a truly un-color-conscious society is only skindeep (if that). The debate over assimilation—to what extent the immigrant communities should be asked to surrender their own collective identities—still rages: should schools in Bradford, where a majority of pupils are Moslems, base their moral precepts on the Koran rather than the Bible; and should the history of the Caribbean islands be taught to young blacks in South London as being "their culture," for example?

The British are clearly torn between their traditions of tolerance on the one hand and their quest for fair play and equality before the law on the other: should Sikhs be compelled to wear motorbike crash helmets—like everyone else—and remove their turbans in defiance of their religion? (The courts decided that road safety laws should take second place to religious devotion.) And what about Jewish and Islamic slaughtering of animals; is this compatible with animal cruelty legislation (that great touchstone of Britishness)? The jury's still out on that question. The potential for real conflict is obvious and, in fact, questions such as these usually lie behind the race riots that are sparked off from time to time. Until a clear line is drawn—either rigorous assimilation, which implies full acceptance of black Britons, or multiculturalism which implies a new respect for alien cultures taking root in their towns and cities—the British will be constantly wrong-footed, embarrassed and occasionally very frightened by the newcomers in their midst.

The Old Order Changeth

Making a decision on what sort of relationship to promote between the immigrant and indigenous communities isn't the only important issue facing Britain's political leaders as the society gets ready to enter the '90s. The whole question of the balance of rights and duties between the state (and other expressions of man's collective identity) and the individual still needs to be sorted out.

In the 1970s, the main threat to individual liberty appeared to come from Britain's over-mighty labor unions, but by the latter half of the 1980s, strikes—long considered the "British disease"—had dropped in frequency to a level not seen since the '30s. This in turn has led to a remarkable revival in industrial confidence and contributed to the return of profits—both at a low ebb in the '70s. What is more, the whole concept of enterprise seems to have come back into fashion. The withdrawal of the state from the business of owning and attempting to run large parts of British industry (a process awkwardly dubbed "privatization"), allied to the rise in the number of private stockholders and small businesses willing to "have a go" all suggest that the tide is turning away from large, unresponsive "collective" solutions toward greater reliance on individual adaptability and risk-taking. Thus far, the results—in terms of falling unemployment rolls—have been patchy; but there's hope that the '90s will see free markets and daring British entrepreneurs delivering the goods—and the jobs—as they did in the last century.

A more disturbing threat to liberty may well have arisen in the '80s, however: the State itself. The fact that Britain has no written constitution, no bill of rights and no entrenched legislation protecting the individual that may not be overturned by a simple majority vote in Parliament might have seemed, until recently at least, yet another pleasant quirk—and probably entirely superfluous—in what is undoubtedly a very tolerant and liberally minded country. Not only do the British carry no government identity cards, their drivers' licenses bear no photographs, preventing the surreptitious importation of identity checks *à l'américaine.* There are no laws prescribing what names parents may bestow on their children (as in France and Spain) and there are no restrictions on the number of occasions during the year when storekeepers may put "sale" prices on their wares (as in Germany): yet citizens of these other "less liberal" countries are protected by a well developed array of constitutional safeguards of their liberty. Admittedly, all three countries, unlike Britain, have played host to decidedly illiberal regimes within the last half-century—but that's surely no cause for complacency.

The pervasiveness of secrecy within British officialdom (it's a crime for a civil servant to tell you what's on the ministry's lunch menu) leaves many citizens wondering whether their democratically expressed wishes really are being carried out by their representatives. The question of "answerability"—so well defined under the American constitution—in areas like internal security, policing and (nuclear) energy policy might well have been dismissed as irrelevant a few years ago: but in an era of spy trials, urban riots and nuclear leaks it takes on a new significance.

So is British society—torn by uncertainties and incapable of resolving key social problems—really in terminal decline and fading away like the mighty Empire itself? The answer is quite simply no. As a skeptical American observer remarked during the Falklands War, "The British can be relied upon to fall at every hurdle—except the last." When the chips are down, the British come up trumps. This can't be explained rationally; what was it that sank the Spanish Armada or defeated Goering's Luftwaffe? It certainly wasn't superior economic resources or disciplined social organization. Maybe there is more in the souls of a collection of free people united in a common purpose than generations of economists and sociologists could ever hope to understand. The British are such a collection; and their quirkiness, their social "distance," and their habit of driving on the left are inseparable parts of a greater whole. But without such a people, the world would be a poorer place.

A MINI-HISTORY

Kings and Queens and All That

The British have monarchs the way other people have mice, as Thurber might have said. It is impossible to visit the country, to tour historic houses, even to walk down the street, without coming face to face with more than a thousand years of kings and queens. In order to help you sort them out and place them in their right order, we give here a brief run down of those who have sat on the throne (before 1603 the throne of England, after that the joint throne). Even if a monarch was not very important as a ruler, he or she may have given the name to an age—Queen Anne, for example—so, getting them in perspective can be very helpful.

Reigning Monarch	Dates	Important Events
	50 B.C.	Julius Caesar arrives with expedition
	43 B.C.	Emperor Claudius invades Britain
	A.D. 410	Romans withdraw from Britain to help defend Rome
	5th cent.	Angles and Jutes arrive
	597	St. Augustine arrives at Canterbury to Christianize Britain
	9th cent.	Invasions of Vikings at peak
Various Saxons and Danes, including:		

48

Reigning Monarch	Dates	Important Events
Alfred the Great 871-901		
Athelstan 925-40		
Canute 1017-35		
Edward the Confessor 1042-66		
Harold 1066		
House of Normandy		
William I, 1066-87	1066	William of Normandy invades, defeating Harold at Battle of Hastings
William II (Rufus) 1087-1100 (probably murdered)		
Henry I 1100-35		
Stephen 1135-54		
House of Plantagenet		
Henry II 1154-89	1170	Archbishop Thomas à Becket murdered
Richard I (Lionheart) 1189-99 (killed in battle)	1189	Richard the Lionheart embarks on Third Crusade
John 1199-1216	1215	King John forced to sign Magna Carta at Runnymede
Henry III 1216-72	1265	Summoning of the first parliament
Edward I 1272-1307		
Edward II 1307-27 (murdered)	1314	Robert the Bruce routs English under Edward II at Bannockburn
Edward III 1327-77	1337	Edward III claims French throne, starting Hundred Years' War
	1348-49	The Black Death (plague) sweeps Europe, killing one-third of population
Richard II 1377-99 (deposed, then murdered)	c.1362	John Ball preaches scriptural egalitarianism
	c.1376	John Wycliffe presages Reformation with his preaching
Henry IV 1399-1413	1381	The Peasants' Revolt, defused by 14-year-old Richard II
Henry V 1413-22	1415	Henry V's victory at Agincourt
Henry VI 1422-61 (deposed)	1431	Joan of Arc burned
	1455-85	Wars of the Roses
	1460	Lancaster defeats York at Wakefield
House of York		
Edward IV 1461-83	1461	York wins with victory at Towton, biggest battle yet on English soil
Edward V 1483 (probably murdered)		
Richard III 1483-85 (killed in battle)	1485	Henry Tudor defeats Richard III at Battle of Bosworth Field

Reigning Monarch	*Dates*	*Important Events*
House of Tudor		
Henry VII		
1485-1509		
Henry VIII	1530s	Reformation and dissolution of the monasteries by Henry VIII
1509-47		
	1534	Henry VIII divorces Katherine of Aragon (mother of Mary I)
	1536	Anne Boleyn (mother of Elizabeth I) executed at Tower of London
1537		Jane Seymour dies in childbirth giving birth to Edward VI
	1540	Henry VIII marries Anne of Cleves
	1542	Katherine Howard executed in Tower
	1543	Henry VIII marries Katherine Parr, who outlives him
Edward VI		
1547-53		
Jane		
1553-54 (beheaded)		
Mary I	1554	Mary marries Philip II of Spain
1553-58		
Elizabeth I	1568	Mary, Queen of Scots, flees to England (executed 1587)
1558-1603		
	1588	Spanish Armada fails to invade
House of Stuart		
James I (James VI of	1605	Guy Fawkes tries to blow up Parliament
Scotland) 1603-25	1611	Authorized version of the Bible published
	1620	Pilgrim Fathers sail from Plymouth on the *Mayflower* and settle in New England
Charles I	1640s	Civil War between royalists and parliament
1625-49 (beheaded)		
Commonwealth		
Oliver Cromwell,		
Protector 1653-58		
Richard Cromwell		
1658-59		
House of Stuart (Restored)		
Charles II	1665	Plague sweeps London
1660-85	1666	The Great Fire of London
James II		
1685-88		
(deposed and exiled)		
William III and Mary II	1690	William defeats James II at the Battle of Boyne
(joint monarchs)		
1689-95		
Williamn III		
(reigned alone)		
1695-1702		
Anne	1706-9	Marlbrough's great victories over the French
1702-14		
	1707	Act of Union unites England and Scotland as Great Britain

Reigning Monarchs	*Dates*	*Important Events*
House of Hanover		
George I 1714-27	1721-42	Robert Walpole, Prime Minister
George II 1727-60	1745-6	Bonnie Prince Charlie lands in Scotland and tries to regain his throne, but is defeated and flees again to France
	1755-63	Seven Years' War
George III 1760-1820	1776	Americans declare their independence
	1783-1801	William Pitt, Prime Minister (and again, 1804-06)
	1805	Nelson killed at victorious Battle of Trafalgar
	1811	Prince Regent rules during his father's madness
George IV 1820-30	1815	Wellington defeats Napoleon at Waterloo
William IV 1830-37	1832	Reform Bill extends the franchise, ending rule of great landowners
House of Saxe-Coburg		
Victoria 1837-1901	1861	Prince Albert dies
	1868-86	Disraeli and Gladstone, Prime Ministers (latter also 1892-94)
	1887	Victoria proclaimed Empress of India
Edward VII 1901-10	1899-1902	Boer War
House of Windsor		
George V 1910-36	1914-18	First World War
	1926	The General Strike
Edward VIII 1936 (abdicated)		
George VI 1936-52	1939-45	Second World War; Churchill, Prime Minister (also 1951-55)
	1945	Labour Party wins election
	1947	India becomes independent, followed by nearly all of the Empire
Elizabeth II 1952	1973	Britain joins the European Economic Community
	1981	Marriage of Prince Charles and Lady Diana Spencer
	1982	Britain regains Falkland Islands
	1987	The Conservatives under Margaret Thatcher win a third term in office

HISTORIC HOUSES

Precious Stones in Peril

by
MARK LEWES

Visiting historic houses has become a national hobby in Britain and, luckily, it is one national interest which visitors to the country can share without being raised in it from birth—unlike cricket. The statistics are formidable. The total of visitors to historic buildings in general is in the millions—around 30 million.

Curiosity as to how the other half lives is undoubtedly one of the most deep-seated traits of human nature, and it's extremely comforting to be able to satisfy such a healthy desire to snoop for the payment of a very small amount of conscience money. The fact that you will see some of the greatest of the world's treasures at the same time is a happy bonus.

But even the most highly developed sense of curiosity isn't enough to explain the fact that millions of people have surged on to the Stately Home Trail. They have been urged to move by a great deal of exposure, both involuntary and intentional, on the part of the owners of historic houses themselves. Some, like Lord Montagu of Beaulieu, have brought a Madison Avenue talent for promotion to the job of selling their heritage to the public. Some, like the Earl Spencer, have found that events have conspired to help them in the task of broadcasting their household wares. Althorp, the Spencer family home—and therefore the home of the Princess of Wales—suddenly found itself very much in the news during 1981, which certainly has not hurt the gate receipts. The Mountbatten home, Broadlands, benefited similarly from the royal wedding, since the happy couple spent the first two nights of their honeymoon there and Prince Charles has taken a personal interest in helping to promote the house in memory of his favorite uncle.

Another propaganda weapon that has appeared in the stately home arsenal has been the television historical serial. Royal biopics of Henry VIII, Elizabeth I, the Prince Regent and Edward VII, have been sold around the world. Dramatizations of famous novels—*Brideshead Revisited,* for instance, was filmed at Castle Howard—created a desire on the part of viewers to visit for themselves the splendid locations they have seen on their small screens. There has been a spin-off to this "historical industry" in the touring costume displays of the clothes made for the more popular serials, which visit many of the larger historic houses in turn, coming to rest in such appropriate surroundings as Hampton Court.

The Price of a Patrimony

But why should families, many of whom have a lineage going back well over a thousand years, put themselves in the humiliating position of having droves of visitors plowing around their homes? Things were done so much more elegantly a couple of hundred years ago. Devotees of *Pride and Prejudice* will remember Elizabeth Bennet and the Gardiners visiting Pemberley during the absence of Mr. Darcy and being shown round by the housekeeper. Nor is it necessary to go back two hundred years. I had exactly the same kind of private tour myself in 1945 around Eastnor Castle, a house that is now open to the general public for a moderately small fee.

The reason for the pressing need for the owners of stately homes to throw them open is simply that they need the ready money. Spiritually rewarding as it must be to own vast tracts of countryside, paintings by Rembrandt and Gainsborough, a house designed by one of the Adam brothers and furnished by Chippendale, tapestries by the mile and porcelain by the ton—it is all a dead loss as far as cash flow is concerned. Of course the great tracts of countryside can be farmed, and many of the estates are profitably managed along those lines, but that does not really provide enough money to keep the vast pile in a proper state of repair or pay for the electric light bills or the insurance on the Rembrandts. Nor, and here the real crunch comes, does it pay for the tax which is levied by an ever-hungry State at the death of the head of the family—a tax which is ironically called Death Duty.

It is a dilemma with epic-sized horns. There are really only three ways out. One—is to open the house to the public and try to make a going concern of it as a tourist goal. Two—is to sell it lock, stock and Adam fireplace, and move into a nice manageable little apartment in Kensington or Paris. Three—is to sell small bits and pieces of the patrimony, trying all the time not to damage the basic historical entity by such piecemeal tactics.

Method One is the one that most concerns both the curious vacationers of Britain and the millions of visitors from abroad—and forms the balance of the rest of this chapter.

Method Two has had one spectacular exemplar. Warwick Castle is one of England's loveliest medieval buildings. Perched on its cliff over the River Avon, it is everyone's idea of a romantic castle. The Warwicks, a family name that has echoed throughout British history from the Middle Ages to the slightly dubious days of Edward VII, sold the castle to Madame Tussauds in 1977. It was a move that shook traditionalists to the core. But in the event, the imaginatively staged displays of wax figures, recreating a weekend house party spent by Edward VII with his mistress— Daisy, Countess of Warwick—gives the family rooms of the castle a unique interest.

Yet another famous house came on the market in 1983 when Lord Astor put Hever Castle up for grabs. The sale of the collection of armor alone created a stir, when a suit made for Henry II of France brought nearly two million pounds. It had formed part of the collection created by the ultra-romantic William Waldorf, 1st Viscount Astor, who bought Hever in 1903 and gathered together quantities of material with either real or imagined historic associations.

Method Three (which is usually run in tandem with Method One) has had an impressive exponent recently, too. Holkham Hall, in Norfolk, is one of the better examples of the Palladian style in England, designed by the architect William Kent in the mid-18th century, at the height of that style's popularity. It was the result of a collaboration between Kent and Thomas Coke, first Earl of Leicester, who had met each other in Rome. Coke was not only an inspired patron, he was also a considerable art collector, and Holkham Hall was designed to be the treasure house of a rich and talented man of taste, at a time when there were treasures in plenty available to someone with an eye for them and a deep purse.

Little by little the deaths of one Earl after another have whittled away at the contents of this Aladdin's cave. The death of the third Earl cost the family around 6,000 acres of land. In 1949 the fourth Earl died and an ever-hungry Treasury took the proceeds from about 10,000 acres and 170 rare books and manuscripts. The trustees of the estate then found themselves trying to meet the death duties due on the passing-on of the fifth Earl, and the additional possibility of the duties which would fall in jeopardy when the Dowager Countess finally died. They could either sell treasures in the market place and get the full going rate on them, or they could pass them over to a national institution such as the British Museum in lieu of part of the taxes due—but if they took that course they would have no cash left over to meet other pressing demands. They went for a combination of the two options. They passed over to the nation at least seven wonderful manuscripts for the credit figure of around £250,000, although their value on the open market would have been four times that amount. But they also decided to sell some manuscripts on the open market, among which were the Leonardo da Vinci pages known as the Leicester Codex. By mid-1981 these sheets of Leonardo's notes and drawings were on view in the west end of London under their new name—the Hammer Codex. Armand Hammer being an internationally renowned man of taste, with a very deep purse. He paid well over £2 million for the Codex.

The above Three Methods are, of course, over-simplified. There are a lot of complexities, including ever-shifting legislation to aid in the handing over of parts of an inheritance in advance of death. The whole subject of death duties is a social and political hot potato.

In Trust for the Nation

The end of the Victorian Age in Britain brought a palpable threat to the existence of open countryside. Creeping encroachment by industry and vast housing schemes were rapidly eating into land which had always been devoted to recreation and of great scenic appeal. After ten years of discussion and preparation, the idea of a National Trust came to fruition and was registered in 1895.

The function of the Trust was conceived as the preservation of places of historic interest or natural beauty in England, Wales and Northern Ireland, (Scotland has its own National Trust). Currently the Trust owns and opens to the public more than 250 buildings of architectural or historic importance, many of them with their contents—paintings, furniture, statuary, porcelain and all that has made them such treasurehouses for centuries. It also owns much of the most beautiful countryside—one acre in every hundred—including woods and moorland, lakes and hills, 1,100 farms and over 480 miles of unspoilt coastline. The Trust manages many fine gardens, Sissinghurst and Stourhead (a stunning garden which is perennially near the top of the Trust's popularity poll) among them, and some of Britain's most splendid examples of landscape; nature reserves, including islands and fens; prehistoric and Roman antiquities; lengths of canal, wind- and water-mills, bridges and other industrial monuments—even whole villages.

The term "national" does not mean that the Trust is in any way run by the government, on the contrary it is an independent charity, operated by central and regional committees. Although it is, of course, extremely wealthy in terms of property, it is property that cannot be sold or mortgaged, so finance is a perpetual problem. It currently costs in the region of £75 million a year for the Trust to function. Largely, it has to rely on membership subscriptions, although it does receive rents, legacies and outright gifts. But it has been very successful in its role as conscience to the nation—it started with 100 members in 1895 and enrolled its millionth member in 1981.

The Trust acquires its properties largely through the generosity of individuals, some have been bought after appeals to members and to the public, or have been given to the Trust by their former owners with endowments to provide for their permanent maintenance. In fact, the Trust finds it almost impossible to accept property unless it *is* accompanied by sufficient funds for its upkeep. It is rather interesting that the first historic building the Trust acquired was the 14th-century half-timbered and thatched clergy house at Alfriston in Sussex. It was bought in 1896 for £10!

Blue Blood and Bureaucracy

Apart from the National Trust, there are two main organizations which represent the Historic House scene. One is English Heritage, and the other the Historic Houses Association.

English Heritage was set up by an Act of Parliament in 1984 to transfer the historic conservation functions formerly carried out by the Government to an independent public body. It manages about 400 nationally significant properties, such as Stonehenge, Hadrian's Wall, Dover Castle, Rievaulx Abbey, and Tintagel Castle—many of the sites of English myth and legend. English Heritage also advises the Government officially on conservation legislation, and is the major source of public funds for historic buildings and towns, ancient monuments and rescue archeology. Its Chairman is Lord Montagu of Beaulieu who, we mentioned before, is one of the most successful owners of a historic family house and estate. There is an organization of American Friends of English Heritage—contact Ann Webster Smith, 3233 Klingle Rd. NW, Washington DC 20008 (202–337–0577). In Britain the contact point is Rebecca Waterhouse, PO Box 1, Bromley, Kent BR1 1LB. For £10 you can have a year's membership and free entry to all the English Heritage sites.

The Historic Houses Association is a combination pressure group and managerial caucus. Its membership, naturally, reads like *Debrett's Peerage* and *Burke's Landed Gentry* rolled into one. Its function is to try to influence the government of the day into making tax concessions and generally easing the burden of the historic house owner. At the same time it is a clearing organization for providing information to the membership on the day-to-day running of buildings open to the public, insurance, catering, legal advice, even how to draft contracts for films and television. It is possible for a member of the public to become a Friend of the Association, though there is not very much advantage in doing so.

A last mention should be made, while we are looking at organizations, of the regional Tourist Boards, which have made a special feature of producing really informative literature about the historic buildings within their areas.

Tea and Topiary Work

What you get for your entrance fee differs enormously from one house to another. The fee itself lies within a range varying from 50 pence to £3, less for children and the elderly; there is often a charge for parking your car. Once within the house you will find that the variation in the way you are treated is quite remarkable. In some stately homes you are left completely free to wander at will, soaking up the atmosphere. In some you are organized into groups which then process through the house like bands of prisoners behind enemy lines. Some—indeed most—guides are enthusiastic volunteers, brimming over with information and goodwill. Occasionally you may find that your mentor is a member of the family, who will gleefully relate stories of uncles, aunts and cousins back to the Crusades. Those are often the best, for they can give a sense of your being welcome guests.

Some houses have converted a stable or old kitchen into a small restaurant, where you can rest your aching feet and enjoy a cup of tea and a bun. Some, though sadly few, have a full-scale restaurant; usually these are in the largest houses only, such as Blenheim or Warwick Castle.

There are two things to remember when planning a historic houses tour—one is that many of them are very difficult to find and often totally ungetatable except by car; the other that nearly all of them close a full half-hour before the stated time, to allow the last parties to make their way round the house.

It is my impression that the more clearly the house's owner has understood that he is running a serious business and not merely playing at it, the simpler and more easily understood are his opening hours. Naturally, since so many of the guides and other staff employed are local volunteers, rosters are very difficult to draw up and even more difficult to keep to. But the complexity of the opening hours of some historic houses defies belief. The matter is made even worse when you realize that if there is a crisis on any particular day the house may not open at all and you will be left, after a difficult journey, standing on the doorstep. My advice is to check up in advance—*always.*

Virtually all historic houses have gardens, some incredibly lovely; some have huge parklands, cleverly landscaped and dotted with other interesting buildings. A visit to these houses is really a double event, partly to the house and partly to the grounds. You need not do both unless you want to, but you should always remember that the two have been planned as a unit, the architecture of the one complementing and being complemented by the design of the other. It is always worth asking about the layout of the grounds, and from which points the best views of the house can be obtained.

Mosaics and Moats

If you tour British stately homes—and, indeed, some not so stately— without trying to take a little history on board, you will find yourself condemned to an increasingly confusing voyage, where tapestries, ornate carvings, gilded ceilings and Greek statues will gradually swim together into a richly-colored fog. Much as I would like to settle down to a cozy five-hundred page discourse on *History and the British House,* I will have to postpone the pleasure in favor of a few brief, but hopefully useful, pointers.

There were stately homes scattered around the English landscape two thousand years ago. The Romans, like the British themselves in their empire-building mood, took their way of life with them wherever they settled. They imported the concept of "the villa" into the areas which they had more or less pacified. For them a villa was more than just a building, it was a complete farming complex with a central focus on a quite sophisticated house, equipped with all the latest modern conveniences, including central heating—which the Romans must have blessed in the temperamental northern climate. These fairly large estates were scattered mainly in the southern half of the territory over which Rome held sway, and some of them were magnificent. Remains can still be seen in a few places, notably Fishbourne in West Sussex, where there has been a shot at recreating a Roman garden *in situ,* and Lullingstone in Kent, which shows clear traces of the way a villa would have been adapted by the resident Britons after the Roman family had left. In various parts of the country mosaic pavements have been excavated which give a very good idea of how the wealthier villas must have looked inside.

The Romans left little behind them that has survived intact, and only by intelligent and resolute digging has that little been revealed. The period from the time the Romans left Britain (around A.D. 410) to the arrival of the Normans in 1066 is one of the slow emergence of the use of indigenous building materials and methods on a large scale. Wood and thatch predominated, with only a minimum use of stone (and that in such buildings as churches or royal halls). Naturally wood and thatch were perishable and so very little of these structures remains, either.

The earliest buildings that can be enjoyed today date from around the time of the Normans' arrival, or are built on a pattern that was set then and did not change for two to three centuries. The name *manor* was an import by William the Conqueror's clerks, who conducted the first great survey of the country, which we know as the Domesday Book. The manor, which became the basic unit of British country life, was very much the same as the Roman villa, a farming complex centered on a main house where the "lord of the manor" lived. This agricultural unit was peopled by tenants, both free and serf, who owed various rents and duties to the lord.

English landowners frequently preferred to live in the country on their estates rather than in the cities, and this preference fixed a pattern which became one of the chief influences on the spread of houses, great and small, throughout the land for the next seven hundred years. In other European countries, especially France, the nobility and land-owning class chose to live in the center of things, near to the warmth of royal power and favor. But in Britain the fact that they actually lived "above the shop," meant that they built their houses with care and thought for their own comfort, and designed their gardens and farmed their lands with the same consciousness that these were the elements that made up their day-to-day world. The richness of so many country houses, great and small, stems from this one central fact.

The Great Halls of both castle and manor were the medieval focal point of planning. It was only as life began to relax and the country became safer did privacy for the lord and his family grow and its effect spread downwards through the household, creating separate rooms not only for sleeping but also for carrying on the various tasks of daily life. The gradual change can be seen in Cotehele, near Calstock in Cornwall, a National Trust property, started in the 14th century but built mainly in the 15th and 16th. It is a building full of romance and atmosphere, constructed round a network of small courtyards and well worth visiting.

At first the houses and castles of the landowners were both built to be defensible, with stout stone walls and moats around them. There are a few such manor buildings left. Ightham Mote in Kent is a wonderful example. Dating from the 1300s and surrounded by a moat, it is nonetheless a very attractive house, whose severe effect is softened by the additions that were made in Tudor times. It even has some 18th-century Chinese wallpaper, just to make the bridge across the centuries complete. Naturally, some of the most striking examples of architecture left from these early days can be found in the great castles which dot the landscape. Even here the fact that they were often the main residence of great families had a definite effect on their design. The great hall of Oakham Castle, for example, in Leicestershire, has a lot of carved decoration which gives a very good idea of how rich landowners of the time—around 1180—tried to soften the massivity of their fortresses and introduce into them something of the relaxation of a home.

Monks Out, Merchants In

The 1300s and 1400s brought continuing chaos to Britain. The nobility struggled with the Throne; the Black Death raged, killing about half the population by the end of the period and eventually releasing the peasants from their serfdom; as the grip of the great feudal families weakened slowly, so the merchant class began its rise to power; imperceptibly the land relaxed, turning away from the rampant bloodshed of the great internecine Wars of the Roses and blossoming into the prosperity of thriving trade.

The stage was set for the arrival of the Tudors.

The Tudor dynasty was cunning, ruthless, sometimes flamboyant, often despotic, in theory tyrannical but in practice the most brilliantly successful series of monarchs England ever had. Under their successive reigns the country was turned from a backward island, concerned only with its petty politics, to being one of the great powers of Europe and, finally, a greater empire builder than Rome.

Their regime was begun by Henry VII, who ruled like an accountant of genius, consolidating the peace he had so hardly won, promoting discovery abroad and trade at home. In him the self-seeking nobility finally found their match.

With the Tudors at the helm, English architecture finally broke away from the influences of France—which had been imported by the Normans and continued by their successors—and settled down to a style entirely native to these islands, firstly with a kind of Tudor Gothic, then with a style which echoed Italy—Elizabethan Italianate. The land began to relax during the reign of Henry VII, so very few castles were built; of those few, Hever was one, the childhood home of Anne Boleyn. The style of this first Tudor King can best be seen in his magnificent Lady Chapel in Westminster Abbey. With the accession of his son, Henry VIII, building took off like a rocket. Easily the most accessible to the visitor is Hampton Court, started by Cardinal Wolsey who was bullied into giving his overly-ostentatious palace to his domineering master. The plan is still medieval, as were the plans of many houses built under the first two Tudors, but the spirit was already very different. You only have to look up at the exotically twisting brick chimneys to see the new feelings at work.

The single major act of Henry VIII's reign which was to change the face of England and create a totally new climate for the building of country houses, was the Dissolution of the Monasteries. Not only did the dispossession of thousands of monks and nuns from their centuries-held homes speed the release of England from the domination of Rome, it also threw vast tracts of land onto the market and turned abbeys and priories into private houses. Among them are Lord Byron's home, Newstead Abbey in Nottinghamshire; Lacock Abbey in Wiltshire; Longleat, once an Augustinian priory, also in Wiltshire, rebuilt in 1567 after a serious fire, and so now a marvelous example of Tudor design—all these the direct result of the Dissolution. It also gave the newly monied class, merchants who were favored by the crown, a chance to obtain land and status to go with the titles that grateful monarchs were showering on them. Begun by the two Henrys, this policy of creating a new aristocracy based on wealth and intelligence to counteract the old aristocracy based on birth was greatly extended by Elizabeth, the most influential of whose ministers were just such men.

Montacute House in Somerset is one of the masterpieces of Elizabethan architecture, and was built in 1598 by Sir Edward Phelps with money made out of his law practice. It is now owned by the National Trust, and has doubled its interest as a place to be visited since the National Portrait

Gallery lent a fine series of Elizabethan and Jacobean portraits for display in its perfectly-suited rooms.

Phelps was one of the "new men" who were able to invest their fortunes in stone and brick. These rising magnates built in the effervescent style coming into fashion, and their houses positively dance with extravagance and over-decoration. But one of the most famous builders of the age was not a "new man" but a "new woman," Bess of Hardwick, who rose from being the humble daughter of a yeoman farmer to become Countess of Shrewsbury. Her monument is Hardwick Hall (1590) in Derbyshire, which called forth the rhyme "Hardwick Hall, more glass than wall," for it is a miracle of lightness and grace, embodying many daring design ideas that must have astonished her contemporaries. Of all the National Trust properties, this is definitely one not to miss.

Two other great houses in which Elizabethan artistry can be seen are Penshurst Place in Kent, and Knole, also in Kent. Penshurst has a Great Hall, dating from around 1340, splendid in its opulent medieval design, but it is the long gallery with a fine plasterwork ceiling that best shows the Elizabethan element in the house. Knole, once home of the Sackville family and now owned by the National Trust, is richly Tudor, its vast complex of buildings ranging from different eras of the 150 years from 1456 to 1508—with decorations and furnishings from the 17th century. It is estimated that nearly half a million pounds have been spent from public funds to preserve this house and its contents in the last twenty years, and any visitor wandering through the rooms will think it money well spent.

For a slightly earlier, and infinitely more startling, building, you should visit Cheshire to see Little Moreton Hall, part of which was built in 1539, and is surrounded by a moat and a knot garden. It is built out of black-and-white timbering which gives it the appearance of a huge geometrical construction toy. Although the house is nearly empty inside, the little furniture there is, the simple paneling and the great windows, give it a unique atmosphere.

A knot garden was laid out in formal patterns (rather like designs for knots) with little hedges and a stress on plants that were useful in medicine or cooking. Many period houses have such gardens recreated alongside, to give the correct atmosphere; there are good examples both at Hampton Court and at Stratford upon Avon.

Jacobeans

The death of Elizabeth brought about the end of the Tudors and the accession to the throne of the first Stuart, James I and VI, son of Mary, Queen of Scots. The trends which had begun under the Virgin Queen were continued under him, and Hardwick Hall became the forerunner of many great country houses in the style called Jacobean—after the Latin name for James—*Jacobus.*

Any list of country houses will contain several Jacobean masterpieces high in its ratings, and one of the greatest is Hatfield House, in Hertfordshire. The home of the great Salisbury family, the Cecils, it was built by Robert Cecil, the first Earl whose father had been one of Elizabeth's leading ministers for most of her reign. The house is a mixture of richly complex Jacobean carving, 18th-century furniture and pictures, and Victorian renovations. The third Marquess was a prominent Prime Minister three times under Victoria.

The mishmash of periods at Hatfield is very typical of the great houses you will visit during any historic tour. The possession of wealth and high office does not ensure taste, and frequently succeeding generations have lavished more money than sensitivity on their homes. This is not true of Hatfield, where there are some remarkable treasures.

Burton Agnes Hall in Humberside is a less ornate Jacobean mansion, but still very typical of its time. Built of red brick it is the work of the same architect as Hardwick Hall. It has been the home of the Boynton family ever since 1654, and the lovely paneling and carving inside is complemented by some very good modern paintings which have been collected by the present owner.

A last dip into the highly-decorated Jacobean jackpot brings forth an oddity, Bolsover Castle, in Derbyshire. This was the home of the Cavendish family and was built during the reigns of James I and his son Charles I. It is partly derelict and wholly desolate, but full of strange details, not least the huge, impressive fireplaces.

It is one of the sad facts of English history that we have so little left of the golden age created under the influence of Charles I. He was a man of great artistic taste though very poor judgment in political matters. The fine art collection which he amassed, sometimes by purchase, sometimes as the result of his direct patronage of such artists as van Dyck, was dispersed, though parts of it can still be seen in national galleries and the royal collection. Of the vast Palace of Whitehall, which contained much of his collection, now only the Banqueting Hall designed by Inigo Jones is left. Inigo Jones, who died in 1651—sometimes called the "English Palladio"—was one of the country's greatest architects, singlehandedly introducing the glories of classical design, freeing English architecture from any lingering medievalism it might have had under the Tudors, and preparing the way for a fully-fledged Italianate invasion later. He became a kind of tutelary deity to subsequent architects.

Wren and "Capability" Brown

As the 17th century wore on, so the rich contentment that the houses displayed grew. After the bloody and bitter period of the Commonwealth—one of the few times that religious bigotry managed to gain a stranglehold on British life—the Stuarts were restored to the throne (or it was restored to them, depending on your point of view). From the Restoration, in 1660, a feeling of security gained ground in the country, reflected in the expansive house building that went on. From this period date— Eltham Lodge, in Woolwich (1665); Ham House, Richmond, begun in 1610, but greatly extended in the 1670s; Hanbury Hall, Droitwich in Hereford & Worcester, completed around 1710 in the style of Queen Anne, with some fine murals and plasterwork; Honington Hall, near Shipston on Stour, Warwickshire, built in 1682, again with quite magnificent ceiling and staircase decorations, this time in a well-lived-in house; and Belton House in Lincolnshire, built between 1685 and 1688, gracious but solid, with some fine period furniture and carving. This last is yet another victim of the auctioneer's hammer.

These are only a few of the many buildings of this rich time, and of these few it is Ham House that may be the easiest for visitors to see, as it can be included in a visit to Hampton Court Palace, not far away. Ham House is run by a combination of the National Trust and the Victoria and Albert Museum, with the result that it is superbly furnished with all the warmth and richness of good late-17th-century furniture—whose fabrics have been either carefully preserved or as carefully copied—to give an idea of how people of the period lived.

Hampton Court itself, on the outskirts of London, is a magnificent example of the evolving taste of the royal families and of Britain in general. The Tudor part of the palace was added to by Sir Christopher Wren for William and Mary, whom the English love to call Willium'n'Mary, more like Siamese twins than a pair of equal monarchs. They were husband and wife with equal claims to the throne, and so ruled jointly. Although the two monarchs wanted to build a rival to the palace of Louis XIV at Versailles—this was the time when Britain was at war with the Sun King—the result of Wren's artistry was to produce a building which is mercifully free of the grandiose rhetoric of the French palace, and seems to harmonize with the warm brick solidity of Henry VIII's original, adding an almost bourgeois touch that may well come from William himself, who, as Prince of Orange, was Dutch. Hampton Court, by the way, is full of pictures from the royal collections, hung in the endless galleries of quiet stately rooms that open out one from the other. The furniture, too, is splendid, with great four-poster beds, chairs whose upholstery was embroidered by Queen Mary, the present Queen's grandmother, and huge and magnificent kitchens. Unfortunately, the amount of the Palace that can be visited will be curtailed for a few years while repairs are carried out following a serious fire at Easter, 1986. The grounds, too, are wonderfully kept, with recreations of Elizabethan knot gardens, a maze and much else to walk around. It is not the most cheerful place in the world to walk around on a winter's day as there is not very much artificial light. If you can choose to go there in spring or summer you will see both the rooms and the gardens at their best.

Two of Britain's most magnificent houses, palaces in every sense, belong to this period, Chatsworth and Blenheim. Chatsworth, the home of the Cavendish family, started as an Elizabethan building, but, since the Cavendish of the period, then Earl of Devonshire, threw in his support with William of Orange, during that prince's first uncertain days in the country, he was raised to a dukedom as a reward. This first Duke of Devonshire was a descendant of Bess of Hardwick, and he shared his ancestress's obsession with bricks and mortar, and turned immediately to converting Chatsworth into a vast classical structure, surrounded by superb grounds which include fountains and a lovely cascade. The decorations inside have been added over the years, and it is crammed with paintings and furniture.

Blenheim had a different genesis. The great hero of the wars with Louis XIV was John Churchill, created Duke of Marlborough. A grateful queen, Anne, sister of Mary, rewarded him with the gift of the wherewithal to build a palace, though no one can have expected the fantastic size of the final building, which cost a staggering sum. It was by no means beside the point that Sarah, Churchill's wife, was Queen Anne's bosom buddy at the time and had a quite unnerving ascendency over the lonely lady. The architect was Sir John Vanbrugh, also a very gifted playwright, whose theatrical Baroque inventiveness is stamped all over the place. He quarreled with the domineering Duchess and was replaced by another dramatic architect, Nicholas Hawksmoor, who had been his assistant. There is a sad story of the banished Sir John standing on some boxes to peek over a wall to see how his brainchild was growing. The interior of this sprawling complex of buildings is as opulent as the exterior is striking, and the whole is vast. You could quite easily spend the day at Blenheim, walking in the grounds, crossing the lake by the beautiful half-submerged bridge to see the column with its statue of the first Duke. The grounds were redesigned by "Capability" Brown in 1765. If ever there were a palace in Britain that could rival Versailles it is certainly Blenheim.

Lancelot Brown, 1715–83, gained his nickname of "Capability" because he used to say, when called in to consider a project for landscaping some nobleman's park, "Well, my lord, there are great capabilities here." He worked on a huge number of projects during his very successful life, recreating the landscape of over ninety houses and castles, and almost single-handedly taming the look of the British countryside, bringing out the capabilities inherent in every view. You will come across his name endlessly as you go around the country and soon acquire a sense of just what it was that he brought to his feats of landscaping. The passage of so many years has brought his landscape designs to full realization. But, in the southeast and south of England, the terrible gale of October 1987 destroyed many of his trees that had grown to maturity over two centuries.

Greeks and Goths

The artistic consciousness of Britain from the middle of the 18th century was dominated by two consuming interests, the balanced order of the classical world of Greece and Rome, and the wild romantic obscurity of the Gothic Age (or, as they liked to spell it, "Gothick"). Men of taste who had been round Europe on the mandatory Grand Tour, bringing home statues and pictures, memories of the villas near Venice designed by Palladio and volumes of designs for the building of classically-influenced houses, could hardly wait to sweep away their antique family homes and replace them with modern Italianate houses. This Mediterranean impulse was one side of a coin whose obverse was the enjoyment of mountain scenery, the taste for wild woodlands, a passion for the "picturesque" carved arches and ivy-clad towers of the Gothic world. The linking word between the two seemingly disparate tastes is "picturesque." They were both foreign and exotic. Which type of house you built just depended on which bug bit you first.

The world following the victories of Marlborough was a secure one and there is nothing like a secure world for persuading people to build for the future. The 18th-century landowners in Britain were certain of their taste and certain of the security of their future, they could plan ahead and plan big. The schemes they conceived involved sometimes sweeping away whole villages to realize the "capabilities" of the terrain and planting strategic trees which would not mature for a hundred years. This was a golden age for building in Britain. As so frequently men and events came together. To meet the grandeur of concept, hey presto, there were the architects needed—William Kent, whom we mentioned earlier in connection with Holkham Hall, one of the great innovators of his time; the brothers Robert and James Adam, who visited Italy and Yugoslavia and brought home a deep-seated understanding of the balance and order of classical building; James Wyatt, the great rival of Robert Adam, and a man of, if anything, even richer genius; these, together with William Chambers, were five of the men who stamped the indelible impression of their age on whole townscapes.

For visitors to London there are two excellent examples of the work of this time, and both are easily visitable—Chiswick House, echoing the country houses around Venice, and recently restored to something of its former grandeur, although virtually unfurnished; and Kenwood House, nestling at the edge of Hampstead Heath in north London, and attractively containing pictures and furniture belonging to the Iveagh Bequest. Especially notable at Kenwood is the Adam library, a singularly delicate and beautifully shaped room.

A little further out from London, though still in easy reach, is Syon House. This was one of Robert Adam's masterpieces of adaptation, full of classical design and gorgeous adaptation of antique motifs to modern use. Adam himself talked of part of the building being "furnished in a style to afford great variety and amusement," and the effect of the house is indeed one of high spirits and happiness.

Although the classical and Gothick were often to be found cheek-by-jowl—a classical house, say, with the grounds full of Gothick ruins and hidden hermitages with live hermits living in them—sometimes the Gothick inspiration created the impetus for the whole house. Strawberry Hill was just one such. It is now a Roman Catholic Teachers' Training College, but part of it can be visited by arrangement. It was the creation of that strange diarist, novelist and feline wit, Horace Walpole. It was a deliberate attempt to translate the jumbled nature of what the period understood by medieval—or Gothick—architecture to the needs of a contemporary house. It resulted in a charming, but frankly jokey structure.

The Gothick passion surfaced all over the country with some striking results, such as the castle at Downton in Herefordshire, built by Richard Payne Knight (a writer on the "picturesque"). Nor was the Gothick world the only exotic realm to be plundered for ideas. The Royal Pavilion in Brighton, the dream palace of the Prince Regent, later George IV—built around 1818 by yet another prolific and talented architect, John Nash—contains a certain amount of Gothickery, topped by Islamic domes and Indian arches, while the interior is a riot of Chinoisery and flying dragons. Furnished, as it now is, with many of the original pieces from the royal collection (Victoria had dispersed them in disgust), it is a sheer delight to visit.

Hearth and Home

The Victorians spent vast sums on building, for this was the age of another wave of "new men," the industrialists and imperialists who brought great wealth pouring into the country. But the majority of the houses that these *nouveau riche* barons lavished so much care and industry on were deeply derivative. The tail end of the Gothick revival produced bastard medieval halls; William Morris and his followers tried to revive medieval crafts; theorists like Ruskin and Pater created a new interest in Italianate architecture, and buildings piebald with Siena-stripes rose everywhere, and were promptly turned a uniform black by the appalling smog that choked the Victorian atmosphere.

One early-Victorian pile, Belvoir Castle, is a spectacular version of 19th-century excess; Waddesdon Manor, based on French models in the 1870s, is another; Scarisbrick Hall, Lancashire—now a school, but which can be visited if you are particularly interested in Victorian design—is yet another, incredibly over-decked mishmash of styles, topped off by a grotesquely out-of-proportion tower. Scarisbrick was the creation of the Pugin family, whose younger and most famous member, Augustus, was also responsible for the infinity of detail on and in the Houses of Parliament, and who died insane at the early age of 40 in 1852.

Cardiff Castle, now in the heart of the modern city, was originally built by the Romans, developed by the Normans, and completely worked over by a strange Victorian genius called William Burges. Supported by the 3rd Marquess of Bute, a patron to be proud of, Burges created a world of medieval fantasy, not only with his architecture, but by designing the total interior, frescos, carving, furniture, the lot. Anyone who is interested in what the Victorians could achieve when they employed both money and talent should not miss Cardiff Castle.

These, and many more, were the prodigious country houses built by the aristocracy, old and new, to accommodate the leisured weekend parties who lazed away the long Victorian and Edwardian summers, attended by an army of servants without whom these monstrous palaces could not function.

To see the ideal Victorian home, the lair of that archetypal materfamilias, Victoria, visit Osborne House on the Isle of Wight, which is almost claustrophobic with its swarms of knicknacks, photographs and useless furniture. This house is in a very real sense a time machine, since it was kept exactly as it had been on the death of Prince Albert in 1861, a shrine to his memory—and is still that way today.

Which has brought us to the last great houses which were built in Britain, built for the Edwardian sunset of Britain's greatness. Although there were several fine architects around the turn of this century, the most popular was Sir Edwin Lutyens who is noted internationally for his designs in New Delhi, but whose English country houses gathered together many threads from the past and seem to grow naturally from their native woods and fields. Perhaps his most striking building is Castle Drogo, in Devon, which was originally conceived as a vast and complex structure, a castle in every way, but which was constantly curtailed as it was built and as money ran out, so that less than half of the first scheme was actually finished. Built in the years immediately before the First World War, it was the last great idiosyncratic house to be built in Britain. Cold and severe in many ways, reminding one of a medieval stronghold at every turn of the smooth stone walls, it is almost totally without fussy carving, relying on mass and line to accomplish its effects. Though now owned by the National Trust, Lutyens designed it for Sir Julius Drewe, the founder of a chain of grocery stores. There is something keenly appropriate about the fact that the last great castle built in Britain was created for a shopkeeper. Napoleon would have approved.

For further details of Historic Houses see the relevant section in Facts At Your Fingertips *and the lists in each regional chapter's* Practical Information.

THE PERFORMING ARTS

An Insubstantial Pageant

One of the main reasons for so many people wanting to visit Britain is its enviable reputation in the performing arts. The country is exactly what Shakespeare described, an "isle full of noises, sounds and sweet airs that give delight and hurt not." In music and drama, opera and ballet, there are endless opportunities for visitors to enjoy themselves to the hilt.

There is a heavy concentration of the performing arts in London as is only natural, but the rich scene there represents only part of what is available in Britain as a whole. Naturally, for someone with limited vacation time London can provide a concentrated experience, but if it is at all possible to venture outside the capital, the rewards both in variety of performance and, especially, in variety of locale are tremendous. Even in the present constrictive economic situation, the arts are managing to flourish, though with great difficulty and deeply-felt complaint. In fact, as so often in the past, times of financial testing seem to call up reserves of imagination and devotion that produce superlative work.

There is a strength and fluidity about the performing arts in Britain which make them very difficult to pin down. An actor playing Lear with the Royal Shakespeare Company one day could quite possibly appear in a television farce the next; an opera that has played to the small exclusive audience at Glyndebourne, who have paid the earth for their evening's entertainment, reappears the next week at the Albert Hall as part of the B.B.C.'s Promenade Concerts, delighting not only the vast throng—around seven thousand—there in person, but millions more by radio. The performing arts largely transcend the social barriers that bedevil most aspects of British life to provide cultural nourishment for the widest spectrum of people. This generalization applies to music as well as to drama, but since the visitor to Britain will probably be most conscious of the theater, let us start there.

Rock of Ages

Like the true church, Britain's theater is founded on a rock. Shakespeare. There was a time when theater managers believed that "Shakespeare spelled ruin." Nowadays he spells big business. And, more importantly, he supplies a backbone to the theatrical life of the country. There can hardly have been a day since the one on which the Bard breathed his last, when one of his plays, in some shape or form, was not being performed. They have survived being turned into musicals (from Purcell to Rock), they have made the reputations of generations of famous actors (and broken not a few), they have seen women playing Hamlet and men playing Rosalind, they have been staged as archeological reconstructions and science fiction; in fact they have proved as near indestructible as anything made by mortal man.

They provide, too, a touchstone by which actors can measure themselves, and by which other people can measure them. About once a decade the theater-going public is sorely tempted to ask for an Act of Parliament to forbid the production of *Hamlet,* so many versions are being staged at the same time (in 1988 it was *The Tempest* that kept cropping up). But that protracted procession of princes gives a fascinating lesson in the richness of talent available. All the Hamlets have something to offer which seems to shed a new light on the weary text. And that is the secret of Shakespeare's perennial success and of his inestimable value to the British theater. However his plays are twisted and reshaped by directors and actors, they always seem to reveal a new facet of some eternal truth about Man.

While on the subject of actors, it is important to mark the strength of acting talent available in Britain. However poor the play, the motive power of the performers rarely fails. Going to the theater in Britain is almost as much an *aficionado* exercise as bullfighting in Spain or opera in Italy. Quite apart from the joy of seeing a star actor playing at the top of his bent, almost every play on view offers character actors and actresses playing endless variations on eccentric types, or stripping bare a personality with instantly recognizable truth.

Stratford-upon-Barbican

The two main institutions of the British theater are firmly based on the foundation of Shakespeare, namely the Royal Shakespeare Company and the National Theater. The history of drama at Stratford-upon-Avon has interestingly mirrored theater trends in general. During the 19th century the town was just another whistle-stop on the round of provincial tours. The mock-Tudor Victorian theater there provided a not-very-rewarding date for actor managers touring their blood-and-thunder versions of the bard. In the early 1930s the theater burned down and another, designed in contemporary style, with some very incovenient features, rose in its

place on the banks of the Avon. For a long time Stratford was largely ignored as a serious theatrical locale by metropolitan theatergoers and critics
alike, but gradually, especially after World War II, more adventurous policies and star names such as Gielgud, Olivier, and Redgrave began to pull
in the crowds. In the '50s—under the directorship of a young Peter Hall—
the whole character of the place changed. An ensemble company was
born, and the Royal Shakespeare Company—R.S.C. for short—entered
the mainstream of international drama.

Now the Company has five permanent theaters—three in Stratford and
two in London. In Stratford there is the main auditorium, badly designed
for staging and undergoing almost annual attempts to make it a more successful playing area; The Other Place, a small studio locale, little better
than a glorified hut, though mounting vibrant performances; and a magnificently effective recreation of an Elizabethan playhouse, created in 1986
and appropriately called The Swan. The cost of converting the building
left over from the burned-out theater of the '30s into this imaginative
space, was borne by a highly anglophile and inspired American millionaire. In London there is the custom-built Barbican auditorium, excitingly
conceived and the one part of this vast and awkwardly designed arts center
that really works; and The Pit, also in the Barbican, which is London's
answer to The Other Place.

The range of the company's offerings in amazingly wide, with experimental, newly-written works sharing company time with classics from all
periods and, primarily of course, Shakespeare. Productions move from
Stratford to London and occasionally in the other direction. They are also
frequently transferred to the West End, tour round the country, and indeed the globe. Performances of drama—*Cyrano de Bergerac, Nicholas
Nickleby, Les Liasons Dangereuses*—and musicals—*Les Misérables*—have
carried the message of the R.S.C.'s quality to Broadway and beyond.

If there is one criticism of today's R.S.C., it is that since the core of
reliable actors is spread so thinly over so many productions, the players
brought in to fill the lower ranks tend to be only just adequate and sometimes less than that. This shows especially in poor verse speaking, and the
consequent watering-down of dramatic impact. But, that cavil apart, the
R.S.C. can still provide, on a good evening, one of the most gripping theatrical experiences to be had anywhere in the world.

The New Nationalism

The National Theater (housed in its complex concrete fortress on the
South Bank) was born originally as the Old Vic Company, only a short
distance away. And, since the Old Vic also gave birth to the English National Opera and the Royal Ballet, it is worth taking a brief look at how
that remarkable institution came about.

In 1912 Lilian Baylis, a dynamic little woman, came to London from
South Africa to take over the running of the Royal Victoria Music Hall
from her aunt, Emma Cons. The "Old Vic" as it was popularly known,
was a reclaimed gin palace, which the worthy Emma Cons ran on strictly
teetotal, improving, high-minded lines. Lilian Baylis was not satisfied with
drawing room ballads as entertainment and began the slow, slippery descent from *Abide With Me* to *Your Tiny Hand is Frozen*. God, however,
stayed on as a firm partner in the enterprise and Miss Baylis could often

be found on her knees in her office, chiding the Lord for not being more financially adroit. Her cry was always "Oh Lord, send me good actors—cheap!" She was in the direct line of great English eccentrics. The battlements of Elsinore or Dunsinane were frequently perfumed by the odor of sausages cooking on the gas-ring in her stage-side office. But, like many another eccentric, she had a vision which she pursued against incredible odds. Her dream was to bring the best in culture to the London poor ("My People") for the price of a packet of cigarettes. From early, amateurly-staged, productions of Shakespeare and opera she gradually advanced to better and better standards. Eventually she was attracting all the best young names in the theater of the day to act for her for, of course, almost nothing.

After a few years, in the early thirties, Lilian Baylis opened Sadler's Wells, a second "people's theater" in the north of London, intended as a supplement to the work of the Old Vic, south of the Thames. The experiment of running the two houses as if they were one, with productions shuttling across the river, was not a success. Audiences never knew at which theater any particular show might be seen; actors became confused and, on more than one occasion, scenery became unmanageable in the high winds on the bridges over the river. The result was that Sadler's Wells became the permanent home for the opera company, performing always in English, and also for the infant ballet company which, under the direction of Ninette de Valois, had grown out of the dancing needs of the opera. Shakespeare ruled at the Old Vic, undisturbed by temperamental tenors.

The Old Vic, by due process of time and, especially, under the aegis of Laurence Olivier, attained the kind of stature which inevitably turned it into the National Theater. The Sadler's Wells Ballet migrated in the mid-'40s to Covent Garden where, again by that naturally inevitable process of change that marks all British institutions, it became the Royal Ballet. Later, in the early '60s, the opera company, finding Sadler's Wells Theater too small for the pressures of modern opera financing, transferred to the Coliseum in St. Martin's Lane, where it finally changed its name to the English National Opera. Thus, by the whirligig of Time, did the children of Lilian Baylis become powers in the land. Needless to say, seats now cost a great deal more than a packet of cigarettes and God would be rather surprised if He began to hear again from any of Miss Baylis's successors.

The National has three auditoria in its South Bank home, the Olivier, the Lyttelton and the Cottesloe—which range from the impossibly spacious to the more nearly intimate. Their span of productions is rich and varied, with plays culled from most countries plus occasional new works that might better have been tried out in a less expensive milieu. Of recent seasons musicals have appeared on the bill—most notably *Guys and Dolls* in a superb presentation. The main problem from a visitor's point of view is that the National's repertory system means that a play, however successful, may only appear a few times in any month, and may also disappear completely, leaving the public thirst unslaked. Planning ahead when wanting to visit the National is a frustrating business.

It is frequently possible to catch up with the more popular of the National's productions if they transfer to the West End. Many have done so over the years, *Amadeus* and *Guys and Dolls* being but two of them. The invasion of the commercial sector by state-subsidized theater creates a completely new situation in the frequently tense relationship between the two.

Lifeblood from the Provinces

But, to return to the theater in general. It would be a serious mistake to think of the British stage simply in terms of the two central institutions of the R.S.C. and the National Theater. Indeed, were it not for the variety and richness of the rest of the theater, the R.S.C. and the National could not possibly exist. Britain is a very small country, comparatively speaking, and there is a great deal of busy traffic between the regional theaters and London. Most provincial cities, and some smaller centers, have excellent repertory theaters.

From the mid-70s to the early 80s no less than 40 professional provincial theaters were opened and only 18 closed. One of the interesting features of the provincial theatrical scene is the refurbishing of attractive old theater buildings so that they can once more contribute that indefinable quality which is such a feature of ornate old auditoria—the feeling that something special is on the way before the curtain even rises. Among the towns with such resurrections are Peterborough, Hereford, Norwich and Winchester. Unfortunately, the current financial stringency enforced by government policies makes the life expectancy of the smaller companies very doubtful. With so much of the budget of the central Arts Council eaten up by the huge metropolitan companies (Covent Garden especially) it is extremely difficult for provincial groups to find adequate support.

There are some 40 provincial companies that do interesting work, and of that 40 some 20 which are to be relied on for an exciting evening in the theater. In one week recently it was possible to see several Shakespeare plays, a couple by Russian playwrights, the first production of an Elizabethan tragedy in this century, plays by O'Casey, Peter Shaffer *(The Royal Hunt of the Sun)*, Alan Ayckbourn, Tom Stoppard, Brecht, Christopher Hampton, Shaw, and a plethora of others, and all of them performed to enthusiastic audiences far from the lights of the West End.

Not all the provincial companies are housed in attractive old buildings, more of them perform in new civic centers, sometimes with the latest concept of open staging (as does the Sheffield Crucible company). They are subsidized by a combination of local government money and grants from the Arts Council, and are usually obliged by such public investment to be both adventurous and educational. The recent cutback of public spending has seriously affected provincial repertory companies, who have rarely been able to make ends meet from their box office receipts alone. But there is a backbone of steel underneath the volatile exterior of committed theatrical people and, though the future does look particularly bleak, no one doubts that they will survive.

The standard of performance in the best of the repertory companies is very high indeed, as a visit to the Bristol Old Vic, the Birmingham Repertory, the Northcott Theater, Exeter, the Liverpool Playhouse, the Belgrade, Coventry, The Royal Exchange Theater in Manchester or the Glasgow Citizens will show. This last is a complete maverick in the British theater, and, if it's wild and vital performances you're after, don't miss it.

It is interesting, too, that it is in these outlying bastions of British theater that some of the most valuable socially-conscious experiments are being carried out. The theater in the West End of London has such high overheads to meet, that it is rare indeed to find any really experimental work being done. But, with lesser financial risks at stake, small local theaters can try out ideas which, in time, percolate through and color West End presentations.

Drama by Starlight

If you are traveling round the country, it is also worth your time to find out what is on in any spot you may hit; especially in summer. Summer is the time when Britain's acting fraternity take to the open air, and strive to out-do passing planes, vociferous birds, the fading light and nearby traffic. Although it is often closer to penance than art, the results can occasionally be exciting. Almost anywhere in Britain you are within reach of openair theater.

There are a few spots where openair theater flourishes that are especially worth the trip. One is York, where the famous medieval cycle of mystery plays is performed every three years in surroundings which add incalculable richness to an already moving text. Then there is Ludlow Castle, which houses classics in the summer against the evocative stones of the fortress. In Cornwall the Minack Theater, perched on a cliff, with the sea providing a wonderful backdrop, stages Arthurian and other plays.

Often, especially in May or June, you can catch plays performed in the ancient gardens and courtyards of the colleges of Oxford or Cambridge by undergraduates, many of whom will go on to make the stage their careers. These students frequently resurrect plays which might never be seen anywhere else and, for the theater buff, this represents a chance to add rare items to his playgoing collection. Performances in the newer universities are more likely to be in winter.

Perhaps the best of all the openair theaters is the one in Regent's Park in London. There, in a semi-permanent setting, you can watch Shakespeare, after having wandered in Queen Mary's rose garden. To sit in the gathering dusk, as Puck and Oberon plot their magic, and the secret lights gradually create a new world of fantasy, is to take part in an essentially British rite.

Opera

Dr. Samuel Johnson, who was a notable grouch, accused opera of being an exotic and irrational entertainment, and it certainly is a maverick element on the British scene, socially acceptable, but never completely taken to the nation's heart. Sir Thomas Beecham, another famous eccentric and wit, spent most of his life fulminating against the lack of interest that the British showed in opera. Unfortunately he did not live quite long enough to see the current upsurge of popularity that the art is enjoying.

Of course opera *is* irrational. It was born in the royal and ducal courts of Europe, where expense had no meaning. All efforts to circumscribe the form within the belt of economic rule are doomed to failure. It is essentially a spectacular and extravagant entertainment. There are small-scale, chamber works, that catch the imagination and fulfill the ideal of music drama, but they have never had really wide public appeal. It is the grandiose, throat-catching works, *Aida, The Ring, Fidelio,* and (though not so grandiose, of course) the works of Mozart, that the public at large want to see, and it is those works that any opera house worth its salt eventually has to stage.

Britain is lucky to have five major opera companies, presenting a vast range of works. In London there is the Royal Opera at Covent Garden and the English National Opera at the Coliseum. There is Opera North, based in Leeds. In Wales there is the Welsh National Opera and in Scotland the Scottish National Opera, with its own home in Glasgow.

The Royal Opera's home, the Theater Royal, Covent Garden, is a splendid building with a massive Corinthian portico, situated, somewhat surprisingly, at the edge of what used to be London's flower and vegetable market. Its red and gold Victorian interior is on the small side for a major opera house these days, but is brimming with atmosphere. The backstage areas have been considerably enlarged by a multi-million-pound extension, carefully designed to fit into its surroundings—none of your Pompidou Center nonsense for the Royal Opera—and greatly relieving the pressure on rehearsal and dressingroom space. But if the atmosphere of the theater is still old-world, there is nothing old-world about the seat prices which have a touch of the stratosphere about them. The casts are a mixture of local and international singers, following the practice of most leading houses and, as most leading houses discover, this is a mixed blessing. The opera company shares the stage with the Royal Ballet, which rather cuts down on the number of opera performances which can be mounted in a season.

An evening at Covent Garden is something of an event, and although there is much less formality than there once was, tuxedos are still not out of place in the best seats, although conservative lounge suits are equally in keeping. There is an heretical feeling abroad in Britain that the standards of the Royal Opera do not always justify the rocketing prices, and that the snob value of the performances counts for more than the artistic achievement. Certainly, it is increasingly difficult for opera buffs to be able to afford to visit "the Garden" when one considers that the top ticket price is now around £75—and that the standard of both singing and staging cannot be guaranteed, even at that price. The new management team that has recently taken over may well manage to cure some of the ills that have bedevilled the Garden for years.

This situation is thrown into relief by contrast with the English National Opera, only a few blocks away at the Coliseum Theater in St. Martin's Lane. Opera is sung here mostly in English, and the repertory is much broader and more experimental than at the Garden. The English National has given helpful stimulus to the development of many British singers and conductors, setting them on the way to international status. The seats are about a third of the cost of those at Covent Garden, and easier to book. The company pursues a valuable middle course between the popular classics and modern works. Exciting performances of standard operas and virtually unknown ones are the order of the day. Though the vocal caliber of the company does not always quite match up to its sense of adventure, for sheer theatrical enterprise the E.N.O. is among the best in Europe.

Opera Outside London

The Welsh National Opera Company was founded on the secure foundation of a national mania for choral singing. Some of the greatest successes of the company have been in slightly unusual works like Berlioz' *The Trojans,* Verdi's *Nabucco,* and Boito's *Mefistofele.* For anyone who has heard a football crowd in Wales rolling *David of the White Rock* forth into the afternoon air, the popularity of Verdi operas will come as no surprise. In order to satisfy the Welsh craving for music, the company tours a lot, and reached the Valhalla of British opera in 1987 when it presented a single cycle of its English-language *Ring* at Covent Garden.

The Scottish National Opera, in its comparatively short history, has already secured a solid international reputation for imaginative staging and expert casting of lead singers. An offshoot of the Edinburgh Festival—itself operatically inclined from the beginning—it is now an entity on its own with its own home base in Glasgow, and is led by an American conductor, John Mauceri.

Opera North was born as the northern branch of the E.N.O., but is now fully weaned. The idea of founding a professional opera in the north of the country—south of Hadrian's Wall, that is—has succeeded beyond all hopes. At first productions were imported from London, but the home-grown article has almost completely taken over and is being exported to other parts of the country.

Before leaving the British operatic scene there are three other regular companies that should be mentioned, all integral parts of British musical life. One is Glyndebourne, the creation of John Christie and his wife back in the '30s, another example of English eccentricity triumphing against huge odds; another is the Aldeburgh Festival, the creation of Benjamin Britten, and deeply rooted in that haunted part of England which is the setting for his own opera *Peter Grimes;* and the third is the Kent Opera.

The opera house at Glyndebourne exactly corresponds to the courtly settings in which opera originated. True, it is the creation of a merchant prince rather than a prince of the blood, but the end result is the same. Tucked in a fold of the Sussex Downs near Lewes, Glyndebourne provides as nearly perfect a setting as can be imagined for the fully concentrated distillation of operatic perfection. The theater is small, the time given to rehearsals long, the stage designs full of interest—with artists ranging from Hockney to Maurice Sendak—and the grounds a summer epitome of the English country garden. Nowadays the leading singers tend to be young, with their careers ahead of them, but they provide an experience just as compelling as their older colleagues once did. The performances start during the afternoon and have long leisurely intervals. The whole ambience is of a lost world. Mark you, the total cost of a visit approaches the astronomic, but if you love music, you will have a memory to treasure.

Aldeburgh is another kettle of fish entirely and one with the ever-present tang of the sea. This is a center for dedicated music-making by some of the country's finest performers. It is not by any means confined to opera (indeed, these days opera has become a rarity there), nor solely to the works of Lord Britten—the Festival's presiding genius when he was alive—but throws its net wide, resurrecting works by neglected composers and re-interpreting works by well-known ones. It is, like Glyndebourne, a small-scale venture, but one which ranges far in expression and in accomplishment. Nor will it cost you the earth to go there, but book tickets and accommodations well ahead.

Yet another facet of Britain's rich operatic life is the work of the Kent Opera, a small company which spends most of its time touring. It has resurrected, in extremely actable modern versions, works by Monteverdi and other rarely seen composers. With exciting productions by such directors as Jonathan Miller, and a small but professional orchestra, the company has rapidly carved out a niche for itself. Sadly, this vital young company is under constant threat of closure by the cancellation of its Arts Council grant.

Ballet

It is one of the most unlikely facts of modern artistic life that ballet—an exotic and irrational entertainment if ever there was one—not only took root in Britain, but grew into a flourishing plant. Anyone who knew the British would have said that ballet was a totally alien art form to them, but the miracle is that it has, over the last seventy years, taken such deep root in the country that missionaries have gone out into all lands, preaching the gospel according to de Valois, Rambert and Ashton.

Ballet in Britain can be dated almost exactly from 1911 when Diaghilev brought his Ballets Russes to London. Somehow, against all possible expectation, they caught the public imagination. There were some English dancers in the company, who stayed on to found British ballet.

Like so much that is of any worth in British cultural life, ballet struggled very slowly up the ladder from near-amateur beginnings to the massive structures of today's companies. The Royal Ballet, which shares Covent Garden with the Royal Opera, and provides more than its share of the box-office receipts (although the top price for a ballet seat is half that for an opera one), began tentatively as the dancing interludes in Sadler's Wells' operas. It moved to Covent Garden after World War II and never looked back. Which is not entirely true, for the smaller company of the Royal Ballet, which tours Britain and manages to do some of the experiments that the parent company is too unwieldy to encompass, re-established a home base at Sadler's Wells during the fall of 1976, and now works out of this theater for its tours of Britain and abroad. The problem of a home base is an ever-present nightmare to the smaller touring companies.

The Royal Ballet now represents the Establishment of British dance, and it could be argued very seriously that the eminence it has attained has brought with it a slight hardening of the arteries, perhaps not too surprising in a body half-a-century old. Companies in other countries have followed in the wake of the Royal Ballet, and have often been created by dancers and choreographers from the Royal Ballet. These companies challenge the Royal Ballet on its own ground and, so far, the Royal has not managed to create a new image to replace the remnants of its days of greatness. But, this said, it has to be admitted that an evening spent watching the Royal Ballet at work can still be an evening of nostalgic enchantment.

The Ballet Rambert, now well launched on its second half-century, is roughly the contemporary of the Royal Ballet, but, because it has remained a small company, and has always reflected the dedication of its founder, the late Dame Marie Rambert, to the cause of experiment, it has also remained youthful and vibrant. Like many of the country's smaller companies, it is always on the move, and visitors to Britain are as likely to catch it performing in a small town as they are to see it in London.

The other major company is the Festival Ballet. Although it does have its London seasons, the policy of the Festival Ballet is to bring all the major works of the ballet repertory to the country at large. It has a few near-experimental works, but its staple diet is the same, basically, as Diaghilev's. Indeed, the company has revived one or two of his ballets, such as *Sheherazade,* which would not otherwise be seen.

The ballet scene in Britain is not so rich in fringe companies as is drama, but there are a fair number. An excellent time to see them and taste their experimental work is during the period of the *Dance Umbrella* held in London each year, six weeks or so when events take place all over town in major venues and tiny halls.

Music

While drama and opera and ballet are all fairly easily segregated facets of the artistic life of Britain, the same cannot be said of music. Britain's amazingly rich musical life fills every hall and theater, church and chapel through the length and breadth of the land. The sheer immensity of the task of confining such incredible performing endeavor within the frame of a brief survey is an impossible task. It is not just the Welsh who can say, in Dylan Thomas's words, "Thank God we are a musical nation."

Quite what impelled the upsurge of interest in music from the '50s onwards would be hard to say. Previous to that time there was only the merest suggestion of the possibility that music could burgeon into such an integrally important part of everyday life. Certainly Britain has produced few great international composers to vie with Italy, Germany or even France, though she has had a steady trickle from Purcell onwards. Her greatest, Handel, was only a naturalized Briton, though fiercely proud of it. Sullivan, Elgar, Vaughan Williams and, most recently, Britten and Tippett, have all achieved moderate fame abroad.

It is not so much composition which has raised Britain to the rank she enjoys today, but execution, scholarship and sheer enterprise. It is possible to hear a vast variety of works performed every day of the year in all the cities and towns of the country, and London leads the parade with half-a-dozen superb concert halls going full tilt. It would be the easiest thing in the world for anyone who really loved music to plan a holiday in Britain, traveling round the country from cathedral to university to concert hall, enjoying some thrilling and unexpected delights.

The comparatively short distances which link all the major cities and towns mean that no one in Britain is far from a performance locale. Apart from the national orchestras located in London, many of the regional centers have their own symphonies—Bournemouth, Liverpool, Manchester, Birmingham—which is gaining an international reputation under its dynamic young conductor, Simon Rattle—among them; there are national orchestras for Wales and Scotland; the B.B.C. has fine regional orchestras as well as its chief one in London; and, of course, foreign orchestras frequently visit throughout the country, coming from places as diverse as Oslo, Moscow, Amsterdam, Paris, Chicago, Prague and Tokyo. Specialist orchestras, performing Baroque music for instance, are flourishing, with groups springing up in the most unlikely places.

But if instrumental work is thriving, even allowing for the extreme expense of keeping the larger groups afloat in a period of severe cutbacks, it is nothing when compared with the popularity of vocal music. Britain has had a strong tradition of singing, especially in church, for many centuries and the fruits of that long tradition are now being harvested. We will look in a moment at the Festival scene in the country, and it is there, perhaps most clearly, that the variety and scope of performances of vocal music can be seen. But every week of the year you can attend performances of great choral works in concert halls, recitals of *lieder* in stately homes by candlelight, strange modern pieces on remote Scottish islands in the rich Celtic twilight of ancient buildings, lively madrigals from boats on a moonlit river. All you have to do is keep your eyes open for posters plastered in market towns, on the notice boards of country churches, outside university cafeterias—or ask the local tourist office for news of up-coming events. The thing that you can be sure of, if you do seek out local performances, is that you will be welcomed by the organizers and made to feel at home.

Since the origin of much of the British love of choral music can be traced to religious music, you could do much worse than drop into a cathedral or large parish church or chapel when one is handy, especially on a Sunday, and hear the music there. You will frequently be amazed at the quality of music which the local choir will be singing. Many cathedral choirs are still manned—or perhaps that should be "boyed"—by the pupils of the choir school, who are chosen for their voices, and are trained by expert teachers.

The Festival Scene

Just as the British dearly love a lord, so they go ape for a festival. Once the worst of the winter chill seeps out of everyone's bones, festival fever sets in. From the Edinburgh Festival at one end of the scale to the tiniest celebration in a forgotten village, the land is simply crawling with artists all doing their thing—local artists, national artists and international artists. The summer air is clangorous with the sound of bandwagons going into high gear.

The idea of a festival goes back a long way. David Garrick held one in 1769 to celebrate Shakespeare in Stratford-upon-Avon, though he called it a Jubilee. The Three Choirs Festival—when the cathedral choirs of Hereford, Gloucester and Worcester get together to sing their heads off in each cathedral in turn—began back in 1724 and has been going strong ever since. The Edinburgh Festival, which is in many ways the archetype of the present-day wing-dings, began just after World War II, in 1947, and immediately demonstrated one of the vital attributes for a successful festival—the interaction of place and event.

Anyone can hold a festival anywhere, of course, but for the idea to take root and settle down into a successful annual event, there has to be some attraction about the location, some *genius loci* at work, which can add an extra dimension of associated glamour to the bare bones of the program. Such a glamour is most clearly in evidence in Edinburgh, where the auditoria are not all that marvelous, and where the sheer dramatic beauty of the town comes into play, especially when the Tattoo is on. Buxton and Harrogate are both very pretty, old spa towns which can bring the elegance of the past to the highjinx of the present, as can Bath, that granddaddy of all watering holes. An interesting town plus a local celebrity can provide the excuse; Stratford-upon-Avon and Shakespeare, Rochester and Dickens, Aldeburgh and Britten, Malvern and Elgar. Sheer beauty of a region can be reason enough for locating a festival there—as with Pitlochry in Scotland, now blessed with a brand-new Festival Theater after years under canvas; or Glyndebourne, tucked into the Sussex Downs and surrounded by lovely gardens.

Another pleasant place to visit both for the town and for the festival performances is Chichester, which has a summer Festival Theater, where quite famous players appear in fairly undemanding plays and musicals, tailored for a moderately conservative country audience. Chichester can be taken in as a day out from London, or included in a round tour. The surrounding region is full of fascinating spots to see.

There are, quite literally, dozens of festivals every year, right down to very small, local ones. How's this for a perfect description of a festival of purely local interest? "Festival of Wild Flowers and Music in Church and Exhibition of Village Activities in Hall. St. Peter's Church and Village Hall, The Street, Westleton, Near Saxmundham, Suffolk." If it's the performing arts you are after, though, you should aim at something a little larger. All the medium-sized and large festivals have mixed programs, music, drama, jazz and dance almost always represented, with exhibitions and perhaps lectures thrown in for good measure. Many nationally-known artists spend most of their summers touring the festivals, and such famous groups as the English Chamber Orchestra or the Academy of St. Martin's in the Fields turn up again and again in festival programs. Mark you, since hotel accommodation is limited in the smaller centers, it is as well to try and plan a little ahead of time so that you can book a room for the days you fancy.

Not all festivals take place in summer, though most of them do—for obvious reasons, when you consider the irrationality of the British weather—and are well spaced from May to September, which means that you could easily take in a couple or more in one trip. Visiting a festival kills several birds with one stone—it is a great way of combining tourism with entertainment, it provides an excellent chance to see how the arts in Britain really function, and it gives a chance to meet local people when they are at their most relaxed.

FOOD AND DRINK IN BRITAIN

The Bad Food Myth

So much mud has been thrown at British food that its defenders almost feel a crusading fire in their veins. The best advice to the visitor is to forget the stories; the myth of bad food in Britain is outdated and is very far removed from the present reality. The problem is not so much bad food as expensive food nowadays. If you avoid certain pitfalls, and they will be mentioned here, you can eat in Britain almost as well as anywhere else in the world.

It is not very difficult (and quite amusing) to trace the origin of the bad food legend, which must stem less from the quality of food than the British attitude to eating. The British, it used to be said, eat to live, while the French live to eat. This was a state of mind which is clearly a hangover of 19th-century Victorian primness. This disdainful attitude towards the pleasures of eating was still present in certain age groups and strata of society in Britain before the Second World War—the world of tweeds, sweaters, pearls and sensible shoes, of stodgy, steamed puddings and over-boiled vegetables.

With the war and its food shortages, the non-caring attitude became a necessity, a cover-up for the inevitably scarce food. So the myth was fully grown, and after bouncing about for some thirty years could well still be lurking in the subconscious of many visitors to Britain. Although it may take another thirty years to destroy the myth, let's make a start.

It is no longer shameful or sinful to enjoy good food, so the ethical aspect has been cleared up for British moralists. Further, the yearly mass

emigration on vacation to the sunny parts of the continent has successfully
eliminated most of the insular attitude about "that greasy foreign mess,"
so small restaurants and even unsophisticated private homes might easily
today serve guests *coq au vin*. Finally, the sophisticated *avant-garde* has
long passed the *coq au vin* stage and is now back to happily feasting on
Basic British Perennials, like steak-and-kidney pie or boiled silverside of
beef.

Food Fit for Knights of Old

The outstanding feature of all British cooking is that it is straightforward, unfussy, good food, entirely dependent on top quality and *fresh*
raw materials. Nothing could be simpler than a large hunk of roast beef—
juicy, succulent and tender—served with crisp and light Yorkshire pudding and a bit of horseradish sauce. Yorkshire pudding is a baked pancake
mixture, originally meant for serving before the meal to take the edge off
your appetite. Now it is generally served with the meat, except in private
homes in the north of England. The roast "joints" are excellent and always
served with two or three vegetables and gravy. Roast young English (or
Welsh) lamb with mint sauce is a culinary feast in itself. The quality of
the home-produced meat is very high, so if the meat you are going to eat
is either English or Scotch, you can be sure it will be among the best you
have ever had.

Strangely, though, some of the most typical, traditional British foods
depend on exactly the opposite of fresh produce. Dating from the medieval
days when food had to be preserved in some basic, simple way in order
to survive through the lean winter months, come the various ways of
smoking and curing meat and fish that are still around today. Smoked
salmon is, of course, a delicacy all over the world, but there are many other
kinds of fish preserved by smoking. From Scotland comes the Arbroath
Smokie, a delicious little fish; more readily available are bloaters and kippers; smoked mackerel and smoked eel, both well-filleted, add to the variety. Meat, hung in the chimney and cured in the curling fumes, was also
a medieval solution to the lack of cold storage. It is still possible to buy
delicious York ham, prepared in Northumbria in the traditional way,
while smoked chicken or turkey often appear on menus.

Another survival, which sometimes seems odd to visitors from the
States, is the eating of fruit and herb concoctions with meat—mint sauce
and mint jelly with lamb, redcurrant with hare, horseradish with beef—
even though the tradition was carried across the Atlantic to survive in
cranberry sauce with the Thanksgiving turkey. These frequently pungent
sauces originally helped to disguise the flavor of meat that was sometimes
more than a little rank. In fact, the greatest of all British sauces comes
from a county called Cumbria, in the extreme north of England. This
sauce alone should give British cooking a better reputation. Made of a piquant mixture of lemon and orange peel and juice mixed with port wine
and redcurrant jelly, it is served with either game or ham.

One of the other major throwbacks to the more opulent days of vast
medieval banquets is the love that the British have for meat pies. Not just
the ubiquitous shepherd's pie, which can be eaten in nearly every pub in
the land—though, sadly, not made according to the song from *Sweeney
Todd,* "with real shepherd in it"—but pies which recall the times when

a "pasty" might be made to look like a castle, or like the nursery-rhyme pie which, when cut, released four-and-twenty blackbirds to sing for the king. These pies, which can be eaten either hot or cold, are usually filled with a mixture of meats; veal and ham, steak and kidney (or steak, kidney and pickled walnuts), beef and oyster, or the delicious game pie, which can contain whatever wild animal happens to have failed to run fast enough.

Of Venison, Haggis and Muffins

The increased awareness of good food has been stimulated not only by the British traveling abroad more avidly of recent years, it has also been egged on by the powers-that-be in the British tourist authorities, who have successfully promoted schemes called "A Taste of England," "A Taste of Scotland" and so on, digging out long-forgotten recipes and persuading commercial restaurants to include them in their menus. Thus you may happen upon "Tweed Kettle," a salmon hash from 19th-century Edinburgh, "Rob Roy's Pleasure" (venison served with chestnut purée and redcurrant jelly), Sussex pudding (blackberries cooked in cider), Dorset apple cake, Cornish burnt cream or roast leg of lamb filled with fresh crab (an 18th-century recipe). Who said the British kitchen was austere and unimaginative?

Added to the national dishes there are any number of regional specialties, many of which are available everywhere. Most of the south of England specialties seem to be tea-time delicacies: chelsea buns, brandy snaps filled with fresh cream and cream darioles (small custard tarts topped with redcurrant jelly and whipped cream). Similar to the English muffin in America, but with holes drilled through (looking a bit like gruyère cheese), are crumpets—luscious, round tea breads, toasted and soaked with lashings of butter. They are a winter-time food, traditionally meant to be toasted on a long toasting fork by the open fire.

The other regional specialty, which you can get wherever you go, is a savory pie called Cornish pasty. These are individual, half-moon-shaped pies filled with meat, onions and other vegetables; you will find them in pubs and snack bars, or you can buy them freshly-baked at small bakers' shops.

Cheesecake, which many think is a typical Austrian or German specialty, is a long-time favorite all over the country. It has no particular regional associations. On the whole, except for places like Mayfair in London, North Country cake and pastry shops are much more interesting than those in the south, and the farther north you go the better the baking gets. The Scots are famous for the lightness of their pastry.

As a wild generalization, one can say that the further north you go in England, the more plain cooking and catering standards in ordinary hotels, and especially guest houses, improve. In the Midlands and the north of England, and in Scotland, you can often find farmhouses serving teas of such quality and quantity that you will have no thought of food till next breakfast time. In these regions, the term "tea" or "high tea" really means "supper." If you don't want a big meal, ask for "afternoon tea."

Crossing the border into Scotland, you should taste the famous Celtic *wurst,* the haggis, of course. But don't be too surprised when, if offered "a drop of gravy," you find a small glass of whisky poured over the dish!

It's the nicest way of learning about Scotch we know! The most likely other national specialty you are bound to encounter is the richest of fruit cakes, called Dundee cake. All are well worth trying. The other Celtic inhabitants of the British Isles are the Welsh, whose cooking has vastly improved in the last few years.

Melting-Pot Cookery

Britain's long association with India left its mark on the national cuisine. You will sometimes find types of curries on the menu. But don't expect a routine restaurant curry to be very hot. They are usually extremely gentle affairs. "Translated" curries are led by a soup called mulligatawny, part of the established British cooking. It is a highly-spiced, rich vegetable broth. Kedgeree is also adopted from India; it contains rice with flaked smoked fish and hard-boiled eggs. Usually served for lunch or even breakfast, it looks as though it might be heavy, but is usually as light as a feather.

Britain's long presence in so many parts of the globe has resulted in additions to the cuisine dating back as far as the time of the Crusades. But, more recently, the enormous influx of Asian and other immigrants has meant the opening up of ethnic restaurants all over the country. For dining-out the choice is no longer restricted to just Italian and French, if you are bored with straight beef and pudding. Now Iranian, Greek, Chinese, Romanian—the list can stretch out to the crack of doom—restaurants vary the possibilities. And many of them serve superb examples of their national cooking. Backing them all up are still the French and Italian restaurants, which have for so long been solid pillars of the British food scene.

The Urban National Dish

Once upon a time your gastronomic education in the British Isles would have been incomplete without tasting that famous grab-and-gulp dish called fish and chips. You would have been unlikely to find a fish-and-chip shop in Knightsbridge or Princes Street—you would have had to go a short distance from the smart shops and restaurants, into less elegant residential districts (or places like Soho) to find them. There are still a few dotted along the shopping parades of middle-income-group districts, and some of them flourish in working-class areas. But the sad stupidity of the "cod war" hit them very hard. As often as not, now, they will be selling fried chicken and chips, rather than fried fish and chips.

The drill is to make your choice of fish (there are always at least five different ones chalked up on their blackboard), ask for it and a portion of chips to take out, and, exiting hurriedly, to rush to your car or taxi, where you consume it elegantly with your fingers. You may not believe it, but fish and chips taste best wrapped in newspaper, but a spoil-sport health bureaucracy has decreed in most places that it's not sanitary, so the days of peeping at the latest murder news through a coating of tasty oil are also past. If you are in a seaside town, make sure you look for fish and chips. Perhaps "look" isn't the word—follow your nose!

Cheeses

With a few exceptions, the British have the same self-deprecating attitude towards their cheese as towards their entire national cuisine. Don't let them feed you on foreign cheese all the time, however, because you will miss a real treat if you don't taste the home-produced ones. Wensleydale looks pale and wan, but has a subtle, delicate taste, with a slightly honeyed aftertaste. It comes from Yorkshire, where they say "An apple pie wi-owt tha cheese is like a kiss wi'owt a squeeze." Cheddar, Leicester, Lancashire and Caerphilly are all subtly different in taste and all excellent. The king of them all is blue Stilton. It is truly a connoisseur's cheese. Sip a glass of port with your Stilton. It's good with coffee too.

If you really want to find yourself part of the most delightfully fragrant mystery of modern times, ask someone to tell you all about the hunt for "Dorset Blue Vinny," a cheese as fascinating and elusive as the Hound of the Baskervilles. Scottish cheeses are one of the gastronomic discoveries of the post-war era, and it is also generally true that many country restaurants offer much better cheeseboards than they did a few years ago. Do not be afraid to ask for "just a taste" of two or three unfamiliar ones.

When to Get Hungry

Meal times ought to be engrained firmly on your memory if you go anywhere outside the big towns and large seaside resorts. Generally, they are breakfast: 8.30 to 9.30; lunch: noon to 2 P.M.; tea: 3.30 to 5.00 P.M.; and dinner, 7.30 to 9.30 P.M. (up to 10.30 if the staff is keen).

Meeting the Natives in Their Local Habitat

Even today, when television keeps so many people glued to their own hearth and home, the public house, the pub, the local—it has many aliases—is still a vital part of British life. We mentioned a while back the Victorianly puritan attitude that bedevils some aspects of food. And this seems as good a time as any to develop the theme a little. You will constantly meet with a great deal of what will seem like hypocrisy in matters such as opening and closing times of pubs, the fact that it is extremely difficult to get a meal after midnight in the West End of London, and the almost total emptiness of country towns after about ten in the evening. Like Parliament and the Law, all these things grew slowly, by long accretion. British life is barnacled over with regulations and traditions and habits, a lot of them excellent, many bad, and some just plain ludicrous. The real secret is that there is a way round each and every one of them, if only you know how. Don't take anything at its face value in Britain or, as they say (proving their vital interest in matters of the stomach) "never judge a sausage by its skin."

For the past 50 years we have been moaning about the absurd opening times for pubs, but in mid-1988 the law was changed. Now publicans can keep open, if they so choose, from 11 in the morning to 11 at night. There were dire predictions that the population would immediately turn into helpless alcoholics, but, in the event, the change passed almost unnoticed. It has certainly made life much easier for the visitor, who can now have a rest and a pint between museums or shops with no problem at all.

Luncheon Is Served

One of the most attractive, and cheapest, ways of lunching is to find a pub, order a pint of whatever you fancy, and attack the section of the bar devoted to food. Pub food is plentiful, usually good, and filling. Most pubs these days have both hot and cold dishes, and here are a few of the ones that are most common.

On the hot side of the menu you are most likely to find shepherd's pie, a foundation of ground meat in a rich gravy, topped off with crusty mashed potatoes. Steak and kidney pie usually comes next on the list of filling foods, with bangers and mash running a close third. "Bangers" are sausages, grilled and piping hot; the "mash" part consists of mashed potatoes. On the cold buffet you will find veal-and-ham pie, or one of the other pies that are very popular. In these more sophisticated days you are also likely to find a quiche, and beside it may well be a pile of Scotch eggs, which are apt to catch the unwary unprepared. They are hard-boiled eggs wrapped in sausage meat and then cooked and served cold. A mite on the heavy side.

There are some dishes which you probably only see in London pubs, but as these are often excellent it's worth looking out for them. If you see eel pie and mash in an East London pub, give it a try. It's a mixture of fish (mainly eel), lemon, parsley and shallots covered with puff pastry and usually served with mashed potatoes. The most authentic places serve it with a so-called green liquor, which is made of parsley. Then there is faggots and peas, which is pork pieces mixed with liver and kidney and onions and seasoned with sage—served with peas. And jellied eels, though increasingly expensive and less frequently found, are very much of a traditional East End Londoner's favorite and should be tried, even if they don't appeal at first taste.

Outside London, especially in the depths of the country, the most likely midday food in a pub will be the Ploughman's Lunch. This varies a little from place to place, but is usually a wedge of Cheddar cheese, a hunk of crusty bread, pickled onions or other pickles to choice . . . washed down, of course, with a pint of the best.

Stirred, Not Shaken

Cocktails are still regarded as an amusing diversion by the British, and you should specify the exact ingredients of what it is you want to drink if you order a cocktail in a bar or restaurant—or at least gently ask if the barman knows how to create your chosen poison. It is not only English as a language that divides the British from the Americans, the correct way to make a martini has been the cause of breaking up many a longterm friendship. Just what you mean by "whisky" can be a source of embarrassment, too. To anyone in the British Isles "whisky" will mean Scotch—though in Ireland it could mean Irish whiskey. So if you are dying for a real Manhattan, just check if there is anything around other than Scotch.

Heroes like 007, with his "shaken not stirred," have made a fair impact on the vocabulary of barmen. And, by and large, you will be able to get whatever you want. Britain isn't all *that* different in the experience of its barmen. The one thing that will strike you (usually with a dull thud) is the wild variety in prices of drinks. We cannot give much advice on this, except to say that if the barman has his coat on instead of being in shirt sleeves then the prices will also be well-clothed. Regulations ensure that prices are displayed in bars. There are some places, like theater bars, where you will be stirred *and* very shaken indeed by what you are charged for a drink.

Liquid Gold

Britain's crowning glories (spiritually speaking) are Scotch whisky and English gin. Gin is very much a matter of personal taste, here as in the States, but books, poems, epics indeed, have been written about scotch. Although North Americans have boosted the sales of the very light Scotch whiskies (which were specially distilled for the U.S. market) to amazing heights, your stay in Britain should be a good opportunity to sample the wide variety of whiskies. Though a bottle of good whisky costs from £9.00 up, you can get a single shot in a pub for about £1. You therefore have no economic excuse to avoid sampling the heavy tangy Scotches as well as the light ones (and all those in between). When ordering, try at least to drink one each of the two basic types, *malt* whisky and *grain,* or blended, whisky. The former is made only from malted barley. Grain whisky, however, is made from malted barley, unmalted barley and maize (corn). About 100 different firms produce malt whisky, about one dozen manufacture grain whisky. The more you sample, the more you'll appreciate the delicate differences and the fanaticism various brands or blends have engendered.

One drink which really must be mentioned, if only for its antiquity, is cider. This is the original folk drink of a lot of the countryside, especially south-western England. If you approach it thinking you are drinking simple apple juice, you may wake up several hours later under a nearby bush. It can be very potent indeed and, since its manufacture is not controlled by the same kind of regulations as most alcohol, it may be strong enough to take the paint off a barn door.

There is a whole new world of wines grown in Britain. It is useless to pretend that they are perfect yet. But, like Dr Johnson's dog who walked on its hind legs, it's not so much what the wines are like, but that there are wines at all! Vine growing was imported into Britain by the Romans, flourished during the Middle Ages and then totally disappeared. The new vineyards are moving slowly, and concentrate mainly on white wines, the lack of sufficient sunshine inhibits the proper ripening of the red wine grapes. If you are in a part of the country where there is a vineyard, do drop in and find out what is happening. Local tourist offices will be able to supply information on visitable vineyards in their area. Some have cafes or restaurants, but all offer tastings and, of course, the chance to buy.

The Bitter End

The names of some of the most popular beers drunk in English pubs need explaining, too. "Bitter" is the drink most frequently ordered, and although this is right at the center of a controversy among male pub-goers (since there is a flourishing movement to bring back the traditionally prepared ale that is much less gassy), bitter is basically the standard English draught beer. The most popular bottled beers are brown ale, which is dark and fairly sweet, and light or pale ale which is a little closer to, say, American or Scandinavian beer, though often rather metallic in taste. It is of a slightly darker color than lager, which is increasingly popular.

"Mild" is a drink which used to be popular, and which may strike the average visitor a little like cold or lukewarm tea, and, although at many places it is not available at all, it still has some devotees. "Guinness" is a universal drink, and found even in pubs that are allied to a particular brewer, where the landlord is a manager or tenant basically under the control of the brewery. Guinness is Irish in origin, though most of the stuff that is drunk in Britain is made in West London. Guinness comes in draught form or bottled, and the bottled drink is slightly less pungent in flavor as well as appearance than the draught variety. A sweeter version of stout, which is what Guinness is, is Mackeson.

Britain's membership in the Common Market has meant that beers—especially lagers—from the Continent have flooded into the country. There is always a bewildering variety of brands available, though many of them are actually brewed in Britain under license. There are even a couple of diet beers, with the sugar brewed away.

When you think you have sorted out the more arcane details of drink and drinking, then it's time, as the British would say, to pop off to a pub and order a pint in your very best man-of-the-world manner. Turn to your neighbor, raise the glass and utter that most pleasant of toasts, "cheers." Your drinking in Britain, with a little bit of luck, will then undoubtedly be "cheers" all the way.

EXPLORING
BRITAIN

LONDON

"The Flower of Cities All"

London has changed. The great open spaces are still green and filled with flowers; there are still wildfowl in St. James's Park and boats on the Serpentine. But behind them, the skyline has assumed a new profile, with familiar shapes set in a new perspective of towering office buildings. Some of these changes have alarmed not only reactionaries, but also people who would have preferred less faceless, more tasteful monuments to the age. But enough of old London survives to make the city still congenial, and sometimes the newer constructions, like the Post Office Tower (or British Telecom Tower, as it is now officially known) and the mammoth NatWest Tower, are quite dramatic.

The enforcement of smokeless zones across the middle of London has had two effects. The deadly fall fogs have been eliminated, and a sweeter atmosphere has inspired a wholesale cleaning of the city's older, more remarkable buildings. The visitor will see St. Paul's Cathedral riding high and white over the rooftops of the City (financial district) of London, just as it does in the painter Canaletto's 18th-century views of the Thames. The great cathedral, cleaned, glows honey-gold, breathtakingly floodlit by night, making Sir Christopher Wren's detail and proportion evident once again.

But even though those choking fogs have gone and the mists no longer wreathe the street lamps on winter evenings, London is still essentially a place where the quality of the light, diamond-hard or softly opalescent, governs the city's mood. It is a mood which the visitor can share with complete enjoyment. For London is a city which loves to be explored; it only reveals its real self to those who are prepared to wander into its back streets and investigate its hidden squares. Under the modern gloss and hectic bustle, London is still the city that it has been for centuries, though, perhaps, the sad prevalence of garbage in the streets more closely reflects the medieval days of the city than is altogether to be welcomed.

The biggest city in Europe, London sprawls over more than 600 square miles. Through its center curls the River Thames, bending and twisting from beyond Richmond and greener fields, past the seat of government, and alongside the docks towards Greenwich and the sea. Sometimes London is criticized for not making more of its river; a strong and beautiful attraction, it is the most spectacular throwaway in the country, and the farther one moves away from it, the less interesting London becomes. Yet you can enjoy its drama, real and potential, anywhere from London Bridge itself up to Chelsea, by walking alongside it.

There is one point that should be made about visiting London, before we launch into the details of our *Exploring* section. Currently about fourteen million visitors arrive in Britain every year, and nearly all of these sightseers inevitably want to see London. Now, London is a working city. Its residents have to get to and from their jobs every day; they have to eat lunch and generally do all the things that you would do yourself back home. Fourteen million visitors makes it a little bit more difficult for them to do these things; and the situation is exacerbated by the fact that the influx of tourists is concentrated in the summer months, when the buses and the underground (subway) are at their least attractive. Londoners are among the most hospitable people anywhere, but the vast number of travelers who surround them for so many months in the year does create a new situation to which they have to adapt. The message is, therefore, try to travel during the out-of-peak periods when sightseeing (it's often cheaper anyway!), and remember that if you ask a Londoner the way somewhere, he may have been asked the same question already a dozen times. Our bet is that he will still answer in a helpful way.

Piccadilly Circus

Since explorations all have to start somewhere we have chosen Piccadilly Circus as the point from which to begin exploring central London. That is about its only useful function, for Piccadilly Circus these days is noisy and rather sordid. The plans for its rehabilitation, which were years maturing, are now beginning to show signs of the shape of the future. Cleaning and rebuilding are going on hand in hand, both on the Circus itself and in the streets roundabout.

Piccadilly Circus is always crowded, sometimes with very dubious characters, especially on the evenings of big football matches, national events and Guy Fawkes Night (November 5), when the crowds are singing, dancing and generally having fun. (Until a few years ago Piccadilly was *the* place to go if you wanted to celebrate New Year's Eve outdoors, but Trafalgar Square has taken over.) The statue of the Angel of Christian Charity, designed in 1893 and mistakenly called Eros (the God of Love), has been rejuvenated and occupies a new home on the south side of the Circus. The statue actually commemorates Lord Shaftesbury, a philanthropic Victorian nobleman—hence the choice of subject—who also is remembered by Shaftesbury Avenue. The arrow (shaft) of Eros is a play on Shaftesbury's name.

Select whatever area of Central London you want to explore, go to Piccadilly Circus, face in the appropriate direction and start. To the north runs Regent Street, curving up one side of Mayfair. To the south is Lower Regent Street, leading towards Whitehall, the parks and the palaces. To the east are Shaftesbury Avenue and Leicester Square, for theaters and Soho; to the west is Piccadilly itself, heading off for Hyde Park, Knightsbridge and, eventually, Land's End. Piccadilly Circus is also one of the embarkation points for the London Regional Transport round-tour bus, which is a very good way of seeing the center of London quickly, so as to get your bearings and choose those parts that you want to return to and investigate in greater detail.

St. James's

Looking south from Piccadilly Circus, down the wide stretch of Lower Regent Street, you will see the Duke of York on his column (he was the one in the children's rhyme who had ten thousand men he didn't know what to do with), and beyond him the towers and spires of Whitehall. The area bounded on the north by Piccadilly, on the east by Lower Regent Street, on the south by The Mall and on the west by St. James's Street, is known as St. James's after the palace that lies at its heart. It is one of the very few areas of London whose plan has barely changed from the time it was laid out in the late 17th century.

Pall Mall (pronounced usually "Pal Mal") has dignity and elegance brought about by the presence of many important clubs. These are not open to the public, but it's always possible you'll meet someone who is a member and may invite you to lunch. The exclusive Reform Club, at No. 104, is a favorite with many famous writers and was where Jules Verne's Phineas Fogg made the wager that he could go around the world in 80 days. The even more prestigious Athenaeum, with its frieze copied from the Parthenon, embellishes a corner. Pall Mall ends up by St. James's Palace, which has a delightful Tudor gatehouse facing up St. James's Street. St. James's Street itself emerges on Piccadilly near the great and recently superbly remodeled Ritz Hotel.

St. James's is an essentially masculine area; Jermyn Street cuts across, parallel to Piccadilly, and contains splendid shops, many offering men's clothing and accessories. There is little enough to attract the explorer's particular attention here, but the area is historically interesting in a general way and exudes a slightly pompous elegance, which is ideal for the discriminating shopper.

Tucked away in the center of this area is St. James's Square, one of the oldest of London's squares. The square is lined by attractive buildings, mostly from the 18th century, which are worth spending a moment looking at. For those interested in books the narrow facade of No. 14, in one corner, will be specially fascinating, for behind it lurk the many thousand volumes of the London Library, one of the best private lending libraries in the world. The equestrian statue in the middle of the square is of King William III (William of Orange).

On the west, St. James's is fringed by Green Park, while Piccadilly forms another side of this triangular parkland. In the summer Green Park

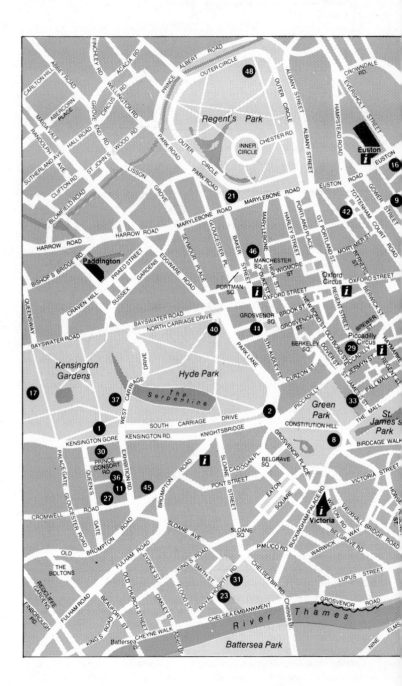

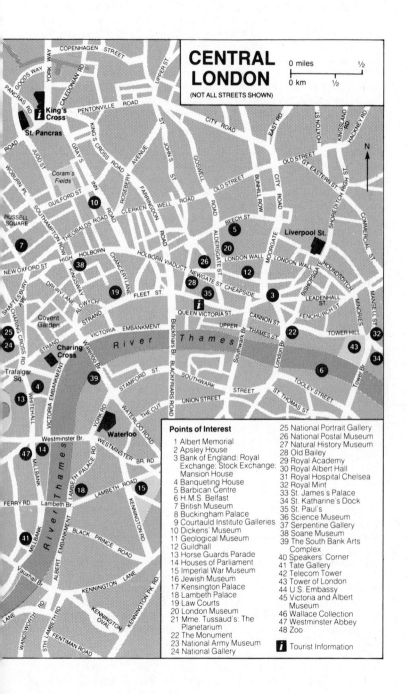

CENTRAL LONDON
(NOT ALL STREETS SHOWN)

0 miles ½
0 km ½

Points of Interest

1 Albert Memorial
2 Apsley House
3 Bank of England: Royal Exchange; Stock Exchange; Mansion House
4 Banqueting House
5 Barbican Centre
6 H.M.S. Belfast
7 British Museum
8 Buckingham Palace
9 Courtauld Institute Galleries
10 Dickens' Museum
11 Geological Museum
12 Guildhall
13 Horse Guards Parade
14 Houses of Parliament
15 Imperial War Museum
16 Jewish Museum
17 Kensington Palace
18 Lambeth Palace
19 Law Courts
20 London Museum
21 Mme. Tussaud's: The Planetarium
22 The Monument
23 National Army Museum
24 National Gallery
25 National Portrait Gallery
26 National Postal Museum
27 Natural History Museum
28 Old Bailey
29 Royal Academy
30 Royal Albert Hall
31 Royal Hospital Chelsea
32 Royal Mint
33 St. James's Palace
34 St. Katharine's Dock
35 St. Paul's
36 Science Museum
37 Serpentine Gallery
38 Soane Museum
39 The South Bank Arts Complex
40 Speakers' Corner
41 Tate Gallery
42 Telecom Tower
43 Tower of London
44 U.S. Embassy
45 Victoria and Albert Museum
46 Wallace Collection
47 Westminster Abbey
48 Zoo

_i_ Tourist Information

is peaceful and shady (called Green Park because, simply, there are virtually no flowers); in the winter the bare trees make a striking frame for the
towers of Westminster and Victoria. St. James's Park, across The Mall,
has a lake, flowerbeds and captive birds. Laid out by a Frenchman, Le
Nôtre, in the 17th century and then worked over by the English architect
John Nash early in the 19th, it is much prettier than Green Park and especially attractive at night when the illuminated fountains play and the skyline beyond the trees looks like a floating fairyland. St. James's Park is
the epitome of the strange ability Englishmen have to translate what are
essentially private gardens into public domains.

The Mall is a wide triumphal way from Buckingham Palace to Trafalgar
Square, decorated with gilded crowns, and banners whenever there is a
State visit or any other excuse for a procession. It is the site of several
great houses occupied by various members of the Royal Family. The most
important of these is Clarence House, where the Queen Mother lives. At
the eastern end of The Mall is Carlton House Terrace, a fine row of Georgian houses with colonnades, in the basement of which are the Institute
of Contemporary Arts galleries, often occupied with shows that are at extreme odds with the dignified terrace rising above. Across The Mall from
Carlton House Terrace is the formidable bulk of the Citadel, Churchill's
World War II headquarters, built in 1941–42 and now shrouded in ivy.

Buckingham Palace itself is so fixed as a symbol in England one rarely
pauses to think how dull it is. (It won't be dull trying to cross the street
to see it, however; the authorities refuse to put traffic signals or pedestrian
crossings in front of the Palace as they don't want to "spoil the beauty
of the place"—so lots of luck en route!) The Palace was built in the 18th
century for the Duke of Buckingham, who sold it to George II for £21,000.
Initially it stood on three sides of a courtyard, the east-facing end open
to St. James's Park. The heavy façade of the east front, which the tourist
sees through the iron fence, was added later (the present one in 1913) and
is less attractive than the west front, which the public cannot see. The interior and the gardens are never open to the public (except for the lucky
few who are invited to Garden Parties or attend formal investitures at
which the Queen confers knighthoods and lesser awards).

The Queen's Gallery (adjoining the Palace on its south side) is one of
the best small galleries in Europe, and regular exhibitions drawn from the
vast and spectacular royal collections are on display. The royal standard
flying above the east front indicates that the Queen is in residence. The
Changing of the Guard is one of London's most important tourist attractions. Since a guardsman had an unfortunate altercation with an importu-
nate tourist a few years ago, the sentries have been moved inside the Palace
railings.

The large monument in front of the Palace is the Queen Victoria Memorial, an epic recapitulation of Victorian ideals, with Motherhood, Truth,
Justice, Peace and Progress all represented. The best thing that can be said
for this mammoth celebration of everything but Virginity and The Right
To Vote, is that it makes a wonderful grandstand from which to view processions and the Changing of the Guard. From the Palace, a street named
Constitution Hill leads alongside Green Park, back to Hyde Park Corner.

Cross St. James's Park, entering from The Mall, and pause on the bridge
across the lake to look at the unexpected and vaguely Oriental profile of
Whitehall through the trees. Leave the park by turning left onto Birdcage

Walk, which leads directly into Parliament Square, with the Houses of Parliament and Westminster Abbey. To the left, Whitehall leads up to Trafalgar Square; to the right, Millbank leads south along the Thames towards the Tate Gallery and Chelsea.

The Houses of Parliament

Parliament Square was designed partly to give a good view of the Houses of Parliament and partly as a kind of garden linking them with Westminster Abbey. The square is fringed with statues, including Victorian prime ministers such as Peel, Palmerston and Disraeli; more distantly historical figures such as Richard the Lion-Hearted and Oliver Cromwell; and illustrious foreigners like Lincoln, while above all broods a powerful rendering of Churchill.

Seen across Parliament Square, the Houses of Parliament seem at first an incoherent complex of elaborate spires, towers and crenelations. But their medieval look is quite spurious. Many people are surprised to discover that they were built between 1840 and 1850, the exception being the genuinely ancient core of the complex, Westminster Hall, which was first built in 1097. The designer of the New Palace of Westminster, Sir Charles Barry, who also designed Tower Bridge, selected the richly decorated Perpendicular style, probably in order to harmonize with Henry VII's chapel opposite. If you view them from across the river, you will see that the Houses of Parliament are planned with a basically classic simplicity, the towers and roofs just giving an impression of confusion from some viewing angles.

Westminster was the first major settlement outside the City of London; Roman remains have been found and King Edward the Confessor built a palace here between 1050 and 1065 in order to be close to the abbey which he refounded. William Rufus, son of William the Conqueror, in 1099 completed the vast Westminster Hall, and his medieval successors made many further additions. The present Houses of Parliament, therefore, occupy the site of a palace and so still rank as such (hence the term, the "Palace of Westminster," in occasional references to Parliamentary news). English kings resided here up to the time of Henry VIII, but from the extensive constructions of that time only a few buildings have survived. Westminster Hall stands in the center, facing across Parliament Square; it has a fine hammerbeam oak roof, put there by Richard II in 1399, and to its east is the crypt of St. Stephen's Chapel (14th-century), still used occasionally for weddings and christenings by Members of Parliament and their families. Across Old Palace Yard is the moated 14th-century Jewel Tower.

The Houses of Parliament and Westminster Hall can be visited (see page 138 for details). If you are fortunate enough to know, or to meet socially, a tame M.P., persuade him to take you around places not shown to the general public. Tea on the terrace with a Member is most prestigious. The palace covers eight acres, and has two miles of corridors and more than 1,000 rooms. The large, square Victoria Tower is supposed to be the tallest square tower in existence, while the 320-foot clock tower, "Big Ben," is the famous symbol of London. Actually, this is the name of the 13½-ton bell on which the hours are struck, named after Sir Benjamin Hall, First Commissioner of Works when it was hung. When Parliament is sitting, a flag flies from the Victoria Tower by day and a light shines by night. Watching the House of Commons or the House of Lords at work, from the Strangers' Gallery, is probably the best free show in London, staged in the world's most renowned ego chamber. Apply in advance for tickets from your Embassy. If you want to watch Prime Minister's Question Time—the liveliest hour in the Commons day, taking place on Tuesdays and Thursdays—you will need tickets. But when the Commons is sitting late, you will usually have no trouble getting in.

Westminster Abbey

Across Parliament Square stands Westminster Abbey. As with most Christian edifices that become the focus for the whole history of their nations, the Abbey is packed with monuments to the great, the famous, and the totally forgotten. Visitors should not allow their search for great names to blind them, however, to its overall beauty—a fine example of Early English Gothic architecture.

The first authenticated church on this site was a Benedictine abbey, established in 970, dedicated to St. Peter. "Westminster" means "western monastery," indicative of its geographical relation to the City of London. Here, most British monarchs since William the Conqueror have been crowned. A focal point inside the Abbey is, therefore, the Coronation Chair, made by the order of Edward I, which has been used ever since. The chair encloses the Stone of Scone (pronounced "Skoon"), or Stone of Destiny, which has long been a source of friction between England and Scotland. The kings of Scotland were crowned on it and it was used for the coronation of Macbeth's stepson at Scone Palace in Scotland, in 1057. It was carried away from Scotland by Edward I in 1297 but has, over the centuries, become a symbol of Scottish independence. It has been removed from the Abbey only three times—once to Westminster Hall for the installation of Oliver Cromwell as Lord Protector; once for safety from German bombers in 1940; and finally, by Scottish nationalists in 1950, who took it far north. (It was returned six months later.)

The Abbey has been much altered and enlarged over the centuries; some additions are recent, such as the western towers, built in 1740. Edward the Confessor did a great deal of rebuilding and Henry III carried on this work. Reconstruction was finished in 1528. Edward the Confessor's Chapel is the center of the Abbey, around which Henry II built a series of chapels.

Many kings and queens are buried here: Henry III, Edward I, Edward III with his queen, Richard II and his first consort, Henry V, and Anne of Cleves, one of the wives of Henry VIII. There are some fine tombs near the sanctuary, and the finest chapel in the Abbey is undoubtedly Henry VII's where several kings and queens are buried, with two of the most lovely tombs being those of Elizabeth I and Mary, Queen of Scots. Nearby is the Battle of Britain Chapel, with its impressive stained-glass windows.

Westminster Abbey has witnessed many splendid coronation ceremonies and royal weddings. Monuments to great figures in many fields of endeavor are scattered throughout the body of the Abbey; statesmen such as Disraeli, Palmerston, Gladstone, and Robert Peel, together with scientists such as Newton and Darwin. In Poets' Corner, among those honored are Chaucer, Shakespeare, Lord Byron (whose memorial was delayed owing to his "scandalous" life), Kipling, T.S. Eliot, Dylan Thomas and Noel Coward. Elsewhere there are memorials to Americans such as Longfellow, Henry James, James Russell Lowell and Franklin Roosevelt.

The finest architectural aspects of the Abbey, and most impressive views, can be obtained from outside by wandering through the cloisters, which are full of atmosphere.

In the Norman Undercroft, just off the Cloisters, is an excellent small museum. Among the treasures it contains are some effigies that used to be carried in funeral processions; these are mainly of monarchs, clothed in their robes and, since the faces were mainly taken from death masks, they give an impressive idea of how their originals actually looked. The figure of Nelson (not a funeral one, but made to attract visitors) is especially striking. The Chapter House dates from the 13th century, but the oldest relic is the 11th-century Pyx Chamber, a stern Norman place contrasting with the bright courtyard beyond, now open for the exhibition of Abbey treasures.

Nestling near the Abbey is the church of St. Margaret where Sir Walter Raleigh is buried. After he had been beheaded in nearby Old Palace Yard his wife kept his head in a velvet bag to show to visitors. The east window, made in Flanders in 1509, was a gift from Ferdinand and Isabella of Spain. The church has an intimate atmosphere and has been the scene of many notable weddings over the centuries; the poet John Milton and Sir Winston Churchill were married here.

A thorough study of both Westminster Abbey and the Houses of Parliament takes time and is exhausting. But if you have the energy, or on another day, take a side trip to Westminster Cathedral near Victoria Station, approached down Victoria Street from the Abbey. This is the premier Roman Catholic church in England; quite enormous, it was built between 1895 and 1903. Inside, some of the brick walls are covered with sumptuous marble and mosaic, but the job was never finished and is now unlikely to be. The tower is 284 feet high with a marvelous view from the top, accessible by elevator. Once the Cathedral was hidden, but the new buildings which line Victoria Street were specifically designed to allow a small piazza, giving an excellent view of the cleaned façade of the exotic, Byzantine church.

Millbank and the Tate Gallery

After leaving the Abbey, turn once more towards the Houses of Parliament and continue to the right, parallel with the river. This will lead you past the Victoria Tower Gardens, where stand the statue of Mrs. Emmeline Pankhurst—who suffered prison and hunger-strike for the cause of women's suffrage—and the noble group, *Burghers of Calais,* by Rodin, now placed on a low plinth in accordance with the sculptor's wishes.

Off to the right (turn up Dean Stanley Street) is the renovated church of St. John, Smith Square. It represents a perfect solution to the mammoth problem of disused churches which is increasingly afflicting Britain as it slowly swings away from a total involvement with the Established Church. The church was burned down during World War II and rebuilt in the mid-'60s. It is now used as a concert hall, and a more delightful ambience for hearing music, particularly Baroque music, could hardly be imagined. The BBC holds frequent lunchtime concerts here. The streets in this area, especially Lord North Street, which leads out of Smith Square, are largely inhabited by Members of Parliament who want to be near their work. Lord North Street is a delightful example of the domestic architecture of Georgian London.

Farther along Millbank (passing Lambeth Bridge and looking across the river at Lambeth Palace, the London home of the Archbishop of Canterbury) you will find the modern bulk of the Vickers' Building, a strangely light and sweeping construction, much favored by movie makers as a background. Just beyond is the Tate Gallery, a must for all lovers of modern art as well as those who want to find out more about British art in general.

The Tate, like so many great galleries, reveals more gems the more you explore. The works of William Blake and Turner, two English artists poles apart and yet bringing visionary skills to their craft, hang here in profusion. Elizabethan and Edwardian portraits contrast the 16th-century and early 20th-century Briton. Dégas, Giacometti, Rodin, Whistler, Van Gogh, the cream of European creativity is here; so much so, in fact, that the gallery was for years unable to show more than a fraction of its wealth. Then, in the spring of 1979, with a fireworks display and a flourish of trumpets, the Queen opened the long planned extension. This building considerably expands the gallery's exhibition space, and also provides that controlled environment necessary to protect delicate paintings from climatic changes. It may not be the most beautiful modern gallery, but it is one of the most scientifically advanced. There is a restaurant, as well as a cafeteria in the basement.

Whitehall

Returning to the Parliament-Abbey complex, our walk goes up Whitehall, passing the end of Westminster Bridge. Once, this whole area from the river to about where Trafalgar Square now is, was an extensive and fascinating palace which has simply disappeared, most of the buildings having been destroyed by fire in 1698. It was a series of courts, lawns, walks and buildings wonderful in conception, but never fully completed. According to a historian, it was "a glorious city of rose-tinted Tudor brick, green lawns, and shining marble statues." Today Whitehall is a dull, wide, but not quite straight, street.

The big government buildings that line the first part of the street are slightly brutal, but impressive. To the right on Whitehall is New Scotland Yard, its rather quaint brick exterior familiar from a dozen detective and police movies set in London. The headquarters of the Metropolitan police was moved in 1967 to a vast modern building off Victoria Street. Off to the left is Downing Street, a pleasant row of 18th-century houses; No. 10 is the official residence of the Prime Minister.

In the middle of the road stands the Cenotaph, a simple memorial to the dead of two world wars; here, once a year, the sovereign lays the first tribute of Flanders' poppies. The next item of interest is the Banqueting Hall on the right; this was designed by Inigo Jones in 1622, as part of the extensive Palace of Whitehall, to replace one burned down in 1619 and is the only part left of the former palace. In front of the hall, Charles I was beheaded in 1649. The whole building has been cleaned to reveal the Palladian beauty of its form.

Opposite is the Horse Guards, designed by William Kent, a not very tall, but beautifully proportioned, building with a clock tower. Here, the Changing of the Queen's Life Guard takes place every morning, and in the Horse Guards Parade beyond the forecourt, the ceremony of Trooping the Colour is held annually on the Queen's official birthday in June. It is one of London's most spectacular military pageants, with the Queen taking the salute; seats are hard to obtain but it makes an excellent subject for color television.

At the north end of Whitehall, just before Trafalgar Square, is the equestrian statue of the martyr king, Charles I. It was hidden during Cromwell's regime and surfaced again when Charles II was restored to the throne in 1660. As a piece of poetic, if macabre, justice, it is sited on the spot where several of those who signed the execution order for Charles I—the Regicides—were themselves done to death.

Trafalgar Square rivals Piccadilly Circus as the tourist center of London and does so in an infinitely more dignified way. Laid out in 1829, it was finished in 1841. In the center is another celebrated London landmark, Nelson's Column, erected in the 1840s to celebrate the victory of Nelson at the Battle of Trafalgar in 1805. Four huge bronze panels commemorate scenes from naval battles and were cast from French guns captured in the very battles they depict. Stretched out from the base are four vast lions. The fountains are fairly modern, the old ones having been sent around the globe as presents to Commonwealth governments. One is happily ensconced in Regina, Saskatchewan. There are pigeons everywhere, and also many photographers, equipped with birdseed to entice the semi-tame birds to settle on snap-happy tourists. Trafalgar Square is a focal point for rallies, marches and political meetings; on evenings of high jinks and celebrations, crowds throng the square, and even on cold winter nights—like Guy Fawkes Night or New Year's Eve—some students strip and climb on top of the still-flowing fountains. At the northeast corner of the square is a statue of George Washington erected in 1921.

The north side of the square is formed by the long, low National Gallery, housing the national collection of art and containing some of the world's greatest paintings. A modern extension allows for more of the priceless collection to be put on show and yet another extension is now in the works. It was the subject of the usual architectural brawl that is part of the baptismal rites for any British public building. An artistically inclined visitor should set aside a fair chunk of time for the National Gallery, which is rich in surprises. Just around the corner is the National Portrait Gallery, where British men and women through the centuries are gathered together in oils, drawings, sculpture and photographs. It is a parade of the famous—often in unexpected guise—that can be very rewarding to anyone interested in what makes the British tick.

Across the road from the entrance to the National Portrait Gallery is the delicate spire of the church of St. Martin-in-the-Fields, the work of James Gibbs. Running north from the church is the interesting St. Martin's Lane, with its theaters, Victorian pubs and historical associations. On the right-hand side is the Coliseum, home of the English National Opera Company and London's largest theater, with 2,558 seats. Watch for a very narrow opening on the right into Goodwin's Court, with a row of bow-fronted windows, once shops. On the other side of the road are two or three other alleys, Cecil Court is one, where there are a series of excellent secondhand bookshops.

Below St. Martin's is the Strand and below that Northumberland Avenue, which leads down to the Embankment. If you have a car, Northumberland Avenue is convenient for free parking out of office hours.

Soho

Slightly northwest from St. Martin's Lane lies Soho, which can be conveniently regarded as being bounded by Shaftesbury Avenue, Charing Cross Road, Oxford Street and Regent Street, making a small, nearly square area, its geometry emphasized by the way in which the streets run east to west or north to south, crossing each other neatly. It is associated with food, foreigners and sin, the last much overrated.

There is very little about Soho that is architecturally interesting, but the atmosphere is intriguing. There is a high density of Continental residents, which means a variety of food shops, delicatessens and, naturally, some of London's best foreign restaurants. There is, too, a Continental feeling, with cosmopolitan newsdealers. At night comes the neon, when slouching figures in doorways tout for strip shows. There are many such dives and clubs, most of them squalid and unattractive, run by a collection of characters rejoicing in the collective name of The Vice. There are reputed to be more porno movie houses in Soho than there are legitimate ones in the West End generally.

Just off the Regent Street side of the area is Golden Square with perhaps one house indicating its 18th-century grace. Nearby is Carnaby Street, which in the 1960s became a world-wide synonym for swinging young attire. It has recently acquired a new incarnation, '60s psychedelia having been belatedly forsaken in favor of sober gray paving and old-fashioned black-and-gold lampposts, the ultimate intention being to create a shopping environment to rival that of the Covent Garden Piazza.

The other main square is Soho Square, near the Oxford Street side— again fairly dull. Elsewhere, the main part of the church of St. Anne, on Wardour Street, was destroyed by bombing in 1940, but the tower remains. There are some interesting pubs and picturesque, daytime street markets selling fruit, meat and vegetables.

Shaftesbury Avenue cuts through the southern part of Soho; this is the main street for theaters. Between here and Coventry Street, Soho still runs but a small Chinatown changes the atmosphere from Mediterranean to Oriental.

Below Shaftesbury Avenue lies Leicester (pronounced "Lester") Square, another center of entertainment, this time movies. The square has been converted into a chiefly "pedestrians only" area but, however stylish the new paving is and however pretty the flower beds, it is impossible to avoid the impression that the square is more than a little bit insalubrious these days, with hot dog stands, cheap bars and a general air of honky-tonkiness. Shakespeare stands on his plinth in the middle of it all, chin on hand, clearly wishing he were somewhere else. On the north side of the square is the Swiss Center, definitely an exception to the pervading atmosphere. The center is a very convenient rendezvous, with several restaurants serving good Swiss food.

Mayfair

Broadly speaking, Mayfair is bounded by Regent Street, Oxford Street, Park Lane and Piccadilly. The main interest of this area lies in its fine shops, beautiful residential houses and squares. As it represents all that is gracious in London living and shopping, there is an air of wealthy leisure, even on the busiest days. In the 17th century, Mayfair was a quiet country spot, popular as a residential area away from the bustle of Westminster and the City.

Regent Street is perhaps London's most impressive shopping strip, running wide and straight after the initial bend out of Piccadilly Circus. The street was originally planned to run in a direct, triumphal line from Pall Mall to Portland Place, but as with most of the great planning schemes attempted in London, bends and deviations were forced on the builders. Running parallel to Regent Street farther west are New Bond Street and Old Bond Street, equally famous for their even more luxurious and expensive shops. Old Bond Street was created in 1686 and New Bond Street followed some 14 years later, forming a neat snobbish distinction among residents of both streets.

Slightly to the west is Berkeley (pronounced "Barkley") Square, with its trees and garden, which was once one of London's most distinguished residential centers. Three English statesmen, Sir Robert Walpole, Charles James Fox, and Clive of India lived here.

A few streets to the northwest lies Grosvenor Square, one whole side of which is taken up by the American Embassy. It is interesting to study the names of London's streets and squares, which often reflect earlier—or even current—aristocratic landowners. British noble families frequently have two names associated with them; the title that they hold and the name of their family. Here is a case in point, for much of this area still belongs to the Duke of Westminster, whose family name is Grosvenor. This large, graceful square, laid out in 1695, has in its center Sir W. Reid Dick's memorial statue of President Franklin D. Roosevelt, erected in 1948. The British had an especially soft spot for Roosevelt, and his statue was paid for by public donations, large and small. Eero Saarinen designed the embassy, often called "Little America" by Londoners. When the building first went up, there were some wry comments about the huge eagle poised over the façade as if waiting to pounce. But it has long since become the big brother of the London pigeons. John Adams, first American ambassador to Britain and second President of the United States, lived in the house at the corner of Brook and Duke streets here.

Piccadilly

Walking westward from Piccadilly Circus along Piccadilly itself, you will see, again, famous shops. On the left is St. James's Church, severely damaged in the Blitz, but worth visiting to see how its elegant interior was beautifully restored. On the north side is Burlington House, home of the Royal Academy of Arts, where the celebrated summer exhibition and top international shows are held. A statue of Sir Joshua Reynolds stands in the courtyard. Before you reach Burlington House, watch out for a narrow turning on the right, in which stands the Albany, a fine Georgian house behind which is a long alleyway, bordered by apartment suites where some highly distinguished people live. On the other side of Burlington House is the Burlington Arcade, a covered shopping alley with some of the loveliest little shops in London. An excellent place to wander in on a wet day.

Following St. James's on the south side are a series of famous shops, Simpson's, Hatchard's and Fortnum and Mason's, as well as the offices of several top airlines. Then, just after the end of St. James's Street, comes the Ritz. Past the Ritz the south side of Piccadilly is bounded by the quietness of Green Park, while the north side stretches along to Hyde Park Corner in a series of sedate offices and good hotels. Tucked away here is a spot of considerable charm, Shepherd Market, lying between Piccadilly and Curzon Street, a network of narrow alleys with some attractive houses and fascinating shops. There are no sheep here, but there are a couple of rousing pubs, as well as indications that the area is making strong efforts to reassert itself as the capital's premier red-light district.

The last house on Piccadilly—formerly known as address No. 1, London—is Apsley House, built by Robert Adam in 1771 and later the residence of the Duke of Wellington. (Opened in 1952 as the Wellington Museum.) It faces Hyde Park Corner, a busy traffic circle with a large island of green tranquillity on which stands the Wellington Arch.

The western limit of Mayfair is Park Lane, which faces Hyde Park, and which once was synonymous with high living and beautiful houses. Most have now been demolished to be replaced by hotels. Here are the Inter-Continental (opposite Apsley House), the Inn on the Park, the Hilton, the Dorchester, Londonderry House and Grosvenor House. These tall buildings have created an entirely new problem for the royal family, whose secluded garden lying just the other side of the Hyde Park Corner traffic circle is now not quite as private as it used to be. At the north end of Park Lane is Marble Arch, another traffic whirlpool, where you will find, on the park side, Speakers' Corner, a space specially reserved for anyone with anything to say that they *must* say publicly. Great entertainment for a Sunday afternoon.

Marble Arch itself is not particularly impressive; it used to stand in the forecourt of Buckingham Palace, until brought here in 1850, near the place where once stood the public gallows known as Tyburn Tree.

Oxford Street

The north limit of Mayfair is Oxford Street, a long straight shopping thoroughfare containing many department stores and shops of all kinds. It begins on the west at Marble Arch and runs all the way eastwards to Tottenham Court Road. Turn north at the western corner of Selfridges, one of the department stores on Oxford Street, and you soon come to Baker Street, a place of pilgrimage for admirers of the greatest detective of all, though you'll look in vain for the apartment (221B) in which Sherlock Holmes "lived." The Abbey National Building Society, now at Holmes' "address," however, still deals with many letters every year addressed to the sleuth from all over the world.

In Manchester Square, off the end of Baker Street to the east, was the town house of the Marquis of Hertford, now home of the Wallace Collection. It contains some of the most delicate and beautiful things in any London museum and is frequently overlooked by visitors. A lot of the items on display are French rococo masterpieces, but there are some superb medieval works of art and much else besides. As a permanent collection it is London's answer to the Frick.

Turn back down to Wigmore Street and walk east to Harley Street which is mainly devoted to medicine; most of Britain's greatest specialists have their consulting rooms there. A few blocks to the east is the British Telecom (once Post Office) Tower, at 620 feet one of London's tallest buildings. This is a landmark that can be seen from all over London, and can act as a useful pointer if you manage to get lost. It will peep out unexpectedly from behind even the tallest building, but for a complete view of the whole tower stand at the junction of Great Portland and Clipstone Streets.

Lying just north of Harley Street is Regent's Park, generally considered the most splendid park in London. It contains the Zoological Gardens, an open-air theater and the Regent's Canal, and it is surrounded by row houses and town houses of great distinction. The Zoo is a fascinating place to visit, although not cheap, especially for a family. Its various animal houses offer a fascinating cross-section of architectural styles, of which perhaps the most famous piece is the Aviary, designed by Lord Snowdon, former husband of Princess Margaret.

Part of the park is devoted to Queen Mary's Rose Garden, one of the most beautiful public gardens in the world, and a showcase for British roses. The open-air theater is a favorite summer recreation, offering fine productions of Shakespeare in a magical setting. No matter how warm the day, it is a good idea to take a blanket, for, as night falls, the breeze may turn chill.

It is possible to take a trip on one of the old traditionally painted canal barges along the Regent's Canal, which goes through the Zoo; apart from being a pleasantly relaxed way of lazing away the summer hours, it offers charming views of this part of London. There is also a launch from Camden Lock that stops at the Zoo before continuing to Paddington's Little Venice.

Hyde Park and Kensington Palace

Having seen one of London's green spaces—her "lungs"—return to Hyde Park Corner, just by Apsley House at the end of Piccadilly to visit another, even bigger, park.

London has developed, over the centuries, a keen awareness of the importance of having wide, green spaces in the center of the city. St. James's Park, Green Park and Buckingham Palace Gardens make an open swathe across the middle of central London; this is continued westwards by Hyde Park and Kensington Gardens, which taken together make more than 600 acres of space in which to play, walk babies and dogs, lie in the sun, boat, swim, make love and generally romp about. London takes full advantage of this opportunity and Hyde Park is a focal point for relaxation. You can walk steadily for two or three hours among trees and flowers, all the way from Kensington Palace to the Houses of Parliament (or vice versa), with only a couple of ventures into the real world of London traffic, and be all the time in the very heart of the metropolis.

The main gate to Hyde Park is Decimus Burton's screen at the south end of Park Lane. To the left is Rotten Row, a sand track for horse riders who use it daily, while the paths either side of the Row have always been a popular strolling place. You may row on and swim in the Serpentine, and enjoy open-air refreshment in the cafés you'll find among the trees—though be warned that these cafés, though attractive from outside, serve rather depressing food.

Kensington Gardens, once the private territory of Kensington Palace, has lovely walks and trees. Cutting across both parks is a crescent of water called in Hyde Park, the Serpentine, and in Kensington Gardens, Long Water. Peter Pan, the hero of J. M. Barrie's play, lived on an island in the Serpentine, and on the bank of Long Water is the famous statue of him.

On the south side of the park is the Albert Memorial, a Victorian concoction that greatly resembles a medieval reliquary. There Albert sits, looking pensively towards the great circular Albert Hall across the road, and beyond that to the whole complex of museums and colleges that was conceived as a tribute to him (see South Kensington below).

Kensington Palace, at the western end of Kensington Gardens, was the residence of the reigning sovereign until 1760, when George II died. It has been altered by two great architects, Wren and William Kent. Queen Victoria was born here and also Queen Mary II. Present residents include the Prince and Princess of Wales (Charles and Diana) and Princess Margaret. The state apartments and Court Costume Museum are open to the public.

South Kensington

Although it is not generally recognized by visitors as such, partly because it covers such a large area, the district that runs southwards from Kensington Gardens to Cromwell Road, is a huge cultural complex, probably the most extensive and comprehensive in the world; and it was planned as such by the Victorians.

It is perhaps best to begin from Brompton Road, having, with unlikely self-discipline, passed Harrods. On the right is the Brompton Oratory, a very Italianate Roman Catholic church, inside and out. It was built in that mid-Victorian period when the English Catholics, who had suffered eclipse and worse for centuries, were emerging into the light of tolerance.

The next building is the Victoria and Albert Museum, cliff-like and surmounted by cupolas and a structure like a cross between a crown and a wedding-cake. This is the heart of the whole area. It would seem strange that there can be two museums such as the British Museum and the V&A in the same city, but they really do serve two fairly distinct purposes. In some realms they overlap a little, as with drawings and watercolors, but the main function of the V&A is to act as a "Museum of Ornamental Art," with the object of "the application of fine art to objects of utility and the improvement of public taste in design." It is essentially a teaching museum, heavily committed to design from every age and country. Arm yourself with a floor plan when you go in; if you don't you may feel utterly bewildered.

The collection is so vast, and so rich, that it is difficult to pick out some of the most exciting elements. The paintings of Constable, perhaps the greatest English landscape artist, rank very high on any list; the jewel rooms, especially the massive Baroque jewels; the delicate miniatures, with some of the loveliest painted in Elizabeth I's reign; the medieval church art, with its elaborate workmanship and occasional glimpses into a world haunted by the fear of death and damnation; a profusion of Renaissance art, especially a series of magnificent Raphael cartoons; costumes from many periods, excellently exhibited in the Costume Hall; musical instruments bewildering in their complexity and craftsmanship, and frequently played in fascinating recitals; Chinese, Islamic, Indian art . . . the list is endless. A wing around the corner in Exhibition Road gives a chance for even more of the collection to be displayed, especially the photographic riches. This is a museum in which to wander and ponder, taking time off, if needed, for refreshment.

Next to the V&A come the three museums devoted to science, the Natural History Museum, the Geological Museum and the Science Museum itself. These are extremely informative especially for youngsters, who find the working models and the detailed explanatory displays absorbing. If you go there with children of school age be fully prepared to spend the rest of the day!

Exhibition Road, the wide road beside the V&A, will take you back to Kensington Gardens through the heart of this cultural area. On the left is the Imperial College of Science, now part of London University. On the right hand side of Exhibition Road is a large Mormon Chapel, with a thin spike covered in gold leaf.

To the left runs Prince Consort Road, and, above it, the Royal Albert Hall, scene of the summer series of Promenade Concerts.

Chelsea

Begin your exploration in Sloane Square, where stands the Royal Court Theater. Behind it are the quiet, rich residential streets of Belgravia, such as Eaton Square–*Upstairs, Downstairs* territory—and, on Sloane Street, the Cadogan Hotel, where Oscar Wilde was arrested and taken to prison. Ahead lies King's Road—packed with boutiques, bistros and antique shops. This is the road to visit on Saturdays from about noon onwards, when the pavement is crowded with a trendy army, among which the psychedelic glory of pink-headed punk stands out. Streets leading south from King's Road bring you to the Chelsea Embankment; those to the north lead to Kensington. Chelsea was traditionally the artists' quarter and is still a chic—and expensive—address to have.

The most interesting part of the King's Road is not the section from Sloane Square to the Town Hall, but the stretch beyond that. Here there are good small restaurants, lots of excellent antique shops and places to browse in endlessly. The walk could well be a long one, for the road continues all the way to Putney Bridge.

For the visitor the joys of Chelsea lie in the area south of King's Road, and the chief of these joys is the Chelsea Hospital. The easiest way to reach it is to turn left down Cheltenham Terrace, just past the Duke of York's Barracks, and continue down Franklin's Row until you see the hospital straight ahead. It was built around 1690 by Sir Christopher Wren as a refuge for old and disabled soldiers. It had the seal of approval of Charles II, and there is a fine statue of the Merry Monarch in the grounds. The statue is decked with oak leaves on 29 May each year, Oak Apple Day, in commemoration of the time when Charles hid in an oak tree to escape the troops of Oliver Cromwell. The Hospital is a peaceful place, and one can understand why it is that old soldiers never die but only fade away; it would be a fine spot to fade in. The building itself is worth visiting, it is open to the public in the mornings and afternoons, and the manicured grounds are ideal for strolling in. Each spring, the Chelsea Flower Show is held here. Garden-lovers (who rival dog-lovers in Britain for their ubiquity) troop to the Show to see the latest improvements in gardening and to carry away samples and ideas.

The comparatively new National Army Museum is just past the Hospital, on Royal Hospital Road. This museum celebrates the exploits and achievements of the Army from 1485 to 1982. The sad thing about it is that the outside of the building is monumentally ugly, and, since it stands in close proximity to the work of one of the world's greatest architects, uncharitable thoughts about the army's taste not being what it once was are unavoidable.

One of the most intriguing parts of Chelsea, especially for the visitor who is attracted to houses with histories, is the long riverside walk from just past the Chelsea Hospital, westwards beyond Battersea Bridge. This street of houses overlooking the river is called Cheyne Walk and has been the haunt of many poets, painters and other assorted notables. Among such famous literary names as George Eliot, Thomas Carlyle and Henry James, is that of Sir Thomas More, the Man for All Seasons, who was one of the area's greatest residents. You will suddenly come face to face with his statue, seated and looking out across the river; it is modern, set up in 1969, but has a strongly Tudor look to it, square, gilded and hierarchic. It portrays More the saint, rather than More the richly humorous, warm human being. The statue stands outside All Saints' Church, which was badly damaged in the Blitz, but has been rebuilt and contains many interesting memorials that survived nearly untouched. More's first wife is buried in the church, part of which he designed.

One of the most attractive sights here is the spider's-web Albert Bridge, built in 1873 and quite beautiful when lit up at night.

Bloomsbury

Before the redivision of London by the now defunct Greater London Council, Holborn was a borough. It is now joined with others into the much bigger area called Camden. An important part of Holborn, to the north of Holborn underground station, is called Bloomsbury, associated with students, the university and the self-centered literary set of the 1920s (of which Virginia Woolf was the leading light). Bloomsbury consists mainly of a series of linked squares and streets of 18th-century origin, some of them preserving the old houses intact, some sadly botched with modern replacements. Not the least remarkable thing is the fact that Bloomsbury Square itself, lined with huge trees, was excavated to a great depth a few years ago and now hides a vast underground parking lot. Close by can be found the London University, the British Museum and the Courtauld Institute Galleries (which contain a fine collection of Impressionist paintings).

It is a district of neat squares. In Bloomsbury Square, the Victorian philosopher Herbert Spencer wrote his *First Principles,* and Sir Hans Sloane started the collection that was to be the nucleus of the British Museum. Steele, the 18th-century writer, entertained his friends in one of the prim houses—employing the bailiffs who had just arrested him for debt as waiters. In his youth Disraeli was a resident. And other Bloomsbury squares—Russell, Bedford, Woburn—have had almost equally distinguished pasts.

A suggested itinerary for a walk around Bloomsbury: starting from Holborn underground station, cut north through Red Lion Square (not so pretty, but the Victorian painter and poet Dante Gabriel Rossetti lived there) into Theobalds Road. Walk east, past Great James Street (a narrow street built in 1722 and a fine example of domestic Georgian architecture—many of the original glazing bars and fanlights remain) until you reach the pleasant greenness of Gray's Inn. Opposite, turn north on John Street, which also contains some good 18th-century houses. In John Street's continuation, Doughty Street, is Dickens' House, where the writer lived from 1837 to 1839. It contains a good library and museum.

At the end of Doughty Street, turn left along Guilford Street past Coram's Fields, a children's play area on the site of the Foundling Hospital which was started by Captain Coram, a friend of Handel. The composer gave proceeds from early performances of *The Messiah* to help support the work of the orphanage. Turn left into Lamb's Conduit Street, in which is a pub called The Lamb, interestingly decorated and very crowded indeed in summer. From Lamb's Conduit Street, turn right into Great Ormond Street, with its famous Hospital for Sick Children, through Queen Square (surrounded by hospitals), and through a little passage westward into Southampton Row. Turn right until you reach Russell Square, very large and full of trees, lawns and fountains. In Montague Place, on the west side, is the back entrance to the British Museum.

The British Museum

There are two ways of approaching the British Museum, either through the wide forecourt on Great Russell Street, where the huge columns of the portico dwarf the mere mortals scurrying around below, or through the more homey backdoor on Montague Place (though getting through to the front from here isn't easy). The main shop, where you can buy posters, postcards, slides and other mementos, is just inside the Great Russell Street entrance. As we suggested for the V&A, pick up a free pamphlet with a floor plan.

For the culture vulture, serious or not, the British Museum is a must. Not only is it one of the world's really great museums, but it also houses the British Library, one of the great libraries, and on both scores has been enriched by the natural acquisitiveness of the British over two hundred years. While the average visitor is unlikely to be using the Library for study purposes, the displays of manuscripts, bindings and rare printed and illuminated books are always fascinating. The Library benefited from a gesture made by George II, in 1757, when he gave the Royal Library to the Trustees. Along with the priceless volumes went the right to have a free copy of every book published in Britain. This means that the Library has been the recipient of well over ten million books, and the stream is still in full spate!

A description of a few highlights will introduce the museum's wealth. First and foremost come the Elgin Marbles, brought from Greece by the seventh Earl of Elgin at the beginning of the 19th century. Today they are at the center of a growing international quarrel following demands for their return to Greece by the Socialist Greek government. The British Museum (and the British government) are naturally reluctant to part with what has now become part of Britain's heritage and it is unlikely that the marbles will leave London in the foreseeable future. The display techniques now employed at the British Museum have banished for ever the old "junk shop" feeling that the place used to have. Especially notable is the Egyptian Collection, whose subtle lighting throws the details of carving into relief, while the chronological arrangement helps to emphasize the rich variety and sheer length of ancient Egyptian history—from 3000 B.C. to the 2nd century A.D.

Upstairs, one of the most intriguing displays is that of the Mildenhall Treasure, a cache of Roman silver found in a field in Suffolk in 1942. On this floor, too, are delightful displays of Greek and Roman art, the grisly mummies and the delicate jewelry found on the site of Ur of the Chaldees by Sir Leonard Woolley.

It is not the slightest use thinking that you could cover the British Museum in one short visit, so don't try to. See what you can, and savor what you see in the hope that you can return again.

North of Russell Square are Woburn Square (where the Courtauld Galleries are), Gordon Square and Tavistock Square, pretty, green places with some attractive town houses. Running along the western side of Gordon Square is University College, London, founded by the Utilitarian philosopher, Jeremy Bentham, whose preserved body is still on the premises. The college was the first in England to admit Jews, Catholics and women. For anyone interested in modern architecture, there are several examples in this area, both of university buildings and of apartment buildings.

Holborn

Two major highways link central London with the City: the Strand and Holborn (pronounced "Hoburn"). Strand here means "beach," as it was originally a riverside road along the Thames. Holborn derives from Hole Bourne, or "stream in the hollow," as it lies along the route of the little Fleet River (it runs underground now). Between these two arteries lie the great Inns of Court, and around them, the first urban development outside the cities of London and Westminster took place; so while much ugly rebuilding has been done, there are still quiet streets of genuine historical charm.

Begin once more at Holborn underground station, at the north end of Kingsway (a wide, dull street linking Holborn with the Strand) and walk eastwards. At first, the street is unexciting: shops, big office buildings, a pompous insurance company building. Soon, on the right, comes Chancery Lane. A detour along this narrow street leads you to several interesting and unusual places. On the right are old arched gateways that take you from the roar of the traffic into the cloistered 18th-century hush of Lincoln's Inn, part of London's legal quarter. Here, too, is the Soane Museum. Farther down on the left is the Public Record Office, whose archives include Britain's national records since the Norman Conquest—including the Domesday Book.

Back in Holborn now, just past the entrance to Chancery Lane is Staple Inn, a romantic-looking half-timbered building. It is not original (having been blown up by a German bomb in 1944), but has been rebuilt so that it looks exactly as it did in Elizabeth I's London; the original dated from 1586. Inside are two pleasant courtyards, on one of which Dr. Johnson lived for a while. Here, too, in the street, are Holborn Bars, two small obelisks that mark the western limits of the City of London (the originals were placed here in 1130).

Farther along is Holborn Circus, in the center of which is an equestrian statue of Prince Albert. On the left is Hatton Garden, occupied by diamond merchants. A little way along Hatton Garden, on the right, is The Mitre, a small historic pub hidden away down a narrow alley (well signposted outside). Just off Holborn Circus, too, is Ely Place where the Bishops of Ely had their London house from the late 1200s to 1772. The place is still a private road with its own security guard (the police can only enter on invitation). Described by Dickens, Ely Place contains Ely Chapel (St. Etheldreda's), a noted example of 13th-century Gothic, which has a vaulted crypt standing on Roman foundations.

But let us continue along the main street, now called Holborn Viaduct. On the right is Wren's church of St. Andrew, whose tower interior dates from 1446. Wren did not alter it. It was here that Dickens' David Copperfield married Dora Spenlow. The street now really becomes a viaduct, constructed in 1867 to take the road across the Fleet valley. It is an impressive construction with elaborate bridges. At the end of the viaduct on the left is the 12th-century church of St. Sepulchre (where Captain John Smith, "sometime Governor of Virginia and Admirall of New England," whose life was saved by Pocahontas, is buried), which had its bells rung when there was an execution at Newgate. Newgate Prison stood opposite, on the site now occupied by the Central Criminal Court (the "Old Bailey"), topped by the symbolic statue of justice. There are five courts, open to the public and usually crowded, especially when a sensational case is in progress.

To the left of this corner (up Giltspur Street) is St. Bartholomew's Hospital, built by James Gibbs in 1730, though founded in 1123. Just past the hospital (Smithfield Meat Market is on the left), is the church of St. Bartholomew the Great, well worth visiting. Apart from the chapel in the White Tower, it is the oldest church in London, being part of the priory founded in 1123. The church is approached through a charming gateway with an Elizabethan, half-timbered façade, revealed when a bomb explosion in 1915 shattered its covering. The interior is beautiful; the heavy roundness of Norman architecture is fully evident. The church is the setting, every Thursday lunchtime throughout the year, of some delightful concerts—as are many old buildings in the city—and to hear Bach and Handel superbly performed in these surroundings is a memorable experience.

At the junction by the Old Bailey, Holborn becomes Newgate Street, leading to St. Paul's Cathedral and Cheapside.

The Strand

The other major highway linking the center of London with the City is the Strand, which runs from Trafalgar Square eastward to Temple Bar—main gate to the City of London—where it becomes Fleet Street, finally ascending to St. Paul's as Ludgate Hill.

Between Trafalgar Square and St. Mary-le-Strand—a Gibbs church is-landed by traffic—the Strand is little more than a reasonably interesting shopping street with three theaters, the Adelphi, the Vaudeville and the Savoy. Off to the north, however, up Southampton Street, is Covent Gar-den, definitely *the* "in" place in London today. Until the early 70s, Covent Garden was home to an enormous fruit, flower and vegetable market. This has been moved to a new site south of the Thames and since then the area has been—and still is being—extensively redeveloped. After a period of sad dereliction, the area has been taken up in a big way by all sorts of adventurous firms and is now an exciting mixture of shops, restaurants, a few building sites and pot-holes and some genuinely attractive buildings. The centerpiece is the old 19th-century market itself which has been re-stored and turned into an elegant and spacious shopping center. It has some of London's trendiest and newest shops, and not at the outrageous prices one might have thought likely. There is a regular program of street entertainers of all kinds who perform in and around the market buildings, and these, together with pubs, a wine bar and restaurants, have turned the lovely old colonnades into a lively spot. Opposite the market is Inigo Jones' rather forbidding and austere church of St. Paul, whose main en-trance is a block away in Bedford Street. It is the church which the acting profession use for their memorial services and houses a fine selection of stage commemorative tablets. The network of streets nearby contains the Royal Opera House and Drury Lane Theater. The latest newcomer to Co-vent Garden is the long-awaited Theater Museum.

To the south of the Strand lies the Adelphi area, originally built by the Adam brothers, though not much of the original 18th-century architecture remains (one exception: the *Lancet* offices, 7 Adam Street). Along the side of the Thames here there is an attractive garden, excellently maintained and providing a pleasant spot to listen to a brass band or sit in the summer sun.

The Embankment along here is probably at its best by night, when the lights twinkle on the water, but there is much of interest around here in the day. Cleopatra's Needle, downstream towards Waterloo Bridge, first erected 1450 B.C. in Heliopolis on the Nile, has nothing whatever to do with Cleopatra. It is one of a trio given by Egypt to the western democra-cies in 1875; the other two are in the Place de la Concorde in Paris and in New York's Central Park. The two sphinxes at the base of the Needle are pitted with holes resulting from a bomb in 1917. There are frequently interesting ships moored along this stretch of the river, downstream to-wards the Tower of London.

While Lancaster Place leads off the Strand to the right to Waterloo Bridge, on the left is the Aldwych, a crescent containing the theater of that name which was for quite a few years the London home of the Royal Shakespeare Company until their move, in 1982, to the new Barbican Cen-ter. Beyond is St. Clement Danes, a Wren church with a Gibbs tower and a statue of one of its regular worshippers, Dr Johnson, outside the choir. The original "oranges and lemons, say the bells of St. Clement's" church, it is now dedicated to the R.A.F. To the south is Somerset House, whose spectacular façade built in 1776, is best seen from the river. Next door, under King's College, are the so-called Roman Baths.

Just before Temple Bar (now marked by a rather uninteresting memorial with statues of Queen Victoria and Edward VII—though it is unlikely that any statue of Victoria could ever be called interesting) are the Royal Courts of Justice or Law Courts, amazingly Gothic in the Victorian style. It is possible to listen to cases in the courts, but, as they are mainly civil actions, they quickly become tedious to the inexpert. To get a better idea of how British justice deals with the man in the street, drop in at a magistrates' court, the main central one being in Bow Street across from the Royal Opera House or, even better, visit the Old Bailey.

On the other side of the road is The Temple, approached by many unlikely-looking alleys. This is the legal quarter, with linked courtyards and a quiet atmosphere. The name derives from the Knights Templar, a powerful medieval order created during the Crusades. It was dissolved in 1312, and in 1346, the ground belonging to the Knights Templar was leased to law students; it has been, ever since, the home of lawyers. The Temple Church dates from the 12th-century and was badly damaged during World War II but has now been restored. The Middle Temple Hall provides one of those rare glimpses of Elizabethan times, remaining just as it was when built. Explore this area one afternoon, using Wren's gatehouse in Middle Temple Lane (off Fleet Street) to enter.

The Strand becomes Fleet Street at Temple Bar, where traditionally, the Lord Mayor of London must challenge the reigning monarch when she (or he) enters the City. Sir Christopher Wren designed the old gate that stood here, but it was removed in 1878.

Fleet Street, of course, was until recent years the home of the British national press industry. Though one or two diehards remain, several of the major national titles have moved out of Fleet Street and the center of London to new premises down river, a trend that seems likely to continue.

Just north of Fleet Street (turn down Bolt Court) is Gough Square, where, at No. 17, Dr. Johnson compiled his dictionary. At Ludgate Circus, Ludgate Hill rises to St. Paul's Cathedral. To the right is Blackfriars Bridge and, at Puddle Dock, the Mermaid Theater.

St. Paul's Cathedral

The great cathedral was cleaned completely in 1965–66 and now looks even more spectacular from this approach, though as one gets nearer an office building masks part of the façade. Illuminated at night, the cathedral is then at its most splendid.

The area immediately around St. Paul's was devastated during the Blitz. Now, decades of careful planning and rebuilding are just beginning to yield results, not all of them happy. To the left of the cathedral is Paternoster Square, a pedestrian complex of plazas with shops, restaurants and pubs. It has been cunningly designed to afford unexpected views of Wren's cathedral, which stands as if moored like a vast ship among the smooth surfaces of concrete and glass. Just behind the cathedral is the new Choir

School, but to the southwest, much still remains to be done. The scheme for St. Paul's precinct was devised by William Holford, with the intention of framing the cathedral from various angles, among paved courts, flights of steps and lawns. Some voices argued for wide open spaces around the cathedral, and today a stroll around the new developments quickly indicates that this might have been preferable to some of the ugly crowding buildings that have been erected.

In the crypt of this great monument is the tomb of Sir Christopher Wren, bearing the epitaph: *Lector, si monumentum requiris, circumspice.* ("Reader, if you want a memorial, look around you.") Perhaps the most potent comment on London's largest and most famous church, this tribute refers to a living entity, the cathedral of the Bishop of London. It was begun in 1675 and completed during the reign of Queen Anne, in 1710, when Wren was almost 80, replacing an earlier cathedral destroyed in the Great Fire of 1666. The Renaissance-style building is 520 feet long (the nave is 125 feet long), and the marvelous dome is 112 feet across; the top of the cross is 365 feet above the pavement of the church. The Whispering Gallery around the base of the dome is a source of fascination; it is 112 feet across but words whispered on one side can be distinctly heard on the other, as in the dome of the Capitol in Washington, D.C.

It is an enormous and impressive church and crowded with memorials, some indifferent, some good, most of them large and elaborate. Dr. Johnson, the poet and preacher John Donne (who served as the cathedral's dean from 1621 until his death in 1631), the painters Reynolds and Turner and even George Washington are commemorated here. In the crypt, too, is a commemorative tablet to one of the American pilots who "died that England might live." The Jesus Chapel, in the Apse, is dedicated to the 28,000 Americans who fell in operations based in Britain during World War II.

Some of the memorials are gigantic, especially the monument to the Duke of Wellington, who became a national hero after defeating Napoleon at Waterloo in 1815. The funeral of the Iron Duke, in 1852, was, with that of Sir Winston Churchill in 1964, among the most impressive ever staged in London for anyone outside the royal family. The memorial was erected in 1875. Lord Nelson, the victor of Trafalgar, was given a statue, as was Lord Kitchener, drowned off the Orkney Islands in 1916.

St. Paul's, being modeled on the great masterpieces of Italian church architecture, lacks the atmosphere of intimacy that strangely invests most British cathedrals, even the most splendid. It is enormously impressive, but might be happier bathed in the rich warmth of a Mediterranean sun. It does provide, however, a splendid setting for the pageantry of great state occasions such as the wedding of the Prince and Princess of Wales in 1981, which was seen around the world.

While you are here, it is well worth having a look at the Barbican, an area just to the north of St. Paul's, which after 1940 was reduced to 35 acres of complete devastation. Slowly it is being rebuilt along the most modern lines. High-rise buildings march two abreast down London Wall (a street so called because it follows the route of the Old Roman Wall, remains of which are incorporated into the new scheme) and are connected by walkways, above traffic level. The complex includes many apartment buildings, offices, the occasional hidden Roman remains and, most interesting to the visitor, the Museum of London and the Barbican Center.

The Museum is one of the most exciting in the capital, and is worth visiting for the imaginative way in which it handles London's history. The new Barbican Center houses conference facilities, a concert hall, exhibition areas, a library, two notably undistinguished restaurants, a movie theater, and the two theaters of the Royal Shakespeare Company, the larger of which is one of the most comfortable and best equipped anywhere in the world. The atmosphere of the Center is that of a plushly-cushioned air-raid shelter, but it should be visited if only for a performance by the RSC. You should be warned that is almost impossible to find your way there without a compass and a bloodhound. However, the stories of tourists lost for days in the maze are quite without foundation.

The City

Known as "The Square Mile," the City of London is an irregularly defined crescent stretching from Temple Bar to the Tower of London. Its heartbeat is at the giant crossroads, a meeting of seven streets, where stand the Bank of England, the Royal Exchange and the Mansion House, official residence of the Lord Mayor. On-the-spot information about the City is obtainable from the information bureau across the road from St. Paul's in St. Paul's Churchyard.

From behind St. Paul's, the most immediate approach is a walk along Cheapside, past the Cockneys' church of St. Mary-le-Bow to the big seven-way intersection. Memories of Saxon times haunt the streets near Cheapside; indeed, the very name Cheapside is of Saxon origin, *ceap* meaning *barter*. The earliest Saxon (if not Roman) relic in the City is claimed to be the famous London Stone. The stone was formerly embedded in the wall of St. Swithin's Church, in Cannon Street, but the church, damaged by bombing, was demolished in 1958. The stone is incorporated in a new office building on its old site. All around Cheapside and east of St. Paul's Cathedral, street names (Bread Street, Ironmonger Lane, Wood Street) indicate that busy markets flourished there in medieval times. In Pudding Lane, the Great Fire of London started on September 2, 1666.

Buried in the entrails of Bucklersbury House are the remains of the Temple of Mithras. If you visit the Museum of London, you will be keenly aware of the Roman past of the city, and here is one of the major evidences of that past. If you walk along Queen Victoria Street, you will find the temple in the side of Bucklersbury House—not that there is very much of it, but what there is serves as a reminder of the antiquity of life on this spot.

Off Cheapside to the left down King Street, is the Guildhall, the seat of the City's town council and of the City guilds. Only the porch and one 15th-century window survive; otherwise, it is a mass of replacements. It was destroyed by the Great Fire of 1666 and again by German bombs in 1940. This impressive building is the scene of major City events, such as the Lord Mayor's Banquet.

Behind the Mansion House is the church of St. Stephen Walbrook, considered to be one of Wren's finest works. The Bank of England, another citadel of Britain's financial power, faces the Royal Exchange. Farther east, near London Bridge, stands a towering 200-foot monument built between 1671–7 as a memorial to the Great Fire of 1666. For a small fee you can climb its 311 steps for a view of London's most historic area (a view rather restricted by high-rise buildings).

The City is full of noise and bustle during the day, but at night and weekends becomes quiet and deserted, so if you want to wander at will, looking up at the buildings and not having to worry about traffic, then Saturday or especially Sunday would be the best time. To the east of Mansion House is London Bridge and, beyond it, the Tower.

The Tower of London

The Tower celebrated its 900th birthday in 1978, taking that date from the year that William the Conqueror began to build on the site. But in reality the foundations he laid were solidly placed on fortifications that were even then a thousand years old. The Tower is the root of London's history, with the constructions of the centuries from the Normans onwards well preserved. Seen at night when floodlit it becomes a setting more evocative than any designer could create.

The White Tower, in the center, is the oldest part of the fortress, having been built for William the Conqueror. Wren, who had a hand in many of London's buildings, made some alterations to the exterior, but inside, the Norman origins are still self-evident. The Bloody Tower is the most infamous, for here most of the important prisoners in bygone days were confined and tortured. One particularly nasty cell was called Little Ease, an ironic name, since the unfortunate inmate couldn't stand, sit or lie down. Some years ago a well was found in the lower part of the tower—filled nearly to the top with human bones!

This main tower is surrounded by fifteen others, each individually named, the whole complex resting across the ancient wall of the City of London. A Roman fortress, mythically ascribed to Julius Caesar, certainly occupied the site, and later a Saxon castle stood there. Since it was built (William the Conqueror wanted to frighten the Londoners), the Tower has never been seriously attacked and has served more as a state prison than a fortress. Innumerable famous people have been immured here and many have lost their heads on the block.

A good three hours is needed to do the Tower full justice (there are a cafe and restaurant here). Things to see are the Gun Floor, St. John's Chapel—the oldest church in London—the armories, with a collection begun by Henry VIII, and the site of the scaffold on Tower Green. You may see the Tower's tame ravens hopping about on the Green. There have always been ravens here, and legend says the Tower will crumble if they should ever leave. Since their wings are clipped, that's unlikely.

The Beauchamp Tower has had a most distinguished list of prisoners—from Sir John Oldcastle (possibly the model for Shakespeare's Falstaff), who was executed on Tottenham Court Road in 1418 for his religious beliefs, to the Earl of Leicester, who was later a favorite of Queen Elizabeth I. Inscriptions on the walls of the tower total nearly a hundred. The list does not, of course, comprise all the victims, most of whom were buried in the Chapel of St. Peter ad Vincula, or in the burial ground close by (now part of the Green). The great English historian, Macaulay, said of the Tower that "in truth there is no sadder spot on earth."

Of the famous people who were beheaded in the Tower at least four should be mentioned: the philosopher, author of *Utopia,* statesman and saint, Sir Thomas More; two wives of Henry VIII, Anne Boleyn and Catherine Howard; and that versatile courtier and hot-headed lover of Queen Elizabeth, the Earl of Essex. When the axe fell for the last time in 1747, it was upon a rebel's head. The axe, execution block and instruments of torture can still be seen in the White Tower.

Elizabeth I (while still a Princess) knew something about the Tower from personal experience. Her half-sister Queen Mary imprisoned her in the Bell Tower. She arrived by barge at Traitors' Gate; it was raining, but she sat on the steps and refused to budge. Looking at the grim place, you'll scarcely blame her.

Perhaps the most famous part is the Bloody Tower—the name seems to sum up the history of the place. Some inmates, however, must have found it tolerably comfortable, as jails go. Sir Walter Raleigh spent thirteen years there—for seven of them his wife was permitted to be with him, and his son, Carew, was actually born there. He received visitors and worked on his *History of the World.*

Of course, you'll want to see the Crown Jewels, and doubtless you'll be impressed by the elaborate precautions taken to ensure their safety and by the striking way in which they are displayed. Formerly they were kept in the Martin Tower, and while they were there a Colonel Thomas Blood made a determined effort to steal them, actually getting as far as Traitors' Gate before he was stopped. Instead of being punished, he received a royal pension. Understandable perhaps, when rumor said that Charles II, being short of ready cash, had connived with Blood over the attempted theft. Since most of these jewels were scattered during Cromwell's Commonwealth, the ones you see today are largely post-Restoration (after Charles II). Since 1967, the jewels have been kept in the Jewel House, a depository below the Wakefield Tower. Be prepared for quite a long wait, since there is always a line during the height of the tourist season.

There are two recent additions to the attractions of the Tower. One is the Herald's Museum, opened by the College of Arms Trust in the Waterloo Building. The exhibits are changed annually, but they always include various aspects of heraldry, with documents, painted shields, coronets and crests and much of the panoply that makes this such an intriguing subject to so many people. The other new attraction is the walk along the battlements, opened in 1983 with due pomp by the Queen. It gives a completely new dimension to viewing the Tower as a whole.

The Tower is a peaceful enough place today, and it is pleasant to sit in the gardens near the ancient cannon and watch the Thames roll by. Remember, however, that the Tower is still a military fortress. You'll see the troops of crack regiments as well as the Yeoman Warders—popularly called "Beefeaters"—in their picturesque Tudor-style uniforms.

Tower Bridge, nearby, is frequently mistaken for London Bridge, upstream. Tower Bridge is new, having opened to traffic only in 1894. It has now been turned into an unusual museum, with the walkways open for the public to use; there is a wonderful view from on top.

Near the Tower is All Hallows church, important to American visitors as it was the site of both William Penn's baptism in 1644 and the marriage of John Quincy Adams, sixth president of the U.S.A.

St. Katharine's Dock

You can reach St. Katharine's Dock by using the system of pedestrian underpasses from Tower Hill tube station. This is an intriguing area, strongly reminiscent of the small harbors that fringe the coast of Cornwall. Once a busy dock, with cargoes arriving from all over the world, it fell, with most of this part of the Port of London, into disrepair and decay. But little by little it has found a vivid new life.

Part of the dock is now a marina for small craft, with several historic boats preserved there. One of the old warehouses, the Ivory House, which got its name, very simply, from the kind of cargo that was stored there, has been converted into a magnificent suite of apartments, imaginatively using the resources of the old building. There are a series of shops and bars and, across the dock, the Dickens Inn, a completely reborn building—even its site has been moved—which hosts evenings of rather rowdy Dickens-inspired entertainment. The whole of St. Katharine's Dock is a pleasant change from the bustle and noise around the Tower, just a few hundred yards away.

The South Bank

The south bank of the Thames in London is usually only seen by visitors when they pass through, catch trains at Waterloo Station, or attend performances at the Royal Festival Hall, the Queen Elizabeth Hall, the Purcell Room, the National Film Theater or the National Theater. (Temporary membership of the National Film Theater, where club rules apply, is available.)

But you can walk all the way along from Lambeth Palace, the London home of the Archbishop of Canterbury (on the south end of Lambeth bridge), past the new buildings of St. Thomas's Hospital; across the end of Westminster Bridge, having admired the Houses of Parliament across the river; past the massive County Hall, seat of the Greater London Council until its abolition in 1986, and so to the front of the Festival Hall, and then under Waterloo Bridge to the National Theater. It is a walk lined with trees and revealing very photogenic views of London's riverscape. At the end of it you can drop into the Festival Hall for refreshment, which you can enjoy still looking out over the river, or visit the National Theater where there is usually something going on in one of the foyers, and where the bars and cafeterias also look out over the Thames. In 1988 the Museum of the Moving Image opened next to the National Film Theater.

Part of the South Bank complex houses the Hayward Gallery, now one of the leading exhibition galleries in London. It is topped by a tall, skeletal sculpture made of neon tubing. At night rather hectic colors run up and down this erection, their speed and intensity being governed by the velocity of the wind playing on a small device at the top.

Among the other sights immediately south of the river, pride of place is shared between Southwark Cathedral, a proud 13th-century Gothic building with a chapel honoring John Harvard, founder of Harvard University, and the Pilgrim Fathers' Memorial Church in Great Dover Street.

If you feel in need of a drink after this make for the George (with restaurant) in Borough High Street, the only galleried inn left in London. At

No. 103 in the same street is a Georgian House on the site of John Harvard's family tavern. Another interesting old pub and restaurant is the Mayflower Inn, down in Rotherhithe Street. Now modernized, this was the 17th-century tavern called The Shippe, frequented by the owners of the *Mayflower,* one of whom, Captain Christopher Jones, is buried at nearby St. Mary's Church. Or you could try the Anchor, at the corner of Clink Street, which affords fine views across the Thames of St. Paul's Cathedral. The notorious but thankfully long-vanished Clink Street Prison once stood here; hence "clink," the slang expression for jail. Look out for two plaques: on Wren's house at 49 Bankside from which he watched the building of St. Paul's, and on a powerhouse standing on the site of Shakespeare's Globe Theater.

Hampstead

Hampstead lies to the northwest of central London, high on a hill; it has a clean, refreshing, country atmosphere (rather like a particularly charming English county seat). It also has literary associations, some beautiful houses, good shops, interesting pubs and several first-class restaurants.

If you go by underground, you will emerge at Hampstead tube station in the middle of old Hampstead, halfway up the hill. This is the most picturesque part, not far from delightful streets like Flask Walk and Keats' Grove, where the poet once lived. Also nearby is Church Row, with some grand Georgian houses; the streets behind the main roads also offer many architectural delights.

Hampstead flanks the Heath, a vast stretch of parkland, mainly rough (that is, not divided into formal walks), from which there are spectacular views over London; this is where kites are flown, swimming is done and where, on national holidays, a fair is held.

By the Heath, at the top of the hill, is Jack Straw's Castle, a big, plush pub with a Victorian ambiance; farther along is the 18th-century inn called The Spaniards, which contains, among other literary and historical associations, the pistols that Dick Turpin the highwayman supposedly used.

A little farther along to the east is Kenwood, a house with a library designed by Robert Adam, set in a fine park and possessing an excellent collection of paintings and furniture. In the summer, open-air concerts are held by the lake.

Near Hampstead, also topping a hill, is Highgate, again retaining a village atmosphere and some pretty houses. Highgate Cemetery is known as much for its elaboration of memorial and tombstone as for the famous buried here—the latter including George Eliot, Karl Marx and Michael Faraday. Often used as a film location (especially for *Dracula* movies), the cemetery is open to visitors except for some restricted areas which can be seen only at certain times. A society has been formed to help with its rehabilitation.

DAYS OUT FROM LONDON

The places that are easily visited from London, but will consume most or all of a day, divide themselves into two sections. The first includes the closer-in locations, among them Greenwich, Kew, Chiswick, Hampton Court and Richmond. The second includes the ones farther afield, which we cover in the appropriate regional chapters, but which we will discuss briefly here, to give an outline of the kind of destinations possible from London.

Greenwich

If you have managed to catch a sunny day, and London summers can occasionally be blazingly hot, you should take the trip by boat from Westminster on Tower Pier down river to Greenwich. Not only will you see the remains of what used to be one of the busiest ports in the world as you chug along, but at the end of the voyage you will be in for a delightful surprise.

For Greenwich (pronounced "grenitch") is yet another spot where British history has coalesced. The heart of the historical area on the banks of the Thames is the Royal Naval College, housed in a former palace. This is some of the most splendid architecture and interior decoration anywhere in Britain. The Painted Hall is a triumph of breathtaking illusionism, painted by Thornhill. The Chapel is more restrained, but in its serious, 18th-century way, equally lovely. The whole complex was the work of several of Britain's greatest architects, Vanbrugh, Hawksmoor and, of course, the ubiquitous Wren among them. Here, too, is the National Maritime Museum, a treasurehouse of the days when Britain ruled the waves, with paintings, models, maps, intriguingly mysterious globes and sextants, relics of dead heroes, and all that will fascinate anyone who has a taste for the sea. It is currently the subject of a £5½ million appeal to finance a five-year restoration program.

The work of another great architect, Inigo Jones, can be seen in the Queen's House, which he built for Charles I's queen, Henrietta Maria. This is one of the earliest, and best, flowerings of classicism in Britain, mathematically perfect, with a lovely central hall and staircase.

Actually on the edge of the river are two real ships, each of great historical interest. The *Cutty Sark* was the last of the tea clippers, ships that raced from the East with their holds full of tea for the tables of England. Beside her is *Gipsy Moth IV,* the small boat in which Sir Francis Chichester sailed alone around the world.

On the hill a little inland, with the sweeping grass of Greenwich Park leading up to it, is the Royal Observatory. It was here that Greenwich Mean Time was born. The work of the Observatory is now carried on at Herstmonceux Castle, away from the obscuring atmosphere of London, but the building remains as a museum of the astronomer's science. The prime meridian runs through the center of the courtyard, so this building commemorates the establishment of two universal standards, time and longitude. It was also designed by Wren . . . who else!

If you can stay for the evening, there is a lively theater where classics and modern plays are performed in a near-repertory way, with well-known actors doing their thing away from the West End. You can return to town either by river (though not at night), bus or train.

Kew

Just to get out of the built-up conglomeration of London for a few hours and to take an opportunity to experience a world of rare plants, exotic flowers and strange trees, try the Royal Botanic Gardens (known as Kew Gardens) which are especially popular during the spring and summer. The gardens cover 300 acres and contain more than 25,000 varieties of plants. There are strong Hanoverian associations here, as the gardens were actually begun (in 1759) by Princess Augusta, George III's mother. The Georges (of the German royal line of Hanover) and their queens spent much time here and Kew Palace (the Dutch House), which has been restored to its former state, contains plenty of their relics. The gardens have beautiful walks and the plants are housed in a series of sometimes spectacular buildings, such as the Orangery, the Palm House, built by Decimus Burton, and various hot-houses. Another feature is the pagoda, built in 1761 by Sir William Chambers—a delicious extravagance that can be seen for miles around. Kew itself is on the river, with a village green fringed with 18th-century houses; the painters Gainsborough and Zoffany are buried in the churchyard.

Chiswick

Quite close to Kew is Chiswick House, built by the 3rd Earl of Burlington in 1725 in the full flush of the Palladian craze. It is best reached by taking the tube to Hammersmith and then the 290 bus, which will drop you at the entrance to the House, on Burlington Lane, not far from the complex of the Hogarth's Corner cloverleaf.

The interior of the house is quite lovely, designed by William Kent and magnificently restored. Pope, the poet who most closely echoes this period in his verse, was a frequent visitor here. The grounds are laced with delightful walks and avenues. There are temples, lakes, a bridge built by James Wyatt and a gateway designed by Inigo Jones. If you can time your visit to coincide with the flowering of the camellias in the large conservatory, you will be rewarded by a really striking sight.

While in this area it is worth visiting Hogarth's House, at the back of Chiswick House, which, though there is not all that much to see, does give one an insight into the way the great painter lived. He and his family are buried in St. Nicholas' Church, back across the huge superhighway intersection (take the underpass again), near the river. This is a pretty little enclave of houses, and one can spend a long time wandering along the side of the Thames here.

Hampton Court

Farther upriver, lies Hampton Court—a delightful boat ride, though much longer, in the opposite direction from Greenwich. On a loop of the Thames beyond Richmond is a mellow redbrick palace, bristling with turrets and twisted chimneys in the very best Tudor tradition. It is one of the spots that should top every visitor's list of what to see near London and can easily be reached by train, bus or even by boat, perhaps the best way of all though it takes up to four hours.

The house was begun in 1514 by Cardinal Wolsey, who intended it to surpass in size and opulence all other private residences. Henry VIII coveted it and made the Cardinal an offer he couldn't refuse. The king added a great hall and chapel and lived much of his rumbustious life here. Further improvements were made by James I, but by the end of the 17th century the place was getting rather run-down. William III, the husband of Mary II and equal monarch with her, was a Dutch Prince of Orange who decided that England should have its own Versailles to rival that of France. There was an epidemic of Versaillesmania at this time. In order to build a massive new palace, the existing Tudor one would have had to have been demolished, but money was short and the architect, Wren, had to produce a simpler, and in the event more effective, scheme. William and Mary, Mary especially, loved the palace. A lot of their life there is still in evidence, especially the collections of delftware and porcelain.

The site beside the slow-moving Thames is perfect, set in its great park full of dappled deer and tall ancestral trees, with magnificent ornamental gardens, an elegant orangery, the celebrated maze, and the old palace itself, steeped in history, hung with priceless paintings, and full of echoing cobbled courtyards and cavernous Tudor kitchens, now restored to their original splendor—not to mention a couple of royal ghosts (the shades of Jane Seymour and Catherine Howard, two of Henry's unfortunate queens).

In a very real way Hampton Court not only enshrines some of the best architecture that England can show, but also is a microcosm of much that was good in three centuries of English art and art collecting. To progress from the Tudor part of the palace, with its roundels of Roman emperors, its allegorical tapestries, its ornate Jacobean woodwork, its tiny, almost claustrophobic, panelled chambers, into the endless series of elegant rooms of later periods, opening one out of the other like a chain of airy boxes, with spacious views over the gardens and the park, is to walk through a central part of English history.

The rooms are furnished with many excellent pieces, especially the bedrooms, with their rearing four-poster beds like ornate catafalques surmounted by plumes. A great deal of fine art is hung here, too, including royal portraits and a fair number of Dutch still lifes. Try, however, to choose a sunny day as the rooms are dark and rather somber when the weather is overcast.

Royalty ceased to live here with George III. He, poor man, preferred the seclusion of Kew, where he was finally confined during his madness. However, the private apartments which range down one side of the palace are occupied by pensioners of the crown. Unfortunately, there was a serious fire at Easter, 1986, when part of Wren's work was destroyed and one of the elderly pensioners died. Reconstruction work will take several years, and during that time only part of the palace will be open to visitors.

In the same area is the town of Twickenham, where the poet Alexander Pope lived—he is buried in the parish church. Turner and Tennyson both lived here for a while, and among the notable houses are Marble Hill House, a Palladian mansion built for George II, and Strawberry Hill, Horace Walpole's villa in the most delicately fanciful "Gothick" style of the mid-18th century. It is now a Roman Catholic teacher-training college, but admission can be obtained on written application.

From Hampton Court, the River Thames bends and winds its way to Windsor.

Richmond

A little closer in to London, and the stop before Hampton Court on the upriver boat, is Richmond, which has been a favorite residential town since Henry VII (Duke of Richmond, in Yorkshire, before he became king) changed its name from "Sheen." It is picturesquely sited on the slope of a hill, at the top of which is Richmond Park. The hill commands a celebrated and fine view of the Thames and the park (2,350 acres), which is stocked with deer. The trees, especially the oaks, are ancient, the last vestiges of the once vast medieval forests that crowded in upon London. There are several private (and originally, royal) residences in the park. White Lodge, for example, was once the home of the present Queen's parents and is now the Royal Ballet School.

Richmond is particularly rich in fine houses and literary associations, Leonard and Virginia Woolf, Dickens, George Eliot and Sir Richard Burton, the explorer, secret agent, and translator of *The Arabian Nights,* all lived here. On the southwest side of Richmond Green is all that remains of Richmond Palace and on its site is now a series of interesting houses. The side streets of Richmond well merit exploring for their quaint alleyways. The town has a number of pleasant pubs and a lively theater (the Orange Tree).

An extension of Richmond Park is Ham Common, and just outside Richmond is Petersham, a delightful riverside village and more 17th- and 18th-century houses, including Ham House. This Jacobean house is most notable for its contents, which are almost totally original, giving a vivid impression of the life of the time. The house is managed by a combination of the National Trust and the Victoria and Albert Museum, with enviable results. The 17th-century grounds will interest avid gardeners, as it is one of the very few gardens to survive from that period.

Farther Afield

A great deal of southern England is reachable from London on a "Day Excursion" basis. You can either do this by taking one of the many coach trips available, most of which will include several places on their itinerary thus giving you a taste at least of what is available—or you can plan to see one major town and take an InterCity train there, or, if closer to London, a local train.

You would be surprised how far afield you can go on a day basis. Bath, in Avon, is quite possible, as are Winchester, Chichester (go there in summer for a performance at the Festival Theater, even, and be back in London for a very late bedtime), Brighton, Hastings, and Canterbury—all those to the southeast, south and southwest. To the northwest, north and east lie Oxford, St. Albans, Cambridge, Bury St. Edmund's, Norwich and Colchester—all destinations with much to see.

Those are only some of the main points that lie within easy reach; there are, of course, many smaller ones that are possible (see also Map 6 at the

end of the book), but you should be warned that the many cutbacks in
train timetables have meant that it is not always easy to get to a place and
away again within a few hours. You should be sure to consult the latest
schedules while planning your trips. For example, while Stratford-upon-
Avon is theoretically reachable by train for a day's outing, in practice the
nature of the scheduling makes it a difficult trip—and indeed the station
at Stratford is closed in winter on Sundays!

You will find more information about these destinations under their
places in the regional chapters, with a little help on how to reach them
from London in the appropriate *Practical Information* sections.

PRACTICAL INFORMATION FOR LONDON

HOW TO GET AROUND. Heathrow Airport is conveniently linked
to the Underground (London subway) on the Piccadilly Line, with trains
to and fro about every five minutes, 20 hours a day (slightly fewer Sun.).
It takes only 40 minutes into central London and the fare is around £1.70
one-way. "Travellators" (moving walkways) link the station with Terminals 1–3; the new Terminal 4, being some distance from the other terminals, is connected with them by bus, and has its own branch of Heathrow
Underground station.

London Regional Transport (LRT) Airbuses are available at all terminals and between them stop off at 18 points throughout the main hotel
areas of central London. The trip usually takes about 50 minutes, depending upon traffic conditions. If you decide to go by taxi, check first with
the driver as to the fare, which should not be more than about £18 to Hyde
Park Corner or equivalent, depending on traffic conditions; most cabbies
you can trust, but there are always a few unscrupulous characters (as in
every city) who prey on unsuspecting tourists, so keep your eye on the
meter. *Avis, Hertz* and *Godfrey Davis* are also available at both Heathrow
and Gatwick.

From Gatwick, rail is the quickest method (about 30 minutes to Victoria), with trains running around the clock, four an hour 5.30 A.M. to 10
P.M., costing £5 one-way.

By bus. London is served by fleets of LRT single- and double-decker
buses, and bus travel is easy and cheap, although the pressure of traffic
can make it a very slow means of getting around. Route numbers and maps
are listed on signs at bus stops and as the bus arrives, quickly check its
destination window to make sure you're going in the right direction!

Buses will stop only at the clearly indicated bus stops, of which there
are two types. All main stops are indicated by a plain white background
with a red London Regional Transport symbol emblazoned upon it; these
are the stops at which the buses will stop automatically so you needn't
bother to signal. At other stops (those with a red background and white
symbol, together with the word *request*) the buses will only stop if you
signal for them to do so—stick out your arm! When paying, simply state
your destination, "Oxford Circus, please," or "Two to Trafalgar Square."
If you are not sure where to get off, ask the conductor or driver to help
you.

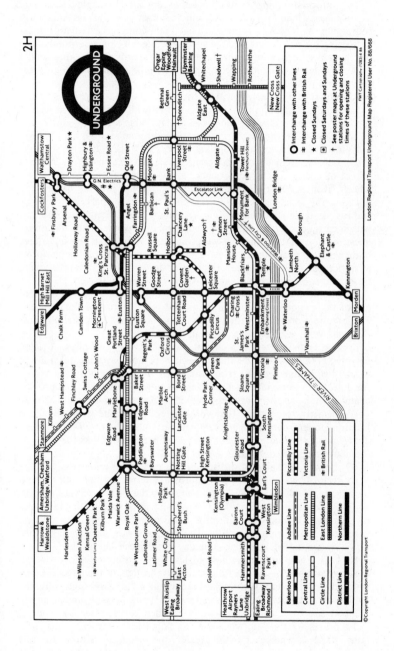

This information applies to all buses except the red single-decker *Red Arrow* buses which operate a fast, almost non-stop service on some busy routes. On the Red Arrow there is a fixed fare and you obtain your ticket by putting the right coins into the automatic machine on entering the bus. For longer suburban or country routes, take speedy Green Line single-deckers which maintain services within a 30-mile radius of London, cutting across town.

A useful introduction for visitors staying in London is the *Visitor's Travel Card,* providing unlimited travel on virtually all LRT buses, as well as the London Underground. The passes are available for 1, 3, 4 and 7 days at any Travel Information Center or Underground station.

By underground. Colloquially known as the "tube," London's underground train system is a bit more comfortable than the New York subway, except of course during rush hours, when it becomes a sardine can on wheels. Routes cover all inner London, and you'll find it's usually the quickest way to get about. The various lines are clearly marked in stations, and easy-to-understand maps of the system are found along platforms and within carriages. Ticket offices also supply handy pocket maps free on request, or you can use the one we print here. About half the lines have branches; electrically operated signs, usually suspended over the platforms at stations on these lines, show the branch destination of the approaching train, and sometimes how long the train will take to arrive.

We should warn you that the simplicity of the system breaks down at one or two major exchange points, such as King's Cross or Baker Street. These stations are, frankly, hell if you don't know them intimately. Follow the signs very carefully and, when in doubt, ask.

London is divided up into separate zones with set unit fares. A ticket covering both Central and Inner zones is 80p. You buy your ticket at the station before starting your trip, from either the ticket office or (avoiding the lines) the automatic ticket machines, most of which will provide change if necessary (try to keep some 20p, 50p and/or £1 coins handy).

We heartily recommend that you find out about the latest LRT and London Underground budget offers—in particular, the *One Day Off-Peak Travelcard* (which allows use of most LRT buses as well as the tube) or the above-mentioned *Visitor's Travel Card.*

By the way, a "subway" in Britain is a pedestrian underpass.

By train. If you want to visit suburbs not served by the underground (and many, like Kew and Richmond, are), try the electric services of British Rail. To places like Croydon (10 miles in 15 minutes), Ilford (7 miles in 15 minutes), Woolwich (10 miles in 25 minutes), this is the quickest way. For a round trip, ask for a return ticket, or for the cheaper day return if you're coming back on the same day out of rush hours.

By taxi. These unmistakable vehicles—in a variety of colors, though most are still black—are liberally scattered throughout the streets of central and west London. If their flags are up, or a "for hire" sign is lighted on the top, just hail them. Be warned though: you can rarely find an empty one between 5 P.M. and 7 P.M.—which is when you so often want one.

Taxi fares start at 80p when the flag falls then, after 990 yards (or 3 mins. 30 secs., whichever is the greater) the meter clicks up at the rate of 20p per 495 yards (or 1 min. 45 secs.). After 6 miles it becomes 20p per 330 yards (or 60 secs.). Weekday nights 8 to midnight, and Sat. up to 8 P.M. there's a 40p surcharge; Sat. after 8, all day Sun. and public holidays, there's a 60p surcharge; while over Christmas and New Year's Eve, the surcharge is £2. Luggage is carried in the driver's compartment. Extra passengers also mean surcharges. If, after reading all that, you still want to—tip the driver 10%! These were the rates as we went to press.

By car. Driving in London is not recommended for anyone. It is a very, very, big city, and whereas in New York, for example, there is some logic in the street planning, in London there is none. A minute grid system bequeathed to us by the Romans and extended in all directions in a crazily haphazard manner over roughly the last 2000 years, has in no way been clarified by the modern passion for one-way systems. Drivers who get lost and think to retrieve the situation by returning to base through a series of left-hand turns invariably find themselves quite somewhere else.

For those who must drive in London, however, the speed limit is 30 m.p.h. in the Royal parks as it is theoretically in all streets, unless you see the large 40 m.p.h. signs—and small repeater signs attached to lamp-posts—found only in the suburbs. Pedestrians have absolute right of way on "zebra" crossings. These have black and white stripes between two striped beacon poles topped with orange bowls (that flash) and have zig-zag road markings on both sides. It is an offense to park within the zig-zag area on either side, or pass another vehicle on the approach side.

The red, yellow and green traffic lights sometimes have arrows directing left- or right-hand turns. It is therefore important not to get into the turn lane if you mean to go straight on (if you can catch a glimpse of the road markings in time). The use of horns is prohibited in all built-up areas between 11.30 P.M. and 7 A.M. You can park at night in 30 m.p.h. limit zones provided that you are within 25 yards of a lit street lamp, but not within 15 yds of a road junction. To park on a bus route, side (parking) lights must be shown—but you'll probably be fined for obstruction. In the day time it is safest to believe that you can park nowhere but at a meter or in a garage. The basic cost of transgression is a £12 parking ticket, and you can't soft-soap a traffic warden. If the car is towed away it could cost a total of £69—plus sweat and tears—to get it back (the retrieval points are situated in the most out-of-the-way places imaginable!). Then there's the Denver Boot wheelclamp, which sets you back £37 in all to get released, as well as a wait of up to four hours.

Car rental. Among the leading firms in the London area supplying both chauffeur-driven and self-drive cars are: *Avis Rent-a-Car,* 68 North Row, off Park Lane, W.1 (tel. 629 7811) or 35 Headford Place, S.W.1 (tel. 235 3235); *Hertz Rent-a-Car,* 200 Buckingham Palace Rd., S.W.1 (tel. 730 8323) or 35 Edgware Rd., Marble Arch, W.2 (tel. 402 4242); and *Godfrey Davis,* Wilton Rd., S.W.1 (tel. 834 8484). (For information on rates and terms, see *Traveling in Britain* section of *Facts at Your Fingertips.*) Or, you can contact *Car Hire Center International*; it has contacts in all the main rental centers in Britain, including at 23 Swallow St., Piccadilly, London W.1 (tel. 734 7661). *Camelot Barthropp Ltd.,* Headfort Place, Chapel St., S.W.1 (tel. 245 9171), operates exclusively chauffeur-driven Rolls-Royces, Bentleys, Daimlers and Mercedes, etc., by the hour, the day, etc. To rent a self-drive Rolls-Royce, contact *Guy Salmon Car Rentals,* Cumberland Garage, 23 Bryanston St., London W.1 (tel. 408 1255).

By cycle. A novel, if somewhat nerve-wracking, way of seeing London is by renting a bicycle, by the day, by the week, or longer. Try *Savile's,*

97 Battersea Rise, S.W.11 (tel. 228 4279). Most will require a deposit and some form of identification—best bring your passport.

By river. From Easter through to October, large excursion boats cruise on the Thames, starting mainly from the piers at Westminster Bridge, Hungerford Railway Bridge (opposite the entrance to the Embankment Underground station) and the Tower of London. They go up river to Kew, Richmond and Hampton Court. Trips down river to the Tower and Greenwich operate all year round, from Westminster Pier. All have running commentaries.

An interesting new venture was launched recently by *Thames Line:* fast catamaran riverboats run between Chelsea Harbor and the West India Dock Pier, every 15 mins. at peak time (7–10 A.M., 4–7 P.M.), and every 30 mins. other times (10 A.M.–4 P.M., 7–10 P.M.).

Capital Cruises, based at Lambeth Pier and Tower Pier (tel. 350 1910), offer a four-hour Disco Cruise including two-course buffet; boarding is at Temple Pier at 8 P.M.; however, reservations are vital. *Capital* also have a sailing barge transformed into a wine bar/restaurant moored on the Thames at Temple, just along from Charing Cross, which specializes in summer barbecues, and is open both lunchtime and evenings. Their main operation these days, though, is in catering to private parties wishing to partake of the joys of the Thames, good food and refreshments.

Full information on these and other river trips from the information kiosks at the piers mentioned or the London Tourist Board.

By canal. In order to experience a totally different side of London, you might enjoy a cruise down Regent's Canal. *Jason Trips,* in Little Venice opposite 60 Bloomfield Rd., W.9 (tel. 286 3428), offer just such an experience. Daily trips from Easter through early October. Luncheon cruises are available. It's advisable to make reservations; reservations are mandatory for any trips requiring food. On Sat. and Sun. it is possible to disembark at Camden Lock and wander about the craft shops and flea market before returning by a later boat. A 12-seater boat/restaurant, the *Lace Plate,* is available for private luncheon or dinner parties.

All trips begin at Little Venice, about 15 minutes up Edgware Rd. from Marble Arch. Tube: Warwick Ave.

Canal Boat Cruises, based at 250 Camden High St., N.W.1 (tel. 485 4433/6210), ply the Canal from Camden Lock to Little Venice, with the *Jenny Wren* and the floating restaurant *My Fair Lady.* Dinner (£16.95) and lunch (£12.75, Sun. only) are available on the latter all year round; prices include everything but drinks. Reservations strongly recommended.

The *London Waterbus Co.,* also at Camden Lock (tel. 482 2550), have four launches that travel up and down the Lock, via the Zoo (where you can disembark for optional entrance) to Little Venice. Available year round, but no meals.

HOTELS. London's hotels have become among the most expensive in Europe. This trend may ease off in the next year or so as hoteliers become increasingly concerned about the effect high prices are having on their business. Needless to say, you should make sure you know exactly what your room will cost before you check in. In common with most other European countries, British hotels are obliged to display a price list on the reception desk. Study it carefully. The general custom used to be for rates to be quoted for both bed and breakfast; but more and more London hotels, especially the top-class ones, now give rates for room only. Again, check if this applies in your case. The prices we quote are inclusive of both VAT and service (except where this is optional) and are based on those of summer 1988.

Fluctuations in exchange rates directly affect the tourist scene in London, as elsewhere—creating an inflow when the dollar is riding high, an ebb when the rate is low—but that is not the only factor to be watched; seasonal events, trade shows or royal occasions can fill hotel rooms for sudden, brief periods. We give suggestions on reservations in the *Facts at Your Fingertips* section. If you haven't reserved your hotel room before you arrive, the following organizations can help you find a room: *Room Center (U.K.) Ltd.,* Kingsgate House, Kingsgate Place, London N.W.6 (tel. 328 1790); *Hotel Reservations Center,* by Platform 8 at Victoria Station, S.W.1 (tel. 828 1849) and the *London Tourist Board,* also at Victoria Station, S.W.1. The last named cannot accept reservations over the telephone. Please note, however, that one of the main complaints lately of visitors to London has been about the exorbitant charges exacted by certain accommodation agencies for their "services."

It should also be emphasized that we have graded the hotels listed here according to the *cheapest* rooms available—in some establishments you can pay considerably more. In the Super-Deluxe category, "£150 and up" means just that—in some cases above the £200 mark!

SUPER-DELUXE (Double room £150 and up)

Berkeley, Wilton Pl., S.W.1 (tel. 235 6000). An English hotel experience akin to staying in the finest country house; impeccable decor, service and fairy-tale banqueting facilities. No one will ever afford to build like this again. *The Buttery* restaurant features live guitar music from about 9 onward, and with its superb cuisine has everything for the ideal celebratory evening. Tops every list.

Churchill, Portman Sq., W.1 (tel. 486 5800). A success ever since they opened the doors to that large Regency style lobby and those splendidly comfortable bedrooms. A good management team helps, but the position is very convenient.

Claridge's, Brook St., W.1 (tel. 629 8860). Don't be discouraged by the usual clichés. True—this hotel is the home of dignity, royal or otherwise (it can boast 3 Royal Suites), but the staff are friendly and not in the least condescending while the rooms are luxurious. A living hotel legend.

Dorchester, Park Lane, W.1 (tel. 629 8888). This hotel will be closed during 1989 for refurbishment.

Dukes, 35 St. James's Pl., S.W.1 (tel. 491 4840). Quietly but centrally located in a small backwater redolent of old London. An excellent choice for those who relish small-scale, sedate accommodations backed by friendly service.

Grosvenor House, Park Lane, W.1 (tel. 499 6363). Completely renovated as a well-appointed conference hotel, with hardly a trace of the former Grosvenor style remaining. Restaurants include the luxurious *Ninety Park Lane.*

Hilton, 22 Park Lane, W.1 (tel. 493 8000). Not the best of the chain, but keeps the Hilton flag flying. Refurbished in 1988. Fine views and plenty of variety in bars and restaurants.

Howard, Temple Pl., W.C.2 (tel. 836 3555). Beside the Thames, and convenient for both City and West End. Opulent bedrooms, with fine reproduction antiques.

Hyatt Carlton Tower, Cadogan Pl., S.W.1 (tel. 235 5411). Handily situated for West End or Chelsea. Elegant accommodations suited particularly to guests who like a touch of Bohemia nearby. *Very* Super-Deluxe, pricewise! The *Chelsea Room* is an excellent restaurant for serious gourmets.

Hyde Park, 66 Knightsbridge, S.W.1 (tel. 235 2000). Facing Knightsbridge for shopping and backing onto Hyde Park for relaxation. Fairly sumptuous in a distinctly Victorian way, with marble and chandeliers, but reasonably priced for the category.

Inn on the Park (Four Seasons), Hamilton Pl., Park Lane (tel. 499 0888). Not much change out of £200 for a double, but an opulent interior, eminent situation, and high standards help to compensate. Rooms are all beautifully furnished and ultra-comfortable.

London Inter-Continental, Hyde Park Corner, W.1 (tel. 409 3131). Cool and modern, with flawless rooms and service—and fantastic views straight over Hyde Park Corner. *Le Soufflé* restaurant is elegant but over-priced.

Meridien Piccadilly, Piccadilly, W.1 (tel. 734 8000). Reopened 1985 after £16 million "overhaul," and the last word in 80s-style luxury. Aimed principally, though not exclusively, at the executive (male or female), facilities are health-oriented—including solarium, sauna, Jacuzzi, massage, swimming pool, squash, dance studio, etc.

Ritz, Piccadilly, W.1 (tel. 493 8181). César Ritz's elegant landmark provides sumptuous decor and fine service. Recent change of ownership and the ensuing refurbishment have seen public rooms return to their former splendor. Restaurant continues to make gastronomic news.

St. James Court, Buckingham Gate, S.W.1 (tel. 834 6655). Recently refurbished.

Savoy, Strand, W.C.2 (tel. 836 4343). Synonymous with old-fashioned luxury, yet pleasurable also for those small corners of happy informality. A grand hotel of brilliant contrasts, personalities and mood.

Seven Down Street, 7 Down St., W.1 (tel. 493 3364). Fairly recent addition to the London scene, and somewhat out of the ordinary. Just six double suites, each reflecting a particular theme—includes an Indian room, a Blue Room (with original Tudor four-poster), and Kalahari (a "desert" room decorated in shades of sand and rust).

Sheraton Park Tower, 101 Knightsbridge, S.W.1 (tel. 235 8050). Luxurious bedrooms sport fine views from this circular tower, now an established part of the Knightsbridge scene. Casino.

LUXURY (Double room £120–£150)

Athenaeum, 116 Piccadilly, W.1 (tel. 499 3464). Renovated with a strong dash of originality and managerial flair. Rooms are first class and well positioned at the "right end" of Piccadilly. Malt-whiskey bar here is a fashionable hang-out.

Britannia Intercontinental, Grosvenor Sq., W.1 (tel. 629 9400). Top marks for a modern hotel facade blending unobtrusively with the Square. Inside, restrained decor and comfort. Central location with friendly service.

Blakes, 33 Roland Gdns., S.W.7 (tel. 370 6701). Chic and trendy, mainly show business clientele. Its 55 rooms include 11 suites. Renovated in

'87; make reservations at least 2 weeks ahead to be sure of getting what you want.

Brown's, Dover St., W.1 (tel. 493 6020). Very British, very Victorian, with moderately modern comfort. Try their afternoon tea, before a stroll down Dover Street—but don't forget their excellent restaurant later. Bedroom sizes vary.

Cadogan, 75 Sloane St., S.W.1 (tel. 235 7141). This rejuvenated hotel has original Adam ceilings in the bar. Before it became a hotel, Lillie Langtry, who numbered King Edward VII among her admirers, lived here. Bedroom standards and amenities vary.

Capital, 22 Basil St., S.W.3 (tel. 589 5171). Small, tasteful, and near Harrods. Excellent personal service and decor. Make reservations well ahead—for the restaurant as well as the hotel. Highly recommended.

Connaught, Carlos Pl., W.1 (tel. 499 7070). With only 90 superb rooms and a worldwide reputation, here is true quiet luxury. Among the best bases for touring London. Their famous kitchen is splendidly dominated by one of the world's best chefs.

London Marriott, Duke St., W.1 (tel. 493 1232). Extensively refurbished in 1984. Facilities include air conditioning and some double glazing. *Diplomat* restaurant.

Lowndes, 21 Lowndes St., S.W.1 (tel. 235 6020). Deep within the residential heart of Knightsbridge. Adamesque decor and picturesque people.

May Fair Intercontinental, Stratton St., W.1 (tel. 629 7777). Animated lobby scene reflects Mayfair bustle outside. Has undergone massive refurbishment to emerge with every conceivable luxury facility—including a health club and the near-compulsory Jacuzzi. Still has tiny theater.

Montcalm, Great Cumberland Pl., W.1 (tel. 402 4288). Encased in an elegant Georgian crescent and centrally placed. An extremely civilized house, admirably suited to those of sybaritic taste.

Park Lane, Piccadilly, W.1 (tel. 499 6321). Most rooms were upgraded two years ago, but hotel still retains its original character, with Victoriana triumphant.

Portman, 22 Portman Sq., W.1 (tel. 486 5844). Older brother of the *London Inter-Continental* (see above), this hotel has quietly established and maintained a high reputation.

Royal Garden, Kensington High St., W.8 (tel. 937 8000). Crisp modern hotel, convenient for shopping. Some rooms with stunning view of the Park.

Selfridge, Orchard St., W.1 (tel. 408 2080). Attached to the famous store for obvious shopping possibilities. Modern and attractively conceived, with well-fitted bedrooms and willing staff.

Stafford, 16 St. James's St., S.W.1 (tel. 493 0111). In a secluded courtyard complete with gaslights, yet only five minutes from Piccadilly. Excellent choice for small-hotel fans; attentive service and pleasing decor.

Westbury, New Bond St., W.1 (tel. 629 7755). The first of the American-style hotels in London, now part of the Trusthouse Forte group. The bar's one of the coolest places in London on a hot summer's day. Rooms are good and the location very handy, but the hotel is beginning to show its age.

White's, Lancaster Gate, W.2 (tel. 262 2711). Old building, refurbished, overlooking Hyde Park. Very friendly staff.

EXPENSIVE (Double room £90–£120)

Basil Street, 8 Basil St., S.W.3 (tel. 581 3311). Traditional style and elegance—an ideal spot for the well-heeled single woman.

Cavendish, Jermyn St., S.W.1 (tel. 930 2111). Centrally located for St. James's shopping and theaters; functional hotel despite its tenuous Edwardian associations with Rosa Lewis ("The Duchess of Duke Street"). Public rooms include some striking modern art. Coffee shop open until 3 A.M.

Chelsea Hotel, 17–25 Sloane St., S.W.1 (tel. 235 4377). A former Holiday Inn hotel, now run by Sorava. Basic facilities expected to remain unchanged. Swimming pool.

Clifton Ford, 47 Welbeck St., W.1 (tel. 486 6600). Splendid location, plus very reasonable prices for this category. (Basic rate includes early morning tea and cookies, as well as a newspaper!)

Cumberland, Marble Arch, W.1 (tel. 262 1234). Massive central hotel offering good value.

Flemings, 10 Half Moon St., W.1 (tel. 499 2964). Attractive period hotel, just off Piccadilly and so extremely handy. Recently refurbished; restaurant and pleasant staff.

Gloucester, 4 Harrington Gdns., S.W.7 (tel. 373 6030). At bottom end of price category. Modern hotel close to hectic Gloucester Road and tube station.

Goring, 15 Beeston Pl., S.W.1 (tel. 834 8211). Family-run Edwardian hotel in immaculate condition and recently redecorated. Try for a quiet room overlooking the garden. Close to Victoria Station and Buckingham Palace.

Holiday Inn, 134 George St., W.1 (tel. 723 1277). Marble Arch branch, so centrally located. Completely refurbished in 1987.

Holiday Inn, Berkeley St., S.W.1 (tel. 493 8282). Mayfair locale close to Bond Street. A comfortable place, with a marked French decor. Fourth floor dedicated to "business travelers throughout Europe."

Holiday Inn, 128 King Henry's Rd., N.W.3 (tel. 722 7711). Swiss Cottage-based and handy for Hampstead and north London, but a bit far from the center (though tube station nearby). Well-appointed and with modern indoor pool.

Ladbroke Westmoreland, 18 Lodge Rd., N.W.8 (tel. 722 7722). Overlooking Lord's cricket ground and popular with our readers for its friendly staff, good rooms, and value-for-money *Carvery* restaurant.

Norfolk, 2–10 Harrington Rd., S.W.7 (tel. 589 8191). In popular one-room apartment area. Recently refurbished.

Royal Court, Sloane Sq., S.W.1 (tel. 730 9191). Well-located and highly convenient for Chelsea sorties.

Royal Lancaster, Lancaster Terrace, W.2 (tel. 262 6737). Excellent views from a well-decorated hotel with everything for an enjoyable stay.

Royal Trafalgar Thistle, Whitcombe St., W.C.2 (tel. 930 4477). Very handy for Trafalgar Square and almost everywhere else.

St. George's, Langham Pl., W.1 (tel. 580 0111). Near Oxford Circus, this hotel occupies the top floors of an office building beside the BBC.

Waldorf, Aldwych, W.C.2 (tel. 836 2400). Midway between theaterland and the City, with a blend of both—plus a strong element of Edwardiana.

MODERATE (Double room £45–£90)

Alexander, 9 Sumner Pl. S.W.7 (tel. 581 1591). Comfortable bedrooms in an attractive establishment.

Barkston, 36 Barkston Gdns., S.W.5 (tel. 373 7851). Very bottom end of this price category.

Bloomsbury Crest, Coram St., W.C.1 (tel. 837 1200).

Charing Cross, Strand, W.C.2 (tel. 839 7282). Gaunt exterior but a friendly heart, beside theaterland with excellent restaurant and interesting architectural features preserved. Rooms are comfortable.

Clive, Primrose Hill Rd., N.W.3 (tel. 586 2233). Quiet Hampstead location with great views.

Durrants, George St., W.1 (tel. 935 8131).

Ebury Court, 26 Ebury St., S.W.1 (tel. 730 8147). Considerable charm and friendly staff. Good restaurant and elegant Belgravia location. Make reservations well in advance.

Gore, 189 Queen's Gate, S.W.7 (tel. 584 6601). Personally run, with a friendly atmosphere.

Grafton, 129 Tottenham Court Rd., W.1 (tel. 388 4131). A member of the Edwardian group, who reopened it in 1982 after a multimillion-pound refurbishment program.

Great Western Royal, Praed St., W.2 (tel. 723 8064). Huge bedrooms and lofty ceilings remain in this imposing and well-modernized Victorian hotel, joined to Paddington rail station.

Kensington Close, Wrights Lane, W.8 (tel. 937 8170). Facilities include two squash courts and a swimming pool.

Leinster Towers, 25–31 Leinster Gdns., W.2 (tel. 262 4591). 170 rooms. Modern interior.

London Embassy, 150 Bayswater Rd., W.2 (tel. 229 1212). Handy for Hyde Park and the colorful Greek Queensway scene.

London International, 147 Cromwell Rd., S.W.5 (tel. 370 4200). Large, modern, and slightly anonymous—but well-placed for the South Kensington museums.

London Metropole, Edgware Rd., W.2 (tel. 402 4141). In a dull area, but comfortable and efficiently run.

London Ryan, 10–12 Gwynne Pl., W.C.1 (tel. 278 2480).

London Tara, Wrights Lane, W.8 (tel. 937 7211). Good-value accommodations on 12 stories—factory-style but competently run. Just off Kensington High Street.

Londoner, Welbeck St., W.1 (tel. 935 4442). A well-placed small hotel within strolling distance of shops, pubs, and quiet residential London.

Mount Royal, Bryanston St., W.1 (tel. 629 8040). Big and central, beside Marble Arch. Reasonable rooms—and their English breakfast is definitely top-notch.

Number 16, 16 Sumner Pl., S.W.7 (tel. 589 5232). 32 rooms. Winner of 1984 Kensington and Chelsea Chamber of Commerce Award for Excellence.

Pastoria, St. Martin's St., W.C.2 (tel. 930 8641). Small, relaxed establishment off Leicester Square, with well-maintained bedrooms at reasonable prices for prime location.

Pembridge Court, 34 Pembridge Gdns., W.2 (tel. 229 9977). 27 rooms (some recently enlarged) at this friendly Victorian house. Near Portobello Road and the market.

Portobello, 22 Stanley Gdns., W.11 (tel. 727 2777). An unconventional and enjoyable small hotel, sporting potted palms and military furnishings. In antique-land.

Royal Horseguards, 2 Whitehall Ct., S.W.1 (tel. 839 3400). Part of the reliable Thistle chain; massively renovated in '88; in a good "historical" situation for touring town.

Rubens, 39–41 Buckingham Palace Rd., S.W.1 (tel. 834 6600). Near to Palace; recently refurbished.

Russell, Russell Sq., W.C.1 (tel. 837 6470). A good choice (if you don't mind the decor on the ground floor). Handy for the British Museum.

Strand Palace, Strand, W.C.2 (tel. 836 8080). Comfortable, but without fuss or frills, and good value for the category.

Tower, St. Katharine's Way, E.1 (tel. 481 2575). Vast modern hotel overlooking the Thames with suitable riverside ambience. Nearest tube is Tower Hill.

Vanderbilt, 68–86 Cromwell Rd., S.W.7 (tel. 584 0491). Another member of the Edwardian group, with all that that entails in terms of atmosphere and facilities.

Wilbraham, Wilbraham Pl., S.W.1 (tel. 730 8296). Rather like a rural hotel translated to London. Convenient for Chelsea and Knightsbridge shopping.

INEXPENSIVE (Double room under £45)

A good budget chain of hotels is run by **Ladbrokes,** from Watford in Hertfordshire (tel. 0923 38877). Prices for a double start at around £45, rising to about £60, and in all they have some 60 properties in and around London.

The following brief selection includes but a few of London's many guest houses and smaller private hotels, offering reasonable accommodations for the most part. The majority are converted 19th-century row houses.

Averard, 10 Lancaster Gate, W2 3LH (tel. 723 8877).

Camelot, 45–47 Norfolk Sq., W2 1RX (tel. 723 9118).

The Claverley, 13–14 Beaufort Gdns., SW3 1PS (tel. 589 8541).

Elizabeth, 37 Eccleston Sq., SW1V 1PB (tel. 828 6812).

Morgan House, 120 Ebury St., SW1 9QQ (tel. 730 8442).

Parkwood, 4 Stanhope Pl., W2 2HB (tel. 402 2241).

Prince, 6 Sumner Pl., SW7 3AB (tel. 589 6488).

Prince William, 42–44 Gloucester Terr., W2 3DA (tel. 724 7414).

Regent Palace, Piccadilly Circus, W1A 4BZ (tel. 734 7000).

Ridgemount, 65 Gower St., WC1E 6HJ (tel. 636 1141).

Ruskin, 23 Montague St., WC1B 5BN (tel. 636 7388).

The Vicarage, 10 Vicarage Gate, W8 4AG (tel. 229 4030).

Willett, 32 Sloane Gdns., SW1W 8DJ (tel. 730 0634).

LONDON AIRPORT (HEATHROW)

Expensive (E), £90–£120; Moderate (M), £45–£90

Ariel (M), Harlington Corner, Bath Road, Hayes (tel. 759 2552). Unusual circular hotel with well-maintained bedrooms for an overnight airport stopover.

Excelsior (M), Bath Road, West Drayton (tel. 759 6611). Located at the north entrance to airport, with a businesslike atmosphere for stopovers.

Heathrow Penta (M), Bath Road, Hounslow (tel. 897 6363). Luxury hotel at very top end of price category, actually within the airport borders and filled with every jet-set facility; getting known for good eating.

Holiday Inn (M), Stockley Rd., West Drayton (tel. 0895 445555).

Post House (M), Sipson Rd., West Drayton (tel. 759 2323). Comfortable, though some of the facilities are a bit on the small side. Good food.

Sheraton Heathrow (M), Colnbrook Bypass, Longford, West Drayton (tel. 759 2424). Quite adequate for the one-night stopover. Downstairs can be good for drinks and dining, prior to catching the next flight.

Sheraton Skyline (E), Bath Rd., Hayes (tel. 759 2535). The really bright airport spot with lovely bedrooms and lively entertainment. Caribbean temperature patio guarantees easy acclimatization.

Skyway (M), Bath Rd., Hayes (tel. 759 6311). Low rates for its category.

For hotels at **Gatwick Airport** *see* The Southeast chapter.

APARTMENTS

Many people prefer the freedom and convenience of having an apartment to living in a hotel when on vacation. It can work out cheaper, too. Here are a few of the many possibilities available, admittedly at the luxury end of the market. You should apply for the latest price list.

Embassy Apartments, 24 Queen's Gate Terr., S.W.7 (tel. 584 7222). Five apartments, handy to tube and buses. Well decorated and equipped. Maid service.

Lambs Service Flats, 21 Egerton Gdns., S.W.3 (tel. 589 6297), in quiet elegant houses only a couple of hundred yards from Harrods.

One Carlos Place, W.1 (tel. 491 4165). Absolutely exclusive and better value than most hotel suites of similar standard. Refurbished in 1986.

CURRENT INFORMATION. The useful weekly publication, *What's On in London* (sold at newsstands), supplies information on theater and movie programs, nightclub floor shows, soloists appearing at dining clubs, and sports events (including those not usually announced in the daily newspapers, such as baseball and basketball). *Time Out* and *City Limits* are similarly comprehensive, though aimed at a radically chic readership. Listings also appear in London's evening papers, the *London Evening Standard,* the *Evening News* and the *London Daily News.* A new daily, *The Independent,* is already known for its detailed arts coverage.

If you ever need directions, the best person to ask is a policeman; traffic wardens (with the yellow and black uniforms) are also very helpful. Post

Offices or shops usually know the area, but you'll find that most people you approach in the street will help if they can.

The **London Tourist Board** provides information on all you may want to know about London. Head office is at Victoria Station, S.W.1 (tel. 730 3488), and during the summer months this is open every day from 9 to 8.30 P.M.; in winter, to 7 P.M. There is an Information Center at Heathrow Airport tube station, as well as at Harrods and Selfridges during normal store opening hours, and within the Tower of London Apr. through Oct. For nationwide information, check with the *British Travel Center,* 12 Regent St., S.W.1 (tel. 730 3400).

City of London Information Center has detailed information about the City as well as general information, and it is located across the street from St. Paul's Cathedral (tel. 606 3030).

SIGHTSEEING. London Regional Transport issue special tickets such as the *Visitor's Travel Card,* the *One-Day* and *Weekly Travelcards,* in addition to their joint ticket with British Rail, the *Capitalcard.* Perhaps the best way to see the main sights is by bus. London Regional Transport offer their *Original London Transport Sightseeing Tour,* which covers some 18 miles of the West End and the City. This tour can be picked up at a variety of central London locations.

Other companies offering guided tours of London include *Evan Evans,* 25A Cockspur St., S.W.1 (tel. 930 2377—24 hours a day); *Frames Rickards,* 11 Herbrand St., W.C.1 (tel. 837 3111); and *Harrods* (tel. 730 1234) whose tour includes commentary in eight languages, as well as stewardess-served refreshments, and lasts two hours. Harrods' prices are £12 per head (£7.50 for children). Three tours a day.

GUIDES. For a guide registered with the London Visitor & Convention Bureau, contact your travel agent or *Prestige Tours* (see below). *Tours and Charters Dept.,* London Regional Transport, 55 Broadway, S.W.1 (tel. 222 5600) also offer some interesting possibilities.

One of the best and most easily accessible ways of getting a guided tour of London is to phone *Prestige Tours,* 13–16 Jacob's Well Mews, W1H 6BD (tel. 584 3118). These are normal London taxis, but driven by qualified guides. A day's notice is usually enough to lay on a really expert and comfortable tour around town. £130 will pay for a full day's tour of London for four people; shorter trips also available, such as half-days costing £80, or the two-hour tour for £55. You can use the service for a whole range of out-of-town trips, too. Stratford combined with Oxford, for example, costs around £200.

WALKING TOURS. The City Corporation have laid out an interesting walk around the City of London, taking in buildings and monuments of particular interest. Visitors are guided by means of directional studs set in the sidewalk. The Heritage Walk, as it is known, includes Bank, Leadenhall Market and Monument. A map of the walk appears within *A Visitor's Guide to the City of London* (25p), available from the City Information Office opposite St. Paul's Cathedral, who will also be able to supply further details.

If you want to know more about the life and times of Winston Churchill, Ghosts in the City, Jack the Ripper, and the Belgravia of *Upstairs, Down-*

stairs (there are about 80 tours in all), Alex and Peggy Cobban, of *Discovering London,* 11 Pennyfields, Warley, Brentwood, Essex (tel. 0277 213704), are the people to contact. £2.50 for adults, £2.25 senior citizens and students; under-16s free if accompanied by an adult. Available all year—always weekends, weekdays vary though. Working in the same field, and highly recommended, *London Walks,* 139 Conway Rd., N.14 (tel. 882 2763), offer their excursions at about the same rates and on the same days.

MUSEUMS AND ART GALLERIES. London is one of the two or three most important centers of western civilization, and many of its museums are incomparable in their scope, variety and imaginative presentation. Here is a brief selection. Admission is free (unless otherwise indicated), and museums are usually open daily including national holidays, except Good Friday, Christmas Eve, Christmas Day, Boxing Day (Dec. 26) and New Year's Day and except where otherwise stated. The best times to visit are between 10 and 4, or Sunday afternoon. Information about public transportation is included. Note that we have given the popular name of each institution, the one you would use when asking for information. Some of them have official names which are slightly different.

Bethnal Green Museum of Childhood, Cambridge Heath Rd., E.2 (tel. 980 2415). Excellent collection of dolls' houses and toys. Near the Underground station. Mon.–Thurs. and Sat. 10–6, Sun. 2.30–6. Closed Fri. Tube: Bethnal Green.

British Museum, Great Russell St., W.C.1 (tel. 636 1555). The single most important institution of its kind in the world. Among the various departments are prints and drawings; coins and medals; Egyptian and Assyrian antiquities; Greek, Roman, British, Medieval, Oriental antiquities; and The British Library. Try to find time to take in some of the excellent modern display techniques which have given new life especially to the Egyptian Collection. Weekdays, 10–5, Sun. 2:30–6. Tubes: Russell Square, Tottenham Court Road, Holborn (Kingsway).

British Museum/Museum of Mankind, Burlington Gardens, W.1 (behind Royal Academy) (tel. 437 2224). Exhibits of tribal life and culture areas throughout the world, excitingly displayed. Same times as British Museum. Tubes: Piccadilly Circus, Green Park.

Costume Museum, Kensington Palace State Apartments, Kensington Gdns., W.8 (tel. 937 9561). Opened 1984. Court dress from the late 17th century to 1936, complete with appropriate accessories. Admission of £2.60 also includes Kensington Palace. Daily 9–5, Sun. 1–5. Tubes: Queensway, Kensington High St.

Courtauld Institute Gallery, Woburn Sq., W.C.1 (tel. 636 2095). The outstanding collection of French Impressionists was for the most part on display in the States in '87, but should be back by spring of this year. Also to be seen are varying modern works, and the munificent bequest of the Prince's Gate collection of Old Masters. Admission £1.50. Daily 10–5, Sun. 2–5. Tubes: Goodge St., Russell Square, Euston Square.

Design Museum, Butler's Wharf, tel. 403 6933. Due to open in mid-1989. Explores design in consumer products like furniture, cars, clothing and electrical or electronic goods. Probable admission £1.80. Probable open times Tues.–Sat. 11–6.30.

Dickens' House, 48 Doughty St., W.C.1 (tel. 405 2127). Occupied by the author from 1837 to 1839, during which he worked here on *Pickwick*

Papers, Oliver Twist, Barnaby Rudge, and *Nicholas Nickleby.* Fragments of manuscripts are on display, also letters, first editions, portraits etc. Admission £1.50 (£3 for family of 2 adults and 1 or 2 children). Mon.–Sat. 10–5. Closed Sun. Tube: Russell Square.

Dulwich Picture Gallery, College Rd., S.E.21 (tel. 693 5254). Newly-restored gallery (but originally built in 1813) with small but superb collection of paintings. Admission £1.50. Sat. and Sun. most of year there are free guided tours at 3.00. Tues.–Sat., 10–1, 2–5, Sun. 2–5. Closed Mon. Bus: 3. Train: British Rail from Victoria Station to West Dulwich.

Fan Museum, 10–12 Crooms Hill, tel. 305 1441. Due to open summer 1989, this unique collection of over 2,000 fans will include history, art and manufacture of fans. Phone for admission charges and opening times.

Freud Museum, 20 Maresfield Gardens, Hampstead, tel. 435 2002. Located in the house occupied by the founder of psychoanalysis during the last year of his life. Presents Freud's study just as he left it, including the famous couch. Admission £2. Wed.–Sun. 12–5.

Geffrye Museum, Kingsland Rd., Shoreditch, E.2 (tel. 739 8368). Furniture and furnishings arranged chronologically from 1600 on. Daily 10–5, Sun. 2–5. Closed Mon. Tube: Liverpool Street, Old Street.

Geological Museum, Exhibition Rd., S.W.7 (tel. 938 8765). Collections of gemstones and exhibitions of basic science and geology. Admission £1 (but see *Natural History Museum* entry). Daily 10–6, Sun. 1–6. Tube: South Kensington.

Hayward Gallery (Arts Council of Great Britain), Belvedere Rd., South Bank, S.E.1 (tel. 928 3144). Major art exhibitions. Admission £3 (£1.50 Mon. and after 6 Tues. and Wed.). Mon.–Wed. 10–8, Thurs.–Sat. 10–6, Sun. 12–6. Tube: Waterloo.

ICA Gallery (Institute of Contemporary Arts), Nash House, Carlton House Terrace, S.W.1 (tel. 930 3647). The latest "happenings" in art and art forms. Admission 75p for non-members (under-14s free). Daily noon–11. Tube: Charing Cross.

Imperial War Museum, Lambeth Rd., S.E.1 (tel. 735 8922). Comprehensive collection of the Commonwealth during two world wars, including an art collection and a library of films, photographs and books. Admission charges to be introduced in 1989; rates not available at press time. Daily 10–5.50, Sun. 2–5.50. Tubes: Lambeth North, Elephant & Castle.

Jewish Museum, Woburn House, Upper Woburn Place, W.C.1 (tel. 388 4525). Entrance in Tavistock Square. Fine collection of Jewish antiquities. Voluntary contributions box. Open late Oct.–late Mar., Tues.–Thurs. 10–4, Fri. 10–12.45; late Mar.–late Oct., Tues.–Fri. 10–4, Sun. 10–12.45. Closed Sat. and Mon. Tube: Euston, Euston Square, Kings Cross or Russell Square.

Dr. Johnson's House, 17 Gough Sq., E.C.4 (tel. 353 3745). Home of the great lexicographer from 1749 to 1759. Admission £1.30. May–Sept., Mon.–Sat. 11–5.30; Apr.–Oct., Mon.–Sat. 11–5. Closed Sun. Tube: St. Paul's, Chancery Lane, Blackfriars.

Keats' House, Keats Grove, N.W.3 (tel. 435 2062). The home of the poet during the most creative years of his brief life. Mon.–Fri. 2–6, Sat. 10–5, Sun. 2–5. The house may be closed in 1989 for lack of finance. Tube: Hampstead or Belsize Park.

Kenwood House, Hampstead Lane, N.W.3 (tel. 348 1286/7). Fine paintings, Adam decoration. Lovely location in scenic Hampstead Heath.

Daily Apr.–Sept. 10–6; Oct. 10–5; Nov.–Jan. 10–4; Feb.–Mar. 10–5. Tubes: Archway or Golders Green, then bus 210.

Lloyds of London, Lime St., E.C.3 (tel. 623 7100). Opening its doors to the public three years ago, this exhibition traces the history of this august organization from its beginnings in a 17th-century coffeehouse to today's international institution. Mon.–Fri. 10–2.30. Tube: Bank or Monument.

London Dungeon, Tooley St., S.E.1 (tel. 403 0606). Authentic exhibitions of the Great Plague, Tyburn and other gruesome aspects of Britain's history. Admission £3.50. Daily 10–5.30, Oct.–March 10–4.30. Tube: London Bridge.

London Toy and Model Museum, 21–23 Craven Hill, W.2 (tel. 262 9450). Collection for children of all ages, including model cars display, the Paddington Bear collection, and other items involving visitor participation. Admission £2.20, children 80p. Tues.–Sat. 10–5.30, Sun. 11–5.30. Closed Mon. Tube: Queensway.

London Transport Museum, The Piazza, Covent Garden, W.C.2 (tel. 379 6344). Relics from London Transport's better days. Admission £2.40. Daily 10–6 (last admission 5.15). Tube: Covent Garden.

Madame Tussaud's, Marylebone Rd., N.W.1 (tel. 935 6861). World's best-known waxworks of famous and infamous. Often crowded but the long lines move fast. Admission £4.20. Open Easter–end Sept., daily 9.30–5.30; Oct.–Easter, daily 10–5.30. Next door is the **Planetarium** (tel. 486 1121), with its breathtaking visual display of the night sky. Admission £2.20. Star show presentations daily from 11–4.30. Laser light concerts performed most evenings from 6; tel. 486 2242 for details. Admission £3.75. Closed Mon. Tube: Baker Street.

Note: Combined ticket, giving admission to both Mme. Tussaud's and the Planetarium, £5.60.

Museum of Garden History, St. Mary-at-Lambeth, Lambeth Palace Rd., S.E.1 (tel. 261 1891). Interesting garden exhibits in old church next to Lambeth Palace; especially in spring and summer. Mon.–Fri. 11–3, Sun. 10.30–5; closed Sat. and from 2nd Sun. in Dec. to 1st Sun. Mar. Tube: walk upriver from Westminster and over Lambeth Bridge.

Museum of London, London Wall, E.C.2 (tel. 600 3699). Devoted to the history of London, from prehistoric times to the present day. Based on the combined collections of the former Guildhall and London museums. Open Tues.–Sat. 10–6, Sun. 2–6. Closed Mon. Tubes: St. Paul's, Barbican, Moorgate.

Museum of Mankind (see **British Museum**).

Museum of the Moving Image, next to the National Film Theatre, Waterloo, S.E.1. Largely financed by philanthropist J. Paul Getty, Jr., and a must for all movie-buffs, it opened in 1988. Admission £3.25. Open Tues.–Sat. 10–8, Sun. 10–6 (last admission 1½ hrs before closing time). Closed Mon. Tube: Waterloo.

National Army Museum, Royal Hospital Rd., S.W.3 (tel. 730 0717). The story of the British Army from Tudor times up to 1982. Daily 10–5.30, Sun. 2–5.30. Tube: Sloane Square.

National Gallery, on Trafalgar Sq., W.C.2 (tel. 839 3321/3526). Collection of Italian, Dutch, Flemish, Spanish, German and French paintings up to 1900, plus British painters from Hogarth to Turner. In effect there is at least one masterpiece by every major European painter of the last

600 years. Daily 10–6, Sun. 2–6. Tubes: Charing Cross or Leicester Square.

National Maritime Museum, Romney Rd., Greenwich, S.E.10 (tel. 858 4422). Superlative collection of ship models, navigational instruments, charts, uniforms, medals, portraits and paintings of naval scenes. The museum buildings themselves are lovely to see. Admission £1.20; combined ticket for Museum and Observatory £2.20. Daily 10–6 (10–5 in winter), Sun. 2–5.30 (2–6 in winter). Train: Cannon Street, Charing Cross or Waterloo to Greenwich (change at London Bridge).

National Portrait Gallery, at St. Martin's Pl., Trafalgar Sq., W.C.2 (tel. 930 1552). Paintings, drawings, busts of famous British men and women from Tudors to the present. Admission charge for special exhibitions (about £2). Open Mon.–Fri. 10–5, Sat. 10–6, Sun. 2–6. Tubes: Charing Cross, Leicester Square.

National Postal Museum, King Edward St., E.C.1 (tel. 432 3851). Vast collection of stamps from all over the world. Open Mon.–Thurs. 9–4.30; Fri. 9–4. Closed Sat. and Sun. Tube: St. Paul's.

Natural History Museum, Cromwell Rd., S.W.7 (tel. 589 6323). Animals, plants, minerals, fossils (nearly 15,000,000 specimens). Admission £2 (£2.50 for combined ticket including Geological Museum too). Daily 10–6, Sun. 2–6. Tube: South Kensington.

Percival David Foundation of Chinese Art, 53 Gordon Sq., W.C.1 (tel. 387 3909). Chinese ceramics and a library of Chinese and other books. Mon.–Fri. 10.30–5. Closed weekends. Tubes: Goodge St. or Russell Sq.

Public Records Office Museum, Chancery Lane, W.C.2 (tel. 876 3444). Fascinating documentation of British history, including one of the original copies of the Magna Charta. Mon.–Fri. 9.30–4.45. Tube: Chancery Lane.

Queen's Gallery, adjoining Buckingham Palace, S.W.1 (tel. 930 4832). Selection of paintings and masterpieces from the Royal Collection. Admission £1.20. Tues.–Sat. 10.30–5, Sun. 2–5. Closed Mon. Tubes: Green Park, Hyde Park Corner, Victoria.

Royal Academy, Burlington House, on Piccadilly, W.1 (tel. 734 9052). The temple of traditional art. Mounts some of the largest exhibitions, including the annual summer one (May–Aug.) of works by living artists. Admission varies depending on exhibition. Daily 10–6. Tubes: Piccadilly Circus, Green Park.

Science Museum, Exhibition Rd., S.W.7 (tel. 589 3456). Illustrates the development of mathematics, physics, chemistry, engineering, transportation, mining, communications (an operating radio station), and industry as a whole. Originals of many famous locomotives, aircraft and cars. Many working displays; children's gallery. Daily 10–6; Sun. 2.30–6. Tube: South Kensington.

Shakespeare Globe Museum, Bear Gardens (tel. 602 0202). Advance guard of Sam Wanamaker's ambitious project to re-create Shakespeare's riverside playhouse, as well as to build an additional theater. New theaters scheduled to open in early 1990's; meanwhile museum presents historical background. Admission £1. Apr.–Sept., Mon.–Fri. 10–5, Sat. 10–5.30, Sun. 2–6. Phone for winter opening times.

St. Thomas's Hospital (*not* the modern St. Thomas's Hospital near Westminster Bridge), St. Thomas St. (tel. 739 2372). 19th-century operating theater closed and blocked off in mid-century. Rediscovered in 1921, it has now been restored to show pre-antiseptic and pre-anaesthetic practices. Admission £1. Mon.–Sat. 10–6, Sun. 2–6.

Sir John Soane's Museum, 13 Lincoln's Inn Fields, W.C.2 (tel. 405 2107). Early 19th-century museum of art and antiquities. Tues.–Sat. 10–5 (lecture tours Sat. 2.30). Closed Sun. and Mon. Tube: Holborn.

Tate Gallery, Millbank, S.W.1 (tel. 821 1313). Some modern foreign paintings and sculpture, but primarily dedicated to British artists, especially Turner, Blake and the Pre-Raphaelites. Restaurant and café. Admission charge for special exhibitions (£2). Daily 10–5.50, Sun. 2–5.50. Clore Gallery of Turner paintings open Tues.–Sat. 12–5. Tube: Pimlico.

Theater Museum, Tavistock St., W.C.2 (tel. 831 1227). All the performing arts—grand opera to pop, classical drama to circus—are represented here. An offshoot of the V&A. Admission £2.25. Tues.–Sun. 11–7. Closed Mon. Tube: Covent Garden.

Victoria and Albert Museum, Cromwell Rd., S.W.7 (tel. 938 8500). Displays fine and applied arts of all countries and styles, British, European and Oriental; a magnificent collection. Voluntary donation (£2). Mon.–Sat. 10–5.50, Sun. 2.30–5.50. Tube: South Kensington.

Wallace Collection, in Hertford House, Manchester Sq., W.1 (tel. 935 0687). Exceptionally fine works of Dutch, Flemish, French, Spanish, Italian and British painters together with sculpture, furniture, china, armor and work in gold. Daily 10–5, Sun. 2–5. Tubes: Baker St., Bond St.

Wellington Museum (Apsley House), Hyde Park Corner, W.1 (tel. 499 5676). The London home (its address used to be "Number One, London"!) of the famous duke, containing uniforms, trophies and some paintings. Admission £2. Tues.–Sat. 11–5. Closed Sun.–Mon. Tube: Hyde Park Corner.

Wesley's House and Museum, 47 City Rd., E.C.1 (tel 253 2262). Shrine to John Wesley and museum of Methodism. Admission £1.20. Daily 10–4, Sun. 1–3. Next door to Wesley's Chapel. Tube: Old Street.

Wimbledon Lawn Tennis Museum, The All England Club, Church Road, S.W.19 (tel. 946 6131). The history of lawn tennis and its antecedents. Includes a library and an audio-visual theater. Admission £1.50. Closed during Championship Fortnight (2 weeks) each June; otherwise, Tues.–Sat. 11–5, Sun. 2–5. Closed Mon. Train: Victoria or Blackfriars to Wimbledon, then 93 bus.

PLACES OF INTEREST Banqueting House. Whitehall, S.W.1 (tel. 930 4179). This is the only part of the old Whitehall Palace to escape the fire of 1698. Designed by Inigo Jones in 1619. The painted ceiling by Rubens was commissioned by King Charles I, who in 1649 was executed on a scaffold outside this building. Open to the public when not in use for official functions. Admission 70p. Tues.–Sat. 10–5, Sun. 2–5. Closed Mon. Tubes: Charing Cross or Westminster.

H.M.S. Belfast, Symon's Wharf, Vine Lane, Tooley St. (tel. 407 6434). A chance to tour a famous World War II cruiser, saved from the scrap yard in 1963. Mess decks, engine room, brig, bridge, battle stations, etc. Admission £3. Mid-Mar.–mid-Oct., daily 11–5.30; late Oct.–mid-Mar., daily 11–4.30.

Buckingham Palace, The Mall, S.W.1 (tel. 930 4832). The official royal residence is best approached down the Mall from Trafalgar Square. The statue of Queen Victoria in front provides a good vantage point for Chang-

140 EXPLORING BRITAIN

ing of the Guard. The only parts open to the public are the Queen's Gallery (see under *Museums,* preceding) and the Royal Mews (admission 60p; open Wed. and Thurs. 2–4). Tubes: Green Park, Hyde Park Corner or Victoria.

Cabinet War Rooms, Clive Steps, King Charles St., S.W.1, edge of St. James's Park, just behind Admiralty Arch (tel. 930 6961). Churchill's World War II underground Cabinet rooms. Memorabilia; famous "lavatory" telephone room for hot line to Roosevelt. Admission £2.50. Daily 10–5.50. Tube: Westminster.

Chelsea Royal Hospital, Royal Hospital Rd., S.W.3 (tel. 730 0161). Charming home for old soldiers ("pensioners"), founded by Charles II and designed by Wren. Daily 10–12 and 2–4, Sun. 2–4 only. Tube: Sloane Square.

Chiswick House, Burlington Lane, W.4 (tel. 995 0508). Lovely restored Palladian villa. Admission £1. Apr.–Sept., daily 9.30–6.30; Oct.–Mar., Mon.–Sat. 9.30–4, Sun. 2–4. Tube: Turnham Green; or Hammersmith, then 290 bus.

The Commonwealth Institute, Kensington High St., W.8 (tel. 603 4535). Permanent displays, art gallery, movie theater, library and information center. Daily 10–5.30, Sun. 2–5. Tube: High Street, Kensington.

Covent Garden Market, The Piazza, Covent Garden, W.C.2. Beautifully restored 19th-century building, former home of London's fruit and vegetable market. Now bustles with some of the capital's trendiest shops. Tube: Covent Garden.

Cutty Sark, Greenwich Pier, S.E.10 (tel. 858 3445). Part of the National Maritime Museum as the last of the famous tea clippers. Nearby is *Gipsy Moth IV,* Sir Francis Chichester's around-the-world yacht. Admission £1.30 (*Gipsy Moth* alone, 20p). In summer, daily 10.30–5.30, Sun. 12–5.30; winter, daily 10.30–4.30, Sun. 12–4.30. By boat from Westminster, Charing Cross or Tower Piers, or by train to Greenwich (from Charing Cross).

Guildhall, King Street, E.C.2 (tel. 606 3030). The 15th-century council hall of the City, scene of civic functions. It has an extensive medieval crypt. Mon.–Fri. 9–5—except when in official use. In the new West Wing is the **Museum of the Worshipful Company of Clockmakers.** Mon.–Fri. 9.30–5. Closed Sat. and Sun. Tubes: Bank, Moorgate, St. Paul's.

Guinness World of Records, The Trocadero (tel. 439 7331). Housed in the Trocadero Center, an entertainment and shopping complex, this is an exhibition of wonders drawn from *The Guinness Book of Records.* Other attractions in the Trocadero Center include world's largest exhibition of holograms, and electronic-media history of London. World of Records: admission £3.50. Daily 10–10.

Hampton Court Palace, Hampton Court, East Molesey (tel. 977 8441). The former residence of Cardinal Wolsey and Henry VIII. Staterooms, tapestries and pictures. Access limited after fire damage. Set in beautiful grounds with the famous maze. Admission £2.80. Open summer, daily 9.30–6, winter, daily 9.30–4. Easily reached by boat from Westminster Pier (summer)—though can take 3–4 hours!—or train (from Waterloo).

Houses of Parliament, Westminster, S.W.1 (tel. 219 3000). House of Commons sits from 2.30 onwards, Mon.–Thurs.; from 9.30 on Fri. To hear debates in the Strangers' Gallery, join the line outside St. Stephen's Hall (but foreign visitors are advised to apply to their embassies in London). House of Lords (to hear debates in Strangers' Gallery apply as for House

LONDON

141

of Commons), sits from 2.30 onwards, some Mons., Tues.–Thurs., occasionally 11 on Fri. No sittings during main holiday periods—plus Aug. and Sept. Tube: Westminster.

Kensington Palace State Apartments, Kensington Gdns., W.8 (tel. 937 9561). The official residence of the Royal Family before Buckingham Palace. Paintings from Royal Collections, early Georgian and Victorian furniture and objects d'art. Admission £2.60 (includes Costume Museum—see under *Museums* preceding). Daily 9–5, Sun. 1–5 (last admission 4.15). Tubes: Queensway or Kensington High St.

Kew, Royal Botanic Gardens, Kew Rd., Richmond, Surrey (tel. 940 3321). One of the oldest and loveliest botanical gardens anywhere. Admission 80p. Open daily all year from 9.30 to around dusk. Within the gardens are **Kew Palace** (Apr.–Sept., daily, 11–5.30) and **Queen Charlotte's Cottage** (Apr.–Sept., Sat., Sun., Bank Hol. Mon. only, 11–5.30). Admission 80p and 40p respectively. Tube: Kew Gardens. By boat from Westminster or Charing Cross in the summer.

Law Courts, Strand, W.C.2 (tel. 936 6000). The legal enclave called the Temple at the entrance to Fleet Street comprises the Inns of Court or Courts of Law, built by Street c.1882. The surrounding area is Old London at its most charming. Seating is usually available in the back two rows of the court; sessions at 10.30–1, 2–4, Mon. to Fri., except during Law Vacations. Tubes: Chancery Lane, Temple.

Monument, Monument St., E.C.3 (tel. 626 2717). Commemorates the Great Fire of 1666, which broke out in Pudding Lane 202 ft. from the monument—its height. Apr.–Sept., Mon.–Fri. 9–5.40, Sat.–Sun. 2–5.40; Oct.–Mar., Mon.–Sat. 9–3.40, closed Sun. Admission 50p. Tube: Monument.

Old Bailey, Old Bailey, E.C.4 (tel. 248 3277). Central Criminal Court. (More what you would expect if you get a kick out of watching a trial, than is offered by the Law Courts.) To attend session: Public Gallery opens 10–1 and 2–4. Line up at door in Newgate St. Tube: St. Paul's.

Royal Britain, the Barbican (tel. 588 0588). "You are there" audiovisual show brings to life royal history from Arthur and Guinevere to Charles and Di. Admission £5. Daily 9–5.30.

St. Paul's Cathedral, E.C.4 (tel. 248 2705). The masterpiece of Sir Christopher Wren, built after the Great Fire of London. Contains memorial chapel to the American forces in Britain. Tours of the Cathedral take place daily at 11, 11.30, and 2.30; cost £3.50. Admission charges to special areas include 80p to Crypt and £1 to Dome. Open daily except when in use. Tube: St. Paul's.

Southwark Cathedral, Borough High St., S.E.1 (tel. 407 2939). Across the river from St. Paul's, and several centuries older, Southwark Cathedral is one of the finest Gothic buildings in London. Open daily, 9–6. Tube: London Bridge.

Thames Barrier, Eastmoor St., off Woolwich Rd., S.E.7 (tel. 854 1373). Opened 1984, and not to be missed for a unique view of the river. Audiovisual and other displays. Admission £1. Mon.–Fri. 10.30–5, Sat.–Sun. 10.30–5.30. By British Rail train from Charing Cross to Charlton.

Tower of London, Tower Hill, E.C.3 (tel. 709 0765). Outstanding collection of armor, uniforms, historic relics. Admission £4.50 all year except Feb., when Jewel House closed for cleaning. Mar.–Oct., Mon.–Sat. 9.30–5, Sun. 2–5; Nov.–Feb., Mon.–Sat. 9.30–4, closed Sun. The Tower gets very crowded so try to avoid mid-day and weekends. Tube: Tower Hill. Buses: 35 or 40 to Monument, then walk, or 23 to Tower Hill. **Tower Bridge** (tel. 403 3761) is open to view daily 10–6.30 (summer), 10–4.45 (winter). Admission £2.

Trafalgar Square is a well-known landmark, with Nelson's Column, the fountains and pigeons—there is an excellent view of the area from the steps of the National Gallery. A huge tree is erected each Christmas, and crowds gather on New Year's Eve to celebrate en masse. Tube: Charing Cross.

Trocadero Center (see **Guinness World of Records**).

Wesley's Chapel, City Rd., E.C.1 (tel. 253 2262). One of the focal points of Methodism. Includes attractive 18th-century chapel as well as the house where Wesley lived and worked. House open weekdays 10 to 4. Snack lunch available after morning service on Sundays. Tube: Old Street or Moorgate.

Westminster Abbey, Broad Sanctuary, S.W.1 (tel. 222 5152). Daily 9.20–4, Sat. 9.20–2 and 4–5 (nave 7.30 A.M. to 6 P.M.), except when in use. Closed Sun. Admission £1.60 (free Wed. 6–8). Tube: Westminster or St. James's Park.

Westminster Cathedral, Ashley Pl., S.W.1 (tel. 834 7452). Most important Roman Catholic church in England. Daily 7 A.M.–8 P.M. except when in use. View London from 284 ft. tower, open daily 9.30–4.30 (April–Sept.); closed winter. Admission to tower 70p. Tube: Victoria.

Zoo. Situated in Regents Park, N.W.1 (tel. 722 3333). The huge London Zoo contains one of the world's largest collections of mammals, reptiles, and birds. Children's Zoo includes farm animals and offers rides for the youngsters. Admission £3.90 (less in winter). Apr.–Sept., daily 9–6; Oct.–Mar., daily 10–dusk. Tubes: Baker Street then 74 bus, or Camden Town, then 74 bus or walk. Buses: 74, 74B from Marble Arch or Baker Street to Gloucester Gate, Regent's Park. Zoo Water Bus from Little Venice, Paddington, March to early October.

CHANGING OF THE GUARD. This colorful ritual takes place in two ceremonies—*Queen's Life Guard,* daily at 11 A.M. (10 on Sun.) lasts about 25 minutes and is held at the Horse Guards, Whitehall. *Queen's Guard,* daily at 11.30 A.M., Apr.–July; alternate days at 11.30, Aug.–Mar. Ceremony lasts about 30 minutes; subject to cancellation without notice, held at Buckingham Palace. Tube for Whitehall: Charing Cross. Tube for the Palace: Victoria, Hyde Park Corner, or Green Park.

PARKS AND GARDENS. Londoners are proud of their precious green breathing spaces, abundant throughout the bustling city. They are popular for picnics, tennis, rowing, swimming, riding, or just walking the dog. You can also listen to music, watch open-air plays or do almost anything except pick the flowers. You can visit private gardens in London through the *National Gardens Scheme,* 57 Lower Belgrave St., S.W.1 (tel. 730 0359).

Battersea Park, S.W.11, covers 200 acres, with lake. Borders the Thames.

Blackheath, S.E.3. A big sweep of open common covering 268 acres, is an open space where fairs are staged, also cricket matches.

Dulwich Park, S.E.21 (72 acres). Famous for its rhododendrons and azaleas. The western gate leads into semi-rural Dulwich Village, and the superb Dulwich Picture Gallery, London's first public art gallery.

Green Park, smallest (53 acres) of the Royal Parks, between Piccadilly and St. James's Park.

Greenwich Park (which adjoins Blackheath—see above) is a Royal Park of 200 acres beside the river, containing the Royal Naval College, and the Maritime Museum.

Hampstead Heath covers 800 acres and is north London's favorite national holiday playground, with fairgrounds and other open-air attractions. Also Kenwood House, plus atmospheric pubs Bull & Bush, Jack Straw's Castle and the old Spaniards Inn.

Holland Park, W.8 (off Kensington High St.). 55 acres, once the private grounds of old Holland House, this lovely area contains part of the Elizabethan mansion, now a youth hostel, and an orangery. Charming gardens, open-air theater in summer. Excellent chic restaurant.

Hyde Park, W.1. Most famous of the Royal Parks, 340 acres stretching from Park Lane to Kensington Gardens. Swimming and boating in the Serpentine lake, Rotten Row for horse-riding, Apsley House, and the Achilles Statue, and quite famous for "Speakers' Corner" near Marble Arch.

Kensington Gardens, W.2. A 275-acre Royal Park adjoining Hyde Park and extending to Kensington Palace. Contains the Albert Memorial and Round Pond (famous for model yacht sailing), and part of the Serpentine. Carefully tended flower-beds are a picture in summer (along the south edge).

Kew, Royal Botanic Gardens. 300 acres about 10 miles west of the center of London. World-famous botanical gardens with many fine examples of rare plants. Gorgeous grounds. Open 9.30–dusk. Admission now 50p to gardens themselves; additional charges to Kew Palace and Queen Charlotte's Cottage (80p and 40p respectively).

Parliament Hill, N.W.3. 271 acres adjoining Hampstead Heath, with swimming lakes. Popular with kite-flyers.

Regent's Park, N.W.1. Royal Park stretching from the Marylebone Road to Primrose Hill, covers 464 acres, and dates from the days of the Prince Regent. Surrounded by beautiful houses. Contains the Zoo, Regent's Canal, lake, Queen Mary's Rose Garden (a wonderful sight when the roses are in bloom), and an open-air theater with Shakespearean productions.

Richmond Park, Richmond. Largest (2,470 acres) of the Royal Parks, with many deer as well as fine trees, ponds and mansions.

St. James's Park, S.W.1. Small (93 acres), but most attractive and oldest of the Royal Parks. Lake with many species of ducks, swans, and pelicans. Fine view of Buckingham Palace and the towers and spires of Whitehall from the bridge over the lake. Ideal for an after-theater summer stroll, when the fountains in the lake are illuminated.

Waterlow Park, N.6. A small park of 26 acres on the southern slopes of Highgate Hill, containing Lauderdale House, formerly occupied by Nell Gwyn, Charles II's favorite mistress. Open-air concerts.

SPORTS. Cricket is the traditional summer game, played daily all over the country. The first-class matches in the London area are those played at the Oval ground, where Surrey have their headquarters, and at Lord's, the Middlesex ground at St. John's Wood. The best way to get a taste of cricket without being bored to tears is to attend a one-day match of the

NatWest Trophy, the Benson and Hedges Cup or the Refuge Assurance Sunday League. Other matches worth seeing are the Test Matches between England and overseas teams, or the Eton *v.* Harrow public schools game at Lord's in July—the latter for crowd watching, too.

Football (Rugby Union) is played between October and the end of March. Big matches are staged at the Twickenham ground, within easy reach of Waterloo station, about six times during the season. Otherwise, rugby matches are club ones in the London area.

Football (Soccer) is the leading British winter game. Best first-class matches, held on Saturday afternoons in the London area, are to be seen at Chelsea, West Ham, Tottenham, and Highbury. The daily newspapers will give details of forthcoming matches. *Note:* Certain grounds have experienced considerable problems with crowd violence in recent years, which may make you think twice before deciding on a visit.

In May the Cup Final is played at Wembley Stadium when thousands of fans watch the last two survivors of an 8-month-long knock-out competition battle for honors. Tickets for this popular event are virtually unobtainable at short notice, but it is fully televised on British networks.

Golf. Although most golf clubs in the Greater London area are private, visitors are often able to play on them by payment of a green fee, which varies widely according to the course. It is best, especially with private courses, to telephone in advance to find out what the fee is and the restrictions (if any) for visitors. A letter of introduction from your own course at home is always valuable.

For a complete run-down of all of the area courses (as well as those throughout England), a good source is the *Golf Course Guide,* from Telegraph Publications, 83 Clerkenwell Rd., London E.C.1 (tel. 242 0747, Ext. 473). Some of London's larger bookstores also carry the guide.

Racing. You can watch speedway racing at Wimbledon Stadium on occasion, cycle racing at Herne Hill Stadium several nights a week during summer months, and both motorcycle and car racing at Brands Hatch, which is 30 minutes by train from Victoria Station to Swanley.

Horse Riding in Hyde Park, Richmond Park or Wimbledon Common is a lovely experience, and there are still a number of stables from which you can hire horses, prominent among them *Lilo Blum,* 32 Grosvenor Crescent Mews, S.W.1 (tel. 235 6846).

Rowing. You can row on the Serpentine in Regent's Park, and on the Thames from Kew and other places. For more formal rowing, the four-day *Henley Royal Regatta* is a colorful high-society occasion held at Henley-on-Thames in the first week of July. The regatta dates from 1839 and is world-famous.

Another well-known event is the annual boat race between Oxford and Cambridge Universities, which takes place on the Thames, from Putney to Mortlake, in late March.

Skating (Ice and Roller). Rinks usually have two sessions during the day including weekends. Check with the rinks for the hours and charges for the day you wish to go. The nearest to central London is *Queen's Ice Skating Club,* Queensway, W.2 (tel. 229 0172), which actually has three sessions a day, seven days a week. Tubes: Queensway and Bayswater.

Streatham Ice Rink, 386 Streatham High Rd., S.W.16 (tel. 769 7771), is also open daily. Take the B.R. Southern Region train to Streatham or Streatham Common.

Swimming. London's major outdoor swimming place is the Serpentine, in Hyde Park. Among the municipal pools are: the Oasis, 32 Endell St., Holborn, W.C.2; Great Smith Street Baths (near Westminster Abbey); and Swiss Cottage Baths, Winchester Road, N.W.3. Open-air swimming is also possible at Parliament Hill Fields, on the edge of Hampstead Heath. For further information try the *Amateur Swimming Association,* Harold Fern House, Derby Sq., Loughborough, Leicester (tel. 0509–230431).

Tennis headquarters for not only London but the world is Wimbledon. This is a large suburban center reached by train from Waterloo in 12–15 minutes or by District Line underground from Kensington and Earls Court. Many tennis clubs exist all over London, and thousands of public courts are available in the parks by the hour for modest fees.

The tennis tournament season in Britain starts early in April on hard courts, and changes to grass toward the end of May. The Surrey Championships are held at Surbiton, 12 miles from Waterloo, and the Kent Championships at Beckenham, 10 miles from Victoria. The Stella Artois Championships at Queen's Club, West Kensington, are the traditional curtain-raiser to the All-England Championships at Wimbledon in late June. Obtaining tickets for Wimbledon is a matter of luck and perseverance. Write to the *All England Lawn Tennis Club,* Church Rd., S.W.19, enclosing an International Reply Coupon, from early August through January. You'll be sent an application form, but tickets are finally allocated by ballot once all applications have been received. Reserved tickets cost anywhere from £15. Some tour operators (e.g. American Express) run special package tours (details from travel agents).

If you can't get tickets for any of the show courts, you can always just pay your £5 entrance fee (£3 after 5 P.M.), or £4 in Finals week (£3 after 5), and wander around the outside courts where you will often find some excellent games and plenty of big names, especially during the first week. However, it can get extremely crowded and unfortunately many of the subsidiary attractions are both expensive and tawdry. For the really keen there are also a number of standing places available on the center court every day. But these are issued on a first-come, first-served basis and as the demand is incredible you must be prepared to camp out at least half the night and stand in line for a very considerable time.

THEATERS AND CONCERT HALLS.

To find out what is on in the entertainment world in London, consult *What's On in London,* published weekly, or *Time Out,* which is better for the unconventional events. The evening papers *(London Evening Standard, London Daily News* and *Evening News)* carry listings, as do the major Sunday papers. Most of the theaters have a matinee twice a week (Wed. or Thurs. and Sat. usually), and an evening performance which begins at 7.30 or 8. Sunday drama performances are rare in London, though there is a movement towards them.

Prices for seats vary a lot, but you should expect to pay within a range from about £5–£6 up to around £20 for a ground-floor or first-balcony seat, depending on the theater and the production. For opera the prices will be higher—up to £75 a head for the best Covent Garden can offer, and around £20 at the Coliseum (higher if the present financial situation deteriorates), though there are cheaper seats at both houses. Concert tickets are still very moderate, ranging from about £3 to around £12.50,

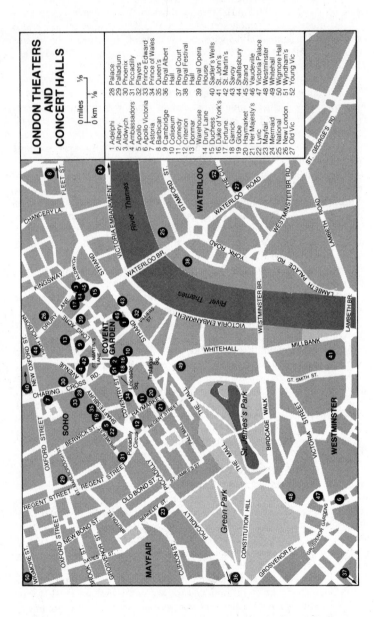

LONDON THEATERS AND CONCERT HALLS

0 miles   ⅛
0 km   ⅛

1 Adelphi
2 Albery
3 Aldwych
4 Ambassadors
5 Apollo
6 Apollo Victoria
7 Astoria
8 Barbican
9 Cambridge
10 Coliseum
11 Comedy
12 Criterion
13 Donmar Warehouse
14 Drury Lane
15 Duchess
16 Duke of York's
17 Fortune
18 Garrick
19 Globe
20 Haymarket
21 Her Majesty's
22 Lyric
23 Mayfair
24 Mermaid
25 National
26 New London
27 Old Vic
28 Palace
29 Palladium
30 Phoenix
31 Piccadilly
32 Players
33 Prince Edward
34 Prince of Wales
35 Queen's
36 Royal Albert Hall
37 Royal Court
38 Royal Festival Hall
39 Royal Opera House
40 Sadler's Wells
41 St. John's
42 St. Martin's
43 Savoy
44 Shaftesbury
45 Strand
46 Vaudeville
47 Victoria Palace
48 Westminster
49 Whitehall
50 Wigmore Hall
51 Wyndham's
52 Young Vic

though a visiting celebrity such as Von Karajan can command much higher prices. Most theaters will accept credit cards at the box office.

There is a reduced-price ticket booth in Leicester Square, open 12–2 for matinee tickets, 2.30–6.30 for evening ones. Reductions can be as much as 50% (plus 80p service charge). Personal application only (no phone), but be prepared for a long line.

The excellent *Fringe Theater Box Office,* Duke of York's Theater, St. Martin's Lane, W.C.2 (tel. 379 6002), handles bookings for some 40 fringe productions (the London version of Off Broadway).

Be very careful indeed of scalpers outside theaters and concert halls. They have been known to charge £200 or more for a sought-after event. Unless you *really* have money to burn, don't encourage these touts.

There are many theatrical ticket agencies, of which *Keith Prowse* is probably the leader with about a dozen branches around the West End (look under *Keith* in the phone book—not *Prowse*). All the big hotels have desks at which you can book for an entertainment. If you are coming from the States and want to book seats in advance, Keith Prowse have a New York branch—234 West 44th St., Suite 902, New York, N.Y. 10036, (212) 398–1430, (800) 223–4446.

Here are the main London theaters and concert halls:

Adelphi, Strand, W.C.2 (tel. 836 7611)
Albery, St. Martin's Lane, W.C.2 (tel. 836 3878)
Aldwych, Aldwych, W.C.2 (tel. 836 6404)
Ambassadors, West St., W.C.2 (tel. 836 6111)
Apollo, Shaftesbury Ave., W.1 (tel. 437 2663)
Apollo Victoria, Wilton Rd., S.W.1 (tel. 828 8665)
Barbican Center, Silk St., E.C.2 (concerts and Royal Shakespeare Company, tel. 628 8795, 638 8891)
Coliseum, St. Martin's Lane, W.C.2 (tel. 836 3161)
Comedy, Panton St., S.W.1 (tel. 930 2578)
Covent Garden, (see Royal Opera House)
Criterion, Piccadilly, W.1 (tel. 930 3216)
Donmar Warehouse, 41 Earlham St., W.C.2 (tel. 379 6565)
Drury Lane (Theater Royal), Catherine St., W.C.2 (tel. 836 8108)
Duchess, Catherine St., W.C.2 (tel. 836 8243)
Duke of York's, St. Martin's Lane, W.C.2 (tel. 836 5122)
Fortune, Russell St., W.C.2 (tel. 836 2238)
Garrick, Charing Cross Rd., W.C.2 (tel. 379 6107)
Globe, Shaftesbury Ave., W.1 (tel. 437 3667)
Haymarket, Haymarket, S.W.1 (tel. 930 9832)
Her Majesty's, Haymarket, S.W.1 (tel. 839 2244)
Lyric, Shaftesbury Ave., W.1 (tel. 437 3686)
Lyric Hammersmith, King St., Hammersmith, W.6 (tel. 741 2311)
Mayfair, Stratton St., W.1 (tel. 629 3036)
Mermaid, Puddle Dock, E.C.4 (tel. 236 5568)
National Theater (Cottesloe, Lyttelton and Olivier), South Bank Arts Centre, S.E.1 (tel. 928 2252)
New London, Drury Lane, W.C.2 (tel. 405 0072)
Old Vic, Waterloo Road, S.E.1 (tel. 928 7616)
Palace, Shaftesbury Ave., W.1 (tel. 437 0909/8327)
Palladium, 8 Argyll St., W.1 (tel. 437 7373)
Phoenix, Charing Cross Rd., W.C.2 (tel. 836 2294, 836 8611)

Piccadilly, Denman St., W.1 (tel. 437 4506)
Players, 173 Hungerford Arches, Villiers St., W.C.2 (tel. 839 1134)
Playhouse, Embankment Place, W.C.2 (tel. 930 4594)
Prince Edward, Old Compton St., W.1 (tel. 734 8951).
Prince of Wales, 31 Coventry St., W.1 (tel. 930 0844)
Queen's, 51 Shaftesbury Ave., W.1 (tel. 734 1166)
Regents Park (Open-Air), Inner Circle, Regents Park, N.W.1 (tel. 935 5884, 486 2431)
Riverside Studios, Crisp Rd., Hammersmith, W.6 (tel. 748 3354)
Royal Albert Hall, Kensington Gore, S.W.7 (tel. 589 8212/9465)
Royal Court, Sloane Square, S.W.1 (tel. 730 1745); **Theatre Upstairs,** tel. 730 2554
Royal Festival Hall, South Bank, S.E.1 (tel. 928 3191)
Royal Opera House, Covent Garden, W.C.2 (tel. 240 1066)
Sadler's Wells, Rosebery Ave., E.C.1 (tel. 278 8916)
St. George's, 49 Tufnell Park Rd., N.7 (tel. 607 1128)
St. John's, Smith Square, S.W.1 (tel. 222 1061)
St. Martin's, West St., W.C.2 (tel. 836 1443)
Savoy, Strand, W.C.2 (tel. 836 8888)
Shaftesbury Theater, Shaftesbury Ave., W.C.2 (tel. 379 5399)
Strand, Aldwych, W.C.2 (tel. 836 2660)
Theater Royal, Stratford East, E.15 (tel. 534 0310)
Vaudeville, Strand, W.C.2 (tel. 836 9987)
Victoria Palace, Victoria St., S.W.1 (tel. 834 1317/8, 828 4735/6)
Westminster, 12 Palace St., S.W.1 (tel. 834 0283)
Whitehall, 14 Whitehall, S.W.1 (tel. 930 7765/6)
Wigmore Hall, 36 Wigmore St., W.1 (tel. 935 2141)
Wyndham's, Charing Cross Rd., W.C.2 (tel. 836 3028)
Young Vic, 66 The Cut, S.E.1 (tel. 928 6363)

MOVIES. There are major cinemas all over the West End, with a concentration around Leicester Square. In most of them you can reserve a
seat in advance, with prices starting at around £3–£3.50. In the suburbs,
which can mean only a short bus ride away from the center, prices are
a pound or so lower, sometimes more. (Mondays and matinees in many
movie houses cost a flat £2).

The West End cinemas and their suburban brothers generally show popular entertainment films, the type of which is denoted, approximately, by
the censor's rating. This appears in small print alongside the title of the
film. Films with a U (for Universal) rating are considered acceptable for
all audiences; those rated PG will require parental guidance; a rating of
15 means the film has been passed for those 15 and over; and lastly, replacing the infamous X-rating comes an 18 which is meant only for the eyes
and ears of those 18 and over.

In addition there are such specialty cinemas as the *Screen on the Green*
in Islington, the *Gate,* Notting Hill Gate, the *Everyman,* Hampstead, or
the *Lumière* on St. Martin's Lane in the heart of theaterland. There are
two important cinema clubs, the *National Film Theater* which is in the
Festival Hall complex, and the *Institute of Contemporary Arts* on the Mall.
The N.F.T. screens movies from its vast library, and specializes in series
highlighting the films of famous directors or the work of a particular studio; temporary membership 80p weekly, £3.30 monthly.

There is a handful of all-night cinemas; otherwise, showings finish around 11 P.M. But there is a growing popularity for late night shows, starting about 11.30, on Friday and Saturday nights.

HORSE AND DOG RACING. Several horse and greyhound racing tracks are to be found in the London area, where you'll find both tote and bookmaker betting. Visitors will have no trouble placing bets for horse races or dog races (as greyhound races are called). Bookie establishments are on every other corner, almost as common as pubs.

Horse Racing. For general information about racing events, phone the *Jockey Club* on 486 4921.

Ascot. Flat (without obstacles) and jump racing. Reached by Southern Region electric trains from Waterloo (28 miles) or by Green Line bus. Royal Ascot is the very fashionable meeting attended by the Queen during the third week in June. Ascot course stages 1-day, 2-day and 3-day meetings each season. For information phone Ascot (0990) 22211.

Epsom. Flat racing only. Scene of the Derby, held first week in June. Reached by electric trains from Victoria to Epsom Downs or Charing Cross to Tattenham Corner in about 35 minutes (21 miles). 2 days in April; 4-day Derby and Oaks event in June; 2 days at end of August.

Kempton Park. Steeplechasing and flat racing. At Sunbury-on-Thames train station is Kempton Park, reached by electric train from Waterloo in 35 minutes. Three 2-day and three 1-day steeplechase events in the winter; four 2-day and four 1-day meetings on the flat in summer.

Sandown Park. Steeplechasing and flat racing. Train to Esher station, Surrey, from Waterloo, in 21 minutes. Ten winter jump events and 16 races on the flat in the summer.

Windsor. Steeplechasing and flat racing. A mile west of Windsor. Seven steeplechase and 14 flat meetings each year, including popular evening meetings.

Dog Tracks. Most tracks have meetings twice during the week, and then on Saturday or Sunday. Weekday races tend not to overlap, so you can usually find a meet at one track or another any day of the week. Evenings, the dogs come under starter's orders around 7.45; during the day it varies with the track.

Main tracks include: *Wimbledon, Catford, Wembley, Hackney Wick, Romford* and *Walthamstow.*

SHOPPING. Despite the ravages of inflation, the effect of soaring rents on prices, the get-rich-quick merchants, the crowds and the alarming increase in sheer shabbiness of so many of London's streets, shopping still ranks high among the delights of the British capital. For one thing, as you might expect in a great metropolis, many of the best shopping streets are in some of the most interesting and fashionable areas of London. So if the constraints of your budget won't allow you to do more than window shop, you can combine this in itself frequently enjoyable process with an exploration of London. But if you do feel a little more flush, you'll find that the quality of traditional English goods has declined not at all; cashmere scarves, sweaters and skirts, hand-made shoes, classic rain-wear, silk shirts and, above all perhaps, the incomparable Savile Row suit still rule the roost in their respective fields. At the same time, London has consistently reaffirmed its position as a (if not *the*) leader of the fashion world, as the glittering shops in Mayfair and upbeat boutiques around Covent Garden make only too clear.

If high fashion is not your thing, however, how about antiques? London probably has more antique shops per square mile than any other city in the world and in all price ranges. Or books? You'll find a number of strikingly excellent specialist and general book shops. And then there are the department stores, covering the entire scale of quality and price, all the way from atmospheric Liberty's to everyday Marks and Spencer.

One word of advice, however. Do remember that London is a sprawling place and that its center alone is the same size as any number of respectably sized cities. So try to confine your shopping activities to no more than one or perhaps two areas at a time.

Oxford Street. Oxford Street, the most famous shopping street in London, is unfortunately also one of the least appealing. Not only is it long and crowded, it is also home to some of the most nondescript and drab shops in town, for the most part selling over-priced jeans. However, to its credit, it does have a number of department stores, all of which are reasonably priced. The best, or at any rate the best known, is *Selfridges,* a splendid pile of grandiose, 1920s architecture dominating the whole of one block toward Marble Arch, and London's equivalent of Macy's in New York. Running from west to east the other principal department stores are *C&A* at no. 505 (there are two smaller branches further along at 376 and 200) for very reasonably-priced clothes for all the family and some surprisingly bright fashions; at no. 458 there's a huge branch of *Marks and Spencer,* one of Britain's best-loved main street stores. It is inexpensive and the service is almost legendary for its friendliness and reliability. Grouped together, just before Oxford Circus, are *Debenhams, John Lewis* (excellent for yard goods) and *British Home Stores,* all of them reasonably priced if perhaps also a little unexceptional. At Oxford Circus itself, however, and occupying the whole of one corner of this great junction formed by the meeting of Oxford Street and Regent Street is *Top Shop,* a department store with a certain farouche style in comparison with its companions in Oxford Street.

While Oxford Street itself may not offer much to the shopper other than the prospect of blisters and exhaustion many of the streets that lead off it rank among London's prettiest and best shopping areas. St. Christopher's Place is on the north side of Oxford Street and practically opposite Bond Street tube station. It's very tiny but well signposted so you shouldn't miss it. Pedestrian-only since 1980, St. Christopher's Place has convincingly established itself as one of the most attractive of London's chic shopping streets, full of boutiques. South of Oxford Street this time and right beside the Bond Street tube is South Molton Street, currently London's most chic and expensive shopping street. It's also a pedestrian-only street, and perfect for window shopping if you have a champagne taste but a beer income. It is one of London's trendiest areas.

Bond Street (New and Old). Returning to Oxford Street and backtracking a little, you'll come to New Bond Street, a street that has consistently maintained its reputation. It's a little less stylish than, say, ten years ago, but it still has a certain glamorous quality. Aside from travel agents and airline offices, the bulk of the shops that dot its length—from Oxford

Street down to Piccadilly—are ultra-sophisticated clothes shops, gift shops and jewelers. There are also a number of art galleries, some of great distinction (including the home of *Sotheby's,* the prestigious art auctioneers at 34 New Bond Street). Needless to say, prices around here are not for those with high blood pressure and anyone subject to dizzy spells should stay well away.

Parallel to Old Bond Street, and on the east side, runs a charming covered alley built in 1819, the Burlington Arcade, linking Piccadilly with Burlington Street and running up one side of the Royal Academy; it's the perfect place to prowl on a wet day. The atmosphere here is terribly English, though in the nicest possible way and, not surprisingly, many of the shops sell mainly British goods, many of them of the highest quality.

Jermyn Street and St. James's. Leading south from Piccadilly roughly opposite the southern end of the Burlington Arcade is Duke Street, St. James, a small road that slants steeply downhill and plunges into the heart of St. James's, still an exclusive enclave of discreet gentlemen's clubs, art galleries and London's most traditional gentlemen's accessory shops. The major shopping street is Jermyn Street, which runs parallel to Piccadilly and is crossed at right angles by Duke Street. Apart from hand-made shirts and hand-lasted shoes this area still sells cheese from all over Europe, excellent perfume, and briar pipes; and it has several art dealers, with a good line in things like English watercolors. The second major art auction house, *Christie's,* is at 8 King Street.

Regent Street. Like Oxford Street which it crosses, Regent Street is one of the great thoroughfares of London. It was built originally by John Nash for the Prince Regent (hence the name) and cuts a majestic swathe through Mayfair to the west and Soho to the east as it runs down to and across Piccadilly Circus and thence to Pall Mall, where it finally comes to an end. However, it offers greater style and elegance than Oxford Street, though it too has a tendency to suffer from the overcrowding and, occasionally, the tawdry bustle that so conspicuously bedevils Oxford Street.

The most splendid store in Regent Street is *Liberty's,* at no. 200. Its principal facade on Regent Street is a magnificent Hollywood-style classical structure of the sort that makes one suspect that the hand of Cecil B. De-Mille has been at work. Around the side of the building, however, the style changes quite unexpectedly to an equally magnificent—and inappropriate—Tudor idiom, all plaster work and gnarled beams.

Liberty's are famous principally for their fabulous fabrics, which they design and print themselves, but they also have an Oriental department full of gorgeous and mysterious saris and Arabian jewelry; on the ground floor there is a small department selling original Art Deco jewelry. It is an excellent spot for searching out that original gift.

Covent Garden. Covent Garden, for long the home of London's fruit and vegetable market, seemed to be proving all the theories about inner-city decay absolutely right a few years ago. The market, up until then the area's principal raison d'être, had moved to a new site south of the Thames, leaving the old central buildings and warehouses empty. But suddenly the whole area sprang to life again as the result of the decision to renovate the elegant mid-19th-century market building and its attendant flower and fruit markets. Today Covent Garden means shops, restaurants, publishers, public relation firms, and the Opera House (of course)—but the heart of it all is the lovingly-restored market, a semi-open arcaded building on two levels watched over by Inigo Jones's austere church of St. Paul's. Its light and airy interior is perfect for window shopping and walking around the stalls and many small shops selling dolls' houses, herbal soaps, toy theaters and many more attractive quirky items.

The Covent Garden complex is now the center of an area of streets bursting with crafts shops and other fascinating venues—mostly lying west, east and north of the market. Even the narrowest alley around here can hide an exciting boutique.

Westward from Covent Garden lie the main secondhand book shops. Near Leicester Square tube station is *Dillons,* at 8 Long Acre. This is a great place for postcards and posters as well as for catalogs of countless exhibitions. You'll also find art books on all subjects and in all price ranges.

Knightsbridge. On the corner of Knightsbridge and Sloane Street is *Harvey Nichols,* considered by many to be London's most attractive department store and rivaled only by Liberty's. One major plus here is that unlike most department stores it is small and comparatively uncrowded. It also has some of the most elegant and desirable clothes in town as well as an atmosphere of well-heeled plush that conspires to make it good fun simply to walk around and look, as well as, of course, to shop.

Knightsbridge is also home to the most famous store in London, and one of the most famous in the world, *Harrods.* Its gaudy Edwardian bulk, all delicate red brickwork and gold detailing, dominates the stretch of the Brompton Road in which, serene and plush, it rules supreme. Times change, though, and Harrods changes with them. The problem is that success has bred success, and in pursuit of incredible profits, the store has sacrificed the quiet dignity on which those profits were originally built. It is still an experience to shop here, with a pause for refreshment at one of the excellent restaurants or coffee shops, but anyone who knows the lavish splendors of Bloomingdale's or Neiman Marcus is in for a disappointment.

A few blocks down from Harrods is Beauchamp (pronounced "Beacham") Place. It is small and pretty and full of interesting and attractive little shops. Running off Beauchamp Place at right angles is Walton Street, a charming little road of pink, yellow and blue Victorian villas that is absolutely perfect for browsing.

Chelsea. For long one of the prettiest areas of London, Chelsea has always enjoyed a rather raffish reputation. This quality came into its own during the heyday of the swinging sixties when Chelsea reigned supreme as the beating heart of all that was most modern and daring in London. Those days are past now, but the place still retains a vigor and spontaneity that can be hard to resist. Nowhere is this more evident than in the King's Road, an endlessly long road that runs from Sloane Square all the way to Putney. However, the part that is most Chelsea-like occupies only the first quarter of its total length. To see it at its most amusing and enjoyable, full of outrageous fashions and wonderfully bizarre characters, walk down it on a sunny Saturday afternoon, when the whole place buzzes and hums with movement and color.

Quite a bit along the King's Road lies World's End, an area that does its best to live up to its name. But if you can bear to continue on through its dreary council buildings and drab shopping complexes, you'll come to perhaps the most interesting stretch of the whole King's Road. It is only

300 or 400 yards long, but a pub or two, a lovely 19th-century arcade and a refreshing mixture of shops, some grand, some rather sheepish and run-down, contrive to give this little area an irresistible flavor.

Kensington. Though primarily a residential district of considerable charm and chic, Kensington nonetheless has a certain amount to offer the shopper. But the principal shopping street, Kensington High Street, is little more than a scaled down version of Oxford Street with very little for the visiting shopper.

The real charm of this area, however, is to be found in Kensington Church Street, a long winding street that snakes uphill from High Street, Kensington toward Notting Hill Gate. Aside from one or two good clothes shops, Kensington Church Street is notable principally for the endless array of antique shops that line both sides. You'll find jewelry, clothes, paintings, glass, ceramics, furniture, clocks, brass rubbings, carpets, dolls and just about anything else you can think of. It is an excellent place for both window shopping and dreaming.

Markets. Fun as it is to wander around the formal shops of London, there is nothing like a street market for stimulating the acquisitive juices. The difference between this kind of shopping and the more sedate kind is that you would be wise to get to the markets as early as you can, both to watch how they gather impetus during the day, and to find those worms that are most tasty for early birds. You should also remember that you can't make mistakes in purchasing as long as you don't spend too much. You will have to be very certain of your own taste and knowledge to spend more than, say, £25. But, above all, it isn't the bargains that really count with street markets; it's the unbeatable atmosphere. Here are the major markets, with a few helpful facts about them:

Bermondsey (New Caledonian), one of London's most extensive. Hundreds of booths and stalls, with a wealth of junk from the attics of England. A special stamping-ground for dealers. Take the 15 or 25 bus to Aldgate, then the 42 over Tower Bridge to Bermondsey Square. But get there early and remember, you may have to walk a lot. The market can start as early as 4 in the morning and runs until about midday *on Fridays only.*

Camden Lock (Dingwalls Market), (Tube or buses 24 or 29 to Camden Town). Antiques and crafts market. Open Saturday and Sunday, 10–5.30, though individual and craft shops are open weekdays around the picturesque lock.

Camden Passage, Islington (Tube or buses 19, 38, to "The Angel"). Mainly open-air antique market, Saturdays. Fascinating antique shops in Camden Passage and Pierrepont Arcade, particularly for silverware. Stick to Association of British Antique Dealers members here. Shops open daily, 10.30–5.30; market Wednesday and Saturday. Also a good spot for a Sunday morning wander.

Leadenhall Market, E.C.3. A Victorian arcade with food and plants; lots of atmosphere. Monday to Friday, 7–3. Tube to the Bank.

Leather Lane, Holborn E.C.1. A blend of traditional fruit, vegetable and crockery stalls with newfangled wares like spare Hi-Fi parts. Monday to Friday, 11–3 P.M. Tube to Chancery Lane.

Petticoat Lane, in Middlesex St., E.1. Open on Sunday mornings (9–2) only, for pets, clothes, fabrics and curios of all descriptions. (Watch your wallets!) Tube to Liverpool St., Aldgate or Aldgate East.

Portobello Market, Portobello Road, W.11. (Take 52 bus or tube to Ladbroke Grove or Notting Hill Gate.) Best day is Saturday, 8–5, (though it is open during the week—not Thursday afternoon) for all kinds of curios, silverware, antiques, etc. Several dealers with shops in other parts of London have booths here. No bargains and sometimes can be a trap for tourists, but is bursting at the seams with local color.

RESTAURANTS. Once upon a time, when the world was young, eating in London was an experience to be endured rather than enjoyed. Things are very different now. There are restaurants offering cuisine from all over the world—and even, be it said in reverent tones, from Britain. There have always been Italian and French restaurants, some dating back for fifty years or more; solid reliable places, with solid reliable menus. But now there are literally dozens of possibilities with exciting, adventurous cooking served in intriguing surroundings.

It is difficult to say what brought about this complete volte face. One of the more obvious reasons is the great influx into Britain in the last decade of new citizens who have brought their own cooking with them. That might explain the opening of what seems like endless Tandoori restaurants, but in no way deals with the fact that Britons are becoming more conscious of what they eat. And not just conscious but downright pernickety. The *Good Food Guide* (that gastronomic bible without which no visitor to Britain who enjoys eating can consider himself equipped), has developed over the years of its existence into a kind of public diary in which contributors can record their dissatisfaction with the amount of vinegar in a sauce or the callousness of a waiter.

That diners do write in to the *Good Food Guide,* by the thousand apparently, shows that food is now taken very seriously in Britain, and such high-seriousness can only benefit the visitor to the country. Whatever your taste, it is likely to find satisfaction in London. The same cannot necessarily be said for your purse which might well not be so happy. Rents and local taxes being what they are, restaurants find that they have to charge more than they would otherwise, just to make ends meet. The result has inevitably been that fewer and fewer Londoners are able to eat out, unless they are on expense accounts or celebrating. It has also meant that restaurants which have reasonable prices and still give value-for-money and courteous service are treasured. So, unless you are the kind of traveler who is not bothered by the size of a check, look very hard before you eat. Most restaurants post their menu, with prices, outside.

We have divided our main listings here by price, rather than by culinary type. The pricing system we have used is explained previously, but here it is again, this time with London prices. All the grades cover an approximate price for a dinner for two, including wine and V.A.T. (Wine in the Budget category means carafe.)

Luxury, £90 and up—way up, you could find yourself faced with a £120 check for two in the upper reaches of this grade with no difficulty at all; Expensive £60–£90, Moderate £30–£60, Budget £30 and below.

We would be wrong to convey the impression that the picture is entirely rosy. There are some serious defects still to eating in London. The main one is that it is difficult to do so on Sunday or late at night. You should always check if a restaurant is open on Sundays; it could save you a trip. See "Late Meals," further on in this section, for a list of London restaurants with late-night hours.

A law obliges all U.K. restaurants to display their prices, including V.A.T., outside their establishments along with their menus. At the time of writing, not all restaurants are conforming to this sensible piece of consumer legislation. But most do now display their prices, and if you are on a very tight budget, it's wise to read them carefully. Look for the hidden extras such as service, cover and minimum charge which are usually at the bottom of the menu—and make sure the menu inside is the same!

LUXURY (L)

A l'Ecu de France, 111 Jermyn St., S.W.1 (tel. 930 2837). Elegant and well-established near Piccadilly Circus, with wide-ranging menu and a notable wine list. Good value set pre-theater menu. Closed lunch Sat., all day Sun.

Athenaeum Hotel Restaurant, 116 Piccadilly, W.1 (tel. 499 3464). Reliable international menu with excellent wine list.

Berkeley Hotel Restaurant, Wilton Place, S.W.1 (tel. 235 6000). Superb classical cuisine perfectly served by friendly professional staff in elegant surroundings. Closed Sat. *Berkeley Buttery,* in the hotel, offers popular lunchtime buffet, and an evening change of mood to serious dining and music. Both consistently among London's best. Closed Sun.

Le Boulestin, 1A Henrietta St., W.C.2 (tel 836 7061). One of London's grand old French restaurants with its kitchens brought up to date and its decoration lavishly redone in its original late-'20s style (by current owners Grand Met), Boulestin remains one of London's most elegant dining rooms. Classic and modern cuisine from its first British chef Kevin Kennedy; the set lunch is excellent value. Closed Sat. lunch, Sun. and 3 weeks in Aug.

Café Royal, 68 Regent St., W.1 (tel. 437 9090). Lavishly painted ceilings and memories of Oscar Wilde in the "grill". The next door *Le Relais* has metamorphosed brasserie-style, is now called *The Nicols Restaurant* and is open throughout the day for breakfast, snacks, teas and a set table d'hôte.

Capital Hotel Restaurant, 22–24 Basil St., S.W.3 (tel. 589 5171). Redecorated in Louis XV style, with stupendous pale pink curtains, pretty lighting and Limoges china. Short menu of well-prepared modern French food augmented with char-grilled dishes for the plainer palates. Outstanding value set lunch.

Cecconi's, 5A Burlington Gdns., W.1 (tel. 434 1500). An elegant Italian restaurant which attracts a chic set. Try any of their fresh pasta dishes and mouthwatering desserts. Closed lunch Sat., all day Sun.

Claridges Hotel, Brook St., W.1 (tel. 629 8860). The *Causerie* is one of the best buys in town, with a mouthwatering lunch or dinner buffet.

Closed Sat. *Claridges Restaurant,* a 1930's-style room decorated in pastel colors, depends upon fellow diners to create the right ambiance. Food similarly can be dull, but generally well worth a visit.

Connaught Hotel Restaurant, Carlos Place, W.1 (tel. 499 7070). London's current gastronomic temple presided over by high priest Michel Bourdin; befitting its status, it has more than a touch of hierarchical tradition. The range of dishes is vast and the wine selection extremely good value. Dine either on traditional British fare or classical French cuisine. The British breakfast is outstanding. Top of the category; reservations essential. Fine wine list. Closed Sat.–Sun.

Le Gavroche, 43 Upper Brook St., W.1 (tel. 408 0881). Albert Roux presides over the kitchen of one of London's legendary restaurants (brother Michel does the same in the Waterside Inn, Bray) and maintains very high standards from both the kitchen and service staff. Faultless food and fine wine list. Reservations essential; it's easier to get a table at lunch—which is a set all-in "bargain." Closed Sat., Sun.

Grosvenor House Hotel, Ninety Park Lane, 90 Park Lane, W.1 (tel. 499 6363). A grand luxury restaurant with a menu devised by famous South-of-France chef, Louis Outhier. Closed lunch Sat. and Sun.

Hyatt Carlton Tower Hotel, Chelsea Room, Cadogan Place, S.W.1 (tel. 235 5411). Dining room has delightful views across Cadogan Square. *Soigné* French cooking and agreeable service. Elegant teas in the *Chinoiserie.*

Hyde Park Hotel, Grill Room, 66 Knightsbridge, S.W.1 (tel. 235 2000). A hold-over from the palmy days of Edwardian London with its marble and plush well-maintained. Popular lunchtime buffet. Closed Sat.

Inigo Jones, 14 Garrick St., W.C.2 (tel. 836 6456). Close to gaslights and the Bow Street Runners' narrow street, this Covent Garden venue offers original bar-brick and stained-glass décor and a tempting well-cooked menu. A fine spot for a reasonable lunch or an expensive dinner. Reservations essential. Closed lunch Sat., all day Sun.

Inn on the Park Hotel, Four Seasons, Hamilton Place, Park Lane, W.1 (tel. 499 0888). An expensive restaurant in this range, but one with imaginative cooking and pleasant service. **The Lanes** is much less pricey, but maintains the same high and attractive standards, with a *prix fixe* lunchtime menu, including wine. Lanes closed dinner Sun.

Inter-Continental Hotel, Le Soufflé, 1 Hamilton Place, Hyde Park Corner, W.1 (tel. 409 3131). '20s decor is the backdrop here to first-class food, expertly served, from one of London's top chefs. For the budget-minded there's a set-price lunch. Closed lunch Sat.

Keats, 3 Downshire Hill, N.W.3 (tel. 435 3544). Hampstead locale. Named after the poet, with decor to simulate his study. Famous with Hampstead literati for its fine classical food, cellar and seasonal gourmet dinners; phone for details.

Leith's, 92 Kensington Park Rd., W.11 (tel. 229 4481). Prue Leith is also a well-known writer on food, a teacher and fine cook herself, so you'd expect the food here to be interesting. Her restaurant is a converted row house—food mixes nouvelle and classical cuisine. Dinner only. Open Sunday.

Ma Cuisine, 113 Walton St., S.W.3 (tel. 584 7585). Reservations weeks in advance are essential in this tiny (11 tables) restaurant that lives up to its enviable reputation. Closed Sat.–Sun. and 4 weeks July–Aug.

Rue St. Jacques, 5 Charlotte St., W.1 (tel. 637 0222). Run by graduates of Carrier's and Boulestin's, with three different mood dining rooms. Expect rich food and a serious wine list. Be sure to ask about the set lunch.

Savoy Hotel, Grill Room and **Restaurant,** Strand, W.C.2 (tel. 836 4343). A well-founded reputation for classic French cooking and impeccable service at this splendid ornately decorated restaurant overlooking the river. The Grill, though, remains a top place for British roasts, grills and regional fare. Closed Sat. lunch and Sun.

Scott's, 20 Mount St., W.1 (tel. 629 5248). Luxurious landmark in the heart of Mayfair. English menu of classic fish dishes; the catch of the day being the highlight. Also plain grills and oysters. Light meals can be had at the oyster bar. Closed Sun. lunch.

Simply Nico, 48A Rochester Row, S.W.1 (tel. 630 8061). Fine flavored and finely presented modern French food from famed chef Nico Ladenis. Phone for details of the new address of sister restaurant **Chez Nico.** Excellent value set lunches. Fine wine list. Mon. to Fri. only.

Suntory, 72 St. James's St., S.W.1 (tel 409 0201). Elegant, chic Japanese restaurant. Specialties include tempura, teppanyaki and shabu shabu. Closed Sun.

La Tante Claire, 68 Royal Hospital Rd., S.W.3 (tel. 352 6045). Enlarged and redesigned in a light and pretty style, this restaurant with kitchens run by Roux graduate, Pierre Koffman, serves classic French food with a bias to variety meats and fish. Fine wine list. Closed Sat., Sun., 3 weeks Aug.–Sept., and 10 days at Easter.

Trader Vic's, Hilton Hotel, Park Lane, W.1 (tel. 493 7586). Still one of London's best spots for a touch of the South Seas exotic. Menu large and variable. Closed lunch Sat.

Waltons, 121 Walton St., S.W.3 (tel. 584 0204). A pretty restaurant specializing in 18th-century English dishes. 300-item wine list. Sunday lunch and after-theater dinner are exceptional value.

Wiltons, 55 Jermyn St., S.W.1 (tel. 629 9955). Wilton's retains its original Edwardian charm and discreet, efficient staff, plus a menu of British food with seafood and game seasonal specialties. Closed Sat. and Sun.

EXPENSIVE (E)

Alcove, 17 Kensington High St., W.8 (tel. 937 1443). Good, fresh, quality fish is best sampled here unadorned (branch of Wheeler's). Closed Sun.

Alastair Little, 49 Frith St., W.1 (tel. 734 5183). Stylish Anglo-French, *nouvelle cuisine*-inspired food from London's most esteemed young British chef. Lunch and dinner menu changes daily. Closed weekends and 3 weeks in Aug.

Bagatelle, 5 Langton St., S.W.10 (tel. 351 4185). Art deco restaurant offering light, beautifully cooked French dishes. Summer garden behind. In farthest Chelsea. Closed Sun.

Baron of Beef, Gutter Lane, Gresham St., E.C.2 (tel. 606 6961). A popular lunchtime venue for traditional English fare. The cellar stocks some exceptional claret. Closed Sat. and Sun.

Bentley's, 11 Swallow St., W.1 (tel. 734 6201). Traditional seafood restaurant with a downstairs bar. Classic spot. Closed Sun.

Brinkley's, 47 Hollywood Rd., S.W.10 (tel. 351 1683). Dinner only—by candlelight or in the courtyard. Competent and highly original. Excellent wines. Reservations essential. Closed Sun.

English House, 3 Milner St., S.W.3 (tel. 584 3002). Lovers of traditional English food can enjoy a taste of the past in this charming dining room in a private house. Reservations essential.

L'Etoile, 30 Charlotte St., W.1 (tel. 636 7189). Small and tasteful French place with the true touch of Paris. Great wine list and generally good to know. Closed all day Sat. and Sun.

Fisherman's Wharf at the Belvedere, Holland Park (behind the Commonwealth Institute), W.8 (tel. 602 1238). The attractive location of this restaurant in Holland Park (in the evening it's floodlit) has always made it a popular rendezvous, but now its new fish bias has raised the food to new heights. 90 malt whiskeys. Closed Sun.

Le Français, 529 Fulham Rd., S.W.3 (tel. 352 3668). A gastronomic *tour de France* with a choice of either a fixed carte of well-chosen dishes or specialties of French regional dishes complemented by the wine of the area (the region changes weekly). Closed Sun.

Frederick's, Camden Passage, N.1 (tel. 359 2888). An imaginative menu served beneath high ceilings with a lovely conservatory too. *The* time to visit is Sat. lunch, when the nearby antiques market is in full swing. Closed Sun.

Greenhouse, 27A Hays Mews, W.1 (tel. 499 3331). Airy setting for interesting range of dishes in this stylish restaurant. Closed lunch Sat., all day Sun.

Hilaire, 68 Old Brompton Rd., S.W.7 (tel. 584 8993). The latest "in" spot for *cuisine eclectique.* Closed Sat. lunch and Sun.

Khun Akorn, 136 Brompton Rd., S.W.3 (tel. 225 2688). Sumptuous Thai restaurant serving the rich and elegant Thai Royal cuisine as served at their hotel, the Imperial, in Bangkok. Open Sun.

Langan's Brasserie, Stratton St., W.1 (tel. 491 8822). Delightful Edwardian premises whose walls are lined with contemporary art; the well-run kitchen maintains a high standard of everyday French food. The mix of owners (cook—Richard Shepherd, actor—Michael Caine, champagne-guzzling restaurateur—Peter Langan) ensures that it's the most fashionable eatery in town. Reservations essential. Open late, though. Closed lunch Sat., all day Sun.

Leoni's Quo Vadis, 26 Dean St., W.1 (tel. 437 9585). Heart-of-Soho, old-fashioned, long-established, reliable and good Italian cooking. Very highly regarded. Karl Marx lived upstairs. Closed lunch Sat. and Sun.

Locket's, Marsham Court, Marsham St., S.W.1 (tel. 834 9552). Close to the Houses of Parliament and one of a small number of restaurants that sounds the Division Bell (summoning Members of Parliament to a vote in the House of Commons). Staunchly English food. Closed Sat. and Sun.

Ménage A Trois, 15 Beauchamp Pl., S.W.3 (tel. 589 4252). The hors d'oeuvres-and-desserts-only place ("no inter-course" says chef/patron Antony Worrall-Thompson) made famous by a visit from Princess Diana. Closed Sat. and Sun. lunches.

Mijanou, 143 Ebury St., S.W.1 (tel. 730 4099). Intricate, delicate food from a woman chef, Sonia Blech, served in what resembles a private dining room. Fine wine list; good set lunch. Closed Sat. and Sun.

Mr. Chow, 151 Knightsbridge, S.W.1 (tel. 589 7347). Modern decor and contemporary paintings cover the walls of this top class Chinese restaurant.

Mr. Kai of Mayfair, 65 South Audley St., W.1 (tel. 493 8988). On two levels, this is a modern, stylish restaurant with a mock blossom tree bearing flowers on each floor. High standard of cooking and efficient service with exotic Chinese ladies serving drinks.

Neal Street Restaurant, 26 Neal St., W.C.2 (tel. 836 8368). Prized spot for that business lunch or dinner. Trendy but cool Conran (Habitat) decor. High in this price range. Closed Sat. and Sun.

Odins, 27 Devonshire St., W. 1 (tel. 935 7296). Unusual and original food with a good wine list. Reservations essential. Closed lunch Sat., all day Sun.

Pier 31, 31 Cheyne Walk, S.W.3 (tel. 352 5006). Oriental and French food plus char-grilled dishes from a Japanese chef, served in stylish art deco room with a view across the Thames. Traditional British Sun. lunch. Sushi bar and restaurant.

Pomegranates, 94 Grosvenor Rd., S.W.1 (tel. 828 6560). Comfortable club-like basement; interesting menu of dishes from around the world, based on the owner's travels. Excellent wine list. Closed Sun.

Le Poulbot, 45 Cheapside, E.C.2 (tel. 236 4379). Popular with gourmet businessmen who get privacy (the tables are set in semi-booths) and a daily-changing menu of top, modern French food. Part of the Roux empire. Mon.-Fri. lunch only, closed weekends.

Read's, 152 Old Brompton Rd., S.W.5 (tel. 373 2445). Small, charming and pretty; offering superb value and quality French-inspired food from a young British female chef. Well-explained and chosen wine list. Traditional British Sun. lunch is one of the best in town. Closed Sun. dinner.

Ritz Hotel, Louis XVI Restaurant, Piccadilly, W.1 (tel. 493 8181) Good food and an excellent wine list in magnificent surroundings, recently restored to their original glory. Top of this price range. Late cabaret with all-in supper.

Rules, 35 Maiden Lane, W.C.2 (tel. 836 5314). Since 1798, they have been serving truly English food here in great style. Recently its new owners have cleaned the place up and shaken up the kitchen so that the food is once again the Great British Fare as is Rules tradition. Reservations advised. Closed Sun.

St. Quentin, 243 Brompton Rd., S.W.3 (tel. 589 8005). Brightly lit, and very stylized French restaurant with a short, imaginative menu and outstanding set lunch. On weekends they serve Continental breakfast and tea.

Sheekey's, 29 St. Martin's Court, W.C.2 (tel. 240 2565). Traditional haunt for good pre-theater fish meals of large proportions. Closed Sun.

Simpsons, 100 Strand, W.C.2 (tel. 836 9112). An English institution for roast beef or saddle of mutton; this is a place for atmosphere and tradition rather than exciting food. Closed Sun.

Le Suquet, 104 Draycott Ave., S.W.3 (tel. 581 1785). Excellent French shellfish and fish restaurant with decor and style of its origins—the South of France. Closed lunch Tues., all day Mon.

T'ang, 294 Fulham Rd., S.W.10 (tel. 351 2599). Mixed Oriental food served in a chic setting and prepared by some of London's leading Chinese chefs. Late last orders.

Trattoo, 2 Abingdon Rd., W.8 (tel. 937 4448). Friendly service for well cooked Italian dishes in this bustling appealing restaurant. Consistently good, with obliging staff.

Turners, 87 Walton St., S.W.3 (tel. 584 6711). The noted chef of the Capital Hotel has gone it alone here; sound modern cooking, set lunch at excellent value.

Wheelers, 12A Duke of York St., S.W.1 (tel. 930 2460), 19 Old Compton St., W.1 (tel. 437 2706) and others. Long-established seafood chain, with interesting atmosphere—especially the Duke of York St. one, which is in a tall narrow house with each room barely the width of two tables. Most close Sun. See also the **Alcove.**

The White Tower, 1 Percy St., W.1 (tel. 636 8141). Reputed to be London's oldest Greek restaurant and certainly one of its finest in style, service and—if you choose carefully—food. Amusing menu. Closed Sat.–Sun. and 3 weeks in Aug.

MODERATE (M)

Ajimura, 51 Shelton St., W.C.2 (tel. 240 0178). Not particularly elegant, but simple, excellent Japanese food at very reasonable prices. The tonkatsu is especially good. Handy for Covent Garden area; sushi bar for light meals. Closed lunch Sat., all day Sun.

L'Artiste Assoiffé, 122 Kensington Park Rd., W.11 (tel. 727 4714). This purposely "Bohemian" restaurant near the Portobello Road is always entertaining and good value. Summer dining outside. Closed Sun.

Auntie's, 126 Cleveland St., W.1 (tel. 387 1548). Superb British food from a chef trained by Anton Mosimann. Closed Sat. lunch, Sun., and 2 weeks in Aug.

La Bastide, 50 Greek St., W.1 (tel. 734 3300). Various menus of assorted modern and classic French food; ideal for after-theater. No minimun charge. Comfortable, luxurious but relaxed. Closed Sat. lunch and all day Sun.

Blooms, 90 Whitechapel High St., E.1 (tel. 247 6001). Jewish restaurant particularly popular for that East End Sunday excursion, but excellent anytime. Enormous portions, reasonable service; totally Kosher; takeout also. Closed Sat.

La Brasserie, 272 Brompton Rd., S.W.3 (tel. 584 1668). London's first brasserie; open from breakfast through the day for snacks, lunch, tea and late suppers.

Bubbs, 329 Central Market, E.C.1 (tel. 236 2435). Characteristic French restaurant, well praised for food and wine—small selection but excellent quality. Next to Smithfield meat market. Closed Sat.–Sun. and 2 weeks in Aug.

Cafe Flo, 205 Haverstock Hill, N.W.3 (tel. 435 6744). Very *relais routiers;* a French cafe offering steak, *frites* and salad for a modest sum or a choice from a short but varied menu of French country food. Country wines to match. Open Sun.

Camden Brasserie, 216 Camden High St., N.W.1 (tel. 482 2114). Unpretentious and reliable French café where everything is homemade and they cater as much to meat lovers as to vegetarians. Sun. brunch is popular; reservations advised.

La Capannina, 24 Romilly St., W1 (tel. 437 2473). Good home-cooked pasta served at this crowded Soho *trattoria.* Closed Sat. lunch.

Le Caprice, Arlington House, Arlington St. (just behind the Ritz), S.W.1 (tel. 629 2239). Stylishly run media haunt, successful artists, et al.

Short menu of fashionable French food and an equally good Sun. brunch menu. Reservations essential. Closed Sat. lunch and Sun. dinner.

Le Cellier du Midi, 28 Church Row, N.W.3 (tel. 435 9998). Open evenings only, and worth traveling out to Hampstead for. Provençal cooking with slightly more variety of menu than you might expect. Prices at the top end of this range.

Champagne Exchange, 17C Curzon St., W.1 (tel. 493 4490). Cool, elegant champagne bar and restaurant. Short menu of good and in some cases very modestly priced fish dishes. Delicious caviar on blinis or baked potatoes. Closed Sat.–Sun.

Le Champenoise, Cutler's Gdns. Arcade, Devonshire Sq., E.C.2 (tel. 283 7888).Large, stylish and chic basement champagne-and-wine bar, with restaurant. Only open Mon. to Fri. for lunch and dinner.

Chez Gerard, 8 Charlotte St., W.1 (tel. 636 4975). French steakhouse with both atmosphere and quality. North Soho. Closed Sat. lunch.

Chez Solange, 35 Cranbourne St., W.C.2 (tel. 836 0542). Satisfactory basic French cooking and character. Closed Sun.

Chuen Cheng Ku, 17 Wardour St., W.C.2 (tel. 437 1398). One of Soho's largest Cantonese cafés with one of the longest and most interesting menus. At lunch dim sum is wheeled around on trolleys. Open daily and late.

Como Lario, 22 Holbein Pl., S.W.1 (tel. 730 2954). All the family works to run a very happy restaurant below Sloane Square, with a particularly good zabaglione. Closed Sun.

La Cucaracha, 12 Greek St., W.1 (tel. 734 2253). Mexican food in a delightful atmospheric vaulted cellar. Guitar music completes the mood-Mexicana. Closed Sat. lunch, all day Sun.

English Garden, 10 Lincoln St., S.W.3 (tel. 584 7272). A very pretty restaurant off the King's Road, designed like a conservatory and decorated in white and pink with lots of plants. Currently "in." Prices at the top of this range.

Gavvers, 61 Lower Sloane St., S.W.1 (tel. 730 5938). Related to the famous La Gavroche, with expertly cooked French food. There is a useful fixed price menu, which is altered daily. Open for dinner only. Closed Sat. lunch and Sun.

Gay Hussar, 2 Greek St., W1 (tel. 437 0973). A long-standing favorite with an atmosphere that's always dynamic. Hungarian cooking at reasonable prices. Make reservations well in advance. Closed Sun.

Good Earth, 91 King's Rd., S.W.3 (tel. 352 9231). Cantonese and Pekinese dishes, with delicate flavors. Chelsea favorite.

Hungry Horse, 196 Fulham Rd., S.W.10 (tel. 352 7757). Stands out in an area of small interesting restaurants. Friendly service and well-prepared traditional English dishes make this busy basement the place for a relaxed, enjoyable meal. Closed Sat. lunch and Sun.

Au Jardin des Gourmets, 5 Greek St., W.1 (tel. 437 1816). Attractive Soho stalwart serving modern French food from a chef trained by Paul Bocuse. Famous for its outstanding cellar; wood-panelled private rooms for party hire. Closed Sat. lunch and Sun.

Kalamaras, 76–78 Inverness Mews, W.2 (tel. 727 9122). Relaxed and informal Greek restaurant (incorporating two dining rooms next door to each other) with imaginative house specialties. Closed Sun.

Ken Lo's Memories of China, 67 Ebury St., S.W.1 (730 7734). An elegant, modern spot with a reputation as one of the best Chinese restaurants in the U.K. Closed Sun.

Ley Ons, 56 Wardour St., W.1 (tel. 437 6465). Long-established and still serving excellent Chinese food. Especially good for a dim sum meal.

Lou Pescadou, 241 Old Brompton Rd., S.W.5 (tel. 370 1057). Atmospheric and authentic South-of-France cafe serving traditional French fast foods such as pizza, oysters, soups and plainly cooked fish dishes. Owned by Pierre Martin of *Le Suquet* and *La Croisette.* Closed Aug. but otherwise open until 2 A.M.

Luigi's, 15 Tavistock St., W.C.2 (tel. 240 1795). This Italian bistro on three floors is well worth a visit before or after the theater. Closed Sun.

Manzi's, 1 Leicester St., W.C.2 (tel. 734 0224). A happy fish spot; value is good and the helpings generous. Always crowded to the gunwales, so reservations essential. Very central for theaterland. Closed Sun. lunch.

Mon Plaisir, 21 Monmouth St., W.C.2 (tel. 836 7243). A bustling French bistro in the heart of theaterland. The menu may be small but the portions are reasonably priced. Their cheeseboard is among the best in London and the Gallic ambience is hard to beat. Reservations essential. Closed Sat. lunch and Sun.

New World, 1 Gerrard Pl., W.1 (tel. 734 0677). Huge, bright and modern Cantonese spot related to its popular neighbor, *Chuen Cheng Ku.* Dim sum at lunch or long and explained menu.

Orso, Basement, 27 Wellington St., W.C.2 (tel. 240 5269). Snappy staff, glitzy showbiz clientele and an Italian menu. Best late.

Rodos, 59 St. Giles High St., W.C.2 (tel. 836 3177). Just beside Centre Point, off the top of Charing Cross Rd., this small family-run Greek café serves the best *mezedakia* (eight courses) in town. Everything cooked to order before your eyes. Closed Sun.

The Rossetti, 23 Queen's Grove, N.W.8 (tel. 722 7141). This hybrid pub trattoria near St. John's Wood tube excels for its hors d'oeuvres table and excellent food. Good for summertime dining. Must book.

RSJ, 59 Coin St., S.E.1 (tel. 928 4554). Useful modern French restaurant south of the river and close to National Theater. Closed Sun.

San Frediano, 62 Fulham Rd., S.W.3 (tel. 584 8374). Basic Italian with excellent specialties (especially the homemade pasta) and good, fast service. Comfortable and with a regular clientele. Closed Sun.

Soho Brasserie, 23 Old Compton St., W.1 (tel. 439 9301). Snack at the bar or dine on fine *nouvelle cuisine* at this well-converted pub. Short but good wine list. Closed Sun.

South of the Border, 8 Joan St., S.E.1 (tel. 928 6374). Convenient for the National Theater, dining among the bricks and rafters in this converted factory. Frequently changing menu; usually a vegetarian dish is available. Closed lunch Sat., all day Sun.

Sweetings, 39 Queen Victoria St., E.C.4 (tel. 248 3062). Small, 150-year-old fish restaurant with a charming atmosphere. Drinks from a good short wine list. Lunches only, Mon. to Fri. Closed weekends.

Swiss Centre, 2 New Coventry St., W.1 (tel. 734 1291). A very handy place to meet friends. Has four restaurants, all with a different Swiss accent, so you can take your pick—the price range varies too. All have straightforward mass Swiss catering, but good value.

Throgmorton Restaurant, 27 Throgmorton St., E.C.2 (tel. 588 5165). Beside the Stock Exchange; excellent value for traditional English beef, pies and fish. A city institution. Lunch only. Mon. to Fri.

Le Tire Bouchon, 6 Upper James St., W.1 (tel. 437 2320). Good-value, brasserie spot just off Golden Square. Simple menu. Closed weekends.

Trattoria il Carretto, 20 Hillgate St., W.8 (tel. 229 9988). Candlelit restaurant with music and good steaks.

Viceroy of India, 3 Glentworth St., N.W.1 (tel. 486 3515). Something special in the way of Indian restaurants. Imaginative elegance in the decor, subtly spiced food, discreet service.

BUDGET (I)

London has many hundreds of budget eating places, which often do better than their expensive relations. Remember that pubs can provide an excellent cheap midday meal, while the West End is chock-a-block with sandwich shops for light picnics in the many parks and squares.

Ark, 122 Palace Gdns. Terr., W.8 (tel. 229 4024). Unbeatable for excellent value and really good cooking. Reservations advised. Closed Sunday lunch. Highly recommended.

Bahn Thai, 21A Frith St., W.1 (tel. 437 5194) and 35 Marloes Rd., W.8 (tel. 937 9960). Authentic and charmingly run Thai restaurants. Clearly worded menu.

Bistro Vino, 303 Brompton Rd., S.W.3 (tel. 589 7898). Good value at a busy bistro.

Brasserie des Amis, 27 Basil St., S.W.3 (tel. 584 9012). Light and cheerful brasserie, with popular French dishes.

Bumbles, 16 Buckingham Palace Rd., S.W.1 (tel. 828 2903). Original cooking at reasonable prices; self-service also available at lunchtimes.

Café des Amis du Vin, 11–14 Hanover Pl., W.C.2 (tel. 379 3444). Tucked down an alley beside the Opera House, this very popular establishment in Covent Garden includes wine bar (basement), café (ground floor) and salon (upstairs) and offers authentic French bistro food and well-chosen wines (bin ends by the glass). Closed Sun.

Café du Jardin, 28 Wellington St., W.C.2 (tel. 836 8769). Bright and cheerful brasserie-style restaurant with a large plant-filled basement. Excellent value pre-theater meals. Closed Sat. lunch and Sun.

Café Fish des Amis du Vin, 39 Panton St., W.C.2 (tel. 930 8769). French and English seafood served café-style with basement wine bar. Open from 11.30 A.M. to midnight, Mon. to Sat.

Café Pelican, 45 St. Martin's Lane, W.C.2 (tel. 379 0309). Along with La Brasserie, this is London's closest thing to a genuine French brasserie, serving breakfast, bar snacks, set meals and tea at the bar—superb modern French cooking from a talented chef in the back restaurant. Open late and daily.

Chicago Meatpackers, 96 Charing Cross Rd., W.C.2 (tel. 379 3277). Sound American favorites from an ex-Chicagoan, Bob Payton. 200 seats.

Chicago Pizza Pie Factory, 17 Hanover Sq., W.1 (tel. 629 2669). Hectic and crowded, purveying the "deep" pizza species to enthusiastic customers.

Covent Garden Pasta Bar, 30 Henrietta St., W.C.2 (tel. 836 8396). Stand in line for a table at this busy and hectic fresh pasta bar. Choose the sauce and pile on the salad.

Cranks, 11 Covent Garden Market, W.C.2 (tel. 379 6508). Vegetarian and wholefood fare served in rustic ambiance. Closed Sun. There are three other branches in W.1: at 8 Marshall St., 196 Tottenham Court Rd. (in Heal's) and 214 Oxford St. (in Top Shop).

Daquise, 20 Thurloe St., S.W.7 (tel. 589 6117). Haunt of mid-European emigres, this restaurant serves specialties such as stuffed cabbage and goulash.

Food for Thought, 31 Neal St., W.C.2 (tel. 836 0239). Menu changes twice daily at this simple, whitewashed health restaurant. It is so popular that rare is the day when there is no line outside at lunch-time. Closes 8 P.M.

Fountain Restaurant, Fortnum and Mason, 181 Piccadilly, W.1 (tel. 734 4938). Delicious food and ice-cream sodas, in an unhurried atmosphere. Best for light snacks like Welsh Rarebit, or pastries. The restaurant is open until 11.30 P.M., but closes on Sunday.

Hard Rock Café, 150 Old Park Lane, W.1 (tel. 629 0382). A loud-rocking favorite with burgers and juke box. Unfortunately, you must always stand in line.

Joe Allen's, 13 Exeter St., W.C.2 (tel. 836 0651). Not so much the food as the people, piano, and theatrical flavor of this basement haunt—it's one of the best places in town to see showbiz personalities relaxing. Particularly good late night. 7-day opening. Normally budget range, but watch the menu.

Joy King Lau, 3 Leicester Sq., W.C.2 (tel. 437 1133). Authentic Cantonese—full of Chinese at lunchtime and early evening.

Justin de Blank, 54 Duke St., Grosvenor Square, W.1 (tel. 629 3174). Delicious food, mainly of the salad type with a different range of hot dishes every day. Mouthwatering desserts. A takeout service is available. Closed Saturday evening and Sundays. Justin de Blank also runs the restaurant in the **General Trading Co.** store at the bottom end of Sloane St. (no. 144). Light lunches and great teas (light afternoon meals) at normal store hours. Good for shopping in the King's Rd. area.

Luba's Bistro, 6 Yeomans Row, S.W.3 (tel. 589 2950). Russian Bistrovitch with a long-established reputation for good portions. No liquor license—so bring your own bottle. Cramped but fun. Closed Sun.

Mandeer, 21 Hanway Pl., W.1 (tel. 323 0660). A relaxed Indian restaurant with an accent on health-conscious dishes. It forms part of a cultural center devoted to poetry, music and other art forms. Closed Sun.

Melange, 59 Endell St., W.C.2 (tel. 240 8077). Interesting, budget French-ish food served by a young team in their own design '50s-style *tabac* (downstairs) and restaurant (upstairs). Closed Sat. lunch and Sun.

Michel's Bistro, 343 Kensington High St., W.8 (tel. 603 3613). Though it looks like an Italian *trattoria,* you'll find excellent quality and reasonably-priced French food here.

Mildred's, 135 Kensington Church St., W.8 (tel. 727 5452). Informal restaurant with simple, well-cooked food like steak and kidney pie.

Minogue Bar and Dining Rooms, 60 Liverpool Rd., N.1 (tel. 354 4440). An Irish pub with delicious, soundly cooked food and that's not just potatoes! Also Irish whiskeys, beers and Guinness. Handy for Camden Passage antiques market. Wonderful Irish brunch at the weekends.

Mykonos, 17 Frith St., W.1 (tel. 437 3603). Reasonably priced Greek food in the right surroundings. Try the Mykonos Mixed plate, which gives you a taste of all the grilled specialties.

Pizza Express, 30 Coptic St., W.1 (tel. 636 3232). Our favorite branch of our favorite pizza place. Stylishly and plainly decorated, with pizzas cooked on the spot.

Pollyanna's Bistro, 2 Battersea Rise, S.W.11 (tel. 228 0316). Extremely reasonable and well-run with friendly service and atmosphere. Their wine bar around the corner makes a suitable rendezvous. Closed lunch Mon. to Sat., open all day Sun.

Poons, 4 Leicester St., W.C.2 (tel. 437 1528). Authentic Chinatown restaurant for cooking rather than comfort. The expensive branch in King St., W.C.2 (tel. 240 1743) has the reverse order of priorities. Closed Sun.

Porters, 17 Henrietta St., W.C.2 (tel. 836 6466). Another welcome budget spot in the new Covent Garden area. Meat pies and other goodies with wrap-around sound. Open Sunday, too.

Rebato's, 169 South Lambeth Rd., S.W.8 (tel. 735 6388). Authentic Spanish tapas bar that is worth tracking down. Restaurant at rear is outstanding value.

Le Renoir, 79 Charing Cross Rd., W.C.2 (tel. 734 2515). The first of a chain of fast French restaurants with a cheap all-in menu. Stick to the plain dishes and you can't go wrong. Last orders 1 P.M. daily.

Rouxl Britannia, Triton Court, 14 Finsbury Sq., E.C.2 (tel. 256 6997). Sophisticated vacuum-packed food served with élan in ultra fashionable cafe (seating for 400) from Britain's front rank brother cooks (you have to say the name aloud to get the pun). Lunch only. Closed Sat.–Sun.

Saigon, 45 Frith St., W.1. (tel. 437 7109). Cool and pleasant Soho restaurant serving delicious and spicy Vietnamese food. Wonderful combinations and help on hand with the menu. Open late and daily.

Topkapi, 25 Marylebone High St., W.1 (tel. 486 1872). Turkish restaurant that won a local radio restaurant-of-the-year competition. High standards prevail.

LATE MEALS. London is not a late-night city but, if you know where to go you need never be hungry or thirsty throughout the night. *Sunrise* has metamorphosed into *Mexican Zona Rosa* at 3 Long Acre, W.C.2 (tel. 836 2816), open until 1 A.M. but trying for a 3 A.M. license. *Harry's,* 19 Kingly St., W.1 (tel. 734 8708) opens at 10.30 P.M. and serves steaks, salads and breakfast foods until 6 A.M.

In Soho there are numerous all-nighters, but our favorites are the 4 A.M.-closing *Diamond,* 23 Lisle St., W.C.2 (tel. 437 2517) and *Mayflower,* 68 Shaftesbury Ave., W.1 (tel. 734 9207), which both serve good Cantonese food.

In the West End it's useful to know of the excellent brasserie *Café Pelican,* 45 St. Martin's Lane, W.C.2 (tel. 379 0939) which serves snacks and meals until 2 A.M., while, around the corner from Covent Garden, *Frère Jacques,* 37 Long Acre, W.C.2 (tel. 836 7639), a French fish spot stays open until 1 A.M. *Le Renoir,* 79 Charing Cross Rd., W.C.2 (tel. 734 2515), is also useful for a late West End meal; they take last orders at 1 A.M.

Lebanese restaurants always stay open late and both Queensway and the Edgware Road have more than their share of them. Our favorite Lebanese restaurants are—the *Phoenicia,* 13 Abingdon Rd., W.8 (tel. 937

0120), open until 2 A.M. (sometimes later), and *Fakhreldine,* 85 Piccadilly, W.1 (tel. 493 3424), which stays open until 5 A.M. *Lou Pescadou,* 241 Old Brompton Rd., S.W.7 (tel. 370 1057), a delightful French fast-order restaurant, serves food and booze until 2 A.M.; closed Mon. Finally, London has a 24-hour restaurant, *Le Casino,* 77 Lower Sloane St., S.W.1 (tel. 730 3313), which serves interesting international food. Eat as much breakfast as you can for an all-in price.

WINE BARS. Wine bars, scattered all over central London, provide a slightly raffish—and not usually cheap—way of having a bite to eat and a glass or two of wine in crowded, often noisy, surroundings. Recommended for atmosphere and sometimes for the chance to taste good vintages.

Archduke, 153 Concert Hall Approach, S.E.1 (tel. 928 9370). Attractive decor, good food with international sausage specialties. Handy for after Festival Hall concerts or a visit to the National Theater. Always packed.

L'Artiste Musclé, 1 Shepherd Market, W.1 (tel. 493 6150). A typical French bistro bar with tables on the pavement. Good food and excellent house wines.

Bill Bentley's Wine and Oyster Bar, 31 Beauchamp Pl., S.W.3 (tel. 589 5080). Excellent seafood restaurant upstairs with fluent service, or enjoy the crowded main bar and cellar below. Closed Sun.

Blushes, 52 King's Rd., S.W.3 (tel. 589 6640). French cafe-style singles bar. Mirrored interior with a profusion of palms and potted plants.

Boltons, 198 Fulham Rd., S.W.10 (tel. 352 0251). Small and tastefully designed bar with good homemade food and well-chosen wine list.

Bow Wine Vaults, 10 Bow Churchyard, E.C.4 (tel. 248 1121). Sandwiches and excellent set lunches frenetically available; just behind Bow Church.

Brahms and Liszt, 19 Russell St., W.C.2 (tel. 240 3661). Good value food supported by funky decor, very loud music and the latest American bands. The odd name is Cockney rhyming slang for . . . well, drunk.

Bubbles, 41 North Audley St., W.1 (tel. 499 0600). A comfortable bar handy for Oxford Street shoppers. The wine list is varied and the food nicely presented.

Charco's, 1 Bray Pl., off Anderson St., S.W.3 (tel. 584 0765). Their peerless buffet presents a superabundance of delicacies, complemented by a solid wine selection; just off the King's Road. Tables outside are pleasant in warm weather.

Chez Solange, 11 St. Martin's Court, W.C.2 (tel. 240 0245). In the lane beside Wyndham's Theater, this wine bar is an extension of the same-name restaurant. Relaxed spot for good food, better wine and congregating, especially in summer.

Cork and Bottle, 44 Cranbourne St., W.C.2 (tel. 734 7807). A welcome civilized downstairs oasis, sandwiched between sex shops and the cinemas of Leicester Square.

Crusting Pipe, 27 The Market, Covent Garden, W.C.2 (tel. 836 1415). Good spot to refresh yourself after a visit to the new market at Covent Garden. In the former vegetable storage vaults.

Daly's, 210 The Strand, W.C.2 (tel. 583 4476). Frequented by lawyers, it's right opposite the law courts; excellent food.

Downs, Down St., W.1 (tel. 491 3810). Top-drawer bar for huge portions and excellent wines, especially from the Loire. Convenient for Park Lane and Mayfair.

Draycott's, 114 Draycott Ave., S.W.3 (tel. 584 5359). Popular wine bar with a good list (from the Ebury Wine Co.) and food. Upstairs is less chaotic, and boasts a "cruover" machine which enables *premier cru* wines to be sold by the glass.

Ebury Wine Bar, 139 Ebury St., S.W.1 (tel. 730 5447). Menu of homemade food such as squab pie and lamb cutlets complementing a fine wine list that includes 30 wines by the glass.

El Vino, 47 Fleet St., E.C.4 (tel. 353 6786). Famous watering hole for journalists, lawyers, and press barons—a discriminating and expert clientele. They don't serve women at the bar, a rule which has made them the subject of frequent (so far unsuccessful) court cases. Closed Sun.

Fino's Wine Cellar, 12 Mount St., W.1 (tel. 492 1640). The discreet Mayfair address conceals a vaulted cellar for candlelit dining. Good also as friendly meeting spot. Also at 37 Duke St., W.1 (tel. 935 9459), 12 North Row, W.1 (tel. 491 7261) and 104 Charing Cross Rd., W.C.2 (tel. 836 1077). Quieter and more relaxed.

Jimmy's Wine Bar, 18 Kensington Church St., W.8 (tel. 937 9988). This converted section of the barracks becomes more enjoyable as the evening lengthens, particularly when guitar music is featured.

Julies, 137 Portland Rd., W.11 (tel. 727 7985). Good food in the cellars of no. 135, or wander with wine upstairs; atmosphere abounds.

The Loose Box, 135 Brompton Rd., S.W.3 (tel. 584 9280). This large wine bar on two levels is usually bustling, often with shoppers from Harrods. A modest selection of wines and good choice of food. Closed Sun.

Le Metro, 28 Basil St., S.W.3 (tel. 589 6286). The menu is overseen by the Capital Hotel chef from next door and it's more like brasserie food; expect sophisticated salads, smoked meats and ripe cheeses, plus a dish or two of the day. "Cruover" machine and good wine list.

Mildred's, 135 Kensington Church St., W.8 (tel. 727 5452). A stylish bar where the walls are often hung with the work of young artists. Food good but expensive.

Motcomb's, 26 Motcomb St., S.W.1 (tel. 235 6382). A smart Mayfair bar with "Old Masters" on the walls. An imaginative choice of wines, which can be expensive. An attractive display of bar food and a restaurant in the basement.

Mother Bunch's Wine House, Arches F&G, Old Seacoal Lane, E.C.4 (tel. 236 5317). Worth the search underneath the arches for the Victorian charm plus good wines. Services can be erratic. Reservations essential for lunch.

Reams, 34 Store St., W.C.1 (tel. 631 4918). Outstanding good food; game in season, homemade sausages and fresh fish daily.

Shampers, 4 Kingly St., W.1 (tel. 437 1692). A relative of the *Cork and Bottle* and *Bubbles,* with similarly excellent food and wide ranging wine list.

The Vineyard, International House, St. Katharine's Way, St. Katharine's Dock, E.1 (tel. 480 6680). Handy for recovering from visits to the docks. Steaks.

Whittington's Wine Bar, 21 College Hill, E.C.4 (tel. 248 5855). Vaulted cellar reputed to have been owned by Dick Whittington. Buffet food at the bar or you can lunch in their small restaurant. No food in the evening. Closes 7 P.M.

NIGHTLIFE. In London, nightclubs usually put more emphasis on cuisine than elsewhere. They are really clubs, and most people join them for the exclusive atmosphere, for the floor shows, and for an opportunity to dance way into the small hours. To join a nightclub, telephone the secretary, and then take your passport along to be shown at the door. Most Americans will be made temporary members for a nominal subscription fee right on the spot. Commonwealth or foreign visitors resident in London will have to join normally, and annual subscriptions vary. Establishments requiring membership on the following list are indicated by "sub" after the name.

Nightclubs come and go, so we list only a few well-established ones, together with some good dinner-dance spots. Evening dress is optional in most, desirable in a few. Expenditure for two could easily hit £100, though the average should be a fair bit lower. At some clubs there's a special low-price dinner-dance arrangement available before midnight. Clubs have more freedom in alcohol serving hours than formerly—but the liquor licensing law is still complicated so you'll have to check before you go.

For the latest "in" spots, consult *What's On* or *Time Out.* You may find it impossible to *get* in. Always phone in advance to see what the state of war is. Most of these places are incredibly expensive.

Annabel's, (Sub.) 44 Berkeley Sq., W.1 (tel. 629 2350). Very elegant *boîte* below *Clermont Club,* London's poshest gambling den. Hard to get in (huge sub.), but members can bring guests if they can afford the rates. Disco.

Barbarella's, 428 Fulham Rd., S.W.6 (tel. 385 9434). One of the few discos where you can also eat in reasonable comfort, and hear each other talk. Suitable for all ages.

La Bussola, 42 St. Martin's Lane, W.C.2 (tel. 240 1148). Convenient and elegant for a post-theater dinner-dance but prices require caution.

Dorchester Terrace Restaurant, Park Lane, W.1 (tel. 629 8888). An exceedingly good choice for that special evening, where you want to enjoy the food as well as the company.

The Gaslight, 4 Duke of York St., S.W.1 (tel. 930 1648). Much advertised nightclub, working hard at living up to Edwardian image. Cabaret has replaced striptease routines. Open 8–2.30/3 A.M. Entrance £9.80.

Hilton Hotel Roof Restaurant, 22 Park Lane, W.1 (tel. 493 8000). Cooking is surprisingly consistent, and of course the view sets the mood from this top-of-the-hotel nightspot.

Hippodrome, Hippodrome Center, Leicester Sq., W.C.2 (tel. 437 4311). The very latest thing in nightspots. Reputed to have cost around £3 million for the original conversion, this is a spectacular place to spend the evening. Entry fee £6 Mon. through Thurs., £7.50 Fri. and Sat. up to 11, £10 thereafter; closed Sun. Membership comes in two grades: Silver (allowing one guest) at £175 p.a., Gold (three guests) at £350 p.a. Monday being "gay night," members can bring guests Tues. to Sat. only. As this is strictly a *jeunesse* joint and style is vital if you want to get in, it is perhaps not a spot for the older, staider visitor—but if you can get through Checkpoint Charlie then the laser shows and general concept spawned by nightlife boss Peter Stringfellow may well make your trip. Live music most nights, plus disco, to 3.30 A.M.

Raymond's Revuebar, Brewer St., W.1 (tel. 734 1593). Two shows a night, Mon. through Sat., of super-sexy striptease; the only one we can list as good value for money.

The Roof Garden, (Sub.) 99 Kensington High St., W.8 (tel. 937 7994). Fantastic roofgarden with magical views, restyled and revamped a few years back. Thurs. and Sat. nights only; members only (membership £100). Please check.

Royal Roof Restaurant, Royal Garden Hotel, Kensington High St., W.8 (tel. 937 8000). Terrific view from this 10th-story nightspot with dance band music and an ambitious menu.

Savoy Hotel Restaurant, Strand, W.C.2 (tel. 836 4343). This granddaddy of all London's nightspots comes into its own for a special dinner out with dancing.

Stringfellow's, 16–19 St. Martin's Lane, (tel. 240 5534). One of London's brightest—the first-born of Hippodrome's Peter Stringfellow. Open daily 8 P.M.–3.30 A.M. (but closed Sun.). Entrance to non-members, £6 on Monday, rising to £12.50 Saturday. Membership comes in three grades: Silver at £200 p.a. (one guest); U.K./U.S.A. Silver at £250, which provides entry to the club in either country; and Gold membership, at £500 (three guests). Operates a strict dress code—smart and chic. Cocktail bar and restaurant (upstairs) from 8, disco from 11.30.

Tiddy Dols, 2 Hertford St., W.1 (tel. 499 2357/8). English food with French influence, 18th-century setting, great wines, nightly pianist and strolling minstrels. Open from 6 (last orders 11.30, bar closes midnight). Reasonably priced.

Xenon, 196 Piccadilly, W.1 (tel. 734 9344/5). A laser-lit trendy hangout.

La Valbonne, 62 Kingly St., W1 (tel. 439 7242). Stylish dining, dancing, and the inevitable disco. Open Mon. to Sat. for disco and nightclub—plus à la carte restaurant. Admission £5 (but women, accompanied or not, free Tues. night, and men, £8 Sat. night).

PUBS. There are at least 5,000 pubs (public houses) in London ranging from tiny back-street bars to loud, noisy places; from the unutterably squalid to the suavely opulent. Opening times are basically 11 to 11 but, at the discretion of the landlord, some may close for the afternoon. Shorter hours on Sundays. All serve beer (over £1 for a pint these days), spirits, wine and soft drinks, and a great many of them offer excellent budget meals at lunchtime. Here is a brief selection.

The Anchor, 1 Bankside, S.E.1. Shakespeare drank in the original. Excellent restaurant and good views of St. Paul's.

Antelope, 22 Eaton Terrace, S.W.1. Popular watering hole with good food and beer.

City Barge, Strand-on-the-Green, W.4. Very popular for Thames towpath drinking.

The Dove, Upper Mall, Hammersmith, W.6. Old and small, with Thames views as painted by Turner and Brangwyn. Excellent beer, but it's very strong.

The George Inn, 77 Borough High St., S.E.1. Originally a Victorian coaching inn, it now has a wine bar serving food. Excellent food is also available upstairs in a restaurant complete with beamed ceiling, leaded windows, and fox-hunting prints.

Lamb, 94 Lambs Conduit St., W.C.1. Small, atmospheric and popular. Recommended, but crowded at lunchtime.

Lamb and Flag, 33 Rose St., W.C.2. Home-made game pie and good beer in this tiny, enjoyable haunt.

Nag's Head, James St., W.C.2. Next to the Royal Opera House and a favorite spot with the theater crowd.

Olde Cheshire Cheese, Fleet St., E.C.4. Once a favorite with all the literary lights—Congreve, Thackeray, Dickens, Conan Doyle and—just possibly—Dr. Johnson himself. Close to the newspapers and law courts, so it's still frequented . . . but now mostly by tourists. Steak-and-kidney pie a specialty.

Prospect of Whitby, 75 Wapping Wall, E.1. Right on the riverside and named after an old sailing ship. Full of character; good for lunch.

The Salisbury, St. Martin's Lane, W.C.2. Fine Victoriana, excellent cold food and lots of actors.

Scarsdale Arms, 23 Edwardes Sq., W.8. Lively and attractive pub in an elegant 19th-century square. Good beer; can be crowded.

Star, Belgrave Mews, S.W.1. Good beer and plenty of atmosphere in this small mews pub.

Steam Packet, Strand-on-the-Green, W.4. A warm friendly pub with huge helpings of home-cooked food at reasonable prices and fine beer.

Sun in Splendour, 7 Portobello Rd., W.11. Small, attractive pub with good beer and excellent food. Tiny garden at the back. Close to the market.

Surprise, 6 Christchurch Terrace, S.W.3. Small, lots of character and strong beer. Just around the corner from where Oscar Wilde lived.

Windsor Castle, Campden Hill Rd., W.8. A large garden makes this stylish but friendly spot perfect for a relaxed summertime drink.

USEFUL ADDRESSES. Airlines. *Air Canada,* 140–144 Regent St., W.1 (tel. 759 2636/439 7941); *British Airways* (Intercontinental), Victoria Terminal, Buckingham Palace Road, S.W.1 (tel. 897 4000); *Pan Am,* 193 Piccadilly, W.1 (tel. 409 0688); and *TWA,* 200 Piccadilly, W.1 (tel. 636 4090).

Clubs. The *English-Speaking Union,* 37 Charles St., W.1 (tel. 629 0104), is a meeting-place for the people of Britain, the Commonwealth, and the Americas. Although it is open to members only, it is accessible to all American (and other visiting) E.S.U. members and their guests. *American Chamber of Commerce in London,* 75 Brook St., W.1 (tel. 493 0381). *YMCA,* 112 Great Russell St., W.C.1 (tel. 637 1333) and the *YWCA,* Central Club, 16–22 Great Russell St., London W.C.1 (tel. 636 7512).

Reciprocal arrangements have been made between some clubs in London and those abroad so that overseas visitors may be able to experience the genteel life in exclusive—and usually men's only—clubs: The Savile with the Players and Coffee House in New York, the Cosmos in Washington, the Tavern in Boston; Brooks' with the Knickerbocker in New York; The Garrick with the Century, the Players, and the Lotos in New York, and St. Botolph's in Boston; The Travellers' with the Cosmos and Georgetown in Washington, the Harvard Club of Boston, and the Rittenhouse in Philadelphia; Boodle's with the Somerset in Boston and the Knickerbocker in New York.

Reciprocal arrangements usually need a letter of introduction from the home club and allow entrance to the reciprocating club for up to nine months.

Embassies. *American Embassy,* 24 Grosvenor Sq., W.1 (tel. 499 9000); *Canadian High Commission,* Canada House, Trafalgar Sq., S.W.1 (tel. 629 9492).

Lost property. Anything found in the street should be handed in to the police. Items lost in trains, tubes and buses should be inquired for at the London Regional Transport Lost Property Office, 200 Baker St., London, N.W.1 (only tel. is 486 2496 for recorded message). Office hours are 9.30–2 Mondays through Fridays. For property lost in taxi-cabs check with the Public Carriage Office, 15 Penton St., N.1 (no tel.), open 9–4 Mon.–Fri.

Religious services. There are hundreds of churches in London; check national daily or Sunday newspapers for details. Here are just a few of the famous, or conveniently located ones: Church of England centers, with Holy Communion service at 8 A.M., morning service at 10 or 10.30, include *St. Paul's Cathedral,* City E.C.4. *Westminster Abbey,* S.W.1. *St. Martin-in-the-Fields,* Trafalgar Sq., W.C.2. *St. George's,* Hanover Square, W.1. *Southwark Cathedral,* S.E.1. For more information, tel. 222 9011.

Leading Roman Catholic churches, with weekday and Sunday Mass, include *Westminster Cathedral,* Ashley Gardens, Victoria St., S.W.1 (tel. 834 7452), and *Brompton Oratory,* Brompton Road, S.W.3 (tel. 589 4811).

Leading synagogues include *Central Synagogue,* Great Portland St., W.1; *Marble Arch Synagogue,* 32 Great Cumberland Place, W.1; *West London Synagogue* (Conservative), 34 Upper Berkeley St., W.1; *The Liberal Jewish Synagogue* (Reform), 28 St. John's Wood, N.W.8. Also the *Spanish and Portuguese Synagogue* (Abraham Lopez Dias Hall), the oldest still in use in London, 2–4 Heneage Lane, E.C.3 (tel. 289 2573). For information on other London synagogues, tel. 387 4300.

Travel. *American Express* has offices at: 6 Haymarket, S.W.1 (tel. 930 4411) and 89 Mount St., W.1 (tel. 499 4436). *Hogg Robinson Travel/Diners Club,* is at 176 Tottenham Court Rd., W.1 (tel. 580 0437). *Thomas Cook* offices at: 45 Berkeley St., Piccadilly, W.1 (tel. 499 4000); 1 Marble Arch, W.1; 378 Strand, W.C.2; 108 Fleet St., E.C.4; and other addresses.

British Airways, above their booking office at 75 Regent St., and *Cooks* at 45 Berkeley St., both have *immunization centers* where you can get that last minute shot that you have forgotten. But try to get there Monday to Friday, normal office hours (appointments possible at 2–3 days' notice).

USEFUL LONDON TELEPHONE NUMBERS

Dial

123	for the correct time.
142	for assistance with London telephone numbers.
192	for assistance with telephone numbers outside London.
730 0791	*Teletourist Service* giving information on the principal events of the day. (If from a telephone booth refer to the instruction notice.)
246 8021	for road conditions within 50 miles of London.
246 8026	*Financial Times* Index and Business News Summary.
222 1234	*London Regional Transport* travel inquiries.

387 7070   Euston/St. Pancras railway stations for train information.
278 2477   King's Cross railway station train information.
283 7171   Liverpool St. railway station train information.
262 6767   Paddington railway station train information.
928 5100   Victoria/Waterloo railway station train information.

HELP!

Real emergencies are taken care of by dialing 999 (fire, police or ambulance). But what about other situations which seem like emergencies—for example, when you want to buy aspirin at midnight? Here's a little helpful miscellany.

Hospital emergency wards. The following hospitals have 24-hour emergency wards: Guy's, Royal Free (Hampstead), St. Bartholomew's, St. Thomas's, University College, Westminster.

Chemists (Drug stores). *Bliss Chemist,* 50–56 Willesden Lane, N.W.6 (tel. 624 8000), is open 9 A.M. to 2 A.M., seven days a week, with another branch at 5 Marble Arch, W.1 (tel. 723 6116), open from 9 A.M. to midnight, daily.

Money. Banks are the best bet for changing money, as they charge the least commission. However, when they are shut there are change bureaux at main hotels, airports and air terminals. Also: *Thomas Cook* (Exchange) at Victoria railway station, open daily until 10 P.M. In central London there were 25 branches of *BCCI* at the last count, open Mon.–Fri., business hours only; and some 16 branches of *Cheque Point,* most open from around 8.30 A.M. until midnight.

THE SOUTHEAST

History in Every Corner

A great deal of British history has been forged in southern England. Since the Norman invasion was secured by the Battle of Hastings in 1066, there have been alternating periods of rural peace and wars or threats of wars. The Cinque Ports stood guard, their ships, the "Wooden Walls" of England, setting sail on voyages of discovery and conquest. From Dover Castle and from the Martello towers of Romney Marsh, the soldiers stood watch as Napoleon brooded over his invasion fleet at Boulogne only 21 miles away.

From Dover, Portsmouth and Southampton, the "Old Contemptibles" of 1914 embarked for the trenches of Flanders. A generation later their sons came back to Dover in the little ships that rescued them from the Dunkirk beaches in 1940. The English beaches, accustomed to the happy laughter of children, became strangely silent. Barbed wire, concrete pill boxes and anti-aircraft guns scarred the promenades all round the southeast coast. Across the Channel big guns threatened, and in the skies above the Weald of Kent and Sussex the Battle of Britain was fought. From a tiny airstrip at Biggin Hill, the gallant "Few" made history.

The scars of all the wars have long since healed. In spring, the bluebells and primroses brighten the woods and hedgerows, while in summer, the beaches are thronged with families.

In an era when it has become fashionable to have everything as small as possible—from miniature transistor radios to cameras—the southern counties will inevitably have great appeal to overseas visitors. From the air, the tiny fields, neatly hedged, look like a patchwork quilt. Motoring (once away from the fast motorways), one can drive through narrow lanes between the orchards and hop fields of Kent. The acres of apple and cherry blossom with their massed pink-and-white blooms have easily earned Kent its title "Garden of England." Turn west and you find the expanse of the Downs, starting at the white cliffs of Dover and terminating at the Hog's Back in Surrey. In between, there are cathedral towns to be explored and sleepy villages discovered. It may be fun to conjecture, for instance, why the bell tower of the church at Brookland on Romney Marsh stands on the ground apart from the main building. You may be lucky enough to watch the ancient game of stoolball, which still survives in parts of Sussex.

KENT

It must be right to say that Canterbury is the star of the Southeast. It is also very easy to get to or from London once you have struggled free of the suburbs. It was through that same gently rolling countryside of Kent that the early pilgrims went on their way to Canterbury and caught their first sight of the cathedral. The mother church of England, the seat of the Primate, it is a magnificent achievement of Gothic architecture (with remains of an earlier Norman structure), some rare early stained glass and a wonderfully serene crypt.

Canterbury

This is indeed an historic center. Even in prehistoric times, this part of England was relatively well settled, as we know from the plentiful archeological evidence around, including an important Iron Age hilltop camp at Bigbury, two miles west of Canterbury. In the first century A.D., Kent was a kingdom with Canterbury as its capital. The Roman conquerors settled in these parts, and Canterbury's magnificent mosaic pavement remains are one of the reminders of their stay. Saxon settlers, Norman conquerors and the folk who lived here in more settled late medieval times all left their mark—as you will see on a tour of the compact central area, which is now easier to explore than ever thanks to the pedestrianization of the city center.

At the heart of everything is the celebrated cathedral, the nucleus of worldwide Anglicanism. The history of Canterbury Cathedral goes back to the days of Ethelbert, King of Kent, who in 597 granted the site now occupied by the cathedral to St. Augustine, the Christian missionary from Rome. St. Augustine's church, despoiled by the Danes in 1011, was destroyed by fire in 1067. The oldest stones in the existing fabric of the cathedral belong to the church built by Lanfranc, who in 1070 became the first Norman archbishop of Canterbury. In 1175, William of Sens, a renowned French architect, was called in to design a splendid new choir and presbytery to house the tomb of Archbishop Thomas à Becket, who was murdered in the church in 1170. His tomb became a shrine, the focus of pilgrimages from all over Europe. Stone for the tomb was shipped from Caen, Normandy, and brought up the River Stour, at that time navigable as far

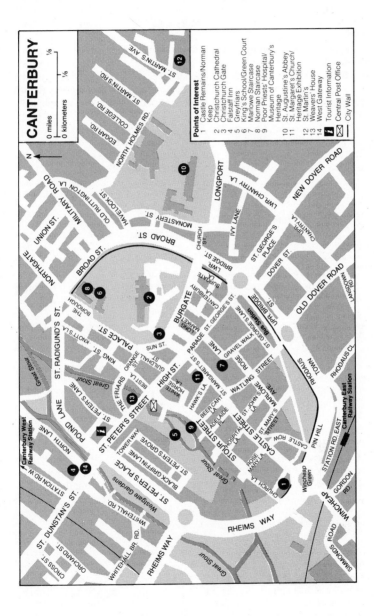

CANTERBURY

0 miles 1/8
0 kilometers 1/8

N

Points of Interest
1 Castle Remains/Norman Keep
2 Christchurch Cathedral
3 Christchurch Gate
4 Falstaff Inn
5 Greyfriars
6 King's School/Green Court
7 Marlowe Staircase
8 Norman Staircase
9 Poor Priests' Hospital/ Museum of Canterbury's Heritage
10 St. Augustine's Abbey
11 St. Margaret's Church/ Heritage Exhibition
12 St. Martin's
13 Weavers' House
14 West Gateway
i Tourist Information
⊠ Central Post Office
City Wall

as Fordwich. The shrine was destroyed by Henry VIII. Beside the spot where Thomas was martyred now stands a commemorative altar of a dramatic jagged design.

Behind the high altar in the Trinity Chapel is the tomb of the Black Prince, that redoubtable fighter who won his spurs at the Battle of Crécy in 1346. The high vaulted nave and beautiful choir, one of the longest in England, are among the most striking features. Other treasures include its truly magnificent medieval stained glass, intricate carvings, ancient paintings and memorials. The whole of the cathedral is open free, though the cathedral authorities exhort visitors to place offerings in boxes placed at different points in the cathedral.

Directly outside, in the cathedral precincts, there is more to see; notably, the peaceful Green Court, beside King's School (England's oldest public— i.e. private—school), the Norman Staircase, and the elaborate Christ Church Gate which guards the precinct entrance. This gate was built to commemorate the death of Henry VII's son in 1502. A traditional curfew bell is still rung here every night, after which the great wooden doors of the gate are shut to safeguard the peace of the cathedral.

The city still retains much of its medieval character with the West Gateway, part of the ancient walls, old churches, houses and inns. It is also a modern town with plenty of diversion for the holiday-maker; excellent shops, cinemas and the Marlowe Theatre, which produces plays of a high standard and is one of the venues for the Canterbury Festival of the Arts at the end of September, which also stages performances in historic buildings including the cathedral. If you are interested in cricket, you can certainly watch it here. The students of the university help give color to the snack bars and pubs of the town. For the authentic atmosphere of medieval Canterbury, there are such inns as the 15th-century Falstaff, originally the parish clerk's house.

Canterbury contains many other ancient and lovely buildings; the Norman keep; the Church of St. Martin, one of the historic gems of British Christianity, which claims an unbroken pattern of worship lasting nearly 1,500 years; Greyfriars, the only remaining 13th-century building; and the Weavers' House, where the Huguenots plied their trade at the end of the 17th century; and many other buildings of great historic interest. The Poor Priests' Hospital has been recently restored and now houses the Museum of Canterbury's Heritage, which tells the story of the city's history from Roman occupation to the present day and is worth putting on your list as the first place to stop, as it will give you an excellent grounding in Canterbury's past. The converted medieval church of St. Margaret's also has dynamic displays of Canterbury's long history, as well as exhibitions on modern themes. This is the new Canterbury Center.

Canterbury is rich in literary associations, Chaucer's *Canterbury Tales* (c. 1380) being the most famous. Elizabethan poet and playwright Christopher Marlowe was born in Canterbury and Joseph Conrad (1857–1924), writer of stirring sea tales, is buried in Canterbury Cemetery. Somerset Maugham was among the famous alumni of the King's School in the cathedral precincts.

There are endless excursions to be made through the varied countryside of Kent, pink and white with apple blossoms in the spring, the woodlands pale with primroses and wood anemones and, later, deep in a mist of bluebells. It is a county of orchards, market gardens and the typical round, red-roofed oast houses (for drying the hops), lovely villages and small towns.

Rochester, on the Medway and back toward London, is noted for its fine cathedral and massive Norman castle keep. There are many fine buildings here, but the general atmosphere is of a busy town, without the peace you might expect to find in a cathedral city. Charles Dickens is associated with Rochester. Indeed Kent is Dickens' country: he not only lived here for many years at Gad's Hill on the outskirts of Rochester, but several local inns keep his memory alive, as does the annual Dickens-oriented Festival. The ambitious Charles Dickens Center is certainly worth a visit. It is situated on the High Street, at Eastgate House, a building featured in two of Dickens' novels, and is designed to show what conditions were like in those days. Life-size models of scenes from his books, as well as sounds of jollity and moans of misery bring the period to vivid life.

Almost next door to Rochester is Chatham, associated with the Navy for centuries. The former Royal Navy dockyards are being developed as a tourist attraction, and will appeal to anyone interested in Britain's maritime heritage. Various historic buildings and a visitor center are open, and there are boat trips (by vintage paddle steamer) down the river.

Chilham, to the west of Canterbury on A252, has a castle set in a park and gardens designed by Capability Brown, which overlooks the Stour valley. The castle is now given over to the strange combination of conferences and re-enactments of medieval jousting.

Farther west again from Chilham stands Leeds Castle. It has been called the "most beautiful castle in the world," and there cannot be many who would disagree. Its setting on two islands in the middle of a lake by the River Len is stunning, and its historical connections, especially with royalty, impressive. Its role as an occasional conference center—sometimes with very impressive delegates indeed—means that it can shut at unexpected times. It is also a rather long and steepish walk from the car park.

Ightham Mote, near Sevenoaks, is also surrounded by water, but there the similarity ends. This idyllic medieval moated manor house is one of the National Trust's latest acquisitions, willed by its American owner Charles Henry Robinson on his death in 1985. The odd name is pronounced "Eye-tam."

For those who want to stray into the depths of rural England and seek out unfamiliar places, Barfreston, well to the southeast (off the A2 midway between Canterbury and Dover), and difficult to find in a maze of secondary roads (it is also spelt in a variety of ways), has one of the finest examples of a Norman village church in England. It has a wealth of carvings, a rose window and a bell oddly hanging in an old yew tree.

Immediately north of Canterbury, Whitstable stands at the mouth of the River Swale, which might well be mistaken for part of the Thames Estuary. The town has been famous for its oysters since the days of the Romans. In September, at the beginning of the oyster season the waters are blessed at an open-air service. The town, which was once a small fishing port, has become a popular sailing center and resort, but it still has character.

Farther along the coast you come to the Isle of Thanet with Margate, Broadstairs and Ramsgate competing for visitors. Dickens spent many summers in Broadstairs (1837–1851) and a number of houses record the fact that he lived in them. Bleak House is not the setting for the novel of that title, but is open to the public in summer, and each year in June a Dickens Festival is organized in the town. Local people dress up unself-consciously in Dickensian costume. Just to the south of Ramsgate lies a long stretch of beach between Pegwell and Sandwich Bays.

Dover

Dover can be reached by continuing round the coast through Sandwich and Deal—which both are attractive old towns, with many picturesque streets from the days when they were still fishing harbors—or from Canterbury down the history-soaked Dover Road (A2) which was there at the time of the Romans. Dover, chief of the ancient Cinque Ports (meaning five and pronounced "sink") is the busiest passenger terminal in Europe, handling the second largest number of passengers after Heathrow. But do not let that put you off. It is basically old, dating from the 12th century, and has an elegant Regency shore line. Owing to the fact that the ships which constantly enter and leave the port are small, they do not impinge on the town in such a manner as you would find, for instance, on the Tyne; in fact their bright colors and swift movement enliven the seascape. The Channel Tunnel, which is being built at a great rate, will almost certainly take away part of Dover's ferry trade.

Dover has always been England's chief link with France and the Continent; in fact Richard II decreed that it should be the sole port through which pilgrims and official visitors might enter, so the list of people and processions that passed through Dover and traveled up towards Canterbury is prodigious. Chief among the many places to visit in Dover is, of course, its castle perched high on the White Cliffs and built soon after the Norman Conquest. Standing in its courtyard is a Roman Lighthouse or Pharos; the top part is a reconstruction, but the base is original, very early Roman work.

Sissinghurst and Penshurst Place

Leaving Folkestone, a genteel resort and small port, by the new brief stretch of motorway, M20, one is very quickly transported into a really lovely area of Kent characterized by its villages with names ending in "den"—Tenterden, Rolvenden, Smarden, Biddenden, Newenden, Frittenden, Marden, Ingleden and Dashmonden. All enchanting, and all connected by delightful small roads in idyllic scenery.

Within this area, on A262, is the lovely garden at Sissinghurst, at its best in spring. Created by the author and poet, Vita Sackville-West, and her husband, Sir Harold Nicolson, it is maintained by the National Trust. For a splendid view, climb the tower of the old church at Tenterden or ride, at weekends, on the idyllic steam-hauled railway and, if you are interested in theatrical shrines, go on to 15th-century Smallhythe Place, with its relics of Irving's leading lady, the actress Dame Ellen Terry.

Further on again along the same road lies Royal Tunbridge Wells, butt of humorists who make it out to be unbelievably strait-laced. The main attraction here is the charmingly laid-out parade called the Pantiles, paved and free from traffic, with fascinating antique shops and a band playing on summer evenings. Just to the south is Frant, resting place of Colonel John By who, between 1826 and 1832, built the Rideau Canal in Canada. He also laid out the town that was eventually to become Ottawa.

Nearby Penshurst Place retains its Great Hall dating from the 14th century, but is mainly Elizabethan, with gardens laid out in the 16th century. It has a long history of literary associations, having been in the Sidney family for centuries and still is. The most famous Sidney was the Elizabethan poet, Sir Philip. This family continuity brings a particular richness to the Place. The Baron's Hall, for instance, contains two medieval trestle tables thought to be the only ones existing today, while the state dining-room, sometimes still used by the family, has its great table laid with a beautiful as well as priceless Rockingham dinner service. There is a collection of 18th-to-19th-century toys in the Buttery. The whole stands in a splendid garden, itself in parkland, while the village is still part of the estate. There's also a vineyard here. English wines are becoming increasingly popular, and at Penshurst visitors can see the vineyards and modern winery before tasting the final product.

SUSSEX

Sussex is now divided into two parts for administrative purposes, East and West, and is the one county of this area that claims for itself the distinction of being "by the sea," though it is really no more so than is Kent. It is also a sad fact that there is now little of the Sussex shore line which has not been tamed, even corsetted in concrete promenades and endless ribbon developments of retirement bungalows. However, if you follow the county boundary from just west of Tunbridge Wells towards the coast you arrive at one of the wildest bits of the southeast where the strange, flat Marshes of Walland and Romney link East Sussex and Kent. The coast, and the old inns on it, are associated with smuggling, nowhere more so than Rye, one of the two "Ancient Towns" above the marsh, deserted by the sea and now patterned with dykes and innumerable sheep. This once fully-walled and, even today, gated town, with its lovely old church, still has some cobbled streets and almost all its houses are either half-timbered or 18th-century. Henry James lived at Lamb House from 1898 until his death in 1916. Some distance towards Winchelsea Beach lies the 16th-century Camber Castle and, to the east, are the broad Camber Sands, overlooked by a famous golf course. Nearer at hand, most of the Rye fishing fleet moor near the town saltflats in the Rother.

A few miles away, Winchelsea, standing on a wooded rise, is also entered through a fortified gateway, and has a splendid church built, like Canterbury, with stone from Normandy. Another "Ancient Town," it too has been left high and dry by the receding sea. The original five Cinque Ports were Sandwich, Dover, Hythe, Romney and Hastings, all ports that had to supply ships to the fleet in return for special rights. The system started before the arrival of the Normans and continued for centuries, with other towns, such as Rye and Winchelsea, being associated with the original five as the years progressed.

Hastings

Hastings has little of the smartness or architectural elegance of its neighbor to the west, Eastbourne. There's a ruined castle, a fishermen's quarter,

underground caverns and a good amateur theater club. First-class concerts
are given at the White Rock Theater. On the sandstone cliff above the Old
Town are the ruins of England's first Norman castle. The victory of William the Conqueror over the Saxons is commemorated in the name of the
town of Battle, where William erected an abbey (a stone in the grounds
of the ruined abbey, which is open to visitors, marks the spot where the
Saxon King, Harold, was killed) and Battle Museum tells the 1066 story
in a diorama of the conflict, together with other local history of the time.
Another interesting visit to make is to the complete shell of the 14th-
century Bodiam Castle, built to protect the approaches up the Rother and
now standing reflected in a moat surrounded by trees.

There is little enough of old Bexhill left, with St. Leonard's slotted in
between it and Hastings, but for elderly people who like their entertainments close at hand and sheltered, the De La Warr Pavilion provides varied entertainments and an inexpensive glassed-in cafeteria overlooking the
sea; plays of the "family" type are also produced by a resident repertory
company and there is old-time dancing on a terrace in summer as well
as more modern dancing for younger people. There is an annual Festival
of Music.

The silver grey stones of Pevensey Castle turn the main road to Eastbourne into a narrow lane for a few yards before it approaches this attractive and popular resort with its great cliffs and Beachy Head rivaling those
of Dover. It naturally has all the diversions of a popular seaside town. The
climate along this part of the coast through Seaford and the Channel port
of Newhaven to Brighton is very good, with a large share of the English
sunshine and little of its cold and rain, although it cannot claim to be always free from gales.

Newhaven to Lewes

But before going on to Brighton, spare the time to explore the Ouse Valley from Newhaven to Lewes, on A275. In a matter of only seven miles
is Piddinghoe, a tiny riverside village given over to messing about in boats
beside its round towered, Norman church; Telescombe, an unbelievably
picturesque downland village; Southease, with another Norman church,
and Rodmell where Virginia Woolf lived with her husband Leonard until
she tragically drowned herself in the Ouse. Their house, known as Monk's
House, is now run by the National Trust.

And thus to the ancient town of Lewes, with its castle perched on a
hill with a good view all around—so that, originally, the Normans could
keep a more efficient eye on the conquered English. Today Lewes is a place
to walk in rather than drive in, not least so that the period architecture
can be appreciated and the secret lanes behind the castle with their huge
beeches can be enjoyed. Among the points of interest worth visiting are
the castle itself, with its 13th-century keep and 14th-century barbican; a
Tudor house that belonged to Anne of Cleves, one of the three wives of
Henry VIII who survived the experience; the 15th-century home of Thomas Paine; the 16th-century house of John Evelyn, one of England's best
diarists; the ruins of a once-lovely priory; and, just to round it off, a long
climbing street of Georgian houses. The picturesque narrow streets are
noted for antiques and secondhand-book shops; and for a pleasant stroll
away from town attractions, at the bottom of Cliffe High Street a footpath

gives access to the Downs, with fine views over the town and the valley of the River Ouse.

For music lovers, Lewes is also a good overnight resting place when attending Glyndebourne which, in the summer season, offers some of the finest opera productions in the world, in an incomparable garden setting.

Only four miles southeast of Lewes, on the Eastbourne road (A27), is Firle Place. It is of interest to U.S. visitors, through its association with General Gage, Commander-in-Chief of the British forces at the beginning of the War of Independence. The house has been the home of the Gage family since the 15th century, though the original Tudor building was largely altered in the middle of the 18th.

Brighton

Just eight miles down the A27 from Lewes lies Brighton, the self-proclaimed belle of the coast. For anyone who does not mind a busy, lively resort, now developed into a big town with a broad coast road, Brighton and its continuation, Hove, can provide a delightful holiday. Quite apart from the obvious attractions of the huge new marina, and good shops and restaurants, there is the maze of little alleys full of antique shops known as the Lanes. There is also the new entertainment and shopping center and some of the finest Regency architecture in the country. Brighton, in fact, developed from the impetus given it by the Prince Regent, later George IV, in the late 18th century, when he took up sea bathing there. Appropriately, it is his "house"—the Brighton Pavilion—which seems to be the epitome of the town. Built mainly by John Nash in a mock Oriental manner with domes and pinnacles abounding, it has never failed to shock and delight in equal measure, particularly against a background of the lovely little Regency houses that the Prince's more seemly friends built themselves. The Chinese décor of the Pavilion's rooms is almost as astonishing as its exterior. Today it is used for public functions and is well worth visiting, especially since the rooms have been refurnished with many pieces of Regency design from the Royal Collection. The interior has been refurbished, and work on the exterior should be complete during 1989. The nearby Dome which was once the stables, is a concert hall. Besides its elegant center, Brighton has its brash area facing the sea where there are fun fairs and two piers—one sadly dilapidated and now closed—and cheap eating places, deckchairs on the beach and winking colored lights. The "beach" along this part of the coast is composed of ankle-breaking pebbles, not sand.

For wet weather days, the King Alfred Leisure Center at Hove—Brighton's genteel neighbor—caters for all kinds of indoor sports. There are three swimming pools, one with islands and a water slide, and there's a Solarium. You don't have to go outside for refreshments: a cafeteria and a licensed bar serve snack meals or just drinks. Shrubs, flowers and palms thrive in the warm temperature. If you feel more like watching than taking part, there is ample seating for spectators. If it is too much for you there are wonderfully quiet places to walk on the Downs just outside the town. These are the low, rolling hills beloved of Kipling, Chesterton and Belloc who did not, however, have to walk so far as we now do to get outside the town which has spread in all directions.

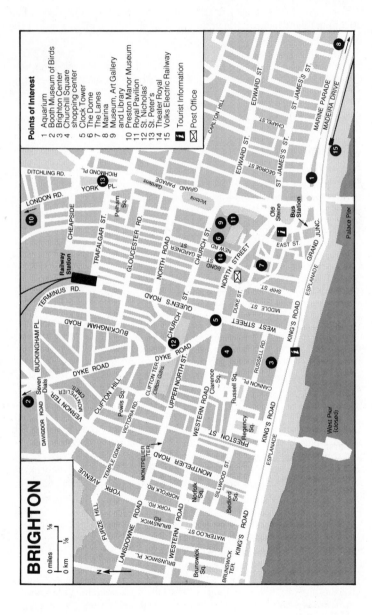

BRIGHTON

0 miles   ⅛
0 km   ⅛

N

Points of Interest

1 Aquarium
2 Booth Museum of Birds
3 Brighton Center
4 Churchill Square
   shopping center
5 Clock Tower
6 The Dome
7 The Lanes
8 Marina
9 Museum, Art Gallery
   and Library
10 Preston Manor Museum
11 Royal Pavilion
12 St. Nicholas'
13 St. Peter's
14 Theater Royal
15 Volks Electric Railway

i Tourist Information

⊠ Post Office

Chichester and Beyond

Westward from Brighton, a number of resorts, Worthing, Littlehampton, Bognor Regis, enjoy equally good weather. Inland lies Chichester, with its Norman cathedral, fine old 18th-century houses and beautiful 16th-century market cross. The waters of Chichester harbor are always animated with small boats and yachts. But the town is best known for its Festival Theater's summer season, which combines classical productions with modern. Like Glyndebourne, it has an international reputation and can provide an evening focus for a day out from London. You can just get back to London after the theater by a late train. Essential short side-trips from Chichester are to Bosham (pronounced "Bossum"), a yachting village with a church depicted in the Bayeux Tapestry. It was here that King Canute is said to have ordered the sea to recede; his daughter is allegedly buried in the local church.

At Fishbourne, one mile west of Chichester, a grand Roman palace, the largest found in Britain, has been excavated, and catwalks have been built from which visitors can see the extravagant marble mosaic flooring. It is open daily from March through to November.

Arundel Castle, near Chichester, has been much restored and the great park with its attractive lake is always open to the public, though no cars are allowed in. Nearby is the Wildfowl Trust Reserve on the banks of the Riven Arun. Racing enthusiasts may like to visit Goodwood Park and racecourse, where fashionable meetings take place at the end of July. The motor racing circuit is no longer used for public meetings. Goodwood House is open to the public.

To many people the best of Sussex, both East and West, is to be found between the A27, which runs parallel with the coast from Pevensey Bay to Chichester, and A272, following the same line but further inland from Heathfield, due north of Eastbourne, to Winchester in the neighboring county. Just prior to where this road starts, Burwash stands on a ridge overlooking the Weald. Burwash was Kipling's village and his house, Bateman's, is open to the public.

This road is quite splendid from the moment it sets out in the east, but the first gem strung on it is tiny Cowfold with its almshouses and church of considerable interest. Next look out for Wisborough Green, a near-perfect picture-postcard village, leading to Petworth, where the House is one of the National Trust's treasures. Set in a 700-acre park designed by Capability Brown, the rooms are full of works by van Dyck and Turner, Holbein and Rembrandt, set off by the rich carvings of Grinling Gibbons. Next the road passes through Cowdray Park where you can watch polo-playing royals, and so to Midhurst, with its many 16th- and 17th-century inns. Just west of Midhurst an ancient bridge spans the Rother, at Trotton, effectively keeping juggernauts off the road. Petersfield offers very little now, but who cares with Winchester waiting at the end of the road.

In the gap between the A27 and the A272 run the South Downs, round and between which little side roads meander enchantingly to lead to such places as Alfriston, whose Star Inn is one of the oldest in England, and which can also boast a 14th-century church and the Clergy House, the first ancient building to be acquired by the National Trust. Nearby, and within sight, is the Wilmington Long Man, a giant figure cut in the chalk

Downs. It also has, in contrast, one of the tiniest churches in England. All this is in the Cuckmere Valley, and in it, too, is Michelham Priory, notable mostly for its huge Barn and collection of farm carts.

From around here the A22 will take you northwards to one of the strangest parts of Sussex, Ashdown Forest. Strange because it is untrammeled, wild, a great common land largely devoid of trees, but rich in history and nature. It is a place that arouses the strongest passions—of dedication or disinterest. You can drive right across it on A22, criss-cross it on minor roads, or walk endlessly on it. Driving off the roads is strictly forbidden, and so is horseriding without the requisite license. The highest point is Crowborough Beacon, near the busy little town of Crowborough. The famous Christopher Robin and Winnie-the-Pooh children's stories by A. A. Milne were set in this area near Forest Row. Looking at the forest from one of the higher roads you might think it went on forever, which is why it is so unlike the rest of Sussex which is essentially cosy.

SURREY

The landscape of Surrey is distinguished by its woods, heaths and commons, many of which link up and provide a chain of wild, free "Green Belt" country or National Trust land which can never be built on. It is easily accessible from London by excellent roads, by train or by bus. Guildford, which is Surrey's county town and its most interesting center, is an excellent base from which to explore Surrey's gentle and well-manicured "Home Counties" countryside. Fast electric trains will take you there direct from London (Waterloo) in 35 minutes.

Quite close in to Central London are the gardens of the Royal Horticultural Society, a must for devoted gardeners, lying just off the Portsmouth road, between Cobham and Ripley. (See *Practical Information* for more details.) These 200 acres of gardens are run by horticultural experts who grow a huge range of plants, many of them very rare. Not only are the collections very attractive, but they are also extremely educational, and it is impossible to come away without a renewed interest in one of Britain's greatest achievements—the art of the garden.

Guildford

Above the town of Guildford stands the modern cathedral designed by Sir Edward Maufe, begun in 1936, consecrated in 1961, and completed in 1964. This structure is built of rose-colored brick and the architect relied more on the skilful disposition of the masses and the simple grace of Gothic lines than on elaborate decoration. The statue of St. John the Baptist, in the transept, is by Eric Gill, an early-20th-century sculptor and typographer—he created the Gill Sans typeface—whose fame is likely to endure.

Guildford is an ancient city which has suddenly become an important center. The Royal Grammar School, in the High Street, was founded in the early 16th century, but the actual structure was built in the reign of Queen Elizabeth I. Bibliophiles should visit the library to inspect the 80 chained books that include the original version of Sir Walter Raleigh's *History of the World.* Other historical buildings in this beautiful thoroughfare include the Abbott's Hospital, founded in 1619 by George Abbott, Archbishop of Canterbury, who collaborated in the translation of the Authorized Version of the Bible.

Also built in the 17th century, but fifty years later, the timber-faced Guildhall is easily discernible from afar because of the clock that projects over the street. The courtroom, with its Georgian paneling, is worth visiting if only because of the 17th-century portraits of monarchs and the superb silver plate used by the town corporation on state occasions. This visit can only be made by prior application in writing to the Mayor of Guildford, at Millmead House.

To the south of the Guildhall, the ruins of a Norman castle stand on a mound not far from the museum, which exhibits objects found in burial grounds of all periods in the vicinity of the city. Lewis Carroll (Charles Dodgson), author of *Alice's Adventures in Wonderland,* died at The Chestnuts, a house near to the main entrance to the castle.

Despite the flood of traffic that fills parts of the steep, cobbled High Street, and the tortuous one-way traffic system, it is still possible to admire the 17th- and 18th-century houses, as well as the ancient inns, such as the Angel.

Since it has become a satellite city (to London), Guildford has developed in the modern manner, but with its own individuality. The Yvonne Arnaud Theatre, by the river, presents good plays, both classical and avantgarde. Surrey University, transferred and re-created here in 1965, is growing rapidly.

Around Surrey

Farnham, due west of Guildford, is also in the process of becoming a satellite town, but it has a castle inhabited for centuries by the bishops of Winchester. The streets of the center are still filled with splendid examples of English architecture of most periods. There are 18th-century mansions with doorways in the Adam style, as well as one or two Tudor inns and Tudor houses. Castle Street and West Street are particularly notable and elegant, with good shops. William Cobbett, the 18th-century horseback travel writer, was born and buried in Farnham; Charles I spent a night here on his way to execution, and James Barrie wrote *Peter Pan* in a house nearby. Do not be put off by the brash new commuter housing.

Godalming, to the south of Guildford, is yet another of these country towns, growing rapidly because it is within easy distance of London by rail. It was the birthplace of Sir James Oglethorpe, founder of the state of Georgia. The High Street still has some fine old houses—a few of them half-timbered—and a church with a Saxon chancel and a Norman tower. To the west of Godalming lies Frensham Common, with its expanses of heather and pinewoods, and its broad ponds, in which you may sail or bathe in the summer-time, but even before you reach Frensham Common there are Loseley House—an Elizabethan gem built in 1562, where Elizabeth I stayed three times, and which is still a fascinating home—and the Winkworth Arboretum.

Further south on A3 from Hindhead Beacon (nearly 900 feet high), there are views of this green countryside in every direction. Still further south again is Shottermill Common (near to Haslemere), where George Eliot lived in a small cottage. Haslemere is an elegant little town to which people come to hear old English music during the annual Dolmetsch Festival. It has an individualistic shopping center and a number of acceptable eating places.

To the north of Haslemere is the village of Chiddingfold, the center of glass-making in the early Middle Ages. One maker, Lawrence by name, was responsible for creating many of the stained glass windows in Westminster Abbey. Because this industry prospered, there are many old houses round the broad village green. About the year 1281, Cistercian monks here began to build a travelers' rest house, laying the foundations of the 13th-century building which is now the oldest inn in Surrey, the Crown. The Crown was already thriving in the 14th century and it was here that King Edward VI stayed on one of his royal progresses.

Though the population of Surrey is exploding, a lovely stretch of countryside with a number of ancient villages has been preserved in the area that lies to the southeast of Guildford, and to the southwest of Dorking. There are beechwoods thick with bluebells in May, heathery commons, and meadows with Hammer Ponds, used by the blacksmiths who forged the guns for Elizabeth's fleet. Friday Street, Holmbury St. Mary, Abinger Hammer—their names ring out like a poem. Possibly the loveliest of the Surrey villages is Shere, on the banks of the Tillingbourne stream. Then there is Wootton, where the 17th-century diarist John Evelyn spent most of his life, laying out the garden round his house, which is still standing. And there is Gomshall, where you can eat a real English country tea in a converted watermill, called simply The Mill, that is mentioned in the Domesday Book.

All of these lovely villages are on the A25, now thankfully relieved of heavy traffic by the new M25 Outer London Orbital Motorway.

PRACTICAL INFORMATION FOR THE SOUTHEAST

HOW TO GET THERE FROM LONDON. To help you plan visits to some of the centers in the Southeast that are reachable in one day we list some of the main towns/tourist centers and the relevant travel information. For rail travelers British Rail have introduced the *Network Southeast Card* which gives 1/3 off standard Single, Cheap Day Returns, and Saver fares in the Southeast. The card may be used by the single traveler or groups. It is valid for a year and costs £10; valid for travel after 10 A.M. on weekends, and any time at weekends. The card holder can take up to three other adults at the discounted rate. Take a passport-sized photo with you.

Arundel. By train: served by one train an hour from London Victoria, the fast trains only take 1 hour 20 minutes. The railway station is a good ten-minute walk from the town itself. **By coach:** no through service—go by rail! **By car:** A24, A29, A284.

Battle. By train: one through train an hour from Charing Cross which can be joined also at Waterloo East and London Bridge. The journey time can be as little as 1 hour 30 minutes. **By coach:** National Express run three coaches a day in summer from Victoria coach station, but they are not suitable timed to allow a day return trip. **By car:** A21, A2100.

Brighton. By train: an excellent service of three or more trains per hour from London/Victoria with the fast train taking under 1 hour for the 51 miles. **By coach:** National Express operate an hourly service from 9 in the morning to 9 in the evening. The coach takes 1 hour 45 minutes for the journey. **By car:** A23, M23.

Canterbury. By train: basic frequency of two trains an hour from London Victoria to Canterbury East station. The fast service takes 1 hour 20 minutes. An alternative hourly service is available from Charing Cross running via Waterloo East and London Bridge and taking 1¾ hours for the journey to Canterbury West. Going this way—the long way round—you will usually have to change at Ashford. **By coach:** National Express run about every 1½ hours from Victoria Coach Station, journey time just under two hours. The best bets for a day's excursion leave at 08.00 or 10.00, arriving in Canterbury in good time for lunch. Return at 16.25 or 17.55. Several coach tour operators including Evan Evans and Thomas Cook, run day excursions to Canterbury, also including Dover in their itinerary. **By car:** A2, M2.

Chichester. By train: one through train an hour from London Victoria railway station. This completes the journey in 1 hour 38 minutes, and usually includes a buffet car. **By coach:** National Express run services every two hours from Victoria Coach Station, a delightful though longish journey taking 3¼ hours. The 08.30 departure and 18.30 return allow nearly five hours Chichester. **By car:** A24, A29, A27.

Eastbourne. By train: one direct service an hour from London Victoria railway station, taking 1 hour 25 minutes. A light refreshment service is available on these trains. It is also possible to travel to Eastbourne via Brighton, from whence there is an excellent connecting service. This route takes 1 hour 43 minutes including changing trains. **By coach:** National Express run every two hours from Victoria Coach Station, taking 2¾ hours—a pleasant run through the Ashdown Forest and Uckfield. The 09.30 from Victoria and 18.15 return allow almost six hours in Eastbourne. **By car:** A22 throughout.

Hastings. By train: served by two main rail routes. Firstly from London Charing Cross—also calling at Waterloo East and London Bridge—there is an hourly electric service which takes a little over 1½ hours. Secondly there is another hourly service from London Victoria which runs via Eastbourne (where the train reverses—no need to get off) in just over 2 hours. **By coach:** Same service as Battle, the round trip being impracticable in a day. **By car:** A21.

Lewes. By train: direct service of one train per hour from Victoria and the journey time is just over 1 hour. So no problems over a day trip. It is also possible to go via Brighton which has an excellent train service, and there change onto the connecting train to Eastbourne which calls at

Lewes en route. **By coach:** Lewes is served by three National Express coaches daily from Victoria Coach station, but timings are not really convenient. The last two return coaches leave in the late afternoon and early evening. **By car:** quickest route is as for Brighton, then take the A27. More scenic route: A22, A275—perhaps calling in at the Bluebell Railway en route.

Rochester. By train: two routes are available and both have a half-hourly service. From Charing Cross, also calling at Waterloo East and London Bridge the journey time is 62 minutes. From Victoria it takes 53 minutes. **By coach:** the *Invictaway* service 991 runs from Victoria Coach Station every hour from 9.00, journey time 1 hour 20 minutes. Return journeys every hour until 17.04, then 19.04. All coaches also serve Chatham. **By car:** A2.

Tunbridge Wells. By train: travel from Charing Cross, Waterloo East, London Bridge to Tunbridge Wells Central station. The journey takes around 1 hour, with some trains taking slightly less, and there is an hourly service. **By coach:** Green Line from Victoria, takes 2½ hours. Irregular on weekdays (take the 10.15 for a day return trip), but more frequent on Sundays when some coaches also run via Winston Churchill's home, Chartwell. **By car:** A21, A26.

HOW TO GET AROUND. British Rail's Network Southeast operate fast services throughout this part of England, with some express trains which offer much reduced journey times to the major centers compared with the suburban trains. Due to road congestion in central London and on the approaches to the capital, the train offers the quickest and most comfortable means of transport. Regional coach services are cheaper and quite comfortable, but cannot compete on journey time or the number of departures per day—however, they are well worth considering. The *National Express* coaches depart from Victoria Coach Station which is about ten minutes walk from Victoria British Rail/Underground station. *Green Line* coaches, serving many of the principal towns and tourist attractions within 35 miles of London, leave from Eccleston Bridge (between Victoria rail and coach stations).

HOTELS AND RESTAURANTS. All around this coast resort towns stretch along beaches, their hotels cheek by jowl. Holiday hotels usually quote all-inclusive rates for a week's stay, which works out cheaper than taking room and meals by the day. Prices usually rise in July and August, but some hotels offer reductions for short stays and in the off-season—well worth enquiring.

Details about our grading system, telephoning, plus other relevant information about hotels and restaurants, will be found at the beginning of the book in the *Facts at Your Fingertips* section.

Alfriston (E. Sussex). *Star Inn* (E), tel. (0323) 870495; 34 rooms with bath, preserves some 13th-century features and is well recommended. *Deans Place* (E–M), tel. (0323) 870248; 46 rooms with bath, lies close to the river, long-established solid reputation.

Restaurant. *Moonrakers* (M), tel. (0323) 870472. A restaurant as picturesque as its name with beams and low ceilings. Imaginative, fixed-price
menu changes regularly. Dinner only. Closed Sun., Mon., and mid-Jan.
to mid-Feb.

Arundel (W. Sussex). *Norfolk Arms* (M), tel. (0903) 882101; 34 rooms
with bath, 18th-century coaching inn near the Castle. Narrow passages
and cozy rooms, with a modern annex.

Ashford (Kent). *Eastwell Manor* (E), tel. (0233) 35751; 24 rooms with
bath. Luxurious 19th-century reconstruction of manor house dating to
Saxon times. Magnificent central staircase and public rooms. Elegance
with period character. Good restaurant with French cuisine.

Bagshot (Surrey). *Pennyhill Park* (L–E), tel. (0276) 71774; 50 rooms
with bath. Edwardian mansion in magnificent tailored grounds; tennis,
fishing, croquet, golf and riding; evening dancing in delightful restaurant.
Wise to book.

Battle (E. Sussex). *Netherfield Place* (E–M), tel. (042 46) 4455. 12
rooms with bath. Georgian-style mansion in 30 acres of private park. Elegant restaurant.
Restaurant. *Pilgrim's Rest Inn.* Reader recommended for lunch.

Bosham (W. Sussex). *Millstream* (E–M), tel. (0243) 573234; 29 rooms,
all with bath, friendly and comfortable. There really is a millstream. 3
miles west of Chichester.

Brighton (E. Sussex). *Grand* (L), King's Rd., tel. (0273) 21188. 166
rooms with bath. Rebuilt and completely redecorated after the bomb attempt on Mrs Thatcher five years ago, the grand Grand still has pride of
place along the sea front. The decor, especially of the public rooms, is of
the marble and chandelier variety. But it can rely on its reputation a little
too much. *Ramada* (L), King's Rd., tel. (0723) 206700. The latest on the
scene. The Ramada is built around a huge atrium, with sea views. Very
popular with Arabs and conference delegates. Well designed, with carefully color-schemed rooms—but on the pricey side for what it offers. *Topps*
(M), 17 Regency Sq., tel. (0273) 729334. Two Regency houses have been
turned into this excellent hotel, run by the owners, Paul and Pauline Collins. All the rooms are attractive, and the atmosphere relaxed and friendly.
The restaurant, *Bottoms,* is worth a visit all on its own. The interesting
English menu is prepared by Pauline Collins, but the place is small, so
book.
Restaurants. *English's Oyster Bar* (M), 29–31 East St., tel. (0273) 27980.
A genuinely old-fashioned seafood haven. Some of the most succulent oysters in Britain. *Mangetout* (M), 34 Ship St., tel (0273) 770298. A new eatery on the Brighton scene, right beside the Lanes. Excellent, mainly
French, dishes and good, reasonable, wine. *Orchard* (M), 33 Western St.,
tel. (0273) 776618. On the border with Hove, this prettily decorated restaurant has imaginative food, largely French inspired, good wine, and a
friendly staff. There are three other good restaurants within two blocks,
should the Orchard be full. *Les Bouchons* (I), 85 St. James St., tel. (0273)

683152. A tiny neighborhood place, run by a French husband and wife team. The limited menu depends on the availability of market produce. A genuine find. Must book.

Canterbury (Kent). *County* (E–M), High St., tel. (0227) 66266; 74 rooms with bath. 16th-century building with a family atmosphere. *Canterbury* (M), 71 New Dover Rd., tel. (0227) 450551; 28 rooms with bath or shower. Friendly and comfortable hotel, with good service. *Chaucer* (M), 63 Ivy Lane, tel. (0227) 464427; 45 rooms with bath. Pleasant and efficient, with good restaurant. *Slatters* (M), St. Margaret's St., tel. (0227) 463271; 30 rooms, 28 with bath or shower. Modern exterior, but retains some old features inside. *Abbeygate Guest House* (I), 7 North Lane, tel. (0227) 68771. A central Victorian house, comfortably converted.

At **Chartham Hatch,** 1 mile southeast. *Howfield Manor* (M), tel. (0227) 738294; 5 rooms with bath. Friendly and comfortable with some fine antiques.

Restaurants. For dinner, try *Restaurant 74* (E), 74 Windcheap, tel. (0227) 67411 for adventurous cooking. *Waterfields* (E–M), 5A Best Lane, tel. (0227) 450276. Ambitious French and English influenced dishes. *Falstaff Inn* (M), St. Dunstan's St., tel. (0227) 462138. *Tuo e Mio* (M), 16 The Borough, tel. (0227) 61471. An excellent Italian restaurant.

At **Pett Bottom,** 3 miles south, visit the *Duck Inn* (M), tel. (0227) 830354. Excellent dining room in quiet country pub. Also recommended, especially for its buffet lunches, is the *George and Dragon Inn* (M), tel. (0227) 710661, at **Fordwich.**

Chichester (W. Sussex). *Goodwood Park* (E–M), tel. (0243) 775537; 50 rooms with bath. Modernized hotel at Goodwood House, the stately home; incorporates the historic Richmond Arms. *Dolphin and Anchor* (E), Wesr St., tel. (0243) 785121. 54 rooms with bath. Immediately opposite the cathedral, for sightseeing convenience. Fine restaurant, too. *Chichester Lodge* (M), Westhampnett, tel. (0243) 786351; 43 rooms with bath. Modern motel-style hotel. 3½ miles northeast on A27.

Restaurant. French and English platters are available at *Christopher's* (M), tel. (0243) 788724. Closed Sun., Mon. and Christmas week.

Chiddingfold (Surrey). *Crown Inn* (M), tel. Wormley (042 879) 2255; 8 rooms with bath. Top notch for atmosphere—beams, antiques, and a log fire—service and an enjoyable stay, and their restaurant is highly recommended with an excellent wine list.

Chiddingstone (Kent). **Restaurant.** *Castle Inn Restaurant* (E), tel. (0892) 870 247. Central in beautifully preserved (and very alive!) National Trust village. Solid selection of enjoyable English fare. Closed Tues. all day, Wed. lunch and Jan.

Climping (W. Sussex). *Bailiffscourt* (E), Climping St., tel. (0903) 723511; 19 rooms with bath, some with four-posters. Best of both worlds with oak-beamed ceilings and open fires in large stone fire places; also tennis and outdoor swimming pool. Above average restaurant serves good range of interesting dishes.

Cranbrook (Kent). *Kennel Holt* (E–M), Goudhurst Rd., tel. (0580) 712032; 8 rooms, 4 with bath, 2 with shower. Authentic Elizabethan manor house in the Weald of Kent with beautiful gardens. Serene atmosphere, with library and *cordon bleu* cooking.

Cuckfield (W. Sussex). *Ockenden Manor* (E), Ockenden Lane, tel. (0444) 416111; 10 rooms with bath. 16th-century, well-restored building with restaurant featuring French food and wine. Only 10 miles from Gatwick airport.

Dover (Kent) *Dover Moat House* (M), Townwall St., tel. (0304) 203270; 80 rooms with bath. Modern, comfortable and convenient if en route to the Continent. *White Cliffs* (M), Seafront, tel. (0304) 203633; 62 rooms, 42 with bath or shower. In a Regency terrace on the seafront. *Number One Guest House* (I), 1 Castle St., tel. (0304) 202007; 5 rooms, most with bath or shower. Well-equipped, good budget alternative.

Eastbourne (E. Sussex). *Grand* (E), King Edward's Parade, tel. (0323) 22611; 164 rooms with bath. The essence of Victorian Eastbourne elegance, with fine cuisine and new leisure facilities. *Queen's* (M), Marine Parade, tel. (0323) 22822; 112 rooms with bath. Impressive, late Victorian, facing the sea.
Restaurant. At **Jevington** (7 miles northwest on A259) the *Hungry Monk* (M), tel. (03212) 2178, serves carefully considered food and excellent wine in remodeled Tudor building. You must book.

East Grinstead (W. Sussex). *Gravetye Manor* (L), Vowels Lane, tel. (0342) 810567; 14 rooms with bath. This stone Elizabethan mansion offers superb vistas in every direction; wonderful surroundings for a stroll before or after dinner. Excellent restaurant, but it is essential to book first (a *Relais de Campagne* hotel).
Felbridge Hotel and Country Club, (M), London Rd., tel. (0342) 26992; 50 rooms with bath. Pool and restaurant. Adjacent health club and leisure center.

Egham (Surrey). *Great Fosters* (E), Stroude Rd., tel. (0784) 33822; 44 rooms with bath. Magnificent moated Tudor mansion set in formal gardens. Splendid public rooms with antique decor. Outdoor swimming pool, tennis.

Folkestone (Kent). *Burlington* (M), Earl's Ave., tel. (0303) 55301; 59 rooms with bath. Good sea views and a certain elusive touch—could it be gentility? *Clifton* (M), The Leas, tel. (0303) 41231; 58 rooms, 46 with bath. With sea views from its clifftop location. A solidly traditional place.
Restaurants. *Emilio's Portofino* (M), 124A Sandgate Rd., tel. (0303) 55762. Solid Italian fare. Closed Mon., best to book. *Paul's* (M), 2A Bouverie Rd. West, tel. (0303) 59697. French influenced cuisine with local seafoods. Closed Sun. *La Tavernetta* (M), Leaside Court, tel. (0303) 54955. Excellent Italian food; overlooks seafront gardens. Closed Sun. and Bank Holidays.

Gatwick Airport (W. Sussex). *Copthorne* (E), Copthorne Rd., Crawley, tel. (0342) 714971; 221 rooms, all with bath or shower. Beautiful location. Just across M23, but well worth the short trip (see also East Grinstead). *George* (E), High St., Crawley, tel. (0293) 24215; 75 rooms with bath. Modern rooms in well-adapted 15th-century inn. *Hilton International* (E), tel. (0293) 518080. 552 rooms with bath. When Hilton does it well, they do it well. This is a comfortable stopover spot, with all the comforts needed to prepare you for the horrors of the air. *See also* Lower Beeding.

Guildford (Surrey). *Angel* (E), tel. (0483) 64555; 34 rooms with bath. Ancient coaching inn, complete with minstrels' gallery and inglenook fireplace.

Restaurant. *Café de Paris* (M), 35 Castle St., tel. (0483) 34896. Both a bistro and a formal restaurant, this totally French spot is good for a quick lunch or a leisurely dinner.

Haslemere (Surrey). *Lythe Hill* (E), Petworth Rd., tel. (0428) 51251; 38 rooms, 34 with bath. Combines 14th-century farmhouse with modern accommodation; its restaurant, *L'Auberge de France* (E), has an excellent wine list and serves authentic French cuisine of the highest standard. Closed Sat. lunch, Mon. evening. *Georgian* (M), High St., tel. (0428) 51555; 21 rooms, 12 with bath. Originally built by Sir James Oglethorpe, who founded the American state of Georgia. Squash and sauna.

Restaurant. *Morels* (E), 25 Lower St., tel. (0428) 51462. Superb, authentic French cooking. Cheeseboard brought over from France. Should book.

Hastings (E. Sussex). *Beauport Park* (M), Battle Rd., tel. (0424) 51222; 23 rooms with bath. 3 miles north on A2100. Spacious country house in 33 acres with Italian formal garden overlooked by the restaurant. Heated pool, squash, billiards, sauna.

Herstmonceux (E. Sussex). **Restaurant.** *Sundial Restaurant* (E), tel. (0323) 832217. French cuisine of high quality. Fish specialties. Closed Sun. eve, Mon., last 3 weeks in Aug.–first week in Sept., Christmas–mid-Jan.

High Halden (Kent). **Restaurant.** *Hookstead House* (E), Durrant Green, tel. (023385) 670. Noteworthy food in pleasant old manor near Ashford. Some accommodation.

Lewes (E. Sussex). *Shelley's* (E), High St., tel. (0273) 472361; 21 rooms, 9 with bath, 12 with shower, and *White Hart* (M), High St., tel. (0273) 474676; 29 rooms with bath. Both for vintage atmosphere and overnighting after Glyndebourne.

Restaurant. *Kenwards* (M), Pipe Passage, tel. (0273) 472343; imaginative English dishes served in historic building. Closed Sun. and Mon. Must book.

Lower Beeding (W. Sussex). *South Lodge* (E), tel. (040376) 711; 39 rooms with bath. Magnificently renovated Victorian country mansion with oak paneling and open fires. 10 miles from Gatwick.

Midhurst (W. Sussex). *Spread Eagle* (E–M), South St., tel. (073 081) 2211; 37 rooms with bath. Splendid 15th-century, black-and-white timbered showplace building, comfortable, with good food and "authentic" beer. *Angel* (M), North St., tel. (073 081) 2421; 18 rooms, 12 with bath, 4 with shower. Somewhat younger (16th-century) but also charming, with walled garden.

Rochester (Kent). *Crest* (M), Maidstone Rd., tel. (0634) 687111. Brand new 106 bed hotel.

Rushlake Green (E. Sussex). *Priory* (E–M), tel. (0435) 830553. 15 rooms with bath. Restored early 15th-century monastery set in 1,000 acres of pasture and garden. Homely atmosphere. Some rooms may exceed (E). Particularly noted for its excellent *Restaurant* (E), specializing in masterfully presented classic dishes; also excellent wines and English cheeses. Closed end of Dec.–mid-Jan.

Rusper (W. Sussex). *Ghyll Manor* (L), tel. (029 384) 571. Lovely Elizabethan house with 28 rooms, including one with four-poster. Some (E) and (M) rooms. Heated pool, park, tennis. Excellent restaurant (E), good varied menus.

Rye (E. Sussex). *George* (M), tel. (0797) 222114. 16 rooms with bath or shower. Characterful. *Mermaid* (M), tel. (0797) 223065; 30 rooms, 27 with bath or shower. Ancient lovely building, bursting with history (the cellars are Norman).
Restaurants. *Simmons* (E–M), 68 The Mint, tel. (0797) 222026. Pretty cottage restaurant serving French-inspired dishes. Closed Sun. evening and Mon. *Flushing Inn* (M), Market St., tel. (0797) 223272. Medieval inn with restaurant. Fresh fish specialties. Closed Mon. evenings and Tues.

Sevenoaks (Kent). **Restaurant.** *Royal Oak* (M–E), Upper High St., tel. (0732) 451109). Both a hotel (21 rooms) and a fine restaurant. Very handy for visitors to Knole—it's close to the entrance—its fixed-price menus bring it well within the (M) grade.

Storrington (W. Sussex). *Little Thakeham* (L–E), Merrywood Lane, Thakeham, tel. (090 66) 4416. Lutyens house on South Downs with beautiful gardens and highly original architecture. 9 rooms with bath. Excellent restaurant with English specialties, (E).
Restaurant. *Manley's* (E), Manley's Hill, tel. (090 66) 2331. Superb menu featuring original creations, with good wine list. Traditional oak beams, leaded windows.

Tunbridge Wells (Kent). *Spa* (E), Mount Ephraim, tel. (0892) 20331; 75 rooms with bath. Impressive 18th-century house in large gardens. Comfortable hotel with leisure center and good restaurant.

Uckfield (E. Sussex). *Horsted Place* (L), tel. (0825) 75581; 15 rooms with bath. Formerly a country house, which, in its former incarnation, hosted members of the royal family. Potentially an exceptional place to stay, but expensive.

Wrotham Heath (Kent). *Post House* (E), tel. Borough Green (0732) 88331; 119 rooms with bath. New, comfortable and well-equipped—pool, health club, sauna. On London Road near Sevenoaks. Handy for a visit to Ightham Mote.

Wye (Kent). **Restaurant.** Dine at the *Wife of Bath* (M), 4 Upper Bridge St., tel. (0233) 812540, for charm and reliably excellent food. Closed Sun., Mon.

PLACES OF INTEREST. While Britain has a rich heritage of stately homes scattered all over the landscape, there is, perhaps, a greater concentration in the southern regions than elsewhere. Here is a listing of some of the major houses in the southeast. There are further notes on seeing Historic Houses in *Facts At Your Fingertips,* and a discussion of the problems of the Historic House situation in the chapter *Historic Houses— Precious Stones in Peril.*

Kent. Canterbury Centre, St. Alphege Lane (tel. 0227 457009). Historical and environmental exhibitions in converted church. Tues.–Sat. 10.30–5.

Canterbury Heritage Museum, Poor Priests' Hospital, Canterbury (tel. 0227 452747). An imaginative "time walk" experience through the long history of the city. Open all year, Mon.–Sat. 10.30–4.

Chartwell, Westerham (tel. 0732 866368). Home of Sir Winston Churchill, now run by the National Trust as a permanent memorial. Open Mar. and Nov., Sat., Sun. and Wed., 11–4; Apr.–end of Oct., Tues.–Thurs., 12–5, Sat., Sun. and Bank Holidays 11–5. Closed Good Fri. and Tues. after Bank Holidays. Gets very crowded. (NT)

Chatham Historic Dockyard, Chatham (tel. 0634 812551). 18th and 19th-century docks once used by the Royal Navy. Open Apr.–Oct., Wed.–Sun. 10–6; rest of year Wed., Sat. and Sun. 10–4.30.

Chiddingstone Castle, near Edenbridge (tel. 0892 870347). Royal Stuart and Jacobite relics. Open Easter through Oct., Wed.–Sat. 2–5.30, Sun. and Bank Holidays 11.30–5.30 (also Tues. July–mid. Sept.) Oct., weekends 2–5.30. Check, times may change.

Dover Castle, Dover (tel. 0304 201628). The keep was built by Henry II in 1180–6; the outer curtain was added in the 13th century. Open daily, except Christmas and New Year.

Hever Castle, near Edenbridge (tel. 0732 865224). Home of Henry VIII's second wife, Anne Boleyn. Contains new exhibition with lifesize models of Anne and other historic figures. Splendid gardens and lovely house renowned for its treasures bestowed by William Waldorf Astor in 1903. Open Good Fri.–early Nov., daily, castle from 12 noon, gardens 11–6.

Ightham Mote, near Ightham (tel. 0732 810378). Superb medieval moated manor house, continually inhabited since the 14th century. Recently given by its American owner to the National Trust. Open Easter through Oct., Mon., Wed., Fri. 11–5.30, Sun. 11–5. (NT)

Knole, Sevenoaks (tel. 0732 450608). Home of Lord Sackville. Built in 1456. Open Apr.–Oct., Wed.–Sat., Bank Holiday Mon., 11–5, Sun., 2–5. Last admission 4. (NT)

Leeds Castle, near Maidstone (tel. 0622 65400). One of the most outwardly impressive castles in Britain, standing in the middle of a lake. Once a palace of Henry VIII's. Recent additions include a maze, in classical 18th-century style, with an underground grotto at its center. Open Apr.–Oct., daily 11–5; Nov.–Mar., Sat. and Sun., 12–4. (Castle is sometimes used for conferences, when it may be closed.)

Penshurst Place, Tunbridge Wells (tel. 0892 870307). Dating from 1340, one of England's great houses, home of poet Sir Philip Sidney. Now the residence of the Rt Hon. Viscount de L'Isle. Has a unique Toy Museum. Open Apr.–early Oct., every afternoon, exc. Mon. (open Good Fri. and Bank Holiday Mon.). House 1–5.30, grounds 12.30–6.

Quebec House, Westerham (tel. 0959 62206). Early 16th-century in origin, but mainly 17th-century. Relics of General Wolfe. Open Apr.–Oct., daily (except Thurs. and Sat.), 2–6. (NT)

Sissinghurst Castle Garden (tel. 0580 712850), the famous gardens of Vita Sackville-West and Sir Harold Nicolson; a gardener's joy. Open Apr.–mid-Oct., Tues.–Fri., 1–6.30; Sat., Sun., Good Friday, 10–6.30. (NT)

Smallhythe Place, The Ellen Terry Museum, Tenterden (tel. 058 06 2334). Mementoes of Ellen Terry, David Garrick, Mrs. Siddons, Henry Irving and others famous in the British theater, in Ellen Terry's former home. Open Apr.–Oct., Sat.–Wed., 2–6 (or dusk). (NT)

Tyrwhitt-Drake Museum of Carriages, Mill St., Maidstone (tel. 0622 54497). Claimed to be the largest display of horse-drawn vehicles in the country. All the coaches on display are in original unrestored state. Open Mon. Sat., 10–1, 2–5; also Sun. afternoons and Bank Holidays (Apr.–Sept.).

Surrey. Clandon Park, near Guildford (tel. 0483 222482). Beautiful 18th-century Palladian house. Open Apr.–mid-Oct., daily (except Mon., unless Bank Holiday, and Fri.), 1.30–5.30, last admission 5. (NT)

Farnham Castle, Farnham. Former bishop's palace, mainly Norman, with Tudor and Jacobean additions. All year, Wed., 2–4. Closed Christmas week.

Loseley House, near Guildford (tel. 0483 571881). Noble Elizabethan mansion, built 1562. Open end May–late Sept., Wed., Thurs., Fri., Sat., 2–5.

Polesden Lacey, near Dorking (tel. 0372 58203). Regency house (altered in Edwardian period) in charming surroundings. Open Apr.–Oct., Wed.–Sun., 1.30–5.30 plus Bank Holiday Mon. Mar. and Nov., Sat. and Sun., 1.30–4.30. Gardens open daily all year, 11–sunset. (NT)

Thorpe Park, near Chertsey (tel. 09328 62633). Britain's first purpose-built theme park (500 acres), illustrating British heritage from the Stone Age to Magna Carta; also rides and water gardens. Open mid Apr.–late Sept. Complex opening times, so please check.

Wisley Gardens, near Ripley. These magnificent gardens of the Royal Horticultural Society show British gardening at its very best. Open daily year round, Mon.–Sat. 10–7, Sun. members only. (Closes at sunset, if earlier).

Sussex (East and West). Arundel Castle (tel. 0903 883136). Home of the Duke of Norfolk. Ancient castle rebuilt in the 18th century and altered at the end of the 19th century. Open Apr.–Oct. daily (not Sat.), 1–5 (12–5 June–Aug.). Also Bank Holidays 12–5. Check before going. Nearby is a *Wildfowl Trust* of 55 acres, open daily year round 9.30–6.30 (or dusk).

Batemans, near Burwash (tel. 0435 882302). Built 1634. Delightful house of Rudyard Kipling. Open Apr.–end Oct., Sat.–Wed., 11–6, and Good Fri. (NT)

The Blue Idol, Coolham near Horsham (tel. 040387 241). Ancient timbered building and Friends Meeting House, founded by William Penn and colleagues some 300 years ago. Spacious garden and orchard. Open all year during daylight hours.

Bodiam Castle, near Robertsbridge (tel. 058 083 436). Build 1386–9 for protection against the French, this moated castle is among the best-preserved and most beautiful in the country. Open daily, Apr.–Oct., 10–6 (or sunset); winter, Mon.–Sat., 10–sunset. (NT)

Charleston Farmhouse, Firle, near Lewes (tel. 032183 265). 17th/18th century farmhouse, a favorite retreat of the famous literary Bloomsbury Group, house and contents decorated by Bloomsbury artists. Recently opened to the public, Apr.–end Sept., Sats and Bank Holiday Mon., 2–6 (last admission 5). Check before visiting.

Firle Place, near Lewes (tel. 079159 335). Has important collection of pictures and many items of particular interest to visitors from the U.S.A. Open June–Sept., Wed., Thurs. and Sun., and all Bank Holidays, 2–5.

Glynde Place, near Lewes (tel. 079159 248). Splendid 16th-century house. Open June–Sept., Wed., Thurs., also Bank Holidays, 2.15–5.30.

Goodwood House, near Chichester (tel. 0243 774107). Built by Wyatt. Fine collection of pictures and Louix XV furniture. Open May–Oct., Sun. and Mon., also Tues.–Thurs. in Aug., 2–5. Closed on all horse event days.

Great Dixter, Northiam (tel. 07974 3160). Medieval half-timbered manor house with fine gardens. House and gardens open Apr.–mid Oct., daily (except Mon.) but open all Bank Holiday Mons., 2–5. Gardens open at 11 on Sun. in July and Aug.

House of Pipes, Bramber (tel. 0903 812122). Quirky, award-winning museum with thousands of exhibits relating to the history of smoking. Daily, 9.45–6.30.

Lamb House, Rye. Home of American writer Henry James from 1898 to 1916. Some of James' personal possessions on view. Open Apr.–end Oct., Wed. and Sat. 2–6. (NT)

Leonardslee, Horsham (tel. 040376 212). Notable spring and fall gardens with ornamental lakes and spectacular views. Open mid Apr.–mid June, daily 10–6; July–end Sept., weekends only 12–6; Oct. weekends 10–5.

Michelham Priory, near Hailsham (tel. 0323 844224). Tudor farmhouse, originally an Augustinian Priory. Surrounded by medieval moat. Special exhibitions and events; Tudor barn; watermill for grinding grain recently restored. Open Easter through Oct., daily 11–5.30.

Monks House, Rodmell. Formerly the home of Virginia and Leonard Woolf. Open Apr. and Oct., Wed. and Sat. 2–5, May–Sept., Wed. and Sat. 2–6.

Parham, Pulborough (tel. 09066 2021). Magnificent Elizabethan house. Fine gardens, 4-acre walled garden, herb garden and orchard, also 18th-century garden with statuary and lake. Open Easter–early Oct., Sun., Wed., Thurs. and Bank Holidays, 2–6; Gardens 1–6.

Petworth House, Petworth (tel. 0798 42207). Palatial mansion rebuilt 1688–96 by the 6th Duke of Somerset. Fine collection of paintings. Impressive park. Open Apr.–Oct., daily except Mon. and Fri., plus Bank Holiday Mon., 1–5. (NT)

Preston Manor, Preston Park, Brighton (tel. 0273 603005). Georgian house with rich Edwardian interior and furnishings. Open all year, Tues.–Sun., 10–5.

Royal Pavillion, Brighton (tel. 0273 603005). A dazzling and exotic folly built for the Prince Regent in the early 19th-century. A "must" sight. Open daily, 10–5; June–Sept., 10–6.

Standen, East Grinstead (tel. 0342 23029). 1894 house with Morris decorations and fine Pre-Raphaelite feel. Lovely views from the garden. Apr.–Oct., Wed., Thurs., Fri., Sat. and Sun., 1.30–5.30. (NT)

Weald and Downland Open Air Museum, Singleton, near Chichester (tel. 024 363 348). A fascinating collection of historic buildings saved from destruction and re-erected on a magnificent 40-acre site; woodland nature trail. Open Apr.–Oct., daily 11–5; Nov.–Mar., Wed. and Sun., 11–4.

THE SOUTH

Wild Ponies and Great Stones

English counties have a tendency to group themselves in threes or fours to form regions which have marked dissimilarities from their neighbors. Thus, there are characteristics in common between *Sussex* and *Hampshire* which, together with *Dorset, Wiltshire* further to the west, and the *Isle of Wight,* make up what is known as the South.

HAMPSHIRE

Many centers in Hampshire can easily be reached by train from London (Waterloo) because they are so conveniently arranged that one line can serve many towns without having to divert to east or west. Likewise, now that the M3 is complete for 49 miles, through to Winchester, and the exit from London the easiest there is, one can reasonably expect to be in Hampshire within 90 minutes. Alternatively, the lovely A272 road from East Sussex enters Hampshire just east of Petersfield and continues on its enchanting way westwards to reach a climax near Telegraph Hill, 533 ft., whence you can get your first exciting glimpse of Winchester.

Winchester

Hampshire has a lot to offer the visitor, but nothing greater than Winchester which besides being one of the most ancient is also one of the most graceful and unspoilt of English cities. It reflects the history of England from earliest times, and was a capital city before London assumed that dignity. It was from Winchester that King Alfred, the first great king of England, and its savior from the Danes, reigned from 871 to 900. Under Alfred, Winchester became a great center of learning, and in late Saxon times Winchester was the home of the finest school of calligraphy and manuscript illumination in Europe. It was from here that William the Conqueror compiled the *Domesday Book*.

The cathedral, set in a peaceful Close with a partly 13th-century deanery, the Pilgrims' School and the Tudor Cheyney Court, has early Norman Perpendicular features, the Gothic roof being supported by clusters of pillars. There are seven richly carved chantry chapels as well as carved choir stalls and a Norman font. Outside, the cathedral presents a sturdy, chunky appearance in keeping with its Norman origins, so that its Gothic lightness within is even more than normally breathtaking. So is the knowledge that at the beginning of this century much of the flooded foundations of the cathedral had to be renewed by a diver working twenty feet below ground. Look out for the little bronze statue of "William Walker the diver, who saved this cathedral with his two hands, 1905–1912".

Of the nearby castle, the birthplace and abode of many kings, all that remains is the Great Hall, finished in 1235. In it hangs the supposed Round Table of the legendary King Arthur. It was the meeting place of many medieval parliaments and the scene of many notable trials, including that of Sir Walter Raleigh who was there sentenced to death, and the "Bloody Assizes" held by Judge Jeffreys in 1685.

In College Street stands Winchester College, founded in 1382 and probably the oldest boys' public (private) school in the country. There are guided tours from April to September daily, except Sunday morning.

A walk of about a mile to the south of the cathedral will bring you to the ancient charitable institution of St. Cross Hospital, where the Wayfarer's Dole of a horn of beer and a portion of bread has been handed to travelers through the porter's doorway for more than six centuries.

The New Forest

Although walkers will say that only on foot can you see the New Forest at its best—which is probably true—it is very accessible by car, with many car parks from which way-marked forest trails originate. The New Forest has many small, twisty roads leading to delightful little villages, mere clusters of cottages with the semi-wild ponies cropping round them; to specially planted "drives"; and to great houses standing alone as they have for years. A lot of the forest is rich in splendid trees, but much more of it is barren heathland. At Stoney Cross in Canterton Glen, near the Cadnam-Ringwood road (A31), a stone commemorates the death of William Rufus, mysteriously killed by an arrow when out hunting. It is not very likely that you will see many deer here, however, but there are still large numbers of ponies. Great care is needed when driving as, being free, they are very vulnerable and many are killed every year. Pony sales are held twice a year at Beaulieu Road on the B3056. One of the most relaxing ways of seeing the New Forest must be from the horse-drawn wagons that run from Balmer Lawn Road, near Brockenhurst, into peaceful wooded enclosures.

Six miles from Southampton, on the way to Beaulieu—pronounced *Bewley*—and not far from Ashurst, is the New Forest Butterfly Farm. Situated on a 2,000 acre estate, the 3-acre farm site is open daily from April to October, 10 to 5, with over fifty different species flying freely in a vast glasshouse. It is a spot especially interesting to camera buffs, who should appreciate the chances to photograph such lovely creatures in exotic surroundings.

One of the most famous places in the forest is Buckler's Hard, an almost perfectly restored 18th-century hamlet which was formerly a shipyard, where some of Nelson's three-deckers were built. It now has a maritime museum. The village is situated on the river some two miles from Beaulieu. Nearby is Beaulieu Abbey, founded in the early 13th century, and Palace House, originally the abbey's great gate house. Here lives Lord Montagu of Beaulieu who created the Montagu Motor Museum, now the National Motor Museum, with its collection of over 200 vehicles and vintage cars. A new attraction is the ingenious "Wheels" exhibition on the history of motoring, featuring a ride on an electrically-powered "pod." His enterprise has helped to make this one of England's most visited stately homes.

Buckler's Hard is on the Beaulieu River, immediately east of which is the great Southampton Water, fed by the Rivers Test, Itchen, Hamble and the comparatively tiny Meon, all on the east side. The west side has to be avoided as it is one huge oil refinery. Each of these rivers is interesting.

The Test runs from its source near Overton to flow into Southampton Water near Totton. A few miles to the northwest of Southampton it passes the Norman abbey of Romsey, founded in the 10th century; here, the carved abbess's doorway is Norman and, beside it, a most moving crucifix, believed to be Saxon. Nearby is Broadlands, which is now widely-known as the spot where the Prince and Princess of Wales spent the first two days of their honeymoon in 1981—as had the Queen and Prince Philip before them. Broadlands was the home of Prince Charles's uncle, Earl Mountbatten, and is now open to the public. There is a Mountbatten Exhibition, commemorating the Earl, who was killed in a terrorist bomb attack in Ireland, and memorials to the Mountbatten family in Romsey Abbey.

Stockbridge is where the Danes had their ship repair yards, but now there is a trout hatchery to help stock one of the most expensive stretches of fishing in the country. The town itself is very attractive with a long, wide main street with many antique shops, and is an excellent place to stop for lunch or tea. The Grosvenor Hotel, still with its huge porch built out across the pavement is a feature, and, naturally, the focal point of anglers. Westwards, the three Wallops, Middle, Nether and Over, lie close together and, quite apart from their fascinating shared name (the origin of which is unknown), they are very attractive. Nether Wallop has early wall paintings in the church, and Over Wallop has a 15th-century font.

The River Itchen rises northeast of Winchester and is equally famous for trout fishing. The Hamble, which has a long indented estuary is given over to sailing and boat building. It is here that many of the great sea-going yachts are built. Finally, the Meon emerges over flat land below the delightful village of Tichfield—and then we are at Portsmouth, seriously naval, last landfall for Nelson's flagship, *H.M.S. Victory,* which has been restored to the condition it enjoyed when it made history at the Battle of Trafalgar, and is open to visitors.

The city is rich in associations with England's maritime heritage, much of which is remembered at the naval base. Near to *H.M.S. Victory* are the remains of Henry VIII's favorite ship, the 15th-century *Mary Rose,* subject of a recent famous salvage operation. The public is allowed to view the restoration work on the hull, and can visit the Mary Rose Exhibition Hall, which contains artifacts from the ship. The Royal Naval Museum, devoted entirely to the history of the Navy, is also located here. *H.M.S. Warrior,* launched in 1860 as Britain's first iron-hulled battleship, joined this wealth of naval memorabilia in 1987.

Victorian statesman Lord Palmerston had Portsmouth's Fort Widley built in the 1860s; it commands fine views and contains a maze of subterranean passages. Spitbank Fort, its foundations sunk into the sea-bed a mile offshore, is another Victorian coastal defence. This sturdy, circular fort is now open to the public. The Victorian novelist Charles Dickens was born in Portsmouth's Commercial Road. Mementos are displayed in his house in a reconstructed period setting.

The cathedral, a mixture of ancient and modern, was originally founded in the 12th century in honor of St. Thomas à Becket. The city has its own seaside resort at Southsea, home of the prestigious D-Day Museum which commemorates, in an imaginative and exciting way, the 1944 Allied landings in Normandy. It is situated near Southsea Castle, a fort built by Henry VIII in 1539. More military history is to be found at Southsea's Royal Marines Museum.

Southampton is another city whose past revolves around the sea. Armies left the port for the Crusades and it was from here that the Pilgrim Fathers departed on the first stage of their voyage to America in 1620. Harbor cruises take visitors past such liners as the *QE2* and *Canberra.* On dry land, the 14th-century Wool House is now a maritime museum. Other places of interest include the 16th-century Tudor House, traces of the old town walls and the new Southampton Hall of Aviation, which contains a giant flying boat.

THE ISLE OF WIGHT

There are car ferries plying to the Island from Portsmouth, Southampton and Lymington, the latter lying southwest of Beaulieu. Southampton is a convenient route to take, using the M3 and A33. You embark on the Red Funnel car ferry at Royal Pier. The crossing takes you down Southampton Water—if you are lucky you may see the QE II or another famous liner—past the awe-inspiring Fawley oil refinery to land at the renowned yachting center of Cowes. The Sealink service from Lymington to Yarmouth is a shorter sea-crossing. It is advisable to book space, especially at weekends in summer, but the ferries are efficient and space can sometimes be found.

The Island used to be part of Hampshire, but is now on its own. It has a very pronounced atmosphere, quite distinct from that of the mainland.

To begin with it is essentially Victorian. This is only reasonable since, although the Island was known to the Romans and, indeed, the ill-fated Stuarts, it was Queen Victoria who put it on the map by choosing to build there, live there as much as she could, and ultimately die there. Clearly she must have created a great vogue, because most of the domestic architecture is exclusively Victorian. Another curious thing about it is that the islanders are fiercely chauvinistic, and none more so than the retired people who could be counted as newcomers. They, it seems, greatly resent the tourists and the day-trippers, although without them the Island's economy would collapse.

Yachts and a Poet Laureate

The Island, some 22 miles long and 13 wide, is dominated by its resorts, Ryde, Bembridge, Sandown, Shanklin, Ventnor—all on the east side—and to a lesser extent Totland and Freshwater in the west. Cowes, famous all over the world for its regattas, lies on the north coast opposite Southampton, while the Needles—the lovely chalk monoliths rising out of the sea to the extreme west—are seen by many travelers arriving in England from distant ports. The changing coastline combines semi-tropical vegetation to the east with sheltered coves and dramatic ravines called "chines" and, on the west coast, the strange colored sand of Alum Bay can still be collected beneath the four-hundred-feet-high cliffs.

Inland, you will find many typical peaceful villages and small towns. The whole history of the Isle of Wight centers round Carisbrooke Castle, which has a fine church and which was once the chief Roman settlement in the Island. The well-preserved fortress has a museum, where the exhibits include old maps, coins and paintings, as well as relics of Charles I, who was a prisoner in the castle in 1647 and 1648.

Queen Victoria and Prince Albert built Osborne, and though she was happy there, there is an underlying sadness to the place. Here one sees the engineer manqué of Prince Albert with his clever innovations—even central heating—and the desperate attempt of Victoria to give her children a normal but disciplined up-bringing. For anyone drawn to the domestic side of history, Osborne is enormously interesting.

Yarmouth is a small attractive town, a yachting center with a year-round character—it is no summer-on, winter-off resort. Be sure to visit St. James's church, which contains a marble statue, begun as Louis XIV, but, after being captured at sea, finished off with the head of Sir Robert Holmes, a 17th-century governor of the Island, who also had the distinction of taking New York from the Dutch in 1664. The George Hotel, with a famous bar, was once the Governor's mansion.

Tennyson was an inhabitant of the island until he was driven away by tourist harassment. He lived at Farringford, near Freshwater, and today his house is an hotel. Many things in it remain to remind one of the poet, including a study with a secret staircase, and a way out of the house onto the Downs which was not overlooked by trippers. In those days, Cowes in particular was the center of high society during the summer months, especially during the Cowes Regatta, when millionaires' yachts jostled for moorings and the fashionable ladies strolled on the lawns of the Royal Yacht Squadron. Cowes Week is still patronized by royalty, the Duke of Edinburgh being a regular participant.

But yachting in the 20th century is no longer the prerogative of millionaires. Small-boat enthusiasts from all walks of life throng the yacht harbors of Cowes, Bembridge and Yarmouth, and the busy jade-green waters of the Solent are flecked with the scudding sails of British yachtsmen displaying their passion for a life on the ocean wave.

But don't be put off by all this talk of sea and sails. There is some splendid gentle motoring to be done in the interior of the island over such places as Brading Down, Ashey Down and Mersley Down, while villages such as Kingston, Brighstone, Shalfleet and Mottistone should not be missed. Try to go in the spring or fall, or you may find yourself driving behind motorcoaches most of the time.

DORSET

Dorset is a county that the visitor to Britain frequently passes through but overlooks, as though it were nothing more than a length of railway line or highway. This is a grave error, shared by many Englishmen who have never seen Dorset. Consequently this green and hilly county is very largely unspoilt and is, in fact, one of the last remaining corners of the old, rural England. Many of the finest stretches of the Dorset coast are preserved by the National Trust, and large areas of the county are designated "Areas of Outstanding Natural Beauty."

Nowhere are the hills higher than 1,000 feet, yet this is a county of astounding views. There are no great stately homes, but instead countless historic manor houses, each with a special charm. While a good deal of the county is devoted to agriculture, the quarrying of stone ranks high, colors ranging from off-white, grey and amber, to green, blue and purple. These are used locally, sometimes all at the same time, forming a sort of checkerboard design on houses and churches.

Internationally famous for its stone is Portland, a five-mile spit jutting out from Weymouth Bay. It is a grey-white world of limestone, the supply seeming inexhaustible, the demand endless. St. Paul's Cathedral and many of Christopher Wren's other churches were built from it; Buckingham Palace, Whitehall, and further afield, the White House, and the United Nations Headquarters in New York. Stone apart, it is a small area with a strong character. There are two churches, one built by prisoners, a nice hotel, and from the top of a hill ridge, incomparable views along the great curve of the Chesil Bank.

If you have a chance to read some of Thomas Hardy's novels before visiting Dorset, you'll already have a feeling for it, and indeed, you'll recognize some places immediately from his descriptions. The countryside surrounding Dorchester, in particular, is lovingly described in *Far from the Madding Crowd,* and Casterbridge, in *The Mayor of Casterbridge,* stands for Dorchester itself.

Bournemouth and Surroundings

The interior of east Dorset shows distinct signs of being a neighbor of Wiltshire, which lies north of it, but its coastal area is very much its own thing, except for the large seaside town of Bournemouth which was re-moved from Hampshire—where it belongs temperamentally—to Dorset at the time of the boundary reorganization. It is a large and popular resort, verging on the smart, which has everything to offer in the way of good beaches, all kinds of entertainment, sport and an extremely mild winter climate.

Between Bournemouth and the Hampshire boundary is Christchurch, a place of picturesque walks, old buildings and the modern Saxon Square shopping centre. The Priory Church, the longest parish church in England, is a great attraction. There is also a pleasant little harbor that offers sailing, fishing and boat hire in the summer.

Poole, once Dorset's largest town, has been an important port from medieval times onwards. Its enormous natural harbor, almost 100 miles around, has no less than seven islands and a multitude of channels through shallow flats that dry out at low tide. The historic cove of Poole is now a well-restored conservation area. It is worth exploring the many alley-ways and fine old streets in the center, such as Blue Boar Lane, Malet Street, West Street and New Street, where you can see the proud 18th-century homes of the prosperous merchants and shippers of Poole. The small Guildhall Museum is interesting.

Along the rest of the coast, bright white chalk mingles with darker rocks, and many small bays and inlets provide natural harbors for fishermen and sailors. Indeed it would be fair to say that the Dorset coast is the first shore line between the Thames and the west which offers natural, unharnessed beauty for those who care to go down the little lanes to find it. It is also richly varied geologically and has such curious things to show the visitor as the unique Chesil Bank, the Durdle Door, Kimmeridge Bay, the Isle of Purbeck and chalk Downs that reach 900 ft. The Chesil Bank is indeed unique: 18 miles of smooth, high-banked stones at which the tide drags noisily, all perfectly graduated from fist-size at the Portland end to pea-size at Abbotsbury. It is claimed that boatmen, landing in the dark, can tell precisely where they are by the size and shape of the stones.

Another Dorset curiosity is the Swannery at Abbotsbury where, in a lagoon trapped behind the Chesil Beach, hundreds of swans come to breed, as they have done since the 14th century. Before Henry VIII seized so much church land, Abbotsbury was one of the most important monasteries in England. Today all that is left is a huge tithe barn and a tropical garden.

At nearby Portesham, a surprise awaits you. Here there is a monument to a *second* Thomas Hardy, who also lived in Dorset: Admiral Sir Thomas Hardy, Nelson's captain at the Battle of Trafalgar. As a monument it's not much to look at—rather like a chimney stack—but with tremendous views from the hill on which it stands. This was the Thomas Hardy who was with Nelson at his death, and there is some controversy as to whether Nelson said "Kiss me, Hardy", or *"Kismet, Hardy."*

Weymouth and Dorchester

At one end of the Chesil Bank stands Weymouth, resort and small port from which ferries sail to France and the Channel Islands. It has a most beautiful, curving sea-front of Georgian houses, and within the town many little ancient alleyways. It became fashionable as a resort during the 18th century when George III and members of the royal family made frequent excursions there, the monarch emerging from his bathing machine to take dips in the sea to the strains of the National Anthem. A brightly painted statue of him, flanked by the lion and unicorn, overlooks the promenade. Another royal tribute is at Osmington, a few miles east, where a chalk-cut figure of the king on horseback is carved on the hill. Osmington, one of Weymouth's many surrounding countrified villages, is worth a special visit. Constable spent his honeymoon here in 1816, and painted his famous picture, *Weymouth Bay.*

Immediately north of Weymouth is Dorchester, the Casterbridge of Hardy's novels, and a thriving county town which becomes especially animated on market day, Wednesday. On these days the streets are thronged with farmers and people from the outlying villages all around. The center of the town is basically Georgian, interspersed with Victorian churches and modern shop fronts. But the modern intrusions are not as blatant as in other similar places; old inns, tea rooms and antique shops abound, and St. Peter's Church, built in the Perpendicular style and possessing a fine tower, is worth seeing. The founding of Massachusetts was the idea, originally, of a former parson of St. Peter's, John White, who started a settlement on the coast of America for fishermen, who later moved to Salem. He is buried in the porch of the church.

Archeologists will tell you that Dorchester is situated at the intersection of a number of Roman roads and that its Roman name was Durnovaria. To support that claim, remains of a Roman amphitheater are shown near the town; the place where the remains were excavated is known by the strange name of Maumbury Rings. Evidence of a pre-Roman settlement can be seen at the fortified earthwork called Maiden Castle and at the vast entrenchment known as Poundbury. Relics from these and many other ancient sites are on view in the County Museum, near St. Peter's Church. Dorchester is well blessed with museums—the Dorset Military Museum and the Dinosaur Museum are also located here.

It is difficult to imagine this cheerful little town as the place of the infamous Bloody Assizes of 1685, presided over by the sadistic Judge Jeffreys. It's even harder to think of these gruesome connections when one takes tea and scones in Judge Jeffreys' Lodgings, which today is both a tea shop and a restaurant. The actual trials, at which men were sentenced to hang for taking part in the ill-fated Monmouth Rebellion, were held in the oak-paneled back room of the Antelope Inn. The room can still be seen today.

Dorchester and other little towns of Dorset have some excellent antique shops, and prospective buyers of good furniture are advised to make a tour of those places.

Thomas Hardy actually lived about two and a half miles from Dorchester at Higher Bockhampton, where the gardens of his home are open to visitors. The Thomas Hardy Memorial Room in the Dorset County Museum has a reconstruction of his study at his later home, Max Gate, along with various other memorabilia—including an outstanding collection of his manuscripts. A little farther away, at Clouds Hill, the adventurer and chronicler T. E. Lawrence (Lawrence of Arabia, as he is better known) spent several years writing his *Seven Pillars of Wisdom.* Lawrence considered Clouds Hill as "one of the most English and most wonderful places in the country."

A few miles from Dorchester runs the river Piddle, its name changed on some reaches to Puddle, to suit the Victorians who thought Piddle was undignified. Variations include village names such as Piddletrenthide, Puddletown, and Tolpuddle. The latter was made famous in the early 19th century by the Tolpuddle Martyrs, six Dorset farmers who banded together and asked for a shilling a week rise. They were charged with mutiny and sentenced to deportation (to Australia). It was the beginning of Trade Unions, and the courage of the farmers is commemorated by cottages built by the Trade Union Movement, dedicated in 1934, and visited annually by T.U.C. officials.

The chalk hills that run southeast through the county from Shaftsbury contain some of the most perfect prehistoric earthworks in the world. Maiden Castle near Dorchester is the most famous, but the most spectacular site is Eggardon Hill, crowning an 800-ft chalk escarpment near Bridport. The site is best reached by taking the A356 and diverging at Maiden Newton. Equally extraordinary is Britain's earliest full-frontal nude; the enormous 180-foot prehistoric hill carving known as the Cerne Giant was restored in 1983 and stares down on you from miles around. Both the village of Cerne Abbas (north of Dorchester on A352) and the giant should be visited.

Guns and Hounds

To the east of Dorchester the Purbeck Hills stretch away towards Wareham, in whose Saxon church there is a fine marble effigy of Lawrence of Arabia. The Purbeck coast is magnificent, with soaring white cliffs and unusual rock formations at Lulworth Cove and Durdle Door. Although much of the area is an Army gunnery range, the coast paths are cleared in the summer and the roads opened for visitors.

This whole coast is notable for its high, rugged cliffs, and along Lyme Bay, near the Devon border, are some of the most spectacular. Here people still dig for fossils, an occupation dating back at least to the 18th century. Mary Anning was the daughter of a humble family who lived at the charming old port and resort of Lyme Regis. They set up The Fossil Shop, and Mary, from an early age, helped her parents scour the cliffs for fossils which they sold as their livelihood. At the age of eleven, she unearthed the bones of several prehistoric monsters, authenticated by experts; a window in the parish church is dedicated to her. You can still dig for fossils, but it is a good deal easier to buy them in today's Fossil Shop or look at them in the local museum. Lyme Regis is now famous not only for its fossils and The Cobb, its 13th-century curving, stone breakwater, but also for the movie *The French Lieutenant's Woman* which was filmed here. John Fowles, the author of the novel on which this movie was based, is Lyme's most prestigious resident.

However it was not the Army's guns that created the spectacular ruins of Corfe Castle, whose thick gray walls have guarded a strategic gap through the Purbecks since Saxon times. The damage was done by Cromwell blowing up the place after it had been betrayed in the Civil War. Even in ruins, the Castle is awe-inspiring; best seen from nearby Kingston village.

Wimborne Minster, in the eastern corner of the county, is a small market town whose glory is its ancient Norman Minster, or church. From

Wimborne, B3082 follows the placid River Stour northwest to Blandford Forum, which, despite its Roman-sounding name is very much an 18th-century town, with a wealth of Georgian architecture.

Not far from Blandford, at Sturminster Newton—a charming market town encircled by the River Stour—is yet another sign of the kind of punishment handed out to delinquents in earlier days. A fine stone bridge spans the river, and at one end an old plaque has been preserved: "Anyone found defacing this bridge will be instantly deported."

In North Dorset, buried among the lush foxhunting landscapes of Cranborne Chase and the Blackmoor Vale, are two more venerable towns, Shaftesbury (the "Shaston" of Hardy novels and location of the cobbled Gold Hill, one of England's most photographed historic streets) and Sherborne. In Sherborne there are two castles, one founded in 1107, the other begun by Sir Walter Raleigh, with its 70 rooms and wealth of fascinating domestic details, gathered over the centuries by the Digby family. But the town's most imposing building is the Abbey Church. Built of honey-hued local stone, it contains within its weathered walls the tombs of ancient Saxon kings of Wessex.

WILTSHIRE

Although the east of Dorset has something about it of Wiltshire, notably thatched and color-washed cottages in neat little villages, there is nothing anywhere in England that can be compared to Salisbury Plain. This is largely because of its color and the quality of its light. Although such a lot of it is apparently empty, it is never dull. The little clumps of trees could not be better placed had they been planted by landscape design, and the turned earth or crops according to season, only add to a fascinating pattern.

White Horse Country

Wiltshire has another distinction. Part of King Alfred's Kingdom of Wessex, often now known as White Horse Country, Wiltshire has more of these huge figures cut into the chalky hillsides than any other county. Four are particularly impressive: Cherhill carved in 1780, Marlborough in 1800, Alton Barnes in 1812, and Westbury in 1778. This latter horse, the oldest of the four, is cut high above Westbury on a shoulder of the Bratton Iron Age camp, all grassy banks and ditches. It measures 180 feet from nose to tail, and 107 feet high to its shoulder. It was re-designed on a site of a much older figure thought to mark the spot where King Alfred scored one of his biggest successes against the invading Danes, historically pinpointed as Ethandune or Edington, in the year 878. This earlier figure was considered a bit too cart-horsey for 18th-century tastes. More chalk-cut figures decorate the hills near Salisbury Plain, this time regimental badges carved by soldiers stationed at nearby camps during World War I.

Stonehenge and Avebury

If you are a push-over for prehistoric remains, this is your county.
Stonehenge, of course, takes first place; a lone, eerie collection of stones
so placed that the sun does all sorts of odd things with them on certain
days of the year. Stonehenge is the best example in Britain of these groups
of ancient stone relics known as Druids' circles, although almost certainly
not erected by that mysterious sect, about whom almost nothing definite
is known. Stonehenge has been so intensely the object of modern tourism,
so obsessed are we today by cults and unexplained phenomena, that it has
had to be fenced off for its own protection. Seen thus, like a captive animal,
decrepit and encaged, Stonehenge loses much of its impressive impact. But
even if it takes an effort of the imagination to picture these monoliths as
they once were, it is an effort worth making. A number of waymarked
trails have recently been laid out here, linking Stonehenge to nearby archeological sites.

Avebury, west of Marlborough, and even older than Stonehenge, is a
complex monument consisting of several huge stone circles inside 4,000-
year-old grassgrown banks and ditches, while a mile-long avenue of these
great bulky stones leads off in the direction of Overton Hill. Largest of
its kind in Europe, and seeming to engulf the little village of the same
name, some of the stones have since fallen and some are missing altogether, having been filched and broken up long ago and used as building material. In the museum on the site, among the many finds on show, are the
scissors of a 14th-century barber on whom one of the four-ton stones toppled. Naturally he didn't survive: they found his remains as well as his
more durable scissors.

A mile from Avebury is an enormous prehistoric mound called Silbury
Hill, an example of the tumuli that are scattered all over Wiltshire. Silbury,
however, is unique in that it's the largest artificial mound in Europe, being
450 yards round at the base, and 120 feet high. Why it was built or what
purpose it served is a mystery.

Circuiting the county west and northward, we come to Swindon, a busy
rail center, with a small railway museum, and not far away Wanborough
and its 400-year-old Harrow Inn, in which is an ancient wooden pulley
allegedly used to string up customers who misbehaved themselves. A more
likely use was to hoist contraband to the attic. Exhibit No. 2 is an old "dog
grate," a relic of days when the landlady put a dog in a cage in the chimney
to drive a spit. Some venerable inns are linked with a past even older than
themselves. The Angel, Chippenham, was built on part of the site of the
ancient palace of King Alfred; it still exhibits a sentry look-out.

Four miles south of Chippenham is one of the most beautiful villages
in southwest England—Lacock—where in 1839 Fox Talbot conducted his
early photographic experiments. The village is now owned by the National
Trust, a delightful place to wander in—shops, cafes and pubs all handy—
the whole place impeccably cared for. Lacock Abbey, where Fox Talbot
once lived, is a 13th-century convent converted to a private house in the
16th century; the medieval cloisters are still in good order and can be visited.

Level with Lacock and a little to the east is Bowood Park, standing on
Derry Hill in superb grounds which can never have been better kept than

they are now. Just a small number of rooms in the house, containing art pieces and family heirlooms most imaginatively arranged, are open to the public. Its smallness is very much in its favor.

Another dream village is Castle Combe, also near Chippenham, though it has been slightly spoiled by American film-makers, who "redecorated" it for *The Story of Dr. Dolittle*. Bradford-on-Avon not only has one of the most perfect small Saxon churches in England, but also an interesting example of a type of bridge that the medieval monasteries used to build, erecting a chapel at its end to remind wayfarers of the industry of these religious foundations.

Longleat and Salisbury

A little farther on—beyond Warminster, itself lying astride a scattered miscellany of ancient battlegrounds—rise the noble outlines of Longleat House, home of the Marquess of Bath, with a name all to itself on the map. The house is the country's prize gem of Elizabethan architecture and is approached by a long, leafy drive of towering rhododendrons. Started in 1568, it was completed during Elizabethan times. Its leather-lined library contains one of the largest private collections in Europe. Good Queen Bess was served in its banquet hall where a Sèvres dining service stands ready for another royal visit. A costume museum displays breakfast bonnets, wedding garments, and other rare period robes. More recently, Longleat has been making a name for itself as the stately home where lions roam free in the grounds—a brilliant stroke of showmanship by the Marquess of Bath, who was the first of the aristocratic entrepreneurs in this field. His enterprise has attracted thousands of visitors to the house, who now have the added fun of mingling with cheetahs, giraffes, and roaming monkeys (keep your car windows closed if you don't want them to climb inside).

South of Longleat, near the village of Mere, is Stourhead. Although the house is attractive, it is the grounds that must draw anyone interested in the art of landscape gardening. Around an elongated lake are arranged forests of rhododendrons, variegated trees, classical temples, all the ingredients of a gardener's dream. The effect, especially when the flowering bushes are out, is breathtaking. The house is separated from the grounds by a small hill.

In fact, Wiltshire is enormously rich in houses and gardens that can be visited, quite apart from all the Ancient Monuments which are there for the finding. And none has more than Salisbury where the cathedral and its setting must surely rank as one of the most beautiful in England. The spire can be seen from almost any approach to the town where you choose to pause, while the first sight of the cathedral as a whole is most impressive through St. Anne's Gate. It is unique in that it was conceived as a whole and built throughout in early English style between 1220 and 1258, although the spire was added in the 14th century. Inside are lancet windows, a 14th-century clock of wrought iron, tombs of Crusaders and of those who died at Agincourt. Don't overlook the beautiful octagonal chapter house with sixty wondrously carved 13th—century friezes upheld by a single pillar and a fan-span to the roof. One of the four existing copies of the Magna Carta is kept here, where it was brought for safe-keeping shortly after 1265.

The cathedral Close provides an impressive setting, with its smooth lawns and splendid examples of architecture of all ages (except modern) creating a harmonious background. The town of Salisbury itself was also conceived as a whole, on the grid system, which to a large extent remains. It is a town full of interest. Wherever you look there is something to delight or instruct, and the local tourist office organizes walks—of different lengths for varying stamina—to lead visitors to the treasures. Even if you are normally slightly allergic to this sort of thing, you will find a two-hour walk highly rewarding, discovering things which you would never have found alone.

Close to Salisbury is Wilton House, the splendid home of the Earls of Pembroke, with an incomparable art collection—including 16 van Dyck canvases hung in the famous double cube room where General Eisenhower planned the Normandy invasion. Here too, close to Wilton House, is the home of the Wilton Carpet factory—a great inducement to buy since it, too, can be visited.

Old Sarum and Marlborough

Immediately north of Salisbury is Old Sarum, the original site of the Bishop's see and now above all a spot from which to view Salisbury and tune in to the past. From there an unclassified road delightfully follows the course of the River Avon right up to Pewsey where a famed white horse is cut in the downs. The Kennet & Avon Canal passes nearby. For any canal buff this is happy hunting ground because the canal is repeatedly crossed by small roads which supply access and view points, while outside Devizes is the 29-lock Caen Hill Flight—a series of locks like a staircase.

Following the road north of Pewsey one reaches Marlborough, a singularly attractive small town perched on the A4. This road, forerunner of the motorway M4, is the old Bath Road, well known in coaching days and now much to be recommended to tourists. If you join it at the M4 junction 12, after about 23 miles into Berkshire you emerge just west of Savernake Forest, a strange place well worth visiting, and so to Marlborough, Avebury, Calne, Chippenham, with endless places to left and right worth a detour. Because the old, historic road has been superseded by the motorway, it is almost devoid of heavy traffic, and well-primed with good, ancient inns.

Marlborough should not, however, be regarded simply as a point on the A4. Besides having an almost uniquely wide High Street, it has a history which goes back well before the Romans and has been pretty lively ever since. It was fought over during the Civil War, and nearly destroyed by fire in 1653, again in 1679 and yet again in 1690. As a result of this the general aspect is Georgian, but there are much older houses to be found here and there, including at least one of the houses of Marlborough College, the famous public school.

PRACTICAL INFORMATION FOR THE SOUTH

HOW TO GET THERE FROM LONDON. All the large towns of the south and inner southwest are easily accessible by train from London—as far west as Bournemouth for days out. It is well worth enquiring at British Rail Travel Centers to see if there are any special offers to places of interest which include rail travel, admission and coach travel to and from the place to be visited—all at a discount price. For example there are often special offers for days out to the Salisbury/Stonehenge area. The majority of the region is covered by the *Network Southeast Card*—see page 186. Many of the important towns can also be reached almost as easily by the services of National Express. Unfortunately deregulation has drastically reduced the bus services to the smaller rural towns and villages. In many cases by setting off early you can have time to explore as well as a leisurely lunch. But be sure to check the bus times carefully and if in doubt ask. At the main railway stations there are usually notice boards which give details of local public transport—where the buses go, when and where to catch them. If not, ask at the information office and they will tell you where you can find out.

Bournemouth. By train: two trains an hour from Waterloo, with the fast service taking about 1 hour 40 minutes for the 108 miles. All fast and semifast trains have a buffet car. A good bus service connects the railway station to the town center. A very pleasant ride, especially through the New Forest. **By coach:** also a very good service from Victoria Coach Station; as well as hourly coaches via Heathrow Airport and Southampton which take about 3 hours, there are six nonstop journeys a day, taking 2 hours 35 minutes. The 9.30 nonstop from Victoria and 16.50 return allow over 4½ hours in the town for a day return fare of £9.20. The last return coach leaves Bournemouth coach station in the early evening. There are also six nonstop Rapide services each way per day, with a journey time of 2 hours 15 minutes. The outward Rapide coaches are not generally well timed for a day trip. **By car:** M3, A33, M27, A31, A338.

Portsmouth. By train: there are two routes available, but the only one worth using is that from Waterloo via Woking and Guildford. There is a service of two fast trains an hour which run through to the Harbour station. For Portsmouth town center, alight at Portsmouth and Southsea. For the ferry service to the Isle of Wight and harbor tours of HMS Victory and HMS Warrior, stay on to the Harbour station. The run from London takes 1½ hours for the complete trip on the fastest service. **By coach:** the National Express service from Victoria is basically hourly and stops at the Continental Ferry terminal and the Hard (adjacent to Portsmouth Harbour station). The journey takes 2½ hours. **By car:** A3.

Salisbury. By train: the frequency of trains from Waterloo is basically hourly and takes 1 hour 24 minutes for the fast trains, just under 1¾ hours for the semifasts. The railway station is a good 10 minutes' walk from the city center. The rail journey is very picturesque. Train and coach packages are also available, visiting Stonehenge via Salisbury. **By coach:** National Express run a two-hourly service from Victoria Coach Station. The 09.00 departure and 16.55 return allow almost 5 hours in the city. The journey takes 3 hours. Several tour operators, including *Evan Evans* and *Thomas Cook,* offer day excursions to Salisbury, often combining this with a visit to Stonehenge. **By car:** M3, A30.

Southampton. By train: first-class service of three trains an hour from Waterloo—fast, semifast and stopping. The first two do the run in 70 minutes and 85 minutes respectively. The railway station is close to the city center. Do not get off the train at Southampton Parkway. In order to visit Broadlands, the home of the late Lord Mountbatten of Burma at Romsey, change onto the local service at Southampton. The semifast train from London offers the best connection onto this service, and it only takes 13 minutes for the short journey to Romsey. **By coach:** an excellent service of one coach an hour from 08.30 to 23.30. The coach travels via Heathrow Airport, calling at the Bus/Underground interchange and takes 2 hours. There are several conveniently timed return services in the late afternoon. Much cheaper than the parallel rail service. **By car:** M3, A33.

Swindon. (Good for getting to Malmesbury, Avebury etc. Change here for Stroud, Gloucester and Cheltenham.)
By train: an excellent InterCity 125 service from London Paddington station of one, sometimes two trains an hour. The fast trains cover the 77 miles in under 1 hour, sometimes as little as 48 minutes. From Swindon there is an hourly service along the very picturesque line to Stroud, Gloucester and Cheltenham. Connections to and from this service onto the mainline trains are very good with little waiting. **By coach:** there is at least a two-hourly service (from 08.00 to 20.00) from London/Victoria. It runs mostly on the M4 motorway, calling at Heathrow Central Bus/Underground interchange en route, and takes 1 hour 50 minutes for the trip. **By car:** M4.

Winchester. By train: trains every hour from Waterloo, takes just over 1 hour, with all trains having a buffet service. **By coach:** every 2 hours from Victoria Coach Station. Coaches take exactly 2 hours for the run.

HOW TO GET AROUND. The Southern Region of *British Rail* operate fast services throughout this part of the country from Waterloo Station. Some of the InterCity trains cut travel time considerably with the suburban trains serving the same route. On most Southern routes there is usually one fast train per hour, and they normally depart at the "same minutes" past each hour, making it simple to remember times. Regional Coach and Bus services—there is a dense network of coach and bus routes in Southern England. The coach system is continually expanding and more frequent services are being run. So you are well advised to check with National Express at Victoria Coach Station or an appointed agent. See *Facts at Your Fingertips.*
New Forest. Horse-drawn wagon rides make a happy change from public transport. They plod slowly through unfrequented ways, with a chance to see the countryside and wild life at close quarters. Details from *New Forest Wagons,* Balmer Lawn Rd., Brockenhurst, Hants., tel. (0590) 23633.

HOW TO GET TO THE ISLE OF WIGHT. There are 4 main routes to the Island.
1 Lymington Pier-Yarmouth: car ferry operated by *Sealink-British Ferries.* Rail travelers from Waterloo should change at Brockenhurst onto the branch line train to Lymington–Pier.

2 Southampton–Owes: car ferry and passenger only hydrofoil. Both *Red Funnel* services from Royal Pier. There is a connecting bus from the railway and coach stations in Southampton; also connecting buses from Cowes to Newport.

3 Portsmouth–Ryde: passenger only service. *Sealink-British Ferries* from Portsmouth Harbour to Ryde pierhead. Trains from Waterloo terminate at the Harbour station and it is only a very short walk to the ferry. National Express coaches to Portsmouth call at the ferry terminal. Ryde Pierhead is connected by rail to Ryde Town and Shanklin, and by direct bus to Newport.

4 Portsmouth–Fishbourne: *Sealink-British Ferries* car ferry reaches the Island a couple of miles west of Ryde.

National Express run services from London Victoria Coach Station to Southampton for the Red Funnel hydrofoil/ferry to Cowes, and to the Hard in Portsmouth for the ferry to Ryde. The interchange is easy at both points.

HOTELS AND RESTAURANTS. Many of the hotels and restaurants listed here are not open in the winter months and it is advisable to check through the National Tourist Board or Regional Tourist Office if you travel out of season. Details about our grading system, plus other relevant information about hotels and restaurants, will be found at the beginning of the book in the *Facts at Your Fingertips* section.

Abbotsbury (Dorset). **Restaurant.** *Manor Hotel* (M), Beach Rd., West Bexington, tel. (0308) 897616. English and French cuisine in restaurant with rooms (10) for overnighters.

Amesbury (Wilts). *Antrobus Arms* (M), tel. (0980) 23163; 20 rooms, 12 with bath. A former vicarage with walled garden and restaurant. 1½ miles from Stonehenge.

Basingstoke (Hants). *Red Lion* (M), London St., tel. (0256) 28525; 63 rooms, 31 with bath, 32 with shower. 17th-century coaching inn in the town center, with pleasant, beamed restaurant.

At nearby **Rotherwick,** *Tylney Hall* (L–E), tel. (025672) 4881; 37 rooms with bath, some with four poster beds. Refurbished historic country house in spacious grounds, with restaurant as well.

Beanacre (Wilts). *Beechfield House* (M), tel. (0225) 703700. 8 rooms plus 8 in adjacent coach house, all with bath and shower. Victorian mansion, beautifully restored and with excellent restaurant. Garden, coarse fishing, tennis, croquet, heated swimming pool. Near Bath, Badminton, Lacock Abbey and Longleat.

Beaulieu (Hants). *Montagu Arms* (M), tel. (0590) 612324; 26 rooms with bath; creeper-clad, redbrick hotel, traditional atmosphere, restaurant, pleasant garden.

Bembridge (I.O.W.). *Highbury* (M), tel. (0983) 872838; 9 rooms, 7 with bath, 2 with shower. Small, homely villa-style hotel, with Victorian decor. Garden, swimming pool, croquet, sauna, solarium. Renowned for personal service and its *Restaurant* (M), with traditional copper pans and white rough-cut walls. Reasonably priced continental and local cuisine.

Blandford Forum (Dorset). **Restaurant.** *La Belle Alliance* (M), tel. (0258) 52842. Restaurant with rooms (4). French bias to carefully selected menu, making full use of fresh produce. Closed Sun eve.

Bonchurch (I.O.W.). *Lake Hotel* (M–E), Shore Rd., tel. (0983) 852613. 21 rooms, 17 with bath. Georgian-style, village hotel which offers excellent food and relaxing views.

Bournemouth (Dorset). *Carlton* (L), Meyrick Rd., East Overcliff, tel. (0202) 22011; 66 rooms with bath. Justly treasured by its many devotees as a hotel-home away from home. *Royal Bath* (L), Bath Rd., tel. (0202) 25555; 135 rooms with bath. Much more impressive inside, with enjoyable Buttery restaurant. Both have heated pools, plenty of leisure amenities and good views.
Langtry Manor (M), Derby Rd., East Cliff, tel. (0202) 23887. 30 rooms with bath. Built by Edward VII as a love nest for his mistress Lily Langtry, this hotel has retained its romantic, Edwardian ambience. 8 rooms with four-posters. Fine restaurant with Edwardian banquet every Sat.
Normandie (M), Manor Rd., East Cliff, tel. (0202) 22246; 70 rooms, all with bath, and *Palace Court* (M), Westover Rd., tel. (0202) 27681, 107 rooms with bath, are reasonably priced alternatives. Both have sauna, solarium and gymnasium.
Restaurants. *La Taverna* (M), Westover Rd., tel. (0202) 27681; comfortable restaurant with good service and French-inspired menus. Closed Sun. *Henry's* (I), 6 Lansdowne Rd., tel. (0202) 297887. Imaginative vegetarian cuisine.

Brockenhurst (Hants). *Ladbroke Balmer Lawn* (M), tel. (0590) 23116; 58 rooms, 54 with bath, 4 with shower. In the peaceful heart of the New Forest, with good sporting amenities.
Restaurant. *Le Poussin* (M), tel. (0590) 23063. Interesting French and English cuisine. Also rooms (5) available.

Bucklers Hard (Hants). *Master Builders House Hotel* (M), tel. (059 063) 253; 23 rooms, 17 with bath. Beautiful location. Beside Beaulieu river with nautical interior. Ideal yachting/walking center. Booking essential.

Burley (Hants). *Burley Manor* (M), tel. (042 53) 3522; 22 rooms with bath. Elegant country manor house set in spacious parklands. Good leisure amenities.

Castle Combe (Wilts). *Manor House* (E), tel. (0249) 782206, 32 rooms with bath. Provides traditional English comfort; a superb setting in splendid parkland. Its restaurant (E) is noted for the variety of dishes based on fresh local produce.

Charmouth (Dorset). *White House* (M), tel. (0297) 60411; 6 rooms with bath. Most attractive, friendly guest house providing reasonably priced meals.

Chideock (Dorset). *Chideock House* (M–I), tel. (029 789) 242. 15th-century stone house, 9 rooms, 8 with bath or shower. Restaurant. Service with a personal touch. *Clock House* (I), tel (029 789) 423. 6 rooms, 1 with bath. Bedrooms with sloping floors and low ceilings are typical of this thatched cottage-style hostelry in the town center.

Cowes (I.O.W.). *Holmwood* (E), tel. (0983) 292508; 19 rooms, 7 with bath, 7 with shower. French cuisine. Overlooking the Solent. Be sure to reserve well ahead for Cowes Week.
Restaurant. *Gisaine's* (M), Bath Rd., tel. (0983) 297021. Intimate, candlelit French restaurant, with covered terrace for alfresco eating.

Dorchester (Dorset). *King's Arms* (E), 30 High East St., tel. (0305) 65353. 34 rooms with bath. Quiet comfort and excellent service. Setting for parts of Hardy's *Mayor of Casterbridge. Antelop* (M), tel. (0305) 63001; 18 rooms, 7 with bath or shower. 17th century coaching inn with memories of the infamous Judge Jeffreys.
Restaurant. *Embers* (M–L), North Sq., tel. (0305) 67679. Friendly brasserie-cum-restaurant. *Mock Turtle* (M), 34 High West St., tel. (0305) 64011. Unusual French or West African cooking at this popular restaurant.

Droxford (Hants). *Coach House Motel* (M), Hambledon Rd., tel. (0489) 877812. 9 rooms with bath. Converted coach house with modern accommodation and fine views of the Meon Valley.

Ferndown (Dorset). *Dormy* (E), tel. (0202) 872020; 133 rooms, 128 with bath, 5 with shower. Bungalows in spacious grounds, indoor pool, tennis and championship golf course next door. Good leisure facilities.

Freshwater (I.O.W.). *Farringford* (M), tel. (0983) 752500; 15 rooms with bath. 200 year old stone house, formerly Tennyson's home. Park and gardens, outdoor pool, tennis. Also self-catering bungalows. Good sea fishing and golf (9-hole course at hotel and 18-holer nearby).

Lacock (Wilts). *Sign of the Angel* (M), tel. (024 973) 230; 6 rooms with bath; 14th-century hostelry in National Trust village. One of the best for traditional English food, setting and service. Book well in advance.

Lulworth (Dorset). *Castle Inn* (I), tel. West Lulworth (092 941) 311; 16 rooms, 10 with bath. A picturesque thatched inn; comfortable port of call with hot and cold buffet lunches and small separate restaurant which serves seafood. *Lulworth Cove* (I), tel. West Lulworth (092 941) 333; 11 rooms, 3 with bath, 7 with shower. Some rooms overlook Cove. A la carte restaurant.

Lyme Regis (Dorset). *Alexandra* (M), Pound St., tel. (029 74) 2010; 26 rooms, 22 with bath. Wide views over the bay. *Mariners* (M), tel. (029 74) 2753. Characterful old coaching inn with 16 rooms, overlooking the harbor, with excellent restaurant. *Royal Lion* (M), tel. (029 74) 2768; 25 rooms, 15 with bath, 10 with shower. Charming 16th-century coaching inn.

Lymington (Hants). *Passford House* (E), Mount Pleasant, tel. (0590) 682398. 56 rooms with bath. In own parkland, comfortable. Croquet, putting, tennis, snooker, sauna, solarium, swimming pool. *Stanwell House* (M), tel. (0590) 77123. 33 rooms, 30 with bath. Georgian building on High St. Good restaurant.

Restaurant. *Limpets* (M), Gosport St., tel. (0590) 75595. French-inspired menu in small, simple bistro. Closed Sun. and Mon.

Lyndhurst (Hants). *Beaulieu Hotel* (M), Beaulieu Rd., tel. (042129) 2141. 8 rooms, 3 with bath. Relaxing 18th-century country hotel in the heart of the New Forest. A la carte restaurant. *Parkhill House* (M), Beaulieu Rd., tel. (042 128) 2944. 22 rooms, 20 with bath, 2 with shower. Set in own park. Coarse fishing available. Reliable restaurant (M). *Pike's Hill Forest Lodge* (M), Romsey Rd., tel. (042 128) 3677; 20 rooms, 11 with bath, 4 with shower. Friendly Georgian country house with good standard bedrooms, and an interesting à la carte menu. Heated outdoor swimming pool.

Malmesbury (Wilts). *Whatley Manor* (E), Easton Grey, tel. (066 62) 2888; 25 rooms with bath. Cotswold stone manor house with elegant restaurant. *Old Bell* (M), Abbey Row, tel. (0666) 822344; 19 rooms, 15 with bath or shower. Delightfully old-fashioned with lovely gardens, rooms and friendly staff. New garden annex.

Marlborough (Wilts). *Castle & Ball* (M), tel. (0672) 55201; 38 rooms, 7 with bath, a coaching inn. 5 miles away in peaceful countryside at Burbage is the *Savernake Forest* (M), tel. (0672) 810206; 12 rooms with bath. Well worth the detour; family-run with wine-bar and traditional English fare. Coarse fishing available and beautiful forest nearby.

Restaurant. *The Loaves and Fishes* (M–E), Rockley Chapel, Rockley, tel. (0672) 53737. 3 miles from Marlborough. A converted country chapel specializing in English cooking. Closed Mon. and Tues.

Mere (Wilts). *Old Ship* (M), tel. (0747) 860258; 24 rooms, 14 with bath, 2 with shower. Famous for its superb hospitality and quiet charm.

New Milton (Hants). *Chewton Glen* (L), tel. (042 52) 5341; 44 rooms with bath. Stands in lovely woods and gardens and offers the feel of 18th-century life, combined with high contemporary standards. Recommended for comfort and cuisine (a *Relais de Campagne* hotel), but remember that it *is* a very expensive spot. Their *Marryat Room* (L) is one of the finest restaurants in the country, with a distinguished French chef and superb wine list.

Piddletrenthide (Dorset). *Old Bakehouse* (M–I), tel. (03004) 305. 9 rooms with bath. Friendly, family-run country hotel. Outdoor heated pool and gardens. Receives praise for excellent pheasant in season.

Portsmouth (Hants). *Holiday Inn* (E), tel. (0705) 383151. 170 rooms with bath. Good leisure facilities. Views over harbor and castle. *Portsmouth Crest* (E), tel. (0705) 827651; 165 rooms with bath. *Hospitality Inn* (E–M), South Parade, Southsea, tel. (0705) 731281. 115 rooms with bath.

Pendragon (E–M), Clarence Parade, Southsea, tel. (0705) 823201; 49 rooms with bath.

Restaurant. *Bistro Montparnasse* (M), 103 Palmerston Rd., Southsea, tel. (0705) 816754. Candles, prints and pink tablecloths help create the intimate atmosphere of a traditional French restaurant.

Ryde (I.O.W.). Popular resort with sandy beaches overlooking the Solent. *The Ryde Castle* (E), The Esplanade, tel. (0983) 63755. 17 rooms with bath. Ivy-clad walls, battlements and four-poster beds set the scene at this first-class hotel. Two restaurants. *Yelf's* (M), tel. (0983) 64062; 21 rooms with bath. Informal and friendly.

Restaurant. *Biskra House* (M–E), 17 St. Thomas St., tel. (0983) 67913. High standard Italian and international cuisine in an elegant dining room with sea views. Also less formal Fondue Cellar.

Salisbury (Wilts). *Red Lion* (E), Milford St., tel. (0722) 23334; 59 rooms, almost all with bath. Former coaching inn dating from 14th century. *Rose and Crown* (M), Harnham Rd., tel. (0722) 27908; 27 rooms with bath. Combines idyllic views of the river and cathedral with low-beamed atmosphere.

Restaurant. *Harpers* (M), Market Sq., tel. (0722) 333118; good value, particularly at lunchtime. Closed Sun.

Shaftesbury (Dorset). *Royal Chase* (M), tel. (0747) 3355; 32 rooms, 27 with bath, 3 with shower. Converted Georgian country house, once a monastery. Traditional food. Friendly atmosphere.

Shanklin (I.O.W.). Sea fishing and golf available. *Cliff Tops* (M), tel. (0983) 863262; 96 rooms with bath. Modern, refurbished hotel with good views and new leisure complex. *Luccombe Hall* (M), tel. (0983) 862719. 31 rooms, 27 with bath, 3 with shower. Overlooking the bay.

Restaurant. *Punch's Bistro* (M), tel. (0983) 864454. French-style cooking—dinner only. Closed Mon.

Southampton (Hants). (*See* also Lyndhurst—8 miles.) *Dolphin* (E), High St., tel. (0703) 26178; 74 rooms, 68 with bath, 5 with shower. Has charm and good service. The modern *Post House* (M), Herbert Walker Ave., tel. (0703) 228081; 132 rooms with bath, overlooks the docks, with magnificent view down Southampton Water. Outdoor heated swimming pool.

Restaurant. *Jeeves* (E), Terminus House, Terminus Ter., tel. (0703) 221021. *Nouvelle cuisine* complemented by soft lighting and art nouveau decor. Closed Sun. and Mon.

Studland (Dorset). *Knoll House* (M), tel. (092 944) 251; 79 rooms, 56 with bath. Delightful rambling hotel amidst pine trees, with heated pools and golf. Handy to beach. Closed Oct.-March.

Ventnor (I.O.W.). *Winterbourne* (M), tel. (0983) 852535, 20 rooms with bath. One of the most beautiful hotels in the country, overlooking the sea with a stream running through the terraced garden. Where Charles Dickens wrote much of *David Copperfield*. Restaurant.

Wareham (Dorset). *The Priory* (E), tel. (092 95) 2772; 19 rooms, 17 with bath. Stands in beautiful gardens beside the River Frome. Finely furnished, good breakfasts and cellar restaurant.

Warminster (Wilts). *Bishopstrow House* (L), tel. (0985) 212312; 26 rooms with bath. Ever-improving hotel run like a private house. Charming decor, excellent service, set amidst 27 acres, underpass leading to river frontage.
Restaurant. *La Petite Cuisine Belge* (M), 60–62 East St., tel. (0985) 215052. Pine-furnished dining room with patio. Belgian specialties. Closed Sun. and Mon. lunchtime.

Wickham (Hants). *Old House* (M), tel. (0329) 833049; 10 rooms with bath or shower. Attractive Georgian house. The restaurant is excellent and the bedrooms charming. Staff friendly. Must book.

Wimborne Minster (Dorset). *King's Head* (M), tel. (0202) 880101; 28 rooms, 17 with bath. On the Square, and covered with creepers.

Winchester (Hants). *Lainston House* (L), Sparsholt, tel. (0962) 63588. 32 rooms, 31 with bath. In listed 17th-century house. Well-thought-of restaurant providing classic continental fare. *Wessex* (E), Paternoster Row, tel. (0962) 61611; 94 rooms with bath. Modern and very comfortable beside the cathedral.
Restaurant. *Old Chesil Rectory* (M), tel. (0962) 53177, offers traditional English cooking in a 15th-century rectory.

PLACES OF INTEREST. This is one of the regions of England which contains a rich mixture of historic buildings—with one or two of the greatest. Wiltshire, especially, has Longleat and Wilton House, as well as the breathtaking gardens of Stourhead. One of the intriguing points is the survival of medieval buildings, for this was an area rich in abbeys and monasteries, as well as containing the once-vastly-powerful Winchester.

There are further notes on visiting historic houses in *Facts At Your Fingertips,* and a discussion of the subject in the *Historic Houses—Precious Stones in Peril* chapter.

Dorset. Athelhampton, near Puddletown (tel. 030 584 363). Splendid stone-built medieval house with enchanting gardens. Open Easter–mid-Oct., Wed., Thurs., Sun., Good Fri., Bank Holidays, 2–6; also Mon. and Tues. in Aug.
Clouds Hill, near Wareham. Home of Lawrence of Arabia after World War I. Open Apr.–Sept., Wed., Thurs., Fri., Sun., Good Fri., Bank Holiday Mon., 2–5; Oct.–Mar., Sun. only 1–4. (NT)
Forde Abbey, near Chard. 12th-century Cistercian monastery with beautiful tapestries and gardens. Open Apr.–mid-Oct., Sun., Wed., 2–6. Also all Bank Holiday Mon., 2–6. Gardens open all year, daily 10.30–4.30.
Hardy's Cottage, Higher Bockhampton (tel. 0305 62366). The author's birthplace and home until 1928. Interior open by appointment, garden, Apr.–Oct., daily except Tues. morning, 11–6. (NT)
Kingston Lacy House, Wimborne Minster. 17th-century house with 19th-century alterations. In 250-acre wooded parkland. Open end of Apr.

through Oct., Sat.–Wed., 1–5; park 12–6. Access to house may be limited on busy summer days. (NT)

Purse Caundle Manor, near Sherborne (tel. 0963 250400). Medieval manor house. Open Easter Mon.–Sept., Thurs., Sun. and Bank Holidays, 2–5.

Russell-Cotes Art Gallery and Museum, Bournemouth (tel. 0202 21009). Victorian pseudo-Italian villa with an admirable collection, strong on watercolors, but including Henry Irving memorabilia and Bournemouth's last bath chair among other attractions. All year, Mon.–Sat. 10–5.30. Gardens, June–Sept.

Sherborne Castle, Sherborne (tel. 093581 3182). Interesting 16thcentury house lived in by the Digby family since 1617. Open Easter–Sept., Thurs., Sat., Sun., Bank Holiday Mon., 2–6.

Wolfeton House, Dorchester (tel. 0305 63500). Magnificent Frenchlooking, medieval and Elizabethan house, full of interest. May–Sept., Tues., Fri., Sun., Bank Holiday Mon., 2–6; also daily (except Sat.) during Aug. 2–6.

Hampshire. Jane Austen's House, Chawton (tel. 0420 83262). Open daily Apr.–Oct. plus Wed.–Sun. in Mar., Nov. and Dec. Closed Jan. and Feb. All 11–4.30.

Beaulieu, Beaulieu (tel. 0590 612345). Fascinating National Motor Museum as well as the Palace House and Gardens, The Abbey and Exhibition of Monastic Life. Lots to see and do for all tastes. Easter–Sept., daily, 10–6; Oct–Easter, daily, 10–5.

Breamore House, near Fordingbridge (tel. 0725 22270). Fine Elizabethan Manor House. Also Countryside and Carriage Museums. Open Apr., Tues., Wed., Sun. and Easter Hol.; May–July and Sept., Tues., Wed., Thurs., Sat., Sun. and Bank Hol.; Aug., daily. All 2–5.30.

Broadlands, Romsey (tel. 0794 516878). Former home of Lord Palmerston and Earl Mountbatten. Adam interior and Capability Brown park and gardens close to the River Test. Open Apr.–Sept., daily (except Mon. Apr.–Jul., unless Bank Holiday), 10–6 (last admission 5).

D-Day Museum, Portsmouth (tel. 0705 827261). Exciting new museum incorporating the Overlord Embroidery depicting the Allied invasion of Normandy. Displays D-Day in action. Open daily 10.30–5.30.

Mary Rose, Portsmouth (tel. 0705 812931/750521). The famous rescue of this Tudor warship remembered. Reconstruction and conservation of the ship itself in the Ship Hall. Exhibition displays the ship's treasures. Open daily 10.30–5.

The Pilgrims' Hall, Winchester Cathedral Close. 14th-century hall. Open daily year round, 10–6, except when privately booked.

Southampton Art Gallery, Southampton (tel. 0703 832769). British painting (much contemporary), French 19th century. Open Tues.–Fri., 10–5; Sat., 10–4; Sun., 2–5. Closed Mon.

Stansted Park, near Havant (tel. 0705 412265). A neo-Wren house, ancient walled gardens, arboretum and theater museum, all set in forest surroundings. Open Easter Sun. and Mon., May–Sept., Sun.–Tues., 2–6.

Stratfield Saye House, Reading (tel. 0256 882882). Dating from the reign of Charles I, home of the Dukes of Wellington since it was presented to the Great Duke in 1817. Wellington Exhibition, State Coach, Great Duke's Funeral Carriage, paintings, furniture, personal effects etc. Open

Easter weekend, Sat. and Sun. in Apr., then daily (excl. Fri.) May–Sept., 11.30–5.

Isle of Wight. Arreton Manor, near Newport (tel. 0983 528134). 17th-century manor house with early and late Stuart furniture. Fine pictures and a good Folk Collection. Open Easter–end Oct., Mon.–Fri. 10–6, Sun. 12–6.

Carisbrooke Castle, Newport (tel. 0983 522107). Seven acres of castle and earthworks. Contains the island's museum which features the history of the Isle of Wight plus relics of Charles I, who was imprisoned in the castle. Castle open daily, mid-Mar.–mid-Oct., 9.30–6.30; in winter, 9.30–4; opens Sun. Apr.–Sept. at 11, otherwise at 2.

Golden Hill Fort, Freshwater (tel. 0983 753380). Craft center and military museum within one of Lord Palmerston's forts (an intriguing architectural folly). Open daily all year, 10–6.

Osborne House, near East Cowes (tel. 0983 200033). The favorite residence of Queen Victoria. Open Apr.–Oct., Mon.–Sat. 10–5; Sun. 11–5.

Wiltshire. Alexander Keiller Museum, Avebury (tel. 067 23 250). Pottery and other Neolithic objects from excavations in the area. Open mid-Mar.–mid-Oct., weekdays 9.30–6.30, Sun. 2–6.30 (9.30–6.30 Apr.–Sept.); mid-Oct.–mid-Mar., weekdays 9.30–4, Sun. 2–4.

Bowood House, Calne (tel. 0249 812102). Marvelous gardens, plus exhibition rooms. Open Apr.–Sept., daily, 11–6.

Corsham Court, near Chippenham (tel. 0249 712214). Elizabethan and Georgian house with lovely furniture and paintings. Fine park and gardens. Open mid-Jan.–mid-Dec., daily (except Mon., unless Bank Holiday, and Fri.), 2–4.30; June–Sept., 2–6. Otherwise by appointment.

Lacock Abbey, near Chippenham. 13th-century abbey, converted 1540. Later Georgian "gothick" additions. In one of the most beautiful villages in England. Open Apr.–Nov., daily (except Tues. and Good Fri.), 2–6. In a 16th-century barn at the abbey's gates is the **Fox-Talbot Photographic Museum** (tel. 024 973 459). Open daily, Mar.–Oct., 11–6 (closed Good Fri.). (NT)

Longleat House, near Warminster (tel. 098 53 551). Home of Marquess of Bath. Built 1566–80, superb Renaissance building, lavishly decorated. One of the great houses of the world. Also lions and children's zoo. Open all year, daily 10–4; Easter–Sept., 10–6.

Stonehenge, 2 miles west of Amesbury. One of the world's greatest engineering feats, and Britain's most popular ancient monument. Open daily except Christmas and New Year.

Stourhead, Stourton, near Mere. 18th-century house with gorgeous gardens; house and gardens are quite separate. House open Apr. and Oct.–mid-Nov., Sat.–Wed. 2–6 (or dusk); May–Sept., daily (excl. Fri.), 2–6 (or dusk). Gardens daily all year, 8–7 (or dusk). (NT)

Wilton House, Salisbury (tel. 0722 743115). Noted for its double-cube room. Partly the work of Inigo Jones. Ancient lawns and cedars of Lebanon. Palladian bridge. Dollshouse, model soldier exhibition. Open Easter–early Oct., Tues.–Sat., Bank Holiday Mon., 11–6, Sun. 1–6.

THE SOUTHWEST

England's Sunshine Region

If you do have time to leave London for more than a few days, the southwest of England is one of the most rewarding and relaxing places to visit. The three counties that make up the long southern peninsula are *Somerset, Devon* and *Cornwall,* and each has a distinct individuality. In the peninsula you'll be surprised to discover a regionalism that amounts almost to patriotism. Each county has a local dialect and accent—although the former is often limited to the older inhabitants—and in some cases a local cuisine.

Somerset is noted for its rolling green countryside; Devon's wild and dramatic moors contrast with the restfulness of its many sandy beaches and coves. And Cornwall has managed to retain something of its old insularity, despite the annual invasion of thousands of holidaymakers.

The southwest is one of England's largest agricultural areas, and although industry is by no means absent, the skyline is rarely ruined by smoking chimneys and factory architecture. Devon and Cornwall have long coastlines, and have always had strong connections with the sea. Indeed, many of England's most famous sailors were born in the southwest. Then, because the new county of Avon refuses to sit comfortably anywhere, we have tacked it for convenience sake onto Somerset where most of it belonged, with Bristol and Bath playing lead.

SOMERSET AND AVON

If you care to progress from the southeast by car or local buses you can get to Bristol quite easily from Winchester via Salisbury, but most visitors will probably be starting from London, which is simplicity itself. Just follow the M4 to junction 19, then the M32 spur right into the city, 125 miles in all. There is also a super InterCity train service taking just over the hour from Paddington.

Bristol can be called the "birthplace of America" with some confidence, for it was from the old city docks of Bristol that John Cabot and his son Sebastian sailed in 1497 to the discovery of the American continent. Furthermore, Bristol was the home of William Penn, developer of Pennsylvania, and haven for John Wesley, whose Methodist movement played such a large part in the settling of Georgia.

Brunel's famous Suspension Bridge spans the beautiful Avon Gorge and is only a short bus-ride from the city center. His equally famous vessel, the S.S. *Great Britain,* the world's first ocean-going, screw-propelled iron ship, made its maiden voyage to New York in 1845. Now returned to its original dock in Bristol, it is in the process of restoration and open to the public. Next to it is the city's Maritime Heritage Center with its rare collection of relics, drawings and models.

Bristol, besides being a treasure-house of great historic interest, is well supplied with entertainment of all kinds. The famous Theater Royal, one of the oldest theaters in the country, is the home of the Bristol Old Vic. In the little back streets, with a bit of exploring, you will find the alleys devoted to the selling of secondhand books.

If you leave Bristol on the A4 to go to Bath, seek out the church of St. Mary Redcliffe, described by Queen Elizabeth I as "the fairest, goodliest and most famous parish church in England." It is to be found on Redcliffe Way, southeast of the city and its harbor, probably not without difficulty because of the complicated one-way system.

You can get to Bath from Bristol on A4, the last leg of the old coaching road which starts in London; or on M4 from junction 18 or, again, by Inter-City train from London. The problem with Bath is to know just where to begin. Its city status belies its size, for it is not a large place. Yet within modest confines, Bath manages to pack in a treasure chest of history and architecture unmatched in Britain. As an added bonus, the city has—again considering its size—an amazing range of shops, hotels and restaurants.

You should abandon the car when you come to Bath. The city is made for strolling. In the summer, the flower-decked streets throng with tourists from all over the world (one-quarter of Bath's two million annual visitors are from the United States). The famous Roman Baths are the main magnet. Next to the Tower of London, they are now reputedly Britain's top tourist attraction (in summer, you may wish that the place was not so popular).

, Bath's history really begins with the Romans. To them, Bath was known as *Aquae Sulis,* named after their goddess Sulis Minerva. In about A.D. 75

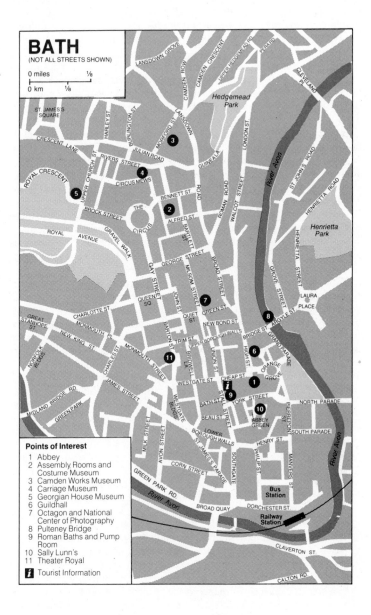

BATH
(NOT ALL STREETS SHOWN)

0 miles 1/8
0 km 1/8

ST. JAMES'S SQUARE

CRESCENT LANE

Hedgemead Park

Henrietta Park

River Avon

Points of Interest

1 Abbey
2 Assembly Rooms and Costume Museum
3 Camden Works Museum
4 Carriage Museum
5 Georgian House Museum
6 Guildhall
7 Octagon and National Center of Photography
8 Pulteney Bridge
9 Roman Baths and Pump Room
10 Sally Lunn's
11 Theater Royal

i Tourist Information

they founded a sacred temple around the only place in Britain which has a natural hot spring. The Romans, to whom hot baths were an essential ingredient of a civilized life, were delighted to discover thermal waters (bubbling to the surface at a constant temperature of 116 degrees Fahrenheit) around which they constructed an elaborate bathhouse complex that served as a partly religious, partly social center. Their baths, wonderfully intact in places, are amongst the greatest surviving Roman relics in Europe. Recent excavations on site have revealed even more about Roman life in Britain, while the remarkably complete Great Bath, its greeny, hot waters steaming in the open air, must look almost as it did 2,000 years ago.

Bath's other great glory is its Georgian architecture, a reflection of its fashionable status amongst English society from the 18th century onwards. The finesse and uniformity of building are largely due to architect John Wood and his eponymous son, who between them created a Palladian Bath inspired by visions of Rome. The city became a fashionable spa resort where the genteel English, presided over by Master of Ceremonies Richard "Beau" Nash, took the waters, promenaded by day and danced by night. Gainsborough, Lord Nelson and Queen Victoria, amongst many other luminaries, traveled here to sip the waters, which Dickens described as tasting like "warm flat irons." Jane Austen lived here and captured Bath in two of her novels, *Northanger Abbey* and *Persuasion.*

Bath's achievement—possibly unique in Britain—has been the preservation of this sense of period through its architecture. There are modern developments, of course, and although the marriage of old and new can never be an entirely happy one the city, more than most, has retained its integrity. 20th-century intrusions are muted through the use of the same warm, honey-coloured local stone with which Georgian Bath was built. Visitors are taken back in time in the sumptuous Pump Rooms, where tea is served amongst elegant surroundings and Chippendale furnishings to the strains of a trio of musicians (the adventurous can even try the spa water).

Surrounded by the bustling main streets and narrow shopping alleyways (selling everything from Antiques to books, craftware to high fashion) is the imposing, medieval edifice of Bath Abbey. Of the many museums and galleries here, don't miss the Royal Photographic Society's National Center of Photography and, on the hillside above the center of town, the Museum of Costume (in the grand Assembly Rooms), the Bath Carriage Museum (Britain's coaching past remembered), the unusual Camden Works Museum (perfectly preserved Victorian workshops), and Sally Lunn's (reputedly the oldest house in Bath—while there, sample the famous bun named after her).

The city's architectural high spot is undoubtedly found along its Royal Crescent, a semi-circle of 30 Georgian houses overlooking the city. Treat yourself to a stay at the superb Royal Crescent Hotel, or visit Number One, a house furnished in the style that recreates Bath's golden era. In the evening, take in a performance at the restored Theater Royal, a regional base for the National Theater. A summer music and arts festival usually lasts for two weeks from late May to early June, when opera, symphonies, choral and chamber music are performed (information in the U.S.A. is available from Edwards and Edwards, 1 Times Square, New York, NY 10036; tel. 212–944–0290).

Two miles away, in Claverton Manor, there is an American Museum, where each room is arranged by region and by period. The Georgian house is set in a splendid 55-acre estate. Eight miles further south and we are in Somerset proper. Like the whole of the southwest, it is intensely rural in character, but nowhere else does the countryside appear so rich and well-tended as in this serenely beautiful county. The secret of exploring Somerset is to ignore the main highways and just follow the signposts through the leafy narrow country roads that lead past miles of buttercup meadows and cider apple orchards to countless mellow villages of stone and thatch. The village names are music to the ears. There's Tintinhull, Midsomer Norton, Huish Episcopi, Bower Hinton, and dozens more, each with its architectural treasures.

In the center of Somerset is the strangely secretive lowland region known as Sedgemoor, criss-crossed with long dykes and reed beds, where King Alfred once hid from the marauding Danish armies of the ninth century. This was part of Alfred's Wessex, and memorials to him are widespread. Close to the Somerset/Wiltshire border is Alfred's Tower, a tall three-sided monument with a statue of the king in a high niche—a landmark for miles around. Athelney, to the south of it, is where—if you want to believe it—he hid with local sympathisers and, brooding over his lot, burnt their cakes.

To the east lie the Mendip Hills, slashed through at one point by the Cheddar Gorge, a miniature Grand Canyon of gray limestone riddled with miles of spectacular caverns. To the west rise the lovely wooded Quantocks, and beyond, finest of all, are the heathery heights of Exmoor, bounded by great cliffs that tumble headlong into the sea between Minehead and Porlock.

Taunton, more or less in the middle of Somerset, is the county town, a pleasant place, with a market and a fine shopping center. As a touring base Taunton is ideal, as it is set in the pleasant Vale of Taunton Deane, enclosed by the Quantock and Blackdown hills, and within easy reach of the Somerset, Devon and Dorset coasts, and Exmoor. This part of Somerset is an area of exceptional scenic beauty, and also has many historical associations. It is also famous for its potent apple cider. Taunton's Castle, dating from Norman times, houses natural history and archeological displays and a fine Roman mosaic.

People who come to Somerset by car will find the county's roads excellent. In autumn, when the beaches are deserted and the trees turning to golden brown, you should go to Exmoor and ride the lonely paths, catching glimpses of deer silhouetted on the crest against the timid blue of the sky, or go to the Quantocks and watch the sun setting.

Visit Muchelney Abbey, a medieval Benedictine abbey with lovely 15th-century cloisters and a carved stone fireplace beside the foundations of a seventh-century Saxon church. (Until lately, the cloisters were used by a local farmer as a cider cellar.) If Druids and prehistoric circles fascinate you, see Stanton Drew Circles and cove.

Old Cleeve, near the charming village of Washford, is an example of a noble building becoming derelict after being ravaged by fires and the hostility of men. But even in its dilapidation, this sunny skeleton of Cistercian cloisters, surrounded by ancient trees, bears witness to the enormous labors of monks who settled here not only to praise God but also to teach the art of cultivating the land.

King Arthur's Country

Wells, which lies about 27 miles northeast of Taunton, has the first completely English Gothic cathedral. This glorious cathedral derives its beauty from a perfect harmony of all its component parts, from the gamut of colors of its splendid stained-glass windows to the peaceful setting among aged trees and lawns. Its great glory is the west front, decorated with some 356 carvings of statues in ornate niches, and recently undergoing much needed repairs. Wells has one of the few medieval clocks to have survived, the figures performing every quarter of an hour: four knights on horseback joust, while a seated man, Jack Blandiver, rings bells with his hands and feet. More carved figures decorate the interior, showing aspects of life in the 12th and 13th centuries: a farmer chasing a fox, a man with toothache, another with a thorn in his foot, fruit thieves pursued by farmers who finally catch them.

Although Wells has the status of a city, the atmosphere is more like that of a small country town. When you have seen the cathedral, make your way from the market square through the curiously-named Penniless Porch to the moated Bishop's Palace and its famous bell-ringing swans. Hanging from the wall beside the moat is a rope attached to a bell, which the swans ring when they want to be fed.

Two miles from Wells are the Mendip Hills and Wookey Hole Caves, with their strange stalagmite-stalactite formations. Visit also the three-mile-long Cheddar Gorge, with the fantastic Gough's and Cox's caves. All these caverns were once the home of Prehistoric Man.

Glastonbury is probably the town that most people think of when they think of Somerset, simply because it is steeped in legends that seem to intensify with the passage of years. Briefly, the story goes that Joseph of Arimathea buried the chalice used at the Last Supper under a spring on the slopes of a Tor (hill)—which, strangely enough, does exist in the town, with a chapel on its top: that when he thrust his thorn staff into the ground on another hill, it took root and produced the distinctive Glastonbury winter-flowering thorn—which also exists; and that on what subsequently became the site of a great abbey, he built a daub and wattle church in which he made the first conversions to Christianity in Britain. Certainly Glastonbury later had a monastery which was bigger than Wells' cathedral is now, and it is said that King Arthur and Queen Guinevere were buried there. One of the many legends has it that the monks discovered a tomb, on which were carved the words, in Latin, "Here lies Arthur, the Once and Future King."

The current obsession with legend and myth has made Glastonbury one of the most popular meccas for the many people who take the tales of Arthur and the Matter of Britain as a kind of gospel. But even if you are sceptical about the stories, you will find the beauty of St. John's church and a walk up the Tor to see the superb view, very rewarding.

In an endeavor to establish the Arthur story, South Cadbury, the site of a high hilltop prehistoric fort, was excavated over several successive years by teams of archeologists, hoping to prove that this was Arthur's Camelot, his seat of power. They found clear indications of a palace with a grand hall of the period, but since wood was then the main building material, little remained except post holes indicating its size. The conclusion was that an important chieftain ruled here, certainly of the Arthurian period. You believe what you like in these parts.

Dunster is a market town that lost much of its old importance as English history shifted from both western and eastern counties towards the center, to concentrate more and more on London. Less than 1,000 people live there now, but visitors are fond of the place, for it has preserved in its lovely mellowed walls a warmth and an intimacy that some towns of south Germany and Provence have kept. In the market you are greeted by a picturesque, octagonal building with a deep sloping roof, built about 1600, that looks like a creation of Scandinavian architecture.

The streets of the little town rise sharply towards the castle, built between the 13th and the 15th centuries. The castle, long the residence and seat of the Luttrell family, gives Dunster a great house of rare distinction. The view from its ramparts is grand, the eye having room to play on the spacious polo field beneath, where deer are lazily wandering, or upon the beige sandy heights of the moor, or to repose on the cornflower blue of the sea near Blue Anchor. The southern, sun-exposed wall of the castle might be from Sicily, with its lemon and orange trees, and the layout of the grounds and building has a generosity matched only by such magnificent residences as Warwick Castle, near Stratford-upon-Avon. After 600 years of continuous occupation, the Luttrell family gave the house with its treasures to the National Trust, who now look after it for posterity.

If, after visiting Dunster, you feel like a trip to the sea, go to nearby Minehead, a center for the Exmoor National Park. Beaches are good here, and the sea is bracing and refreshing. There is a very pretty little bay at Porlock, dwarfed almost by the hills that surround the town. Indeed, Porlock Hill is one of England's steepest, with a gradient of 1 in 4. So be warned, if you intend to drive up Porlock Hill—be sure your car will make it, and be sure to have enough gas in the tank.

There are two Porlocks. Lively Porlock village, between Exmoor and the sea, has a fine church dating from the 13th century which, from the outside, may appear slightly flawed. Its tall steeple is blunted, the top having been destroyed by lightning and blown down in a great gale. Porlock Weir is beside the sea and a mile-and-a-half westwards. From it, a leafy cliff walk brings you to Culbone and the lovely little church dedicated to St. Culbone, one of the smallest of its period in England, measuring only some 35 feet long. Its steeple is perfectly in keeping with its size—it is the top of the steeple blown down from Porlock church!

For an Atlantic City-type resort, try Weston-super-Mare, down the coast from Bristol. But you will probably find it more rewarding to turn away from the coast and explore the soft green hinterland. Nether Stowey, at the foot of the Quantock Hills, has many memories of the poets Wordsworth and Coleridge, and you can visit the cottage in which Coleridge lived. Also well worth a visit are the cluster of picture-book villages that lie to the southwest of Minehead. Selworthy, Luccombe and Allerford are the loveliest. Not far from here is Dunkery Beacon (1705 feet), the highest point on Exmoor, which can be reached on foot by way of a beautiful walk through Horner Woods. On Dunkery's summit you can lie in the heather, listen to the skylarks and look out across the Bristol Channel to the distant hills of Wales.

Most of Exmoor is within Somerset, and much of its splendid scenery can be seen from roads which criss-cross the moor. It is a place of many moods—quiet heathland where sheep and ponies graze, wooded slopes and rushing streams giving way to wilder uplands. But Exmoor, to some, is a place of pilgrimage, following in the footsteps of R. D. Blackmore's characters in his novel *Lorna Doone:* the Valley of the Rocks, where Jan Ridd consulted the White Witch, the Doone Valley and lovely Badgworthy Water; and Oare church, claimed to be the church through whose window the villainous Carver Doone shot Lorna on her wedding day.

Five miles northwest of the ancient market town of Dulverton is Tarr Steps, a prehistoric clapper bridge made of huge boulders.'

Do not be afraid of the little roads in Somerset. You will probably get lost on them, but there are no longer any dragons. And watch out for the smaller houses open to the public. These are manors, and yeoman residences, not grand, but very revealing of the social mores of past centuries.

Montacute is one of the finest of these, with landscaped gardens and topiary hedges. Somerset is also notable for its magnificent churches with high, lacey towers; and for its many prehistoric forts—high hills dug out into a series of ditches and steep embankments for protection against invaders. Now grassgrown, some planted with rings of trees, these are easy to walk to and are natural viewpoints. One such hill is Ham Hill, near Montacute House. Old quarrying here has produced a strange, lumpy landscape. No need to walk this one: a motorable road leads to the top where, improbably, there's a pub—handy for a snack lunch with a view.

DEVON

Devon is one of England's biggest counties, exceeded in size only by Yorkshire, under its pre-1974 boundaries, and Lincolnshire. But the total population is only just under a million, with most people living in or near the few large towns. Consequently there are great tracts of Devon that are relatively empty and utterly peaceful. The beautiful Dartmoor National Park, whose bare heathery hills fill the southern half of the county, can be one of the loneliest places in Britain, seemingly inhabited only by hill sheep and shaggy wild ponies. But *only* if you leave the roads big enough for cars, do you get away from it all.

Once you leave the Moor, however, the countryside is unbelievably green and luxuriant, the rich red soil adds to the color of the Devon scene, and there is nowhere you can more easily get lost when motoring. The lanes are narrow, cut deep within high banks, and weave about in all directions, up hill and down dale. Every now and again a field gate will provide a breathtaking view and maybe a point of reference, but if you mean to stray from the main roads—and it would be a great pity not to—a good map, indeed an Ordnance Survey map, is essential.

Devon is fortunate in having two holiday coasts. The north coast faces the Atlantic and is rugged and invigorating. The south coast is the complete opposite, soft and languid, with red cliffs and south-facing bays that enjoy a mild, almost Mediterranean climate in spring and summer. Because of its close connections with the sea, many of Devon's most famous sons have been sailors and adventurers. Not only was Drake a Devon man, but so was Sir Walter Raleigh. In literature, too, Devon has a place, for it was at Ottery St. Mary that Samuel Taylor Coleridge was born and spent a good deal of his life. And from Plympton came the master of English painters, Sir Joshua Reynolds.

Today Devon is reached in under five hours from London, via the M4 and M5 motorways, and in considerably less time by rail. It is an extremely popular and crowded holiday area during the summer months, so booking of accommodations is essential betwen July and September.

Exeter, undoubtedly the principal historic city here, has managed to preserve some medieval and Tudor character. Roman foundations can be found alongside fragments of Roman mosaics and pavements, and the city, situated on a broad ridge of land overlooking the River Exe, must have been tempting from time immemorial for those who wanted to build a fortress here. Rougemont Castle was a valiant bastion for many generations and held a record in sieges, some of them prolonged and bloody. Today, this menacing citadel, which was considered a key position for the south Devon coast, looks quite domesticated. The mound of the castle is laid out as a promenade lined with trees, and the knights exercising their mounts have been replaced by the ubiquitous student. Only part of the gate tower remains.

Exeter Grammar School (founded by Walter de Stapledon, Bishop of Exeter and founder of Exeter College, Oxford), is one of the chief showplaces of the city. It dates from 1332 and was re-founded 300 years later. Now, Exeter also has a university that is gaining esteem in the academic world.

Exeter Cathedral, built in the theatrical Decorated Gothic style, is an architectural rarity, as there is only one other church in this country that has a similar design, that is, the use of transeptal towers. This is a Norman survival in the realm of the Gothic; the cathedral took about 90 years to build (1280–1370), and its west front is covered with statues. There is no central tower, or lantern, above the long nave of the church. The window tracery is elaborate.

Other buildings of note are the Guildhall, rebuilt in 1330, with a stone colonnaded façade straddling the pavement in the High Street; the Cathedral Library containing the *Exeter Book of Anglo-Saxon Poems, c.* A.D. 50, and the *Exeter Domesday,* 1085–7; the Priory of St. Nicholas, founded in 1080—good undercroft and kitchens; Tuckers' Hall, the craft guild hall of the weavers, incorporated in 1489, with a fine oak-paneled chamber and timbered roof.

Exeter abounds in little red ancient churches, of which the best are thought to be St. Mary Arches and St. Mary Steps. The city also has a unique system of underground aqueducts dating from the 13th century, which can sometimes be visited. Visit also the medieval inns, particularly the White Hart, Turk's Head and Ship, which last is notable for its connections with the admirals of Elizabeth I, especially Sir Francis Drake. It is also interesting to learn that the ancestors of Daniel Boone lived in Bradninch, near this ancient city. His father sailed for North Carolina some time around 1750. Incidentally, the Maritime Museum, a collection of vessels in The Quay, is an excellent addition to the city.

At Topsham, near Exeter, Dutch architecture intrudes itself pleasantly into a mixture of Georgian and Tudor black and white buildings. The whole place is quiet in an almost Dutch way and makes an attractive center for yachting.

South Devon

To add to the architectural interest of this area are Dartmouth Castle and Kingswear Castle, facing each other like sentinels across the mouth of the river. The former is open to visitors.

The most important resort area in South Devon is Torbay, which is an amalgamation of three resorts, Torquay, Paignton and Brixham, all spread around a sheltered east-facing bay. The biggest of the three is Torquay (pronounced *Tor-key*), which is one of the most elegant British seaside towns. Modern hotels, luxury villas and apartments climb the hillsides above the harbor. Palm trees and other exotic semi-tropical plants flourish in the seafront gardens. The sea is a clear and intense blue, and the whole place in summer has an unmistakable continental atmosphere. Small wonder the bay is now known as the English Riviera, and as an additional accolade, the E.E.C. have commended half-a-dozen of its larger beaches as meeting the required standards of Good Beaches.

There are a number of delightful coves tucked away among the red sandstone cliffs, including Anstey's Cove, a favorite spot for scuba-divers, with more beaches farther along at neighboring Babbacombe. Before leaving Torquay you should find time to visit Cockington, on the outskirts of the town, where there is a cluster of old-world cottages, a blacksmith's forge and a beautiful village church, surrounded in springtime by carpets of daffodils.

Paignton has broad sands, a harbor, and unusual grotto gardens at Oldway Mansion, a miniature version of Versailles. Just three miles outside the town is Compton Castle, now owned by the National Trust but once the home of Sir Humphrey Gilbert, founder of St. John's, Newfoundland, the first English colony in America, in 1583.

Much more interesting is Brixham, a bustling fishing port on the southern rim of Tor Bay. Here, with the gulls clamoring and baskets of crabs and lobsters being unloaded from the fishing boats, you can savor the true flavor of Devon. The statue on the quay is of William of Orange, who landed here in 1688 to assume the throne of England.

Salcombe, a town honeycombing a green mount overlooking the Kingsbridge Estuary, sits surrounded by fjord-like scenery. It's a favorite with the nautical crowd—you'll find them in the Ferry Inn, or at Tides Reach. For seclusion, there's nearby Bolt Head and Hope Cove.

There are some marvelous isolated holiday spots on this part of the coast, such as Torcross, a tiny village on a lagoon south of Dartmouth, commanding a causeway and a wide and lonely stretch of beach.

Plymouth and the River Dart

Plymouth, known the world over for its great seafaring traditions, is a proud West Country city with a unique setting on the beautiful south coast of Devon. Plymouth Sound, on whose shores the city has grown, is one of the finest natural harbors in the world. Although badly damaged during the war, Plymouth has been rebuilt and is a pleasant blend of ancient and modern. On the barbican is the Mayflower Stone, commemorating the spot from which the Pilgrim Fathers sailed to the New World, and it was on Plymouth Hoe that Sir Francis Drake lingered to finish his game of bowls before dealing with the Armada. Plymouth is a busy terminus and port. There are more attractive places to stay, though on the plus side it is a well located touring center for Devon and the neighboring county of Cornwall, which can be reached by the splendid road-bridge over the River Tamar.

The 12-mile trip by steamer down the River Dart to Dartmouth is one of the most enjoyable experiences to be found in the southwest. It starts at Totnes, a fascinating old town which has managed to preserve its medieval gateways, 17th-century colonnaded guildhall and Norman castle keep. Situated at the highest navigable point of the Dart, it is an excellent center for exploring south Devon, for Dartmoor, Plymouth and Exeter are all within easy reach. The Dart winds its way down to the sea through thick oak woods, cider-apple orchards and plunging meadows, passing some of the most peaceful hamlets in England. Those who want to learn the secrets of salmon and trout fishing should enroll in a game fishing course run by Charles Bingham. He runs three and four-day beginners courses on the lower Dart—contact him at the Rod Room, Broad Park, Coryton, near Okehampton; tel. Chillaton (082286) 281.

To reach Dartmouth by car, leave the main highway after Paignton. Cut across green fields to Kingswear for the little ferry and a four-minute push by tug across the Dart. Dartmouth is a small port visited by the Pilgrim Fathers in *Mayflower* and *Speedwell* for repairs prior to their journey to America. The town is steeped in history and has recorded associations with Raleigh, the Gilberts and John Davis. Overlooking the town is the Britannia Royal Naval College, famous as the training ground of officers of the navies of Great Britain and the Commonwealth, where tradition is still preserved and where the walls breathe stories of the time when Britain "ruled the waves."

North Devon

Between the two coasts of Devonshire lies the massive expanse of Dartmoor, one of the most romantic and impressive regions in England. The Dartmoor National Park consists of 365 square miles of gaunt moors and hills capped with rugged outcrops of weathered granite known as "tors" and incised by deep valleys in which clear trout streams rush through gnarled and ferny oakwoods; a marvelous area for the horseman, the walker and fisherman, for the naturalist and for anyone interested in the prehistoric sites which litter its wild hillsides. Fit yourself into a comfortable hotel and spend a little time here seeking out the unique sights of Dartmoor: Haytor Rocks, Fingle Bridge, Lydford Gorge, prehistoric Grimspound, the moorland village of Widecombe-in-the-Moor and the lonely little church of St. Michael on the Rock perched on a windy outcrop at Brentor. It is a strange, fey, slightly eerie part of England, frequently wreathed in mist. No wonder Conan Doyle set his *Hound of the Baskervilles* here.

In contrast to the southern coast, the beaches of the north of Devon, facing Wales, are half-rocky, half-sandy, while the promontories between Lynmouth and Ilfracombe are dangerously precipitous. The sea here is the Atlantic, of course, far less friendly than the warmer Channel. However, Combe Martin, situated in a sheltered valley near Ilfracombe, affords the maximum amount of shelter from the cold currents. The surrounding vegetation is rich with geraniums, myrtles and abundant heliotropes.

Ilfracombe is the largest town on the northern coast, its harbor and coves overhung by huge cliffs. This resort is overcrowded in summer but is a good base for exploring this scenically exciting stretch of coast which includes the delightful twin village resorts of Lynton and Lynmouth. There are some interesting walks here up the valleys of the East and West Lyn, two rivers that come bounding down from the lonely heights of Exmoor, the *Lorna Doone* country of R. D. Blackmore's romantic novel.

Clovelly, a village to the west of Bideford, always seems to have the sun shining on its stepped and cobbled streets. The car is no use in Clovelly as the village tumbles down for almost half a mile to the sea at such an angle that walking is the best way to reach the tiny harbor.

CORNWALL

The last 50 years have produced a remarkable change in this southernmost county of England. There was a time in the not-too-distant past when the inhabitants of Cornwall spoke their own language. Indeed, Cornishmen have always considered themselves something of a separate entity from the rest of the country, and almost anyone who lives on the other side of the Tamar River is a "foreigner." Even today there is a flourishing "home rule for Cornwall" movement called *Mebyon Curnow!*

A mild climate and long stretches of sandy beaches are Cornwall's principal attractions. The coastline is, however, remarkably varied. It's much rockier and far more precipitous than the rest of England's coast.

Cornwall's history has always been bound up with the sea, and the coastline, indented with hundreds of coves and bays of all sorts, was a natural favorite for smugglers and pirates.

The building of the Tamar Bridge and the extension of the railway line down to Penzance in the early part of this century brought the greatest changes. Today, Cornwall can be reached in just over three hours by a fast express train from London, or in about seven hours by car. There is a great deal to see and enjoy in Cornwall and it's the ideal place if you need a break from London.

The best months in which to visit the county are, without doubt, May and June, for not only is the weather better than anywhere else in England at that time of the year, but the countryside looks its loveliest, and the tourist season has not yet really got under way. If you want to go in July or August, it is imperative to book both accommodations and train seats in advance (as always, ask about weekend and mid-week bargain tickets), though the M5 and the improved A38 have done much to help motorists.

The Tamar River, the great divide between Devon and Cornwall, is a beautiful, placid waterway. Upstream at Cothele, the old quayside beneath medieval Cothele House has been preserved from the times when the river was a busy trading highway. At nearby Morwellham Quay, "the greatest copper port in Queen Victoria's Empire," old mines and a complete 19th-century village have been recreated and reopened for visitors.

The most interesting part of Cornwall is to the west of Truro. Nowhere are you more than seven miles from the sea in this part of Cornwall, with the Atlantic in the north and the Channel in the south. But both coastlines have totally different characteristics. The Atlantic coast is forever being battered with large breakers that have eroded the coastline into abrupt headlands, high cliffs and sheltered, difficult harbors.

Make a trip along this northern coastline from Morwenstow, not far south from Clovelly (about 15 miles), with its lonely church perched on the very top of a cliff, to Land's End. It can be a most spectacular and rewarding experience if the weather is good.

Tintagel, farther south along A39 and B3263, is reputed to have been the birthplace of King Arthur; the remains of the great castle stand for all to see. All that is left is the outline of the walls, moats and towers, but it is an atmospheric historic site, perched dramatically on a rocky promontory, and it only requires the smallest amount of imagination to conjure up a picture of Sir Lancelot and Sir Galahad riding out in search of the Holy Grail over the narrow causeway above the seething breakers. The ruins themselves are in rather poor shape, with lush green turf growing where rushes probably once covered the floors of the halls and corridors of the castle. A westerly Atlantic wind seems always to be sweeping through Tintagel and the thunder of the breakers is forever in your ears. Even on a summer's day, when visitors swarm all over the battlements, one cannot help being awed by the proximity of the past. (Whether it was Arthur's castle or not, it is a most impressive place.) To see the castle and magnificent cliff scenery properly, be prepared to do quite a lot of walking—or, better still, hire a horse from the local stables.

From Tintagel to Land's End

It's about 70 miles from Tintagel to Land's End, a journey through some of the most remarkable scenery in England. Newquay, Cornwall's busiest resort, is along this coast. There are a number of good hotels here, set on the cliff-tops overlooking nine of the finest beaches in Europe, thronged with summer visitors who come to swim, sunbathe and enjoy the surfing. Still farther west lies the old fishing port of St. Ives. Leave your car in one of the municipal car parks and then proceed on foot to explore what is one of the most popular holiday resorts in Cornwall.

Once an ancient and quiet fishing village, St. Ives today finds its narrow streets always tightly packed with young holiday-makers. For many years, an artists' colony has lived in St. Ives, so there are several galleries where original paintings and sculptures can be bought very reasonably. The hand-thrown pottery of late master potter Bernard Leach is world-famous, and the garden/studio of the late Barbara Hepworth, who lived in St. Ives, is now open to the public.

Although the Atlantic breakers in Cornwall are nowhere like the size of those off the Californian coast, surfing (in rubber suits, naturally) is a very popular sport. The favorite centers for surfing are Newquay, St. Ives, Widemouth Bay and Bude.

The road from St. Ives to Land's End runs through a barren and severe landscape, in which there is little habitation; the dominant color is the cold steel gray of exposed granite. Land's End, as the title suggests, is the most westerly point of the mainland of England, and it offers an unrivaled view of the seas that surround the British Isles. Here, the cliffs come to an abrupt and craggy halt. Centuries ago, the Celts defended the peninsula against raiding Vikings and pirates; to the Romans it was *Belerion*—Seat of the Storms. Then, in the 17th century, visiting began: the preacher, John Wesley, the painter Turner; and in the mid-19th century with the coming of the Penzance railway, it was accessible to everyone. The property has now been bought privately and a new era has already begun in which the necessity for conservation and the demands imposed by visitor pressure will hopefully be reconciled. The development program includes two comprehensive exhibitions, Land's End Heritage, and The Man and the Sea, as well as the New Craft Center/Workshops at the First and Last House in England. Added facilities for visitors include car and coach parking, toilets and gift shop, cafeteria and bar; and a post box. There is an admission charge. Well contained on its spectacular site, all this, it is sincerely hoped, can only represent improvement.

The Southern Coast and Inland

Not far from this remote spot, to the south, is Porthcurno, where, during the summer, there are regular performances of classical and Shakespearean drama in a tiny open-air theater known as the Minack Theatre. Nearby is a delightful cove, Porth Chapel, and in the very opposite direction, the strange natural phenomenon of the Logan Rock, which is an enormous mass of stone balanced on a natural pedestal.

A little further east, at Lamorna, skin-divers are frequently to be seen. Then there is the curious little fishing village of Mousehole (pronounced *Mowzl*), with narrow winding streets and harborside restaurants, reminiscent of St. Ives, but much smaller. At Mousehole there is an excellent hotel and restaurant, The Lobster Pot, which is an ideal base from which to explore the region.

Penzance, just round the headland north from Mousehole, is southern Cornwall's principal town and main shopping center. There are regular helicopter and boat services from here to the Isles of Scilly. Beyond Penzance at Marazion, which was a Jewish settlement in the Middle Ages, is St. Michael's Mount, which rises out of the sea to the height of 230 feet. At low tide you can walk across to the island, as you can to its "sister" of the same name in France. According to legend, it was here that the child Christ was brought by Joseph of Arimathea on their way to Glastonbury.

Between the two sea coasts of this lobster-claw-shaped projection at the foot of the Cornish peninsula, are networks of flower-bordered lanes, green valleys and granite-capped moors. The countryside is rich in prehistoric remains, stone circles, burial chambers and Iron Age settlements such as Chysauster, near Penzance.

Bodmin Moor, unlike Dartmoor and Exmoor, is a somewhat bleak plateau roughly 12 miles square. Because of its relatively poor soil and sometimes poor weather, it has remained essentially wild. Two of its peaks top 1,300 ft.—Brown Willy and Rough Tor—and on the western edge lie rocky valleys, toppling streams and a steep-sided gorge called Devil's Jump. For a bit of legend-cum-history take a look at Dozmary Pool, not an exciting patch of water, but featured in the Arthurian legend as the bottomless lake into which the king's famous sword, Excalibur, was tossed after his death, a hand reaching up to catch it and draw it under. And near Bolventor is Jamaica Inn, made famous by Daphne du Maurier's novel. The interior has been rigorously modernized and bears little resemblance to the grim hostelry in the story; but the inn sign is still capable of creaking ominously in the wind.

Bodmin, the assize and county town of Cornwall, is situated almost exactly at the geographical center of the county, providing an ideal base for touring. The town has free car parks, an attractive central park with children's playgrounds, tennis courts, an indoor heated swimming pool and other recreational facilities. The parish church of St. Petroc is the largest church in Cornwall and contains the battle honors of the old county regiment. The Duke of Cornwall Light Infantry's Museum is situated at The Keep, Victoria Barracks, Bodmin.

Along the south coast, between Penzance and the Tamar river there are fine beaches, especially near small fishing villages-cum-holiday resorts such as St. Mawes on the lovely wooded Fal estuary, and above it, on a steep-banked creek, St. Just-in-Roseland; then picture-postcard Mevagissey, Fowey, Polruan, and the shark-fishing center of Looe.

Inland from Fowey is St. Austell, center of Cornwall's china clay industry. The clay is mainly used for the making of porcelain, but is also valued in paper-making, paint and some medicines. The waste from the quarries is piled high in great white mountains, creating a moonscape. Some of the workings are open to visitors who can see the processes from quarrying to the finished product.

THE ISLES OF SCILLY

The Isles of Scilly are about 30 miles from Land's End; they are a cluster of about 100 tiny islands, of which the five largest are inhabited. The islanders will tell you that however cold and wet England may be, you'll always find the sun here, but you will have to allow for a little local exaggeration. The islands are the last link with land before North America and stand at the entrance of the English Channel with the warm Gulf Stream washing their shores. They are reached by either boat or helicopter from Penzance, and by Brymon Airways operating from Plymouth, Newquay, Exeter, Bristol and London (Heathrow and Gatwick) airports. The difference in climate is noticeable immediately. It's mild and temperate, a fact borne out by the second industry of the islands, which is horticulture (tourism has recently become the biggest money-spinner). In early spring almost everywhere you look, the fields are covered with the narcissi known as Scilly Whites. At harvest time the quays are stacked with boxes of the flowers waiting for export.

Communications between the islands are well organized, so the visitor will have no difficulty in reaching any of them, even the uninhabited ones where only puffins and seals bask in the sun. As most of the regular boat trips leave from St. Mary's, the largest island, this is the obvious place to stay, especially since most of the hotels are located here in the "capital," Hugh Town. Booking, in any case, is essential.

The ideal time to visit the Scillies is in April and May in order to avoid the crowds, and to reap the maximum advantages of the mildness of the climate. Later in the year, in September and October, ornithologists descend on the islands to spot birds (many from America) on their long migrations south to warmer climes.

St. Mary's is all of three miles wide, with about ten miles of splendid coastline. To the islanders it is "the mainland," though in comparison to the British mainland proper it seems like a foreign country. The pace of life drops, and the only noises likely to distract are the sounds of the sea and the birds, although one visitor allegedly claimed to have been disturbed by the munching of a cow.

There is a local bus service; *Vic's Coach Tours,* taking an hour or so, are highly entertaining island excursions, enlivened by hilarious comments from the driver-guide. Favorites among walkers are the coastal paths, with wildflowers wherever you look. For an evening stroll to watch gaudy sunsets, walk the massive ramparts of Star Castle, one-time Elizabethan garrison built in the shape of an eight-pointed star, the inner building converted to an hotel, the dungeons to a bar.

Night life is moderate. There are pubs for after-dinner drinks, and in season a few discos. Wrecks are an endless topic for conversation, since the whole seabed round the islands is littered with the remains of centuries of sunken ships.

The other islands have limited accommodation, mostly in small, quiet guesthouses. Tresco is the exception. Second largest island after St. Mary's—though still only some two miles long and half-a-mile at its widest—it is privately owned by descendants of the great Augustus Smith, who revitalized the island. He and successive generations of his family were responsible for importing the exotic shrubs, trees and flowers that form today's magnificent sub-tropical gardens. The Abbey Gardens are open to the public, as is the Valhalla Museum with its relics from wrecks and ships' figureheads. There are superb white beaches, among them Pentle, noted for its seashells; and landmarks such as King Charles Castle, a fat round tower facing the hilly little island of Bryher.

The other inhabited islands—St. Agnes, Bryher and St. Martin's—are peaceful, charming places, ideal for a boat trip from St. Mary's, and for exploring on foot before taking a later boat back to base.

PRACTICAL INFORMATION FOR
THE SOUTHWEST

HOW TO GET THERE FROM LONDON. The following are some of the towns which can be visited from London for a day. For the more far-flung only the train permits day trips to be made, while closer to the capital many centers can be visited by coach as well. In the mornings the ticket offices at both British Rail stations and Victoria Coach station can become very busy. In order to save waiting in line, you are advised to purchase your ticket in advance from a Travel Center or Travel Agent.

Bath. One of the very best days out from London. There is plenty to see including remains of the famous Roman Baths. **By train:** an excellent service of one InterCity 125 an hour from Paddington station taking around 1¼ hours for the 107 miles. **By coach:** one National Express coach every 2 hours from London/Victoria. The 8 or 10 departures are best for a day trip; return on the 4.05 or 6.05. The journey, via Heathrow Central Bus/Underground interchange takes 3 hours, mostly on the M4. **By car:** M4, A46; or more attractive, leave M4 at junction 12 and take A4 to Bath.

Bristol. By rail: a very good service of one train an hour, sometimes two, from Paddington. The run takes around 1½ hours and nearly all trains are formed of InterCity 125 units and have a buffet or restaurant service. When booking, please bear in mind that Temple Meads (*not* Bristol Parkway) is the station for the city center. **By coach:** National Express operate an hourly coach service from Victoria, commencing early morning and running through to early evening. There are some 14 departures a day all of which call at Heathrow Central Bus/Underground interchange en route and take 2½ hours for the journey. All journeys are Rapide services with hostess, video and refreshments. **By car:** M4, M32 or A4.

Exeter. By train: a good service of one train an hour—sometimes two—from Paddington. Journey time around two hours, depending on the service (most trains are the fast InterCity 125 units), and most have a buffet or restaurant service. By rail Exeter is quite possible as a longer day out: the 8.50 or 10.10 departures from Paddington allow at least six hours to be spent in the City, and still return you to London before 10 at night. Another service from London's Waterloo Station is less frequent and slower, and travels via Salisbury. **By coach:** National Express operate a Rapide coach service from Victoria Coach Station with 7 departures a day; the 08.30 departure is the only one which allows a reasonable amount of time to be spent in Exeter. Journey time is 3¾ hours. In summer and weekends it is essential to book early for the National Rapides. **By car:** M4, M5.

Plymouth. By train: an hourly service from Paddington station (some InterCity 125 trains) with a buffet or restaurant service. The journey time is around 3½ hours. Plymouth is probably the outer limit for possible day trips by train to the southwest, but well worth it, especially for the coastal scenery near Exeter. The 8.50 and 10.10 departures from Paddington allow around five hours in Plymouth, with a late return to London the same evening. **By coach:** National Express operate a direct Rapide service from Victoria Coach Station to Plymouth with nine coaches daily and the journey time is just under 4½ hours. A day trip to Plymouth is only practicable by taking the 8.00 departure, allowing some five hours in the city. Advance booking is essential at weekends and in the summer. **By car:** M4, M5, A38.

HOW TO GET AROUND. British Rail serves the area with fast and frequent trains from Paddington to Exeter and the West Country. Plymouth (225 miles) can be reached in as little as 2 hours 53 mins, and Penzance (305 miles) in around 4 hours 42 mins.

There are unlimited, and good value, travel tickets available, valid for most local bus and coach services throughout Devon and Cornwall, as well as parts of Somerset and Dorset. Enquire at bus company offices in the area.

There are scheduled flights from Plymouth to Newquay and Exeter, and helicopter flights from Penzance to St. Mary's, Isles of Scilly. Brymon Airways operate scheduled flights to the Islands from Plymouth, Exeter, Bristol and Newquay, with regular linking flights to London Heathrow, Gatwick, also to the Channel Islands, Birmingham and the East Midlands. Services by sea to the Isles of Scilly are operated regularly, taking about 2½ hours.

Note: No services by air or sea run to or from the Isles of Scilly on *Sundays.* This does not affect the inter-island boat trips which run all the time.

HOTELS AND RESTAURANTS. Many of the hotels and restaurants listed here are not open in the winter months and it is advisable to check through the National Tourist Board or Regional Tourist Office if you travel out of season. Since this is very much a vacation area, the season itself sees fully booked-up accommodations, and you would be well advised to make sure of advance reservations.

Details about our grading system, plus other relevant information about hotels and restaurants, will be found at the beginning of the book in the *Facts at Your Fingertips* section.

Axbridge (Som.). *Oak House* (M), tel. (0934) 732444; 9 rooms, 7 with bath. Tiny hotel facing ancient market place. The restaurant has original dishes including the 1789 "Rev. Gould's Delight" (pigeon breasts cooked in red wine served in a pastry case). Super desserts; worth a visit.

Barnstaple (Devon). *Downrew House* (M), tel. (0271) 42497; 13 rooms with bath. Queen Anne period residence overlooking hills. Swimming pool, tennis, golf course and great food. Off the beaten track at Bishop's Tawton; closed early Nov.–mid-March. *Royal and Fortescue* (M), tel. (0271) 42289; 61 rooms, 33 with bath. Conveniently situated downtown.

Restaurant. *Lynwood House* (M), tel. (0271) 43695. Enjoy fresh, local fish either in downstairs bistro or more expensive restaurant upstairs.

Bath (Avon). *6 Kings Circus* (L), tel. (0225) 28288; 6 rooms with bath. Charming, unusual little hotel in immaculately restored town house. *Royal Crescent* (L), 16 Royal Cres., tel. (0225) 319090; 45 rooms, 42 with bath in an elegant crescent, a luxurious hotel for sybarites. *Priory* (L–E), Weston Rd., tel. (0225) 331922; 21 rooms, 20 with bath. Personally run, own pool and on edge of town. Superb restaurant. *Francis* (E), Queen Square, tel. (0225) 24257; 94 rooms with bath. Superb 18th-century spot in historic square. *Ladbroke Beaufort* (E), Walcot St., tel. (0225) 63411; 123 rooms, all with bath. *Lansdown Grove* (M), Lansdown Rd., tel. (0225) 315891; 45 rooms, all with bath or shower. Interesting views; quality restaurant. *Fern Cottage* (M–I), Northend, Batheaston, tel. (0225) 858190. 8 rooms in Georgian hotel 3 miles from Bath. Good budget alternative.

At Ston Easton. *Ston Easton Park* (L–E), tel. (076 121) 631/393; 20 rooms, 19 with bath. 18th-century house in own parkland, recently renovated and with excellent restaurant.

Restaurants. *Clos du Roy* (E), 7 Edgar Bldgs, George St., tel. (0225) 64356. Interesting, well-presented French dishes. *Hole in the Wall* (E), 16 George St., tel. (0225) 25242. Small high-quality menu in small high-quality restaurant. Excellent wines. *Popjoy's* (M), Sawclose, tel. (0225)

60494. An excellent choice, with an imaginative menu. *Woods* (M), tel. (0225) 314812. One of the best value restaurants in Bath.

Bideford (Devon). *Durrant House* (M), tel. (023 72) 2361; 58 rooms all with bath or shower. Tennis, dancing and heated pool; open Easter through November. *Rosskerry* (I), tel. (023 72) 2872; 10 rooms, 4 with bath. Perfect setting overlooking the River Torridge; closed Dec.–Feb.

Bristol (Avon). *Holiday Inn* (E), Lower Castle St., tel. (0272) 294281; 284 rooms with bath; heated pool and sauna. *Ladbroke Dragonara* (E), Redcliffe Way, tel. (0272) 260041; 197 rooms with bath. Squash and sauna, dancing most nights. *Grand* (M), Broad St., tel. (0272) 291645; 180 rooms with bath. Renovated Victorian hotel in the city center. *Unicorn* (M), Prince St., tel. (0272) 230333; 194 rooms with bath and shower; overlooking harbor.

Restaurants. *Harveys* (E), Denmark St., tel. (0272) 277665. Long-standing reputation in ancient wine cellar. *Les Semailles* (E), 9 Druid Hill, Stoke Bishop, tel. (0272) 686456. Newcomer with fine reputation; in northern suburbs. *Restaurant du Gourmet* (E), Whiteladies Rd., tel. (0272) 736230. French cooking, consistently good. Closed Sun. and Mon. *Rajdoot* (M), 83 Park St., tel. (0272) 268033. Excellent, authentic Indian restaurant with reasonable prices. Also good value at *Howards* (M), la Avon Crescent, Hotwells, tel. (0272) 262921. Informal bistro near floating harbor. Closed Xmas and 2 weeks in summer.

Brixham (Devon). *Quayside* (M), tel. (080 45) 55751; 30 rooms with bath or shower. Picturesquely situated close to the harbor. Centuries-old *Smugglers Haunt* (M), tel. (080 45) 3050; 14 rooms, 4 with bath. Full of atmosphere.

Bryher (I.o. Scilly). *Hell Bay Hotel* (M), tel. (0720) 22947. Comfortable, converted farmhouse; restaurant with fresh home produce.

Budock Vean (Cornw.). *Budock Vean* (E–M), tel. (0326) 250288; 54 rooms with bath. Pleasant woods and extensive grounds, private beach, indoor heated pool, golf, sea fishing. Near Falmouth. Closed Jan. and Feb.

Chagford (Devon). *Gidleigh Park* (L–E), tel. (06473) 2367. 14 bedrooms with bath in a finely-sited stockbroker's Tudor house in 22 acres of ground with friendly personal service. Superb restaurant serving French cuisine, excellent wines. Off the beaten track, so ask directions when you book. *Easton Court* (M), tel. (064 73) 3469; 8 rooms with bath or shower in 15th-century oak-beamed thatched house. Evelyn Waugh wrote *Brideshead Revisited* here. *Great Tree* (M), tel. (064 73) 2491; 14 rooms with bath. Good restaurant. *Mill End* (M), tel. (064 73) 2282; 17 rooms with bath or shower. Converted water mill with reputation for good food and service.

Colyford (Devon). *Old Manor* (M), tel. (0297) 52862; 11 rooms, 7 with bath. Charming 15th-century thatched house near Lyme Regis; relaxing with good service.

Dartmouth (Devon). *Royal Castle* (M), tel. (080 43) 4004; 21 rooms, all with bath or shower. 17th-century, centrally sited on the quay. Closed Jan.–Feb. *Stoke Lodge* (M), Stoke Fleming, tel. (0803) 770523, 24 rooms, all with bath. Former 17th-century house, now family-run hotel, ideal for children, with indoor and outdoor pools, sauna.

Restaurants. *Carved Angel* (E), tel. (080 43) 2465. Excellent restaurant overlooking the harbor. Specializes in seafood, great wine list. Closed Sun. dinner, all Mon. and Jan. *Bistro 33* (M), tel. (080 43) 2882. Simple decor, but imaginative and varied menu.

Dulverton (Som.). *Ashwick House* (M), tel. (0398) 23868. 6 rooms with bath. On the edge of Exmoor with fine views and gardens. *Carnarvon Arms* (M), tel. (0398) 23302. 25 rooms, 22 with bath. Own shooting and fishing.

Exeter (Devon). *Rougemont* (E), Queen St., tel. (0392) 54982; 76 rooms, all with bath. Situated downtown, in a large Victorian building. *Buckerell Lodge* (M), Topsham Rd., tel. (0392) 52451; 54 rooms with bath. House dates back to the 12th century. *Exeter Moat House* (M), tel. (039 287) 5441; 43 rooms with bath. *Royal Clarence* (M), tel. (0392) 58464; 63 rooms, all with bath. Historic hotel overlooking the Cathedral. *White Hart* (M), tel. (0392) 79897. 60 rooms, most with bath or shower. 14th century, beamed and full of antiques. *Woodhayes* (M), Whimple, tel. (0404) 822237. Country house hotel with elegant restaurant. 7 rooms with bath.

Restaurants. *Golsworthy's* (E), tel. (0392) 217736. French restaurant in the heart of the city. Closed Sat. and Sun. lunch. *Coolings Wine Bar* (M), tel. (0392) 34183. Popular wine bar offering wide range of dishes. Closed Sun. *Herbie's Wholefood Restaurant* (I), tel. (0392) 58473. Typical vegetarian's hangout with standard and unusual dishes. Closed Sun., and Sat. and Mon. lunch.

Exmouth (Devon). *Barn* (M), Marine Drive, tel. (0395) 274411. 11 rooms, 9 with bath. Stone built house in lovely garden with views. Tennis, pool, croquet, good restaurant. *Devoncourt* (M), tel. (0395) 272277; 39 rooms with bath and shower. Overlooks the sea, direct access to the beach, heated pool, hard tennis courts. *Portledge* (M), Fairy Cross, tel. (02375) 262; 24 rooms, all with bath. *Royal Beacon* (M), tel. (0395) 264886; 35 rooms, 32 with bath. A former posting house, overlooking Torbay.

Restaurant. *Drake's* (M), tel. (0392) 279644. Wide range of European cuisine.

Falmouth (Cornw.). The *Falmouth Hotel* (M), tel. (0326) 312671; 73 rooms with bath; imposing tropical appearance, grand interior and swimming pool. *Greenbank* (M), tel. (0326) 312440; 43 rooms with bath. Overlooks the harbor with own landing stage. *Penmere Manor* (M), tel. (0326) 314545; 28 rooms, most with bath. *Hotel St. Michael* (M), tel. (0326) 312707; 70 rooms, all with bath. Set in beautiful gardens, with pool, sauna and jacuzzi.

Restaurants. *La Cucina* (M), tel (0326) 311007. Italian specialties; overlooking harbor. *The Pipe* (M), tel. (0326) 315273. Busy bistro serving snack lunches and more elaborate dinners.

Fowey (Cornw.). *Riverside* (M), tel. (072 683) 2275; 14 rooms, 4 with bath, 2 with shower. Fine views along the river; near car ferry, closed from Dec. to March.
Restaurant. *Food for Thought* (M), tel. (072 683) 2221. Friendly bistro, seafood specialties. Closed Sun.

Frome (Som.). *Mendip Lodge* (M), tel. (0373) 63223; 40 rooms with bath. A Grand Metropolitan Hotel with wide views of the surrounding hills.
Restaurant. *The Settle* (M), tel. (0373) 65975. Family-run; with first-rate specialties.

Glastonbury (Som.). *George and Pilgrims* (M), tel. (0458) 31146. 14 rooms, most with bath; has old-world charm and a few four-poster beds.

Gulworthy (Devon). **Restaurant.** *Horn of Plenty* (E), tel. (0822) 832528. Superb continental cuisine and excellent seasonal variations, with suitably inspiring choice of wines. Hospitable atmosphere; 6 high-standard rooms.

Hatherleigh (Devon). *George* (M–I), tel. (0837) 810454; 12 rooms, 10 with bath. Originally a monks' retreat and 500 years old—even has a resident ghost!

Helford (Cornw.). **Restaurant.** *Riverside* (E), tel. (032 623) 443. Pleasant, out of the way *restaurant avec chambres* (6), with unpretentious menu of outstanding quality. Riverside views.

Helston (Cornw.). *Nansloe Manor* (M), tel. (0326) 574691; 7 rooms, all with bath. Peaceful hotel set in 5 acres of grounds; restaurant with a la carte menu.
Restaurant. *The Yard Bistro* (M), tel. (032 622) 595. Part of an old coach house on a country estate near Helston specializing in local seafood. Closed Mon., and Jan., Feb.

Holbeton (Devon). *Alston Hall* (M), Battisborough Cross, tel. (075 530) 259; 9 rooms with bath or shower, in peaceful, oak-paneled mansion near Plymouth.

Honiton (Devon). *Combe House* (E), Gittisham, near Honiton, tel. (0404) 2756. 12 rooms with bath. 16th and 17th-century house in secluded position. Traditional atmosphere and good cooking. Closed Jan. to mid-Feb. *Deer Park* (M), tel. (0404) 41266; 29 rooms with bath, at Weston, 2½ miles west of town; 200 years old, standing in wide grounds; trout fishing. *Home Farm* (M), Wilmington, near Honiton, tel. (040 483) 278; 14 rooms, 9 with bath. Small, partially thatched, originally 17th-century farmhouse. Walks and golf, sea close by. Booking essential. Closed Jan., Feb. *New Dolphin* (M), tel. (0404) 2377; 14 rooms, all with bath. Modern comforts combine with old-world charm in this former coaching inn.
Restaurant. *Angel* (M), tel. (0404) 2829. Bistro serving fish and traditional English fare.

Hope Cove (Devon). *Cottage* (M), tel. Kingsbridge (0548) 561555; 35 rooms, 19 with bath; at Galmpton with sea views; gardens descend to safe beach. Closed Jan.

Hunstrete (Avon). *Hunstrete House* (L–E), tel. Compton Dando (076 18) 578. Near Bristol and handy for Bath. 18th century manor house has 20 rooms with bath and exceptional classic restaurant. In 90 acres of parkland; pool, tennis, croquet.

Kingsbridge (Devon). Beautifully situated *Buckland-Tout-Saints* (E), tel. (0548) 3055; 13 rooms, 12 with bath. Queen Anne house set in beautiful park and gardens. A superb touring base. Closed most of Jan. *King's Arms* (M), tel. (0548) 2071; 12 rooms, 7 with bath. A 15th-century inn.
Restaurant. *Lavinia's* (E), at Loddiswell, tel. (0548) 550306. Restaurant in country house, French menu. Open Apr.–Oct. Closed Sun. and Mon. Ask directions when booking.

Lamorna Cove (Cornw.). *Lamorna Cove* (M), tel. (0736) 731411; 18 rooms with bath or shower. Family-run hotel with heated pool, sauna and lovely views over the sea; closed Dec.–Feb.

Limpley Stoke (Avon). *Homewood Park* (E), Hinton Charterhouse, tel. (022122) 3731; 15 rooms with bath. Elegant decor; imaginative menu with fine wines. *Cliffe* (M), tel. (022 122) 3226. 30 rooms with bath and shower. Good cooking, friendly ambience. Both hotels are near Bath.

Lynmouth (Devon). *Rising Sun* (M), tel. (0598) 53223; 17 rooms, 5 with bath, 10 with shower, in 14th-century thatched inn overlooking harbor. Closed Jan. to mid-Feb.

Montacute (Som.). *The King's Arms* (M), tel. (0326) 574691; 7 rooms, all with bath. Inn featuring quaint interior; restaurant with a la carte menu.

Moretonhampstead (Devon). *Manor House* (E), tel. (0647) 40355; 69 rooms with bath or shower. In huge park; many sporting amenities, cuisine of high standard.

Mullion (Cornw.). *Polurrian* (M), tel. (0326) 240421; 41 rooms, 38 with bath. Overlooks the sea; tennis, heated pool; closed Nov. to Easter.

Newquay (Cornw.). *Atlantic* (M), tel. (0637) 872244; 80 rooms, 70 with bath. Extensive grounds with sea views, heated pool, live music and dancing weeknights during the season. Closed Nov. *Glendorgal* (M), tel. (0637) 874937; 40 rooms, 38 with bath. Tennis; closed from Oct. to April. *Kilbirnie* (M), tel. (0637) 875155, is fine value, with great views. 69 rooms, 65 with bath, heated indoor pool; live music and discos. Closed Jan.
Restaurant. *La Corniche* (M), tel. (0637) 874251. In Hotel Riviera, competently cooked favorites.

Paignton (Devon). *Redcliffe* (M), tel. (0803) 526397; 63 rooms with bath or shower. Large grounds, private beach and good views; heated pool and tennis. Excellent for families.

Penzance (Cornw.). *The Abbey* (M), tel. (0736) 66906; 6 rooms, 4 with bath. Unconventional, stylish, more like a private house. Closed 2 weeks in Jan. *Higher Faugan* (M), tel. (0736) 62076; 12 rooms with bath; stands in its own grounds 300 ft. above Mounts Bay. Heated pool; closed Oct.–mid-Mar. *Queens* (M), tel. (0736) 62371; 71 rooms, all with bath or shower. Views over Mounts Bay. *Union* (M), tel. (0736) 62319; 28 rooms, 20 with bath. Set in historic 17th-century building, completely refurbished.
  Restaurant. *Abbey Hotel* (M), tel. (0736) 66906. French-style restaurant offering short but intriguing selection. Closed 2 weeks Jan. *Berkeley* (M), tel. (0736) 62541. 1930s decor and Italian cuisine, with after-dinner dancing. *Harris's* (M), tel. (0736) 64408. Hidden on a tiny side street, serving fresh, local fish and good steaks. At **Botallack** *The Counthouse* (M), tel. (0736) 788588. An old tin mining building with English cooking. Closed Mon., Tues. and Sun. evening.

Plymouth (Devon). *Copthorne* (E), tel. (0752) 45756; 133 rooms, all with bath. New, large hotel with Edwardian-style restaurant. *Holiday Inn* (E), tel. (0752) 662866; 218 rooms with bath. One of the finest of the chain in the country; heated pool, sauna, dancing on Sat. *Mayflower Post House* (E), tel. (0752) 662828; 104 rooms with bath, heated pool. Views of Plymouth Hoe. *Hotel Albergo Romana* (I), tel. (0752) 667303; 10 rooms, all with bath. Authentic Italian atmosphere in former 16th-century monastery building.
  Restaurants. *Chez Nous* (E), tel. (0752) 266793. French bistro. Closed Sun. and Mon. and first 2 weeks in Feb. and Sept. *The Distillery* (M), tel. (0752) 224305. High-ceilinged restaurant in former distillery, next door to museum on the history of gin. *Piermasters* (M), tel. (0752) 29345. By the fish quay in old Plymouth; French inspired cuisine with extensive choice of seafood; more informal bistro downstairs. Closed Sun.

Polperro (Cornw.). No cars are allowed in this small artists' colony. Overlooking the village is *Claremont* (M–I), tel. (0503) 72241; 10 rooms, 6 with shower. Open Easter–Oct.

Porlock Weir (Som.). *Anchor Hotel and Ship Inn* (M), tel. (0643) 862636; 24 rooms, 19 with bath. Out of the way hotel with character, comfort and reasonable prices.

St. Austell (Cornw.). *Carlyon Bay* (E–M), tel. (072 681) 2304. 74 rooms with bath. Very comfortable hotel overlooking sea, with private beach, sports facilities. *Boscundle Manor* (M), tel. (072 681) 3557. 9 rooms with bath or shower. At Tregrehan, with good restaurant. *Porth Avallen* (M), tel. (072 681) 2802; 24 rooms, 19 with bath. Good views and comfort.

St. Ives (Cornw.). *Tregenna Castle* (E), tel. (0736) 795254; 83 rooms, 68 with bath. Southeast of town; 100-acre grounds and splendid sea views, heated pool, squash, riding, tennis and golf; excellent cuisine and impressive wine list. *Boskerris* (M), Carbis Bay, tel. (0736) 795295. Country house in grounds; heated pool. 20 rooms, 15 with bath. Open mid-April to Oct. *Garrack* (M), tel. (0736) 796199; 19 rooms, 14 with bath. Quiet spot for a relaxed holiday.

Restaurant. *Pudding Bag Lane* (M), tel. (0736) 797214. Above the market, you can dine alfresco on the terrace.

St. Mary's (I.o. Scilly). At Hugh Town on the main island *Godolphin* (M), tel. (0720) 22316; 31 rooms, 25 with bath, is close to the harbor. International restaurant. *Tregarthens* (M), tel. (0720) 22540; 33 rooms, 24 with bath, a family hotel with a fine view. Both are closed mid-Oct.–mid-Mar.

St. Mawes (Cornw.). *Tresanton* (L–E), tel. (0326) 270544; 21 rooms with bath. Charmingly run hotel in magnificent terraced gardens. Elegant restaurant. *Idle Rocks* (M), tel. (0326) 270771; 24 rooms, 22 with bath. Cooking and hospitality first-rate. Closed late Oct. to late Mar. *Rising Sun* (M), tel. (0326) 270233; 13 rooms, 7 with bath, harborside inn of character.

Salcombe (Devon). *Marine* (E), tel. (054 884) 2251; 51 rooms with bath. Overlooks estuary; heated pool; excellent restaurant, but then so is everything in this luxury hotel. *St. Elmo* (M), tel. (054 884) 2233; 23 rooms with bath or shower. High up with superb views. *Tides Reach* (E), tel. (054 884) 3466; 42 rooms with bath or shower. Fine restaurant. All the above hotels are seasonal.

Sidmouth (Devon). *Victoria* (E), tel. (03955) 2651. 62 rooms with bath. Imposing hotel in elevated position above resort.

Taunton (Som.). *Castle* (E), tel. (0823) 272671; 35 rooms with bath. Centuries-old, turreted hotel; elegant cuisine and a well-balanced wine list. Good touring base for the region. *County* (M), tel. (0823) 337651, 67 rooms with bath. Modernized Georgian coaching inn, in center of town. *Falcon* (M), tel. (0823) 442502; 11 rooms, all with bath. Small, family-run hotel on the road towards Ilminster.

Restaurants. *Castle Hotel Restaurant* (E), tel. (0823) 276671. Specializes in *haute cuisine* dishes, from classic roasts to elaborate seafood dishes. *Porters* (I), tel. (0823) 256688. Lively, crowded wine bar with pianist in the evenings.

Thornbury (Avon). *Castle* (L), tel. (0454) 418511. 16th-century castle with 14 splendid rooms with bath. Superb restaurant—among the best.

Torquay (Devon). *Imperial* (L), tel. (0803) 24301; 164 rooms with bath. One of the archetypal luxury hotels of the country, famous for its amenities, cuisine and impeccable service; pool and sauna. *Grand* (L–E), tel. (0803) 25234; 109 rooms with bath. Tennis, heated pool. *Palace* (E), tel. (0803) 22271; 141 rooms, 112 with bath, 29 with shower. Heated indoor pool, golf, good service and comfortable rooms. Many other excellent smaller residential establishments.

Tresco (I.o. Scilly). *Island Hotel* (E), tel. (0720) 22883. In subtropical gardens with private beach. Boat service from main island. Outdoor heated pool. 32 rooms, most with bath; closed mid-October to mid-March.

Truro (Cornw.). *Brookdale* (M), tel. (0872) 73513; 21 rooms, most with bath. Multinational cuisine. Golf available nearby. *Royal* (M), tel. (0872) 70345; 34 rooms, all with bath. Well-established hotel in downtown Truro, with restaurant. *Carlton* (I), tel. (0872) 72450; 28 rooms, all with bath. Family-run, in Victorian building with modern extension.
Restaurants. *Bustopher Jones* (M), tel. (0872) 79029. Exotic dishes are a specialty. Closed Sun. lunch. *The Green Room* (I), tel. (0872) 73775. Convenient spot in shopping district near Cathedral offering wide selection of vegetarian meals.

Wells (Som.). *Crown* (M), tel. (0749) 73457; 16 rooms, all with bath. Historic coaching inn with some four-poster beds; restaurant. *Red Lion* (M), tel. (0749) 72616; 36 rooms, 30 with bath. Small, comfortable hotel close to the Cathedral. *Swan* (M), tel. (0749) 78877; 32 rooms, 27 with bath, 5 with shower. Attractive, ancient building with close view of the cathedral. *White Hart* (M), tel. (0749) 72056. 26 rooms, 12 with bath or shower. Opposite cathedral. Good food and atmosphere.
Restaurants. *Ancient Gate House* (M), tel. (0749) 72056. Traditional Italian dishes, plus English menu.

Woodford Bridge (Devon). *Woodford Bridge* (M), tel. (040926) 481. 21 rooms with bath. Traditional thatched building in beautiful gardens (some accommodations in luxury cottages). Good sports facilities.

PLACES OF INTEREST. Although this is a region rich in ancient legends, especially those of Arthur and the Matter of Britain, it is not so well-stocked with great houses as are other parts of the country. What there are, though, are interesting—especially those with the longest traditions.

There are more details about visiting historic houses in the relevant section of *Facts At Your Fingertips,* and a discussion of the subject in the *Historic Houses—Precious Stones in Peril* chapter.

Avon. **Claverton Manor,** near Bath (tel. 0225 60503), contains the only American museum in Britain. Open late Mar.–early Nov., daily 2–5 (except Mon.), Bank Holidays and preceding Sun., 11–5.

Clevedon Court, near Clevedon, 14th-century manor house with 18th-century gardens. Open Apr.–Sept., Wed., Thurs., Sun., Bank Holiday Mon., 2.30–5.30. (NT).

No. 1 Royal Crescent, Bath (tel. 0225 28126). Completely restored Georgian house, with main rooms decorated and furnished in authentic period style, on the Crescent described as "the summit of the Palladian achievement in Bath." Open Mar.–Christmas, Tues.–Sat., and Bank Holiday Mon., 11–5, Sun., 2–5. Closed Good Fri.

Roman Baths Museum, Bath (tel. 0225 61111). Adjoins the famous baths and contains extensive Roman artefacts. Open daily in summer, 9–6 (until 7, July and Aug.); in winter, Mon.–Sat. 9–5, Sun. 10–5. Admission includes entrance to Roman Baths and Pump Room.

Cornwall. Barbara Hepworth Museum and Sculpture Garden, St. Ives (tel. 0736 796226). The house, studio and workshops of the famous sculptor. Open daily all year (except Sun., Sept.–June), 10–5.30 (to 4.30 in winter).

Cotehele House, Calstock (tel. 0579 50434). Romantic medieval house and gardens. Open Apr.–Oct. daily, 1–6 (or dusk); Nov.–March, gardens open during daylight. (NT).

Lanhydrock, near Bodmin (tel. 0208 3320). 17th- and 19th-century house, picture gallery and gardens. Open Apr.–Oct., daily, 11–6. Nov.–Mar. gardens open daily during daylight hours. (NT).

Launceston Castle, Launceston (tel. 0566 2365). Panoramic views of Cornwall's ancient capital and surrounding countryside. Open mid-Mar.–mid-Oct., Mon.–Sat. 9.30–6.30, Sun. 2–6.30; mid-Oct.–mid-Mar., Mon.–Sat. 9.30–4, Sun. 2–4.

St. Michael's Mount, Penzance (tel. 0736 710507). Home of Lord St. Levan. Open Apr.–May, Mon., Tues., Wed., Fri., June–Oct., Mon.–Fri., all 10.30–4.45; Nov.–Mar., Mon., Wed. and Fri. by conducted tours only, 11, 12, 2 and 3. (NT).

Tintagel Castle, Tintagel (tel. 0840 770328). Legend has this as King Arthur's birthplace; 13th-century ruins and dramatic scenery. Open. mid-Mar.–mid-Oct., Mon.–Sat. 9.30–6.30, Sun. 2–6.30; mid-Oct.–mid-Mar., Mon.–Sat. 9.30–4, Sun. 2–4.

Wheal Martyn Museum, Carthew, St. Austell (tel. 0726 850362). Outdoor and indoor story of the china clay industry on original restored 19th-century site. Open Easter–Oct., daily.

Devon. Arlington Court, near Barnstaple (tel. 027 182 296). Regency house and Victorian formal garden, once home of Chichesters (including Sir Francis). House open Apr.–Oct., daily (except Sat. but open Bank Holiday Sat.), 11–6; Garden and park open Apr.–Oct. daily, 11–6; Nov.–March, daily during daylight hours. (NT).

Bickleigh Castle, near Tiverton (tel. 088 45 363). With a history dating back to Domesday, an 11th-century chapel, an armory of Cromwellian arms and armor, and an exhibition of treasures recovered from Henry VIII's *Mary Rose* warship. Open Easter week then Wed., Sun., Bank Holiday Mon. to end of May; June–mid-Oct., daily except Sat; all 2–5.

Buckland Abbey, Tavistock (tel. 0822 853607). 13th-century Cistercian monastery, later home of Sir Francis Drake. Open Mar.–Oct. daily (inc. Bank Holidays), 11–6; rest of year, Wed., Sat., Sun., 2–5 (NT).

Castle Drogo, near Chagford (tel. 064 73 3306). Superb Edwardian granite castle built by Lutyens, bold lines and general concept. High above the river Teign gorge, in terraced gardens. Apr.–Oct., daily 11–6. (NT).

Compton Castle, near Torquay (tel. 080 47 2112). Fortified manor house. Open Apr.–Oct., Mon., Wed., Thurs., 10–12, 2–5. Otherwise by appointment. (NT).

Exeter Maritime Museum, Haven Banks, Exeter (tel. 0392 58075). Largest collection of historic, working ships in the country. Open Sept.–June daily 10–5; July–Aug. daily 10–6.

Fursdon House, Cadbury, Thorverton (tel. 0392 860860). Georgian manor house in beautiful setting. Open Easter, then May through Sept., Sun., Thurs. and Bank Holiday Mon., 2.30–4.30; also Wed. in July and

Aug. Sun. and Bank Holidays; June through Sept. Thurs., Sun. and Bank Holidays; tours only at 2.30, 3.30 and 4.30.

Killerton, near Exeter (tel. 0392 881345). Splendid costume collection in 18th-century house; fine gardens. House, Apr.–Oct., daily 11–6; gardens, all year in daytime. (NT).

Knightshayes Court, near Tiverton (tel. 0884 254665). Overpowering Victorian mansion designed by the eccentric William Burges, in beautiful gardens. Open Easter through Oct., daily (except Fri.) 1.30–6; garden open daily from 11. (NT)

Morwellham Quay, near Tavistock (tel. 0822 832766/833808). Large open-air museum based "at the greatest copper port in Queen Victoria's Empire." Open Mar.–Oct. daily 10–5.30, Nov.–Feb. daily 10–5.

Powderham Castle, near Exeter (tel. 0626 890 243). Medieval castle, home of Earl of Devon. Open late May–mid-Sept., Sun.–Thurs., 2–5.30.

Rougemont House Museum of Costume and Lace, Rougemont Gardens, Exeter (tel. 0392 265858). Permament collection includes superb displays of local lace. Open Mon.–Sat. 10–5.30.

Saltram House, Plymouth (tel. 0752 336546). Fine mansion, partly Adam. Pictures, plasterwork and wood carving. Lovely garden with rare shrubs. Open Easter through Oct., Sun.–Thurs., also Fri. and Sat. of Bank Holiday weekends, 12.30–6; garden open daily 11–6, also daylight hours in winter. (NT)

Tiverton Castle, Tiverton (tel. 0884 253200). Medieval fortress of Henry I. Open Easter through Sept. daily (except Fri. and Sat.), 2.30–5.30.

Tiverton Museum, Tiverton (tel. 0884 256295/255446). One of the best and most wide-ranging folk museums in the West Country. Open daily 10.30–4.30. Closed Sun., Bank Holidays.

Somerset. Barrington Court, near Ilminster (tel. 0460 41480/40601). Beautiful 16th-century Renaissance house and gardens. Court open Easter–Sept., Sat. and Wed. 2–5; garden Sun.–Wed. 11–5.30. (NT).

Bishop's Palace, Wells (tel. 0749 78691). Comprising 12th- and 13th-century buildings surrounded by moat with swans. Open Easter–Oct. Thur. and Sun. 2–6, May–Sept. Wed. 11–6, Aug. and Bank Holiday Mon. daily 11–6.

Brympton d'Evercy, near Yeovil (tel. 0935 862528). A lovely house, part 17th-century, part Tudor. Various exhibitions include traditional furniture making. Easter, then May–Sept., daily (except Thurs. and Fri.), 2–6. Open. Feb. through Nov.

Clapton Court, Crewkerne (tel. 0460 73220). A stunning garden with magnificent flowering shrubs. All year, Mon.–Fri., 10.30–5; Sun., 2–5; closed Sat. except Easter and in May.

Dunster Castle, Dunster, near Minehead (tel. 0643 821314). Home of the Luttrells. Open Apr. through Sept., Sun.–Thurs. 11–5, Oct.; Sun.–Thurs. 2–4. (NT). Also nearby restored 17th-century Water Mill; grinds and sells flour.

Montacute House, Yeovil (tel. 093 582 823289). Magnificent Elizabethan house. Permanent collection of Elizabethan and Jacobean paintings (in Long Gallery) from National Portrait Gallery. Open Apr.–Nov., daily (except Tues.), 12.30–5.30. (NT).

THE CHANNEL ISLANDS

England with a French Accent

The Channel Islands are the warmest part of Britain, enjoying a mean temperature of a little over 52 degrees. From April to October, day temperatures usually exceed 60 degrees; sharp winter frosts are rare. The archipelago of which Jersey and Guernsey are the chief islands has been called an admirable blend of France and Britain. It lies just off the coast of Normandy and Brittany, more than 80 miles from southern England. St. Helier, capital of Jersey, is a good center, full of quaint streets, good hotels and bathing beaches. You'll be delighted with this touch of France on British soil. Guernsey's main town is St. Peter Port, attractively built on a hillside and with a fine harbor and excellent shopping. The other islands open to visitors are Alderney, Sark and Herm.

But not only is the climate soothing and the surroundings lush—there's an atmosphere of Continental know-how that appeals to all visitors. The food is better cooked and better served than in higher-priced mainland (English) resorts; drinking laws are not so archaic and the atmosphere is flavored with a touch of the Continent.

Tourism is the biggest industry in both main islands, and to protect this industry the States of Jersey, which govern that island, has a law requiring all hotels and guest houses to register. Tourism officials then grade them according to their standards and inspect them annually to see that the standard is maintained, thus ensuring that the visitor gets a square deal. Guernsey has a similar system, and this, undoubtedly, has been one of the keystones to the islands' perennial success with British and Continental holiday-makers.

Of course, potatoes, tomatoes, flowers and the famous island breeds of cattle still play a vital part in the economy, as do the benefits gained from the many wealthy people from Britain who choose to live in or retire to Jersey (largely because taxation is much lower than on the mainland—income tax, for example, being only 20 per cent, and there being no capital gains tax or V.A.T.).

Jersey's States Assembly is composed of 12 Senators, 12 Connetables, and 29 Deputies, all elected by the people. Presiding over this is a Bailiff appointed by the Crown, who has a casting vote, and there's a Lieutenant Governor as well (representing the Queen), a Deputy Bailiff, Attorney-General, Solicitor-General and Dean, all of whom have no vote. The laws and customs present an interesting blend of Norman French and modern British. This amalgam comes about because the islands have never actually belonged to France. They were part of the hereditary estates of Duke William of Normandy, before he became William I of England—the Conqueror.

All of the other islands form part of the Bailiwick of Guernsey, which has the Bailiff of Guernsey as its civil head and chief of justice, and a 65-man parliament called the States of Deliberation. Again, a Lieutenant Governor represents the Queen.

Legal and parliamentary formalities on the main islands are mostly conducted in English although the official language is French, underlining the islands' historical and geographical connections with neighboring France. Among old people, and in outlying parts of the islands, one can hear the true language of the Channel Islands: a Norman-French *patois* which differs from island to island but is still understood by Breton fishermen.

Although not every visitor to Britain will be able to find the time to detour to these islands, they have an individual character and charm which make them worth a visit.

Jersey

Jersey, with an area of 45 square miles, is the largest of the Channel Islands and has long been a popular holiday resort with both British and French tourists. It now attracts many other European visitors, too. Outside St. Helier you can find almost every kind of holiday scenery: secluded coves for sunbathing, big swimming and surfing beaches, pretty fishing harbors, rugged rocks, dramatic cliff walks, and quiet country lanes leading through lush farmland. In fact, you will soon understand why the French call Jersey *La Reine de la Manche* (Queen of the Channel).

The dominant landmark on the west coast is La Corbière lighthouse. The east coast is overlooked by the massive bulk of Mont Orgueil Castle, whose walls (floodlit in summer) tower over the fishing village of Gorey. Beyond the castle are the beautiful bays of Anne Port, St. Catherine's and Rozel—good areas for sailing or fishing.

The rugged north coast is the best place for walking, although there is also a good inland walk along the route of one of the island's former railways (internal transport is now by hired car, taxi, or the excellent bus services). The west coast consists almost entirely of the four-mile sweep of St. Ouen's Bay, backed by sand dunes and a fine picnic ground in summer. As this bay is open to the Atlantic, it is often good for surfing; while during a winter storm the seas can be very spectacular.

St. Helier

St. Helier has its own sand beach too, for it is situated on the big, south-facing St. Aubin's Bay. It is overlooked by two fortifications—one, Elizabeth Castle, is built on an island in the bay, and can be reached by a causeway at low tide; the other is the Napoleonic Fort Regent, built on a rocky outcrop above the town and recently converted into a leisure center complete with indoor swimming pool, roller-skating rink, sports area, formal gardens, children's playground, picture gallery, conference area and museums.

The harbor area of St. Helier is rather untidy, and the town itself has a cramped layout. But this is compensated for by the magnificent shopping centered around the pedestrianized King Street, Queen Street, and part of Bath Street. Luxury goods are cheaper in the Channel Islands than anywhere else in Britain, while typical souvenirs of Jersey include heavy knitwear, pottery, and walking sticks made from the stalk of the island's famous giant cabbage.

Royal Square is an attractive, tree-lined courtyard with a statue of George II. Here, too, are the main administrative buildings of the island including the States Chamber.

Try, also, the author Gerald Durrell's zoo at Les Augres Manor, the Fishermen's Chapel at St. Brelade's Bay and the German Underground Hospital—one of only a few reminders of the Nazi occupation of the Channel Islands. In Victoria village, a few miles north of St. Helier, one of the world's finest private collections of orchids can be visited.

Guernsey

Guernsey is 26 miles north of Jersey, and rather smaller (24 square miles). It is less commercialized than Jersey, but its rugged coast, indented with sandy bays and smothered with wild flowers in spring and summer, has great scenic beauty. Although principally concerned with agriculture (the Guernsey cows are world famous) and the export of flowers and tomatoes, it has a thriving tourist industry. Anyone visiting Jersey for a fair period should cross over to Guernsey for a few days; the journey takes only two hours by steamer, one hour by hydrofoil or 15 minutes by air.

The chief port and capital is St. Peter Port which, with its terraced narrow passageways and cobblestones, has the appearance of a French fishing port. The granite houses with their mellow red-tiled roofs rise in tiers from the water's edge and make an effective contrast with the grim stronghold of Castle Cornet which dominates the harbor. The parish church of St. Peter Port, which stands at the foot of the High Street, is the finest medieval church in the Channel Islands, and has some unusual 13th-century nave arches. An attractive feature of Guernsey's capital is the number of old market halls where local produce, with the emphasis on live lobsters and crabs, is displayed by the friendly stall-holders, a few of whom still speak the old Norman-French *patois*.

Guernsey has its own independent government under the British Crown, and the opportunity of visiting the Royal Court House while the parliament—or States of Deliberation—is in session should not be missed. Not far from the Court House is Hauteville House, the residence of Victor Hugo when he was exiled from France. The house, which now belongs to the City of Paris, is open to visitors from Easter to September, and remains as it was during the lifetime of the great novelist. It gives a fascinating insight into the life and loves of this autocratic yet deeply sincere 19th-century royalist turned republican, who wrote in a rooftop room from which he could see the coastline of his beloved France. Some of the interior decoration is superbly of its time, especially the ruby-colored drawing room and the ornate Garibaldi Room, carved to within an inch of its life.

St. Peter Port is the largest town on the island, but there are many charming hamlets to which expeditions can easily be made. Torteval Church has a remarkable round tower, and in the grounds of the monastery of Les Vauxbelets is the quaint Little Chapel, studded with shells and broken china, the work of one of the brothers. Try to catch it on a sunny day when it positively glows.

Frequent bus services radiate out from St. Peter Port to the island's beaches. The island's triangular shape, and the high cliffs on the south coast which forms the base of the triangle mean that one or other of the beaches is almost always protected from the wind. Try Fermain Bay, by St. Peter Port on the east coast, a pebbled beach with sand at half tide, while in the afternoon one can visit the sheltered southern bays, like Moulin Huet or Petit Bôt. In calm weather the big, flat, sandy beaches of the west and north are the best: among them Rocquaine, Vazon, Pembroke and Cobo Bay, which is excellent for children.

There are many fine walks, particularly on the south coast and on L'Ancresse Common in the north. Numerous gun emplacements bear witness to the German Occupation of the Channel Islands during World War II, and—as on Jersey—there is a vast German Underground Hospital. Look out, too, for Napoleonic Martello Towers guarding the beaches, and for the "water lanes"—quiet paths which follow the courses of streams down to some of the south coast bays and which in summer are almost overgrown with trees, bushes, and luxuriant ferns. In spring, wild flowers appear everywhere in Guernsey—a rare form of yellow poppy even grows on the shingle at some points along the west coast.

The islanders were once a very superstitious people, with a fear of witches. As a result many houses—even comparatively new ones—have the traditional feature of a large stone sticking out of the chimney where passing witches can sit and warm themselves and (hopefully) will therefore be grateful enough not to harm the inhabitants. In fact Guernsey claims to have held the last witch trial in Europe, in 1912, when a woman was convicted to eight days in the hoosegow for bewitching St. Peter Port's chimneys.

The Other Islands

Smaller islands in the archipelago offer attractive by-ways and beaches and quite a lot of solitude, with little in the way of entertainment.

Alderney has an airport and even a capital town (St. Anne) fitted into its tiny area of 1,962 acres on which live about 1,700 people, three quarters of whom live in St. Anne. Many are retired mainlanders, the others are mostly concerned with fishing or agriculture (shellfish are a local industry and are delicious). Should you cross to Alderney, you'll discover silver sands, some hotels and a few comfortable guest or farm houses to cater for you fairly hospitably but not luxuriously. Among the best beaches is Telegraph Bay, ideal for sunbathing on the rocks, and with lovely sand. There are a number of old castles and forts on the islands, many of them in ruins, and little to do except swim or walk, but there are few better places to do just that.

Sark is an independent feudal fief of the crown and can be visited by boat from any of the main islands, most easily from Guernsey. Dame Sibyl Hathaway, who died in 1974 at the age of 90, was the widow of an American war hero who joined the British Army in World War I while the U.S. was still neutral. Her grandson, an engineer, is now the Seigneur of Sark. An unusual feature is that cars are banned from the island: instead you can tour in a horse-drawn carriage or hire a bicycle, much more in keeping with Sark's leisurely way of life. Again, there are superb beaches, many of which are almost inaccessible, requiring quite an expedition to reach. They are, perhaps, not ideal for really small children.

Getting to Sark is quite an experience. The boat weaves through rocks and swirling currents to an incredible little harbor where entry is through a huge, rock-carved tunnel. Two other harbors are used according to the direction and force of the wind, one entailing a climb of several hundred steps carved out of the rock!

Herm and Jethou are mere islets, the largest of the many rocks—some barely showing above the sea—that comprise the remaining Channel Islands. Herm, which is leased to a farmer, Major Peter Wood, has a good hotel and some self-catering accommodation, as well as shops and a friendly pub. It is a pretty island, with excellent beaches including sheltered Belvoir Bay and the sweeping expanse of Shell Beach, where the Gulf Stream deposits millions of shells from the Caribbean, some of them powdered to the consistency of sand but others still whole. It is, of course, a dream place for a shell collector. The island is very popular with daytrippers from Guernsey, three miles away and, as on Sark, cars are banned.

Jethou, close by, is privately owned, and cannot be visited without special permission.

PRACTICAL INFORMATION FOR
THE CHANNEL ISLANDS

HOW TO GET THERE. *British Channel Island Ferries* operate year-round drive-on, drive-off ferry services to Jersey and Guernsey from Poole (taking from 6 to 9 hours). *Condor* operate a hydrofoil service from Weymouth to Guernsey and Jersey (and to Alderney in high summer) from end March through October. Fast trains link London (Waterloo) with these sailings. *Torbay Seaways* operate a roll-on-roll-off car ferry service from Torquay to both islands, the journey taking slightly over six hours. It is also practical to use boat services to travel between the islands. In addition there is a hydrofoil service, operated by *Condor* of Guernsey, between Jersey, Guernsey and Alderney with varying frequency according to the season. This hydrofoil service also operates to St. Malo in Britanny, while another ferry service (also with drive-on, drive-off facilities) runs on this route. For the smaller islands of Sark and Herm there are boat services from St. Peter Port (Guernsey).

Both main islands have frequent air services from around thirty airports on the mainland in summer, less so in winter. Some examples: From London (Heathrow) *British Airways* fly to Jersey and *Air UK* fly to Guernsey; from London (Gatwick) *British Caledonian* operate to Jersey and *Guernsey Airlines* to Guernsey. Shortest route is from Southampton taking about 40 minutes to Guernsey and 35 minutes to Jersey. This route is operated by *Air Atlantique, Aurigny,* and *British Midland* among others. *Air Atlantique* sometimes use a Dakota! Southampton airport has a fast direct rail link from London (Waterloo), alight at Southampton Parkway Station.

The locally run *Jersey European Airways* flies from Jersey to Stansted (near London), Exeter in Devon and Bournemouth on the south coast (and also to Paris). And the tiny island of Alderney has its own airline, *Aurigny Air Services,* which flies to Southampton as well as to Cherbourg and operates an intensive inter-island service.

HOTELS AND RESTAURANTS. Channel Island hotels are mostly attractive and often have a strong French flavor. Most of them quote favorable weekly, all-inclusive rates, but you *must* book well ahead for summer.

Details about our grading system, plus other relevant information about hotels and restaurants, will be found at the beginning of the book in the *Facts at Your Fingertips* section.

Alderney. *Chez André* (M), tel. (048 182) 2777; 14 rooms, 7 with bath. Pleasant, lively holiday hotel with restaurant serving English and continental cuisine.

Restaurant. *Nellie Gray's* (M), St. Anne, tel. (048 182) 333. Wholesome cooking, wide choice.

Guernsey. St. Martin's. *Bella Luce* (M), tel. (0481) 38764. 31 rooms, 27 with bath, 4 with shower. *St. Margaret's Lodge* (M), tel. (0481) 35757; 42 rooms with bath. *St. Martin's* (M), tel. (0481) 35644; 51 rooms with bath.

St. Peter Port. *St. Pierre Park* (E), tel. (0481) 28282. Fine hotel in 40-acre grounds; 134 rooms with bath. Sauna, gym and all the accessories of healthy living. *Old Government House* (E–M), tel. (0481) 24921; 75 rooms, all with bath. Exactly what its name implies, with impressive views and atmosphere.

La Frégate (M), tel. (0481) 24624: 13 rooms with bath, but especially notable for an excellent restaurant; specialties, of course, French. *Royal* (M), tel. (0481) 23921. Nicely sited in the Glategny Esplanade, 78 rooms, 71 with bath, 7 with shower.

Restaurants. *Carrington of Mill Street* (M), tel. (0481) 710451. Creative French cuisine. *La Frégate* (see above), is best for both food and locale. *Le Nautique* (M), tel. (0481) 21714, down near the marina, for excellent local fish. *Nino's Ristorante Italiano* (M), tel. (0481) 23052. Popular spot serving fish and pasta dishes. *Courts Wine Lodge* (I), tel. (0481) 21782. Excellent lunches. Wine bar in evenings.

254　EXPLORING BRITAIN

Jersey. Bouley Bay. *Water's Edge* (E–M), tel. (0534) 62777; 56 rooms all with bath. Exactly what it says—ideal for a sea holiday.

La Corbière. *Seacrest* (M), Petit Port, tel. (0534) 46353; 7 rooms all with bath. Especially notable for restaurant.

Gorey. *Moorings* (M), tel. (0534) 53633. 16 rooms with bath. Below the impressive castle and overlooking the harbor. *Old Court House* (M), tel. (0534) 54444; 58 rooms with bath.

St. Brelade's Bay. *L'Horizon* (L) tel. (0534) 43101; 105 rooms, all with bath. Right on beach, attracting smart clientele. International menu in smart restaurant. *St. Brelade's Bay* (E), tel. (0534) 46141; 72 rooms, all with bath, in pleasant gardens. *Atlantic* (E–M), tel. (0534) 44101; 46 rooms with bath. Modern hotel in splendid setting. *Château Valeuse* (M), tel. (0534) 46281; 26 rooms, 18 with bath, 5 with shower. Try the restaurant for more excellent fish. *La Place* (M), tel. (0534) 44261; 41 rooms with bath. Comfortable and stylish.

Restaurant. *Panorama* (M), tel. (0534) 41399. Seafood and paella.

St. Clement's Bay. *Ambassadeur* (M–I), tel. (0534) 24455; 41 rooms with bath. Scandinavian decor, overlooking beach, excellent for families.

St. Helier. *Grand* (E–M), tel. (0534) 22301. 116 rooms with bath. Elegant seafront hotel. Its *Victoria's* restaurant (M), tel. (0534) 72255, is very good for seafood. *Beaufort* (M), tel. (0534) 32471; 54 rooms with bath, bright and pleasing. *Pomme d'Or* (M), tel. (0534) 78644. 151 rooms, completely modernized.

Restaurants. *La Buca* (M), tel. (0534) 34283 and *Mauro's* (M), tel. (0534) 20147, are two restaurants specializing in Italian and French cooking.

St. Saviour. *Longueville Manor* (L–E), tel. (0534) 25501; 33 rooms with bath. Luxurious manor house hidden from road. Outdoor swimming pool, riding facilities.

Sark. *Aval du Creux* (M–I), tel. (048 183) 2036; 13 rooms, 11 with bath or shower. Good restaurant. *Dixcart* (M–I), tel. (048 183) 2015; 18 rooms; 7 with bath. *Petit Champ* (M–I), tel. (048 183) 2046; 16 rooms, 11 with bath. All secluded and tranquil.

Restaurant. *La Sablonerie* (M–I), tel. (048 183) 2061. Historic farmhouse; excellent restaurant; also 22 rooms, including some attractive small cottages.

TRAVEL ON THE ISLANDS. All three islands have local bus services, that on Alderney being in summer only. In addition car hiring is easy on all three, the rates and gas being expensive. On Sark and Herm cars are banned, so sightseers must walk or cycle.

USEFUL ADDRESSES. *Jersey Tourism* is at Weighbridge, St. Helier, Jersey, C.I., tel. (0534) 78000. Also a London office at 35 Albemarle Street, London W1X 3FB, tel. 01–493 5278. The *States of Guernsey Tourist Board* is at Box 23, White Rock, Guernsey, C.I., tel. (0481) 23552. *Alderney Tourism Committee,* States Office, Alderney, C.I., tel. (048182) 2994.

THINGS TO SEE AND DO. Three outstanding events are Jersey's Spring Festival in May, the France-Jersey Festival in early June, and the *Battle of Flowers* on the second Thursday in August at St. Helier. Guern-

sey also has a *Battle of Flowers* in Saumarez Park, usually on the third
Thursday in August and a large-scale Guernsey Festival in September.

Guernsey. Castle Cornet, in St. Peter Port harbor, is a fine example
of a medieval fortress. It has been considerably altered since that time and
consequently shows a variety of architectural styles. There is a fascinating
museum inside the castle. Open Apr.–Oct., daily, 10.30–5.30.

The Little Chapel, at Les Vauxbelets in St. Andrew, is believed to be
the smallest chapel in the world. Modeled after the grotto at Lourdes, the
building was the work of one monk. Open daily.

Folk Museum, Saumarez Park. Farming equipment, replica of 19th-
century kitchen, etc. Lovely setting. Open Apr.–Oct., daily, 10–5.30.

German Underground Hospital, near the Little Chapel, is the largest
of its kind in the Channel Islands. It took over three years to construct
and serves as a grim reminder of the German occupation during World
War II. Open May–Sept. daily 10–12 and 2–5; Apr. and Oct. daily 2–4;
Nov., Sun. and Thurs. 2–3. Closed winter.

Guernsey Museum and Art Gallery, Candie Gardens, St. Peter Port.
This is a purpose-built museum with its own audio-visual theater. Collections are concerned with the history of the island and its people. Open
daily 10.30–5.30 (4.30 in winter).

Hauteville House, St. Peter Port. Home of the famous French author
and poet, Victor Hugo, from 1856–70. Collection of Hugo relics. Open
Mon.–Sat., Apr.–Sept., 10–11.30, 2–4.30. Closed Bank Holidays.

Sports. The Beau Séjour Center has modern sports facilities of all kinds.
Also musicals, plays, disco-dancing, exhibitions.

Jersey. Elizabeth Castle, St. Aubin's Bay, reached by causeway or
ferry, according to the tide. A 16th-century, Elizabethan castle, which has
been extensively renovated and repaired. Houses the Jersey Militia Museum, with relics from Napoleonic times. Open Apr.–Oct., daily, 9.30–5.30.

Eric Young Orchid Foundation, Victoria Village. Unique collection of
exotic flowers in glasshouse environment. A breathtaking display. Please
check opening times locally.

Jersey Museum and Art Gallery, Pier Rd, St. Helier, contains collections of local and natural history, silver, photography, a Lillie Langtry
display and four period rooms. The art gallery has paintings by local artists. Open daily, except Sun., 10–5.

Jersey Museum at La Hougue Bie, in Grouville. The prehistoric tomb
is crowned by two medieval chapels. A German Occupation Museum is
housed in a former underground shelter. Nearby is an Agricultural Museum with a good collection of old farming implements. A reminder of the
days when Jersey had a railroad network is the railroad exhibition in a
former guard's van. Museum complex is open mid-Mar.–Nov., daily (except Mon.), 10–5.

Mont Orgueil Castle, Gorey. A powerful, 13th-century fortress, which
is totally inaccessible from the sea. From its walls you can see across to
France. The crypt of St. George's Chapel, the keep and Somerset Tower
are all worth looking at. Inside the castle is a small exhibition depicting
the castle's history. Open Apr.–Oct., daily, 9.30–5.30.

Sports, The Fort Regent Leisure Centre has all the facilities, including
a national-size pool, mini golf course, tennis, badminton, solarium. Also

concert hall, discos; doll and toy, shell, and postal museums; restaurants. Open 10 A.M.–10 P.M.

Zoo, Les Augres Manor in Trinity. Founded in 1963 by the well-known author and naturalist Gerald Durrell, the zoo is the headquarters of the Jersey Wildlife Preservation Trust. Dedicated to the preservation and breeding of endangered species, the 20-acre area contains one of the rarest zoological collections in the world. Open daily.

SHOPPING. A worthwhile pursuit in Jersey and Guernsey, as there is no Value Added Tax (V.A.T.). H.M. Customs allow concessions on perfumes, tobacco and alcohol for personal use only, provided these are declared on arrival in the U.K. Details from any Customs and Excise office.

THE COTSWOLDS AND
THE THAMES

Dreaming Spires and White Horses

The Thames exercises a spell. In London it slides by, almost unnoticed, dominated by the great buildings that line its banks. But even there an atmosphere of the magic of times past seems to rise like an intangible mist from the swiftly moving waters.

To see the river at its best means first going towards its source, to the Cotswolds, and then turning back—no hardship, since the stretch of country that lies between say, Gloucester and London is scenically lovely and historically rich, and most of it is the valley of the Thames.

Although the name "Cotswolds" comes from a range of hills that sweeps diagonally from southeast to northwest across the old county of Gloucestershire, part now falls in the new county of Avon, a nebulous area dreamed up by civil servants and one that few people can take seriously. As a result the name "Cotswold" has become a vaguer, and more imprecise term, especially beloved of house agents who like to take advantage of its aura of smart attractiveness to sell their houses. For our purposes, we will stick to the old, accepted definition of the region, claiming that the highest point of the Cotswolds, 1,000 ft., is at Cleve Hill near Cheltenham; that they fall sharply away to the Severn Vale, where Gloucester is located; and that one gets some marvelous views from various points, notably Birdlip Hill, on the A417, the road from Cirencester and one of the two roads most likely to be used by people coming from London. From Birdlip, too, you are within seven miles of both Gloucester and Cheltenham, and only 100 miles from London.

GLOUCESTERSHIRE

Clearly, the best starting point for a tour of Gloucestershire is Gloucester itself, the county town. There are comfortable hotels and inns in which to spend the night. Before setting out in the morning, pay a visit to the famous cathedral. You may have difficulty finding the cathedral at all, as it is none too well signposted. Within the elegant exterior is an almost complete Norman carcass: the massive pillars of the nave have been left untouched since their completion in 1100. Make sure that you do not miss the miraculous fan vaulting in the cloisters, one of the greatest achievements of the art of the medieval mason. Look for the tomb and effigy of Edward II, imprisoned in Berkeley Castle and murdered there in 1327. The interior has been spared the sterilizing attentions of the modern architectural reformer—the clutter of centuries mirrors the slow growth of ecclesiastical taste.

Unfortunately, the town itself hasn't been so lucky. Most traces of its considerable antiquity have been skilfully removed, leaving the cathedral as a lonely monument to the city's distinguished past. However, Gloucester is revitalizing its old docklands and has plans for a National Inland Waterway Museum. But little remains of the town's former glory. In Roman times Gloucester was an important *colonia,* its name being *Colonia Glevum,* founded by Nerva in A.D. 96. Before the Norman conquest, Gloucester was a borough with a royal residence and a mint, a sign of its highly privileged position.

The A38 road from Gloucester runs inland from the Severn, but its side roads make it an ideal route for sightseeing of a varied kind.

Anyone drawn to strange natural phenomena will be fascinated by the Severn Bore. The wide estuary of the River Severn narrows and curves dramatically toward Gloucester, and the incoming tide sweeping up from the Bristol Channel forces its way against the outward flow of the river, creating a great tidal wave sometimes reaching six feet high and charging along at some 13 miles an hour, roaring like an express train. It occurs many times a year, but is at its most spectacular during the high Spring tides. Good viewing points are from Upper Rea, Stone Bench and Elmore Back on the east bank; and from Minsterworth on the west bank, where the river has narrowed considerably and the bore is therefore higher. Any local information office or hotelier in the district will be able to direct you to the best spot at the right time.

If you are a wildlife enthusiast, Slimbridge and Peter Scott's Severn Wildfowl Trust is about 10 miles down the A38. Another splendid place to visit in this vicinity is Berkeley Castle.

Clamped between the two great rivers, the Severn and the Wye, is the Forest of Dean. Ideally it's for walkers, but car owners have not been neglected, for there are scenic drives to be enjoyed in this 25,000-acre area of secret glades, hills and woodland.

Aim at the Forest center, and you reach the Speech House. In medieval times the forest Verderers held court here, the system of forest rule which they administered dating back to the days of King Canute. The Speech House is now an hotel, and although the area is today administered by the county authorities, Verderers are still elected and meet several times a year to discuss and settle more intimate local problems. Facing the hotel, a pillar marks the geographical center of the forest; and memorial trees date from the acorn planted by Prince Albert, Queen Victoria's much-loved Consort, to today's royal tree sprouting from an acorn grown from Prince Albert's oak.

The Dean Heritage Museum, at Soudley, near Cinderford, tells the story of the Forest in words, pictures and exhibits. As an insight into the history of Dean, its mining for iron and coal which has gone on since Roman times (more private now than commercial) and its development as an enchanting area full of interest for today's visitors, this should be one of your first stops. Also visit the Clearwell Caves for an underground tour of the ancient iron mines, worked for over 2,000 years, until 1945.

Cheltenham has managed to attract an undeserved reputation for Victorian stuffiness, but in fact, it is one of the country's most beautiful towns. It rivals Bath in its Georgian elegance, with wide, tree-lined streets, graceful secluded villas, plentiful gardens, crescents and squares. Nearly every house is an almost unsurpassed example of Regency elegance, an elegance that is sometimes unhappily eclipsed by the architectural monstrosities that were produced later in the century.

Until the 18th century, Cheltenham was simply another Cotswold village, but in 1715 a mineral spring was discovered, and by 1740, the first spa had been built. Over the following 200 years, it became a favorite retiring place for colonial civil servants, who found the waters most effective in relieving the liver and digestive troubles that afflict Europeans living in hot climates. The restored pump room, together with a Gallery of Fashion, is now open to the public.

Chipping Campden is undoubtedly one of the most beautiful of the Cotswold stone villages. Its wide main street, divided by an old market hall, is packed with fascinating early buildings. One of the oldest is Woolstaplers Hall Museum, and its contents are as worthwhile to see as its architecture: packed floor to ceiling in small rooms, the upper floors reached by narrow, twisting stairways, are such extraordinary relics as old sewing machines, man-traps, cash registers, fearsome pieces of early dental equipment, early cameras, and highly amusing posters and postcards, many of which are for sale. The church, too, is a splendid one, with fine brasses and tomb monuments.

Thames Country

In order to find the source of the Thames it is necessary first to get to Cirencester. This can be done from London by leaving the M4 at Junction 15, then A419 for Cirencester; from Cheltenham on A435, or from Gloucester on A417, which is a Roman road. But it might be more rewarding to drift around the Cotswolds a little first, taking in such places as Tetbury, Painswick, Bibury, Chedworth, Sapperton, Northleach, North Cerney, to name at random some outstandingly lovely villages in the warm, Cotswold stone. It would be a pity to hurry in such a picturesque and historic district. Constant pictures emerge of that Old Mill by a Stream, especially obvious at the oddly named village of Slaughter. "Royal" Tetbury, a lovely old market town, is near the home of the Prince and Princess of Wales. And Fairford, between Lechlade and Cirencester, is worth visiting if only for its church, dating from the 15th century, with magnificent 15th- and 16th-century stained glass windows, said to be the finest in England. During World War II they were removed and buried in a secret place for safety, but are back in their original positions to grace an already exceptional building.

Since Cirencester was the hub of three Roman roads, Ermin Street, Fosse Way and Icknield Way, it was obviously important from a very early date. The town's excellent Corinium Museum contains reconstructed Roman domestic rooms and a workshop, and will give you a good idea of how much the Romans valued their creature comforts. This attractive town also has a twice-weekly open market and old brewery buildings that have recently been converted into craft workshops producing exceptionally high-quality gifts. To the west of the town is Cirencester Park, owned by Lord Bathurst, but open daily to walkers who can explore its 3,000 acres and five-mile avenues of chestnut trees. Many of the streets in the town are unchanged from the 16th and 17th centuries; and the parish church, the largest in Gloucestershire, dates from Norman times, but most of the structure was built in the 13th to 15th centuries, by the enormously rich wool merchants.

The actual source of the Thames has in the past been a point of controversy. In 1958, the august body of the Thames Conservancy Board definitely marked the source as a spring which flows out of a meadow called Trewsbury Mead near the village of Coates. There used to be a statue of Old Father Thames beside the source, but vandalism prompted its removal and now it stands beside St. John's Lock near Lechlade. To reach the spot, it is best to leave Cirencester on A429, then take A433, the Tetbury road, and after 4 miles you will come to Thames Head Bridge—the source is off to the right.

The first village on the baby Thames is Ewen, followed by Ashton Keynes, but Cricklade is the first town on the banks of the river. Below Cricklade, the river slowly meanders through an almost undisturbed part of the English countryside. This is the stripling Thames, which the poet Matthew Arnold extolled. At Castle Eaton, there is the first of the countless riverside pubs and the first bridge of any size. All these quiet little villages in the upper reaches of the river look almost untouched by the bustle of the 20th century, and it is hard to remember that London is only three hours' drive away. Just above Lechlade, which is the last Thames town in the county, the river is joined by the first of its tributaries, the Lech, famous for its trout. As the river flows on through Oxfordshire, it has at last become recognizable as the Thames.

OXFORDSHIRE

The River Thames takes on a new graciousness as it flows along the borders of Oxfordshire for 71 miles, and with each mile it increases in size and importance. Four tributaries swell the river as it passes through the county: the Windrush, the Evenlode, the Cherwell and the Thame. Just after Lechlade, which is east of Cirencester on A417, there is the first of the 45 locks which make the upper reaches of the river navigable. The Thames Conservancy Board has the overall responsibility for the locks, as it has for the towpaths which border the river. These narrow, dusty paths were originally used by barge horses pulling their heavy loads; today, they provide excellent riverside walks. The stretch of the river between Lechlade and Oxford is intensely rural, frequently winding out of reach of even the smallest road. After Oxford, the river is sufficiently large for "steamers"; for the last century, Salter Brothers have been running a daily summer service downstream leaving from Folly Bridge in Oxford (you can also catch the boat from other points along this part of the river). This is an excellent, if somewhat leisurely, way of seeing perhaps the most interesting section of the Thames.

Although the river is so important to the county, Oxfordshire is not all meadows, willow trees, locks and boats. North of the river and the city of Oxford, there is some of the most fertile farming land in the country, and the dominant topography of both the western and eastern borders is undulating hills. In the west there are the Oxfordshire Cotswolds, with their yellow stone villages and small towns like Burford and Witney, and to the north, Chipping Norton, and Broughton with its castle.

In the east are the Chilterns, with their colorful beech woods and numerous paths. There are not really many wooded areas, but there is a tiny remaining fragment of an ancient royal forest in Wychwood, which still has a magical air about it.

Naturally, the center of interest for any visitor to the county is Oxford and its university, but there are several other interesting places that should be seen before arriving at Oxford itself.

Following the course of the river as it enters the county after Lechlade, you will soon arrive at Kelmscott, the home of William Morris and, for a time, Rossetti. It was here at Kelmscott Manor that they established the revolution in artistic taste a century ago. Even the most perfunctory look at the surrounding countryside will reveal the principal sources of Morris' inspiration. Some of the clusters of the trees look as if they have stepped straight from one of his textile designs. The house itself is now owned by Oxford University, and is a unique monument to the "Brotherhood." Morris died at Kelmscott and is buried there.

Journey north from here towards the Cotswolds once more and stop at Burford. A model English town built on the slopes of the Windrush, it is still in much the same state of preservation as it was two centuries ago, when it was a popular horseracing town. Most of the buildings are set at right angles to the main street and must be approached on foot up narrow alleys and yards. Look for the Tolsey and its museum, the 15th-century Grammar School, and the 17th-century Great House, in Witney Street. Witney itself, famous the world over for its wool blankets, is a few miles' drive to the east on A40. You will have to pass through it to reach Woodstock and Blenheim Palace.

This imposing palace was granted to the Duke of Marlborough after his victories in the Low Countries in 1704, which included the battle at the town of Blenheim—hence the name. The palace was designed by Vanbrugh, and the impressive gardens and lakes are mainly the fruits of 20 years of work by Capability Brown. This most famous of English land-scape gardeners declared that his object at Blenheim was to "make the Thames look like a small stream compared with the winding Danube in Blenheim Park." At points, he almost succeeds—the scale of these grounds must be seen to be believed. The total cost of landscaping is reputed to have been in the region of £300,000. It was here that Winston Churchill was born, and in the nearby village of Bladon, in the simple churchyard, he lies buried. Due south of Woodstock and Bladon on A34 lies the city of Oxford.

Oxford

Whatever preconceived notions you may have about Oxford, your first sight of the city will doubtlessly confirm them all. Stop on one of the low hills that surround it, to look at the skyline. If you are fortunate, and the sun is shining, the towers, spires, turrets and pinnacles will look like a scene from a medieval fairy story. Here stretched out in front of you is Oxford, the home of erudition and scholarship, of Oxford English and—of Oxford marmalade. From here, time appears to have passed the city by and it must look much the same as it did 200 years or even longer ago.

First appearances are deceptive, however. The last 50 years have seen changes in Oxford that have revolutionized not only the town, but the very basis of university life itself. It is, in fact, one of the fastest-growing manu-facturing towns in England. Although the average undergraduate can spend his three years at Oxford and only once a year, perhaps, pass the two vast industrial concerns that are responsible for the changes, he cannot remain unaffected by them. The Rover Group car works and the equally enormous Pressed Steel factory that are situated in the outlying suburb of Cowley are behind the rapid growth of the city. This burgeoning of in-dustry has brought changes which might not be apparent to the visitor, but which are felt most keenly by the shopkeepers and various trades people, who 50 years ago were totally reliant on the university for trade. Today, they have a vast pool of customers from the outlying housing estates, providing them with business throughout the year.

The exact date of the origins of the city of Oxford is not clear. It was most likely a late Saxon town, that was part fortress, and part market. No doubt the Saxon chieftains were attracted to its central position, and it became a favorite venue for royal conferences, a kind of Saxon conven-tion center. During the early Middle Ages, the city thrived as a center of the flourishing wool trade—the earliest records date back to 1147, and can still be inspected in Oxford town hall.

At some time during the 12th century, Oxford became a meeting place for scholars. Some theories claim that it was founded by English students who had been expelled from the University of Paris in 1167, while others hold that it is an offshoot of the various monastic institutions in the imme-diate neighborhood. Whatever its origins, it is certain that by the end of the 12th century, the Royal Borough of Oxford was the home of the first established center of learning in England.

The earliest colleges founded in Oxford were University College (1249), Balliol (1263), and Merton College (1264). From the 13th century on-wards a succession of royal charters strengthened the position of the uni-versity at the expense of the city; in many instances it was the university

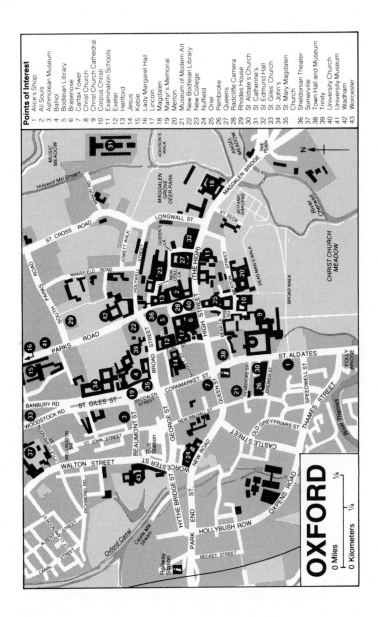

Points of Interest

1 Alice's Shop
2 All Souls
3 Ashmolean Museum
4 Balliol
5 Bodleian Library
6 Brasenose
7 Carfax Tower
8 Christ Church
9 Christ Church Cathedral
10 Corpus Christi
11 Examination Schools
12 Exeter
13 Hertford
14 Jesus
15 Keble
16 Lady Margaret Hall
17 Lincoln
18 Magdalen
19 Martyr's Memorial
20 Merton
21 Museum of Modern Art
22 New Bodleian Library
23 New College
24 Nuffield
25 Oriel
26 Pembroke
27 Queens
28 Radcliffe Camera
29 Rhodes House
30 St Aldate's Church
31 St Catherine's
32 St Edmund Hall
33 St Giles' Church
34 St John's
35 St Mary Magdalen Church
36 Sheldonian Theater
37 Somerville
38 Town Hall and Museum
39 Trinity
40 University Church
41 University Museum
42 Wadham
43 Worcester

OXFORD

0 Miles   ¼
0 Kilometers   ¼

that ruled the town and not the other way round. Oxford became a power in the kingdom, as Canterbury once was, and its splendor was enhanced by new colleges built during the reign of the Tudors and by magnificent buildings of the later era (Sheldonian Theatre, Radcliffe Camera, etc.). There was a good deal of reconstructing and rebuilding of medieval and renaissance Oxford in the 18th century, which destroyed some of the old streets that used to thread their way through the ancient "Latin Quarter" of the university. Many old almshouses, friaries, and houses inhabited in the Middle Ages by various religious bodies were sacrificed in the process, and the city that emerged from all those efforts was less compact, less uniform in its character than before. Nevertheless, even today a visitor will find no difficulty in discovering the real Oxford after wading from the railway station across nondescript approaches of a rather commercial city towards the stern beauty of the colleges.

The presence of the university ensures for the city standards of entertainment and cultural activity unusual in a provincial town. Few evenings pass without a choice of concert and theatrical performance. There is a famous bookshop, as well as schools of widespread renown, while the Clarendon Press is known the world over.

There is such a bewildering display of architectural styles in Oxford that the less good often takes the attention away from the best. You can, of course, just wander around and generally take in the atmosphere, but, assuming you wish to give one of the great cities of Europe its due, it is fairly easy to visit most of the more beautiful and historic buildings and to come away with a feeling for the university.

Start at the Carfax Tower, as this is the center of the city. Walk south down St. Aldate's Street towards Folly Bridge, with the Victorian Town Hall (you can examine the ancient records of the city if you wish to, including the Royal Charter of 1199) and the Public Library on the left. On the other side of the street is the City Information Center, one of the best equipped in the country and ready to advise on all aspects of the city's life and past; during the summer walking tours are organized. Book ahead if possible.

Continuing, you will soon come to the impressive Christ Church, known to its members as "the House." There was a time when the enormous college had only 101 students—Great Tom, its huge bell, can still be heard tolling 101 strokes at five past nine every evening to summon them home. General Oglethorpe, founder of the state of Georgia, studying at the much smaller Pembroke College, opposite, in the shadow of Wren's Tom Tower, must have heard these bells only too often. The chapel of Christ Church existed before the college and is also the cathedral of Oxford. The singing of its choir is justly famous (though keenly rivaled at Magdalen and New College). The college has its own rather splendid picture gallery. Among former members were William Penn (expelled in 1661) and Lewis Carroll. A shop opposite the meadows in St. Aldate's was the inspiration for the shop in *Through the Looking Glass.* The college gardens flanking the Broad Walk are beautiful and the meadows extend to the river Cherwell. If you would rather see Oxford as a distant panorama across a foreground of greenery, continue to Folly Bridge and hire a boat.

On foot it is best to leave Christ Church beyond the cathedral, where you will soon find yourself in Corpus Christi, which introduced Latin and

Greek to the university curriculum. Standing next door is Merton College, one of the richest and oldest. The Chapel and the 14th-century library are notable. T. S. Eliot was a member of this college. Henrietta Maria, the wife and queen of Charles I, was billeted at Merton during the Civil War, to be near her husband, who was staying at Christ Church. Oriel is Merton's neighbor, and is famous for its sons, among others, Sir Walter Raleigh.

Leaving Oriel, make your way up Bear Lane, past the Bear Inn, which boasts the lowest ceiling in Oxford, into the High Street, referred to as "the High." In fact, most streets in the town are known by their nicknames and abbreviations, so Turl Street is never referred to as anything but "the Turl," and then there are "the Corn" and "the Broad," etc. Crossing "the High" then, enter Brasenose College (or BNC for short), named from an ancient bronze nose-shaped knocker that used to hang on the front door.

Across the road from BNC is All Souls, which has no undergraduates. It consists almost entirely of appointed fellows, and is one of the most exclusive and erudite clubs in the world. Radcliffe Square (behind Brasenose), which is the heart of the university, boasts the third largest dome in England in its Radcliffe Camera.

The building at the northern end of the square is the famous Bodleian Library, where a copy of every book published in England must be sent. It takes its name from Sir Thomas Bodley, who presented his own fine collection to the university in 1602 and remodeled the earlier building to accommodate them. A splendid array of books is generally on display under the magnificent vault of the former Divinity School and in a second Exhibition Room, and a glimpse of Duke Humphrey's Library, the oldest part of the Bodleian, can be had above. Beyond, facing "the Broad" stands the Sheldonian Theatre, a fine classical assembly hall by Wren, recently restored with newly sculptured heads of Roman emperors. The corner between the new Bodleian extension and Hertford College is always a scene of flying bicycles and hurrying undergraduates. Hertford has a bridge, modeled on the Bridge of Sighs in Venice, which spans New College Lane. New College—new, that is, in 1379, from which time dates some of the stained glass in the chapel—incorporates a long stretch of the medieval city wall in its gardens. It was the home of the famous Doctor Spooner and his spoonerisms: he is reputed to have told one dilettante student, "You have hissed your mystery lectures and tasted a whole worm."

No tour of Oxford would be complete without a visit to Magdalen—pronounced *Maudlin*—College. To reach it from New College, walk down New College Lane into Queen's Lane, passing on your left St. Edmund Hall, and on your right, Queens. Turn left at "the High," pass the Examination Halls (known as schools), opposite, and find Magdalen College, a few minutes' walk further on. This is one of the richest colleges, with a magnificent main quadrangle and a supremely monastic air. A walk round the Deer Park and along Addison's Walk will lead you to envy the members of the college for the experience of living here. They have included such diverse people as Cardinal Wolsey, John Mason, founder of New Hampshire, Prince Rupert, Gibbon, and Oscar Wilde. Magdalen Bridge is famous for the May Day celebrations after an evening of May Balls. Undergraduates gather in punts under the bridge at dawn to hear the choristers singing the May Day anthem from the tower.

The other principal colleges and the famous Ashmolean Museum all
lie north of Carfax, so that after Magdalen, you should walk up "the High"
back to the Carfax. When you reach Carfax, turn right up Cornmarket
Street, through the main shopping center and soon the massive walls of
St. John's and Balliol loom into sight. The latter's undistinguished 19th-
century buildings do not reflect the fame it acquired at that time in the
world of letters and politics. Opposite Balliol the Martyrs' Memorial
marks the spot where Ridley, Latimer and Cranmer were burned by
"Bloody Mary" in 1555 and 1556. St. John's has colonnades and a garden
front that was designed by Inigo Jones.

Way beyond the north end of St. Giles, in virtual banishment, lie Lady
Margaret Hall and Somerville, the earliest colleges founded for young ladies.

Beaumont Street, on the other side of St. Giles, leads to Worcester College. In this Regency street stands the Ashmolean Museum, with an outstanding collection of archeological finds from Greece, Crete, and the
Near East, as well as famous paintings, prints, porcelain, and scientific
curios. Among medieval items is the Alfred Jewel, found in a context that
suggests a connection with King Alfred.

There remain other landmarks to be visited. The first is Keble College,
unique for its remarkable Victorian architecture. Keble was the only men's
college founded in the 19th century. More interesting and close by is
Rhodes House with unique records of the colonial period in Africa. Much
further out, beyond South Parks Road and St. Cross, lies St. Catherine's
College, one of Oxford's newest.

During the time that it runs through Oxford, the Thames is known as
the Isis. Although it is not much used, according to the Ordnance Survey
maps the river should rightly be called the "Thames or Isis" from Cricklade to Oxford, and then again as far as Wallingford, after which it as-
sumes its single identity—as shown by the next town, Henley-on-Thames.
It seems not to be known where the name Isis came from, but it has been
suggested that it arose from splitting into two parts the Latin name *Tame-
sis, Tame esis* or *Tame isis*. Certainly the confusion seems to have originated round the spot where the River Thame joins the River Thames, just
north of Wallingford.

After leaving Oxford, Abingdon is the first place of interest. It is one
of the most ancient towns in the Thames Valley. Few towns of comparative size have retained so much of their heritage. Its spires and towers loom
above the grassy meadows, so that the unsuspecting visitor might think
he has come upon more Oxford colleges. But Abingdon is considerably
older than Oxford—there was a Saxon abbey here as early as the 6th century (little of it remains today). The town that grew up around the abbey
still has much to offer the visitor. There are beautiful medieval churches,
St. Helens and St. Nicholas, bounded by their ancient alms houses and
guest houses. The Poor House dates from the 13th century and has recently been restored, while the 17th-century County Hall still looks as impressive as it must have done when it was built in the time of Charles II.

The White Horse of Uffington

Some of the most famous landmarks in Oxfordshire and Wiltshire are
the White Horses cut into the sides of the chalk hills. Whereas Wiltshire

has several of these figures, Oxfordshire has just one, in the Vale of the White Horse close to the village of Uffington. Minutes after leaving the village, you will see the gigantic white horse that gallops over the Downs and from which the vale takes its name. It looks northwards into the Cotswolds and is formed by trenches in the chalk, two to three feet deep and ten feet wide. The head, neck and body are drawn in one line, as are the four legs. If you have the energy, climb up and inspect this creature closely—it is supposed to bring good luck if you stand on its eye. It takes four men three weeks to scour and clean it of weeds, a perpetual chore to keep these famous figures clean and bright. Although the origin of the White Horse is uncertain, there is some evidence that it was originally cut to mark the victory of King Alfred over the Danes at nearby Ashdown in the year 871, though it may date from the Iron or Bronze Age.

On the summit of the hill, ancient men raised a massive earthwork which has been called Uffington Castle. Today, it provides a panoramic view into the neighboring counties. The village of Uffington itself has a fine 13th-century church without a spire, which it lost in a storm some two centuries ago. Uffington was the birthplace of the author of *Tom Brown's Schooldays,* Thomas Hughes; there is a brass head to his memory in the church. The downs that surround Uffington along the Oxfordshire/Berkshire border present a refreshing and austere contrast to the lushness of the river valley. The Ridgeway, the ancient road that runs along their northern crest, is as old as any in Britain. It can still be followed across a rolling landscape, and even the shortest walk will be enough to convince you of the beauty of the downs. A few miles north of Uffington, near Faringdon, is the enormous 14th-century tithe barn of Great Coxwell, among the finest in England.

BERKSHIRE

To the south of the Thames lies the peaceful Royal County of Berkshire—"royal" because of Windsor Castle, situated at its eastern border.

Because of its proximity to the capital, and also partly because of its loose topography, the county has always been something of a through route. As early as prehistoric times, men were wearing down the Ridgeway, as it crosses the North Downs, on their way to the great religious center of Wiltshire at Avebury and Stonehenge. During the coaching days of the 18th and 19th centuries, wealthy passengers hurtled through Berkshire on their way to the fashionable watering places of the West Country. Today, every summer weekend, the main roads through this county have a heavy flow of traffic bound for Cornwall and Devon. This transitory mood is further emphasized by the number of commuters who leave their comfortable country homes every morning to work in London. Berkshire is commuter territory as far as Reading, and with commuters have come housing estates, golf courses and all the attendant trappings of suburban life.

Another, rather more bizarre, consequence of being so near the capital has been the establishment of almost every kind of institution imaginable, from the scholastic and scientific to the military and the lunatic. What is more, the spread of light industry (especially in the eastern part of the county) is rapidly turning the county into a garden suburb of London itself.

Newbury, on the southern border of the county, can be reached by a pleasant drive across the downs from Ashbury (near Swindon) on B4000, past Castle Ashdown and through Lambourn. Newbury itself is today a bustling town, but it owes its importance almost solely to one man, Jack of Newbury, an almost legendary figure cast in the Dick Whittington mold. Born John Smallwood, he was sent to Newbury by his father to make his way in the wool industry. According to the 17th-century historian, Thomas Fuller, Smallwood became the most important clothier in Tudor England. It is said that he kept a hundred looms fully employed throughout the year and was the "most considerate and benevolent of employers." The parish church of St. Nicholas was built by him and finished by his son in 1532. Newbury racecourse is one of the most attractive in the country.

Newbury is the natural crossroads of roads leading to Oxford, Winchester, Bath and London, and in the 18th century it was a famous coaching stop. In honesty, it must be admitted that the place has been overtaken by the ubiquitous supermarket and has little left to interest the tourist— apart, that is, from a small museum in an ancient building; an attractive spot where a little bridge spans the River Kennet, shortly to plunge into the Thames; and the fact that the town is now bypassed by the M4 motorway, which may mean that life could return.

West of Newbury lies Hungerford, a small country town that is said to have more antique shops than any comparable town in Britain—a rash claim indeed—and an attractive inn.

Just short of Reading, where the Kennet joins the Thames, is a little-known village called Barkham, in whose churchyard lie several of George Washington's ancestors. His mother's maiden name was Mary Ball and that family owned land at Barkham in the 15th and 16th centuries.

"Wind in the Willows" Country

Because of our detour over the downs, much of the Thames scenery has been missed. A very pleasant way of seeing it is to take a half-day steamer excursion from Reading to Wallingford. This will enable you to see the delightfully-wooded scenery that graces this part of the Thames Valley. On each bank there are fine wooded hills, with spacious houses, greenhouses, flower beds and clean lawns that stretch down to the water's edge. Once again we are reminded of *The Wind in the Willows,* and indeed, it was to Pangbourne, along this stretch of the river, that Kenneth Grahame retired to write that immortal book. E. H. Shepard used the lock at Mapledurham as the model for some of his famous illustrations for the book. Mapledurham House, nearby, is a particularly attractive stately home, but of the essentially domestic kind.

Downstream once more from Reading, there is a whole succession of Thames-side villages, each one more charming than the last. They all have attractive riverside inns and churches that look as if they have not been altered for centuries. If we must be selective, we can choose Sonning as the quintessence of them all. The old bridge spans the Thames with its 11 arches, and the Georgian-fronted houses, the ancient Mill that is mentioned in the *Domesday Book* and the black, white and yellow cottages make it all too perfect a Thames-side village.

Henley

At Henley the river abruptly stops winding, and for just over a mile downstream from Henley Bridge it is almost dead straight. It is on this stretch of water that the famous Henley Royal Regatta is held in the first part of July every year. This is the premier river regatta in the world and attracts thousands of visitors, who watch the races from specially erected stands or from punts and rowing boats that are permitted to be moored on the banks. Competition in this event is between the best oarsmen from all over the world, and many an over-enthusiastic supporter who has forgotten he is standing in a rowing boat has found himself unwittingly in the water while cheering a favorite on. The regatta was started in 1838 by the local townspeople, who initiated the first and most famous of the cups, the Grand Challenge Cup. Very quickly, other awards were donated, such as the Diamond Challenge Plate and the Ladies' Challenge Plate. Henley during Regatta Week is one of the high spots of the social summer, rating with Ascot and Wimbledon as a sports event and a fashionable outing all in one.

Later in the month of July, Henley sees the end of another occasion, hardly as popular as the regatta, but interesting nevertheless. This is the Swan Upping. All the swans on the Thames belong to the Queen, with the exception of those which, by Royal Charter, are the property of the Ancient Livery Companies. The process of Swan Upping is to determine "the ownership of all new cygnets encountered on the Thames between London and Henley." So, once a year, six skiffs set out from London, rowed by oarsmen in red, blue and white jerseys, under the command of the Queen's Swan Keeper, who stands, resplendent in his scarlet livery, while the oarsmen attempt to ascertain the ownership of the parent birds. (If they are unmarked, they are assumed to belong to the Queen.) They then brand the cygnets in the face of what is usually the fierce opposition of their parents. Modern conditions now threaten the very existence of swans, and with them the continuance of the ceremonies.

This is one of the most attractive stretches of the Thames. Soon after Henley comes Medmenham Abbey, famous in the 18th century for being one of the homes of Sir Francis Dashwood's "Hellfire Club"—whose scandalous reputation has gained much in the telling.

Marlow and the lovely Quarry Woods loom into view; Cookham, home of Stanley Spencer, the artist whose work can be seen in the Tate Gallery and other large collections, and who celebrated this area in many striking paintings; and then Maidenhead. This last is perhaps the busiest of all the Thames resorts. It is only 27 miles from London, and can be reached both by train and by a fast motorway. It has several good hotels, a few old inns and quite a lot of riverside atmosphere.

Close to the river bank a couple of miles farther on is the village of Bray. Of its most famous vicar, Simon Alley, it was sung "That whosoever king may reign, I'll still be the Vicar of Bray, Sir." This remarkable man held the post from 1667 to 1709, one of the most changing and troubled times of English domestic history, but was able to adapt his political and religious views to coincide with those of each successive monarch, so enabling himself to keep his post. One visit to Bray will reveal why he was so enthusiastic to stay. Near the church is a well-known inn called the *Hind's Head*. A bridge here gives access to historic Monkey Island; this was built as a fishing lodge for the third Duke of Marlborough and derives its name from the monkey fresco that adorned the domed ceiling of what is known today as the Monkey Room. There is a delightful hotel on the island, based around an old temple building. The island is now privately owned, but the hotel and restaurant are open to visitors.

Shortly after Bray, the river takes a sharp turn to the left, and in the distance you will see the towers and battlements of the Royal Palace of Windsor. If you can see the Royal Ensign flying from the flagpole, the Queen is in residence.

Windsor

Windsor has been the home of English kings, at least since the times of Henry I, and possibly before. It is less than an hour from London by Green Line bus, train or on an organized coach tour. Tour operators make all-day trips, which take in Hampton Court, or, alternatively, very convenient half-day tours.

The gray stone castle dominates the town and looks out over the Thames. Naturally, the Royal Castle and the surrounding parks are the chief focus of interest, but the town round the castle has its own special charm and it is worth wandering in the narrow streets.

The first king recorded as living in the Windsor area was Edward the Confessor, who gave his palace at Old Windsor to Westminster Abbey before he died. William the Conqueror, realizing the military importance of the site, built himself a fortress. Timber fortifications were replaced by stone by Henry II and Henry III, who built the three drum towers.

Most medieval kings resided in Windsor, some for two or three weeks at a time. Edward I lived here and gave the town its royal charter, while Edward III transformed the old castle, building new apartments, the great round tower, the Norman gateway and the two other towers, all of which still stand today. Edward IV began St. George's Chapel, Henry VII completed the nave and Henry VIII set the vault over the choir, and built the castle gateway. Elizabeth I built the north terrace and Charles II restored the state apartments. But it was George IV who transformed the essentially medieval castle into the royal palace you can visit today. Later William IV built the Waterloo Chamber and Queen Victoria (who continued to live here after the death of her husband, Albert, and was commonly called "the widder of Windsor") decorated the Albert Memorial Chapel.

Despite the multiplicity of hands that have gone into the making of Windsor, the palace has managed to retain a unity of style and a very marked character of its own. It is, in fact, the largest inhabited castle in the world. The Round Tower, which is actually not round, rises above the walls to the height of 230 feet, dividing the structure of the castle into two wards—the upper ward with the royal apartments and the lower ward, containing St. George's Chapel, the deanery and cloisters.

A great many famous Englishmen have spent their leisure walking along the castle terraces. Chaucer, for one, is said to have lived here while he was in charge of building improvements. It is from the North Terrace that entry is gained into the State Apartments, which can be visited by the public when the Queen is not in residence. The present Queen, in fact, uses the castle far more than any of her predecessors. It has become over the last decade a sort of country weekend residence, which allows the royal family a few days of relaxation and informality away, as much as possible, from the public eye. On these occasions, Prince Charles often joins a polo team against visiting players in Windsor Great Park.

It is at Windsor, perhaps more than in any of the other royal residences that the public can visit, that one realizes just how incredible is the extent of the Queen's wealth of pictures, furniture, porcelain, in fact of anything worth collecting—all of it housed in buildings of deep historic significance. It makes the Pierpoint Morgans of the world seem like children with their first postage stamps.

Apart from the splendor of the various rooms of the State Apartments, a visit to the Queen's Dolls' House should not be missed. Given to Queen Mary in 1924, it is a perfect, fully-working palace within a palace. Electric lights work, the doors all have keys, the lifts are practical and there is running water. There is even a miniature library, with over two hundred tiny books specially written for the Lilliputian library.

St. George's Chapel is one of the noblest buildings in England. Over 230 feet long, with two tiers of great windows and hundreds of gargoyles, buttresses and pinnacles, it is quite grand. The exterior of the chapel is rivaled only by the interior. Light floods in from the stained-glass windows, and above the dark oak of the stalls hang the banners, swords and helmets of the Knights of the Order of the Garter. Annually in June, new knights are invested here by the Queen at the colorful Order of the Garter ceremonies. Some of the most famous Kings of England lie in St. George's, beginning with Henry VI, and including Charles I, Henry VIII (Jane Seymour, the mother of his only son, is also here) and many others, up to King George VI who has a chapel to himself. This arose from a personal decree by his daughter, the present Queen, and largely commemorates his prowess as a monarch during the Second World War. His brother, Edward VIII, who abdicated in 1936 to marry the woman he loved, and who was known to the world as the Duke of Windsor, is buried in nearby Frogmore Mausoleum, though there is a memorial to him here, before the choir. The Mausoleum is open to the public just three days a year; on a Wednesday and Thursday in May, and on the Wednesday nearest to Queen Victoria's birthday (May 24, 1819). Please check with the Windsor Tourist Information Centre (tel. 0753 852010) for precise dates.

The beauty of the church in the lower ward is matched by the exquisite reception rooms, a guard room, and a picture gallery. The Gobelin tapestries in the reception room are splendid and so is the collection of pictures, with a Rubens and a Van Dyck room. The royal library contains, among an almost unbelievable wealth of treasures, a fine collection of Da Vinci's drawings and 87 portraits by Holbein.

The walls of the castle itself enclose only 13 acres of land, but beyond the battlements are nearly 1,800 acres of Windsor Great Park. Charles II planted an avenue of elm trees, the Long Walk, to join castle and park. On the southeast side of the castle is the smaller Home Park, filled with great oaks, some of which were planted in the time of the first Queen Elizabeth. It was here at Frogmore that Queen Victoria liked to spend her days. An added attraction at Windsor is the 140-acre Windsor Safari Park, situated two miles southwest of the castle on the B3022 road. The park is open all year, from 10 A.M. until dusk, and contains within its grounds a drive-in lion reserve and a dolphinarium. Back in the town itself is the Royalty and Empire Exhibition, run by Madame Tussaud's, which re-creates the pomp and pageantry of Queen Victoria's 1897 Diamond Jubilee celebrations. Also worth a visit is the Royal Mews where the royal horses, carriages and coaches are kept including the one used by the Prince and Princess of Wales at their 1981 wedding.

Only a short walk over the Thames from the center of Windsor is Eton College—open to the public—and beautiful Eton College Chapel, which is impressively austere and intimate at one and the same time. The college has also opened a "Museum of Eton Life" with more than 400 exhibits from both its spartan early days and later, more comfortable times.

The best view of Eton and its famous playing fields is, in fact, from the battlements of Windsor Castle. Eton is an ancient institution (1440, founded by Henry VI) and there is little likelihood that current social pressures and criticisms of an "elitist" training establishment will actually result in the school becoming a state-run affair. Some fond parents believe that their children must have their names put down for a place at birth, and you will meet the current crop wearing their uniform of tailcoats and striped trousers, continuing to create the school's own private history surrounded by its ancient buildings. Also within the College is the Myers Museum of Antiquities, among the finest Egyptological collections in the country, with examples from all periods from the Stone Age to Coptic. Eton town has an attractive High Street with some good restaurants and pubs for lunch.

The Thames, now in full historic flood, passes Hampton Court to reach London, Westminster, the Tower, then on to Greenwich and, finally, the sea.

PRACTICAL INFORMATION FOR THE
COTSWOLDS AND THAMES

HOW TO GET THERE FROM LONDON. A wide range of places of interest in the Cotswolds and Thames area can be visited for a day out from London. In most cases the most convenient way to do this is by train, but for the more distant centers it is essential to check the train/coach times carefully before setting out. For sightseeing by rail the *Network Southeast Card* is well worth obtaining—it covers the area as far west as Oxford—see page 186.

Cirencester. By train: no service. **By coach:** National Express operates one Rapide coach every two hours from Victoria Coach Station. The journey time is 2 hours 15 minutes. Cirencester is easily and most conveniently visited in one day by coach. **By car:** M4, A419.

Gloucester. By train: hourly from Paddington (usually change at Swindon), takes just over 2 hours. An easy day out by train as the local service dovetails into the mainline expresses with little waiting time, and it is a simple cross-platform transfer between trains. **By coach:** National Express operates one Rapide coach every two hours, but an 08.00 departure is recommended to allow sufficient exploration time. **By car:** M4, A419, A417.

Maidenhead. By train: suburban service from Paddington with two through trains an hour. The complete journey takes approximately 40 minutes. **By coach:** an hourly service runs from Eccleston Bridge, Victoria (also available from Kensington)—contact any National Express office or the Eccleston Bridge enquiry office. **By car:** M4, A308.

Oxford. By train: hourly service from Paddington, journey time approximately one hour. **By coach:** a very frequent service operates from Victoria Coach Station—no need to book in advance, just pay the driver. At least every half-hour and scheduled to take 1 hour 40 minutes, but is often quicker. **By car:** M40, A40.

Reading. By train: a very frequent service of at least four trains an hour from Paddington; the fastest journey takes less than 30 minutes. **By coach:** frequent (at least hourly) Londonlink coach from Victoria Coach Station; journey time 1 hour 15 minutes—no advance booking necessary. **By car:** M4, A329M, A4.

HOW TO GET AROUND. The region can be divided into two sections: the suburban fringe, which is well served by a dense net of public transport services, both road and rail; in the outer rural areas, the centers such as Swindon, Gloucester, Oxford and Cheltenham are well served by fast rail services from London. However, local bus routes between the smaller centers are poor. Naturally, in the London suburban area it is best to travel out of the rush hours, and also cheaper since you can make use of cheap day return fares. Oxford is also easy to reach by express coach from Victoria Coach Station. No need to book for this service; just turn up and pay the driver.

HOTELS AND RESTAURANTS. As one of the most popular, and wealthiest, areas of Britain, this one sports plenty of excellent hotels and a good sprinkling of fine places to eat. But, because it *is* so popular, you really must be sure to book ahead whenever possible. You should also brace yourself for some very fancy prices.

Details about our grading system, plus other relevant information about hotels and restaurants, will be found at the beginning of the book in the *Facts at Your Fingertips* section.

Abingdon (Oxon). *Upper Reaches* (E), tel. (0235) 22311; 26 rooms with bath, ancient converted abbey cornmill. Spectacular setting overlooking the Thames.

Ascot (Berks.). *Royal Berkshire* (L), Sunninghill, tel. (0990) 23322; 82 rooms, 81 with bath, 1 with shower. Superb Queen Anne house, tastefully restored as a country house hotel. Indoor pool, squash, sauna, helipad. First-rate cuisine and service in restaurant (L).

Banbury (Oxon). *Wroxton House* (E–M), tel. (029 573) 482. At Wroxton St. Mary, 3 miles northwest of Banbury. Thatched country-house hotel with 15 rooms, most with bath. Candlelit restaurant. *Whately Hall* (M), tel. (0295) 3451; 74 rooms, 65 with bath, 9 with bath or shower. Attractively modernized 17th-century building right by the famous cross; friendly.

Bourton-on-the-Water (Glos.). *Old Manse* (M), tel. (0451) 20642; 12 rooms with bath. Close to the river; good restaurant. *Old New Inn* (M), tel. (0451) 20467; 16 rooms, 8 with bath. Attractive mixture of 18th-century and modern.
Restaurant. *Rose Tree* (M), tel. (0451) 20635. Excellent for value and quality in an area where tourist traps abound. Imaginative home cooking. Closed Sun. eve and Mon.

Burford (Oxon). *Bay Tree* (M), tel. (099 382) 3137; 24 rooms with bath. Tudor house, good food. *Golden Pheasant* (M), tel. (099 382) 3223. 12 rooms, most with bath or shower. A comfortable, recently renovated hotel, partly 14th and 15th century, with some four-poster beds. Beamed restaurant. Tiny *Inn For All Seasons* (M), tel. (045 14) 324; 9 rooms with bath (at the Barringtons, 3 miles west). Delightful stone inn, hospitable hosts and good food.

Chalford (Glos.). *Springfield House* (M), tel. (0453) 883555; 7 rooms with bath or shower. More an elegant English home than a hotel. Reasonably priced, appetizing meals. Marvelous walking country. Must book.

Cheltenham (Glos.). *Greenway* (L–E), Shurdington, tel. (0242) 862352; 19 rooms, all with bath. Superb 16th-century hotel on city outskirts; good dining. *Queen's* (E), tel. (0242) 514724; 77 rooms with bath. Built in classical Regency style; well located on the promenade. *Prestbury House* (M), The Burgage, tel. (0242) 529533; 10 rooms, 8 with bath; in its own parkland, 2 miles out on A6, with well-recommended restaurant.
Restaurants. *La Ciboulette* (M), tel. (0242) 573449. Varied range of French dishes with delicious sauces. Best value at lunchtime. Closed Sun. and Mon. *Moran's Eating House,* 23 Worcester St. tel. (0452) 422024. Friendly bistro in the center of town. Closed Sun. and Mon. lunch.

Chipping Campden (Glos.). *King's Arms* (M), tel. (0386) 840256; 14 rooms, 2 with bath. Central, comfortable with panelled bar and excellent restaurant. *Noel Arms* (M), tel. (0386) 840317; 18 rooms, 15 with bath, 3 with shower (2 with four-poster beds); 14th-century inn beside the market square. Also has a bowling green.

Chipping Norton (Oxon). *Crown & Cushion* (M), tel. (0608) 2533. 17 rooms with bath. Old coaching inn. *White Hart* (M), tel. (0608) 2572; 22 rooms, 6 with bath, a good overnight stop on the way west.

Cirencester (Glos.). *Fleece* (M), tel. (0285) 68507; 25 rooms with bath. Cosy black-and-white inn. English and French cuisine. *King's Head* (M), tel. (0285) 3322; 70 rooms with bath. Pleasant coaching inn with friendly staff. *Stratton House* (M), tel. (0285) 61761. 26 rooms, 22 with bath or shower. Friendly Queen Anne house with antiques; attractive walled gardens. Croquet.

Corse Lawn (Glos.). *Corse Lawn House* (M), tel. (045 278) 479. 10 rooms with bath. Superb cooking in idyllic Queen Anne-style house. Good variety of classic and interesting dishes, excellent seafood. Putting, croquet, helipad.

Dorchester-on-Thames (Oxon.). *White Hart* (E), tel. (0865) 340074. 20 rooms, 19 with bath, 1 with shower. *George* (M), tel. (0865) 340404. 17 rooms with bath. Old coaching inn opposite the Abbey. Good quality, good value food.

Forest of Dean (Glos.). *Speech House* (M), tel. (0594) 22607; 13 rooms, 3 with bath. Historic hotel in heart of this undiscovered, ancient woodland. Traditional English restaurant.

Gloucester (Glos.). *Crest* (M), tel. (0452) 613311. 100 rooms with bath. Modern. *Hatton Court* (M), Upton Hill, Upton St. Leonards, tel. (0452) 617412; 53 rooms, all with bath or shower. Lies just 3 miles out of town with fine views over Severn valley. Recently refurbished with elegant fittings and modern amenities. Garden, outdoor swimming pool.

Great Milton (Oxon). **Restaurant.** *Le Manoir Aux Quat' Saisons* (L), tel. (08446) 8881. Outstanding French cuisine in manor near Oxford. One of Britain's great restaurants in a beautiful setting of gardens and parkland. Also offers superb accommodations (L); 10 rooms with bath.

Henley-on-Thames (Oxon.). *Flohrs Hotel and Restaurant* (M), tel. (0491) 573412. 9 rooms, 3 with bath. Small, elegant Georgian hotel with *cordon bleu* restaurant. *Red Lion* (M), tel. (0491) 572161. 27 rooms, 20 with bath. Traditional hotel overlooking river. Charles I and Dr Johnson stayed here! Views of Henley Royal Regatta from river-facing rooms; but book early.
Restaurant. *Alpenhutte* (M), 41 Station St., tel. (0491) 572984. Austrian specialties with matching decor. Closed Sun.–Mon. and Sat. lunch.

Horton-cum-Studley (Oxon). *Studley Priory* (M), tel. (086 735) 203; 19 rooms with bath. Romantic Elizabethan manor house, 7 miles from Oxford. Tennis, shooting. Formal dining room.

Hungerford (Berks). *Bear* (M), tel. (0488) 82512. 32 rooms, 28 with bath. Parts built in 1279; one of the great inns of England with important historic associations, Good restaurant, imaginative menu.

Hurley (Berks.). *Ye Olde Bell* (E), tel. (062882) 5881. 24 rooms with bath. Built in 1135 as a Benedictine guest house. Elegant rooms.

Lechlade (Glos.). **Restaurant.** *Trout Inn* (M–I), tel. (0367) 52313. Restaurant serving delicious eponymous dishes as a specialty; Thames-side setting accompanies this *compleat* version of the Cotswold inn.

Maidenhead (Berks). *Fredericks* (E), tel. (0628) 35934; 38 rooms with bath or shower. Pleasant, stylish hotel with smart restaurant (also E). *Crest* (E), tel. (0628) 23444; 191 rooms with bath. Modern and very likable for its successful attempt to cope with both business and tourist demands. Good leisure facilities. At the hotel is *Shoppenhangers Manor* (E), tel. (0628) 23444; an elegant, oak panelled restaurant. Closed Sun.

At **Bray.** *Monkey Island* (E), tel. (0628) 23400. 26 rooms with bath. Historic island hotel.

Restaurant. *The Waterside Inn* (L), tel. (0628) 20691. Beautiful setting for masterful restaurant offering outstanding cuisine. One of the best, but always full so book well in advance. Closed Mon.

Middleton Stoney (Oxon). *Jersey Arms* (M), tel. (086 989) 234; 14 rooms with bath. Old Cotswold inn with excellent English cooking.

Minster Lovell (Oxon). *Old Swan Inn* (M), tel. (0993) 75 614; 10 rooms with bath or shower. On River Windrush with all the characteristic charm of an ancient village inn.

Moreton-in-Marsh (Glos.). *Manor House* (M), tel. (0608) 50501; 38 rooms, 36 with bath. 17th-century Cotswold stone exterior, but internally a well-modernized and comfortable hotel with restaurant. Indoor swimming pool, tennis, sauna. *Redesdale Arms* (M), tel. (0608) 50308; 17 rooms, 13 with bath, 4 with shower, is also worthwhile. Recommended restaurant.

At nearby **Blockley,** we recommend the *Lower Brook House* (E–M), tel. (0386) 700286; 8 rooms with bath or shower. 17th-century stone house with superb, well-served food.

Newbury (Berks.). *Chequers* (E–M), tel. (0635) 38000; 62 rooms with bath or shower. *Elcot Park* (M), tel. (0488) 58100. 5 miles west. Country house in own park. 37 rooms with bath, some four-posters. Well-prepared food.

Restaurant. *Spurles* (I), Northbrook St., tel. (0635) 42730. Delightful coffee/lunch shop overlooking canal.

Northleach (Glos.). **Restaurant.** *Old Woolhouse* (E), (04516) 60366. Classic French menu, deserved reputation; very small, so essential to book.

Oxford (Oxon). Central and well-established *Ladbroke Linton Lodge* (E), Linton Rd., tel. (0865) 53461; 72 rooms with bath. A well-converted Edwardian town house. The Gothic style *Randolph* (E), Beaumont St., tel. (0865) 247481; 109 rooms with bath. Full of Victorian grandeur. *Oxford Moat House* (M), Wolvercote, tel. (0865) 59933; 155 rooms with bath. Motel on the outskirts with excellent leisure facilities. Also on outskirts and convenient for a short stopover, is the *Travelodge* (M), tel. (0865) 54301; 100 rooms with bath. Carvery restaurant.

Restaurants. *Elizabeth* (E), St. Aldates, tel. (0865) 242230, has a well-established reputation and a good wine list. Closed Mon. *Le Petit Blanc* (E), Banbury Rd., tel. (0865) 53540, is highly recommended for its classical French cuisine. Closed Tues. *La Sorbonne* (E), High St., tel. (0865) 241320, is consistently good for both food and wine. *Browns* (I), 5–9

Woodstock Rd., tel (0865) 511995. Very popular with both students and townspeople. Wide choice of dishes.

Interesting pubs include *Turf Tavern,* tel. (0865) 243235 (described in Hardy's *Jude the Obscure*). *Victoria Arms,* Mill Lane, Old Marston, tel. (0865) 241 382. The place to go in summer, upriver, for excellent outdoor food—try the Mississippi Mud Pie, made by a local Italian baker.

Painswick (Glos.). *Painswick* (M), tel. (0452) 812160. 15 rooms with bath. Georgian house with good restaurant.

Shinfield (Berks.). **Restaurant.** *L'Ortolan* (E), Church Lane, tel. (0734) 883783. Elegant country restaurant. High standards. Near Reading. Closed Mon. and Sun. eve.

Shipton-under-Wychwood (Oxon). *Lamb Inn* (M), tel. (0993) 830465. 5 rooms with bath or shower. Simple rooms, excellent restaurant and popular beamed bar. *The Shaven Crown* (M), tel. (0993) 830330. 8 rooms, 4 with bath. 14th-century building with fascinating history as a hospice, hunting lodge and inn.

Sonning (Berks.). *White Hart* (M), Thames St., tel. (0734) 692277. 25 rooms with bath. 16th-century inn with fine river views and extensive flower gardens. Period-style and modern rooms. Restaurant.

Stow-on-the-Wold (Glos.). *Fosse Manor* (M), tel. (0451) 30354; 20 rooms, 14 with bath or shower. Lovely surroundings. Recommended restaurant serving home-grown produce. *Royalist* (M), tel. (0451) 30670. Supposedly the oldest building in Stow. 12 rooms, 9 with bath. Lots of beams.

Streatley-on-Thames (Berks.). *Swan* (M), tel. (0491) 873737, 26 rooms with bath. Enviable Thames-side views. Good leisure facilities and fine restaurant (E).

At **Pangbourne** (Berks.). *Copper Inn* (M), tel. (073 57) 2244. 21 rooms with bath. Restored coaching inn. Enjoyable English menu featuring British cheeses.

At **Yattendon** (Berks.). *Royal Oak* (M), tel. (0635) 201325. 5 rooms in delightful 15th-century inn. Privately owned village. Restaurant recommended.

Tetbury (Glos.). *Snooty Fox* (E–M), tel. (0666) 52436. 12 rooms, 11 with bath, 1 with shower. Traditional building in Market Place refurbished to high standard. Good food. *Close* (M), tel. (0666) 52272. 12 rooms with bath. 16th-century stone mansion with excellent restaurant.

Tewkesbury (Glos.). *Tewkesbury Park* (M), tel. (0684) 295405; 82 rooms all with bath. 18th-century mansion, also golf and country club; extensive leisure facilities. The dining room of the *Tudor House* (M), tel. (0684) 297755, was a Jacobean Courtroom; 16 rooms, 8 with bath, 4 with shower.

Upper Slaughter (Glos.). *Lords of the Manor* (E–M), tel. (0451) 20243; 15 rooms, 14 with bath. Mellowed 17th-century house off the well-beaten Cotswold track. Good rooms with views. Friendly service in formal restaurant serving classical cuisine. Ideal touring base. Wise to book.

Wallingford (Oxon.). *The Springs* (L), tel. (0491) 36687. Elegant lakeside hotel and restaurant. 34 rooms with bath. Good sports facilities. *George* (M), tel. (0491) 36665. 39 rooms with bath or shower. Refurbished town center inn with courtyard. *Shillingford Bridge* (M), tel. (086 732) 8567. 36 rooms with bath. Overlooking the Thames.

Weston-on-the-Green (Oxon). *Weston Manor* (E), tel. (0869) 50621. 37 rooms with bath (two 4-poster beds). Extensive gardens and sumptuous accommodation. The restaurant is oak-panelled with a minstrel's gallery and renowned for its cuisine.

Windsor (Berks.). *Castle* (E), tel. (0753) 851011. 85 rooms with bath. Georgian building in town center. *Sir Christopher Wren's Old House* (E), tel. (0753) 861354. 41 rooms with bath. Wren designed and lived in this fine house beside the river. Good restaurant. *Ye Harte and Garter* (M), High St., tel. (0753) 863426. 50 rooms, 43 with bath. Conveniently situated opposite the castle. Originally two Tudor taverns, but now a hotel with a steakhouse and four bars.

At **Water Oakley,** 3 miles west. *Oakley Court* (L–E), tel. Maidenhead (0628) 74141. 91 rooms with bath. Victorian Gothic mansion with modern annex beside the Thames. Good restaurant.

Restaurants. *Bensons* (M), 4 Church Lane, tel. (0753) 858331. Varied set menus in this oak-beamed restaurant with wine bar downstairs. Closed Sat. and Sun. lunch. Just across the river in **Eton,** *House on the Bridge* (E), Windsor Bridge, tel. (0753) 860914. Sophisticated surroundings for traditional English and *cordon bleu* French cooking. Reservations essential.

Woodstock (Oxon). The place to dine after seeing Blenheim Palace, *The Bear* (L), tel. (0993) 811511; 45 rooms with bath. Fine Cotswold-stone inn with lively bars and a good restaurant. A favorite haunt for romantic weekenders. Booking imperative. *Feathers* (E), tel. (0993) 812291. 16 rooms with bath. Charming country house hotel with cobbled courtyard. Highly regarded cuisine in luxurious restaurant. Wise to book.

VISITING THE COTSWOLDS. There is a rather slow rail service from London (Paddington) to Moreton-in-Marsh, often with a change at Oxford. For the southwestern part of the Cotswolds, take a fast train from Paddington to Swindon and change onto a local train for the beautiful ride to Stroud. The National Express buses also visit the region, leaving twice a day for Burford and Northleach, only once a day for Chipping Norton, Moreton-in-Marsh and Broadway. This system, though, will not suit for a day out. For that you would be advised to try one of the tours that visit the Cotswolds, run by *Gray-Green, National Travel* or *Venture Tours.*

TRIPPING UP THE THAMES. Apart from the river buses that operate in the London area, steamers serve the upper and lower Thames throughout the summer. A number of operators contribute to an extensive network of services. Ask at a local tourist information center. Boats make local runs between Windsor, Runnymede, Hampton Court, Kingston and Richmond, while further upriver *Salters Steamers* run services from mid-May to mid-September. Their vessels do return trips between the following points: Oxford–Abingdon; Reading–Henley; Marlow–Windsor; Staines–Windsor. Teas and light refreshments can be obtained on board. There are bus connections. For further information you should contact *Salter Bros. Ltd,* 11 Folly Bridge, Oxford (tel. (0865) 243421/3). Combined coach and Thames riverboat trips usually operate daily in the summer months from Victoria Coach Station. Please enquire at the station for details.

PLACES OF INTEREST. When a region offers Windsor Castle—what else gets a look in? But this region also has Blenheim Palace and Badminton House as competition, to say nothing of the colleges at Oxford. If you are car-borne you would be well advised to keep an eye out for unusual places hidden by the side of the road in the trees, since, even though they may not be visitable by the public, they will offer tantalizing glimpses of out-of-the-way architecture. For further details of visiting historic houses, see the relevant section in *Facts at Your Fingertips,* as well as the chapter, *Historic Houses—Precious Stones in Peril.*

Berkshire. Basildon Park, near Pangbourne (tel. 073 57 3040). Fine late-Georgian house (1776), with interesting Octagon Room; attractive setting. Apr.–Oct., Wed.–Sat., 2–6; Sun. and Bank Holiday Mon., 12–6. (NT).

Eton College and Museum of Eton Life, Windsor (tel. 0753 863593). Guided tours of the Lower School and chapel. Also displays on the school's history. Open daily during college terms 2–5; out-of-term 10.30–5.

Frogmore Gardens, Windsor. Attractive gardens belonging to the Queen, plus the Victorian Royal Mausoleum. Usually open only on first Wed. and Thurs. in May 11–7. Royal Mausoleum also open then and another Wed. in late May.

Littlecote, near Hungerford (tel. 0488 82509). Impressive Tudor mansion with magnificent Great Hall and armor. Enterprisingly run, with a "period village," falconry displays, jousting tournaments also on site. Open daily, Easter–mid-Oct.

Royalty and Empire Exhibition, Thames St., Windsor (tel. 0753 857837). Waxwork recreation of Queen Victoria's arrival in Windsor to celebrate her Diamond Jubilee. Also audio-visual presentation of Victoria's 64-year reign. Open Apr.–Oct., daily 9.30–5.30; Nov.–Mar., daily 9.30–4.30.

Stanley Spencer Gallery, Cookham-on-Thames (tel. 06285 26557). Paintings, sketches, and personalia of the artist, in the village where he lived most of his life. Open Easter–Oct., daily 10.30–1, 2–6; Nov.–Easter, Sat., Sun. and Bank Holidays only, 11–1, 2–5.

Windsor Castle, Windsor (tel. 0753 868286). Royal residence. The world's largest inhabited castle. The Queen owns the greatest collection of treasures in the world, and part of the Aladdin's cave is housed here at Windsor. Open daily except when the Royal Family is in residence. Times vary according to the time of year. Also, **Royal Windsor Safari Park,** 3 miles southwest of Windsor. A drive-in zoo, featuring lion and cheetah reserves among its many attractions. Open Apr.–Sept., daily 9.30–7.30; Oct.–Mar. daily 10–5.30 or dusk.

Gloucestershire. Berkeley Castle, near Bristol (tel. 0453 810332). One of England's most historic homes, the scene of the murder of Edward II in 1327. Open Apr., daily except Mon., 2–5; May–Aug., Tues.–Sat. and Bank Holiday Mon., 11–5, Sun. 2–5; Sept. as Apr.; Oct., Sun. 2–4.30.

Corinium Museum, Cirencester (tel. 0285 5611). Contains one of the finest collections of Roman antiquities in Britain. Open April–Sept., weekdays 10–5.30, Sun. 2–5.30; Oct.–March, Tue.–Sat. 10–5, Sun. 2–5.

Cotswold Countryside Collection, Northleach (tel. 0451 60715 or 0285 5611). Fascinating museum of agricultural history—wagons, tools, etc. Open April–Oct., daily 10–5.30, Sun. 2–5.30.

Cotswold Farm Park, nr. Bourton-on-the-Water (tel. 04515 307). Most comprehensive collection of rare-breed farm animals in Britain. Open Easter–Sept., daily 10–6.

Hidcote Manor Garden, Hidcote Bartrim, near Chipping Campden (tel. 038 677 333). A really lovely garden, one of the most beautiful in England. Open Apr.–end Oct., daily (except Tues., Fri.), 11–8. (NT).

Jenner Museum, Berkeley (tel. 0453 810631). Commemorates Edward Jenner, who discovered smallpox vaccination, in cottage he built for the first patient he treated. Open Apr.–end Sept. and Good Fri., Tues.–Sat. 12.30–5.30, Sun. 1–5.30. Closed Mon. except Bank Holiday Mons. and Oct.–Mar. (During winter months open to pre-booked parties.)

Slimbridge, near Gloucester (tel. 045 389 333). Headquarters of the Wildfowl Trust, with the largest and most varied collection of wildfowl in the world. Also has a Tropical House, cinema, exhibitions. Open mid-Mar.–Oct., daily 9.30–5; Nov.–mid Mar., daily 9.30–4.

Snowshill Manor, near Broadway (tel. 0386 852410). An important collection of musical instruments, clocks and toys, interesting for children. Open Apr. and Oct., Sat., Sun., Bank Holiday Mon., 11–1, 2–5; May–end Sept., Wed. to Sun., Bank Holiday Mon., 11–1, 2–6 (NT).

Sudeley Castle, near Winchcombe (tel. 0242 602308). Dates from the 12th and 15th centuries, and contains tomb of Queen Katherine Parr, who lived here. Plantaganet Society frequently stages battles here; superb art collection; regular falconry displays. Open April–Oct. daily, 12–5 (grounds from 11).

Oxfordshire. Ashmolean, Beaumont St., Oxford (tel. 0865 27800). Britain's oldest public museum houses the university's priceless collections of Egyptian, Greek and Roman artifacts, European silverware and Michelangelo drawings. Open Tues.–Sat. 10–4, Sun. 2–4.

Blenheim Palace, Woodstock (tel. 0993 811325). Birthplace of Sir Winston Churchill (who is buried nearby at Bladon). Built by Vanbrugh for Duke of Marlborough. Magnificent planned gardens. Exhibition of Churchill paintings and memorabilia. Open mid-Mar.–Oct., daily 10.30–6. Park open daily 9–5.

Broughton Castle, near Banbury (tel. 0295 62624). Started around 1300 and developed over the centuries, with some attractive features including paneling and plasterwork ceilings. Open mid-May–mid-Sept., Wed., Sun., Bank Holiday Mon., also Thurs. in July, Aug.; all 2–5.

Cotswold Wildlife Park, Burford (tel. 099382 3006). 200 acres with animals, butterfly house, narrow-gauge railway. Open all year, daily 10–6, or dusk.

Chastleton House, Moreton-in-Marsh (tel. 060 874 355). Built 1603; the box garden is said to be the oldest in England. Open Good Fri.–Sept., Fri., Sat., Sun. and Bank Holiday Mon., 2–5. Best to confirm times.

The Great Barn, Great Coxwell. Huge 13th-century barn, very interesting timber roof. Open daily. (NT).

Greys Court, Henley-on-Thames. Superb gardens with medieval ruins, 16th-century house. Tudor donkey wheel for lifting well water; recently constructed "Archbishop's Maze." Open Apr.–end Sept., house Mon., Wed., Fri., 2–6; garden, Mon.–Sat. 2–6; closed Good Fri. (NT).

Kingstone Lisle Park, near Wantage (tel. 036 782 223). 17th-century house with early 19th-century interiors; dramatic flying staircase; charming wooded grounds. Open Easter–Sept., Thurs. and Bank Holiday Sat., Sun. and Mon., 2–5.

Mapledurham House, Mapledurham (tel. 0734 723350). Elizabethan house, a favorite haunt of the poet Pope; also boasts a working watermill. Open Easter Sun.–end Sept., Sat., Sun., Bank Holidays, 2.30–5.30; Mill 1.30–5. Rest of year, Sun. 2–4.

Milton Manor House, near Abingdon (tel. 0235 831287). Small, handsome 17th-century house with later wings; charming walled garden, spacious grounds; interesting library and chapel. Open Easter–end Oct., Sat., Sun. and Bank Holidays, 2–5.30.

Museum of the History of Science, Broad St., Oxford (tel. 0865 243997). Early scientific instruments, including astrolabes (navigational), and a sizeable display of sundials. The Beeson Room contains clocks and watches. Open Mon.–Fri. 10.30–1, 2.30–4.

Oxford Museum, St. Aldates, Oxford (tel. 0865 815559). Contemporary museum with a multitude of displays illustrating the history of the city. Open Tues.–Sat., 10–5.

Oxford University Colleges. The colleges at Oxford are, as they are at Cambridge, private property. College authorities have found, over the past few years, that the huge increase in tourism has seriously interfered with the life and work of the students and Fellows, and have, therefore, been forced to introduce regulations as to visiting times. As all the colleges have different rules, we would suggest that you acquaint yourself with those applying to the colleges you wish to visit, by enquiring at the Oxford Tourist Information Center, St. Aldate's, tel. (0865) 726871, when you first arrive in the city—or by doing so by phone in advance.

Rousham House, Steeple Aston. Castellated mansion built 1635 and used as Royalist garrison during Civil War. Hanging gardens by William Kent, complete with classical sculpture, waterfalls and cascades. Splendid views above River Cherwell. Open Apr.–Sept., Wed., Sun. and Bank Holidays, 2–4.30; gardens only, every day, 10–4.30.

Stonor Park, near Henley-on-Thames (tel. 049 163 587). Home of the Stonor family for over 800 years, with close associations with Roman Catholicism. The house is set in a wooded deer park amidst the Chiltern hills.

Many fine portraits and furniture. Apr., Sun. and Bank Hol. Mon.; May–Sept., Wed., Thurs., Sun. and Bank Holiday Mon. (and Sat. in Aug.). All 2–5.30 (from 11 Bank Holiday Mon.).

Waterperry Gardens, Nr. Wheatley, tel. Ickford (084 47) 254. Horticultural Center, gardens, alpine nurseries, etc. Saxon village church. 2 miles from Wheatley then 20 mins. walk by footpath. Open Apr.–Sept., 10–5.30 weekdays, 10–6 weekends; Oct.–Mar., daily, 10–4.30.

EAST ANGLIA

Constable Country

The counties of Norfolk, Suffolk, Essex and Cambridgeshire are all lumped under the heading East Anglia for the purposes of administration, although nowhere are county differences more subtly in evidence. If you draw a line from the center of London along the Thames eastward, and then northward from the same point to the most westerly corner of the Wash, a right angle is formed which encompasses all these counties—except for about a third of Cambridgeshire—and emphasizes their affinity with the North Sea.

In some ways this is a cut-off land. When roads lead nowhere, people tend not to use them. The roads leading into East Anglia are ends in themselves. The Romans, who did a lot for Essex when they made Colchester their capital, steered well clear of the rest of East Anglia when they built their important road to the north—which later became the Al. The canal builders in their time also kept away, and so the Industrial Revolution mercifully passed East Anglia by.

The result of being historically a backwater is that the region is enormously rich in the sort of architecture that in other parts of the country has been lost, and it is clear, even to the short-term visitor, that the natives have a strongly regional consciousness. The word "Anglia" constantly appears as a prefix to brand names; hotels feature in their menus not only specialties of the area such as duckling or oysters, Norfolk turkey, hare and partridge, but prepare more universal foods in a regional fashion.

283

Nevertheless, although East Anglia is mostly an agricultural region, much of its scenery has changed dramatically in recent years. Gone are the hedges and ditches. Small—and not so small—farms have amalgamated to form prairie-type, weedless-crop areas which are alleged to be more efficient, but which frighten ornithologists and botanists to death. Because of this rape of the land, maybe, extra efforts have been taken over conservation and East Anglia, besides having a lot of natural secret places full of wildlife, has a glorious proliferation of planned nature reserves to visit. It also proudly puts on display its many crafts—pottery, rushwork, lace, leather work, corn dollies and even rocking horses; also cider and wine making. Norfolk and Suffolk feature Bygones Collections, which is to say informal exhibitions of domestic and agricultural tools and gadgets of the past, items which are not of sufficient significance to be housed in a normal museum, but are immensely informative of the recent past and of essentially human interest.

During and after World War II, East Anglia underwent another change—this time, an invasion by the U.S. Air Force, to whose personnel the region became known as "the 49th state". Now, too, there are nuclear plants, modern factory farming and new technology industries.

Except in the city of Norwich, where the 17th century was outstanding, the 15th and 16th centuries were the period of East Anglia's greatest prosperity and importance. Nearly all the finest of Cambridge's colleges were either founded or generously endowed then; many of the region's most celebrated manor houses and grammar schools were built; in the numerous thatch-roofed, oak-paneled inns and solid stone guildhalls lives the memory of an age when merchants and landed gentry spent their money freely and well. Today Cambridge is still founding new colleges, meeting new scientific challenges; Norwich and Colchester have their own universities and Norwich its own television station.

North of Ely the fens of Cambridgeshire merge without break into the fens of Lincolnshire, discussed in the next chapter. Their broad sluggish rivers, flowing into the Wash, are supplemented by drainage canals in a landscape as reminiscent of Holland as their Dutch engineers' names.

Two main highways, both Roman in origin, link London with Norwich, the undisputed capital of East Anglia. One, A12, runs northeast together with the main railway out of Liverpool Street station to Colchester, Ipswich and the East Coast. The other, A11, runs north and northeast passing east of Cambridge by way of Newmarket.

For part of the way, however, the M11 has superseded the A11. The motorway connects with the M25 London Orbital Route, runs just beyond Cambridge, and can also be used as far as Stump Cross on the borders of Essex and Cambridgeshire where it links up with the A11 for the northeast.

The third Roman road, A10, which used to be the favorite for Cambridge has been superseded by the motorway, but continues to Ely and King's Lynn. At Royston the A14 peels off left for Peterborough, but most people wishing to go there will find it quicker and easier to set out from London on A1 which provides a twenty-mile section of motorway and dual carriageway thereafter.

Two railway lines from London, out of Liverpool Street and King's Cross stations, serve Cambridge; Peterborough, which has lost most of its East Anglian railway connections, is on the main route to York (from King's Cross).

These trunk routes are in many respects and for much of their courses the dullest in the region. They serve for reaching some undeniably superlative goals. But half the attraction of East Anglia lies in its unspectacular but subtle landscapes where the beauties of rural England are seen at their enduring best: to rush in search of one or two highlights is to miss the best, which can be enjoyed only by leisurely journeys along the byways.

The centers best served by public transport (including train) are Cambridge, Norwich and Ipswich. Good accommodation can be found also in Newmarket or Bury St. Edmunds, both central; in Colchester or Woodbridge near the coast; in Cromer and King's Lynn in the north. But a peaceful base for touring may be found in many a small country town or former country house turned hotel.

ESSEX

The southernmost county of East Anglia is Essex, so close to London that it merges with it on an extending band north of the Thames. Highly industrialized and subject to suburban spread, it is a sad area. Fans of industrial history will remember that electronics started in Essex with Marconi, but that is small consolation for today's blight.

In great contrast is the northern, more rolling part of Essex, largely rural still and with villages as beautiful as any in the land. These are to be found in the triangle with one of its three points in Epping Forest on the outskirts of London, one in Saffron Walden, and the third in Colchester. The best way to reach it is to take the A11 and plunge eastwards onto the little roads as soon as Epping Forest has been left behind; or on A12 and leave that on A128 northwestwards from Brentwood. Within this triangle the lanes offer endless inducement to become temporarily lost where plowed fields roll toward the horizon in spring, acres of wheat ripen in summer and cow-pastures are lush and green all the year round. Timber-frame and thatch cottages, which sheltered the purely rural lives of earlier inhabitants, still house both country people and many professional people from the cities, who like to combine old-world surroundings with modern comforts.

Greensted-juxta-Ongar church has a wooden nave of Saxon date. Farther on, two groups of villages, the Rodings and the Easters, have the typical juxtaposition of church and pubs, each with a characteristic but variant echo of the past.

Thaxted is, perhaps, the fairest of the many attractive villages. There you will find a fine church, built of soft yellow-gray limestone, adorned with carved gargoyles, animals and birds, which is a permanent reminder of the days when the little place was a wealthy center for the local wood and cutlery trades. East of Thaxted lies Finchingfield, best-known of the charming group of "field" villages. Others, Great and Little Bardfield, Toppesfield and Wethersfield, are all worth a visit. The immaculately preserved houses and curving lanes of Finchingfield all center on a large green that slopes down to a pond.

Saffron Walden and Colchester

The area's two principal market towns. Saffron Walden (once noted for its culture of saffron) and Braintree, both preserve their lighthearted, haphazard jumble of ancient, historic inns, modern shopping centers, Victorian public buildings, and market stalls bursting with farm produce—although being crossed by two busy main roads does nothing to help Braintree.

Only three-quarters of a mile from Saffron Walden lies Audley End, once a vast manor house, built on the ruins of an abbey. Slimmed down, it now stands an elegant and beautifully proportioned Jacobean building, looked after by the English Heritage organization, and still attractively furnished. The place is full of elaborate carving and fine fireplaces and, best of all, the visitor can wander around unguided.

Colchester is the oldest recorded town in England, dating back to the Iron Age. It is famed for oysters, which the Romans enjoyed so much that they settled there and sent quantities back home. One of the Roman founders was the Emperor Claudius, and the settlement was early attacked by Queen Boadicea, Queen of the Iceni, noted for having used carving knives fixed to her chariot wheels—an early example of dangerous driving. Today the Roman walls still stand, together with a Norman castle, a Victorian town hall and Dutch-style houses built by refugee weavers from the Low Countries in the late 16th century. It is a very interesting, well-cared-for town, a delight to wander in.

In 1989, Colchester celebrates the 800th anniversary of receiving the royal charter from King Richard the Lion-Heart and special events are being planned in the town throughout the year. Also worth a visit is Colchester's Mercury Theatre, one of England's foremost regional theaters with an impressive repertoire of modern and classic plays.

Oyster beds need salt water, and south of Colchester lies a different Essex world where marshes, estuaries, and low meadows lie under the same delicate, pale seaward light that some of the earlier East Anglian artists depicted so surely in their paintings. Maldon, Tollesbury and Burnham-on-Crouch are the main marshland villages, real boating centers where boats are made as well as used. They are haunts of fishermen in thigh boots who tell their fishermen's tales over a noonday pint in the "local" and of birds—black-headed gulls, lapwings and coots—that leave their trails of footprints on the muddy salt flats.

Those who find such quiet, flat spaces bleak and dull need travel only a few miles to find the bright lights. The beaches of the county's most popular resorts, Southend, Clacton and Walton-on-the-Naze, are packed with holiday-makers in the summer. Here are amusement piers, Punch-and-Judy shows, and sand for everyone, though pollution of the coastal waters in this area does not make bathing an attractive proposition. Southend's famous pier is one and one-third miles long—you can take an invigorating walk to the end and back, or ride on the restored pier railway.

SUFFOLK

The ferry port of Harwich lies just south of the River Stour; north of the river, Suffolk begins. Like the rest of the region, Suffolk has its full share of agricultural land, white or strawberry-wash plaster and timber cottages, high-hedged lanes, market towns, beaches and East Anglian dialect, but no one could possibly be unaware when crossing between Essex or Norfolk and Suffolk that they have come to another county. Suffolk is much warmer, rounder, more colorful and gentler.

With flint a significant source of building material (though not as common as in Norfolk), it is no surprise to find that many houses, halls and churches are either built from or decorated with flint stones, some surfaces covered with the entire flint pebbles, others decorated with the shiny split stones, known as flushwork. Outstanding examples are some of the huge churches, built in the days of the flourishing Flemish wool industry, and intended for large congregations. Now, because of a much diminished population, some of these churches stand almost empty, but are spectacular in their structure and enormous bulk. Covehithe is one, grand in ruin, a small thatched church built within its nave for current use. Blythburgh is another, once known as the Cathedral of the Marshes because of its astonishing size.

Characteristic of Suffolk are the windmills—some restored to working order, their spinning sails white-painted—and the crinkle-crankle walls, high serpentine brick walling, ideal for protecting the fruit trees and flowers grown within their generous curves.

The Valley of the Stour on the Essex-Suffolk borders is "Constable Country," so called after the 18th-century artist, John Constable, who was born here in the village of East Bergholt. His paintings (*The Haywain* is perhaps the most famous) reflect the quiet pastoral loveliness of his home surroundings. Flatford Mill, subject of another of his best-known works, still stands here, much the same as in Constable's day and it, together with Willy Lott's cottage, has become a place almost of pilgrimage. This lovely group stands on the Stour just short of the estuary, and from it you can reach East Bergholt on the little road B1070. The church at East Bergholt has a lot in it of interest, not least a 16th-century wooden bell house in which the bells are hung upside down and rung by hand.

Another small road, B1068, leads through lovely land-and-village country to Sudbury, also on the River Stour. On Market Hill there is a statue to Gainsborough who was born here and lived here for some of his life. His house is now both a local art center and a memorial.

Less than four miles northwards the magnificent High Street of Long Melford lines the A134 with its lovely houses and antique shops, almost like a guard of honor leading visitors to the sloping green at the far end, at the top of which stands what is generally considered to be Suffolk's finest church. Mostly rebuilt in the 15th century it is also extremely long, with a nave and chancel measuring 150 feet. Two Tudor mansions close by are open to the public. A little way to the west, Cavendish is a typical and delightful village of thatched cottages.

Bury St. Edmunds and Lavenham

Further up the same road, A134, Bury St. Edmunds contrives, in spite of expanding industry, to retain much of its market-town atmosphere that inspired the 19th-century diarist and politician, Cobbett, to call it "the nicest town in the world." The town's motto, "Shrine of a King, Cradle of the Law" refers to the fact that Edmund, last king of the Angles, murdered in 869, was canonized and later buried at what became known as St. Edmunsbury. In 1215 those much-publicized Barons swore on the saint's altar that they would force King John to sign Magna Carta. The town plan, conceived by an 11th-century abbot, still remains, together with many old houses, though these are often concealed behind Georgian façades. Enough is left of the Abbey, once one of the greatest and richest in Britain, to make it strangely evocative. The ruins are now the site of the Abbey Botanical Gardens where there are various rare trees. There are, besides, a number of splendid public buildings; for example the Town Hall, designed as a theater by Robert Adam; a Queen Anne house on Angel Hill, now containing a collection of old clocks; the 12th-century Moyse Hall Museum, with its macabre display, and the Abbot's bridge across the River Lark. More modern is a statue of Christ by Elizabeth Frink, unveiled in 1976, which stands on a green near the cathedral. This is a town not to be missed.

And neither is Lavenham, which is situated a little to the east, between Bury and Long Melford. Lavenham is unique. It has its own Preservation Society, although it is not unique in that. Its Perpendicular church is of outstanding beauty, erected by the wool merchants who gave so much to Suffolk. The town is rich, too, in 16th-century timber-framed houses with splendid pargeting—a form of decorative plaster work much in vogue during the 16th and 17th centuries—carved angle posts, and with the top stories bulging out beyond those below. Two or three venerable inns and street names, such as Shilling Street and Water Street, contribute to the picture. In the well-known Swan Hotel, now Trust House Forte, there are occasional chamber-music weekends in winter.

From Lavenham it is an easy and delightful run to Ipswich, not forgetting to call in on Hadleigh on the way, where there is another fine church.

Ipswich and A Special Area

Ipswich is Suffolk's county town and its major industrial and commercial center. But it has an ancient history, reflected in its street names and in the very old houses still to be found if you look for them. Chief among these is the Ancient House, probably Britain's oldest and externally most picturesque bookshop, with rich examples of pargeting. The Great White Horse Hotel is noted for the famous Pickwick episode of the "lady in the yellow curl papers." Christchurch Mansion (c. 1550), a fine period building in a park close to the town center, houses a large collection of domestic antiquities and pictures in the Wolsey Gallery (Cardinal Wolsey was born in Ipswich). And do not overlook the docks which present a most lively scene and have, on the quayside, a Palladian-style Customs House built in 1844. It has been said that the docks are at their most impressive at night, when all is still and silent.

On the map, just to the right of Ipswich and at the base of the great bulge into the North Sea, there is an area of outstanding natural beauty. On the bottom edge of it is Felixstowe, opposite Harwich across the confluence of the Rivers Stour and Orwell, and connected with it by a foot ferry.

Felixstowe is an uncommon town, having been built mostly during the last fifty years around a Victorian/Edwardian nucleus. It is a much-liked family resort with exceptionally safe bathing, and is a busy port into the bargain. Townsend Thoresen sail from here to Zeebrugge, which makes it possible to enjoy a day trip to Belgium.

On the inland edge of this special area lies Woodbridge, perched on the River Deben, a small, attractive town with many old buildings, at least three inns worthy of note, a working tide mill, and the distinctive Seckford almshouses. Thomas Seckford was a great benefactor of Woodbridge and his home, Seckford Hall, which lies on the far side of the by-pass, is now an hotel worthy to be his memorial.

The area which stretches from Felixstowe to Lowestoft is very strange. It is flat and bare with heaped-shingle shores. It has curious place names, like Eyke, Iken, Shingle Street and Shane Street. Three rivers meander across it and on one of them stands Orford, where there is a bird sanctuary—the first of thirteen to be found on the Suffolk/Norfolk coasts—a Norman castle keep, and the Butley-Orford Oysterage which sells not only delicious fresh oysters at below London prices, but smoked salmon, trout, eel, over the counter, or by mail order, or—if you can't wait—there is a bustling restaurant of great charm.

Aldeburgh and Framlingham

Just north of Orford is Aldeburgh which has a well-preserved 16th-century Moot Hall on the sea-front. This half-timbered Tudor building once stood half-a-mile inland, but the sea has encroached cruelly in these parts, and the Hall is now only yards from the water.

Here was born the poet George Crabbe, whose character Peter Grimes inspired an opera by Benjamin Britten in which the atmosphere of the Suffolk shore is perfectly caught. Britten lived here until his death in 1976 and the Aldeburgh Festival is held here every June. Many famous musicians take part, and Britten's own works are featured. How well the Festival will survive, now that the inspiring presence of Britten and Peter Pears is slowly fading, is a matter for yearly discussion. Opera and most other Festival events are staged at nearby Snape, where the Maltings has been imaginatively converted to act as an auditorium.

From Aldeburgh, it is an excellent idea to drive unhurriedly west through the very heart of Suffolk, with its comfortable villages, slow rivers and quiet country roads. On the way is Framlingham, a small attractive market town with the picturesque remains of a castle and the late Perpendicular church of St. Michael. Both buildings are steeped in history. The site of the castle was given to one Roger Bigod by Henry I around 1100. On it he built a fortified dwelling house which was subsequently converted into a military castle and later enlarged by the current Roger Bigod of 1213 so that he could entertain King John there. Later the castle came under the direct control of the crown and was accordingly associated with many great names of history until 1665, when it was sold. A hundred years earlier it had been the site of the Proclamation of Mary as Queen of England. It has been said that the church—magnificent as it is—would be remarkable if it contained no more than the tombs of the Howard family. They include that of the Duke of Richmond, reputed bastard of Henry VIII, and of the poet Earl of Surrey who fell victim to Henry's ever-ready axe. The church, however, also has architectural features of interest and there is enough left of the castle to set off the imagination. There are also two fine sets of almshouses and much excellent architecture. At Bruisyard, nearby, is one of England's newly flourishing vineyards.

The Coast Around Lowestoft

Back on the coast, Southwold is an attractive little resort much appreciated by people who like a quiet holiday. Standing on a cliff overlooking the North Sea it has a lighthouse right in its center, groups of flint and color-washed cottages and much greensward for strolling.

Close to Southwold is Dunwich, the scene of some of the worst architectural tragedies. Once the little town had great importance as a port and East Anglian capital, and was graced by nine churches; but the sea, encroaching viciously and overwhelming coastal areas, devoured them all. The last church to fall was All Saints, which toppled over the low cliff in 1919. A new church has now been built well inland. In Dunwich village a small museum tells the sad story in relics and photographs. Not surprisingly, tales are still told of bells tolling mournfully from the sea depths on stormy nights.

Only eleven miles to the north, Lowestoft presents a complete contrast. It is a full-blooded seaside resort, providing vacation-time fun for the thousands who like a traditional break. It is also an attractive fishing port with trawlers and drifters bringing in huge catches of herring, mackerel and halibut which are auctioned, cleaned and packed on the bustling quayside. Another of its attractions is nearby Somerleyton Hall (5 miles northwest), one of the county's finest brick Victorian mansions—with an original 17th-century house buried in its heart. Tapestries and Grinling-Gibbons-style carving vie with stuffed polar bears to adorn the main reception rooms, and there is a maze in the beautiful gardens. Just north of Lowestoft at Corton is Pleasurewood Hills, a "theme park", with fun for all, woodland wildlife and beach walks. Finally, Lowestoft has on its outskirts Oulton Broad, a boat-busy stretch of water that forms a major gateway to the Norfolk Broads.

One of the pleasantest ways to leave Suffolk for Norfolk is through Bungay, which lies fifteen miles from Lowestoft on A1116 and the River Waveney. It is a small market town that weaves this way and that about a church and a butter cross and the remains of a castle which was built by the Bigods of Framlingham. The lower part of the town is on a level with the river, picturesquely bridged on B1132 which is the quiet road to Norwich.

Near the Norfolk-Suffolk border, the Romans built Burgh Castle, one of their so-called Forts of the Saxon Shore, intended as defensive bases to ward off invaders. Parts of its eight-foot-thick walls still stand to 15 feet high or more, with massive circular angle bastions, built from local rubble and flint stones. The west wall has vanished entirely leaving a clear view over the gentle River Waveney with its windmills and marshes.

For a spot of unusual wildlife, visit the village of Earsham close to Bungay, where there is an Otter Trust—a unique collection of these delightful and only-too-rarely-seen little creatures. It lies in the Waveney valley, with lakes, riverside paths, waterfowl and, of course otters; in addition there is a handy cafe and a gift shop.

NORFOLK

Norfolk, extending over 2,000 square miles, is the largest and remotest of the Eastern Counties, but has in Norwich much the liveliest city of the region. As a true provincial capital Norwich was the natural location for the University of East Anglia.

Norfolk's coast juts into the North Sea all the way from Gorleston, near the Suffolk border, to the ancient port of King's Lynn in the north—cargo boats from Copenhagen and the Baltic still call there regularly. This seaward facing bulge gives its inhabitants 100 miles of nearby shoreline, and its visitors an extensive and varied range of seaside towns and villages to investigate. As an added attraction for tourists, Norfolk's annual rainfall is well below the average.

Most popular of the resorts that burst with family holiday entertainment throughout the season are Great Yarmouth, Cromer and Hunstanton; the quietest villages are those that lie along the north-facing coast from Sheringham to Holme-next-the-Sea. During the summer the North Norfolk Railway, a steam line between Sheringham and Weybourne, manned by volunteers, operates on certain summer days.

There is nothing cosy about the villages on this north coast. The houses are as sturdy as the people—both seem to have their shoulders permanently hunched against the wind, are strongly built and indomitable. It is a wild, bleak place with miles of unused sand, and with bird sanctuaries seemingly every few yards.

Blakeney is perhaps the quaintest of these villages. Its narrow main street of fishermen's cottages slopes steeply down to a sudden, open view of the estuary, sailing boats and distant Blakeney Point, now a bird sanctuary. Launch trips to the point are available in the summer. But in choosing to feature Blakeney, one should by no means forget Wells-next-the-Sea and Overy Staithe, or Holkham where there is a gorgeous English-Palladian house standing in a fine park to view, a pottery, a Bygones exhibition, a theater and—guess what—a bird sanctuary. And remember Burham Thorpe, birthplace of Admiral Lord Nelson (its church contains his parents' tomb, and the lectern is made of timbers from *H.M.S. Victory*).

Sandringham and Two Lynns

At Holme-next-the-Sea the land turns suddenly southwards, presenting its beaches to the west, the warmth and the Wash. Just inland from here is where the Queen has her country home, in the parish of Sandringham. The gardens and grounds of the royal estates are surrounded by large areas of heath, rhododendron and pine plantations. Parts of the grounds are open to the public at certain times, and so also is the house. Quite close to Sandringham are the curiously impressive remains of another great household—the Norman castle at Castle Rising.

Close by again is King's Lynn, once known as Bishop's Lynn and now generally called Lynn. It is a typical, energetic country town with a long past. It has two of nearly everything—churches, guildhalls, market places, museums—even the name is doubled. West Lynn lies across the river and is remarkable mostly for the view it provides of King's Lynn. There are remains of a once encircling wall, and the religious houses of Black, Grey, White and Austin Friars. It has a busy little port; the Fermoy Centre is equally busy with music, exhibitions and drama throughout the year, while the Festival is held for two weeks, July-August.

Just beside and above Lynn there are two very attractive tourist traps—the Caithness glass-making establishment, open to casual visits, and Norfolk Lavender (England's largest lavender grower), also open to visitors.

Finally, halfway back towards the north coast is Little Walsingham which contrives singularly well to maintain its own little-village aspect in spite of having been an object of pilgrimage since 1061. Of the original wooden shrine nothing, of course, remains but a new, rather handsome shrine was built between 1931–37, and the pilgrimages continue.

The Broads

A few miles inland from the Norfolk coast, the Broads begin—a name which caused much comment among GIs during World War II. In fact, these innocent Broads are a network of shallow, reed-bordered lakes, many of them linked by wide rivers, which cover about 5,000 acres of the eastern part of the country and offer about 200 miles of navigable waterway. As the Broads are nearly always calm, you can enjoy them as you wish; modern well-equipped cabin cruisers, motor boats and small sailing craft can be hired by the week from all the main Broadland centers, such as Oulton Broad, Horning and Wroxham, and rowboats and small pleasure launches provide day or half-day excursions during the season. The present water pollution has seriously affected the once abundant wildlife, though in remoter parts the prospect is healthier. In high season the Broads are very crowded. They offer some splendid lane and village motoring, but the only way to see them properly is by boat.

Norwich

It is quite easy to sail from the Broads along the River Wensum and into the very heart of Norwich—though more visitors arrive by road or the InterCity train service from London. Seen from many points of approach is the elegant, tapering spire of Norwich Cathedral, soaring 315 feet towards the sky. The cathedral itself is surrounded by a secluded Close of lovely old buildings, including the school where Lord Nelson was a pupil. Among the glories within are the magnificent 15th-century vault above the rich Norman arcades, the Saxon bishop's throne from a still earlier building, and 14th-century paintings of the East Anglian school.

The second building which dominates the Norwich skyline is its castle, a square, stubborn-looking fortress on a steep, grassy mound. Most of the castle's pleasant stone exterior was refaced during the 19th century and to get some idea of its Norman origins one must go inside, where there are plans of the building's original structure and gruesome dungeons. The Castle Museum also contains attractive dioramas of Norfolk wildlife and a comprehensive collection of the Norwich School of Painting. Other museums are The Strangers Hall, in a 16th-century merchant's house; The Bridewell, a square black flint building dating from 1360; and St. Peter Hungate, an ecclesiastical museum in a pre-Reformation church.

Characteristic of medieval Norwich is Elm Hill, a narrow cobbled alley lined with curio shops, picturesque, if a little too tidily restored as a pioneering venture of the Civic Trust. Not far from Elm Hill, down another of the city's narrow alleys, you will come across the famous Maddermarket Theatre, adapted about 60 years ago, with an Elizabethan-type apron stage and a gallery.

In the center of town is the open-air market with its colorful awnings (called "tilts") and multitude of stalls, selling everything from fruit to leather crafts. Between the side of the City Hall and the old Assembly House, which has an exquisite Georgian entrance-hall, stands the new City Library, in part a memorial to men who flew from U.S. 8th Air Force bases in East Anglia.

The Sainsbury Center for the Visual Arts, on the campus of the University of East Anglia, not only has its own permanent collection which is worth seeing, but holds regular and very interesting temporary exhibitions throughout the year. (Open every afternoon, except Mondays.)

Norwich is surrounded by amiable, orderly old villages and market towns. One of the prettiest is Wymondham—pronounced *Windham*—with its Market Cross and overhanging cottages. A few miles to the west lies the parish of Hingham, where Abraham Lincoln's family lived for many generations until they emigrated to America in 1637. A bronze bust of the President can be seen in the fine village church. Routes westward lead on across the rolling heath and forests of Norfolk's Breckland and to Thetford, birthplace (on White Hart Street) of Thomas Paine, author of *The Rights of Man.* Thetford is undergoing large-scale development of housing and industry, but Grime's Graves a short drive away are the most remarkable Stone Age flint-mines in Europe.

CAMBRIDGESHIRE

This last of the counties of East Anglia is something of an acquired taste. Including the Isle of Ely, it divides geographically into Uplands and Fens, the two meeting more or less in Cambridge itself. The Uplands are, roughly, a mixture of Essex and Norfolk, while the Fens are a mixture of black soil and water, dead straight roads, windmills, churches drained of color, and a constantly flat horizon. Given over to a huge acreage of cereals in the Uplands and potatoes in the Fens it is strange country, either depressing or dramatic according to your own disposition.

Cambridge

This peaceful university city, whose Gothic spires are framed by broad meadows and great trees, is within easy range of a one-day excursion from

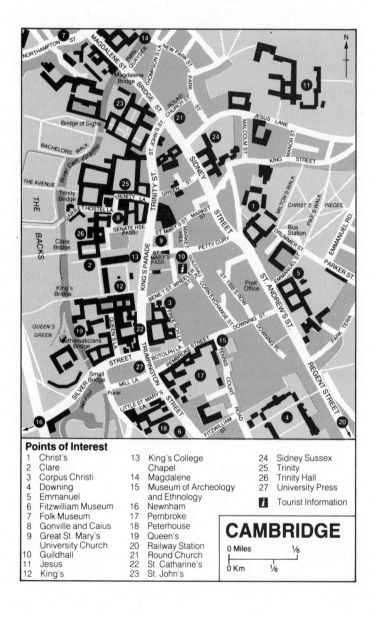

Points of Interest

1	Christ's	13	King's College Chapel	24	Sidney Sussex
2	Clare	14	Magdalene	25	Trinity
3	Corpus Christi	15	Museum of Archeology and Ethnology	26	Trinity Hall
4	Downing	16	Newnham	27	University Press
5	Emmanuel	17	Pembroke		
6	Fitzwilliam Museum	18	Peterhouse	*i*	Tourist Information
7	Folk Museum	19	Queen's		
8	Gonville and Caius	20	Railway Station		
9	Great St. Mary's University Church	21	Round Church		
10	Guildhall	22	St. Catharine's		
11	Jesus	23	St. John's		
12	King's				

CAMBRIDGE

0 Miles 1/8

0 Km 1/8

London and is a convenient starting-point for exploring East Anglia. As the name suggests, from remotest antiquity Cambridge has been the site of a bridge on the river Cam (or Granta). Pre-Roman settlers placed their ford where the bridge is today, at the top of Bridge Street. The town became a market center for the surrounding farms. Over 700 years ago scholars began coming to Cambridge. At first they had no teachers, no organization, and no university. But the 13th century was a thriving period for education and research and universities were springing up all over Europe—in Oxford, Paris, and Salamanca, among other places. The oldest colleges still in existence are Peterhouse (1284), Clare (1326), and Pembroke (1347). The newest is Robinson, a college for both men and women, ceremoniously opened by the Queen in 1977.

"Where is the University?" is a question hard to answer. The colleges are all over town. The oldest women's college, Girton, is three miles out in the Fens; it was originally founded 15 miles away from the male perils of Cambridge, though most colleges are now co-ed, albeit often with just a token force of women.

In recent years the flood of visitors has proved a serious problem to the colleges, and reluctantly they have had to enforce regulations about entrance to their buildings, which are, after all, private property and places of study. Consult the *Practical Information* section at the end of this chapter.

We suggest you begin your tour where Cambridge itself began—at the top of Bridge Street, on the river. After a brief look at Magdalen College— pronounced *maudlin*—which contains the library of Samuel Pepys, walk down to the "Round Church" (dating from Norman times, perhaps founded by Crusaders). Then turn into St. John's College and stroll through its immense courts (quadrangles). Cross the river by the Bridge of Sighs, modeled on its counterpart in Venice.

You are now on the "Backs"—the beautiful green parkland that extends along the river behind several colleges. Here you will feel the essential quality of Cambridge. Resulting in part from the larger size of the colleges, and partly from the lack of industrialization, this atmosphere of broad sweeping openness is just what distinguishes Cambridge from Oxford.

Now make your way to Trinity College. You may see people gliding along the river in punts, long, flat boats propelled by poles. They can be hired from Trinity, or Quayside (next to Magdalene) and the Anchor Inn (near Queen's College). Chauffeurpunt, on Silver Street, will pole you along for about £3 per person, commenting *en route*.

Trinity is Sir Isaac Newton's college; his statue can be seen in the antechapel. The lovely Wren Library is open to the public and contains interesting displays. Outside the Great Gate stands an apple tree said to be a descendant of the one whose falling apple caused Newton to formulate the laws of gravity.

If you are a book lover, be sure not to miss Trinity Street, which contains one gigantic bookshop, almost unsurpassable in most subjects, plus two or three smaller shops.

Then be sure to visit Great St. Mary's, the official church of the University. Cambridge was the scene of considerable controversy during and after the Reformation, and this fact is reflected in the Great St. Mary's pulpit, which moves on rails so that the Protestant-minded can preach from the center and the Catholic-minded can preach from the side.

Clare College, across the street behind the Senate House, is not without its delights, but you will probably prefer to go directly into King's College, whose majestic and huge chapel, dating from 1446, has been called the "finest flower of Gothic in Europe." Attend Evensong; the choir is world-famous.

If you have time, you can now cross the river again, behind King's College (a thing well worth doing for the view), and then look at some of the more controversial pieces of architecture in the University. Behind Clare College's Memorial Court is the University Library, a menacing-looking tower built in the 1930s.

To the south, on the Sidgwick Avenue site, is some quite good modern architecture, including a quadrangular building that stands on great pillars and has no ground floor. The History Faculty building, made of glass panes, is however often referred to as "the greenhouse." Newnham College, across the street, is a women's college with an atmosphere of cultivated elegance.

Return to the river at Queens' College and look at the quaint Mathematicians' Bridge. This is said to have been constructed on geometrical principles to hold together without nails, but a group of curious physicists took it apart one summer to see how it worked and couldn't put it together again. It therefore now has nails. Queens' has some superb Tudor architecture. In one corner of the attractive Pump Court is the Erasmus Tower, where the famous philosopher lived while teaching at the college (1510–13).

The Fitzwilliam Museum in Trumpington Street (closed Mondays) is well worth a visit, having excellent collections of antiquities, paintings and *objets d'art*. The Museum of Archaeology and Anthropology, in Downing Street, is interesting, as is the Folk Museum in Castle Street, which contains objects illustrating everyday life over the past several centuries.

To see the way that a college has grown over the centuries you could not do better than visit Christ's. The Tudor main gateway, bearing a splendid coat of arms, leads into a fine courtyard, with the chapel framed by an ancient magnolia. The unfolding architecture leads you through, past a Fellows' Building credited to Inigo Jones, to the spacious garden (once the haunt of Milton), and finally to one of Cambridge's most modern buildings, a ziggurat-like confection that compels admiration.

If you enjoy walking, you can go to the villages of Coton (behind the University Library) and Grantchester (beyond Newnham) on pleasant country footpaths. Grantchester was immortalized by the poet Rupert Brooke, who lived there in the years immediately before World War I. Cambridge's Tourist Information Office in Wheeler Street provides much useful information, including maps and information about bicycle rentals and guided tours.

There is an American Military Cemetery four miles out on Madingley Road, containing the graves of 3,811 American servicemen who were stationed in Britain during World War II. It is accessible by bus.

Ely and Beyond

Ely, tiny city of the Fens, is built on a patch of high ground above the marshes, one of a series of almost-islands—in fact, its name comes from "Eel Island"—on which stand the towns of northern Cambridgeshire.

Here Hereward the Wake, leader of the Saxons, made his extended stand against the Norman invaders, led by William the Conqueror.

Ely's superb cathedral, which dominates the city and the surrounding countryside, was begun just after the conquest was complete; its octagonal crossing and lantern are unique to Gothic architecture and enormously impressive. The whole of England was searched for oaks large enough to supply the corner posts of the wooden lantern. If you search out the small wooden model of the cathedral in the transept, you can see how the lantern is constructed. The rather gaudily painted ceiling is due to 19th-century restoration, but it does set off the more sombre medieval stonework. On no account should you miss seeing the Lady Chapel, which is almost a separate building. It has some magnificent carvings, especially in the vaulted ceiling. It acted as the Parish Church for four centuries. Another must is the Stained Glass Museum, in the North Triforium, with exhibits dating from the 14th century.

The ancient buildings of the cathedral precincts, the remains of the great monastery, now form the King's School, which claims to be descended from the school which was founded there well before the Norman Conquest. Some of the buildings can be visited, and the lovely chapel is especially interesting.

The new, much larger, Cambridgeshire incorporates both Huntingdon, Oliver Cromwell's birthplace, and the former Soke of Peterborough. Peterborough Cathedral was first founded in the 600s, and so managed the feat of celebrating its 500th anniversary while the Norman building was in construction! The present cathedral is a magnifi-cent work of Norman art, with a fine West Front, built in the early 13th century. This is one of the great buildings of Europe, and worth a side trip to see.

Wisbech, the former port of Peterborough on the River Nene, makes an almost Dutch use of water in its townscape. So it comes as no surprise to find that this is the center of bulb growing, with fields of tulips and daffodils. Many of the towns in this area have great churches with marvelously carved tie-and-hammerbeam roofs. Among them are Tilney All Saints and, especially, the lovely St. Wendreda's Church in March, a little to the south of Wisbech, where the angels seem to form a heavenly choir, frozen in mid-flight.

PRACTICAL INFORMATION FOR EAST ANGLIA

HOW TO GET THERE FROM LONDON. Nearly all the main towns of East Anglia can be visited for a day out by train. The majority of the region is served by trains from Liverpool Street, while a few are served from Kings Cross. If the coach services of National Express are to be used it is essential to check departure times carefully to avoid any danger of being stranded far from home!

Bury St. Edmunds. By train: irregular service from London's Liverpool Street, with at least one train every two hours. It is necessary to change trains at Cambridge or Ipswich—a simple matter. The journey takes about 2 hours 10 minutes, and a day trip is possible allowing at least four hours in the town. **By coach:** National Express operate three coaches daily from Victoria, but timings allow no more than 3 hours' sightseeing. The run takes around 2 hours. **By car:** M11, A11, A45.

Cambridge. By train: hourly service from Liverpool Street, with the fast train taking an hour. Alternatively travel from Kings Cross and change at Royston. One train an hour, and takes a little over 1½ hours. The route from Liverpool Street is the more attractive. **By coach:** National Express run an hourly service from Victoria taking 1 hour 50 minutes. The service is conveniently timed for people wishing to make a day trip. Coaches also pick up at Embankment. **By car:** M11.

Colchester. By train: three trains an hour from Liverpool Street with the fast service—which continues to Ipswich and Norwich—only taking 50 minutes for the run. The expresses have comfortable carriages and usually a light refreshment service. **By coach:** National Express run five coaches a day from Victoria Coach Station (the 11.00, taking just over 2 hours, is suitable for a day trip). **By car:** A12.

Ely. By train: one through train every two hours. Journey time 1¼ hours. **By coach:** two journeys a day from Victoria Coach Station, taking 2 hours 30 minutes, but not suitably timed for day trips. **By car:** M11, A45, A10.

Ipswich. By train: one main-line train an hour from Liverpool Street to this busy town. The journey time is around 65 minutes and most fast trains have a buffet car. **By coach:** National Express run a coach every two hours from Victoria Coach Station. The 11.00, taking 2 hours 30 minutes, is suitable for a day trip. **By car:** A12.

King's Lynn. By train: one train every two hours from Liverpool Street takes just over 2 hours. **By coach:** National Express run three coaches daily, but they are not suitably timed for a day trip. **By car:** M11, A45, A10.

Norwich. By train: this line has been electrified and journey times cut substantially. The hourly fast trains now take around 2 hours for the 115 miles. All expresses have a buffet car. **By coach:** National Express run nine journeys a day from Victoria Coach Station, most of them Rapide services taking 2 hours 40 minutes. The 9.00 Rapide allows over 6 hours in Norwich. **By car:** M11, A11.

HOW TO GET AROUND. This is an area largely isolated from the rest of England, with no large through arteries, an enclave bordered by the sea. But it is within fairly easy reach of London, if you are interested in visiting it on a "days-out" basis, with the major cities of Norwich and Cambridge easily reached. Local bus services have been drastically cut in recent years, and the region is not one of intense activity, so you had better be prepared to move around at a slightly slower pace.

HOTELS AND RESTAURANTS. This is an area of long-settled, rich communities. There are many superb medieval and Tudor inns. Also, since most of the region is easily accessible from London, it tends to have its fair share of people who prefer to live in the heart of the country while working in town. This means that the restaurants and pubs maintain a competitively high standard, while not losing their atmosphere.

Details about our grading system, telephoning, plus other relevant information about hotels and restaurants, will be found at the beginning of the book in the *Facts at Your Fingertips* section.

Aldeburgh (Suffolk). *Brudenell* (M), The Parade, tel. (072 885) 2071; 47 rooms with bath. Victorian hotel with sea views. *Wentworth* (M), Wentworth Rd., tel. (072 885) 2312, 33 rooms, 23 with bath. By the beach; excellent restaurant making full use of local fish and game. *Uplands* (M), Victoria Rd., tel. (072 885) 2420; 20 rooms, 17 with bath. Welcoming 18th century house. At **Snape Maltings.** The *Plough & Sail* (I), tel. (072 888) 413. For real ale, real cyder and good bar food (local game in season).

Blakeney (Norfolk). *Blakeney* (M), tel. (0263) 740 797. 54 rooms, 47 with bath, 2 with shower. Views over harbor. Indoor swimming pool, sauna, solarium. *Manor* (M), tel. (0263) 740376. 26 rooms with bath. Hotel converted from 16th-century farmhouse overlooking fens. English and continental cooking. Good for birdwatchers.

Brockdish (Norfolk). **Restaurant.** *Sheriff House* (M), tel. (037 975) 316. Be prepared to select your menu when you phone to reserve a table. It will be worth taking your meal seriously in this small Georgian village house; fine cooking and wine, Closed Wed. At **Diss.** *Salisbury House* (E), tel. (0379) 4738. Elegant *restaurant avec chambres* (3). Closed Sun., Mon., one week Xmas and two weeks in summer.

Burnham-on-Crouch. (Essex). *Ye Olde White Harte* (M-I), tel. (0621) 782106; 15 rooms, 3 with bath, 3 with shower. A smugglers' inn on the River Crouch.

Restaurant. Try fresh local fish prepared with flair at the *Contented Sole* (M), tel. (0621) 782139. Closed Sun., Mon., last two weeks July and end Dec. through Jan.

Bury St. Edmunds (Suffolk). *Angel* (E-M), Angel Hill, tel. (0284) 3926; 38 rooms with bath. Faces the Abbey gardens; good English dining. Comfortable, well furnished rooms. *Suffolk* (M), 38 Buttermarket, tel. (0284) 3995; 33 rooms with bath. Friendly and reliable. At **Bradfield Combust,** *Bradfield House Restaurant* (E), Subbury Rd., tel. (028 486) 301. Fresh local produce used well in English fare. Closed Sun. evening, Mon.

Cambridge. (Cambs.). Excellent bedrooms at the well-established *Garden House* (E), Granta Place, tel. (0223) 63421; 117 rooms with bath. Well established hotel with lovely riverside setting. *Post House* (E), Lake View, Bridge Rd., Impington, tel. (022023) 7000; 120 rooms with bath. Hotel on spacious grounds north of city. A la carte restaurant. Indoor pool, sauna, solarium. *Cambridgeshire Moat House* (M), Bar Hill, tel. (0954) 80555. 100 rooms with bath. Four miles outside town. Excellent sporting facilities include golf and indoor pool. Modern hotel with that old-world touch. Pleasant restaurant. *Gonville* (M), Gonville Place, tel. (0223) 66611;

62 rooms with bath, also has good amenities. *University Arms* (M), Regent St., tel. (0223) 351241; 115 rooms with bath; well-run central hotel.

Restaurants. *Angeline* (M), 8 Market Passage, tel. (0223) 60305. Friendly and French-inspired. Closed Sun. evening. *Peking* (M), Burleigh St., tel. (0223) 354755. Unpretentious Chinese restaurant with fine authentic Szechuan and Peking dishes at reasonable prices, run by Mr. Mao. Best to book. Closed Mon. *Flames* (I), Castle Hill, tel. (0223) 60723. Fondue specialties in a renovated 18th-century building near the Backs.

Colchester (Essex). *Colchester Mill* (M), East St., tel. (0206) 865022; 70 rooms, most with bath. Victorian mill on site of original mill mentioned in Domesday Book. Restaurant and nightclub. Good for fishing. *George* (M), tel. (0206) 578494; 47 rooms with bath. 500 years old inn on High St. Carvery restaurant. *Rose & Crown* (M), tel. (0206) 866677. 27 rooms, 18 with bath. Half-timbered, flagstone floors, good restaurant.

Restaurants. *Wig and Pen* (M), North Hill, tel. (0206) 41111; the place to go for your oysters (in season). Varied à la carte menu, good lunchtime snacks. Closed Sun. *Pavilion* (I), 7 Culver Square, tel. (0206) 761515. Brand new glass, marble and plant-filled restaurant serving interesting, continental café-style meals.

Cromer (Norfolk). *Cliftonville* (M), Runton Rd., tel. (0263) 512543; 46 rooms, 10 with bath, 4 with shower. Victorian hotel, complete with stained glass windows, minstrels' gallery and sea views. *Hotel de Paris* (M), Jetty Cliff, tel. (0263) 513141. 55 rooms, 33 with bath, 7 with shower. Victorian-style hotel with sea views and restaurant.

Restaurant. At **Aldobrough.** *Old Red Lion* (M), tel. (0263) 761451. Restaurant in lovely old pub 5 miles from Cromer. English cooking. Closed Mon. and Sun. evening.

Dedham (Essex). *Maison Talbooth* (L), Stratford Rd., tel. (0206) 322367; 10 rooms with bath. A truly individual hotel in the country house tradition of hospitality and friendship. Their *Le Talbooth* restaurant (E), tel. (0206) 323150, offers superb flavors, subtly spun in an ancient weaver's cottage beside the river Stour. Gourmet 4-course menu. Half mile from the hotel. (Member of the *Relais de Campagne.*)

Dedham Vale (E), Stratford Rd., tel. (0206) 322273; 6 rooms with bath, also has superbly high standards. Friendly resident owners and fine English and continental cuisine, with some Indian specialties in their *Terrace Restaurant.* Closed Sat. lunch.

Earl Stonham (Suffolk). **Restaurant.** *Mr. Underhill's* (M), tel. (0449) 711206. Small but excellent restaurant. Fine wines. Must book. Closed Sun. evening and Mon. Also provides accommodation (1 room only).

Ely (Cambs.). *The Lamb* (M), Lynn Rd., tel. (0353) 3574; 32 rooms with bath. A superb old Georgian coaching inn well worth a visit. Beautifully refurbished bedrooms with good amenities.

Restaurant. Try the *Old Fire Engine House* (M), St. Mary's St., tel. (0353) 2582, for traditional English fare beautifully cooked. Closed Sun. evening.

Felixstowe (Suffolk). *Orwell Moat House* (M), tel. (0394) 285511; 60 rooms with bath/shower. Traditional, friendly hotel in attractive grounds. English and French cuisine. Dancing on Sat.

Fressingfield (Suffolk). **Restaurant.** *Fox and Goose* (E), tel. (037 986) 247, dates from 1509, but gastronomic pilgrims still gather here; booking and careful ordering in advance essential; fine wines, fresh local produce including pheasant and pike in season. Closed Tues. and Sept.–Mar., Sun. evening.

Glemsford (Suffolk). **Restaurant.** *Barrett's* (E-M), Egremont St., tel. (0787) 281573. Well-presented, quality cuisine in friendly surroundings; must book. Closed Sun. evening and Mon.

Great Dunmow (Essex). *Saracen's Head* (M), High St., tel. (0371) 3901. 24 rooms with bath. Delightful old hotel near market square. Comfortable rooms with modern amenities.
Restaurant. *The Starr* (E), Market Place, tel. (0371) 4321. Good English fare in old beamed inn. Closed Sun. evening.

Harwich (Essex). *Cliff* (M), Marine Parade, tel. (0225) 503345; 31 rooms. 24 with bath or shower. Provides a suitable whiff of sea air from the promenade.
Restaurant. *Pier* (M), The Quay, tel. (0225) 503363; excellent seafood.

Hintlesham (Suffolk). *Hintlesham Hall* (M-E), tel. (047387) 268; 17 rooms with bath. Charming country house hotel dating from 16th century, with 18th-century façade. Completely renovated inside. Excellent restaurant (E). Closed two weeks early Feb.

Ipswich (Suffolk). *Belstead Brook* (E-M), Belstead Rd., tel. (0473) 684241; 33 rooms with bath. Peacocks and stream in the garden. Some luxury suites. *Marlborough* (M), Henley Rd., tel. (0473) 57677. 22 rooms with bath. Good restaurant. *Post House* (M), London Rd., tel. (0473) 690313; 118 rooms with bath. Outdoor swimming pool.

King's Lynn (Norfolk). *Duke's Head* (M), Tuesday Market Place, tel. (0553) 774996; 72 rooms with bath. Busy and welcoming. *Mildenhall* (M), tel. (0553) 775146; 54 rooms, 26 with bath. Pleasant, awning-fronted hotel, centrally located. Both with reasonable restaurants.

Lavenham (Suffolk). *Swan* (E-M), High St., tel. (0787) 247477; 48 rooms with bath. An atmospheric Elizabethan inn, with restaurant. There are very good musical weekends here.

Long Melford (Suffolk). *Bull* (M), tel. Sudbury (0787) 78494; 27 rooms with bath. An ancient half-timbered inn at the village green end of the High Street. Charming and hospitable. *Crown Inn* (M), Hall St., tel. (0787) 77666; praised for good service and food. 13 rooms, 7 with bath. At **Sudbury** *Mill* (M), Walnut Tree Lane, tel. (0787) 75544. 53 rooms with bath or shower in 300-year-old converted millhouse. The old mill-wheel still turns.

Maldon. (Essex). *Blue Boar* (M), Silver St., tel. (0621) 52681. 25 rooms with bath, in an ancient inn. Comfortable and atmospheric.

Newmarket (Suffolk). *Bedford Lodge* (M), Bury Rd., tel. (0638) 663175; 12 rooms with bath. A favorite with the racing fraternity. *Rutland Arms* (M), High St., tel. (0638) 664251; 45 rooms with bath. Coaching inn built around courtyard. English and French cooking.

Just outside at **Six Mile Bottom** is *Swynford Paddocks* (E), tel. (063870) 234. A must for horse fanciers, situated in an actual stud with visits to stables and Jockey Club. 15 rooms with bath, and good restaurant.

Norwich (Norfolk). *Maid's Head* (E), Tombland, tel. (0603) 761111. 80 rooms with bath. Traditional comfort in 700-year-old coaching inn beside the cathedral. *Nelson* (E), Prince of Wales Rd., tel. (0603) 628612. 122 rooms with bath. Modern hotel by the river with sauna and two restaurants. *Castle* (M), Castle Meadow, tel. (0603) 611511; 79 rooms, 26 with bath, is beside the Norman Keep. *Norwich* (M), Boundary Rd., tel. (0603) 410431; 102 rooms with bath. Excellent amenities and friendly host.

Restaurants. *Brasted's* (E), St. Andrews Hill, tel. (0603) 625949. Elegant Regency dining-room for carefully prepared English and French specialties. *Marco's* (E), 17 Pottergate, tel. (0603) 624044; delightful, small restaurant in a cobbled street. Good range of Italian cuisine. *Green's Seafood* (M), Upper St. Giles St., tel. (0603) 623733. Exceptionally varied choice.

Old Hunstanton (Norfolk). *Le Strange Arms* (M), Gold Course Rd., tel. (048 53) 2810. 30 rooms with bath. Country house with views over sea; private beach.

Orford (Suffolk). Near Woodbridge. **Restaurants.** *Butley Oysterage* (M-I), Market Hill, tel. (0394) 450277. Bustling restaurant specializing in home-smoked salmon, eels and local oysters. Also shop. Oct.-Mar. lunch only. Closed Jan. and early Feb. Also in this fishing village is the *King's Head* (M), tel. (0394) 450271. A tiny, family owned and run medieval inn with local produce. Closed Mon., except Bank Holidays, and most of Jan.

Shipdham. (Norfolk). *Shipdham Place* (M), tel. (0362) 820303; 9 rooms, 8 with bath. Pleasant converted 17th-century rectory at end of leafy drive. Worth a visit for the Restaurant (E) alone—which serves superb five-course dinners, with excellent wine list. Closed Sun.-Tues. Jan.-Mar.

Southwold (Suffolk). *Swan* (M), Market Place, tel. (0502) 722186. 52 rooms, 37 with bath. Lovely, 17th-century inn, very close to the beach. Spacious public rooms and comfortable bedrooms. Restaurant.

Thetford (Norfolk). *Bell* (E), King St., tel. (0842) 4455. 46 rooms with bath. Tudor inn by river. *Thomas Paine* (M), White Hart St., tel. (0842) 5631. 14 rooms, 7 with bath, 7 with shower. Historic hotel with *Tom's*

303

Pantry—good restaurant. Reputed birthplace of American patriot Thomas Paine.

Woodbridge (Suffolk). *Seckford Hall* (M), tel. (039 43) 5678; 24 rooms, 22 with bath. Blends original Tudor with modern comfort and personal service. Beautiful grounds in rolling countryside.

Wymondham (Norfolk). **Restaurant.** *Adlands* (E), Damgate St., tel. (0953) 603533. Tiny cottage restaurant in former butcher's shop. Excellent modern cuisine and good wines. Must book. Closed Sun. and Mon.

PLACES OF INTEREST. A region with lovely Regency houses and many fine black-and-white timbered buildings, great churches built on the profits from the wool trade in the Middle Ages and, most important, the county town of Cambridge, rich in university architecture. You will find further details about visiting historic houses in the relevant section of *Facts at Your Fingertips,* and a discussion of the subject in the chapter, *Historic Houses—Precious Stones in Peril.*

Cambridgeshire. **Anglesey Abbey,** near Cambridge (tel. 0223 811200). Tudor manor house and 100-acre gardens. House and gardens open most weekends in Apr. Late Apr.-mid-Oct., Wed.-Sun., Bank Holiday Mon., 1.30–5.30. Closed Good Fri. Gardens open Apr. through June, Wed.-Sun., then daily until mid-Oct., 1.30–5.30. (NT)
Cambridge Colleges. Visiting is only possible to the Colleges, which are, of course, private buildings, during certain hours and the parts that can be seen are also limited—the staircases and students' rooms are not open. Times change from college to college, and all parties of over 10 people have to check in with the **Tourist Information Center,** Wheeler Street (tel. 0223 322640/358977), from which all details of times and guides can be obtained.
Fitzwilliam Museum, Trumpington St., Cambridge (tel. 0223 332900). Classical building with an outstanding collection of art (including paintings by John Constable) and antiquities. Open Tues.–Sun. 10–5, Sun. 2.15–5.
Imperial War Museum, Duxford (tel. 0223 833963). Former Battle of Britain fighter station. Over 90 historic aircraft, including Concorde 01 and tanks. Open mid-Mar. to early Nov., 10.30–5.30 (dusk if sooner). Last entry 45 mins. before closing time. Closed Good Fri.
Kimbolton Castle, Kimbolton. Tudor home of Catherine of Aragon, remodeled by Vanbrugh (1708–20). Now a school. Open Easter Sun. and Mon.; Spring Bank Holiday Sun., Mon.; Summer Bank Holiday Mon.; also late July through Aug., Sun. only, 2–6. Difficult to reach without own transport.
Wimpole Hall, Arrington (8 miles southwest of Cambridge), (tel. 0223 207257). 18th-century mansion, the most spectacular in Cambridgeshire. Stands in 350-acre park. Open mid-Apr. through Oct., daily (except Mon. and Fri. but open Bank Holiday Mon.), 1–5. (NT)

Essex. **Audley End House,** near Saffron Walden (tel. 0799 22399). Magnificent mansion, dating from 1603, remodeled by Vanbrugh with Adam decoration. Impressive Jacobean Great Hall. Open Apr.-mid-Oct.,

Tues.-Sun. Closed Mon. except Bank Holiday Mon. Telephone for further details.

Colchester and Essex Museum, Colchester (tel. 0206 712481). Norman Keep with Roman and prehistoric remains. Castle was built over a Roman temple. Open Apr.–Sept., Mon.–Sat. 10–5, Sun. 2.30–5; Oct.–Mar., Mon.–Fri. 10–5, Sat. 10–4. Closed Good Fri. and Xmas.

The Minories, 74 High St., Colchester (tel. 0206 577301). Two 18th-century town houses converted into an art gallery, with works by Constable and Auguste Rodin. The original ballroom has been arranged as an authentic 18th-century interior, using furniture and paintings from the period. Open Tues.–Sat. 10–5, Sun. 2–6.

Hedingham Castle, Castle Hedingham (tel. 0787 60261/60804). Norman Keep and Tudor bridge, rather bare but very impressive. Open at Easter, May–Oct., daily 10–5.

Paycocke's, Coggeshall. Elaborately decorated merchant's house from about 1500. Open Apr.–Oct., Tues.–Thur., Sun., Bank Holiday Mon., 2–5.30. (NT).

St. Osyth's Prior, St. Osyth. Remains of fine Augustinian Priory, mainly interesting for those who like medieval monastic relics. Also houses an impressive art collection of Old Masters. Open Easter, then May–Sept., daily, 10–5.

Norfolk. Blickling Hall, Aylsham (tel. 026 373 3084). Very impressive Jacobean house, lovely inside and out. Open daily, excl. Mon. and Thurs., Apr. through Oct., 1–5. Also open Bank Holiday Mon.; closed Good Fri. (NT)

Caithness Crystal, King's Lynn, tel (0553) 765111. Guided tours through traditional glassware factory and shop selling seconds. Open all year, Mon.–Fri., 9.30–3.30. Best to telephone beforehand.

Castle Museum, Norwich (tel. 0603 611277, ext 279). Archeology, natural history and fine paintings of the Norwich school. Regular loan exhibitions. Open Mon.–Sat., 10–5, Sun., 2–5. Closed Good Fri.

Holkham Hall, Wells (tel. 0328 710227). One of the world's foremost 18th-century Palladian houses. Paintings by Rubens, Raphael, Gainsborough and other old masters. Also a comprehensive collection of working and domestic appliances from the Victorian and Edwardian eras. Open June-Sept., Sun., Mon., Thurs. (and Wed. in Jul., Aug.), 1.30–5; Spring, Summer Bank Holiday Mon., 11.30–5.

Houghton Hall, east of King's Lynn (tel. 048 522 569). Another great 18th-century house, on the grand scale. Pleasure grounds; heavy horses on show. Open Easter Sun.–late Sept., Sun., Thurs. and Bank Holidays, 1–5.30.

Norfolk Lavender, Caley Mill, nr. King's Lynn (tel. 0485 70384). Colorful lavender fields, herb garden and shop selling natural lavender products. Come in July or August to see the harvest and distillation of pure lavender oil. There is also a teashop. Open Easter–Sept., daily 10–6. Oct.–Easter, Mon.–Fri. (lavender plants and shop only), 9–5.

Oxburgh Hall, Swaffham (tel. 036621 258). Late 15th-century moated and fortified manor house, with outstanding gatehouse tower. Well kept gardens and woodland walk. Open daily, May–Sept. (except Thurs. and Fri.) 1.30–5.30; also weekends and Bank Hol. Mon. for part of Apr. and Oct. (NT).

Park Farm, Snettisham (tel. 0485 41244). Spend a day down on the farm. A working farm with crops and livestock. Tractor tours and farm trails. Open Easter through Oct., Sun.–Fri. 10.30–5.

Sainsbury Center for Visual Arts, Norwich (tel. 0603 56060). Permanent collection of ethnographic, modern and pre-Colombian, ancient and medieval design. Also houses the University of East Anglia's art collection. Open daily (except Mon.), 12–5.

Sandringham House, Sandringham (tel. 0553 772675). Home of H.M. the Queen. Open early Apr.–Sept., Mon.–Thurs., 11–4.45, Sun. 12–4.45. Closed late Jul.–early Aug. and when Royal Family in residence. For specific dates and hours, check with Estate Office, Sandringham.

Walsingham Abbey, between Wells and Fakenham (tel. 032 872 259). 11th-century shrine of Our Lady, later Augustinian Priory. Grounds open Apr., Wed. only; May–Jul., Sept., Wed., Sat., Sun.; Aug., Mon., Wed., Fri–Sun.; also Bank Holidays; all 2–5.

Suffolk. Christchurch Mansion, Ipswich (tel. 0473 53246). Country house collection plus excellent art gallery (works by Constable, Gainsborough). Open all year, Mon.–Sat. 10–5, Sun. 2.30–4.30.

Euston Hall, Thetford. 18th-century, housing famed collection of paintings by Stubbs, Van Dyck, Lely and Kneller, among others. Landscape by John Evelyn and Capability Brown. Open Thurs., June–Sept., 2.30–5.30.

Gainsborough's House, Sudbury (tel. 0787 72958). Birthplace of the great painter, with exhibitions of his work and also contemporary and historic art. Open Easter–Sept., Tues.–Sat., 10–5, Sun. and Bank Holiday Mon., 2–5. Oct.–Easter, Tues.–Sat., 10–4, Sun. 2–4. Closed Good Fri.

Ickworth House, near Bury St Edmunds (tel. 028 488 270). Late Regency house of strikingly original design, a must for architectural buffs. Gardens, orangery, lake, woodland walks. Open May–Sept., daily (except Mon. and Thurs.), 1.30–5.30; also weekends in Apr. and Oct., plus Bank Holiday Mon. (NT).

Kentwell Hall, Long Melford. (tel. 0787 310207). Largely Elizabethan house now being lovingly restored by its occupants. Surrounded by a wide moat; fine gardens with limetree avenue. Open Easter–late June, Wed., Sun. 2–6; mid-July–Sept., Wed.–Sun. 2–6; Bank Holiday Sat., Sun., Mon., 11–6. Telephone for details of June/July historical recreations on site.

Melford Hall, Long Melford. Tudor Mansion with Regency interiors. Gardens with gazebo. Collection of Chinese porcelain. Open Apr.–Sept., Wed., Thurs., Sat., Sun., Bank Holiday Mon., 2–6. (NT).

Museum of East Anglian Life, Stowmarket (tel. 0449 612229). An open-air museum on a 30-acre site. Open Apr.–Oct., Mon.–Sat. 11–5, Sun., 12–5 (June–Aug. 12–6).

Pleasurewood Hills, Corton Road, nr. Lowestoft (tel. 0502 513626). East Anglia's first theme park—American-style. 50 acres with over 50 activities and attractions for the family. Wonderful World of Storybooks, crazy golf, steam railway, etc. etc.; nature walks and beach walks for those who want peace. Open most weekends in late Apr. and May, then daily until mid-Sept., 10–6.

Somerleyton Hall, near Lowestoft. Ancient mansion, mentioned in the Domesday Book, though most of present house is extravagantly Victorian, as are a lot of the contents. Maze and lovely gardens. Open Easter Sun.

through May, Thurs., Sun. and Bank Holidays; June through Sept., Sun., Tues.–Fri. and Bank Holidays; all 2–5.30.

Wingfield College, near Diss. Founded in 1362. A fascinating Gothic timber-framed building hidden behind 18th-century front. Open Easter–Sept., Sat., Sun. and Bank Holiday Mon. 2–6.

HERTS, BUCKS AND BEDS

The Northern Home Counties

The Home Counties are one of those beautifully English inconsistencies. They are supposed to embrace the counties nearest to, in fact adjoining, London and they are traditionally regarded as Middlesex—which has disappeared into Greater London—Surrey, Kent, Essex and occasionally Hertford and Sussex. The fact that Berkshire and Buckinghamshire also lean against London doesn't seem to rate, but in our book it does. We will deal first with Hertfordshire, because it is next to the East Anglia region dealt with in the last chapter; then Buckinghamshire which has its feet in the Thames Valley; and finally Bedfordshire which is wedged in between the upper boundaries of both the other counties. This is a particularly prosperous part of southern England, and country hotels, restaurants and old inns full of character abound.

HERTFORDSHIRE

The jewel of Hertfordshire must be regarded as St. Albans, which lies just over 20 miles to the north of London and is accessible by train from both King's Cross and St. Pancras main line rail stations and by Green Line bus. It is the successor to the tribal capital of Britain called Verulamium, built beside the little river called the Ver. The site of the Roman *muni-*

cipium (which lasted from A.D. 43 to about 410, surviving a sacking by the irrepressible Boadicea) is now occupied by a park and school playing fields, but part of the city wall still stands and archeological work is continuing at the site of the amphitheater. These sites have yielded major Roman relics. Visit the Verulamium Museum, in which most of the finds are collected. Verulamium contains the Roman theater (the only one to be open to view in Britain) and the hypocaust, a Roman heating system of a private suite of baths, which has been excavated and preserved.

The major feature of the city is the 11th-century cathedral, which has one of the longest medieval naves in existence, as well as a fine Norman tower; its west front is an unhappy 19th-century addition. St. Albans has considerable historical associations and was the site of two important battles during the Wars of the Roses. Its name derives from St. Alban, a Roman soldier who was the first Christian martyr in England; he was beheaded here in 303 and his shrine is in the cathedral.

About eight miles north, at Ayot St. Lawrence, is Bernard Shaw's house, Shaw's Corner, open to the public in the spring, summer and autumn. Though only the ground floor rooms and the revolving summer house in which Shaw wrote several of his plays can be seen, the house— unloved by Shaw and his wife—nevertheless has great atmosphere.

Hertfordshire's leading stately home is Hatfield, about 20 miles north of London. Exceptionally large, with a 300 ft. frontage with magnificent windows, domes and towers it was built between 1608 and 1612 by the 1st Earl of Salisbury, Robert Cecil. The Cecil family still live there. The place, inside and out, is sumptuous, beautifully maintained and open to the public between March and October.

Cheek by jowl with Hatfield—well, only 10 miles north of it—lies Knebworth House, another delightful stately home. This one has rich literary associations, since it was the home of Sir Edward Bulwer-Lytton (who wrote a series of historical novels including *The Last Days of Pompeii*) and welcomed many famous Victorian figures there. It began as a Tudor house in 1492 and was "Gothicized" by Bulwer-Lytton in 1843. Among special events held in Knebworth Park are medieval jousting tournaments, American Civil War battle re-enactments, craft fairs and steam and traction engine rallies.

Searching for Villages

It is sad that so much of Hertfordshire has been spoilt because it is too near—and too accessible—to London. For this reason many visitors tend to overlook it. But that would be a mistake. A great deal of it has been carefully preserved, but to find the real gems a car is essential. Hertford, the county town for instance, has cottages and houses of varying periods, and the small remains of the castle built by the son of King Alfred has been turned into a gatehouse now occupied by the county council. It stands in a park running down to the river, and is the place where Queen Elizabeth I lived as a child.

Similarly, there are many, many villages in the county which have, at least, an almost untouched core, such as Aldenham with its village green and ancient church; Barley, with a 300-year-old inn, a Norman foundation church, a Tudor-built town house, and overhanging cottages. Flamstead, too, is small and on the River Ver, with 17th-century almshouses, and the church of St. Leonard, surrounded by lilacs, red and white chestnuts and huge sycamores, besides having what are regarded as the second best wall paintings in the county. Furneaux Pelham—what a name to conjure with—lies in a hollow with a 16th-century manor house at one end and an interesting 13th-century church. Little Hadham is full of timber-framed cottages and farm houses, and also has a windmill. Finally, although it is not the end of the possibilities, is Little Wymondley which can boast in Wymondley Bury a gabled brick building and dovecote surrounded by a moat; Wymondley Hall, a six-gabled, timber-framed house built early in the 17th century; and Wymondley House, Georgian, two-and-a-half stories high with five bays.

Although searching for villages is normally a somewhat time-consuming business, in Hertfordshire it is a good deal easier than in most other counties, because the very roads which have done so much harm to the county as a whole, are a godsend to the tourist in a hurry.

BUCKINGHAMSHIRE

Buckinghamshire is without question the easiest of the home counties to reach from London when driving, because all you have to do is to get onto A40 and stay on it. It starts at the Mansion House, in the City, and goes via Holborn, Marble Arch (it is in fact the old Tyburn Road along which they took wrong-doers, particularly highwaymen, before stringing them up), Notting Hill, then onto Western Avenue and away. Apart from Western Avenue, which is new, this A40 is the old coaching Gloucester Road, which crosses into Buckinghamshire at Uxbridge, now on the boundary of Greater London. From there to where the road passes into Oxfordshire, just beyond Stokenchurch, there are various relics of the coaching days, particularly milestones and inns, to be sought out.

The Chilterns

The rolling Chiltern Hills, which divide the county into two halves, are for many the most characteristic feature of the area. North of the Chilterns, there are many small rivers, streams and marshes that lead towards the sluggish River Ouse, on the northern boundary of the county. The southern escarpment is characterized by leafy forests of beech trees and silver birches, while to the north there are great rolling grass vales, that look from the distance like a checker board. Because of the hills, there are many fine vantage points in the county, such as Coombe Hill near Wendover (over 850 feet) and Ivinghoe Beacon (811 feet). The sharp contrast in the land south and north of the Chilterns is the outward sign of the highly varied geological deposits that go to make up the soil, ranging from hard, dry and infertile chalkland to the rich, fertile alluvial deposits of the Thames Basin.

Like its neighbor, Berkshire, across the Thames, Buckinghamshire has also suffered by being a through route to the west and to the Midlands, the dry valleys of the southern slopes of the Chilterns offering perfect ready-made routes through the hills. (The oldest road in England, the Icknield Way, runs along the top of the Chilterns.) Buckinghamshire has been a center of civilization from prehistoric times onwards. The county has raised more than its fair share of famous sons, and many distinguished people have adopted the county as their home. Milton came to Horton in 1665 to escape the Plague in Cambridge, going on to Chalfont St. Giles where, blind and disillusioned, he completed *Paradise Lost.* His cottage there can be visited. At Olney, William Cowper wrote nearly all the poems and letters that have made him remembered, and it was the churchyard at Stoke Poges that inspired Gray to write his famous *Elegy.* Three prime ministers have been born and raised here, the most famous, of course, being Disraeli, who was later to take the title Lord Beaconsfield, and whose home, Hughenden Manor, near High Wycombe, is open to visitors. William Penn, the founder of Pennsylvania, came from the village of Penn.

Buckinghamshire dwellers will tell you that they may not have much of the Thames, but what they do have is probably the best. "The best" includes the great sweep of the river at Marlow Lock, with the wooded hills of Cliveden dipping down to the river bank, the incomparable view of Windsor Castle, and Eton College. Buckinghamshire claims an equal share of Boveney and Gray, Boulters Lock and Cliveden Reach. The lazy water meadows of Hambleden, which are so often crowded in the summer, are here, as is the equally enchanting village of Medmenham, where incongruously, the Hell Fire Club held its meetings in the ruins of the abbey.

At Cliveden, we remember George Villiers, the powerful Duke of Buckingham, who played such a large role in the country's affairs during the reign of Charles I. Formerly the home of the Astors, Cliveden is now owned by the National Trust, and has also become an exclusive, discreet hotel. A few rooms are open to the public between April and October, and the beautiful formal gardens between March and December.

A little to the east of Cliveden lies Burnham, a fairly large village of ancient origin set within the huge once-pollarded trees of Burnham Beeches which stretch for around 600 acres and are thought by many to be one of the country's loveliest places.

American Timbers and Disraeli

A mile or so north of the A40, near Chalfont Common and tucked away among tall birch trees, lies the Quaker village of Jordans, which for any American visitor is a mandatory stop. Here are preserved the original timbers of the *Mayflower,* which took the Pilgrim Fathers to America in search of religious freedom. The stout black beams of the ship form a great black barn, normally thronged with visitors during the summer months. Here also is buried William Penn, who founded the state of Pennsylvania, and the city of brotherly love, Philadelphia, in an attempt to create a state governed according to Quaker principles.

Surrounding Jordans and nearby Beaconsfield are the magnificent woods that formerly belonged to another well-known Quaker, George Cadbury, of chocolate fame, who generously donated them to the country. Beaconsfield itself is a charming place to wander in, with its broad-timbered inns and hotels. It is the ideal place to break for refreshment. In the large church, you can see the tomb of Edmund Burke and his two sons. Burke was one of England's leading political thinkers, and in the last decade of the 18th century, was one of the most important influences on political thinking in the western world.

The rather dull drive on A40 from Beaconsfield to High Wycombe has been rescued somewhat by the draining of traffic onto the M40, but High Wycombe is still one of the busiest towns in the county. Motorists who are not in too much of a hurry should detour here to see the 13th-century Knights Templar Hostel, and the 18th-century Guildhall at the end of the High Street, with its wooden cupola, on top of which stands a weathervane in the shape of a centaur firing an arrow into the wind.

Just north of High Wycombe is Hughenden Manor, the former home of Lord Beaconsfield, better known to history as the great Victorian Prime Minister, Disraeli. It is now a National Trust property and the parts of it that can be visited have been kept exactly as they were when Disraeli died. It is extremely interesting to be able to catch a glimpse of the way that one of the most intriguing (in both senses of the word) of Englishmen lived. His library is especially noteworthy.

The Hell-Fire Club and Ancient Pubs

The golden ball high on the hill that immediately strikes your eye as you leave High Wycombe is yet another meeting place of the Hell-Fire Club. West Wycombe, lying below the hill, and strung out along the Oxford Road, is one of only a handful of villages in England completely, or almost completely, owned by the National Trust. It is a perfect example of gabled roofs, thatched cottages and old beams. The famous Hell-Fire Caves at West Wycombe are said to be the largest man-made chalk caverns in the world, with an underground river (appropriately named the Styx).

After the rather sinister and magical atmosphere of the caves, the lushness of the surrounding countryside makes a refreshing contrast. Drive northwards through the famous gap at Princes Risborough to Stoke Mandeville, the home of John Hampden, of Civil War fame, and then on to Aylesbury. Famous for the duckling that is said to have originated here, it lies at the very heart of the county. Unfortunately, many of the older inns, which in medieval times used to stand around the market square, have vanished. But there still remain two of interest: the Bell, which boasts a 300-year-old barn for its garage, and the King's Head, a medieval inn in an almost perfect state of restoration. The latter was originally the guest house of the adjoining monastery; its lounge was the old refectory. The leaded glass in the windows is more than 500 years old.

After Aylesbury, the visitor can roam through the villages and towns of northern Buckinghamshire, all of which possess some interest—none is devoid of charm. Try Stowe, for instance, with its famous public school housed in an extraordinarily beautiful building (almost one quarter of a mile long), or Boarstall, with its gatehouse, and Buckingham, small for a county town, with its wide main street and old inns.

At Weedon, a few miles from Aylesbury, is Lilies, a second-hand bookstore in a handsome Victorian house, with about a million volumes. Call (0296) 641 393 for an appointment first (or London, 727 5211).

But if time is limited, drive south on A413 from Aylesbury to Wendover, deep in the heart of the Chilterns, with the Roman Icknield Way as your highroad. There are excellent views from the top of Boddington and Coombe Hill, from which on a fine day you can see St. Paul's Cathe-

dral in London. Drive on to Amersham. This town possesses a very interesting High Street, at each end are watermills and in the very middle is
a 17th-century market hall, with its wooden turret. The building is supported by arches over an old twin lock-up, and nearby, behind a line of
lime trees and grouped around a cobbled courtyard, are almshouses. Within the village, which is really more a small town, are four exceptional inns,
The Crown, The King's Arms, the Elephant and Castle, and the Swan.
All have unique architectural or historical features. At the foot of Gore
Hill which runs steeply into the town, is Bury Farm, where Guilielma
Springett lived before she married William Penn.

BEDFORDSHIRE

Bedfordshire is a county that not only is overlooked, but from its position on the map looks as though it wants to be. Squeezed in between Buckinghamshire and Cambridgeshire, it appears to balance on top of Hertfordshire, holding its breath. It is, however, very easy to reach from
London because the M1 enters it just south of Luton and has four exits
before it goes off into Northamptonshire. There is a fairly reasonable train
service running right up the middle.

Woburn Abbey

Without doubt Bedfordshire's showpiece is Woburn Abbey, family residence of the Duke of Bedford, rebuilt in 1802 and surrounded by 3000
acres of land. To say that it is open to the public is to understate the case.
The public is almost dared not to go there, such are the blandishments
offered by the ducal entrepreneur who could teach Barnum a trick or two.
The attractions include sumptuous apartments, furnishings and paintings
by Holbein, Van Dyck, Rembrandt and Canaletto in the house; a large
wildlife park containing a collection of rare animals; a gift shop, pottery
and antique market; café and restaurant; dolphinarium and pets corner.
The Abbey was first opened to the public by the fourth duke, before any
of the other landed gentry had seized on the idea, and the present duke
is thought still to be ahead of the competition, but no figures are published.

Competition for the Woburn zoo is to be found at Whipsnade, a small
village on the edge of the Dunstable Downs at the southernmost end of
the county. The zoo was the first in Britain to give the animals as much
freedom as is safely possible and enclose them in natural surroundings.
Today it has 2,000 animals and a famous breeding record. It is, of course,
open to the public.

The historic house competition around here is Luton Hoo, designed
originally by Robert Adam with park by Capability Brown. It lies off the
A6129 south of Luton and is said to have been built for the Earl of Bute
when he was Prime Minister. The park, of 1,500 acres, has two lovely lakes
and stables by Robert Adam. For nearly the whole of this century it has
been the home of the Wernher family and contains the great Wernher Collection—porcelain, china, tapestries and furniture, besides robes and mementos of the Russian Royal Family (Sir Julius Wernher's daughter-in-
law was a Romanov), including some pieces by Fabergé.

It has to be admitted that the scenery of Bedfordshire is not exactly breathtaking. It is largely flat, but also has a pastoral individuality which is appealing to many people. Its chief interest lies in its domestic architecture, particularly in the villages. Ampthill, for instance, which lies north of Luton and south of Bedford, is perhaps larger than a village and has gracious Georgian houses, the seven-bay White Hart Hotel, at least three different groups of distinguished almshouses and a connection with Catherine of Aragon, who stayed there during the period of her divorce. It has many buildings worth seeing, and just nearby is Houghton Conquest House which is the model of Bunyan's House Beautiful in his *Pilgrim's Progress*. Bunyan was in fact born a little further up the same road, at Elstow, still a pretty village where there is a Moot Hall which houses a collection of items illustrating his life. It is also said that William the Conqueror's sister founded a nunnery here, which had its own ducking pond, pillory and gallows!

Bedford

Bedford is of course the county town, also a center of industry, but still with plenty in it worth seeing in spite of some rather uneasy modernization. The River Ouse contributes a lot, with its Embankment on both sides, public gardens and two bridges, one Georgian the other late Victorian. The town also remembers with gratitude Sir William Harpur, born in Bedford in 1496, who ultimately became Lord Mayor of London and founded the Bedford Grammar School. It was in Bedford jail that John Bunyan wrote *Pilgrim's Progress* and the Bunyan Meeting and Museum, which is open in summer, displays relics of the writer's life. There are a number of inns, the Swan being particularly interesting because it has a staircase said to have been designed by Wren.

Northwards again from Bedford we come to Bletsoe, a small village lying just off the A6. Here are the remains of a one-time castle, now a farmhouse with a Jacobean staircase and a long, Elizabethan frontage. It was visited by Elizabeth I, and the mother of Henry VII, the formidable Lady Margaret Beaufort, was born there. It has a 13th/14th-century church, and the Falcon Inn down by the river was often visited by Thackeray and his friend Edward FitzGerald of *Omar Khayyam* fame.

When one travels around Bedfordshire, it becomes apparent that the county has one very charming characteristic. In spite of its smallness, and the somewhat overpowering energy of its bigger towns bent on industrialization, it has a large number of small places, villages no more, where the past remains alive in the buildings still in use. Places with such fascinating names as Aspley Guise, Flitwick, Meppershall, Old Warden, Stagsden and Sharnbrook. All of them have architecture of many periods, particularly Jacobean; very old churches, or thatched cottages about village greens. It is a county like a library, designed for browsing.

PRACTICAL INFORMATION FOR
HERTS, BUCKS AND BEDS

HOW TO GET THERE FROM LONDON. This area, which is very closely allied to London yet possesses a distinct charm all of its own, can be visited very easily by a wide range of transport services. Due to road congestion in the capital the best means of access is by rail—either by British Rail or London Regional Transport Underground trains. The whole area is covered by the *Network Southeast Card*—see page 186. Some villages, such as Gt. Missenden or Aylesbury, are particularly suited to outward travel by train and then for exploration on foot.

Amersham. By train: choice of "overland" tube, the *Metropolitan* line from Baker Street—one train an hour—or British Rail from Marylebone, again one train an hour; journey time 38 minutes. **By coach:** not really worth it. Use LRT Red Lines. **By car:** A40, A413.

Aylesbury. By train: British Rail from Marylebone. One train an hour and the journey takes just over 1 hour. **By car:** A40, A413.

Bedford. By train: a choice of routes. British Rail run a fast service which operates with about one train an hour from St. Pancras to Bedford Midland and takes 35 minutes. There is also a slower service leaving every 30 minutes from St. Pancras which takes just under an hour. **By car:** M1, A421.

Hatfield. By train: two trains an hour from King's Cross both taking about 20 minutes for the journey. There is also a service of two trains an hour from Moorgate which take longer, 38 minutes. **By Car:** M1, A1, A1(M).

Marlow. By train: travel first from Paddington to Maidenhead; two trains an hour, but only one connects with the branch line service to Marlow. At Maidenhead change to the second train which runs to Bourne End and Marlow. The complete trip takes 1 hour 15 minutes. **By car:** M40, A404.

St. Albans. By train: four trains an hour from Moorgate, or Kings Cross/Midland City; two trains an hour from St. Pancras; fastest time 18 minutes for the run. **By car:** M1, A1, A6.

HOTELS AND RESTAURANTS. As this is one of the main "stockbroker-belt" regions, the hotels and restaurants available tend to be on the plush side—and ones in which you could very well find an acceptable martini! Pubs will serve good lunches, and there will very likely be good wine available by the glass.

Details about our grading system, plus other relevant information about hotels and restaurants, will be found at the beginning of the book in the *Facts at Your Fingertips* section.

Aston Clinton (Bucks). *Bell Inn* (E), tel. (0296) 630252; 21 rooms with bath. Rustic coaching inn with long consistent reputation for good dining; game dishes particularly memorable. (A *Relais de Campagne* hotel.)

Aylesbury (Bucks). *Bell* (M), Market Sq., tel. (0296) 89835. 17 rooms with bath. An old coaching house, now T.F.H. *King's Head* (M), Market Sq., tel. (0296) 415158. 24 rooms, 8 with bath, 2 with shower. Owned by the National Trust, and said to be one of the very best examples of Tudor architecture. Set menu in restaurant.

Beaconsfield (Bucks). *Santella* (E), 43 Aylesbury Rd., tel. (04946) 6806. Renowned Italian restaurant. Subtle decor and friendly service. The cannelloni is always popular.

Bedford. (Beds). *Swan* (E), The Embankment, tel. (0234) 46565. 100 rooms with bath. Late 18th-century hotel beside the river. New extension and leisure center. *Moat House* (M), St. Mary's St., tel. (0234) 55131. 117 rooms with bath. Modern hotel, recently refurbished, on the edge of the river, overlooking the old town. Functional, with terrace restaurant. *Woodlands Manor* (M), tel. (0234) 63281. 21 rooms with bath. 2 miles north. Regency house in 3 acres. Traditional elegance. Imaginative English cooking.

Buckingham (Bucks). *White Hart* (M), tel. (0280) 815151. 19 rooms with bath, in an interesting building on Market Square.

Chenies (Bucks.). *Bedford Arms Thistle* (E), tel. (09278) 3301. 10 rooms with bath. Elizabethan-style with lots of dark oak. Good restaurant with French classical cuisine, and some very unusual drinks!

Flitwick (Beds.). *Flitwick Manor* (E), tel. (0525) 712242. 15 rooms, 13 with bath, 2 with shower. Lovely 17th-century country house in extensive grounds. Its restaurant (E) is highly recommended for the seafood specialties. Closed Sunday evenings.

Gerrards Cross (Bucks.). *Bull* (E), tel. (0753) 885995. 98 rooms with bath, some in modern annex. Old coaching inn.

Harpenden (Herts.). *Moat House* (M), tel. (058 27) 64111. Elegant Georgian house overlooking the Common. 56 rooms with bath or shower, good restaurant. *Glen Eagle* (M), tel. (058 27) 60271. 51 rooms with bath. Comfortable and quiet.

Hertford (Herts.). *Salisbury Arms* (M), tel. (0992) 583091. 31 rooms, 11 with bath. Ancient inn with beams and wood-paneling. Good restaurant with Chinese chef—chow mein, as well as roast beef, features on the menu.

Restaurant. *Marquee* (E), tel. (0992) 558999. Lavish decor and imaginative cuisine.

Hertingfordbury (Herts). *White Horse Inn* (M), tel. (0992) 56791; 42 rooms with bath or shower. Group owned, but mercifully the management continue to do their own thing. Pleasant restaurant in Victorian-style conservatory; rooms very comfortable and clean.

Houghton Conquest (Beds). **Restaurant.** *Knife and Cleaver* (M), tel. Bedford (0234) 740387. Just south of Bedford, this is a good spot for lunch. The wine list is excellent—if you aren't driving! Closed Sun.

Ivinghoe (Bucks.). **Restaurant.** *King's Head* (E), tel. (0296) 668388. Beamed restaurant offering traditional English dishes.

Jordans (Bucks.). *Old Jordans* (I), tel. (024 07) 4586. Quaker House associated with Wm. Penn. founder of Pennsylvania. 30 rooms, 6 with shower in annex. Also 3 suites (M). Set meals in dining room and afternoon tea.

Little Wymondley (Herts.). Nr. Hitchin. *Redcoats Farmhouse* (M), tel. (0438) 729500. 16 rooms, 10 with bath or shower. Beamed bar, antiques and interesting food. Welcoming.

Marlow (Bucks). *Compleat Angler* (L), tel. (06284) 4444. 46 rooms with bath, in a gracious hotel in busy riverside setting. The *Valasian* restaurant will ensure an excellent meal. All-in-all a delightful spot for a summer evening.
Restaurant. *Cavaliers* (E), 24 West St., tel. (06284) 2544. International cuisine. More informal bistro (M) downstairs. Closed Sun. evening and Mon.

Newport Pagnell. (Bucks). *TraveLodge* (M), tel. (0908) 610878; 98 rooms with bath. Spotless motel-type accommodation on Service Area 3, MI motorway; convenient for north-bound travelers.
Restaurant. *Glovers* (M), tel. (0908) 616398. A very pleasant, atmospheric spot with some intriguing dishes. Closed Sun., Mon. and Sat. lunch.

St. Albans (Herts). *St. Michael's Manor* (M), Fishpool St., tel. (0727) 64444; 26 rooms, all with bath or shower. Very well run in the manor-hotel tradition plus a certain style that brings many guests back. Pleasant conservatory for dining. Attractive garden. *Sopwell House* (M), Cottonmill Lane, tel. (0727) 64477; 30 rooms with bath. Delightful situation, in extensive grounds. South of town just off the A1081.
Restaurant. *Abbotts* (M–E), 17 Holywell Close, tel. (0727) 66067. Beautifully situated overlooking the cathedral. Seafood, Mediterranean and Greek dishes. Also has less formal brasserie with American flavor.

Taplow (Bucks.). *Cliveden* (L), tel. (06286) 68561; 25 rooms with bath. Stately home recently partially converted to hotel where guests enjoy exceptional (and expensive) country house life-style. Elegant dining room

(L) for classy French cuisine. 400 acres of National Trust parkland and many amenities.

Turvey (Beds.). *Laws* (M), tel. (023 064) 213; 11 rooms with bath. Pleasant hotel; rooms recently refurbished with all mod cons. Welcomes children.

Ware. (Herts.). *Briggens House* (M), tel. (027 979) 2416. Georgian country house in 50 acres grounds. 60 rooms with bath. Coarse fishing, tennis, 9-hole golf course, outdoor swimming pool. *Moat House* (M), tel. (0920) 5011. 50 rooms, 44 with bath, 6 with shower. Modern.

Whipsnade (Beds.). **Restaurant.** *Old Hunter's Lodge* (M), tel. (0582) 872228. Good place to eat pre/post- zoo visit; lunchtime bar snacks. English and French food.

Woburn (Bucks). *Bedford Arms* (E), tel. (0525) 290441. 55 rooms with bath. Modernized Georgian coaching inn, close to the abbey.

PLACES OF INTEREST. One of the more settled, fat-cat areas of England, which is reflected in its historic buildings, of which Luton Hoo is a prime example. Woburn Abbey, which is among the leaders in historic-house promotion with an aggressive policy of publicity, lies at one extreme and the quiet dignity of the Victorian Hughenden Manor at the other, with many attractive possibilities in between. For more details about visiting historic houses, see the relevant section in *Facts at Your Fingertips* and the chapter, *Historic Houses—Precious Stones in Peril.*

Bedfordshire. Luton Hoo, home of the Wernher family (tel. 0582 22955). Adam exterior, famous jewel collection, including Fabergé. Open Easter, then Apr.-mid-Oct., daily (except Mon., though open Bank Holiday Mon.), 2–5.45.

Shuttleworth Collection, Old Warden (tel. 076 727 288). Old aeroplanes, motorcycles, cars and carriages with flying displays on the last Sunday of every month in summer and on some Bank Holidays. Open daily 10.30–5 (to 4.30 in winter). Closed Christmas week.

Stagsden Bird Gardens, Stagden (tel. 023 02 2745). Large bird zoo and breeding establishment, with more than 150 rare old species. Fine shrub roses. Open daily from 11–6 (or dusk).

Woburn Abbey, Woburn near Leighton Buzzard (tel. 052 525 666). Ancestral home of the Duke of Bedford (even if he does actually live in a Paris apartment for tax purposes!). 18th-century treasure house, deer park and herd of European bison. Popular attraction: the 350-acre Woburn Wild Animal Kingdom, the biggest drive-thru game reserve in Europe. Open New Year's day and Jan.-end Mar. weekends only; end Mar.–Nov., daily. Times of opening vary slightly according to time of year, but generally 11–5.45.

Buckinghamshire. Ascott, Wing (tel. 0296 688242). House containing important collection of Chippendale furniture and 18th-century paintings. Impressive topiary gardens. House and Gardens open late July–late Sept.,

Tues.–Sun., 2–6. Gardens also open Apr.–late July, Thurs., 2–6, plus last Sun. each month. Check for changes. (NT)

Chenies Manor, Chenies (tel. 024 04 2888). 15/16th century manor with fortified tower, secret passages, beautiful grounds. Original home of the Dukes of Bedford. Open April–Oct., Wed. and Thurs. 2–5; Spring and Summer Bank Holidays, 2–6.

Chiltern Openair Museum, Newland Park, near Chalfont St. Peter (tel. 024 07 71117). Reflects 500 years of life in the Chiltern Hills, set in wooded grounds; Iron Age house, nature trails. Open Easter to end Sept., Wed., Sun. and Bank Holidays, 2–6 (Wed.-Sun. in Aug.).

Cliveden, Taplow (tel. 06286 5069). Country mansion (now partly an hotel) with lovely grounds and formal gardens; fine Thames views. Grounds open Mar.–Dec., daily 11–6 or sunset; some rooms open Apr.–Oct., Thurs. and Sun., 3–6. (NT)

Dorney Court, nr. Windsor (tel. 06286 4638). Beautiful Tudor manor house. Present family has lived here for nearly 400 years. Good collection of furniture and paintings. Open Easter then Sun. and Bank Hol. Mon. until Oct.; also Mon. and Tues., June–Sept. All 2–5.30.

Hughenden Manor, High Wycombe. Former home of the Victorian Prime Minister, Disraeli. Open Mar., Sat. and Sun., 2–6 (or dusk); April–Oct., Wed.–Sat., 2–6; Sun. and Bank Holiday Mon., 12–6. Closed Good Fri. (NT).

Milton's Cottage, Chalfont St. Giles (tel. 024 07 2313). John Milton's home where he worked on *Paradise Lost* and *Paradise Regained;* preserved as it was in 1665. Pretty garden. Open Mar.-Oct., Tues.-Sat., 10–1, 2–6; Sun. 2–6; Spring and Summer Bank Holiday Mon., 10–1, 2–6.

Stowe (Stowe School), Buckingham. 18th-century house, the work of Gibbs, Vanbrugh, etc. Grounds and garden buildings designed by Kent. Open most of Apr. and early Jul.–end Aug., daily from 1.

Waddesdon Manor, near Aylesbury (tel. 0296 651211/651282). Built like a vast French château for a Baron de Rothschild; full of paintings, carvings and French interior design. Really something to see. Open late Mar.-Oct., Wed.-Sun., 2–6 (grounds Wed.-Sat. from 1, Sun. from 11.30); house and gardens both open 11–6 Good Fri. and all Bank Holiday Mon. (NT). Closed Wed. following Bank Holiday Mon.

West Wycombe Park, West Wycombe (tel. 0494 24411). Palladian house and 18th-century landscaped gardens with reconstructed Temple of Venus. Open Apr. and May, Mon.–Thurs; June-Sept., Sun.–Thurs.; also Easter and Bank Holidays; all 2–6.

Hertfordshire. Hatfield House, Hatfield (tel. 30 62823/65159). Home of the Marquess of Salisbury, Queen Elizabeth I lived here. Excellent medieval banquets and annual "Living Crafts" and "Country Fare" exhibitions. Open late Mar.-early Oct., Tues.-Sat., 12–5, Sun. 2–5.30, Bank Holiday Mon. 11–5; Park open daily, 10.30–8; closed Good Fri.

Knebworth House and Country Park, near Stevenage (tel. 0438 812661). Fine "Gothicized" Tudor mansion with deer park, adventure playground for children, picnic sites, narrow-gauge railway and jousting field. Plays, readings and banquets are occasionally held. Open Apr.–late-May, weekends, Bank Holiday Mon. and school holidays; late May–mid-Sept., daily (except Mon.); house 12–5, park 11–5.30.

Shaw's Corner, Ayot St. Lawrence, near Hatfield (tel. 0438 820307). Bernard Shaw's home from 1906–50. Revolving summerhouse in the garden where he retreated to work. Open April–Oct., Wed.–Sat., 2–6; Sun. and Bank Holiday Mon., 12–6. (NT).

THE MIDLANDS

England's Prosperous Heartland

When one thinks of the English Midlands one thinks inevitably in terms of industry. This, however, is a mistake, because of the four counties concerned, only the West Midlands is essentially and almost exclusively industrial, with bits of industry slopping over into the north of Warwickshire and Hereford and Worcester, while all the rest could be regarded as agricultural with a touch of industry here and there.

Away from the towns of this part of the country, and, indeed, within a few miles of their outskirts, there is a sense of permanency not only about the natural landscape but about the works of man. The cottages, the country churches, the layout of the farms, all these and other manmade components seem to have been fashioned with one object, that of fitting in perfectly with their surroundings and in none more so than Northamptonshire, which is not the county that springs to the mind of tourists when they think of England.

NORTHAMPTONSHIRE

Northampton, the county town of one of the loveliest of English counties, dates from pre-Christian times, an iron age fortification at Hunsbury Hill being the first evidence of settlement. There were several periods of

Danish occupation in the 10th and 11th centuries. After the Norman Conquest, Simon de Senlis fortified the town. The castle which he built became famous for the holding of parliaments by Henry I and notable as the place of trial of Thomas à Becket, Primate of England in Henry II's reign. The castle was destroyed by Charles II following the town's support for the Parliamentarians in the Civil War.

The Battle of Northampton (1460), when the Yorkists captured Henry VI, was one of the most decisive in the Wars of the Roses. The town suffered in the mid-17th century from plague and a devastating fire which virtually destroyed it. The town and county are noted for their long association with the footwear industry, an important regional enterprise which is featured in a number of museum displays locally.

Around the county town, there are a number of fine buildings. Althorp, a few miles to the northwest, is the family home of the Princess of Wales. It was partly remodeled in the 18th century, but so successfully as to make it one of the most imposing mansions in these parts. Even lovelier is the Elizabethan facade of Castle Ashby, east of Northampton, the property of the Marquesses of Northampton. There are Saxon churches at Earls Barton and Brixworth.

Sulgrave Manor and Boughton House

Americans may want to make a detour from Northampton to Sulgrave Manor, built about 1560 by Lawrence Washington, a direct ancestor of the first President of the United States. It's a modest Tudor house with a slate roof, about 8 miles northeast of Banbury on a secondary road. It is reached from Northampton on A45 and B4525. Besides various mementos of the family, there's a portrait of George Washington by Gilbert Stuart over the fireplace in the great hall. The manor was purchased on British initiative, restored, and has been endowed by the Colonial Dames of America. In spite of its heavily restored sections, it is now a good example of a small Elizabethan manor house and garden.

On the way back to Northampton from Sulgrave, the minor road passes Canons Ashby, a delightful manor house restored by the National Trust, and then crosses the A5. A canal buff might like to turn southeast and visit the Waterways Museum beside the Grand Union Canal at Stoke Bruerne, near Towcester, which brings to life the 200-year history of canals in Britain. The whole area is rich in canal lore. For train travelers there is at this point a fascinating moment when one can see stretching ahead the canal, the railway, the A5 (in effect the old Roman road of Watling Street) and the M1, five generations of travel. Just to the east of this point, too, is Little Brington, another Washington home, and at Great Brington several Washington brasses in the village church.

Northwards from Northampton the A43 goes to Kettering, passing the village of Pytchley on the way, home of England's top pack of fox hounds. Kettering itself is a market-and-manufacturing town that can boast a charter dating from 1227. North again, just off the A43, is huge Boughton House which has been described as "a vision of Louis XIV's Versailles transported to England" (make sure to take the guided tour, by appointment only, of the State Rooms). The house is reached via the attractive village of Geddington, which has a packhorse bridge and one of the dozen Eleanor Crosses erected by Edward I to mark the places where his queen's body rested on its last journey to Westminster. It is thought to be the most beautiful, although the best known, is, of course, outside Charing Cross station in London (although the present cross there is a Victorian substitute).

Still on the same road we enter Rockingham Forest, once one of the largest in the Midlands. Here lies Deene Park, for the last four centuries the home of the Brudenell family, one of whom, the 7th Earl of Cardigan, led the Charge of the Light Brigade during the Crimean War (1854). Nearby are the ruins of Kirby Hall (Gretton), built in the mid-16th century, updated by Inigo Jones in the 17th, then wickedly abandoned in the 18th. Now nearly derelict, this is a lovely ruin. Finally, using a side road passing north of Corby one comes to Rockingham Castle, above the golden village of the same name, with a breathtaking view into Leicestershire and three other counties. The Castle is an Elizabethan family home within Norman walls, and is open to the public during the summer months.

Northamptonshire is, as will have been seen, well-endowed with open houses and ancient monuments. There are many more than we have space to mention. West of Northamptonshire lies Warwickshire, perhaps the most English county of them all.

WARWICKSHIRE

This is, of course, picture-postcard land, with its sleepy villages, thatched roofs and quiet vistas. But it is also the birthplace of that image of Britain which has been spread over the breadth of the world by the works of Shakespeare. The realm of the yeoman, the wooded land of Arden, the home of the prosperous small tradesman and the wealthier merchant. The region where landowners still pasture deer as they have done for the last nine hundred years. The county of peace and prosperity which is the fire in the heart of "this precious stone set in a silver sea."

Stratford-upon-Avon

Part of the region is indeed Shakespeare's England, and there is a fair number of cottages—now in the $425,000 bracket, if they have more than three bedrooms and all "mod cons"—that resemble the pretty cottage at Wilmcote, a few miles from Stratford, that used to belong to Shakespeare's mother.

Born in a half-timbered early-16th-century building in the town of Stratford-upon-Avon on April 23, 1564, Shakespeare was buried in Holy Trinity Church after he had died (on his fifty-second birthday) in a more imposing house at New Place. Although he spent much of his life in London, where, of course, he became a leading figure of the Elizabethan theater, the world associates him with Stratford. Here, in the years between his birth and 1587, he played as a boy, attended the local grammar school and married Anne Hathaway; here he returned a man of prosperity, to the town with which his name is ineradicably linked.

Today, over three-and-a-half centuries after his death, he remains the magnet that draws hundreds of thousands of tourists each year to this

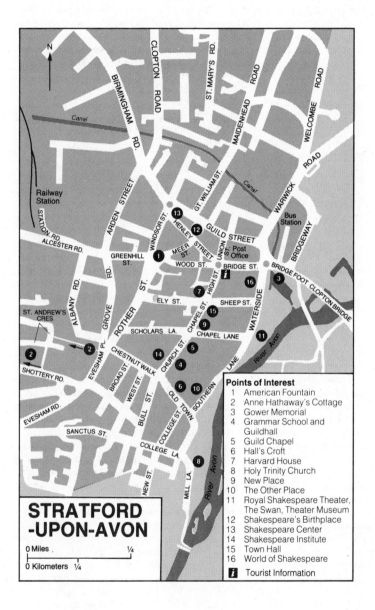

STRATFORD -UPON-AVON

0 Miles   ¼

0 Kilometers   ¼

Points of Interest

1 American Fountain
2 Anne Hathaway's Cottage
3 Gower Memorial
4 Grammar School and
   Guildhall
5 Guild Chapel
6 Hall's Croft
7 Harvard House
8 Holy Trinity Church
9 New Place
10 The Other Place
11 Royal Shakespeare Theater,
   The Swan, Theater Museum
12 Shakespeare's Birthplace
13 Shakespeare Center
14 Shakespeare Institute
15 Town Hall
16 World of Shakespeare

i   Tourist Information

south Warwickshire town. They come to visit the places with which he is identified, and to attend a performance of one of his plays in the Royal Shakespeare Theatre. Stratford has adapted itself to the rising tide of visitors. The town is full of souvenir shops, boutiques selling everything from china to sweaters, quick food outlets, and all the concentrated merchandizing that marks a major tourist destination. To give the town its due, Stratford isn't particularly strident in its search for the quick buck, but if you prefer to seek for surviving traces of history in peace and quiet, you should attempt to hit the town either out of season, or at a time of day either before the bus tours arrive, or after they have left.

The town's historic monuments, as well as charting and celebrating Shakespeare's achievements, give an insight into life in the England of late medieval, Tudor and Elizabethan times. Pride of place goes to the five properties administered by the Shakespeare Birthplace Trust. Three are in the town—Shakespeare's Henley Street birthplace, the New Place/Nash's House property, and Hall's Croft. The others, Anne Hathaway's Cottage and Mary Arden's House, are one and three miles respectively out of town. These five shrines not only give a picture of Shakespeare as writer, actor, man of wealth, status and property, they also help trace the social pattern of Shakespeare's family, following it through a number of generations from quite humble beginnings to a position of eminence.

Shakespeare's ambitious father, John, left farming to set up as a glovemaker in Stratford. The house he rented in Henley Street, in which William was born, is the best known (though not necessarily the most interesting) of the Shakespearean shrines. Next to the modern Shakespeare Centre, with its exhibition of costumes from TV versions of Shakespeare's plays, is the Birthplace, through a garden which is planted with plants mentioned in his works. The house itself is a black-and-white half-timbered structure with three gables. Part of the house has been furnished in 16th-century style, re-creating the comfortable atmosphere of a middle-class home of that period. In addition to the expected Shakespearean memorabilia, there are interesting features such as an original 16th-century window inscribed with the signatures of distinguished visitors—Sir Walter Scott and Thomas Carlyle among them. Scott's signature is dated 1828, by which time the birthplace was already attracting considerable outside attention. By the 1870s, 6,000 visitors a year were turning up, a surprising 1,000 of whom were Americans. Such was the overseas interest that circus impresario P.T. Barnum wanted to buy the property, put it on wheels, and take it around the U.S.A.

Shakespeare's last years were spent at New Place. The site and foundations of this house, demolished in the 18th century, are preserved in replica Elizabethan gardens next to Nash's House, the handsome home of Thomas Nash, husband of Shakespeare's grand-daughter Elizabeth. As well as its period furnishings, the house also contains a museum which traces Stratford's past from prehistoric to medieval times. Hall's Croft was the residence of Dr. John Hall, the Stratford physician who married Shakespeare's elder daughter Susanna in 1607. His career in medicine and the medical practices of the time are featured inside, along with some exceptional items of Elizabethan and Jacobean furniture.

Once a separate village, Shottery is today joined to an expanded Stratford. Here in attractive, leafy surroundings is the most famous cottage in

England, the picturesque thatched home of Anne Hathaway, Shake-speare's wife. Fame comes with a price: be prepared for huge crowds in the peak-season summer months. The building is not really a cottage at all. Dating from 1470, this substantial, 12-room farmhouse preserves its low ceilings, original fireplace, stone-flagged downstairs and creaking floorboards. There is a regular bus service to Shottery, though the best way to see the outlying properties is on one of the round-trip coach tours run by Stratford's enterprising Guide Friday tour company. This short tour also takes in the Tudor farmstead at Wilmcote, home of Shake-speare's mother Mary Arden. Dating from 1409 and the oldest of the Shakespearean properties, it offers a glimpse of the domestic conditions (dirty and unhygienic by today's standards) in which even the prosperous classes lived in late medieval England.

Try to spend at least two full days in Stratford. Quite apart from the properties with direct domestic links with the playwright, there is so much else to see. Many visitors come, of course, for the theater, home of the Royal Shakespeare Company. In 1874, Charles Edward Flower formed the Shakespeare Memorial Association with a view to establishing a per-manent theater here. The forerunner of the present building, opened in 1879, saw the birth of the Shakespeare season which has since grown in both size and stature. In 1926 the original Victorian Memorial Theater was destroyed by fire. A provincial building with a sad tendency towards Tudor-Gothic, it was not mourned (on hearing the news, Bernard Shaw sent a telegram which said simply "Congratulations"). The replacement, the Royal Shakespeare Theatre designed by Elizabeth Scott, rose from the ashes and was opened in 1932. For this, a great deal of money was sub-scribed by—among others—the people of the United States. With frequent internal changes, this is the theater that exists today. Backstage tours are available, and there is a marvelous Theatre Museum on site. The original ornate foyer and gallery survived the fire and now form the entrance to the new Swan Theatre, opened in 1986. This theater-in-the-round is one of the most exciting auditoria in the world, not so much for its design—though that is intriguing—but as an acting space of perfect dimensions. The conversion was funded by an ardent anglophile American philanthro-pist, Frederick Koch. The third theater, the idiosyncratic Other Place (a glorified tin shed), will continue to play to small audiences.

Back in the town, the Guild buildings contain a chapel with a chancel dating from 1450 and incorporating part of the fabric of the original (built in 1269), the early 15th-century Guildhall, and the grammar school at-tended by the bard. There is a fascinating link with the United States in the lovely half-timbered Harvard House (1596), for not only was it owned by the parents of John Harvard, who gave his name to the famous Ameri-can university, but it was actually bought and presented to the university by Edward Morris of Chicago in 1909. Holy Trinity Church, beautifully situated beside the Avon, contains the graves of Shakespeare, Anne Hathaway and other members of his family. The Town Hall, built of lovely Cotswold stone, has a statue of Shakespeare presented by the actor David Garrick on the occasion of a 1769 festival, a forerunner to the theatrical performances of today. A new, non-Shakespearean festival now takes place in Stratford each July, featuring a wide variety of the performing arts. Another fairly recent addition to the scene is the World of Shakespeare, an inventive audio-visual theater that re-creates scenes and episodes from Elizabethan England.

The River Avon, which is the focus for most of the town's activities, is navigable again, after years of disuse, and narrow boats—barges, equipped as floating homes—now line the banks opposite the theater.

As is to be expected, Stratford is well endowed with historic inns and hotels, including the Golden Lion and the Shakespeare which, under a different name, was actually there when the bard was born. North of Stratford, Warwickshire is at its best in the Forest of Arden, where the woodland glades and shady paths through the trees give little indication of the nearness of Birmingham.

The road from Stratford to Warwick passes just north of Charlecote Hall, with its magnificent manor house built on the site of an earlier mansion in 1558 by Sir Thomas Lucy, whose family owned the estate from the 12th century to 1945, when Sir Montgomerie Fairfax-Lucy presented it to the National Trust. It was here that, according to the oft-quoted story, the young Shakespeare was caught poaching deer in the park and was brought before Sir Thomas himself. It was an incident that seems to have left its mark on the mind of the poet-to-be, for there seems little doubt that the builder of the mansion was the protoype of Justice Shallow in *The Merry Wives of Windsor.*

Warwick

History is certainly written all over the face of Warwick, for even a great fire in 1694 failed to erase many of the medieval buildings. Its east and west gates piercing sections of walls that go back to the 12th century; its fine collection of half-timbered buildings, including Lord Leycester's Hospital (originally built as a guildhouse in the time of Henry VI but converted into a hospital by the Earl of Leicester in 1571); and the Church of St. Mary's, largely destroyed by the fire but with parts of the older erection still to be seen, all remain to echo its historic past. St. Mary's is especially worth visiting, to see the floridly ornate Beauchamp (pronounced Beecham) Chapel, containing memorials of medieval and Tudor Earls of Warwick and their families.

Warwick's crowning glory, however, is its great castle, perched conspicuously on a ledge of rock above the River Avon. The Earls of Warwick, as indicated by the term "kingmaker" applied to the holder of the title during the Wars of the Roses, were ever to the forefront in affairs of state; and throughout the castle's long history, it has withstood sieges by hostile armies, held prisoners of high rank, and been the scene of the trials of those who found themselves on the opposite side to the Earls of Warwick.

Doubtless, the Saxons used the mound overlooking the Avon to house a fortification of sorts, and facing the present gatehouse, which is less than 200 years old, is an elevation known as Ethelfleda's Mound, in commemoration of the man who enclosed the town following its destruction by the Danes in A.D. 915.

The first Norman castle was erected soon after the Norman Conquest by Henry de Newburgh, henchman of William I, who was created first Earl of Warwick for his services. Only fragmentary evidence remains of the earliest building; the greater part of the present imposing collection of towers and domestic buildings is of later date.

Caesar's Tower, which rises to a height of nearly 150 feet from the river, was built in 1370 by the first Thomas Beauchamp, who carried out many structural alterations. His son, another Thomas, built the no-less-imposing Guy's Tower, nearly a quarter of a century afterwards.

The family which had fought so many battles for the castle finally acknowledged defeat in 1978 and sold it to Madame Tussauds Ltd., who now run it as successfully as they do their waxworks in London. The attractions of the castle include a torture chamber, the State Apartments and private apartments with the recreation of a Royal Weekend Party of 1898—with wax figures of Edward VII, his mistress Daisy, Countess of Warwick, the young Winston Churchill, and many other figures of the time—a magnificent collection of arms, armor and works of art, a Victorian Rose Garden, and regular special events with an historic flavor.

There are other places of interest in the vicinity of the county town. At Guy's Cliffe, the grounds contain the cave used by the legendary Guy of Warwick who, tiring of the usual pastimes linked with love and war, retired to this beautiful spot to lead the life of a hermit. The nearby priory marks the site of a religious establishment created by the first Earl of Warwick and later converted into a mansion by one Thomas Hawkins. In 1926, however, the mansion was pulled down and shipped across the Atlantic, where it was rebuilt by its new owner.

Almost adjoining Warwick is Royal Leamington Spa, a pleasing town with interesting shops, delightful gardens and medicinal springs which first attracted visitors in the late 18th century. Many of its buildings date from that period of prosperity. The Pump Room, with its Tuscan colonnade, offers refreshments and free tastings of spa water, as well as spa treatments.

Kenilworth and Rugby

Some miles to the north is Kenilworth, where once more the Norman barons successfully used a site previously occupied by the Saxons to build a castle. This romantic, ruined fortress was, of course, the one described by Sir Walter Scott in his novel of the same name. Like nearby Warwick, Kenilworth has had as its owners men who were usually in the forefront of any trouble, including the all-powerful Simon de Montfort, who led his barons in the civil wars of the 13th century.

The keep and some of the outer walls date from the early part of the 12th century, when the original castle was built by one Geoffrey de Clinton (in the time of Henry 1); following the death of Edward II, it was one of the possessions of John of Gaunt, who built the Strong Tower, the Banqueting Hall, and other sections. Then, in the time of Queen Elizabeth I, Kenilworth became the possession of Robert Dudley, Earl of Leicester and strong favorite of the monarch, who showed much extravagance in adding new parts and who frequently entertained his royal mistress here.

The original builder of the castle also founded the Augustinian priory, to which Leamington Spa once belonged, but the greater part of this was demolished after the dissolution of the monasteries and only the gatehouse and some fragments of the original can be seen today.

A few miles northeast of Leamington Spa lies Rugby which quite clearly should belong in West Midlands but somehow contrived to stay in Warwickshire, the only piece of solid industrialization now to be found in the county.

Rugby is the site of engineering works and a famous public school founded in 1567, the scene of the well-known boys' favorite, *Tom Brown's Schooldays*. It was here in 1823 that the game of Rugby football was born. A tablet in the wall of the school close recalls this incident, the inscription reading: "This stone commemorates the exploit of William Webb Ellis, who, with a fine disregard for the rules of football as played in his time, first took the ball in his arms and ran with it, thus originating the distinctive feature of the Rugby game."

WEST MIDLANDS

This is another creation of the 1974 county boundary reorganization, made up of little nibbles taken out of Warwickshire and the old Worcestershire and consisting, in the main, of the major cities of Birmingham, Coventry and the area known as the Black Country, where traditional craftsmanship still flourishes at long-established glass factories. As in other industrial areas, the line between straight industry and the emerging "service" economy is blurring through the opening of industrial-based museums and visitor attractions (such as the Black Country Museum at Dudley). Here lies the complex junction of two expressways—the aptly-named M5/M6 Spaghetti Junction.

Birmingham

In recent years the center of Britain's "second city" has undergone so many structural alterations that, as an official guide book of the local multi-million-pound authority said, "there is more of the future to be seen coming into being than there is of the past left to contemplate." Indeed, its development schemes are resulting in its being a monument to the late-20th-century. Whether you agree that it is a *fitting* monument to the 20th century depends on your feelings towards the 20th century, and the only way to decide is to go to see it.

It is, however, unlikely that anyone could fail to be impressed with the 250-foot circular Rotunda building that rises above the tower of St. Martin's Church, itself severely damaged in an air raid of 1941, but restored through funds raised mainly by local industrialists and businessmen. Neither can one fail to be interested by the uneasy mixture of the old and new at the Bull Ring, where, in keeping with a tradition going back to the 12th century, an open-air market still exists, but with its stalls backed by a center containing supermarkets and stores, restaurants, banks, and one of the busiest bus stations in the land. Traditional Birmingham also lives on in the jewelry quarter, where skills are handed down from generation to generation. The National Exhibition Centre about 13 miles east of Birmingham is beginning to revolutionize this part of the world, giving weight to Birmingham's claims as the convention center for Britain. This mammoth undertaking has taken over some of the functions of Olympia and Earl's Court in London, playing host to trade and other exhibitions, involving international industry. The provision of hotel space for the project is slowly catching up with the other facilities and, by the end of the decade, Birmingham may well be one of the world's major exhibition centers.

Birmingham's permanent symphony orchestra, which gives concerts in the Town Hall, is making an international name for itself under its mesmeric young conductor, Simon Rattle, and regularly tops the recording prize list.

Among the many other facilities is the Museum and Art Gallery in Chamberlain Square, which has a fine art collection, especially rich in Pre-Raphaelites, and also natural history, archeological and ethnographical collections. The branch Museum of Science and Industry is in Newhall Street; and 2½ miles north is Aston Hall, one of the finest Jacobean houses in the country.

One of the unlikely facts that is given about Birmingham, is that it has more canals than Venice. This is actually the case, and some of the stretches of canal have been cleaned up and are used as very attractive areas for fun on and beside the water. You can even have dinner on one of the cruising narrow boats.

Coventry

Eastward is the other big industrial center of Coventry. In spite of Coventry's strong links with industry (and, particularly, the auto industry), there is much evidence of culture in a city that has undergone important structural alterations since it was the victim of Nazi bombing raids. The rebuilding was not entirely successful, either socially or architecturally, and much of the city center looks dated and shabby.

Coventry is a place rich in history. As long ago as 1043, Leofric, Earl of Chester, and his wife, Godiva, founded a Benedictine monastery which was to become one of the richest in the country. Spon Street has timbered buildings of the 14th to 17th centuries, painstakingly re-sited beam by beam to be used as craft shops and cafes. St. John's Church was once used by Cromwell as a prison for Royalists, giving rise to the expression "to send to Coventry," to refuse to associate or speak with someone. The city's industrial heritage is displayed in the Museum of British Transport in Cook Street, where hundreds of vehicles portray the major contribution Coventry has made.

Lady Godiva, is, of course, always associated with Coventry on account of her riding through the streets of the town naked as a jaybird—except for her fine head of hair—and while this incident, if it did take place at all, has often been treated as a joke, it was in reality evidence of the lady's piety and feeling for the poor. Time and time again she asked her husband to relax the taxation which was causing distress in the neighborhood, but he always refused; until one day he said in exasperation the request would be granted if she would ride naked through the town on horseback. This she did, and in all fairness to the Earl, it must be said, the taxes were relaxed. Her ride also gave rise to a new expression in English, when a tailor named Tom peeped through a hole to watch her, in spite of the townspeople's pledge that all would remain behind shuttered windows during her ride. According to the legend, "Peeping Tom" was struck blind for his trouble. Godiva's statue in Broadgate commemorates the famous ride.

The cathedral was destroyed in a terrible air-attack on the night of November 14, 1940, rebuilt and finally reopened in 1962. Many have criticized the architecture of the new cathedral but all who go to the city should see, behind the altar, the Graham Sutherland tapestry, said to be the largest in the world, as well as the brilliant abstract stained glass windows which rise from floor to roof, the Elizabeth Frink sculptures and the giant wall of engraved glass forming the front. The cathedral also has a Visitors' Center with an imaginative audio-visual show highlighting Coventry's medieval and modern history. The burned-out shell of the old cathedral next door preserves a moving memorial to the devastation of war, with the words "Father forgive" on one wall.

HEREFORD & WORCESTER

Hereford & Worcester—once separate entities, now a combined all-purpose and generally unwieldy double-county—is a restructuring which is purely bureaucratic. To all intents and purposes (certainly in terms of character and personality), "old" Herefordshire and Worcestershire remain separate in everyone's mind. Hereford and Worcester are still regarded—by the locals, anyway—as the county towns of their respective shires. When in this part of England, it is best to find out which old county you are really in, and not muddle one with the other, for the natives remain mildly chauvinistic. The individual identities of both areas are especially pronounced in tourism terms, for Herefordshire is an old border county entirely different in flavor from Worcestershire.

For a start, Worcester is the more easterly of the two. Hereford was a buffer state between the unbiddable Welsh and whoever happened to be ruling England at the time. The region was called The Marches, and until well after the Norman Conquest was the scene of enormous turbulence. Both areas have at least one thing in common. Often neglected by tourists in favor of "more exciting" places, they are quiet, gentle regions, outstandingly beautiful in a rounded, undramatic fashion. There are dozens of unspoilt villages and small, friendly towns. It is, in fact, the perfect place for an exhausted tourist seeking a little peace and tranquility.

Worcestershire

The cathedral city of Worcester is in the center of its county, built astride the Severn River. In its time it has suffered, and gained, from the Romans, Anglo-Saxons, Danes and the Welsh. It was the first city to declare for the King in the Civil War, and the last to surrender to Cromwell, thus earning the title of "the faithful city." The cathedral was originally built about 950 and has, of course, its own splendid and not so splendid history, reflected in the tomb of the infamous King John and the lovely chancel in memory of Prince Arthur. There is much of beauty in Worcester and many old houses, but it has suffered greatly from modern road building and traffic management. Among the many points of interest in the town are the Royal Worcester Porcelain Works (a few blocks south of the cathedral), which has a museum showing pieces from the long history of this world-famous factory; also The Commandery, a 15th-century timbered building which contains, amongst other historic exhibits, a dramatic audiovisual display of the Civil War.

Just to the northwest of Worcester is Lower Broadheath, the birthplace of Sir Edward Elgar, whose music is so identified with English national feeling, and who chose to live and work in such an intensely English part of the country. His statue is in Worcester, facing the cathedral where a lot of his music was first performed.

To the south of Worcester, rising suddenly from the level plain, are a range of hills, with Great Malvern, Malvern Wells and Little Malvern all huddled against them as if for shelter from the prevailing west winds. Their two main peaks are the Worcester Beacon, 1395 ft., near the north of the range, and the Hereford Beacon, 1114 ft., at the southern end. Both provide magnificent views for walkers. At the summit of the Hereford Beacon are the remains of a fortified British Iron Age camp. Malvern is, not surprisingly, a town full of steep streets. It houses an annual festival, and has an attractive Priory Church. It also contains what must be one of England's most perfectly located public schools.

Roughly ten miles northwest of Worcester, at the junction of A443 and A451, there is a strangely unsuitable baroque church at Great Witley, well worth a visit. Now the parish church, it stands in what was once a great family estate, and is an outstanding example of rococo work. Close by, at Little Witley, there is a Gothic chapel which was built in 1867 largely by the parson of that period, and his wife, who were both carvers of professional standard.

Look for Bredon Hill, southeast of Worcester, a marvelous viewpoint and landmark, topped by a Romano-British camp. Bredon village, set high on the banks of the Avon, is an archetypally lovely English settlement. The 14th-century tithe barn (National Trust), over 130 feet long, is just one of its treasures. Great Comberton, nearby, is another attractive village which can claim two great dovecots, one round with 500 holes and one square and gabled, with 1425 holes, while just down the road at Little Comberton is a black and white farmhouse with another round, stone dovecote.

Broadway

There are other things to remember about Worcestershire. It contains the Vale of Evesham, and here we are on the edge of the Cotswolds, with Broadway as its lead attraction. Broadway is an enormously popular tourist destination, a stopping-off place for visiting the area. It breathes an air of secure property values and well-manicured period charm. It is extremely attractive, but no more so than many such places—though they must thank their lucky stars that they are not on the over-trodden tourist trail.

There are no great big, roaring towns in this county, and several which were once very busy and less than appealing have slid back commercially . . . to the marked improvement of their tourist value; as, for instance, Bewdly and Droitwich—one once a busy port but now a charming medieval town, the other having more or less lost its spa status but kept its good hotels and one brine bath open to the public.

Herefordshire

The cathedral city of Hereford has also suffered from modernization, though still preserves some of its old character as a country and market town. The city center has predictably dull chain shops, but also the occasional pretty façade and some surviving period architecture. Nothing, however, rivals the cathedral, whose foundation dates from the time of Offa (who built the nearby Dyke, an earthen embankment between his kingdom of Mercia and Wales). Dating from many periods, this lovely cathedral contains the *Mappa Mundi,* one of the oldest maps of the world, the work of an early-14th-century monk, and a rare medieval library of 1,500 chained books (check on its opening times). Very strong in music, the cathedral is host to the Three Choirs Festival once every three years. In the other years, the Festival takes place at Worcester or Gloucester. Also worth taking a look at while in Hereford are the Museum of Cider, which tells the story of traditional cider making, and the St. John's Alms-houses with their small chapel and museum. Another significant survival, Conningsby Hospital, also has the remains of a Black Friars' monastery in the grounds.

The county of Hereford has virtually no tall-chimney industry, and apart from Hereford, which isn't very big, the towns are small. Ledbury, for instance, which stands on the borders of three counties, is absolutely full of architectural interest and minor history.

Anyone interested in oddities would find Kilpeck Church not only architecturally attractive, but some of its decorations highly amusing. It stands in the village of the same name, and is built of local red stone, much of it dating from the 12th century. Both inside and outside are an astonishing number of carved stone corbels—grinning heads, eerie toothy beasts, comic groups. There are obvious gaps, and these were caused by the removal of the more erotic carvings which upset 19th-century proprieties. But look round and you'll find they overlooked some of the most startling.

Another oddity is Pembridge Church bell tower, about halfway between Leominster and Kington. It is completely detached from the church, constructed in three storeys each a different shape—octagonal, square, and a pyramid-shape at the top.

Leominster (pronounced Lemster) was a most important wool center for 500 years, but is now the center of an agricultural area surrounded by hop fields and orchards. Again the town is full of architectural survivals, not excepting the Priory Church, attributed to Earl Leofric, husband of Lady Godiva who, besides her activities in Coventry, also established a convent here.

Kington, which is an ancient market town, stands right on the Welsh border at the foot of the Hergest Ridge, which not only provides shelter but a magnificent viewpoint. Roughly between Kington and Leominster is a spot called Mortimer's Cross which was the scene of the decisive battle between the Yorkists and Lancastrians in the 15th-century Wars of the Roses. Here over 4,000 men were slain in one day in 1461, and the victor, nineteen-year-old Edward Mortimer, Earl of March, was later crowned King of England as Edward IV; also one of the prisoners taken and later executed was an unknown Welshman, Owen Tudor, whose grandson became Henry VII, the first of the Tudor dynasty.

The Wye Valley

Neither should one forget the River Wye, which meanders enchantingly from the Welsh border by Hay on Wye (a small town, beautifully sited and full to bursting with second-hand book shops), to Hereford, to Ross-on-Wye (which overlooks the loveliest sweep of the river), to Goodrich Castle (ruined but built high above the river), to Symond's Yat, where the river makes a five-mile loop in a narrow gorge, before escaping into Gloucestershire. For lovely stretches of countryside, with pretty towns and constantly unfolding views, the Wye Valley is very hard to beat.

SHROPSHIRE

Immediately above Hereford & Worcester is the county of Shropshire. The chief town of tourist interest here is Shrewsbury (pronounced "Shrosebry") which stands within a great loop of the Severn River. Few towns in the country can show a greater wealth of magpie-colored houses. Grope Lane, Fish Street, and Butcher Row, which, appropriately enough, was once occupied by the butchers of Shrewsbury, are packed with treasures in this beautiful form of early domestic architecture. There are also a number of fine old inns, among them the Lion Hotel, a fine Georgian coaching house with Dickensian associations, and the Prince Rupert Hotel, a most attractive timbered building in the town center, dating back to the 15th century. It is named after James I's grandson, who stayed there during the Civil War.

Shrewsbury, however, has sterner things to show. Near the railway station the red sandstone castle built by Roger de Montgomery and added to by Edward I stands on a mound dominating the town, and in the Wyle Cop, up which the coaches clattered on their way from London to Holyhead, is the house where Henry Tudor, soon to become Henry VII, stayed in 1485 before the decisive Battle of Bosworth. If you cross the river by the English Bridge, you'll reach Shrewsbury Abbey Church, almost all that is left of the monastery that stood here from 1083. The abbey is the location for a series of popular medieval whodunits by Ellis Peters, which feature the detective Brother Cadfael, and which give an excellent idea of life in this area in the middle ages. The interest engendered by these books is being harnessed by the Abbey Restoration Project, whose series of medieval walks are worth investigating (tel. 0743 232723).

Southwest of Shrewsbury is Minsterley, where the church contains relics of the maidens' garlands at one time carried on the coffins of young unmarried girls, and, after the funeral, placed over their pews. These consist of thin wooden poles with paper garlands hanging from them. The end of each is carved in the shape of a heart, with the initials of some girl and the year of her burial.

Minsterley lies near the foot of the narrow ridge of the Stiperstones. From the crest one looks eastward into the heart of England; westward, to the heights that mark the border of England and Wales.

The Wrekin, Ironbridge and Ludlow

Eastward, too, one often sees a solitary hill rising above the plains. This is the Wrekin, a hill geologists claim to be the oldest in the land. That may mean little to the average visitor. Far better to record that Housman and others have invested it with some of their poetic charm. Whatever other hill in England is climbed, the Wrekin should not be missed. To stand on its isolated summit and look around is to see what makes up so much of the Midland scene.

During the last few years, however, the Wrekin has taken on a new tourist significance because of the enormous popularity of Ironbridge. Ironbridge has two identities, as a place as well as a thing. The thing is the first bridge made of iron, designed by T. F. Pritchard, smelted by Abraham Darby, and erected between 1777 and 1779. The coke smelting process, of enormous importance to the Shropshire coalfields, together with the availability of iron for the new-fangled machine age, helped usher in the Industrial Revolution. Today, Ironbridge has been largely taken over as a vast industrial museum complex, run by the Ironbridge Gorge Museum Trust.

The six-mile stretch of the Gorge, once an awesome scene of mining, charcoal burning, reeking with smoke and the stench of sulphur, has been completely transformed into a scene of idyllic beauty, scars grassed over, woodland filling the gaps left by tree-felling. The Ironbridge itself is an infinitely graceful arch spanning the river, and can best be seen—and photographed or painted—from the tow path, a charming riverside walk edged with wild flowers and dense shrubs. The original Bedlam Furnaces are there, now very much a visitor attraction; the Elton Gallery has a fine collection of pictures tracing the history of industrial development; the Severn Wharf Warehouses have been turned into a fascinating interpretive center; Coalport china—old and new—is displayed in an enormous original tall brick kiln; and at the Coalbrookdale Museum of Iron, the old, pioneering furnace can still be seen—in all a fascinating excursion into England's past.

Blists Open Air Museum nearby has become a village in its own right, spreading over 50 acres, now described as a "working Victorian community." Here once outdated industries and crafts have been happily revitalized—pottery, plasterwork, saw mill and paper manufacture, candlemaking. Visitors can see how the work is done; products are on show, and many are for sale. There's even a working iron foundry and a reconstruction of a Victorian pub. Some charming old inns stand close to the river not far away—The Boat and Half Moon at Jackfield, and the All Nations at Blists Hill.

Within easy reach, rural Shropshire spreads invitingly. Bridgnorth is well worth a visit. Divided into two parts, its High Town is linked to riverside Low Town by a short funicular railway. Up top, the Norman Keep—all that remains of the original 11th-century castle—rivals Italy's Tower of Pisa in its ability to stay up and to lean over perilously at the same time.

Ludlow has, perhaps, a finer display of black-and-white buildings than even Shrewsbury itself. Worth visiting, too, is the great castle, especially during the Ludlow Festival, held every summer, when Shakespeare's plays are performed in front of the castle ruins. It was in this castle that John

Milton wrote his verse drama *Comus.* There are great hills on either side of Ludlow and its neighboring dales. To the northwest is the heathery mound of Long Mynd, with the ancient track of the Port Way running along its crest; eastward are the higher Clee Hills and, to the north, the wooded ridge of Wenlock Edge.

Within a few miles of Ludlow, northwest, is romantic Stokesay Castle, probably the oldest surviving example of a fortified manor house. Miraculously preserved through all the vicissitudes of civil war, the castle is a near-perfect evocation of medieval England.

West of Stokesay, Shropshire pushed towards Wales to produce a rather curious corner containing Clun Forest and the four villages of Clun, Clunton, Clunbury and Clungunford, as well as the River Clun. They have been described as "the sleepiest places under the sun," but that quiet peace did not set in until after all the border uproar had died down. The number of ruined castles and fortified houses still to be seen make this situation clear. So many places changed hands with monotonous regularity as the fortunes of war ebbed and flowed.

Shropshire is, indeed, very rich in places to visit, such as the Abbeys of Lilleshall and Buildwas, Boscobel House and Shipton Hall; the extensive Roman remains at Wroxeter, the Acton Scott Working Farm Museum, and the enchanting small towns of Much Wenlock, Newport and Bishop's Castle. Many of these are close together, grouped within easy reach of Shrewsbury and the Wrekin.

STAFFORDSHIRE

Staffordshire contains much that is unlovely. No one would visit the Potteries for the sake of their beauty. The literary pilgrim or sociology student, however, may care to see something of the "Five Towns," so well described by Arnold Bennett. Many of the most famous names in china—Wedgwood, Spode, Royal Doulton, Coalport among them—come from this area. It is possible to visit some of the works and watch the creation of these delicate things which, for all their fragility, still manage to bring joy to generations of their owners. One of the best places to go to get a complete idea of the art of the potter, is the Visitor Center at Wedgwood's works, situated a few miles south of Stoke-on-Trent, just off the A34 in Barlaston. Here you will see a film about the firm, re-created 18th-century factory workshops, traditional processes demonstrated, a gallery with treasures created by Josiah Wedgwood and his successors, as well as a well-stocked retail shop.

If fine scenery is your aim, you will find it in Needwood Forest, west of Burton-on-Trent, once a royal hunting ground and still containing many tracts of ancient woodland; in nearby Cannock Chase and at Shugborough, where there is a beautifully furnished 18th-century mansion. The woods and heathlands around Shugborough are ideal for picnics and walks and the estate has an interesting County Museum and Farm Park.

A very good way of seeing Staffordshire from the best possible angle is to take a narrow boat holiday on the canals. On these waterways you see scenery which is not accessible in any other way, much of it truly industrial, but when you are on a waterway that was built to serve the very industry that you are passing, it takes on a different aspect. Staffordshire also shares with Shropshire many stately homes, some of which have interconnecting history.

Lichfield

What no one should miss is Lichfield. There is a dreadful amount of new Lichfield round the old, but as you drive through it you can see the three lofty spires of the cathedral—known as the Ladies of the Vale—all the way, and follow an unerring course towards them. Then, suddenly, one has shaken off the industry, crossed a little stream and has entered the quiet of old Lichfield, with lovely houses, cottages and gardens surrounding the cathedral which, it is surprising to find, stands in a hollow. The little street leading to it has a continental air, and opens onto a turfed close, cupping as it were, the bronze-colored west front. Dedicated to St. Mary and St. Chad, the present building was raised during the 13th and 14th centuries, although the foundation goes back to A.D. 700 The Early Decorated nave is most beautiful, with its clean and repetitive lines and its unusual color, while the subtle red and brass of the choir screen responds to the colors all round it. The great *Gospel of St. Chad* is owned by the cathedral, and pre-dates the Book of Kells. Caught in the evening light with the sun slanting through it into the choir, the cathedral is worth traveling a long way to see.

In the cobbled Market Square there is a statue of Dr. Johnson, sitting facing the house where he was born, now a Johnsonian museum. At the other side of the square there is a statue of James Boswell, and nearby is one of the last men to be burnt at the stake for heresy in England. That was in 1612, and his name was Edward Wightman who came from Burton-upon-Trent. Lichfield was also the birthplace of Elias Ashmole, originator of the Ashmolean Museum in Oxford.

LEICESTERSHIRE

Arguably the most beautiful part of Leicestershire is to be found in its eastern corner, known as Rutland. It is an area of half-hidden lanes, lonely churches, red soil, fox hunting, public schools and aristocratic influences. The schools are at Uppingham and Oakham; the fox hounds at the Cottesmore and Quorn; and the churches and villages are a delight.

Rutland's strong individual identity will not come as a surprise to students of England's past. Before the reorganization of local government boundaries in 1974, Rutland was England's smallest county. Even though it has now been swallowed up by Leicestershire, it still steadfastly retains its own separate identity and personality.

Apart from the administrative changes, the biggest impact on Rutland in recent years has been the creation of the largest man-made lake in the country, filling no less than one-third of "old" Rutland. Built as a reservoir to supply water to nearby towns, Rutland Water has proved to be a most attractive addition to the landscape, providing excellent facilities for sailing and trout fishing and a nature reserve (also bicycle hire).

The name of the former county is remembered not only at the reservoir, but at the Rutland Theater at Tolethorpe Hall, a 16th-century manor house in whose grounds the Stamford Shakespeare Company stage a summer season of Shakespearean plays in the open air. The name also recurs in the title of Rutland Farm Park, with its rare breeds of farm animals in a pleasant landscape, and also at the Rutland County Museum in the former county town of Oakham.

The chief point of interest in Oakham for tourists is undoubtedly the Castle, of which only the Great Hall survives, but that is unique because the walls are hung with horseshoes presented by noble travelers as a sort of toll to the Lord of the Manor. It is believed that one of the shoes was presented by Queen Elizabeth I, another was certainly contributed by Elizabeth II. Besides that, Oakham is a singularly pleasant, well-kept little town, and so is Uppingham, both with busy markets.

Belvoir and Charnwood Forest

Just to the west of the Rutland district is the Vale of Belvoir—pronounced Beaver —overlooked by Belvoir Castle, an early-19th-century Gothic fantasy owned by the Duke of Rutland. The castle is open to the public in summer, with regular medieval jousting tournaments and other special events that draw crowds. The rich grazing on the Vale of Belvoir produces milk to make the local specialty with a national, indeed international, appeal: Stilton cheese. Its production is concentrated in the Vale and the nearby town of Melton Mowbray, also noted for its busy cattle market, its pork pies, and the Quorn Hunt.

At one time, to be said to be "Tip Top Meltonian" was to be tip-top socially. The town, which is not as attractive as it once was, has nevertheless got a very large and splendid church with a 100 ft high tower. To the west, via the A6006 and B676, is Loughborough (pronounced Luffbrer), an engineering town with one of the largest bell foundries in England, which has produced bells and carillons that grace many famous churches and cathedrals around the world. The bell foundry organizes conducted tours, and there is also a museum on site. Steam railway enthusiasts should visit the Great Central Railway, which now runs a regular passenger service to Rothley. Their station, Loughborough Central, is easily reached on foot from the B.R. mainline one.

Just southwest of Loughborough is Charnwood Forest, a miniature mountain district, with its remnants of primeval forest and strange outcrops of the oldest rocks in the land. Newtown Linford, loveliest of all Leicestershire villages, where thatched roofs and half-timbered cottages line the sides of the road, is easily reached on B5327, and bordering the village is Bradgate Park, once the estate of the Grey family. Bradgate Park is certainly unlike the average Midlands park of green pastures and close-cropped lawns. Rather it is a true remnant of ancient forest, abounding in rocky sloped miniature dales and clumps of hoary old oaks. The herds of deer that roam unfettered through the craggy valleys add to the appearance of an old-time hunting chase.

Of special interest to those in search of the historic are the ruins of Bradgate House, where the tragic Lady Jane Grey, the "Tudor Rose," was born in 1537 and lived until her ill-fated marriage to Lord Dudley 16 years later. Only a few weeks afterwards the girl had finished her nine days' reign as

Queen of England by being brought to the scaffold by the vengeful hate of "Bloody" Mary Tudor. On her execution day the oaks around the hall were lopped, and evidence of this can be seen on the old trees.

Bradgate Park is typical of the rest of Charnwood, and go where you will in that compact area, which is wholly contained in a triangle with its points at Leicester, Ashby-de-la-Zouch, and Loughborough, you will find the same areas of fine heathlands and enchanted woods that seem so different from any so far visited in the Midlands.

The Battle of Bosworth, in which Richard III lost his crown to Henry, later Henry VII, first of the Tudors, was fought in 1485 near Sutton Cheney, south of Ashby. The 500th anniversary of the battle saw the opening of the revamped Bosworth Visitor Center, where there are exhibitions, a film theater and waymarked trails.

Leicester

Take the A50 from Ashby-de-la-Zouch and you come to Leicester. Here only the Norman Hall remains of the ancient castle—a pity, because it was from Leicester Castle that the great Simon de Montfort summoned the forerunner of the present British Parliament, the organization that gave birth to democratic government in the mid-13th century. In the vicinity can be seen Trinity Hospital, which was founded in the time of Edward III (parts of the original chapel remain), the Magazine Gateway (now a regimental museum), the Church of St. Mary de Castro, the Newarke Houses Museum which illustrates local history, and some surviving specimens of 17th-century domestic architecture. But all these buildings are mere youngsters when compared with the extensive Roman remains at the Jewry Wall site in the center of the city, thought to date from A.D. 130. Remains which were originally thought to be part of a wall, turned out to be windows of a basilica, with a courtyard, shops and the largest Roman bath yet found in England.

South of Leicester, Market Harborough stands on the border of Leicestershire and Northamptonshire, and its atmosphere is that of both. Corsetry and other local industries are illustrated in the Harborough Museum, which occupies a former factory building. The weekly market attracts dealers and farmers from all over the Midland shires. The two main architectural treasures of the town are the 14th-century parish church, with its fine 161-foot crocketed broach spire, and the 17th-century pillared grammar school, standing adjacent to the church. There is also a wealth of interest in the 17th- and 18th-century coaching inns, namely, The Angel, The Peacock, and The Three Swans.

PRACTICAL INFORMATION FOR THE MIDLANDS

HOW TO GET THERE FROM LONDON. To help you plan visits throughout this region we have listed some of the more important centers mentioned in the text.

Birmingham and Coventry. By train: these two cities have been taken together because they are on the same main line from London Euston and share the same excellent service of at least two trains per hour. Coventry is reached in 73 minutes and Birmingham New Street station in around 100 minutes for the 113 miles. Birmingham International, midway between Birmingham and Coventry, is the station for the National Exhibition Centre. **By coach:** National Express operate a half-hourly Rapide service from early morning to mid evening from London Victoria coach station to Birmingham. The journey, mainly on motorway, takes about 2 hours 15 minutes. Coventry can be reached every two hours from Victoria, journey time 2 hours 20 minutes; there is an additional, slightly slower, two-hourly service via Milton Keynes. **By car:** Birmingham M1, M6; Coventry M1, M6, A46.

Leamington Spa. By train: can be reached by rail from London Paddington (usually change at Reading), taking around 2 hours 50 minutes, though some trains are quicker. Arm yourself with a timetable leaflet—from a BR Travel Center—and study it carefully. **By coach:** National Express provides a coach every two hours to Leamington en route to Stratford, journey time 2 hours 40 minutes. **By car:** M40, A40, A423, A41, A452.

Lichfield. By train: easily visited as a day out from London. Travel from Euston station (making sure you ask for a ticket to Lichfield City) to Birmingham New Street station (see earlier paragraph), where you change onto a local train for the run to Lichfield. The local trains depart at three minutes to the hour and connect with the ten minutes past the hour departures from London. The total journey time works out at just under 2½ hours. **By coach:** There is one through coach a day, but if you want to make a day trip of it you will need to change at Birmingham from Digbeth Coach Station to the Bull Ring Bus Station a half-mile away. The Midland Express Coach runs hourly from here and takes 1¼ hours. **By car:** A5, A38.

Leicester. By train: Leicester enjoys a good service of mainline trains, most of which are InterCity 125s which cover the distance from St Pancras in under 70 minutes. The interval between the trains is uneven, but the service is of one or two fast trains per hour. **By coach:** Leicester has an excellent direct coach service operated by National Express from Victoria. Departures from London are hourly, leaving on the hour, taking 2¼ hours. **By car:** M1, A46.

Stratford-upon-Avon. By train: is accessible by rail—just. The direct route via Leamington Spa is tediously slow and often requires several changes of train. So British Rail operate a rail/coach service called the *Shakespeare Connection*. This runs from London Euston via Coventry and permits the Bard's town to be visited for a day and allows a decent amount of time to be spent in Stratford. Leave London Euston at 10.40 with an additional departure at 08.35 on Saturdays, return from Stratford at 17.20, arriving London 19.30 (or, if you want to catch an evening theater performance and are a real night bird, returning from Stratford at 23.15 to arrive London 02.30). For details contact Guide Friday, 14 Rother St., Stratford-on-Avon (tel. 0789 294466). If you want to see more of the glorious Shakespearean countryside en route, make use of the Britainshrinker tour which also visits Warwick Castle and Coventry Cathedral, as well as taking you for lunch in a country pub! Stratford station is closed on Sundays in winter months, but there are superb steam-hauled Sunday Lunch specials run by British Rail (book well in advance). **By coach:** Oxford Citylink run a special service to Stratford for day visitors, also passing Oxford, Blenheim Palace and Woodstock. It leaves Victoria Coach Station at 9.35 daily and takes 3 hours, allowing 6 hours to explore the town and surrounding area. The two-hourly National Express service from Victoria via Coventry and Leamington takes 3 hours 10 minutes. There are also many coach companies which run day tours to Stratford, taking in Warwick Castle, Oxford and the stone villages of the Cotswolds. Tour operators include Evan Evans, Frames/National Travel, and Thomas Cook. These tours have the advantage that they pick up passengers at several points in central London and the West End, and these are shown in the respective brochures. It is normally possible to book seats as late as the afternoon of the day before you want to go. **By car:** M40, A40, A34.

HOW TO GET AROUND. Large areas of the Midlands are accessible on a day trip from London. The region is served by a wide range of coach and rail services and should you hire a car, roads are excellent.

HOTELS AND RESTAURANTS. You'll most certainly include a visit to Stratford-upon-Avon during a trip to England. If you're touring outside London to the west, or in the Midlands, it's a good idea to make the Stratford area your headquarters. Some of the hotels are pretty busy, especially from March to January, when the Royal Shakespeare Company is functioning. Most hotels are extra busy mid-week. It seems that whatever they charge a well-appointed hotel is full to the rafters with businessmen in this region. So book as far ahead as possible. Weekends, on the other hand, are usually no problem.

Details about our grading system, telephoning, plus other relevant information about hotels and restaurants, will be found at the beginning of the book in the *Facts at Your Fingertips* section.

Abberley (Heref. and Worcs.). *Elms* (E), tel. (029 921) 666; 27 rooms, all with bath. Comfortable country house with picturesque views and piquant cuisine in *Brooke Room Restaurant* (E).

Alcester (Warwicks.). *Billesley Manor* (E), (0789) 400888; 28 rooms with bath; boats beautiful grounds, pool, sauna and four-poster beds. Worth a visit for the excellent restaurant. Recent major refurbishment. Billesley is 4½ miles west of Stratford-upon-Avon by A422.

Birmingham (West Midlands). *Plough and Harrow* (L–E), 135 Hagley Rd., Edgbaston, tel. (021) 454 4111; 44 rooms, all with bath. Comfortable hotel with one of the finest restaurants in town: French food and good wines in elegant surroundings. *Albany* (E), Smallbrook, Queensway, tel. (021) 643 8171; 254 rooms, all with bath. International cuisine in *Four Seasons* restaurant, sports/leisure club, multi-story adjacent car-park. *Holiday Inn* (E), Holiday St., tel. (021) 631 2000; 295 rooms. Comprehensive facilities including a pool and solarium. *Grand* (M), tel. (021) 236 7951, facing the cathedral; 167 rooms, all with bath; good restaurant. *Lad-*

broke International (M), New. St., tel. (021) 631 3331; 194 rooms, all with bath. Recently completely refurbished.

Restaurants. *Lorenzo's* (M), 3 Park St., Digbeth, tel. (021) 643 0541. Cheerful, authentic Italian restaurant. For something different try *Rajdoot* (M), 12–22 Albert St., tel. (021) 643 8805, large luxurious Indian restaurant serving authentic North Indian dishes of the highest order.

Broadway (Heref. and Worcs.). *Lygon Arms* (L), High St., tel. (0386) 852255; 64 rooms, 61 with bath. Renowned for all-around excellence and hugely popular (booking essential). *Dormy House* (E), Willersley Hill, tel. (0386) 852711; 50 rooms with bath. 2 miles east on A44. A tastefully renovated 17th-century Cotswold farmhouse; comfortable and relaxed, with fine food. *Broadway* (M), The Green, tel. (0386) 852401; 24 rooms, 21 with bath. Modernized 16th-century coaching inn.

Restaurant. *Hunter's Lodge* (E), High St., tel. (0386) 853247; excellent French cooking and long wine list, in old stone house.

At **Buckland.** *Manor* (L), tel. (0386) 852626; 11 rooms with bath. Just over 2 miles southwest on B4632. A leading country house hotel, charmingly decorated and set in lovely grounds with views to the Malvern Hills. A great antidote to the commercialism of Broadway.

Bromsgrove. (Heref. and Worcs.). *Grafton Manor* (E), tel. (0527) 31525; 8 rooms with bath in magnificently restored Elizabethan manor. Excellent food.

Church Stretton (Shrops.). *Stretton Hall* (M), All Stretton, tel. (0694) 723224; 13 rooms with bath. Tennis, pool, croquet. Country house in south Shropshire hills.

Coventry (W. Midlands). *Crest* (E), Hinckley Rd., Walsgrave, tel. (0203) 613261; 152 rooms with bath. *De Vere* (E), Cathedral Sq., tel. (0203) 633733; 200 rooms with bath. Central and up-to-date. *Leofric* (M), Broadgate, tel. (0203) 21371; 90 rooms with bath. Modern, popular with local people.

Droitwich (Heref. and Worcs.). *Château Impney* (L), tel. (0905) 774411; 65 rooms, all with bath. Set in lovely grounds, fine restaurant. *Raven* (E), St. Andrews St., tel. (0905) 772224; 55 rooms, all with bath. Bags of atmosphere, lively bars.

Great Malvern (Heref. and Worcs.). *Cottage in the Wood* (M), Holywell Rd., tel. (06845) 3847; 21 rooms, all with bath. Attractively decorated bedrooms. Lovely views from the dining room, well-prepared dishes and good service. *Foley Arms* (M), 14 Worcester Rd., tel. (06845) 3397. 26 rooms with bath. Views of the beautiful Severn Valley. *Holdfast Cottage* (M), tel. (0684) 310288; 9 rooms, 8 with bath or shower. Intimate country house with good food, on A4104 near Welland. *Walmer Lodge* (M) tel. (06845) 4139; 8 rooms with bath or shower. Comfortable and friendly, with good restaurant serving continental cuisine.

Restaurant. *Croque-en-Bouche* (E), 221 Wells Rd., tel. (06845) 65612. Elegant informal atmosphere, superior French cuisine, fabulous wine. Booking and punctuality essential. Closed Sun. and Tues.

Henley-in-Arden (Warwicks). **Restaurants.** *Le Filbert Cottage* (E), 64 High St., tel. (056 42) 2700. French cuisine in attractive beamed cottage. Closed Sun. and Mon.

Hereford (Heref. and Worcs.). *Green Dragon* (M), Broad St., tel. (0432) 272506; 88 rooms, all with bath. Close to the cathedral; friendly, helpful staff.
   At **Much Birch,** 5½ miles south on A49. *Pilgrim Hotel* (M), tel. (0981) 540742. 18 rooms, 16 with bath, 2 with shower. Old pilgrim inn, peaceful, in large grounds; fine views.

Ironbridge (Shrops.). *Telford Hotel, Golf and Country Club,* (M), Sutton Hill, Telford, tel. (0952) 585642; 58 rooms with bath. Hotel-cum-country club overlooking the historic Ironbridge Gorge. Partly in a converted farmhouse.

Kenilworth (Warwicks.). **Restaurant.** *Diment* (M), 121–123 Warwick Rd., tel. (0926) 53763. Excellent French restaurant owned by the chef, with less expensive bistro/wine bar downstairs. Closed Sat. lunch, Sun. and Mon.

Leamington Spa (Warwicks). *Mallory Court* (L–E), Bishop's Tachbrook, tel. (0926) 30214; 10 rooms with bath. Well situated for Warwick and Stratford. Outdoor pool, croquet and putting lawns; interior luxuriously decorated and furnished. Fine restaurant, must book. *Regent* (E–M), The Parade, tel. (0926) 27231. 80 rooms with bath. Traditional service. *Manor House* (M), Avenue Rd., tel. (0926) 23251; 54 rooms with bath. Delightful gardens down to river.

Ledbury (Heref. and Worcs.). *Feathers* (M), High St., tel. (0531) 5266; 11 rooms with bath. 16th-century much-timbered coaching inn. *Hope End* (M), tel. (0531) 3613; 7 rooms with bath. Quiet country house hotel, 2 miles north on B4214. Excellent restaurant with local produce. Dinner only, closed Mon. and Tues.

Leicester (Leics.). *Grand* (M), Granby St., tel. (0533) 555599; 93 rooms, most with bath. Restored Victorian hotel. *Holiday Inn* (M), 129 St. Nicholas Circle, tel. (0533) 531161; 190 rooms with bath, heated pool. Their *Hayloft Restaurant* serves good continental cuisine. *Post House* (M), Braunstone Lane East, tel. (0533) 896688; 172 rooms. 2 miles southwest by A46.

Lichfield (Staffs.). *Angel Croft* (M), tel. (0543) 258737; 13 rooms, 8 with bath or shower; charming Georgian hotel close to the cathedral.
   Restaurant. *Herringbones* (M), 23/25 Sandford St., tel. (0543) 250781. Fresh local fish all along the line, starters and main courses, with a special fish session on the last Tuesday of the month. Reasonable wine, too. Fixed price menus available. Evenings Tues. to Sat., lunch Fri. only.

Ludlow (Shrops.). *Feathers* (E), Bull Ring, tel. (0584) 5261. 35 rooms, all with bath. Magnificent 17th-century building with striking black and white façade. A famous hotel. *Angel* (M), 8 Broad St., tel. (0584) 2581. 17 rooms with bath. Historic, modernized building.

Restaurant. *Penny Anthony* (M), 5 Church St., tel. (0584) 3282. French cuisine. Closed Sun.

Northampton (Northants.). *Northampton Moat House* (E–M), Silver St., tel. (0604) 22441; 135 rooms, all with bath. With Danish coffee shop.

Restaurant. At **Horton,** six miles southeast on B526. *French Partridge* (E), tel. (0604) 870033. High standard, French inspired menu. Closed Sun., Mon.

Oakham (Leics.). *Hambleton Hall* (L), tel. (0572) 56991; 15 rooms with bath. 3 miles east of Oakham on A606. Individually furnished rooms in a beautiful house; fine food and keen service. Overlooks Rutland Water, with access to sporting facilities—fishing, sailing, tennis—and nature walks. *Crown* (M), 16 High St., tel. (0572) 3631; 25 rooms, 23 with bath. Former 17th-century coaching inn, comfortably refurbished.

Restaurant. At **Langham,** 2 miles northwest on A606. *Noel Arms* (M), Bridge St., tel. (0572) 2931. Good beer, restaurant and wine.

Oundle (Northants.). *Talbot* (M), New St., tel. (0832) 73621. 40 rooms with bath. Traditional but stylish.

Ross-on-Wye (Heref. & Worcs.). *Pengethley Manor* (E), 4 miles northwest on A49, tel. (0989) 211. 18 rooms with bath. 15 acres of grounds; handsome interior; keen management and excellent food. Heated pool; musical evenings.

Rothley. *Rothley Court* (E–M), tel. (0533) 374141. 5 miles from Leicester north on A6. 13th-century stone manor with 35 rooms—both modern and traditional. Beautiful grounds.

Rugby (Warwicks.). *Three Horseshoes* (E–M), Sheep St., tel. (0788) 4585. 31 rooms with bath. 16th century coaching inn at center of town with good restaurant.

Shifnal (Shrops.). *Park House* (M), tel (0952) 460128; 38 rooms with bath. Beautiful country house hotel, handy for Ironbridge Gorge.

Shrewsbury (Shrops.). *Lion* (M), Wyle Cop, tel. (0743) 53107; 60 rooms with bath. Ancient inn in the city center. Tapestries and oak beams. *Prince Rupert* (M), Butcher Row, tel. (0743) 52461; 70 rooms with bath. Dates back to the 15th century, full of character.

Restaurant. Try the *Old Police House* (M), Castle Court, Castle St., tel. (0743) 60668. Small and comfortable, with good local and French dishes.

Stratford-upon-Avon (Warwicks). *Alveston-Manor* (E), Clopton Bridge, tel. (0789) 204581; 108 rooms, all with bath. 16th-century manor house. *Moat House International* (E), Bridgefoot, tel. (0789) 67511; 249 rooms, all with bath. High standards and (as a local touch) a private barge to transport guests to and from the theater. *Shakespeare* (E), Chapel St., tel. (0789) 294771; 66 rooms, all with bath. Excellent, and ancient, hostelry (older than the Bard himself); with friendly bars. *Welcombe* (E), Warwick Rd., tel. (0789) 295252; 81 rooms, all with bath. Offers the perfect base for those who can tear themselves away from its setting in vast, classic English grounds.

Falcon (M), Chapel St., tel. (0789) 205777; 73 rooms, all with bath. Elizabethan frontage with modern additions at rear; very central. *Grosvenor House* (M), 12 Warwick Rd., tel. (0789) 69213. 57 rooms. A friendly, reasonable hotel, within easy walk of the theater. Part of the sensible Best Western chain. *Stratford House* (M), Sheep St., tel. (0789) 68288; 9 rooms, 7 with bath. Attractive converted Georgian house close to theater.

Nearby **Wilmcote** (4 miles) is well worth the drive for good value lunch at the *Swan House* (M), tel. (0789) 67030; 8 rooms, all with bath or shower.

At **Broad Marston,** 7 miles away, *Broad Marston Manor* (M–I), tel. (0789) 720252. 7 rooms in old-world country manor—very stylish bed and breakfast.

At **Alderminster,** 6 miles southeast on A34. *Ettington Park* (L), tel. (0789) 740740. 49 rooms, all with bath. Marvelously restored, Victorian-Gothic house, with huge bedrooms, superb restaurant, spacious grounds, and a magnificently-equipped health club.

Restaurants. Good restaurants are surprisingly scarce. *Hill's* (E), tel. (0789) 293563. Good for pre- and post-theater dining; closed Sun. and Mon. There are lots of "eateries." Try the *Dirty Duck* (really the *Black Swan*), which also serves good pre- and post-theater meals. The *Wintner Wine Bar* (I), tel. (0789) 297259 for copious helpings of hot and cold meals. The theater itself has a very useful cafeteria (I) and good restaurant (M) with riverside views.

Symonds Yat (Heref. and Worcs.). *Wye Rapids* (M), tel. (0600) 890366; 16 rooms, 8 with bath. Impressive views of the gorge.

Uppingham (Leics.). *Falcon* (E), High St. East, tel. (0572) 823535; 26 rooms, all with bath or shower. Hospitable 16th-century inn.

Restaurant. *Lake Isle* (M), 16 High St., tel. (0572) 822951. Good-value restaurant with fairly priced wines and convivial Gallic bustle. Also offers accommodation in 8 rooms with bath or shower.

Warwick (Warwicks.). *Ladbroke* (E), Longbridge Roundabout, tel. (0926) 499555; 150 rooms with bath in smart, modern hotel on outskirts of town (A46). *Lord Leycester* (M), 17 Jury St., tel. (0926) 491481. 50 rooms with bath or shower. Get a room at the back to avoid unrelenting traffic. *Woolpack* (M), Market Place, tel. (0926) 496191. 29 rooms, half with bath. Atmosphere and history.

Restaurants. *Randolph's* (E), Coten End, tel. (0926) 491292. Good French cooking; closed Sun. *Westgate Arms* (M), Bowling Green St., tel. (0926) 492362. Reliable English dishes. Closed Sun. Also has 10 (M) rooms.

Weobley (Heref. & Worcs.). *Red Lion* (M), Broad St., tel. (0544) 318220. 7 rooms with bath or shower. Half timbered inn in delightful village.

Wishaw (Warwicks.). Ten miles northeast of Birmingham. *Belfry* (M), tel. (0675) 70301. 170 rooms, all with bath. Ideal spot for golfing holiday in attractive surroundings.

Worcester (Heref. and Worcs.). *Giffard* (E), High St., tel. (0905) 26262; 104 rooms, all with bath. Good view of the cathedral from the dining room.

Restaurant. *Brown's* (E–M), South Quay, tel. (0905) 26263. Interesting selection of dishes in converted corn mill.

PLACES OF INTEREST. A combination of ancient estates and wealthy industrialists makes this one of the richest areas for great houses of all periods. We have included, along with the great palaces such as Althorp, ancestral home of the Princess of Wales, the Shakespeare Birthplace Trust Properties, which are unquestionably historic. Other information on Stratford-upon-Avon will follow this section.

You will find more information on visiting historic houses in the relevant section of *Facts at Your Fingertips* and a discussion of the subject in the chapter *Historic Houses—Precious Stones in Peril.*

Hereford and Worcester. **Avoncroft Museum of Buildings,** Stoke Heath, near Bromsgrove (tel. 0527 31363/31886). Openair museum of historic buildings, with working windmill, cockpit theater, 18th-century ice house. Open daily, June–Aug., 11–5.30; also daily (except Mon.) Apr., May, Sept. and Oct., 11–5.30; and Bank Holidays. Mar. and Nov., Tues.–Thurs., Sat. and Sun. 11–4.30.

Croft Castle, near Leominster (tel. 056 885 246). Continuously inhabited by the Croft family for 900 years. Open April and Oct., Sat., Sun. and Easter Mon., 2–5; May to end Sept., Wed. to Sun., Bank Holiday Mon., 2–6 (NT).

Dinmore Manor, near Hereford. Mainly 14th-century with an interesting chapel, cloisters and rock garden. Open daily 2–6.

Dyson Perrins Museum of Worcester Porcelain, Worcester (tel. 0905 23221). Best collection of old Worcester in the world. Open Mon.–Fri., 9.30–5, Sat. 10–5. Closed Bank Holidays.

Eastnor Castle, near Ledbury (tel. 0531 2305). Fine Regency and Victorian imitation castle with attractive rooms. Open Bank Holiday Mon., also Sun. late-May–late-Sept., also Wed. and Thurs. in July. and Aug. All 2.15–5.30.

Hanbury Hall, near Droitwich (tel. 052 784 214). To be seen for the Thornhill frescoes, though a lovely 1701 house in its own right. April and Oct., Sat., Sun., 2–5; May to Sept., Wed. to Sun., 2–6. Also Bank Holiday Mon. (NT).

Harvington Hall, near Kidderminster (tel. 056 283 267). Moated Tudor house containing priests' hiding places. Open Easter through Sept., weekdays except Fri. 11.30–6, Sun. 2–6 (closed Good Fri); Feb., Mar., Oct. and Nov., daily except Fri. 2–6.

Lower Brockhampton Hall, near Bromyard (tel. 0855 88099). Small half-timbered manor house dating from about 1400. Detached 15th-century gatehouse and ruined 12th-century chapel. Open Apr.–Oct., Wed.–Sun., 10–1, 2–6; also Bank Holiday Mon. (but closed Good Fri.). (NT).

Museum of Cider, Hereford (tel. 0432 54207). Housed in an old cider works, it tells the story of cidermaking through the ages. Open Apr.–Oct., daily 10–5.30; Nov.–Dec., Mon.–Fri. 1–5; Jan.–Mar., Wed. and Sat. 10–5.

Leicestershire. Belvoir Castle near Grantham (tel. 0476 870262). Present building (pronounced "Beever") is stupendous Victorian Gothic. Seat of the Dukes of Rutland since Tudor times. Open late Mar.–Sept., Tues.–Thurs., Sat., 12–6, Sun. 12–7; Bank Holiday Mon. 11–7; Good Fri. 12–6; Oct., Sun., 2–6. Special events include medieval jousting tournaments.

Battlefield of Bosworth Sutton Cheney, Market Bosworth (tel. 0533 290429). On the site of the famous 1485 battle between Richard III and Henry Tudor (later Henry VII). Visitors' Center; outdoor interpretation center. Open Apr.–Oct., Mon.–Sat. 2–5.30; Sun., Bank Holiday Mon. and Tues. (including Good Fri.), 1–6. Battle Trail; functions all year during daylight hours.

Bell Foundry Museum, Freehold St., Loughborough (tel. 0509 233414). Unique exhibition on bells and bellfounding at work—foundry (tour of the works by appointment). Museum open Tues.–Sat. and Bank Holiday Mon., 9.30–4.30.

Northamptonshire. Althorp, Northampton. The family home of the Earl of Spencer and his family, which includes, of course, the former Lady Diana, now Princess of Wales. Started in 1508 it was altered in 1790, and contains some splendid rooms, paintings and other works of art. Successfully commercialized. Open daily Oct.–Jun., 1–5; July–Sept., 1–6, but occasionally closed on short notice.

Boughton House, Kettering (tel. 0536 82248). Originally a church foundation greatly enlarged in the 16th/17th centuries. Huge place with masses of glorious rooms. Extensive grounds with nature trails. House open Aug., daily 2–5, grounds 12–6; grounds also open May–Sept., daily except Fri. 12–5.

Castle Ashby, Northampton (tel. 060 129 234). Elizabethan house, property of the Marquess of Northampton. Superb paintings. Gardens open all year, daily, 10–6. Check locally for house openings.

Canons Ashby House, Canons Ashby (tel. 0327 860044). Authentic 16th-to-early-18th-century manor house with wall paintings and exceptional Jacobean plasterwork. Open Apr.–Oct., Wed.–Sun. and Bank Holiday Mon., 1–5.30. Closed Good Fri. (NT).

Kirby Hall, near Corby (tel. 0533 663230). Richly designed Elizabethan house. Open daily and Sun. afternoon; closed Mon. and Tues. in winter. Check times locally.

Rockingham Castle, near Corby (tel. 0536 770240). Medieval and Elizabethan fortified house. Open Easter Sun.–Sept., Thurs. and Sun. (and Tues. in Aug.), also Bank Holiday Mon. and Tues. following, all 2–6.

Sulgrave Manor, near Banbury (tel. 029 576 205). Home of George Washington's ancestors. Open Feb.–Dec., daily except Wed.: Apr.–Sept. 10.30–1, 2–5.30; other months 10.30–1, 2–4. Closed Jan.

Triangular Lodge, Rushton, near Kettering (tel. 0536 710761). A delightful 16th-century curiosity. Three windows and three gables on each of its three walls. Inspired by the Holy Trinity. Open throughout the year but closed two days a week. Please telephone for details.

Shropshire. Acton Scott Working Farm Museum, near Church Stretton (tel. 06946 306). Agriculture as it was at the turn of the century. Open Apr.–Nov., daily.

Attingham Park, Atcham, near Shrewsbury (tel. 074 377 203). 1785, with fine interiors (pretty painted boudoir). Period atmosphere preserved. Open Apr.–Sept., Sat.–Wed. 2–5.30; Oct., Sat. and Sun. 2–5.30. (NT)

Benthall Hall, Much Wenlock (tel. 0952 882159). Close to Ironbridge, attractive 16th/17th-century house. Easter to end Sept., Tues., Wed., Sun. 2–6; also Bank Holiday Mon. 2–6 (ground floor only). Closed Good Fri. (NT).

Ironbridge Gorge Museum, Telford (tel. 095 245 3522). One of the first—and best—industrial museums in Britain. A fascinating place, mainly open-air and including the famous bridge built in 1779, is a must for anyone interested in the early history of the industrial revolution. This is really a museum complex, with eight separate elements, including an informative Visitor Center. Phone for full information. Open summer, daily 10–6; winter 10–5.

Stokesay Castle, Craven Arms (tel. 058 82 2544). Magnificent and atmospheric not-to-be-missed 13th-century moated manor house. Open Mar.–Oct., daily 10–5 (excl. Tues.); April–Sept., 10–6. Also weekends in Nov.

Staffordshire. Alton Towers, near Stoke-on-Trent (tel. 0538 702200). Huge leisure and theme park with over 70 attractions. Open daily mid-Mar.–end Oct., 10–5, 6 or 7 depending on season.

Cheddleton Flint Mill, Leek, Industrial museum with working water mills. Open all year, Sat. and Sun. afternoons.

Gladstone Pottery Museum, Stoke-on-Trent (tel. 0782 319232). Original bottle kilns and workshops where old pottery is made in front of visitors. Open daily, Mon.–Sat., 10.30–5.30, Sun. and Bank Holidays, 2–6.

Izaak Walton Cottage, Shallowford near Stafford (tel. 0785 760278). Black and white cottage of the famous 17th-century angler and author of *The Compleat Angler.* Period garden. Open Apr.–Sept., Wed.–Sun., and weekends in winter. Please telephone for opening times.

Shugborough, Milford, near Stafford (tel. 0889 881388). Fine 18th-century house in 900-acre park, gardens and woodland; Chinese garden house, classical temple. Seat of the Earls of Lichfield. Open Apr.–Sept., daily 11–5; Oct.–Dec., daily 11–4. **Staffordshire County Museum** and **Shugborough Farm Park,** also located here, are open same times. (NT)

Wedgwood Visitor Center, Barlaston, Stoke-on-Trent (tel. 0782 204218). Pottery and porcelain collection imaginatively displayed in award-winning, redesigned museum; craft demonstration and shop with "seconds." Open Mon.–Fri. 9–5, Sat., 10–4.

Warwickshire. Charlecote Park, near Stratford-upon-Avon (tel. 0789 840277). Elizabethan house and deer park with Shakespearean associations. Open Apr.–Oct., daily (except Mon. and Thurs.), 11–6; Bank Holiday Mon. 11–6. (NT)

Kenilworth Castle, Kenilworth. (tel. 0926 52078). Ruined medieval fortress. Open daily. Please telephone for times.

Leamington Spa Art Gallery, Leamington Spa (tel. 0926 26559). Outstanding collection of Dutch and Flemish masters, as well as English water-colorists. Open Mon.–Sat., 10–1, 2–5; also Thurs. evening 6–8.

Lord Leycester Hospital, Warwick (tel. 0926 492797). Home for ex-servicemen, fine architecture from several centuries starting with 1100. Open all year, Mon.–Sat., 10–5.30 in summer, 10–4 in winter.

Packwood House, Hockley Heath (tel. 056 43 2024). Tudor timber-framed house. 17th-century yew garden representing the Sermon on the Mount. Open Easter through Sept., Wed.–Sun. and Bank Holidays Mon., 2–6; Oct., 12.30–4. (NT).

Ragley Hall, near Alcester (tel. 0789 762090/762455). Stately home of the Marquess of Hertford, with rich art treasures. Complex opening hours, check locally.

The Shakespeare Birthplace Trust Properties, Stratford-upon-Avon (tel. 0789 204016). Inclusive ticket admitting you to all five properties costs around £4.50. Each of these properties can be visited for between £1 and £1.50. **Shakespeare's Birthplace,** Henley St. Open weekdays Apr.–Oct. 9–6 (but check), Sun. 10–6; Nov.–Mar. 9–4.30, Sun. 1.30–4.30. **Anne Hathaway's Cottage,** Shottery. Open same times as for Shakespeare's Birthplace. **Hall's Croft,** Old Town. Open Apr.–Oct. 9–6, Sun. 10–6; Nov.–Mar. 9–4.30 (closed Sun.). **New Place,** Chapel St. Open same times as Hall's Croft. **Mary Arden's House,** Wilmcote. Open same times as Hall's Croft.

Stoneleigh Abbey, Kenilworth (tel. 0926 52116). Grand Georgian mansion, originally a Cistercian abbey. Owned by Lord Leigh. Reopened in 1984—all four wings with private quarters and chapel—after considerable restoration. Extensive grounds with miniature steam railway. Open Apr. and May., Sun. and Bank Holidays; June–Aug. Sun.–Thurs.; Sept., Sun. only. All times: House 1–5; Grounds: 11.30–5. (grounds from 11.30). Please telephone for early season details.

Warwick Castle, Warwick (tel. 0926 495421). A striking combination of fortress and mansion. Now owned by the Madame Tussaud's people. Open daily. March–Oct., 10–5.30, Nov.–Feb., 10–4.30.

West Midlands. Aston Hall, Birmingham (tel. 021 327 0062) Superb Jacobean house (1618–35), almost overwhelmed by modern life (motorways and football). Open Easter–end Oct., daily 2–5.

Black Country Museum, Dudley. A complete village and industrial exhibits are being brought together on a 26-acre site to show the Black Country as it was. Also canal trips through famous tunnel from the wharf. Open daily in summer, 10–5.

Hagley Hall, near Stourbridge (tel. 0562 882408). Mid-18th-century house, beautiful plasterwork and gardens with Greek features. Phone for details.

Lunt Roman Fort, Baginton (2½ miles south of Coventry), (tel. 0203 25555, ext. 2315). Partially reconstructed 1st century turf and timber fort, possibly used againt Boadiceas. Fascinating with museum in granary. Open end May–Sept. daily (except Mon. and Thurs.), 12–6.

Moseley Old Hall, Wolverhampton (tel. 0902 782808). Where Charles II sought refuge after the Battle of Worcester, including the bed in which he slept and the "hide" he used. Complex opening times. Basically Sat.

and Sun., 2–6, Mar.–Oct. 15 July–27 Sept., Sat.–Wed., 2–6. Check locally. (NT)

Museum of British Road Transport, Coventry (tel. 0203 25555). Over 400 exhibits—cars, cycles, commercial vehicles—tracing the history of transport; also "Memory Lanes" period street scenes. Open summer, Mon.–Fri. 10–4, Sat. and Sun. 10–5.30; in winter, Fri. 9.30–4, Sat. and Sun. 10–5.

Oak House, West Bromwich (tel. 021 553 0759). Gorgeous 16th-century timber-framed house, original paneling inside, good period furniture. Open April-Sept., weekdays 10–8 (Thurs. 10–1), Sun. 2.30–8; Oct.–March, weekdays 10–4 (Thurs. 10–1).

Wightwick Manor, Wightwick Bank, Wolverhampton (tel. 0902 761108). A treasure house for those interested in William Morris and the Pre-Raphaelites, the place is bursting with their work. All year (except Feb.), Thurs., Sat., Bank Holiday Sun. and Mon., 2.30–5.30. Also May to Sept., for pre-booked parties. (NT).

ROYAL SHAKESPEARE THEATER. Tickets for the Royal Shakespeare performances cost from £3 to £20. You can use American Express, Mastercard, Visa and Diners Club credit cards by calling the box office at (0789) 295623 (the number is the same for all three auditoria) and quoting the card number. Bookings are confirmed immediately. If you want to book seats before you arrive in Britain, you should pay by sterling check, obtainable from your bank, adding £7.50 to the total (£10 if total exceeds £100). Keith Prowse and Edwards & Edwards also arrange bookings at their New York offices. Alternatively, you can book through Keith Prowse offices in London. The number for 24-hour booking information is (0789) 69191. For details of "Shakespeare Stopover" packages, call (0789) 414999.

THE NORTH MIDLANDS

Tulipland and Sherwood Forest

Lincolnshire, which forms a very large part of the east side of England, is totally unlike any other county. Its southeast corner is flat, with the most magnificent skies. The Fens, formerly a vast region of swamps but now, thanks to a splendidly-kept system of canals and drains which has ensured the reclamation of thousands of acres of land, are among the most important fruit and vegetable districts of England. Here, too, the cultivation of bulbs makes this one of the chief horticultural areas in the country, and no tourist in the vicinity of the East Midlands at the beginning of May should miss the opportunity of paying a visit to the Lincolnshire tulip fields when the colorful flowers present a picture that is unforgettable.

Not all, however, is given over to agriculture. The villages contain much of beauty; this is a land of magnificent churches, with the famous "Boston Stump," the 272-foot-high tower of St. Botolph's Church, at Boston, a landmark for miles. It is right over on the east side, within about four miles of the Wash. It is, of course, of interest to American visitors who like to recall that it was from this Lincolnshire town that, in 1630, Isaac Johnson and John Winthrop showed their disapproval of the then prevailing conditions by crossing the Atlantic and helping to found the Massachusetts town of the same name. The Puritans had tried to set sail for Holland in 1607, but they were arrested, tried and sentenced; the Guildhall cells in which they and their courageous hopes were imprisoned can still be visited.

The Stump, which once housed a light that not only guided ships coming to the old port but also served to direct wayfarers crossing the treacherous marshes, has also its links with the Massachusetts town, for in 1931 funds for its restoration were raised on the western side of the Atlantic. The church itself is of interest as one of the largest parish churches in England, and contains a good deal of splendid architecture. Climb to the top of the Stump on a clear day and you will see 40 miles of fenland stretching away under the open skies, the towers of Ely and Lincoln Cathedrals in the far distance and the ships on the River Witham riding out to sea.

As a port, Boston (originally "Botolph's Town"), which had formerly played a big part in the wool trade with the continent, suffered a period of decline between the middle of the 14th and the mid-18th century as a result of the silting up of the river; but in 1764 the channel was deepened, and since then the construction of docks and a new river bed has meant that a considerable amount of trade is still handled.

Boston's southern neighbor, Spalding, is the capital of "tulipland"; a tulip festival with a multicolored Flower Parade is held every May. More bulbs are grown here than in Holland.

A short distance from Spalding is Stamford, one of the prettiest small towns in England. Burghley House, an architectural masterpiece acknowledged as "the largest and grandest house of the first Elizabethan Age," stands on the outskirts. The town is steeped in history and unspoiled, with three fine churches—St. Martin's, St. Mary's, and All Saints.

While the southern part of Lincolnshire is flat, north of a line taking in the city of Lincoln and the towns of Horncastle and Skegness, the chalk uplands known as the Wolds stretch north to the Humber, beyond which comes their virtual continuation through Yorkshire, with Flamborough Head as one of the extremities. Compared with the heights of the Pennines and the Lake District (and even the Cotswold hills in Gloucestershire and Worcestershire), they are insignificant, yet they give a character to the scene which is entirely different from that of the Fen country and provide fascinating long-range views across to the coast and to Lincoln.

A few miles north of Boston on B1192 is the red-brick Tattershall Castle, built by Ralph Cromwell, Lord Treasurer to the Crown, in the first part of the 15th century. In 1926 it was bequeathed by Lord Curzon to the National Trust, who, of course, permit public access. Americans should notice the lovely stone carved mantelpieces which so nearly found a home in their own country. Indeed, they were actually sold for export in 1911 and had got as far as Tilbury Docks, when they were reprieved and restored to their rightful setting. Nearby, to the north, are the lovely pinewoods in Woodhall Spa, once famous for its rich mineral springs, discovered by chance during exploration for coal. It also has a championship golf course.

A few more miles or so towards Horncastle is the village of Scrivelsby, the home of the King's Hereditary Champion who, in the days when the British monarchs were crowned in Westminster Hall, had the right of riding into the assembly, clad in a suit of armor, and challenging anyone to mortal combat who dared to dispute the titles of the sovereign. Today, he has the honor of carrying the Standard of England at the coronation ceremony in Westminster Abbey. The office of King's Champion was created by the Norman kings and was first held by the Marmions, then passed, by marriage, to the Dymokes. The ancestral tombs of both families are to be seen in the village church.

Horncastle, to the east of Lincoln, is a lovely study of red-brick buildings and gabled inns. In the days before tractors became commonplace on the English farms, this town was the Mecca of farmfolk from a wide area wanting to buy sound specimens of horseflesh at the annual August fair.

Lincoln

Journeying westwards, one sees magnificent stone towers dominating the landscape—those of Lincoln Cathedral, set high on a limestone hill overlooking the town. Like most of the cathedrals in this part of Britain, it was begun in Norman times, suffered fire, natural disaster and pillaging, and has been partly rebuilt, restored and added to at intervals ever since. Inside the cathedral, be sure to look at the intricately carved font, the rose windows at the north and south ends, and its greatest glory—the 13th-century Angel Choir. Lincoln also has its castle, with *two* mounds, and a particularly attractive Guildhall, built above the Stonebow Gateway. The insistent notes of the 14th-century Mote Bell on the Guildhall roof still ring out to summon members to council meetings. One of the 19th century's most famous poets, Alfred Lord Tennyson, was born at The Rectory in Somersby, a quiet Lincolnshire village (house not open), and you will find an extensive and fascinating collection of the Tennyson family's books and correspondence in the Lincoln Central Library. Other sights to look for in this historic city are High Bridge with its medieval houses, and a Roman gateway—the only one in Britain still in use. The city's Museum of Lincolnshire Life is well worth a visit.

Northeast of Lincoln is the National Hunt racing center of Market Rasen, near to which the Tennyson family lived, and between there and the sea is the Georgian town of Louth, where perhaps the greatest of them, Alfred, the Poet Laureate for 42 years, attended the local grammar school. The North Lincolnshire coast has great expanses of sandy beach, as well as holiday resorts at Skegness and Mablethorpe.

From Lincoln make a detour southwards to Grantham before entering Nottinghamshire. Grantham is a fascinating, partly-industrial old town containing much to remind the traveler of its even greater importance in the days of the stage coach. Like so many of the towns in this area, its church is a gem of ecclesiastical architecture, both outside and within, with the bulk of it in 13th-century work.

One of the greatest glories of Grantham, however—apart from being the birthplace of Margaret Thatcher—is its wealth of old inns, including the Angel and Royal, with its lovely 15th-century stone front facing the market place. It was once a hostelry of the Knights Templar and has its links with the English kings—King John holding a court here in 1213 and King Richard III visiting it on the occasion when he signed the death warrant of Buckingham in 1483.

Within easy reach of the town (just 2 miles to the northeast) is one of England's finest historic houses. Belton House, formerly the family seat of Lord Brownlow and now owned by the National Trust, is noted for its fine parklands and Grinling Gibbons carvings.

NOTTINGHAMSHIRE

From Grantham it is but a little way up the A1 to Nottinghamshire. There is a fair amount of industry, mostly mining; not many big towns; dozens of small villages, and it is very well wooded. It has in some ways a secret air, as if it were keeping itself to itself. It is also rich in stately homes.

Just east of Southwell, and by-passed by the Great North Road, is Newark-on-Trent, with its gray old castle still standing solidly above an arm of the River Trent and a general look of well-being befitting a town with a treasured historical past and the center of a thriving agricultural business.

Built by Bishop Alexander of Lincoln in the early part of the 12th century and on the site of an older fortification of sorts, Newark castle maintained its links with the See of Lincoln until 1547, when it passed to the crown. Prior to that, it had often put up a stout resistance to the monarchs during the troubled times that marked the reigns of kings Stephen and John, albeit the last-mentioned king actually died within its walls in October, 1216. When Royalist and Commonwealth armies fought during the long-drawn-out Civil Wars of the first part of the 17th century, however, it stood equally firm in its loyalty to the crown. Three times it had to withstand sieges, and in the end surrender only came at the command of King Charles I himself.

Its church, not only one of the largest but also one of the most magnificent in the whole country, is dedicated to St Mary Magdalene, and although much of its rich interior belongs to the reign of Henry IV, there are parts, such as the Norman crypt and the Early English tower, belonging to an earlier period of history.

With many old inns around the marketplace and several other interesting buildings, Newark is a fine example of the historic Midlands town that retains so much of its past while still playing an important part in the trade and commerce of today.

Eight miles to the west on A612 is Southwell, raised to the seat of a bishopric in 1884 when its truly grand parish church was given the title of a Minster (its Chapter House contains exceptional foliage carving). Yet in spite of this ecclesiastical distinction Southwell could never rank as anything other than a 'small town.' Here Charles I stayed at the Saracen's Head Inn immediately prior to surrendering himself to the Scottish army. The hotel is still fit for a king—comfortable, friendly and well modernized.

Southwest from Southwell on the same road one comes to Nottingham, apparently founded by the Danes in the second part of the 9th century. There is much to be seen in the city, which contains a truly magnificent Council House, a castle perched on the top of a great crag above the city— built by the Duke of Newcastle in 1679 on the site of an earlier erection and now housing the city's Museum of Fine and Decorative Arts—and an ancient inn, Ye Olde Trip to Jerusalem, which claims to have enjoyed the patronage of the Crusaders towards the close of the 12th century. Nottingham has an exciting modern theater, the Playhouse, which presents its plays in a cylindrical auditorium. The Theatre Royal, an older house, presents plays, operas and ballets. Among the several interesting museums, try to see the Brewhouse Yard Museum, depicting daily life in old Nottingham, the Lace Centre and Museum of Costumes and Textiles, and Wollaton Hall, which houses a fine Natural History Museum, and is considered to be one of the finest specimens of Elizabethan architecture.

Sherwood Forest

North of Nottingham is Sherwood Forest, indelibly associated with Robin Hood and his exploits. The road from Nottingham (the A60) passes the grounds of Newstead Abbey (open to the public), which was once a priory of the Black Canons and for many years the home of Lord Byron, whose predecessor, the fifth Lord Byron, seems to have done everything within his power to ruin the estate, cutting down trees, killing the deer, and allowing the hall itself to fall into a state of neglect. Yet Byron's name is still treasured here and no evidence of the destruction is apparent today, thanks to careful restoration by later owners. Now run by the Nottingham City Council, it has lovely gardens.

Mansfield, the next town, is a strange mixture of old and new. The civic authorities have done much to eradicate some of the less savory remains of past years, but there are many old buildings still to be seen, as well as some dwellings cut out of the living rock, said to have been used by British refugees at the time of the Roman occupation of the Midlands. It is a convenient center for exploring Sherwood Forest, the "Dukeries" and Robin Hood country.

Sherwood Forest and the legendary Robin Hood are inseparable. Naturally enough, doubts have been expressed as to the existence of such an outlaw, but although history is largely silent, authentic references are not lacking, and it would seem that the stories are based on something rather more substantial than mere legend. Robin Hood, we are told, died in 1247 at the age of 87—you can see his grave at Kirklees, in the Calder Valley, Yorkshire. That was a time when the Normans imposed harsh laws to govern their forests, and many a Saxon defied them and took his share of venison. Naturally, such men assumed the status of local heroes; stories of their exploits were handed down from one generation to another, and it might well be that Robin Hood is but a composite of all who defied the laws of the Norman overlords and endeavored to preserve the freedom of the forest.

So far as Sherwood Forest is concerned, there is a record of a trial for offenses and trespass being held as long ago as 1160—about the time when Robin Hood seems to have been in action—and it remained a possession of the Crown until the 18th century, when various sections were sold to local landowners. Today, there are still some fine woodland glades and outstanding individual trees, of which the Major Oak, near Edwinstowe, is worth a special visit. Its trunk still has a girth of over 36 feet, in spite of attacks by storm and fire.

The path to the Major Oak starts at the Sherwood Forest Visitor Center, where the Robin Hood story is told in life-size figures and audio, in a series of linked huts, presented as a stage set. The presentation is well done and interesting. There is also a well-stocked gift shop, cafeteria and Tourist Information Center. The Visitor Center forms the focal point of the Sherwood Forest Country Park, from which the County Council carries out its work in caring for the forest and also runs guided walks.

The northern part of the old forest was long given over to various ducal estates and that produced its names of the "Dukeries." Here are the parklands of Rufford, Clumber, Thoresby, and Welbeck, with their grand stretches of woodland, ornamental waters, and spacious areas of turf. Thoresby Hall is still in private ownership and open to visitors in summer (mainly Sundays), but the ruins of Rufford Abbey are being restored by the English Heritage organization. The former stable block at Rufford has become a Craft Center, thanks to the Nottinghamshire County Council. This is a spot for displays and exhibitions, and apart from that you can walk in the grounds. The center has a slot-machine eating place downstairs beside the shop, while upstairs next to the exhibition area there is a particularly pleasant coffeeshop with "proper" food. A major new development near Rufford is the first Center Parcs holiday village in Britain. Its Dutch developers have already proved the popularity of this type of holiday, with extensive all-weather leisure facilities in a domed "village" set in a forest location, at sites in Holland. Welbeck Abbey is now an army training college, while the great house of Clumber has been pulled down, but the park, with its magnificent lime-tree avenue is worth a visit, as is the chapel. Moreover, the park seems always to be open—an ideal spot for a picnic lunch beside the huge lake, although a parking fee may be demanded.

Highways and Byways

Nottinghamshire is perhaps not so well endowed with large, famous places as some other counties, but if you look around in the villages on the little roads there is a lot to be found of interest, and because the county is narrow and not very long, it is possible to visit a number of places in a short time.

Take the A1133 northward to discover Harby, which is right on the Lincolnshire border. It was here, in a manor house, that Queen Eleanor of Castile, wife of Edward I, died, and after being embalmed in Lincoln, began the long funeral journey to Westminster, though there is nothing here today to remind us of this historical episode. In every place en route where her body rested at night, King Edward raised an ornate cross. One, mentioned in the Northamptonshire section, still exists at Geddington, just north of Kettering.

At Laxton, roughly on a level with Harby but to the west of the A1, one can see preserved the old open-field farming system originated by the Saxons. Go from Laxton to Ollerton and down A614 off which is the village of Blidworth. This is what is left of Sherwood Forest—it used to stretch over to Harby at the time of Queen Eleanor's death—and is the place from which, allegedly, Maid Marian came. Anyway, the village makes something out of it. Just south of it is the supposed birthplace of the inventor of the stocking frame, who was an Elizabethan parson, a Mr. Lee. The Queen refused to give him a patent because his machine would make only wool stockings. So he went away and devised another one to make silk stockings, but she refused again because of the possible unemployment among knitters. What happened to poor Mr. Lee we don't know, but his invention put Nottinghamshire on its feet, so to speak, although there are still hand knitters in Calverton today, as there are in some other villages. Their cottages have characteristic wide windows with glass globes hanging in them to catch the light. Framework knitting can be seen in practice at the museum in Ruddington, where some workshops have been restored.

Again level with Calverton, but west of the M1, and by a rather cross-country route, is Eastwood. Not a village, but still peaceful and fairly rural, it is, as D.H. Lawrence fans will know, his birthplace, and the landscape he used for *Sons and Lovers*. Continuing round Nottingham on A6007, one should come to Bramcote, a pocket village saved from the A52, with a fine red-brick manor house and very special views over five counties and the Trent Valley. South of Nottingham on A60 is a pretty little village called Bunny, mostly designed by the eccentric Sir Thomas Parkyns who spent his time making things better for his tenants which was unusual in the 17th century. He also compiled a Latin grammar and passed his spare time wrestling.

DERBYSHIRE

Derbyshire lies to the west of Nottinghamshire, and its chief town, Derby (pronounced Darby), is close to Nottingham. It is one of the most important industrial cities of the country and has many old buildings which are reminders of its historic past, including All Saints' Church, now the Cathedral, with its embattled tower dating from the early 16th century. It has important links with the early development of the woolen and silk trades, as well as the manufacture of exquisite china and Rolls-Royce engines. Lovers of fine china will be interested in the Royal Crown Derby Museum, with examples of the work of the factory dating back to 1725.

Derby has a professional football side, Derby County, and the Derbyshire County Cricket Club plays many of its home games on a ground close to the city center. Plays are presented in the Playhouse, and concerts at the Assembly Rooms.

The Peak District

In the south of Derbyshire the countryside is only a little different from the rolling scene of Nottinghamshire, but there are already indications that if you continue northwards, you are going to come to something quite different. We are, in fact, approaching the Peak District National Park which has Ashbourne as its point of entry. This is the first National Park to have been declared in England, in 1951, and it remains probably the most outstanding. The southern half is known as the White Peak, mild uplands and wooded dales on limestone, while the north, the Dark Peak, is much wilder moorland.

Ashbourne is a small market town which stands on the River Dove and is not given to change. It probably looks much the same as it did to Izaak Walton who fished in Dovedale, and George Eliot who used a nearby village as the setting for *Adam Bede*. Ashbourne has a church that is one of the finest in Derbyshire, and a very fine street leading to it. Like Bakewell, further north, it has its own special food, Ashbourne Gingerbread, and its own spa water which is one of the nearest things to Perrier Water that England has.

Traveling northward towards Chesterfield, one passes through Wirksworth, an attractive small town once a center of lead mining, and so to the Matlocks, where Derbyshire scenery is at its best. Matlock Bath has, as one would imagine, thermal waters. It also has an alpine-style cable car, unique in Britain, that crosses the dramatic Derwent Valley gorge to the wooded landscapes, viewpoints and show caves at the Heights of Abraham. Further up the valley lies Matlock Dale which leads into Matlock Town, also rich in places for leisure and pleasure, while all around the Matlocks is the "area of a thousand views."

A few miles south of the Matlocks is Crich (pronounced as in "cry" with "ch" at the end). Housed on the site of a one-time mineral railway, old tramcars, buffed to sparkling condition, are tight-packed for viewing—horse-drawn, some open-topped with trolley-pole, some steam, some electric. Some are mobilized for tram rides, a chance to sample the alternative to today's bus services.

Travel up A6 from Matlock and one comes to Bakewell, Haddon Hall, Chatsworth House, Eyam village and ultimately to Buxton, an enormously rich area.

Bakewell is a small market town built in brown stone, with a medieval bridge over the River Wye, and set in most beautiful countryside. The recipe for the famous Bakewell Pudding (*never* called "Tart" up here, as are its imitations in other parts of England), was allegedly discovered as a result of a misunderstanding of a cook working in the Rutland Arms Hotel, where Jane Austen once stayed when writing her novel *Pride and Prejudice*. Her room is still preserved. But for a taste of the real Bakewell Pudding, try the Pudding Shop in The Square. You can eat this local specialty in the restaurant as a desert, served either with custard or cream; or buy it in the shop which, incidentally, will take orders and dispatch these "puddings" in any quantity to any part of the world—they have proved great favorites in America.

Haddon Hall, just south of Bakewell, is a 14th-century manor house built on terraced gardens with the River Dove at their feet. A seat of the Dukes of Rutland, like Belvoir Castle, the Hall is simply presented as itself with all the things you would expect to find in such a building; or if you don't expect it, the Hall will unobtrusively teach you to do so in future. There are no gimmicks, no pressures to buy, no interpretation.

Chatsworth

About six miles up B6012 is Chatsworth House—normally just called "Chatsworth"—one of England's great houses, large, sumptuous, overpoweringly rich and belonging to the Dukes of Devonshire. The original house was built by the eccentric Bess of Hardwick, who married four times, acquired estates from each of her husbands, and was a compulsive builder right up to the time of her death. (Her *chef d'oeuvre* is Hardwick Hall, six miles southeast of Chesterfield and now in the hands of the National Trust.) Nothing now remains of her Chatsworth edifice except the Hunting Tower in the woods. The present huge building was mainly built at the end of the 17th century, with a vast addition early in the 19th. Chatsworth attracts hundreds of thousands of visitors a year, so arrive early!

What you will find is a palace that would do credit to many a king. Paintings, tapestries, frescoed ceilings, rich furniture, one of the greatest libraries in Britain, gorgeous fountains, set in seemingly endless gardens—it is quite an experience.

Shortly beyond Chatsworth a T-junction in the road offers a way to Chesterfield to the right or Buxton to the left. Although the twisted spire of the parish church is what has drawn attention to Chesterfield, it is built on a very old foundation, and now also has some outstanding modern architecture.

Going towards Buxton on A623, one is led to the village of Eyam, a place which has a deeply moving story. In 1665 infection of the Great Plague was brought to the village from London in a box of old clothes. The rector, William Mompesson, prevailed upon the people to put themselves into quarantine to prevent the plague spreading into the rest of Derbyshire. He was successful, but it cost the village 75 percent of its inhabitants, including his own wife. An annual commemoration service is held in August.

Buxton

Near the head of the Wye to the west is Buxton, the highest town in England at over 1,000 feet and, like Matlock, renowned for the medicinal qualities of its waters. Indeed, the Romans knew the curative powers of the chalybeate springs and, in all probability, laid the foundations of what has developed into one of the most popular of England's inland spas. Among its notable buildings is the graceful Crescent, built by the 5th Duke of Devonshire between 1780 and 1784. Buxton is a very elegant town, yet friendly, and is making a name for itself with its summer festival, housed mainly in its richly refurbished theater-cum-opera house.

The highly decorative Pavilion Gardens cover some 23 acres of park and woodland, the River Wye meandering through. For loitering or more active pastimes, there are ornamental lakes and walks, tennis courts, putting and bowling greens, indoor swimming pool, a children's playground. There is also good catering in both restaurants and spacious cafeterias.

Buxton makes a fine base from which to explore the surrounding countryside. Buxton Country Park has Poole's Cavern, a fine show cave, and Grin Low Woods, 100 acres of woodland walks. There is a scenic uphill walk to a 19th-century folly with a panoramic view over Buxton. Further afield there are roads and tracks across the uplands to Axe Edge, a breezy expanse of heather upland commanding some of the widest views in the district. Not far away is the renowned Cat and Fiddle, just west of Buxton on A537, one of the highest-situated pubs in the country.

Derbyshire has some charming local customs among which one of the most unusual and picturesque is Well Dressing, a tradition that can be traced back many centuries. Water was of great importance in limestone areas such as this, and many of the little towns and villages continue to hold their Well Dressing ceremonies in the summer as a thanksgiving. Intricate pictures are built up, usually on a religious theme, composed from petals, leaves, bark and other natural materials. The designs usually last for several days, can be seen and admired by visitors and locals alike.

Edale, the approximate center of the National Park, is at the southern end of the Pennine Way, which runs right up to Kirk Yetholm on the Scottish border. Strenuous hiking this, but tackled in short stretches it provides some superb views.

At nearby Castleton, it's descent rather than ascent, as this district is riddled with mines and caverns, mostly converted into tourist attractions. In one of them Queen Victoria ordered an entire symphony orchestra to play, the royal party ranged on one side of an underground lake, the orchestra performing on the other. The Blue John Mine is where the famous, though now diminishing, Blue John stone is found: a sales room at the minehead is a handy place to buy souvenirs, as jewelry and trinkets of all kinds are made from or decorated with the stone. At Cavendish House, in the village main street, the Ollerenshaw Collection is shown in a small, beautifully lit museum, and has one of the finest displays of Blue John in the world with clocks, bowls and goblets, urns and vases made from the colorful stone, some over 100 years old. The craft and jewelry shop adjoins the museum where more souvenirs—cheap and not so cheap—are for sale.

The chilling Peak Cavern, behind the houses, has perhaps the most breathtaking entrance of any cave in Britain—a gaping, gloomy gap at the base of a sheer limestone cliff. Though most visitors come for the caves, the energetic amongst them also end up clambering up the steep slope to Peveril Castle, the ancient stronghold which gave Castleton its name. This dramatically sited ruin, perched on a crag above the village, was built by William Peveril, son of William the Conqueror. North of Castleton, the Derwent Valley is at its loveliest, a blend of lakeland, forest and open, brooding moor—ideal for walking or cycling (bicycle hire is available from the Fairholmes picnic site).

CHESHIRE

From the hills of Derbyshire to the western sea, off the Wirral Peninsula, and to the borders of Wales, Cheshire is mainly a land of well-kept farms, supporting their herds of equally well-kept cattle. Ancient towns, like Sandbach and Tarporley, depend mainly on their links with agriculture. Villages, with Gawsworth in the southeast as one of the gems, contain many fine examples of the black-and-white "magpie" type of architecture more often associated with the Midlands (and every bit as attractive as anything to be found there), and, covering a large chunk of the interior, is Delamere Forest, a region of fine trees and containing some delightful little lakes, or meres.

Chester is its capital, a city steeped in history, with its cathedral, castle, and encircling city walls, as well as a whole host of ancient buildings distributed among its streets, many of them in the bold black-and-white style of Tudor England. The cathedral, originally an abbey dedicated to St. Werburgh, attained its present status in 1536 but still possesses many features, grouped around its cloister, that survive from its monastic past. The castle, built soon after the Norman Conquest and looking across the River Dee to Wales, remains a bastion of strength.

Among the unique features of Chester are the famous "Rows," covered-in footways at first-floor level along many of the main streets, which allow the delights of shopping without fear of any discomfort through wet weather or from traffic. Just how these originated does not seem to be clearly known, although some have it they belong to the time when the Saxons rebuilt much of the city on the older Roman foundations, which were not excavated until a somewhat later date. Most are, however, of the opinion that they served as a most effective means of defense against the incursions of the Welsh raiders.

There is a giant radio telescope at Jodrell Bank with a spectacular planetarium, just the place for a space-age day out. Knutsford is worth a visit too. It is a charming town very little altered since the Victorian novelist, Mrs. Gaskell, lived there and wrote *Cranford.* More literary associations are to be found in the Wonderland village of Daresbury, where Lewis Carroll (The Rev. Charles Dodgson) was born, and where his life story and scenes from his *Alice in Wonderland* and *Alice Through the Looking Glass* are shown in the stained glass windows of the parish church.

Some ten miles south of Manchester, east of the M6, is the impressive Quarry Bank Mill at Styal, part of a country park. The estate is a living and working community of spinners and weavers, with a shop and tea-rooms for visitors, who are also welcome to worship in its chapels. There are 250 acres of woodland and riverside planned by the 18th-century humanitarian Samuel Greg for the benefit of his workforce.

For walkers there are countless marked trails and footpaths: the Sandstone Trail, which runs for 32 miles across the county; and on the Wirral Peninsula, a 12-mile walk along a once-disused and now transformed railway line—the perfect place for superb views across the estuary of the River Dee and into North Wales.

Cheshire is also noted for its "salt towns." Nantwich was one of the biggest producers, and in the 18th century visitors flocked to the town to "take the salts" which were claimed to cure indigestion and rheumatism. There is an outdoor pool fed by the original spring that provided salt for the Romans, and it's open to visitors. In the town itself there are quantities of craft shops, a street market, potteries, and historic buildings.

Middlewich is the second largest salt town in Cheshire. But it is Northwich which has the most to show visitors about the past. This is thanks to the town's Salt Museum, claimed to be the only one in the world which traces its history from Roman times to the present day. For a total change from walking or driving, a canal boat operator—Colliery Narrow Boats, of Northwich—runs relaxing, leisurely trips along the Trent and Mersey Canal (telephone Northwich 44672 for details).

PRACTICAL INFORMATION FOR
THE NORTH MIDLANDS

HOTELS AND RESTAURANTS. Wherever you eat or stay in this area, you will almost certainly find a warmth and friendliness that is the well-known trademark of the region. And you will never be very far from some of the most striking and memorable scenery in Britain.

Details about our grading system, plus other relevant information about hotels and restaurants, will be found at the beginning of the book in the *Facts at Your Fingertips* section.

Bakewell (Derbys.). *Rutland Arms* (M), tel. (062 981) 2812; 37 rooms, all with bath. Jane Austen wrote part of *Pride and Prejudice* here. A good center for touring the Derbyshire dales and historic houses at Chatsworth and Haddon.

Restaurant. *Fischers* (E), Bath St., tel. (062 981) 2687. Tempting menu, superb sauces, served in cottagey atmosphere. Closed Sat. lunch, Sun even, Mon.

Barnby Moor (Notts.). *Ye Olde Bell* (M), tel. (0777) 705121. 55 rooms with bath. Coaching inn with paneling, brass bedsteads and traditional atmosphere.

Baslow (Derbys.). *Cavendish* (E–M), tel. (024 688) 2311; 23 rooms, all with bath. Faces across the Chatsworth Estate. Good, original food and comfortable rooms. Magnificent scenery.

Buxton (Derbys.). *Hartington* (M), 18 Broad Walk, tel. (0298) 2638; 17 rooms, 5 with bath. *Leewood* (M), Manchester Rd., tel. (0298) 3002; 40 rooms, all with bath; pleasant grounds, good views and amenities. *Palace* (M), Palace Rd., tel. (0298) 2001; 122 rooms with bath in large, Victorian hotel with good facilities.

Castleton (Derbys.). *Ye Olde Nag's Head* (M), tel. (0433) 20248. 8 rooms, 3 with bath. Well-situated old inn between Sheffield and Manchester. Grand walking country. Handy for Blue John caves.

Chester (Ches.). *Grosvenor* (L), Eastgate St., tel. (0244) 24024; 90 rooms, all with bath. Luxurious, with elegant dining room and excellent food. Good-sized bedrooms in splendid Victorian surroundings. Wise to book. Recommended. *Mollington Banastre* (E), Parkgate Rd., tel. (0244) 851471. 70 rooms with bath. Expertly run; extensive grounds and superb leisure complex (pool, squash, gym etc.). *Blossoms* (E–M), St. John St., tel. (0244) 23186. 70 rooms with bath. 17th-century coaching inn, now dominated by coach parties. *Redland* (I), 64 Hough Green, tel. (0244) 671024; 10 rooms, 2 with shower. Small, well-appointed private hotel. No restaurant.

Restaurant. *Pippa's "In Town"* (M), 58 Watergate St., tel. (0244) 313721. Wide choice of French dishes. Closed Sun. and Bank Holidays.

Derby (Derbys.). *Midland* (M), Midland Rd., tel. (0332) 45894; 63 rooms, 39 with bath. *Pennine* (M), Macklin St., tel. (0332) 41741; 100 rooms, all with bath or shower.

Restaurant. *Boaters* (M), Friargate. Authentic old-fashioned English food in hospitable surroundings.

Dovedale (Derbys.). *Peveril of the Peak* (E), tel. (033 529) 333; 41 rooms with bath. Modernized rectory in quiet grounds below Thorpe Cloud, 900-ft. peak guarding Dovedale. *Izaak Walton* (M), tel. (033 529)

555; 33 rooms with bath. Trusty old friend, with—naturally—fishing, too. Wonderful views.

Fenny Brook (Derbys.) *Bentley Brook* (M), tel. (033 529) 8 rooms, 3 with bath. In Peak National Park, country inn with good food and real ale.

Grantham (Lincs.). *Angel and Royal* (M), High St., tel. (0476) 65816; 24 rooms, 14 with bath. One of England's most historic inns. 15th-century stone frontage overlooks the market place. *George* (M), High St., tel. (0476) 63286; 44 rooms, all with bath. Charles Dickens worked on *Nicholas Nickleby* here.

Grimsthorpe (Lincs.). *Black Horse Inn* (E–M), tel. (077 832) 247. 4 rooms, all with bath. Georgian coaching inn—lots of character and marvelous English restaurant (M).

Handforth (Ches.). *Belfry* (E), tel. (061) 437 0511; 92 rooms, all with bath. Pleasant, large, modern hotel set in own grounds. International restaurant.
At **Mottram St. Andrew.** *Mottram Hall* (M), tel. (0625) 828135. 95 rooms with bath. Lakeside Georgian house in 120-acre grounds. Fishing.

Knutsford (Ches.). **Restaurant.** *La Belle Époque* (E), King St., tel. (0565) 3060. Good French restaurant in Art Nouveau style; also has 5 rooms.

Lincoln (Linc.). *Eastgate Post House* (E), Eastgate, tel. (0522) 20341; 71 rooms with bath in modern hotel overlooking cathedral. *White Hart* (E), Bailgate, tel. (0522) 26222; 52 rooms with bath. Gracious hotel between the cathedral and castle. Renovated bedrooms furnished with attractive antiques. Friendly staff, good food with local produce. *D'Isney Place* (M), Eastgate, tel. (0522) 38881; 18 rooms with bath in family-run hotel near cathedral. No restaurant.
Restaurant. *White's* (E), The Strait, tel. (0522) 24851. Pleasant, informal restaurant in 12th-century "Jew's House," one of the oldest buildings in Britain. Modern, light dishes.

Matlock (Derbys.). *New Bath* (E), Matlock Bath, tel. (0629) 3275. Off A6, 56 rooms with bath. Indoor swimming pools (thermal springs), sauna. *Riber Hall* (E), tel. (0629) 2795. 11 rooms, all with bath. Restored Elizabethan mansion by the Pennines, antique decor, excellent restaurant with creative menu.

Nantwich (Ches.). *Rookery Hall* (L–E), Worleston, tel. (0270) 626866; 12 rooms, all with bath; tranquil grounds, magnificent food and antiques. Superb French restaurant amidst baronial surroundings.

Nottingham (Notts.). *Albany* (E), St. James' St., tel. (0602) 470131. 150 rooms, all with bath. Good Carvery Restaurant. *Royal* (E–M), Wollaton St., tel. (0602) 414444; 201 rooms with bath in modern, well-designed hotel. *Post House* (M), at Sandiacre, nr M1, tel. (0602) 397800. 106 rooms with bath. *Savoy* (M), Mansfield Rd., tel. (0602) 602621. 182 rooms with bath. Modern hotel with traditional air.

Restaurant. *Les Artistes Gourmands* (M), 61 Wollaton Rd., Beeston tel. (0602) 228288. Popular French spot in a suburban area. Closed lunch Sat., Mon., evening Sun.

Puddington (Ches.). **Restaurant.** *Craxton Wood* (M), tel. (051) 339 4717. On secluded grounds; ivy-clad house with good French food; also has 14 rooms. Closed Sun., Bank Holidays and last 2 weeks in Aug.

Rowsley (Derbys.). *Peacock* (M), tel. (0629) 733518; 20 rooms, 15 with bath. Converted 17th-century dower house of Haddon Hall near Bakewell. Antiques combine nicely with modern furnishings; garden; good food and friendly, efficient service.

Southwell (Notts.). *Saracen's Head* (M), tel. (0636) 812701; 23 rooms with bath. Charles I surrendered here.

Stamford (Lincs.). *George* (E), 71 St. Martin's High St., tel. (0780) 55171; 47 rooms with bath. Excellent old inn with blue-blooded clientèle. Hearty fare in the restaurant.

Woodhall Spa (Lincs.). *Dower House* (M), tel. (0526) 52588. 7 rooms, 6 with bath. Homely and well-run Edwardian Hotel. *Golf* (M), tel. (0526) 53535. 51 rooms, 41 with bath, 10 with shower. Mock-Tudor building by championship golf course.

PLACES OF INTEREST. This region can boast one of the most impressive houses in Britain, Chatsworth, which, in its way, surpasses even Blenheim for magnificence. If you add to Chatsworth the Tudor glories of Hardwick Hall and the black-and-white medieval charm of Little Moreton Hall, then you will find memories that are unlikely to be eclipsed. There are more details about visiting historic houses in the relevant section of *Facts at Your Fingertips,* and another treatment of the subject in the chapter *Historic Houses—Precious Stones in Peril.*

Cheshire. Adlington Hall, near Macclesfield (tel. 0625 829206). Lovely complex of 15th, 16th and 18th centuries; in the Legh family since early 14th. Easter to end Sept., Sun. and Bank Holidays, 2–5.30; plus Wed. and Sat. in Aug.

The Boat Museum, Ellesmere Port, Wirral (tel. 051 355 5017). The biggest collection of inland waterways craft in Europe. Situated where the Shropshire Union and Manchester Ship Canals meet. Open daily, 10–5; Nov.-March, 10–4; Fri. by appointment.

Bramall Hall, Bramhall, Stockport (tel. 061 485 3708). Huge timber-framed house, dating from the late 1400s. Interesting for the structure and 16th-century wall paintings. In large landscaped park. Open daily except Mon. (unless Bank Holiday), Apr.–Sept. 12–5, Oct.–Mar. 12–4.

Dunham Massey Hall and Park, near Altrincham (tel. 061 941 1025). On southwest edge of Manchester in beautiful parkland, an early 18th-century house. House open Apr. through Oct. daily (except Fri.), 1–5 (from 12 Sat., Sun. and Bank Holiday Mon.). Park 12–5.30 (from 11 Sun. and Bank Holiday Mon.). (NT)

Little Moreton Hall, Congleton (tel. 0260 272018). The black-and-white timbered building to end them all, a real stunner, a must for photographers. Open Mar. and Oct., Sat. and Sun. 1.30–5.30 (or sunset); Apr.–Sept., daily (except Tues.), 1.30–5.30 (or sunset). Closed Good Fri. (NT).

Lyme Hall and Park, Disley (tel. 0663 62023). Impressive Palladian house (outside 1720). Fine setting and some attractive rooms. Park and gardens, all year, 8 to dusk. House complex times, liable to change, check locally. (NT)

Quarry Bank Mill, Styal (tel. 0625 527468). This is for those interested in industrial archeology: a model village, and mill, developed as a much-praised working museum with huge Victorian water-wheel. April to Sept., Tues. to Sun., Bank Holiday Mon., 11–5; Oct.–March, 11–4. Closed Mon. and Sat. except in June, July and Aug. (NT).

Salt Museum, Northwich (tel. 0606 41331). Museum of Cheshire's salt industry, from Roman times to the present. Open all year Tues.–Sun., 2–5. Open Bank Holiday Mon.

Tatton Park, Knutsford (tel. 0565 54822). Magnificent country estate with 1813 mansion, farm, deer park, nature trails. House open daily, Easter-end of Oct., afternoons. Park open all year. Times are complex, so please check. (NT)

Derbyshire. Blue John Cavern, Castleton (tel. 0433 20638). Tour through caves which are the source of the rare Blue John Stone. Open daily in spring, summer, autumn and most of winter, 9.45–6 (or sunset).

Chatsworth, near Bakewell (tel. 024 688 2204). Magnificent home of the Dukes of Devonshire, simply bursting at the seams with art treasures. Children's Adventure Playground in Farmyard area. House and gardens open late Mar.–Oct., daily, 11.30–4.30; Farmyard to late Sept., 10.30–4.30 (daily).

Haddon Hall, Bakewell (tel. 062 981 2855). Medieval home of Duke of Rutland and associated with romantic story of Dorothy Vernon. Open Easter–late Sept., daily (except Mon) 11–6 (also closed Sun. in July and Aug.); Bank Holidays 11–6.

Hardwick Hall, near Chesterfield (tel. 0246 850430). Splendid Elizabethan house built by "Bess of Hardwick." Open Apr.–Oct., Wed., Thurs., Sat., Sun., Bank Holiday Mon., 1–5.30 (or dusk); garden daily, 12–5.30. (NT).

Kedleston Hall, Derby (tel. 0332 842191). Splendid Robert Adam House, one of England's finest. Currently in the process of being acquired by the National Trust. Should be open from Apr.–end Sept., Sat.–Wed., 1–5.30 (garden from 12). Best to check.

Royal Crown Derby Museum, Osneaston Rd., Derby (tel. 0332 47051). Traces the history of the only company entitled to use "Crown" *and* "Royal" in its title. Open weekdays 9–12.30, 1.30–4.

Sudbury Hall Museum of Childhood, Sudbury (tel. 028 378 305). A museum *for* children, as well as about them, with every room featuring items that can be played with—such as board games and jigsaws, a doll's house, and copies of period costume that can be worn. Open Apr.–Oct., Wed.–Sun., Bank Holiday Mon., 1–5.30 or sunset.

National Tramway Museum, Crich, near Matlock (tel. 077 385 2565). Unique collection of horse, steam and electric tramcars. Tram rides. Open Apr.–Oct., Sat., Sun., Bank Holidays, 10.30–6.30; also May–Sept., Mon.–Thurs., 10–5.30, plus Fri. late July–Aug.

Lincolnshire. Belton House, near Grantham (tel. 0476 66116). Splendid 17th-century house with fine wood carvings, tapestries and paintings. Orangery, stables, park. Open Apr.–Oct., Wed.–Sun. and Bank Holidays, 1–5.30. (NT).

Burghley House, nr. Stamford (tel. 0780 52451). Huge, ornate Elizabethan mansion built 1587 by William Cecil, first Lord Burghley, and occupied by the Cecil family every since. Magnificent rooms, fine art collection; grounds and deer park by Capability Brown. Open Easter–early Oct., daily 11–5, Good Fri. 2–5.

Doddington Hall, near Lincoln (tel. 0522 694308). Elizabethan mansion with gabled gatehouse. Furniture, pictures, gardens. Open Easter Mon. and May–Sept., Wed., Sun. and Bank Holidays, 2–6.

Fydell House, Boston (tel. 0205 51520). Built 1726; houses Pilgrim College. Open in University term time Mon.–Fri. 10–12, 1–4.30; at other times by appointment (tel. 0205 68588).

Lincoln Cathedral Library and Cathedral Treasury, Lincoln (tel. 0522 44544 for all departments). Important manuscripts and one of the four copies of Magna Carta. Both Library and Treasury are open to the public though appointment may be necessary. Please check. (Note that the Magna Carta is often away on extended tours, and is not on show in winter).

Tattershall Castle, near Woodhall Spa (tel. 0526 42543). One of the finest brick fortified houses; 100-ft.-high keep remains; built around 1440. Marvelous Fenland views from the top. Open end Mar. through Oct., daily 11–6.30 (Sun. 1–6.30); winter, daily 12–6 or sunset (Sun. 1–6). (NT)

Nottinghamshire. Framework Knitters Museum, Ruddington (tel. 0602 846914). Cottages and workshops, original and reconstructed, from the 19th century. Open regularly Apr.–Oct., Tues. and Thur., 10–4. Otherwise by appointment. Best to check.

Newstead Abbey, 11 miles north of Nottingham (tel. 0623 793557). Byron relics in converted priory. Open Easter–Sept., daily 1.45–6.

Nottingham Museums. Nottingham has some excellent museums; opening times are reasonable—please check locally. **Nottingham Castle Museum** (tel. 0602 411881), a 17th-century residence with a huge collection of ceramics, silver and glass, medieval Nottingham alabaster. **Brewhouse Yard Museum** (tel. 0602 411881), where daily life in old Nottingham is depicted in 17th- and 18th century cottages. **Museum of Costumes and Textiles** (tel. 0602 411881), which recalls Nottingham's lace industry. **Natural History Museum** (tel. 0602 281333), with extensive displays in fine Elizabethan mansion. **Industrial Museum** (tel. 0602 284602), lace again, together with printing, engineering and agricultural exhibits.

Thoresby Hall, Ollerton (tel. 0623 822301). Mammoth Victorian pile. Open Bank Holidays and Sun. in May, June, July and Aug.; House 1–5.30, grounds 11–6.30. Tours (prebooked groups) by appointment May to Aug., Wed. and Thurs.

THE INDUSTRIAL CENTER

Great Cities and the Brontë Landscape

It has to be admitted that this is not a region of England into which the tourist would drift by chance. That is not, of course, to suggest that there is nothing there worth seeing. Manchester, for instance, is a cultural center, but it is also a huge commercial hub and the idea of visiting it does not seem irresistible to a stranger. The same applies, even more so, to Liverpool.

MERSEYSIDE

Liverpool used to be in Lancashire. By giving it its own county of Merseyside its commercial aspect has been underlined. It stands, hugely, on the Mersey, looking across at Birkenhead which is on the Wirral peninsula and also now in Merseyside, and there is a coastal strip of Merseyside going up what used to be the Lancashire coast as far as the estuary of the River Ribble. This gives it Southport as its holiday resort with a fine August flower show, six golf courses within its boundaries, and miles of sand where sand yachting is popular.

After Southport, you soon enter Liverpool, the historic seaport on the River Mersey. The busy airport at Speke is some miles outside the city. One of the most important commercial cities in England, it has first-class shopping. In its heyday it was a terminal for the Cunard and White Star liners which took emigrants to America and the Commonwealth, and brought in immigrants from all over, particularly Ireland. Many of these got no further than Liverpool and formed the nucleus of the cosmopolitan society which still flourishes in this rather strange city—strange because today it displays all the trappings of great former wealth while experiencing extremes of poverty. It is, too, unique in possessing two new cathedrals standing almost in sight of each other and no more than half-a-mile apart.

The Anglican cathedral, started in 1904 and eventually completed in 1978, was designed in a modern Gothic style by Sir Giles Gilbert Scott and built in red sandstone. It is the biggest cathedral in Britain. Fortunately for everyone, the Roman Catholics' dream of producing something to compete with St. Peter's in Rome had to be discarded, and instead they have a strictly modern, circular building of enormous appeal, with a lantern tower containing stained glass by John Piper and Patrick Reyntiens. The building was designed by Sir Frederick Gibberd in 1960 and completed in seven years. In 1982, when Pope John Paul II made the first-ever visit of a pope to Britain, he was a guest speaker at the Anglican cathedral, then progressed up the street to the Catholic one to say mass—a deeply symbolic act.

Liverpool gave birth to The Beatles, four young men who revolutionized both pop music and the life-style of the young in the 1960s; ask at the Tourist Information Centre about guided tours around Beatles landmarks. The highly impressive Graeco-Roman edifice, St. George's Hall, completed in 1854, was designed by Lonsdale Elmes who at the time was only 24. The Queensway tunnel beneath the Mersey was, at nearly 3 miles, the longest underwater road when it was opened in 1934. A second tunnel, The Kingsway, 5½ miles, was opened in 1971. Yet another instance of Liverpool's innovative spirit was the huge International Garden Festival held in 1984. Half the site, formerly wasteland, beside the Mersey, remains as a public park.

Meanwhile, Liverpool is not short of culture. The Walker Art Gallery, which has an enormous collection of paintings, was the gift of Sir Andrew Barclay Walker, Lord Mayor in 1873. The Merseyside Maritime Museum recalls the city's great seafaring days and has an "Emigrants to the New World" section. Speke Hall, built between 1490 and 1610 escaped the doubtful attentions of later centuries and is now thought to be one of the best examples of its period in existence. Its furnishings are mostly those of Richard Watt who owned the house in the late 18th century. For entertainment there are two good theaters which have top visiting companies, a repertory theater and nightclubs. The Liverpool Philharmonic Orchestra gives regular concerts in the city.

Just outside Liverpool, and readily accessible by train (to Bebington), is the suburb of Port Sunlight, a model village built by the soap tycoon Lord Lever at the turn of the century for his workers, and the increasingly popular Lady Lever Art Gallery. The gallery contains many fine English 18th- and 19th-century paintings and *objets d'art.*

Manchester

Despite its rather darkened reputation, Manchester has a great deal to offer the visitor. The Opera House has been restored to its former glory

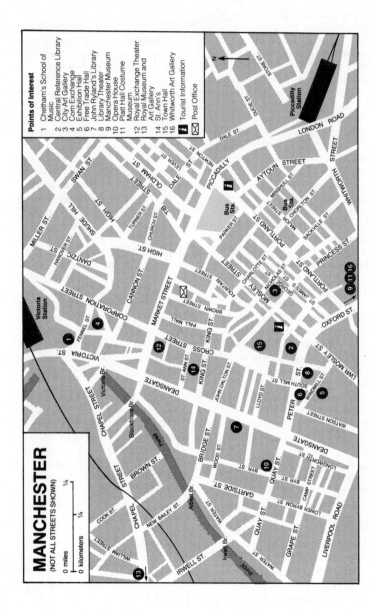

MANCHESTER
(NOT ALL STREETS SHOWN)

0 miles   ¼
0 kilometers   ¼

Points of Interest

1 Chetham's School of
   Music
2 Central Reference Library
3 City Art Gallery
4 Corn Exchange
5 Exhibition Hall
6 Free Trade Hall
7 John Ryland's Library
8 Library Theater
9 Manchester Museum
10 Opera House
11 Platt Hall Costume
   Museum
12 Royal Exchange Theater
13 Royal Museum and
   Art Gallery
14 St. Ann's
15 Town Hall
16 Whitworth Art Gallery

i Tourist Information
⊠ Post Office

and the exciting theater in the Royal Exchange has proved to be one of the most go-ahead in the country. Manchester is probably best known now for its Free Trade Hall, home of the orchestra founded by Sir Charles Hallé. The present hall is the third, rebuilt in the style of the first after World-War II bombing.

There is the important John Rylands Library in a lovely mock-Gothic masterpiece. John Rylands was a rich weaver whose wife, after his death, spent his money founding a library in 1900. Seventy-two years later it was merged with the Manchester University Library, but remained in its original building. Its collection includes many rare, early volumes. A certain Humphrey Chetham also endowed a library, the first free one in Europe, and it was his money that was responsible for what has become the Chetham School of Music for musically gifted children. Its pupils regularly win international competitions.

Manchester's cathedral is a 15th-century Gothic building with a later tower. Superbly carved pew ends were installed by Bishop Stanley between 1505 and 1510. Another building of great elegance is the Barton Arcade with its pretty glass roof. The city can boast no less than five art galleries besides a Gallery of English Costume.

These are just the surface facts, the tourist statistics as it were. Behind them lies Manchester's reputation, and there the city has been much maligned. The Royal Exchange Theater, in a very real way, symbolizes the change that is slowly coming over the city, for it is built in the very heart of the old cotton Exchange, a great hall that, at the height of its power would see over 9,000 dealers packing the building twice a week to fix world prices. The theater presents some of the best work on view in Britain, in a futuristic, imaginative structure that allows for experiment.

You will notice that the buildings which were once dark and not a little satanic, have been cleaned and now glisten in the sun. Many gems of Victorian architecture and decoration—among them, the Town Hall, designed by Alfred Waterhouse, with murals by Ford Madox Brown, the Art Gallery with its fine collection of Pre-Raphaelites—and older buildings, especially the Old Shambles, with its half-timbered buildings, will provide plenty to see during a walking tour. Visit also the Museum of Science and Industry, much of it devoted to transport, and located appropriately on the site of George Stephenson's pioneering railway line to Liverpool (the world's first passenger station has been preserved as part of the museum). There are further historic links. A certain Henry Royce built his first car in Cooke Street in 1904, two years before he went into partnership with C.S. Rolls. The museum is now part of the innovative Castlefield complex, the country's first urban heritage park, which includes other museums and trails.

WEST YORKSHIRE

Brontë Landscape

North of Manchester and north again of the Calder valley and south of that of the Aire, gaunt hills enclose an area that is classical ground, the district immortalized by the writings of the Brontë sisters. Haworth, a few miles south of Keighley, is the mecca of the Brontë enthusiast—a gray West Yorkshire village that certainly might have passed unobserved throughout the years but for the magnetism of the family that lived in the old parsonage, now the museum of the Brontë Society. Every summer thousands of people toil up the steep main street to visit the hilltop church and the museum, where all too often Brontë enthusiasm stops. Nearby, the old mill town of Hebden Bridge is worth a stop, as is the higher village of Heptonstall.

To understand the real spirit of the Brontë books it is necessary to go farther afield. Even to go as far as the Brontë waterfall and beyond that to the ruined farm of High Withens, said to be the inspiration for *Wuthering Heights,* on the crest of the hills, is to see something of the moors behind, but better still is to cross the watershed to Wycollar, over the Lancashire border, or make that fine walk from Withens to the Hardcastle Crags valley.

East of Keighley are Bradford and Leeds, two of Yorkshire's biggest industrial cities. Bradford, generally regarded as the center of the world's woolen industry, in recent years has seen a great deal of development in the heart of the city, but its roots still lie in the charter granted by King Henry II early in the 13th century. Its interesting buildings include the cathedral and the Town Hall, with its 200-foot-high tower built after the style of Palazzo Vecchio at Florence. St George's Hall houses some good entertainment, as does the refurbished Alhambra Theater which preserves its Edwardian splendor. The National Museum of Photography, Film and Television has a giant cinema and imaginative displays.

Leeds is the largest city in Yorkshire and the fourth largest in England outside London. Much of the center has been redeveloped in the functional, modern style. First-class shops, theaters (including the Leeds City Varieties, the only music hall in the country still presenting weekly bills and dating back some 200 years), and night clubs are abundant. The Grand Theatre attracts most of the top English companies each year. Throughout the season there are symphony and other concerts in the Town Hall. The Opera North also has its home in Leeds.

On the west side of the city are the ruins of Kirkstall Abbey, a Cistercian monastery, and an interesting folk museum, and on the other side of Leeds is the mansion-museum of Temple Newsam, where Lord Darnley, ill-fated husband of Mary, Queen of Scots, was born in 1545. Some miles to the north is Harewood House, the home of the Earl of Harewood, cousin of the Queen.

Leeds possesses some lovely parks, many maintained in almost natural conditions, as at Roundhay, formerly a hunting ground of the Norman barons.

SOUTH YORKSHIRE

The chief city of this county is Sheffield, and the word Sheffield is synonymous with steel and cutlery.

Although Sheffield's history is largely that of her major industries it is of interest that in 1569, the sixth Earl of Shrewsbury became custodian

of the captive Mary, Queen of Scots. For 14 years she languished in Sheffield Castle or in the Turret House, which may still be seen at the Manor
Lodge. Try to see the ancient Cathedral Church of St Peter and St Paul,
Church Street, founded early in the 12th century and rebuilt in the 15th.
It has also had modern extensions added, consisting of a tower and lantern, and new glass-and-steel doors. There are also stained-glass windows
by Christopher Webb. Another feature of Sheffield, which must be unique,
is a walk all round the city—10 miles solely over public property, i.e.
through the city's parks. Do not miss the City Museum, in Weston Park
near the University, where the collection of cutlery dates from the 16th
century, and there is, besides, a huge display of Sheffield plate—sheet copper with a silver coating, a cheap Victorian substitute for solid silver. The
Sheffield Industrial Museum, on the historic man-made Kelham Island
site, is also worth a visit. The museum contains artifacts made in Sheffield
over the past 300 years—iron and steel products, silverware and mother-
of-pearl. There is a 12,000 horsepower steam engine still working, and
workshops where traditional crafts and trades are practiced.

   Towards the edge of South Yorkshire are two small places of interest.
The first, Tickhill, has remained a village, although in the middle of a mining area. It once had an extremely important castle, of which some ruins
remain. The second village is Austerfield, right on the border with Humberside, and birthplace of William Bradford who, as doubtless every
American tourist will know, was a Pilgrim Father who sailed in the Mayflower. He was a member of the Brownists, an extreme Puritan group.
Austerfield Manor, where he was born, is a two-story Tudor house. Part
of the village church was rebuilt in 1897 by the Society of Mayflower Descendants.

HUMBERSIDE

   Humberside is another new county carved out of Lincolnshire, on the
south of the Humber, and out of the East Riding of Yorkshire on the north
side. In 1981, at long, long last, the great £80-million Humber Bridge was
finally opened. No one who visits Hull is likely to escape the controversy
that the expensive bridge building aroused.

   Hull, the third of the great ports of England is, alas, not thriving as it
was, but it still has much of historic interest, including Holy Trinity
church, a very early brick building. Wilberforce House is a Jacobean building, where the famous abolitionist was born in 1759. It is now a museum
with relics of Wilberforce himself as well as other historical material, costumes and silver. The garden is delightful. And then there is the Town
Docks Museum, on Queen Victoria Square, where there is also a plaque
marking the spot from which Defoe's Robinson Crusoe set sail.

   From Hull there is easy access to the coast—Withersea, Hornsea (setting of the North Holderness Museum of Village Life, housed in a small
farmhouse), Bridlington—while just north of the city is the noted racing
town of Beverley, once the capital of East Riding. The Minster here is
one of the finest Gothic churches in the whole of Europe. Here, too, is
the beautiful church of St. Mary, with a fine façade, some excellent wood
carving, and a painted ceiling depicting 40 of the kings of England.

Four other notable historic houses that should be visited in Humberside are Burton Constable Hall, Burton Agnes Hall, Epworth Old Rectory and Sledmere House.

Burton Constable Hall, 8 miles northeast of Hull (reached by the B1238 to Sproatley), is an imposing Elizabethan mansion. Its sumptuous rooms contain a superb collection of paintings and furniture, with some fine works by Robert Adam and Chippendale. Other attractions include museums of agricultural machinery and vintage motorcycles, and beautiful grounds around the house.

Burton Agnes Hall, 5 miles southwest of Bridlington on A166, is one of Britain's great Jacobean buildings, dating from the first decade of the 17th century. As it is still lived in by the Boynton family, who have been there since 1654, it has a feeling of comfortable continuity, which extends to the paintings, many of which are fairly recent. Next door is Burton Agnes Old Hall which, while more modest, is also worth seeing while in the vicinity.

Epworth Old Rectory, run by the Trustees of the World Methodist Council, is a mecca for devotees of the Wesleys, since the house is now a memorial to the great founder of Methodism. The place is furnished with period pieces, much of it donated by American Methodists.

Sledmere House is another kettle of fish entirely from the simple Epworth Old Rectory. Although it has been beset by fire and the selling-off of some of its treasures—including a Gutenberg Bible that once belonged to Cardinal Mazarin, now in New York's Metropolitan Museum—Sledmere survived, to show off its rebuilt and refurbished Adam glories. Perhaps the most striking of the many striking rooms is the great library.

PRACTICAL INFORMATION FOR
THE INDUSTRIAL CENTER

HOW TO GET THERE FROM LONDON. Not entirely easy for this region, but as there are quite a lot of express-type trains—especially the InterCity ones—with good planning you should manage a day's trip. It will mean an early start, of course, and a late return.

Haworth. By train: the Brontë Country—combines modern rail travel with a glimpse of the past. Leave London King's Cross on the 8.50 departure to Leeds. At Leeds transfer to the local train for the mill town of Keighley. Here you join the Keighley & Worth Valley train for the climb to Haworth, which is reached at 12.30—just in time for a quick look around before a pub lunch! After lunch there is ample time for sightseeing before the steam train leaves Haworth at 4.10 to return you to British Rail at Keighley. Then you board the local train to Leeds to arrive at around 5.25, in good time for the express train to London which pulls out at 5.45, and returns you to base at 8.16. The train has full restaurant car facilities with a good—though expensive—standard. Note that this entire journey is based on the current Monday through Friday steam train service, which only runs in July and August. However, the service also operates, though at different times, on Saturdays and Sundays from March to October. For further details, call (0535) 43629 or 45214. **By coach:** not possible to make the round trip in one day, though there is a twice-daily service from London (Victoria) to Keighley, and a special 3-day coach tour to the Brontë Country.

Leeds. By train: a good range of through trains—one per hour—from London King's Cross enables Leeds to be visited for a day. The journey time for the 185 miles is around 2 hours 20 minutes. **By coach:** can be visited in a day by a dedicated traveler. First departure of the day at 8.30 (Rapide service) from London Victoria giving over 6 hours sightseeing. Journey time 3 hours 40 minutes. **By car:** too far for a day trip.

Liverpool. By train: well-served by rail from London Euston—but note that the trains do not depart at regular intervals. The journey time is upwards of 2 hours 40 minutes by electric train. All trains have on-train catering (some are high-standard Pullmans), many offering a full restaurant service. **By coach:** a good service from Victoria Coach station by National Express with six daily Rapide journeys. The 9.00 departure makes a day trip possible for the really dedicated (with 4½ hours sightseeing). **By car:** M1, M6, M62.

Manchester. By train: an excellent service of one through express train per hour from London Euston—journey time around 2 hours 56 minutes. All trains have on board catering, including some Pullman services. **By coach:** a useful service of six Rapide coaches a day, journey time 4 hours. The 9.30 from Victoria allows up to 4½ hours sightseeing. **By car:** M1, M6, M62.

Sheffield. By train: connected to London St. Pancras by a good service of one train per hour (most hours). All are high-speed and have reduced the journey time to 2 hours 15 minutes for the fastest service. **By coach:** an excellent two-hourly service of Rapide coaches by National Express from London Victoria coach station, which take 3 hours 20 minutes for the trip. The 9.00 departure makes a day excursion possible. **By car:** M1, A57.

HOTELS AND RESTAURANTS. Wherever you eat or stay will almost certainly reflect the well-known warmth and friendliness that is the trademark of this region. Whether you are in the heart of an industrial city or in a quiet coal-mining village, you will never be far from some of the most attractive and memorable scenery anywhere in Britain.

Birtle (Gtr. Manchester). *Normandie* (M), Elbut Lane, tel. (061) 764 3869. 20 rooms. Well-run family establishment with one of the best restaurants in the area, serving French specialties. Highly recommended. Closed Sun.

Bradford (W. Yorks.). *Stakis Norfolk Gardens* (E), Hall Ings, tel. (0274) 734734; 123 rooms with bath. Central, modern, and with a certain amount of renovation.

Restaurant. *Restaurant Nineteen* (E–M), 19 North Park Rd., tel. (0274)
492559. Subtle cooking and superb service. Booking essential. Closed Sun.
and Mon. 10 rooms also available.

Halifax (W. Yorks.). *Holdsworth House* (M), Holmfield, tel. (0422)
240024; 40 rooms, 28 with bath, 12 with shower. 17th-century country
house in beautiful grounds. Elegant Geogian restaurant (E), serving English regional dishes and game specialties. Closed for lunch Sat. and Sun.
Restaurant. At **Ripponden**. *Over the Bridge* (M), Millfold, tel. (0422)
823722. Attractive, beautifully presented English and French food. Best
to book. Closed Sun.

Huddersfield (W. Yorks.). **Restaurant.** *Weavers Shed* (M), Knowl
Rd., Golcar, tel. (0484) 654284. Good English cooking in converted 18th-
century mill. Closed Sat. lunchtime, Sun. evening and all Mon.

Hull (Humb.). *Waterfront* (M), Dagger Lane, Old Town tel. (0482)
227222; 32 rooms, 25 with bath or shower. Dockside hotel, once a warehouse, with many original features, including attractive loft rooms with
views.
At **Beverley**. *Beverley Arms* (E), North Bar Within, tel. (0482) 869241.
61 rooms, all with bath. Comfortable, historic hotel.
At **Little Weighton**. *Rowley Manor* (M), tel. (0482) 848248. 16 rooms,
12 with bath. Georgian house in parkland. Some four-poster beds.

Ilkley (W. Yorks.). *Craiglands* (M), Cowpasture Rd., tel. (0943)
607676; 73 rooms, 53 with bath, 5 with shower. On lkley Moor with super
views.
Restaurant. *Box Tree* (E), Church St., tel. (0943) 608484. Among the
top eating places in the land. Every dish is virtually unsurpassable, soups
and game particularly fine, wine list impressive. Advance reservations essential. Closed Sun. and Mon.

Kildwick (W. Yorks.). *Kildwick Hall* (E), tel. Crosshills (0535) 32244;
14 rooms with bath. Creeper-covered Jacobean manor house overlooking
Aire valley. Atmospheric period decor. Also has magnificent restaurant,
the *Candle Lite Room,* with chandeliers and ancient portraits; serves excellent continental cuisine and good wines.

Leeds (W. Yorks.). *Ladbroke Dragonara* (E), Neville St., tel. (0532)
442000; 230 rooms with bath. Businessmen's hotel; cabaret twice a week.
Merrion (M), Merrion Center, tel. (0532) 439191; 120 rooms with bath.
Metropole (M), King St., tel. (0532) 450841; 113 rooms, 77 with bath. Both
modern and dependable. *Queen's* (M), City Sq., tel. (0532) 431323; 198
rooms with bath. Central, next to station, sauna.
Restaurants. *Gardini's La Terrazza* (M), 16 Greek St., tel. (0532)
432880. Is worth a visit for its interesting Italian menu (same group as
the London Terrazzas). For less expensive fare try *Rules* (M), Selby Rd.,
tel. (0532) 604564. Pleasant restaurant serving continental cuisine.
At **Guisely**. *Harry Ramsden's* (I), White Cross, tel. (0943) 74641. *The*
fish and chip restaurant—an institution. Plush surroundings for a simple
meal.

Liverpool *Atlantic Tower Thistle* (E), Chapel St., tel. (051) 227 4444; 226 rooms with bath, very modern. *Britannia Adelphi* (M), Ranelagh Place, tel. (051) 709 7200; 344 rooms, 314 with bath. One of England's famous hotels, but choose your room carefully. Heated pool, sauna and squash.

Restaurant. *Jenny's Seafood* (M), Old Ropery, Fenwick St. tel. (051) 236 0332. An excellent spot for seafood dishes. Closed Sun., Sat. lunch, Mon. evening.

Manchester. *Portland Thistle* (L), Portland St., tel. (061) 228 3400; 219 rooms with bath. Central and welcoming, with good restaurant (open Sun.). *Holiday Inn Crowne Plaza Midland* (L–E), tel. (061) 236 3333; 303 rooms with bath. Famous hotel (previously known simply as the Midland). Extensively refurbished and should live up to its new extravagant name. *Britannia* (E), Portland St., tel. (061) 228 2288; 360 rooms, all with bath or shower. Imaginately-converted 19th-century warehouse with 6-story gilded staircase; central, with pool, turkish bath, bistro.

Restaurants. *Sam's Chop House* (M), Blackpool Fold, tel. (061) 834 1526; for solid sensible fare. *Terrazza* (M), 14 Nicholas St., tel. (061) 236 4033. Excellent Italian dishes, one of chain. Closed Sun. *Yang Sing* (M), 34 Princess St., tel. (061) 236 2200. Popular basement restaurant serving excellent Cantonese food (there's quite a Chinese colony in Manchester). Can be crowded, so be sure to book.

Monk Fryston (N. Yorks.). *Monk Fryston Hall* (M), tel. (0977) 682369; 29 rooms with bath. Originally a medieval house. Spacious grounds and ornamental gardens.

Pool-in-Wharfdale (W. Yorks.). **Restaurant.** *Pool Court* (E), tel. (0532) 842288. Excellent restaurant with original, successful food, and a magnificent winelist. Also 4 rooms.

Sheffield (S. Yorks.). *Grosvenor House* (E), Charter Sq., tel. (0742) 720041. 103 rooms with bath. *Hallam Tower Post House* (M), Manchester Rd., tel. (0742) 670067. 135 rooms with bath. Both are Trust House Forte.

Restaurant. Good restaurant at the *Crucible Theater* (I), tel. (0742) 760621. Closed Sun.

Wentbridge (W. Yorks.). *Wentbridge House* (M), Great North Rd., tel. (0977) 620444. 20 rooms, 17 with bath. Fine 17th-century house in quiet grounds. French restaurant.

PLACES OF INTEREST. There's a lot of civic pride around Manchester and Liverpool, in spite of their unemployment. Both have interesting historic houses and fine museums.

Humberside. Burton Agnes Hall, near Bridlington (tel. 0262 89 324). Fine Elizabethan country house with large collection of antique furniture, and Impressionist and modern paintings. Open April–Oct., daily 11–5.

Burton Constable Hall, Sproatley (tel. 0964 562400). Elizabethan house with fine collection of furniture, paintings, porcelain, tapestries. Open July

and Aug., Sun.–Thurs. 1–5.30; Apr., May, June, and Sept., Sun. and Bank
Holiday Mon. only, 1–5.30. Grounds open at noon.

Epworth, The Old Rectory (tel. 8427 872268). Home of the Wesleys
and a Methodist place of pilgrimage. March–Oct., daily, 10–12, 2–4, Sun.,
2–4.

Normanby Hall, Scunthorpe (tel. i0724 720215). Regency mansion furnished in period. Rooms with static models in period dress. Gardens, deer
and country park, craft and countryside center. Hall open Easter–Oct.,
Mon.–Fri. 11–5, Sun. 2–5; rest of year by appointment. Park open daily
throughout year.

Sledmore House, Driffield (tel. 0377 86208). Grand Georgian house
with furniture, paintings, fine library, gardens by Capability Brown. Outstandingly beautiful interior. Open Easter, then all Sun. to May; then daily
(except Mon. and Fri.) to late Sept. (inc. Bank Holidays); also Sun. in Oct.,
all 1.30–5.30.

Wilberforce House, 23–25 High St., Hull (tel. 0482 222737). Birthplace
of the slave emancipator, plus collections of furniture, silver and costume.
Open Mon.–Sat. 10–5, Sun. 1.30–4.30.

Greater Manchester. Castlefield, (tel. 061 832 2244). Britain's first
urban heritage park, comprising Museum of Science and Industry; Air
and Space Museum; Roman Fort; transportation history and heritage
trails. Museums open daily, 10–5, (last admission 4.30).

Manchester City Art Gallery, Mosley St., Manchester 2 (tel. 061 236
9422). English and French paintings. Fine collections of Stubbs, pre-
Raphaelites, Henry Moore. Open Mon.–Sat., 10–6, Sun. 2–6.

Manchester Museum, University, Oxford Road, Manchester (tel. 061
273 3333). University-based museum, specially noted for its superbly displayed Egyptian collections. Winner of the *1987 Museum of the Year*
award. Open Mon.–Sat., 10–5.

Salford Art Gallery and Museum, Peel Park, Salford (tel. 061 736
2649). Mainly 19th- and 20th-cent. paintings, notably a large collection
by famous local artist L.S. Lowry. Museum has a full-scale reproduction
of an old street. Open Mon.–Fri., 10–5; Sun. 2–5.

Whitworth Art Gallery, Oxford Road (tel. 273 4865). Small, impressive
gallery; English watercolors, modern art and textiles. Also Japanese, Spanish, Italian, Peruvian and Near Eastern artifacts. Open Mon.–Sat., 10–5,
Thurs. 10-9.

Merseyside. Lady Lever Art Gallery, Port Sunlight Village (tel. 051
645 3623). Outstanding collection of porcelain, furniture and paintings.
Open Mon.–Sat. 10–5, Sun. 2–5.

Merseyside Maritime Museum, Pier Head, Liverpool (tel. 051 709
1551). Liverpool's great days as a thriving seaport remembered; includes
a new "Emigrants to the New World" exhibition. Located right on the
waterfront. Open daily 10.30–5.30.

Pilkington Glass Museum, St. Helens (tel. 0744 692014). Evolution of
glassmaking techniques in a town famous for the product. Open
Mon.–Fri., 10–5 (Wed., Mar.–Oct., 10–9), Sat., Sun., Bank Holidays,
2–4.30.

Speke Hall, Liverpool (tel. 051 427 7231). Opulent half-timbered Tudor
house with rich interior decoration, carving and plasterwork. Open

Apr.–end Oct., daily (except Mon.); Tues.–Sat. 1–5.30, Sun. and Bank Holiday Mon. 12–6. Nov.-late Dec., Sat. and Sun. 1–5. (NT)

West Yorkshire. Armley Mills, Canal Rd., Armley near Leeds (tel. 0532 637861). The world's largest woolen mill, in unique 19th-century fireproof building on island in the River Aire. Machinery, locomotives, water wheel, etc. Open Apr.–Sept., Tues.–Sat. 10–6; Sun., 2–6. Oct.–Mar., Tues.–Sat., 10–5, Sun., 2–5.

Brontë Parsonage, Haworth (tel. 0535 42323). Shrine of the Brontë family. All year, daily, 11–5.30 (winter, 11–4.30).

Harewood House and Bird Garden, Leeds (tel. 0532 886225). 18th-century home of the Earls of Harewood, with Chippendale furniture. Exotic bird garden in grounds. Open April–Oct., daily. Grounds at 10, House at 11. Limited opening Nov., Feb., Mar., on Sun.

National Museum of Photography, Film and Television, Bradford (tel. 0274 727488). Marvelous new museum which explores all aspects of TV and photography; has Britain's biggest cinema screen. Open daily (except Mon.), 11–7.30.

Nostell Prior, near Wakefield (tel. 0924 863892). Mid-18th-century house, Palladian with lots of Adam work. Open Apr., May, June, Sept. and Oct., Sat. 12–5, Sun. 11–5; July and Aug., daily (except Fri.), 12–5, Sun. 11–5; also open Bank Holiday Mon. and most following Tues. (NT)

Temple Newsam, Leeds. Tudor-Jacobean house, birthplace of Lord Darnley. Rather a mishmash of styles inside, but houses part of the Leeds Museum collections. Open daily all year except Mon. (unless Bank Holiday Mon.), 10.30–6.15 (dusk if earlier).

THE NORTHEAST

Abbeys, Romans and Raiding Scots

It would be unthinkable to visit North Yorkshire without going first to the atmospheric cathedral city of York. Its central location makes it a practical place to start, and it is easily reached by car on the M1 or A1, or by rail to an imposing station outside the city walls. It would take a fat guidebook in itself to do justice to York. Encircled by a three-mile ring of massive walls of creamy-colored stone (you can walk almost around York on them), it is the most completely medieval of all English cities. During the great industrial age, which caused so much havoc in many northern towns and cities, York was a forgotten backwater—hence the survival of so much medieval and 18th-century architecture. Within the walls, still entered by ancient fortified gateways known as "Bars," lies a web of narrow thoroughfares, all leaning gables and crooked timbers, such as Stonegate and The Shambles, the latter an incomparable example of a medieval street built between 1350 and 1450. And at the heart of this maze, dominating the city, stands the biggest medieval cathedral in northern Europe, York Minster.

This vast Gothic cathedral attracts almost as many visitors as London's Westminster Abbey. Inside, the effect created by its soaring pillars, lofty vaulted ceilings and dazzling stained glass windows is quite overpowering. Sadly, the cathedral was damaged by fire in 1984, though not as badly as was initially feared. The damage, which will be fully repaired within the next few years, was mostly confined to the South Transept, and the cathedral is almost entirely open to the public. The Minster's greatest

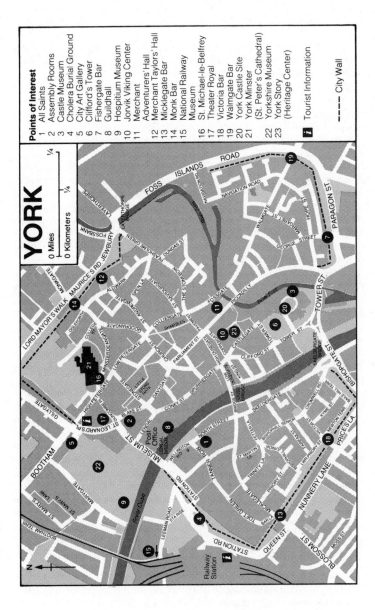

YORK

0 Miles ¼

0 Kilometers ¼

Points of Interest

1 All Saints
2 Assembly Rooms
3 Castle Museum
4 Cholera Burial Ground
5 City Art Gallery
6 Clifford's Tower
7 Fishergate Bar
8 Guildhall
9 Hospitium Museum
10 Jorvik Viking Center
11 Merchant
   Adventurers' Hall
12 Merchant Taylors' Hall
13 Micklegate Bar
14 Monk Bar
15 National Railway
   Museum
16 St. Michael-le-Belfrey
17 Theater Royal
18 Victoria Bar
19 Walmgate Bar
20 York Castle Site
21 York Minster
   (St. Peter's Cathedral)
22 Yorkshire Museum
23 York Story
   (Heritage Center)

i Tourist Information

- - - - - City Wall

glory is its medieval windows in stained glass, glowing with deep wine reds and cobalt blues. Only Chartres Cathedral in France is greater. For a small fee, you can visit the Undercroft where there are substantial Roman remains and ingenious underpinning which saved the central tower from collapse.

Back in the streets, history puts in an appearance around almost every corner. The fine Assembly Rooms, 17th-century Treasurer's House, half-timbered 14th-century Merchant Adventurers' Hall, red-brick Georgian Fairfax House and Judge's Lodging (now a fine hotel) are just some of the many buildings that reflect York's past prosperity as a port, trading center and fashionable place of society. And if that is not enough, the city is also endowed with some of the best museums in the land.

Start at the former Church of St. Mary, converted in 1975 into a museum which tells "The York Story." Then move on to the Castle Museum, housed within a former prison. This award-winning museum merits a visit of many hours. An entire Victorian cobbled street, complete with police station, coaching house, cobbler's and saddler's shops has been re-created in vivid detail within this endlessly fascinating and wide-ranging museum. Amongst its contents are period costumes, a "Coronation Room" depicting a typical working class household at the time of Queen Elizabeth's coronation in 1953, and an exhibition which explains the evolution of the domestic vacuum cleaner!

The Yorkshire Museum has also won awards for its displays of Roman, Anglo-Saxon, Viking and medieval treasures. Railway enthusiasts from all over the world travel to York's National Railway Museum, located a little way outside the city center. The museum's huge main hall, presided over by a statue of George Stephenson, father of "The Age of Steam," contains full-sized locomotives and rolling stock which chart the evolution of the train from earliest times to the experimental vehicles of tomorrow. Yet another museum worth visiting is the Yorkshire Museum of Farming set in a country park three miles from the city.

York's latest attraction, the Jorvik Viking Center, is to be found below ground, beneath the attractive new Coppergate shopping complex. In the 9th and 10th centuries, York was an important Viking stronghold. Excavations beneath Coppergate unearthed a wealth of artifacts, miraculously preserved in the wet, marshy soil, which revealed how the Vikings lived and worked. These form the basis of a "time car" ride on an electric-powered buggy through a Viking settlement with its market place, wharf, smoky houses and workshops, all re-created in painstaking detail and accompanied by the sounds—and smells—of the messy inhabitants. From here, the time car moves through the actual excavations, many items from which are on display in an adjoining hall.

Castle Howard

From York, the Yorkshire coast calls, and there is a good road, A64, across to Scarborough, and one or two small diversions on the way could prove very rewarding. About eight miles out of York and then four miles up a side road is Sheriff Hutton, with the ruins of a massive, five-storey 14th-century castle, and a medieval church containing a number of historically interesting monuments. A few miles from that is the beautiful Castle Howard, the largest house in Yorkshire. It was the first effort at designing by Sir John Vanbrugh, better known as a late 17th-century playwright. His second effort was Blenheim Palace. He had the good sense to form a partnership with Nicholas Hawksmoor, one time clerk to Wren. Castle Howard took thirty-seven years to build, and by that time the third Earl of Carlisle who had commissioned it, Vanbrugh and Hawksmoor were all dead. Besides all the riches one would expect in such a house, there is also a costume museum. Castle Howard will be familiar to TV addicts who have seen Evelyn Waugh's *Brideshead Revisited,* which was filmed here. If you have the time—and energy—take a walk in the grounds to see the Tower of the Winds and the fine Mausoleum.

Rejoining the A64, you will be just opposite the road to Kirkham Abbey, well worth a visit if only for its lovely setting on the River Derwent. But there is more to it than that.

The Coast

Scarborough combines the appeal of a typical North Country resort with much of historic interest. A ruined castle perches on the summit of a rocky headland, beneath which a fine marine drive joins the two bays, and opposite the busy harbor is the 15th-century Richard III House. The south bay has lovely cliff gardens and clifftop walks. Northwards, the paths pass small rough bays. The roads are more inland, but whether one goes by road or path, Robin Hood's Bay, a crazy collection of cottages crammed together in a little declivity of the cliffs, should not be missed.

Whitby is one of the glories of the Yorkshire coast. The River Esk comes down a long glen-like ravine cut through the moors and makes a natural harbor of great beauty. Above it, on either side, red-roofed buildings rise tier upon tier. On top of the cliff is St Mary's Church reached—if you have the stamina—by 199 steps. It is a seaman's church if ever there was one, with fat box pews, pillars resembling ships' masts, painted biblical texts on the walls. The nearby Abbey was built on the site of the original Abbey of St. Hilda where Caedmon, a local herdsman, was miraculously inspired to become the father of English Sacred Song. The Caedmon Cross, named for him, intricately carved with birds and wild creatures, stands by the church steps.

It was this view of the church and abbey that inspired author Bram Stoker to write his most famous story—*Dracula.* No need to go to Transylvania for his setting; he found it where he was staying, right in Victorian Whitby. Today's Whitby has not been slow to profit from the association. A local leaflet, *The Whitby Dracula Trail,* starts the visitor from the Bram Stoker Memorial Seat on West Cliff, follows heroines Mina and Lucy on their dangerous moonlight wanderings, takes in the old disused railway sidings where Dracula left for London in one of his collection of wooden coffins, the Abbey and the church graveyard; and so—safe and sound, you hope—back to base. There's even a Dracula Experience museum here now.

An interesting view of both church and Abbey can be seen through the huge arch on the sea-front, composed of the jaws of whalebone, highly suitable since Whitby has a long history of seafaring, and was once a whaling and jet-jewelry town. The famous explorer, Captain Cook, lived in a house near the harbor, and made his first voyages in Whitby-built ships.

North York Moors National Park

The words North York Moors provoke a vision of somewhat bitter, near-Siberian remoteness. The truth is a revelation. These northern moors which start almost immediately behind the coastal strip—from Scarborough in the south to Staithes in the north—form one of Britain's oldest National Parks, their 550-or-so square miles embracing not only wild, high moorland, but a scattering of picturesque market towns, small villages of remarkable charm, and historic abbeys and castles all the more romantic for their often ruinous state.

Entirely unsuspected is the sharply contrasting scenery: stone-walled farmsteads, massed trees shading the many lanes and masking the lower slopes. And, below the wilder heather and bracken-covered moorland, wind more dales than it seems possible to count.

Even the remoteness is relative. Suddenly, round the next bend in a lane that seems to lead nowhere, there stands an imposing church, a tall monastery, a stately mansion. In the south-western corner of the National Park, below the Hambleton Hills, villages and abbeys lurk in wooded corners or beside deep river valleys, each with a claim on the visitor's time. The market town of Helmsley, for instance, in Ryedale, is easily reached by the main road from the coast at Scarborough, skirting the southern edge of the moors. It is dominated by its ruined Norman castle; and though the Church of All Saints was heavily renovated in the 19th century, inside there are still fascinating survivals of its early medieval beginnings. A few miles southwest, near the miniature village of Wass, are more ruins: the 12th-century Byland Abbey, where patches of beautifully glazed and colored tiles that once paved almost the entire floor in geometric patterns are carefully preserved.

But it is Rievaulx—pronounced *Reevo*—Abbey which is considered to be not only the finest in Yorkshire, but in all England, a claim shared with some justification by other abbeys such as Fountains, near Ripon. Indeed, whether glimpsed from the high terrace above or closer to, beside the River Rye, it has an ageless, jewel-like fascination. Perhaps the best way to approach Rievaulx is gradually, starting from the wide grassy terrace high above, then descending slowly to reach the Abbey.

The village of Coxwold, south of the main Thirsk to Pickering road, is notable for two historic buildings: Shandy Hall, home of the Reverend Lawrence Sterne, author of *Tristram Shandy;* and St. Michael's Church with its surprising octagonal tower, and where Sterne—when he remembered—preached with fine eccentricity. He is buried in the graveyard by the south wall of the nave. Another famous, but in this case unproven nearby burial site, is that of Oliver Cromwell whose body is reputed to be interred in Newburgh Priory.

Eastwards, beyond Bilsdale and Bransdale and Farndale, at the southern end of Rosedale, is the substantial market town of Pickering, complete with Norman castle, and an extensive market place which fills the site of the original village green. The fine church of St. Peter and St. Paul contains an amazing spread of 15th-century wall frescos, accidentally discovered during restoration. Here, too, is the southern terminus of one of the longest privately-owned steam and diesel railways, running throughout the season (early April to end October) to Grosmont, 18 miles north, where it connects with the main British Rail line to Darlington, Middlesbrough and Whitby. At the Pickering end of the line there's a good bookshop and information center; and at the Grosmont end, visitors can see the old Engine Shed and Viewing Gallery. The ride is a rewarding one, through the heart of the Moors National Park at a speed never more than 25 m.p.h., allowing you time to read the names of the stations, and to spot the "golf balls" of the huge Fylingdale Early Warning system on the horizon.

Anyone interested in England's Roman remains, will find a section of slabbed road which runs northeast from ancient camp-sites at Cawthorn, over the Pickering and Wheeldale Moors. A preserved mile of the road is remarkably clear—rough stones overlaying gravel, ditched along the sides. It winds in long bends on either side of a bumpy, just about motorable track, signposted from Egton Bridge, inland from Whitby, and turning off the A171 to Egton. It's a lonely spot—just you and the sheep.

The best of this fascinating countryside can only be seen by walking, and the Park authorities give endless encouragement by the production of leaflets giving details of waymarked routes, guided treks, and information on what to look for on the way. One such walk is from the Dalby Forest Drive, a few miles northeast of Pickering. The starting point is signposted from the car park, from where a snaking path leads upwards to a high ridge where a surprise is in store: The Bridestones—batches of enormous rocks weathered over the centuries into curious, comic shapes. The path continues, dropping down to a bright little stream, over it, and then following its sparkling course through gentle Dovedale, and so back to Staindale Wood and the entrance car park. It's a fine-day walk, ideal for loitering and for camera shots.

Harrogate and The Dales

Moving westwards, either through a series of baffling little roads or doing it the easy way via York on A19 and the A59 (take the signed short cut from one to the other if you want to get through York in less than half-an-hour)—you reach Harrogate, passing on the way through the ancient town of Knaresborough. Here the River Nidd flows through a wide ravine and past the cliff crowned by the ruins of Knaresborough Castle with its grim traditions emphasized by the equally grim dungeons that remain. Two unusual sights are Mother Shipton's Wishing Well, and the Dropping Well, whose dripping waters have petrifying properties that will turn to stone any object placed beneath them.

Before leaving Nidderdale, there is a short worthwhile excursion to another Yorkshire curiosity. From Pateley Bridge, a narrow road leads northwards via the Gouthwaite Reservoir which has all the attributes of a natural lake. Nearby is a tract of National Trust land filled with the most extraordinary volcanic-looking upheavals known as Brimham Rocks, one of the strangest areas imaginable and one of the funniest. Great rock stacks poke up in pinnacles or loll about in grotesque attitudes, looking like ragged mushrooms, giant profiles, even pieces of furniture. It is a landscape which cries out for a camera.

Harrogate, just north of Leeds, between the River Nidd and the forest of Knaresborough, makes a pleasant base for exploring the nearby countryside. It has been a health resort for centuries, due to its mineral springs and its healthy air. It is also one of England's finest floral towns, with numerous decorative parks and gardens, and as a year-round resort it provides such diverse entertainment as music and drama festivals, French Week, and the Great Yorkshire Agricultural Show. As the town's spa activities decline, its popularity as a conference center increases.

Twenty-two miles west from Harrogate along the A59, Skipton stands in a pleasant green setting on the River Aire and a canal. It has a particularly well-preserved castle which has links with Bolton Abbey, about five miles back along the road, where it crosses Wharfedale. Bolton Abbey is always known as an abbey, but in fact is a priory. It dates from 1151, although there was an Anglo-Saxon manor there before that. Its architectural beauty goes hand in hand with loveliness of setting; and from here there are roads (B6160 is best) and riverside paths through the woods to Burnsall, considered by many as the loveliest of Wharfedale villages, standing peaceful and undisturbed beside its spacious green.

Grassington, farther north and just off the B6160, a place ancient in both architecture and setting, marks the entry into wilder scenes, and from here the road continues through Kilnsey (clustered under a great bulge of limestone overhanging cottages and dales), Kettlewell and Buckden, beyond which the Wharfe comes dancing down a narrow mountain-girt valley until, with the river now a series of silver tributaries, only the great fells remain in all their glory.

The Dales have yet another curiosity to surprise the visitor. There are several prescribed routes to reach Malham Cove; it lies north of Skipton or west of Grassington, but either way there is a walk to reach it, worth any effort for the extraordinary view that gradually comes into sight. In stark grandeur, a near-white stratified limestone cliff curves in the shape of a giant amphitheater, rising to a rugged 300 feet, and extending to a length of 900 feet or more. Once the river fell in a great cascade over the near-vertical cliff; now it has retreated underground to re-appear trickling gently at paddling depth over the more or less level ground at the foot of the Cove. Nearby is Malham Tarn, a small lake with pretty waterside walks; a building has been converted into a residential study center for students and devotees of natural history.

B6160 comes down from the hills into Wensleydale, surely the best known of all the dales. Go west as far as Hawes, and then onto the B6255 and you will come to Ingleborough, most outstanding of the Yorkshire hills, with a host of caves to visit and, nestling at its foot, Ingleborough Hall, where the great botanist-explorer, the late Reginald Farrer, father of Alpine gardening, laid out a rock garden that is still visited by enthusiasts the world over. Today thousands who have never heard the name Farrer practice the art he invented.

Or, instead of turning west up Wensleydale, go east. The first turning left will lead to Castle Bolton, where Mary, Queen of Scots was held prisoner for a time. In Leyburn, back on the main road, there is a terrace from which can be seen Castle Bolton and Middleham Castle—to which Mary escaped one afternoon—and a splendid view of Wensleydale. Middleham, which is on the A6108 out of Leyburn, is the great castle where Warwick the Kingmaker had his home during the stirring years of the 15th century when England was torn between loyalties to the Houses of Lancaster and York contending for a country's throne. Richard III spent much of his married life here.

Below Middleham is Jervaulx Abbey—pronounced *Jervo*—its decay arrested but not prettied up. It is privately owned but the public is allowed in. The journey downstream to Ripon passes through some of the fairest scenery. St. Wilfred, Bishop of York, who lived in Ripon, built a cathedral there in 670; only his crypt survives, one of the oldest Christian shrines in England. The cathedral was destroyed, rebuilt, added to and "restored" in later centuries. There are many things worth seeing in Ripon, not least the 13th-century Wakeman's House which is now a museum and Tourist Information Center. A wakeman was one paid to see that medieval householders were not robbed at night. If they were, he had to make good their losses.

About three miles south of Ripon, on a side road, stands Newby Hall at Skelton. Newby Hall was built in 1705, but redesigned and enlarged by Robert Adam between 1765 and 1783. The house is notable for its Roman sculptures, tapestries and gardens, 25 acres of them, and is an experience for those with a taste for history.

Yet another fine example of England's heritage is Fountains Abbey, its truly wonderful ruins standing picturesquely in the valley of the River Skell, four miles southwest of Ripon. William Aislabie, owner of the adjoining estate of Studley Royal, acquired the abbey ruins in 1768.

Now administered by the National Trust, the glorious Abbey itself is part of a great complex which includes other historic buildings such as the Jacobean Fountains Hall and the Victorian Church of St. Mary, as well as the 400-acre deer park, woodland, lakes and gardens of Studley Royal. Incidentally, Friar Tuck is said to have come from Fountains Abbey and to have met Robin by River Skell. Marked there for all to see, is Robin Hood's well.

From Ripon it is an easy trip up the A1 to the cross roads and Catterick whence B6271 leads to Richmond, one of the finest of all North Country towns, with its castle standing on the brink of a great cliff, guarding the entrance to Swaledale. Richmond Castle is one of the noblest examples of medieval fortification in the land, and its keep is generally regarded as being among the most perfect Norman towers in existence. Holy Trinity Church is the only one in England that has shops built into its walls, a reminder of the town's connections with the dukes of Brittany, who introduced much of what was predominantly continental in atmosphere and architecture. The town also boasts one of the oldest and prettiest theaters in the country.

Swaledale, bounded on either side by steep-sided fells and extensive sheep walks, is even wilder than Wensleydale. Here, near the head of the dale, originated one of the hardiest of the black-faced sheep breeds, the Swaledale itself. The villages take on something of the texture of the fells and fit snugly into little pockets looking as though they, like the Pennines, have been here from eternity. All the dales are connected by winding roads going over the moors, climbing maybe to as much as 1,700 ft. They are absolutely breathtaking scenically, but are not designed for the faint-hearted.

NORTHUMBRIA

The creation of new counties under umbrella titles makes little if any difference to visitors to Britain. The boundaries, in effect, are lines on a map and names used in postal addresses—no physical frontiers exist, no barriers to cross, no passports. Information Offices exist throughout the entire region, coping with their own particular county and the region as a whole.

Originally the name "Northumbria" meant "Lands North of the River Humber" when, centuries ago, this region was a strong Anglo-Saxon kingdom. Now the title covers four counties drawn together under the over-all title of "Northumbria": Cleveland, Tyne and Wear, Durham, and Northumberland.

Alike in their numberless historic associations and monuments of a vigorous and often warlike past, in their share of a coastline and their undoubted scenic attractions, they contrast with each other in size—Northumberland is equal to, if not larger than, the other three put together. They also differ in scenery, since the southeast is, in part, monopolized by ports and cities, whereas the north and west, Northumberland in particular, have an attractive emptiness—vast tracts of moorland and hills extending clear to the Scottish border. Again, Northumberland wins in its share of coastal beauty, a shoreline decorated with great castles and off-shore islands.

CLEVELAND AND TYNE & WEAR

These two new counties are another example of the Merseyside-and-Greater-Manchester syndrome. They are areas of enormous industrial, commercial or shipping activity which have annexed most of the country around them and named it after themselves.

Cleveland is actually named after the hills of antiquity which lie along its southern border—but they belong to North Yorkshire, just to confuse the matter. The county of the name consists very largely of Billingham, Thornby-on-Tees, and Middlesbrough, all wrapped about the River Tees, with Redcar out on the coast just south of the river, and Hartlepool with Seaton Carew north of the Tees. Putting it briefly, Billingham is dominated by the chemical industry; Middlesbrough by coal, iron, steel and chemicals; Stockton-on-Tees by ship building and engineering, it still has an enormous twice weekly market dating from 1310, and memories of the first passenger train to steam in from Darlington in 1825. Redcar is a holiday resort for Teesside, and Hartlepool a harbor dating from the 7th century but sadly declined now. There is one seaside resort, Saltburn-by-the-Sea, which has a rather endearing Victorian aspect, but is also somewhat run down. As for the country round about, it is mostly flat with humps—the spoil tips from old mine workings.

Tyne & Wear consists largely of Newcastle upon Tyne, stretching—with Wallsend and Tynemouth—roughly fifteen miles from the Northumberland border to the sea, along the north side of the Tyne, while Blaydon, Gateshead, Felling, Hebburn, Jarrow and South Shields do much the same thing on the south side. In what little scraps of countryside are left, one might manage to find Washington New Town which has been built on and around an old village, and Washington Old Hall, for 400 years until 1613, the home of the George Washington family. So much sweeping away and tidying up has been done in the area that, with its motorway-type roads, it is almost entirely faceless. Some of the rooms are furnished in typical 17th- and 18th-century style, and there are some items of Washington memorabilia. A 100-acre wildfowl reserve, fairly recently established, is nearby. Like everywhere else in the district, it is somewhat nude. But trees have been planted, so one day . . .

Newcastle

Newcastle should not be dismissed as simply a great big commercial complex, however complex its traffic management may be. The fact is it began life as a minor fort at the unfashionable end of Hadrian's Wall. The New Castle was built by the Normans in 1080 in wood, and replaced in stone in 1172, and that really set the pattern for the city—continual growth and improvement. Some bits of these very early buildings survive as relics surrounded by railway lines.

The vestiges of the castle are worth visiting. St. Nicholas church, mainly 14th-century, became a cathedral towards the end of the 19th century. There is also All Saints, in a rare architectural style, art galleries and museums. Museums in this part of the country will yield a lot to interest anybody who wants to know more about the Roman occupation. Finds are being made all the time and they all extend the understanding of this far-flung part of the Roman Empire. One needs really to devote quite a lot of time to Newcastle to get anything out of it. For the evenings there are good theaters and plenty of night life.

DURHAM COUNTY

The two counties of Durham and Northumberland are unusual in that they are very alike. It is quite possible to drive from one to the other without realising that you have done so. Both are very beautiful, and both have one particular specialty. Durham's is the City of Durham; Northumberland's is Hadrian's Wall.

Coming from London on the Great North Road, A1(M), one enters Durham County to by-pass Darlington which seems to have escaped from Cleveland to which it is more suited. The road goes straight up the east side of Durham, keeping a distance of about ten miles from the coast, which is mostly collieries. The country in between is not of much interest to visitors. But on the west side of the road, the County of Durham immediately comes into its own, and on the edge of this, halfway up the county, is Durham city.

The Bastion of Durham

Astride the Wear, the city presents a true bastion to invaders from north to south. Its magnificent Norman cathedral and the castle of the Prince Bishops share the summit of a high, narrow peninsula with steep wooded sides dropping to the River Wear. This is the heart of the ancient city. Around Palace Green are ranged the cathedral, the castle and Bishop Cosin's house and library. The castle is unique among northern fortresses in that it never fell to the Scots. Inhabited for 900 years without a break, it is now a hall of residence for the university, and tourists can stay there, July through September, very inexpensively. The cathedral is a stunningly beautiful edifice, spare and impressive inside, standing on the foundation of the Lindisfarne monks who sought a safe resting place for the body of St. Cuthbert. Note especially the huge bronze sanctuary knocker on the north door. The cathedral museum contains relics of St. Cuthbert dating back to A.D. 698. The city has a quiet, gentle air about it, although it is the county town of a mining region.

A good way to encapsulate Durham County after seeing the city, is to leave it on A690 which goes first to Brancepeth, where there is what Nikolaus Pevsner has described as "one of the most remarkable contributions to English architecture" in St. Brandon's church. It was restored by John Cosin, rector of the church between 1626–44 and later Bishop of Durham, who employed Robert Barker to do the carving, all over the building. The church, considered to be exceptionally good, also contains monuments of the great Neville family, in the grounds of whose former castle it stands.

Wolsingham, some 12 miles further on, is the entrance to Weardale which has some of the finest scenery in the county. The road follows the River Wear all the way to the border with Cumbria, at which point it is the highest classified road in England at 2,050 ft, and is flanked on either side by great wild moors known mostly as commons. Here, the Killhope Wheel Center (at Cowshill, near Stanhope) is a gaunt evocation of the life of 18th-century lead miners. In about the middle of the Dale, Stanhope stands at a crossroads, acknowledged as the "capital" of Weardale and now a place for unusual holiday quiet. The road south, B6278, leads grandly over Bollihope Common to Middleton-in-Teesdale, a terraced town rising from the river with tough, stone houses originally built for lead miners. It also has an interesting church, with many reminders of the lead mining days.

Follow the River Tees southeastwards and you come to Barnard Castle, the Norman remains of which stand on a cliff above the town. Surprisingly, this small town has two main thoroughfares, running at right angles to one another, and even more unexpected is the huge 19th-century French château standing just outside the town on the south. This is now the Bowes Museum, built by John Bowes and his French wife and stocked with a reputed 10,000 beautiful objects, including some very fine paintings. It also has a 21-acre park, and is now owned by the Durham County Council. Not only are its contents and its architecture astonishing, but the views from it are breathtaking.

NORTHUMBERLAND

If, when you are in Stanhope, County Durham, you turn right instead of left and follow B2678 over Stanhope and Muggleswick Commons, you will come quite easily to Blanchland. This is said to be one of England's most perfect villages, and is certainly one of Northumberland's show-pieces, although it misses being in Durham by a whisker. From the south one crosses into the village on a 19th-century bridge over Beldon Brook, which soon becomes the River Derwent, and at the other end of the L-shaped village one leaves on the Hexham road through a medieval gate-house. At one time the village was practically in ruins, but in the 18th century it was rebuilt, using stones from the ruined abbey. Part of the abbey guest house was incorporated in the Lord Crewe Arms, which was built by the Trustees of Lord Crewe, who were also responsible for the model village. North of Blanchland is Blanchland Moor which seems to stretch forever, and over which one travels to reach Hexham and The Wall.

Blanchland, the Moors, Hexham with its Abbey, and Hadrian's Wall are the epitome of Northumberland. It is a county which appears much larger than it is because so much of it is empty. South of the Wall the moors stretch in an uneven, rugged mass to the border of Cumbria; north of it they reach to the Cheviots which form the "frontier" with Scotland, and in this northern area they sweep to within about ten miles of the coast. This is a similar configuration to Durham, but the country in between the sea and that same Great North Road is not only more attractive than it is in Durham, but there is a great deal more of it.

Back, then, to Hexham. Today Hexham is a small, compact market town, a good shopping center, and good place from which to discover Roman Northumberland. And it has an Abbey. The first church, founded by St. Wilfrid, was built of stone taken from the Roman camp near Cor-bridge. The crypt of that church remains. The Abbey of today was built in the 12th, 13th, 14th and 15th centuries, with some rebuilding of ruins in the 20th. It is very beautiful, evocative and rich in possessions, the most notable of which is the Frith Stool—St. Wilfrid's stone chair—standing in the chancel. Just outside the Abbey, like a stage set, is the market place, and just nearby is the Moot Hall, once the gatehouse of a castle, and the Manor Office which was a 14th-century gaol. Nothing could make it more clear how the little town grew up at the knee of the Abbey.

Hadrian's Wall

The Roman wall stretched across northern England from the aptly named Wallsend, near the center of Newcastle, to Bowness-on-Solway, west of Carlisle. It runs along the brink of a whinstone elevation, just north of the main east-west road A69, but for most of the way there is a minor road, B6318, running close beside the Wall. The Emperor Hadrian planned the wall in A.D. 122 as a series of signal stations. Eventually it had 17 forts with Roman mile castles and signal towers in between, linked by a wall, probably 20-ft high and up to 10-ft broad, but 9 ft is the maximum height of what remains. It took some eight years to build, eventually extending to ports on the River Tyne at the eastern end, and the Solway Firth in the west. These extensions increased its over-all length to a final 76 miles (the equivalent of 80 Roman miles, which were shorter than the English measurement).

Today, excavating, documenting, interpreting, repairing, displaying and generally managing the Roman remains is a Northumbrian growth industry, and anyone sufficiently motivated could spend endless time there. There are places—forts—all along the Wall where people can browse, notably at Chesters, Housesteads (the best preserved fort), Vindolanda and at Carvoran Museum near Greenhead, which presents a good introduction to the life led by Roman soldiers on the frontier. It is also possible to walk on the Wall, but no one should imagine that it would entail just an afternoon stroll. It is very hard going, and once you are committed to it it is not possible to get off just anywhere and step back onto the road.

The western part is the most exciting scenically. Here, steep vertical precipices needed little additional fortification save for the parapet wall which originally topped the Wall to protect the look-out sentries. For photographers, one spot above most others produces a memorable souvenir: looking east towards the fort of Housesteads from Cuddy's Crag, the Wall can be seen snaking up and down across the wildest, most inhospitable country imaginable.

Anyone with a special interest in Britain's Roman remains would find it fascinating to follow the main A68 road northwards from Corbridge, just east of Hexham, leading to small villages such as Otterburn and Rochester, built mainly from stones filched from the Wall. Even the old schoolhouse has huge stone Roman ballistae decorating its gable.

At Redesdale Army Camp at Rochester, a path leads through prehistoric remains such as standing stones, to Chew Green Roman camps, whose outlines are clear as you reach the summit of the path. A tangle of enormous grassy ditches and high banks, it is now a pleasant area where sheep graze. One thing is important: at the Army Camp there are regular artillery exercises, indicated by the flying of red flags, and then it's certainly no place for visitors nor would they be allowed to pass. Check before going at Otterburn Camp, by telephoning 0830 20241, extension 201 or 227; if the go-ahead is given, for politeness' sake, mention that you have done so at the Camp Superintendent's hut when you arrive.

Immediately north of the Wall is Wark Forest leading into Kielder Forest, a huge wild place on either side of the North Tyne, now dammed to make a great reservoir, but with its many inlets and wooded arms transformed into a beautiful, entirely natural-looking lake. The project is a highly ambitious one. Already there are sections devoted to water sports, swimming, anchorages for private boats and boats for hire, a lake steamer service, holiday chalets for renting, a peaceful stretch for fishermen. There is provision for camping, picnicking, pony trekking, forest walks; and a nature conservation area has been created to protect the fine variety of plants, trees and wildlife. At Kielder Castle on the site an interpretive center has been set up, with a sales counter for leaflets and literature of all kinds, and refreshments in the very pleasant new cafe.

From Kielder, the Cheviots—pronounced *Cheeviots*—slope northeastwards along the Scottish border providing some of the most beautiful scenery in Britain and cradling, as it were, the rest of Northumberland and out of which such lovely rivers as the Coquet run, past Rothbury and Felton, to emerge at the coast at Warkworth.

Castles and Holy Island

The stretch of land on and near the coast is very rewarding, in fact it is counted by many the best stretch anywhere on the North Sea. Warkworth is a fairytale village, with its castle perched on a hill immediately above, playing the proud border fortress. There is more left of it than of most such castles, and on a sunny day there is just enough light inside to give you a rather dreadful idea of what it must have been like to live in such a place. It belonged to the fighting Percys, lords of Northumberland; and inland is Alnwick Castle, even more spectacular, the centuries-old seat of the Percys and still lived in by the Dukes of Northumberland.

North of the Coquet, the Northumberland coast reveals its finest features. Here and there the hard basaltic rock thrusts itself out into the North Sea, making the grand headland crowned with the ruins of Dunstanburgh Castle and the even more striking stronghold of Bamburgh, which legend declares to have been the Joyous Garde of Sir Lancelot du Lac, one of King Arthur's fabled knights. At Bamburgh, legend is replaced by history, in the creation of the Grace Darling Museum. It commemorates the rescue by Grace and her father of nine survivors from the wreck of the storm-shattered ship, the *Forfarshire.* The museum contains many original relics of Grace, her family and the ill-fated *Forfarshire,* as well as the boat in which the rescue was made.

Off the fishing village of Seahouses, near Bamburgh Castle, however, a seaward extension of this same basaltic rock results in the long line of the Farne Islands, sanctuaries for seals and for some of Britain's rarest sea birds. Go there to see the colonies of gulls, terns, puffins, and most fascinating of all, eider ducks.

Continuing north, the low outline of Lindisfarne, or Holy Island, cradle of northern England's Christianity and home of St. Cuthbert, shows on the eastward horizon. To reach it, one travels by car along a causeway over three miles of tide-washed sand, a journey possible only twice a day. Go there to see the red ruins of Lindisfarne Priory, built on the site of the first Christian edifice in the north, and the fairylike Lindisfarne Castle, a miniature fortress perched on top of a conical-shaped mound of rock. This castle owes a great deal to the imagination of the Edwardian architect Sir Edwin Lutyens, who built its interior before the First World War. Art from an earlier age provided one of the most famous relics of the days when Holy Island was just starting as a great monastic center. The *Lindisfarne Gospels,* glorious manuscripts painted around the end of the 7th century, can now be seen in the British Museum.

Berwick-upon-Tweed marks the approach to Scotland, and is the last town of the Northumberland coast. Wandering round its streets, one feels conscious of being in the presence of history. Berwick bore the brunt of the border wars between England and Scotland so fiercely that many of the really old buildings do not survive intact, though the town has some of the finest walls in England and interesting features such as the old gaol in the Guildhall. Only a few miles from the High Cheviots, in Chillingham Park, roam the unique wild white cattle of Chillingham. Led by a king bull, this herd—unapproachable except with a guide (tel. 066 85 250)—is descended from the primeval aurochs that lived in Britain thousands of years ago.

The guided trek starts from the Warden's cottage, and at the top of the path it's worth a stop, not only to get your breath back, but to admire the fabulous view of forested slopes and the Cheviot hills lining the skyline. The herd diminished tragically during the last war to only eleven animals; but happily numbers have now risen to nearly 50, and with the birth of new calves, are still increasing. It's a matter of luck how many you see, but the Warden is an expert at spotting them. Stay quiet when he says so, and stop when he says stop. The animals know his voice, but bulls have an inborn instinct to charge if the mood takes them, though with an expert around there is little danger. On one occasion it did happen. Thomas Bewick, the wonderfully talented 18th-century artist and wood engraver found this out for himself: he finished his sketch of a Chillingham bull up a tree! Leaflets telling the Chillingham story, as well as picture postcards of Bewick's meticulously drawn bull, are on sale at the Warden's cottage.

PRACTICAL INFORMATION FOR
THE NORTHEAST

HOTELS AND RESTAURANTS. The Northeast, generally, is an area of great historic interest. Some of the places on this side of the Pennine chain are resorts from way back, and have the elegant old hotels to prove it. Food specialties are abundant. Northumbrian beef, game from the woods and moors, Tweed salmon, Brontë Liqueur Cakes, York hams—among the most succulent in the world—and fresh fish all over the area, all make dining a potential delight.

Bamburgh (Northumb.). *Lord Crewe Arms* (M), Front St., tel. (066 84) 243; 27 rooms, 14 with bath. Views of the Castle, Closed from mid-Nov. through mid-March; full board only in season.

Berwick-Upon-Tweed (Northumb.). Good touring center (Holy Island a few miles south). *King's Arms* (M), Hide Hill, tel. (0289) 307454; 37 rooms, all with bath or shower. *Turret House* (M), Etal Rd., tel. (0289) 307344; 13 rooms with bath or shower. Small but good.

Blanchland (Northumb.). *Lord Crewe Arms* (M), tel. (043 475) 251; 15 rooms, all with bath or shower. In one of the loveliest villages in England, this delightful hotel has been converted from the remains of the 13th-century Blanchland Abbey.

Chester-Le-Street (Durham). *Lumley Castle* (E), tel. (091) 389 1111; 68 rooms with bath. A real castle with full room service and candle-lit Elizabethan banquets; heated pool and sauna.

Coatham Mundeville (Co. Durham). *Hall Garth* (M), tel. Aycliffe (0325) 313333. 21 rooms with bath or shower. Country house dating back to Tudor times, in park and woodland. Some rooms in stable block. Simple, good restaurant.

Cornhill-on-Tweed (Northumb.). *Tillmouth Park* (M), tel. Coldstream (0890) 2255; 13 rooms with bath. Beautiful location. Late Victorian country house in vast grounds; salmon fisherman's paradise; fine restaurant.

Darlington (Co. Durham). *Blackwell Grange Moat House* (M), tel. (0325) 380888; 98 rooms with bath. Modernized 17th-century mansion in attractive parkland.

Restaurant. *Bridge Inn* (M), tel. (0325) 50106. An excellent pub-restaurant at Stapleton, near Darlington.

Durham (Durham). *Royal County* (M), Old Elvet, tel. (0385) 66821; 122 rooms with bath. Pleasant modernized coaching inn, sauna and restaurant. *Hardwick Hall* (M), (at **Sedgefield,** 11 miles on A177), tel. (0740) 20253; 17 rooms with bath. Converted stately home in pleasant grounds.

Restaurant. *Traveller's Rest* (I), 72 Claypath (get the right one—there are two of the same name), tel. (0385) 65370; pub with out-of-the-ordinary bar food; good value.

Greenhead (Northumb.). *Holmhead* (I), tel. Gisland (06972) 402; 4 rooms in award-winning farm guest house. Run by enterprising, helpful owners.

Harrogate (N. Yorks.). *Majestic* (E), Ripon Rd., tel. (0423) 68972; 156 rooms with bath (Trust House Forte). *Old Swan* (E), Swan Rd., tel. (0423) 500055; 138 rooms with bath; wide grounds, tennis. *Harrogate International* (M), Kings Rd., tel. (0423) 500000; 214 rooms with bath. New, multistory hotel with well-equipped bedrooms.

Restaurant. *Number Six* (M), Ripon Rd., tel. (0423) 502908. Candle-lit restaurant offers carefully prepared food and good service; extensive wine list. Well recommended, but wise to book. Closed Mon. and three weeks in Aug.

Langley-on-Tyne (Northumb.). *Langley Castle* (M), tel. Haydon Bridge (043484) 8888; 8 rooms with bath in 14th-century castle, recently converted into luxury hotel and restaurant.

Longhorseley (Northumb.). *Linden Hall* (E–M), near Morpeth, tel. (0670) 56611; 45 rooms, all with bath. Stylish Georgian mansion well restored, and set in 300-acre estate.

Newcastle Upon Tyne (Tyne and Wear). *Gosforth Park* (L–E), (3 miles), tel. (091) 236 4111; 178 rooms, all with bath. Fairly new hotel in attractive surroundings with good restaurant. *County Thistle* (M), Neville St., tel. (091) 232 2471; 115 rooms with bath. Recently restored, but retains its Victorian character. *Swallow* (M), 2 Newgate Arcade, tel. (091) 232 5025; 94 rooms with bath. Roof-top restaurant.

Restaurant. At **Corbridge** (Northumberland). *The Ramblers* (M), Tinklers Bank, Farnley, tel. (043 471) 2424. Interesting German menu in country house restaurant. *Blackfriars Restaurant and Brasserie* (I), Monk St., tel. (091) 261 5945. Close to the center, this friendly eatery is sited in the refectory of a 13th-century Dominican friary. Outside tables in summer. 8–5.30, Mon.–Sat. only.

Otterburn (Northumb.). *Percy Arms* (M), Main St., tel. (0830) 20261; 30 rooms, all with bath or shower. Well-recommended; game fishing available.

Powburn (Northumb.). *Breamish House* (M), tel. (066578) 266; 10 rooms with bath in former shooting lodge. Fine service and food. Near Alnwick.

Richmond (N. Yorks.). *Frenchgate* (M), 59–61 Frenchgate, tel. (0748) 2087; 12 rooms, 6 with bath. Stone-built Georgian house. *King's Head* (M), Market Place, tel. (0748) 2311; 29 rooms, 20 with bath. 18th-century building on market square, comfortable.
Restaurant. At **Moulton**. *Black Bull Inn* (M) tel. (032 577) 289. Good food.

Ripon (N. Yorks.). *Ripon Spa* (M), Park St., tel. (0765) 2172; 41 rooms with bath. Victorian house on edge of town.
At **Jervaulx**. *Jervaulx Hall* (M), tel. Bedale (0677) 60235. By the ruined Abbey, early Victorian house in 8 acres. 8 rooms with bath.

Scarborough (N. Yorks.). Hotels match the old-world elegance of this magnificent seaside town. *Holbeck Hall* (E), Seacliff Rd., tel. (0723) 374374; 30 rooms with bath, is truly gracious. *Royal* (M), St. Nicholas St., tel. (0723) 364333; 137 rooms with bath or shower; really grand.
Restaurant. Eat at the *Lanterna Ristorante* (M), Queen St., tel. (0723) 363616; for serious Italiano among crowded tables. Dinner only.
At **Hackness**. *Hackness Grange Country Hotel* (E), tel. (0723) 82345; 27 rooms, 26 rooms with shower. In lovely country by River Derwent. Parkland, tennis, swimming, fishing, golf.

Staddle Bridge (Cleveland). *McCoy's at the Tontine* (M), tel. East Harsley (060 982) 671; 6 rooms with bath. Friendly inn run by three brothers with excellent (E) restaurant; original and tasty food.

West Witton (N. Yorks.). *Wensleydale Heifer* (M), Main St., tel. Leyburn (0969) 22322; 20 rooms with bath. Modernized, comfortable 17th-century inn in the heart of the Yorkshire Dales.

York (N. Yorks.). *Middlethorpe Hall* (L), Bishopthorpe Rd., tel. (0904) 641241; 30 rooms with bath. Restored historic mansion overlooking York racecourse. *The Judge's Lodging* (E), 9 Lendal, tel. (0904) 38733, 13 rooms, all with bath. Lavishly decorated Georgian town house. *Viking* (E), North St., tel. (0904) 59822; 187 rooms with bath. Modern, reliable hotel beside river. *Chase* (M), Tascaster Rd., tel. (0904) 701000; 80 rooms, all with bath or shower. Near the racecourse.
Restaurant. *Giovanni's* (M), 12 Goodramgate, tel. (0904) 23539. Good Italian restaurant. Closed Mon.

At **Whitwell on the Hill.** *Whitwell Hall* (M), tel. (065381) 551; 21 rooms, all with bath. Splendid country house hotel 12 miles from York on 18-acre grounds.

HADRIAN'S WALL. The Northumbria Tourist Board, Aykley Heads, Durham DH1 5UX, can supply publications with information on local transport, car parks, the best maps required for intensive touring, etc.

PLACES OF INTEREST. This region's position, just south of the Border, is reflected in many of the fortified houses which were needed in times of raid and pillage. There is, indeed, a feeling of deeply entrenched history all through the area, starting, of course, with the ancient stones of Hadrian's Wall, snaking away across the landscape, and continuing through the mystic rocks of Holy Isle. But the region is not without its Baroque glories, and none so glorious as Castle Howard, a fantasy of architectural extravagance. For more details on visiting historic houses, consult the relevant section in *Facts at Your Fingertips,* and the chapter *Historic Houses— Precious Stones in Peril.*

Cleveland. Captain Cook's Birthplace Museum, Steward Park, Middlesbrough (tel. 0642 311211/813781). Illustrates Cook's life and adventures. Open all year, daily 10–6 (10–4 in winter).
Preston Hall Museum, Yarm Rd., Stockton-on-Tees. An openair period street, working craftsmen and galleries depict social history of the area. Open Mon.–Sat., 9.30–5.30, Sun. 2–5.30.

Durham/Tyne and Wear. Bowes Museum, Barnard Castle, Co. Durham (tel. 0833 69060). Imposing Victorian "château"; fabulous collection of Spanish pictures, many fine objets d'art; also interesting "life of a leadminer" display. Open weekdays 10–5.30 (Oct., Mar., Apr., 10–5, Nov.–Feb. 10–4), Sun. 2–5 (winter 2–4).
North of England Open Air Museum, Beamish (tel. 0207 231811). A 260-acre site, with pit-workers' cottages, reconstructed town street, a colliery, and a rail station in working condition as it would have been in 1910–1920 (complete with a real train). Winner of Britain's National Heritage Museum of the Year Award 1986 and the European Museum of the Year 1987. Open Apr.–Sept., daily, 10–6; Oct.–Mar., Tues.–Sun., 10–5.
Raby Castle, Staindrop (tel. 0833 60202). Home of Lord Barnard. 14th-century, later alterations. Open Easter weekend (Sat.–Wed.) then May and June, Wed. and Sun., July–Sept. daily (excluding Sat.), and Bank Holidays. All 1–5.
South Shields Museum, Ocean Rd., (tel. 091 4561369). Contains a special exhibition based on the life and work of the famous novelist Catherine Cookson, who grew up here. Open Mon.–Fri. 10–5.30, Sat. 10–4.30, Sun. 2–5.
Washington Old Hall, near Sunderland (tel. 091 416 6879). Jacobean manor house, with portions of 12th-century house of the Washington family—George Washington's direct ancestors lived here from 1183–1288. Open early Apr. and Oct., Wed., Sat. and Sun.; mid-Apr.–end Sept. daily (except Fri.); all 11–5. (NT)

The Wildfowl Trust, Waterfowl Park, Washington (tel. 091 416454). Over 1200 birds can be seen in landscaped hillsides along the River Wear. Open daily 9.30–5.30 (or dusk).

Northumberland. Alnwick Castle, Alnwick (tel. 0665 602207/ 602196). 12th-century home of the Duke of Northumberland. Medieval fortifications. Open May–Sept., daily exc. Sat., 1–5.

Bamburgh Castle, Bamburgh (tel. 066 84 208). Restored castle with 12th-century Norman keep and plenty of atmosphere. Open Easter–Oct., daily, from 1 (check for closing times).

Belsay Hall, Belsay (tel. 066 181 636). Part of the hall plus stables, castle and grounds open to public. Hall early 19th-century, castle 14th-century. Open daily Apr.–end Sept. and winter weekends. Telephone for opening times.

Cragside House and Country Park, Rothbury, near Morpeth (tel. 0669 20333). Magnificent Victorian mansion on dramatic, fascinating site. The first house in the world to have electric lighting. Open May through Sept., daily except Mon., 2–6. Park open Easter–Oct. from 10.30. (NT)

Lindisfarne Castle, Holy Island (tel. 0289 89244). 16th-century original, updated by Lutyens in 1st decade of this century. Open Apr.–end Sept., daily, except Fri. 11–5; Oct. Sat. & Sun. 11–5. (NT)

Wallington House, Cambo, near Morpeth (tel. 067 074 283). On site of a medieval castle, dating from 1688 but refashioned in 1740s by Daniel Garrett. Exceptional plasterwork by Francini brothers; fine furniture from mid-Georgian to late Victorian. Dolls' houses, museum, coach display. Also beautiful woodland, grounds and walled terraced garden. House open Apr.–end Sept., daily (except Tues.) 1–5. Walled garden open Apr.–end Sept., daily 10–7, until 6 in Oct., and until 4 Nov.–Mar.; grounds open all year. (NT)

North Yorkshire. Castle Howard, near York (tel. 065 384 333). Palatial 18th-century house by Sir John Vanbrugh, featured in *Brideshead Revisited,* with pictures, furniture, costume galleries. Open late Mar.–Oct., daily, house from 11 (last admission 4.30); grounds from 10.

Fairfax House, York (tel. 0904 55543). Restored Georgian house, possibly one of the finest in Britain. Mar.–Dec. Mon., Tues., Wed., Thurs., and Sat. 11–5, Sun. 1.30–5.

Fountains Abbey and Studley Royal Country Park, Ripon. Extensive deer park with lake, ornamental gardens, etc. The very beautiful Abbey is a Cistercian monastic ruin. Abbey and grounds open daily, Jan.–Mar., Nov. and Dec. 10–5 (or dusk); Apr.–June and Sept. 10–7; July and Aug. 10–8; Oct. 10–6 (or dusk).

Fountains Hall (which contains exhibition) open daily, Apr.–Sept. 11–6, Oct.–Mar. 11–4, (NT)

Georgian Theater, Richmond (tel. 0748 3021 P.M.). Britain's oldest theater still working (1788). Attractive auditorium, theater museum. Open Easter, then May to Sept., daily, 2.30–5; also Sat., Bank Holiday Mon., 10.30–1.

Newby Hall, Ripon (tel. 0432 322583). Famous Adam house with tapestries, gardens. Open Apr.–Oct., daily (except Mon. though open Bank Holiday Mon.), house 12–5, garden 11–5.30. Garden remains open into late Oct. (house closes early in the month).

Ripley Castle, Ripley (tel. 0423 770152). Mixture of 15th and 18th century. Much used as setting for film locations. Fine grounds. Open June–mid-Oct., Sat., Sun. and Tues.–Thurs., 11.30–4.30 (also weekends in Apr. and May). Gardens, Apr.–mid-Oct., daily 11–5.30.

Skipton Castle, Skipton. A fully-roofed medieval fortress; attractive 15th-century courtyard and a massive gatehouse. Open all year, weekdays 10–6 (or dusk), Sun. 2–6 (or dusk).

York Museums. The city is exceptionally well-endowed with museums; opening times are reasonable—please check locally. **York Castle Museum** (tel. 0904 653611), an outstanding, not-to-be-missed museum in a vast building (previously a prison), with entire re-created period streets and a wealth of unusual exhibits. **Jorvik Viking Center** (tel. 0904 643211), where visitors take a "time car" ride through Viking York, complete with the smells! **National Railway Museum** (tel. 0904 21261), a must for train enthusiasts—everything from early steam locomotives to the trains of tomorrow. **York Story** (tel. 0904 28632), which gives a good background picture of the city's social and architectural history. **The Yorkshire Museum** (tel. 0904 29745), good for Roman, Anglo-Saxon and Viking artefacts. A little way out of the city is the **Yorkshire Museum of Farming** (tel. 0904 489966), with its collection of implements and daily farming demonstrations.

THE NORTHWEST

Mountains, Lakes and Valleys

West of the Pennines are the counties of Cumbria and Lancashire, each of which contains the general pattern of the north in providing a striking variation of scene and character, and out to sea rides the Isle of Man, with its own history and myths.

The roads which cross the Pennine barrier are quite interesting. The most northerly, the A69, keeps south of the line of the Roman Wall which, although so often originally associated with Northumberland (where the best preserved sections are to be found), actually bisected the entire country from the mouth of the Tyne, on the east, to the Solway on the west. (The A69's lesser but straight and well-surfaced partner, B6318, runs right along the wall from Heddon, near Newcastle, to Greenhead, near Haltwhistle.)

Beyond Haltwhistle, where the South Tyne, which has been its nearby consort for many miles of the way, turns abruptly south to follow a long gap into the hills, the westward road goes over the watershed between east and west, passing the stark pile of Thirlwall Castle (at Greenhead), whereabouts the Picts are said to have breached the Roman defenses, and then dropping down into the Irthing Valley and so on to Carlisle, capital of the western borderland. Like Berwick-on-Tweed, on the opposite side of the country, Carlisle has a history full of the bitterness and occasional romance of the long continuing strife between two rival nations.

CUMBRIA

Carlisle

Carlisle is a busy place today, with its industries allowed to flourish un-molested by any thoughts of imminent unrest, yet it has managed to retain much that is reminiscent of the days when kings and military leaders passed through its streets or stayed within its walls as their armies took part in the backwards and forwards surges of warfare. Its history dates from long before Roman times. Slightly to the south of Hadrian's Wall, it became an important Roman settlement (Luguvallium), and the large cavalry camp of Petriana was close by. (The City Museum in Tullie House is particularly strong in Roman remains and information about the Wall.)

The castle and city walls were projected by William Rufus (1087–1100) and the city became English in 1092. It was an important border fortress during the wars between England and Scotland, and changed hands sever-al times. During the Civil War, Carlisle surrendered to the Scots after a siege of nearly nine months in 1644–5. Its stormy history continued longer than any other town in England, and in 1745 the Young Pretender, Bonnie Prince Charlie, entered the town preceded by the famous "hundred pip-ers" and established his headquarters in English Street. Carlisle remained a walled city for 700 years, having but three entrances: English Gate, Scotch Gate and Irish Gate.

Try to see the cathedral, which was started in 1093, the 15th-century tithebarn, the Market Cross, the Town Hall and the new Lanes shopping development.

Carlisle's castle, standing on a mound with two rivers washing two sides, has sufficient majesty to summon an impression of its worth as a northerly bastion of England; and its red sandstone cathedral, though di-minished from its original size as a result of the Civil War between king and parliament in the 17th century, has a dignity in keeping with the seat of a see established as long ago as 1133. Fragments of the walls that once encircled the city are still enough to summon up visions of their former strength.

Carlisle is, of course, the traditional gateway to Scotland on the west, but it is also at the entrance to the Eden Valley, a long, lovely passage from the Cumbrian plain back to the Pennine hills where the old breed of Dairy Shorthorn cattle still have a stronghold.

It is on the Eden that Appleby, which that unrivaled chronicler of local life, the late W. T. Palmer, once described as "probably England's quietest and smallest county town," stands, for although Kendal was until recently the center of administration for Westmorland, Appleby remained its right-ful capital, and there is much that smacks of history, including its castle. Little changed and, perhaps, unfortunately, forgotten by many visitors to the northwest, it is a lovely spot. It is best reached from Carlisle on A6 and A66, south.

Pennine Fairs

Not far away on A66 and B6259 south is Kirkby Stephen, a busy place on market days and even more so on those occasions in autumn when the hardy Swaledale sheep occupy the sales ring and buyers from all parts of the north come to bid for the stout rams reared on the nearby fells. Of almost equal importance are the horse and pony sales of the Cowper Day fair, which falls on September 29 each year (unless, of course, that is a Sunday, in which case the event takes place on either the Saturday or the Monday).

South of Carlisle, the A6 road, the chief communication between England and Scotland before the coming of the M6 motorway, goes on to Penrith, yet another town which bore its share of the troubled times of border strife, retaining its castle as a permanent memorial, and then on to one of the most notorious moorland crossings in the country—the way over the wild and bleak Shap Fell.

Lower levels are reached at Kendal, a major gateway to the Lake District. From here southwards, the road continues to Levens Bridge, with a fine example of a topiary garden beside the ancient hall.

The Lake District

It is impossible to think of a greater "must" for tourists visiting Great Britain than the inclusion of a visit to the Lake District, which is contained within Cumbria, created in the 1970s from parts of the "old" counties of Cumberland, Westmorland and Lancashire.

This part of the northwest, which is now enjoying the protection of National Park status, combines so much that is magnificent in mountain, lake, and dales in a comparatively small space that new and entrancing vistas open out at each corner of the road. Higher mountains there most certainly are even in Britain, but none that are finer in outline or which give a greater impression of majesty; deeper and bluer lakes can be found, but none that fit so readily into the surrounding scene; and while the dales themselves are not so long as many of the glens north of the border, or even those watered by the rivers on the east side of the Pennines, they yield to none so far as beauty is concerned.

In these circumstances it is only to be expected that the area will be much visited—not to say crowded—in the summer and indeed, to a lesser extent, in spring and autumn, because the lakes are especially beautiful in those two seasons. They even have their winter devotees, though the weather then can be very nasty indeed. It is unfortunately true to say that at the most popular times the narrow, winding roads are crammed with slowly moving cars, and the easiest climbs are being worn away by thousands of pairs of feet. So, be guided by anyone who can tell you when and where to go to avoid the crush.

Perhaps it is only natural that so lovely an area should have become linked with so many prominent figures in English literature. The poet William Wordsworth, himself born in the area, lived at Grasmere, and may be regarded as the figurehead of a group which included Samuel Taylor Coleridge and his pathetic son, Hartley, Thomas de Quincey, and Robert Southey, who made their homes in the district in the first part of the last century. Later came Hugh Walpole, the children's artist and writer Beatrix Potter and the poet Norman Nicholson, all of whom made contributions to Lakeland literature which are every bit as rich and important as those of 150 years ago.

As with many regions of England, the Lake District has its own language variations. For instance a lake is a mere, a smaller lake, a tarn; mountains are frequently referred to as fells; a waterfall is a force, a beck is a small stream; and the addition of "thwaite," of Scandinavian origin, to place names implies a clearing.

Kendal, Windermere and Ambleside

Approached from the south, the natural gateway to the Lake District is Kendal. On the way into Kendal, five miles to the south, lies Levens Hall. This is a lovely Elizabethan House, with spacious gardens full of the most fascinating twisty topiary work. The interior of the Hall is the very reverse of most historic houses, it is light and airy, welcoming, and full of interesting details.

Kendal is a study in gray stone, with reminders of the coaching days in its old inns. Its yards, leading off the main streets, could be closed when news that a visit from Scottish raiders was imminent. Here you see the remains of its old castle occupying a green knoll above the town.

Some nine undulating miles of roads (A591) separate Kendal from Windermere, showing something of the grandeur that lies ahead from the tops of the rises, and of the comparative mildness of the dales as the road drops down to the Kent, near Staveley.

An excellent introduction to the Lake District is to be found at the National Park Center at Brockhole on Windermere, a fine wisteria-clad mansion in grounds leading down to the lake shore where you are welcome to wander. Films, slides, lectures and interesting displays give every aspect of the history, geology and customs of this unique region. There is also an excellent book and souvenir shop, and a good cafeteria. An indoor working exhibition shows you how drystone walls are constructed—you'll see plenty of them in the area when touring, dividing up farmland and surrounding estates. In the very pleasant grounds of Brockhole a pile of stones and boulders lie beside a partly constructed piece of wall, inviting you to try your hand.

Windermere town, which has a branch line rail link to Kendal, is a mile or so from the lake, which is reached at Bowness. Bowness, a pleasant open resort, has a 15th-century church with interesting chained books, a "Breeches Bible," and what is probably one of the earliest examples of stained-glass windows in the country. In this window is an illustration of the arms of the Washington family, forebears of George Washington.

Some 10½ miles in length, Windermere Lake may well be regarded as the water passage from the mountain scene to the more tranquil; Bowness comes about midway in the transition. Looking across the water, the general impression is of thickly wooded slopes, rising to no great height, encompassing the waters. The woodlands continue down to the foot of the lake at Newby Bridge and even down the Leven Valley almost to the shores of Morecambe Bay.

The head of the lake at Ambleside, however, is on the threshold of the mountain scene, and although the larger hills themselves are a little too

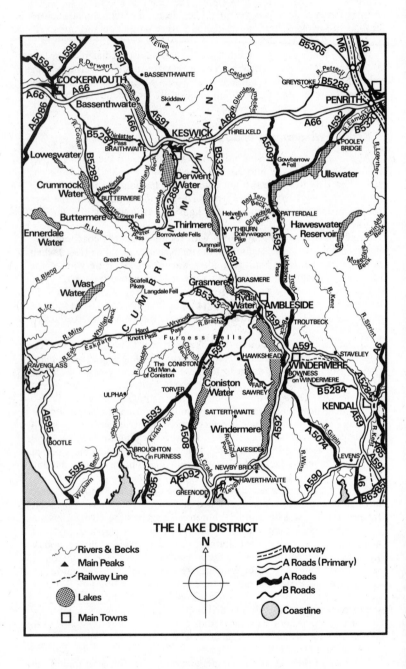

THE LAKE DISTRICT

N

Rivers & Becks

▲ Main Peaks

Railway Line

Lakes

Main Towns

Motorway

A Roads (Primary)

A Roads

B Roads

Coastline

far away from the water to give any sense of overpowering influence, they are still big enough to bring grandeur rather than sylvan beauty to the upper reaches of the lake.

During the summer months there is a regular steamship service from Lakeside, near the southern end, to Ambleside, with calls at Bowness. At Bowness, too, are the headquarters of the Royal Windermere Yacht Club, one of the foremost inland sailing clubs in Britain, which organizes regular races throughout the season.

From Bowness, the road (A591) keeps sufficiently close to the eastern shore of the lake to allow intriguing glimpses of the water, the woods, and the mountains on the way to Ambleside, where suddenly one feels one has arrived at the very heart of things. Kendal and Windermere, in turn, give an impression of something different, but at Ambleside, one feels that the town is itself almost part of the hills and fells. It is not difficult to understand why. Its buildings, mainly of local stone and many built in that local traditional style which forgoes the use of mortar in the outer walls, blend perfectly into their setting.

From Ambleside there is a road (A593, then B5343) leading to thetop of one of the most interesting valleys, Langdale. It goes by the little lake of Elterwater and along the floor of a wide dale until it comes to a halt near Dungeon Ghyll, with its waterfalls, in the very shadow of the mountains of the Langdale Pikes, perhaps the most exciting in outline of all Lakeland mountains, with higher Bow Fell, on the opposite side of the deep dale. Beyond it, there is a foot pass over the hills to Borrowdale and a climbers' way via Rosset Ghyll to the head of Wasdale, from where Scafell Pike—at 3,210 feet England's highest mountain—can be ascended.

Where Langdale used to end as far as motor traffic was concerned, there is a Mountain Rescue Post and a small hotel, the Old Dungeon Ghyll, which is the epitome of the Lakes. A bit shabby, and with the entrance hall full of boots, there is a marvelous atmosphere in which people eat hugely and loll about in front of roaring fires in the evenings, sharing an almost religious dedication to the mountains. The road, or what passes for one, now continues southward to emerge at the bottom of Wrynose Pass which leads onto Hardknott Pass, a lovely motoring road if you don't mind hairpin bends and the occasional gradient that makes it appear that the car is standing on its rear wheels. These passes, one leading almost immediately to the other, are best used when visiting the western lakes from the eastern side.

From Ambleside, too, there is a road (B5284, south) over the fells to the idyllic little town of Hawkshead, a fascinating spot of odd nooks and corners where the poet Wordsworth attended the former grammar school. The B5285 road goes over the ridge to Coniston, beside the lake of the same name, where Donald Campbell met his death when attempting to break the water-speed record in the winter of 1967. Near at hand is Brantwood, associated with yet another literary figure, John Ruskin. Brantwood is a fascinating house to visit for those interested in Victorian art. It has been preserved largely as Ruskin left it, and his many water-colors bear witness to a much-neglected writer and artist. Towering above the village is the Old Man of Coniston, a crag which rises to a height of 2,633 feet.

From Ambleside to Keswick

For most, however, the favorite road from Ambleside is that north to Keswick (A591), perhaps the finest, scenically, of any main highway in the north of England. A short mile from the town and on the right of this road is the place where the famous Vale of Rydal sheep dog trials take place in August.

Rydal Water is the next lake and then comes Grasmere, where the mountains really do exert their influence on the scene, contrasting superbly with the placid lake set in the green hollow.

Grasmere is, of course, packed with Wordsworthian associations. The poet and his family lived at Dove Cottage, on the outskirts of the village, for many years, the house now being a place of pilgrimage for thousands of folk each year. He lies, with the remainder of his family in the quiet graveyard, within a stone's throw of the murmuring River Rothay. Grasmere, too, is the place where possibly the most famous of the traditional Lakeland sports meetings is held in August with the local form of wrestling and races up and down the neighboring fells as leading attractions.

Beyond Grasmere, the Keswick Road begins the steep climb over Dunmail Raise, at the top of which was fought a battle between the Celtic inhabitants of the area and the Saxons and where, legend has it, a big pile of stones marks the place where the local "king," Dunmail, was slain. Much more certain than the legend, however, is the grandeur of the scene, with Grasmere's long dale behind, and the wooded reservoir-lake of Thirlmere ahead.

Thirlmere, which serves as a reservoir for Manchester and other northern centers, covers a once-swampy valley containing a couple of uninteresting shallow pools. Around it, a discerning authority has embarked on a forestry scheme which is a good example of how well-planted trees can be blended into the mountain landscape.

Helvellyn rises to a height of 3,113 feet almost overshadowing the lake from the east. It can be ascended by a well-marked path from Wythburn. There are, however, other longer but more interesting routes to the summit. One leaves Grasmere by Tongue Ghyll and then, by the lonely tarn of Grisedale, there is a mountain track up the slopes of Dollywaggon Pike and on to Helvellyn itself.

The main road keeps to the Helvellyn side of Thirlmere, but there is a quieter and more interesting one (from the point of view of scenery) which branches left after leaving Dunmail and goes along the bottom of the Armboth Fells, commanding more open views of the water and, of course, revealing the full grandeur of Helvellyn itself.

Both roads unite at the north end of Thirlmere before the long drop into Keswick, with commanding views of Skiddaw (3,054 feet) and over Derwentwater to the heights around Borrowdale and Newlands. Older rocks fashion the more urbane slopes of the first, volcanic rocks the more serrated outlines of the second.

Keswick

Keswick, the virtual capital of this part of the Lake District, has catering for the tourist as its summer objective, although there are small industries which provide the local folk with work throughout the year. In the past, a good deal of mining was carried out on the nearby hillsides. There are still slate quarries on the heights above Borrowdale, but the scars of those near Keswick have long since been removed and the quarries well disguised.

It was at Keswick that Coleridge and Southey lived and, at a later date, Hugh Walpole; there are many reminders of all three. In the summer, a festival of plays has become a regular feature.

Only a mile or so from the town is the lake of Derwentwater, often cited as being the loveliest in the area, although in a district like this, where each stretch of water has its own individual appeal, it is difficult to make comparisons. Its immediate setting is one of woodland, but beyond lie England's grandest mountains. From the head of the lake, Borrowdale runs south, deep into the heart of the hills; it is a magnificent dale with two little hamlets, Seatoller and Seathwaite.

Some four miles or so from the head of Derwentwater, the dale is split by a rocky tongue of land coming down from Glaramara and what may be called the "roof" of the area. On the left, there is a way through Langstrath which leads to the Snake Pass, a track crossing that watershed into Langdale. The right-hand branch is wilder, going into what Thomas Gray referred to as "that turbulent chaos of mountain behind mountain," a dale deep-set among the grandest peaks. From the head of the watershed, a foot track climbs skywards to the Sty Head Pass, with an even finer aspect as it keeps to a narrow niche on the flanks of the magnificent Great Gable (with its spectacular "Striding Edge" beckoning the would-be climber), to drop into Wasdale on the other side of the watershed.

The crossings of both the Snake and Sty Head passes are walkers' ways, but the motorist can get the feel of these mountain crossings by taking the road (B5289) over Honister Pass from the lower reaches of Borrowdale to the head of the Buttermere Valley.

The Eastern Lakes

There still remain the eastern lakes of Ullswater and Hawes Water. The first, second in length to Windermere (and also served by steamers in the summer months) is best approached from Penrith, although those coming to it via Kendal and Windermere have a chance to use one of the most interesting of Lakeland passes, the Kirkstone (on A592) winding over the hills and dropping past the lonely tarn of Brothers Water to Patterdale on Ullswater.

Ullswater combines sylvan loveliness with mountain setting, and changes its moods as one goes along A592 from Pooley Bridge, at the outlet, southwest to the top of the lake, which like so many of the others, is deep within a fold of the hills. There are some excellent, not too strenuous walks reached from the road running along the western shore. To Aira Force, for instance, a fairytale waterfall that drops down some 60 feet into a mossy-edged rock pool, overhung by dense trees. Many visitors make this the end of a short circular tour; but continue up-river and you reach the Upper Falls, even more spectacular, great boulders edging the bank above the rushing water. Here, with patience, it is possible to spot the red squirrel, fast becoming a rarity in England.

Nearby is Gowbarrow Park, where Wordsworth's sister Dorothy first saw that "host of golden daffodils." Returning from walking the higher levels above the lake, the views over Ullswater are dreamy and wonderfully romantic.

Hawes Water is another of Manchester's reservoirs, the original lake having been deepened and extended, a change involving the flooding of the entire hamlet of Mardale. Again, the approach is from the east, leaving the road at Shap or Penrith. Whatever changes have taken place, however, the higher reaches of the valley containing the reservoir remain the same—a wild declivity among high fells, over which the Romans had what must have been one of their most exposed roads in the country, the aptly named High Street.

The Passes

There is one south-to-north pass, the **Kirkstone,** by which Ullswater can be reached from Windermere. It starts from the main Troutbeck road, a side fork before the summit dropping steeply down to Ambleside at the northern end of Windermere. Passing lonely little Brothers Water, the pass reaches Ullswater at Patterdale at its southern end. Naturally, visitors to Ullswater can reach Windermere following the pass southwards.

Traveling to the western lakes may involve long detours, since they lie beyond the main central mountain mass. Direct roads climb steeply over the passes, some more difficult than others, but all immensely scenic, especially from their summits, and worthwhile for that alone.

The Wrynose and Hardknott Passes. These are the most southerly and the most difficult. The combination of the two takes you over from Little Langdale into Eskdale. One leads to the other with scarcely a breath between; but it is the Hardknott Pass which needs the greatest care and concentration, parts of its steep snaking bends rising in a gradient of 1 in 2½. Best not try it in wet, misty weather.

The Honister Pass. This is the next pass to the north, running from Borrowdale over to the head of Buttermere. The climb begins at Seatoller at the upper end of Borrowdale, with gradients of 1 in 4 much of the way. The descent to Buttermere is fierce at first, then less so as it drops down the wild Gatesgarth valley to the lake.

The Newlands Pass. Rather less sensational than the previous two, it is reached by side roads from Keswick, passing through the village of Stair, and then up to the Keskadale valley. Here the beck wanders through lonely hills and at the head of the valley, Moss Force crashes down from a considerable height. After this, the road drops steeply towards Buttermere village with fine views of both Crummock Water and Buttermere itself.

The Whinlatter Pass. This pass presents no difficulties. It is approached from Braithwaite (2 miles from Keswick), the road rising smoothly up through Thornthwaite Forest, its highest point passing almost unnoticed. Then it drops quietly down into the village of High Lorton and just beyond, a turn off to the left through Lorton Vale leads to the lakes.

The other approaches to these western lakes are from the coast road, which can be reached in the south from the lower end of Coniston Water, and in the north via Cockermouth.

The Buttermere Valley

The Buttermere Valley, which not only contains the lake of the same name, but also Crummock Water and Loweswater, has a quiet grandeur. From the east it can be reached either by the Honister or the Newlands Pass; but the main roads are from Cockermouth and the western towns, which are somewhat off the beaten track and not nearly so scenic.

The valley is one of the gems of the area, each of its three lakes exhibiting a differing characteristic. Loweswater is gentle and pretty; at Crummock Water the closeness of the high mountains has a telling effect; and at Buttermere the great peaks are in command, exerting their influence in majestic fashion. It is a progression from good to better to best. There are many delightful walks round the lakes, and from the central little plateau joining Crummock to Buttermere, where you can take refreshment at either of the two hotels there—The Bridge and The Fish.

Cockermouth, which is reached from Keswick by roads on either side of Bassenthwaite Lake (A591 or A66), has a castle and several old buildings, including the house where Wordsworth was born in 1770. Beyond it, the Derwent goes through country which swells into the seaward plain to the coast. But, keeping to the hills again, there is the way south to the Buttermere Valley (B5289 again) and, a little further away, to the even wilder one containing the lake of Ennerdale Water, probably the least-visited of all, and yet one of the most arresting in the country (via A5086).

By far the most exciting route to the Wasdale area is by the Wrynose and then the Hardknott Pass, stopping at the summit of the latter to take breath, and to look at the excavated remains of Roman Mediobogdum, surely one of the most inhospitable and cruelly exposed sites ever chosen to house a garrison. Below the steep precipices are unparalleled views into Eskdale, winding peacefully at the bottom of the valley, the skyline crammed with massed mountains.

Wastwater, England's deepest and sometimes most awe-inspiring lake, fills the upper basin, its highest mountain—Scafell Pike—frowning above its head, making an instant appeal to those who wish to see the sheer grandeur of the district. Yet there is no other height in the north quite like Great Gable, which commands the skyline from many parts of the upper dale. Reached by tortuous roads from Gosforth on the A595, no wonder this symmetrical peak was selected by the district's premier climbing club, The Fell and Rock, to be given to the nation as a war memorial to its members. Climbing Gable is another matter: there one moment, its head lost in shrouding mists the next, it presents plenty of hazards to the unwary, though nobody should try it without strictly observing the climbers' code, well displayed in the region and at the little hotel at the head of the lake. At Wasdale Head a small church underlines the warning not only to experienced climbers, but to over-ambitious novices. Many of the gravestones in its little churchyard are memorials to climbers lost on Gable, some of them experts, some who went to the rescue of others.

Wasdale is, indeed, the climbers' dale, with some of the most difficult ascents in the world on the slabs and crags high above the lake. One can watch the experts essaying forth with ropes and other equipment from the farms offering accommodation and from the inn at the top of the dale, but only the skilled can follow them to their fastnesses in the hills. Take heed of that warning. The Fells may not look much compared with the Alps, but they are very tricky and the weather even more so. Do *not* set off on what you think is an easy trek without taking advice from a local expert.

Further south and running parallel with Wasdale is Eskdale, with Muncaster Castle at its approach. Although it contains no lake, it is as wild a dale as any in the land, particularly at the head, where the old Roman way of Hard Knott climbs up the slopes on the way to Ambleside. Today, there is a narrow-gauge railway running from Ravenglass, the former Roman port on the coast, up Eskdale to Boot—the open carriages give fine scenic views in good weather.

South is the Duddon Valley, perhaps softer in aspect than the two to the north. From this river, we cross another ridge or two via A593 to get back to Coniston, and so to the vicinity of the southern approaches to Lakeland.

The Coasts

The seacoasts of west Cumbria, though in places devoted to coalmining and industry, are not to be ignored. From the road at Levens Bridge, south of Kendal, there are roads through the valleys and over the low ridges to Windermere (A5074 and 592) and one which keeps close to the estuary of the Kent to pretty Grange-over-Sands (A590) and then up to the foot of the same lake. While in the vicinity of Grange-over-Sands, be sure to visit nearby Cartmel Priory, dating from 1188, and Holker Hall, set in its own leafy deer park.

Barrow-in-Furness is mainly concerned with shipbuilding and repairing. A bridge here crosses the narrow channel to Walney Island, which, in spite of a lot of building, has fascinating sands on the opposite shore. Close to Barrow itself is the Cistercian ruin of Furness Abbey, and, at nearby Ulverston, most unexpectedly, a shrine to Hollywood's Golden Era of Comedy. Stan Laurel was born here, a fact celebrated in the town's marvelous little Laurel and Hardy Museum.

LANCASHIRE

South from the Lake District is Lancashire. For just a few miles the characteristics of Cumbria slide into Lancashire, as at Silverdale and the villages of Yealand Conyers and Yealand Redmayne, set in a mass of woodlands and as beautiful and unspoilt as their names suggest, and Warton, where ancestors of George Washington once lived. Links survive in the form of a plaque embodying the family coat of arms (said to be the source of the stars and stripes theme), originally incorporated in the masonry of the church tower, but now removed to safer keeping in the building itself. Near to Yealand Conyers are two old houses of particular interest—Leighton Hall which has belonged to its present owner-family for many generations and has good furniture and pictures; and Borwick Hall, an Elizabethan manor house which has not been altered since it was built in 1595.

Beyond Carnforth, the traveler who keeps to the old A6 road rather than taking the modern motorway (M6) which bypasses the old city of Lancaster on the way south, has a sight of the broad expanse of Morecambe Bay, bounded by the hills of the Lake District to the north. Low tide reveals a big area of sand, which in former days had to be crossed by travelers on their way to the peninsulas of Cartmel and Furness.

Lancaster

The main road continues to Lancaster, but there is a way (A589) along the coast to Morecambe, a popular resort which combines the usual attractions of a seaside holiday town with a situation that makes it a fine base for exploring the Lake District and neighboring countryside. A mile or so south is historic Heysham, whose church recently celebrated its 1,000th anniversary of foundation and whose old village street, running down to a cove where St. Patrick is said to have landed, is one of the most picturesque on the northwest coast.

Lancaster, which is the county town, is just about level with Morecambe and on the map there is not much to tell them apart. Unlike York, Lancaster has allowed much that was historic to disappear, but that is not entirely the fault of modern developers. A town which goes back many, many centuries—indeed, was once occupied by the Romans—is bound to have experienced some vicissitudes, especially one so near the Scottish border. A lot of building was done there by King John and later by John of Gaunt, "time-honored Lancaster." Elizabeth I did some repairs. The parish church of St. Mary is full of interest, and survived two burnings of the town by the Scots and devastation by the Black Death. Enough of the castle, too, remains, to be used as a gaol. George Fox, founder of the Society of Friends, the Quakers, spent some time in it, although the Friends Meeting House, dated 1690, is now a school. The town also has an unusually handsome Customs House, and a Town Hall containing two museums—one illustrating the history of Lancaster from the Stone Age, the other a military museum.

Bowland Forest

East of Lancaster there is a vast area of moorland called Bowland Forest, which is without roads, except for very minor ones. Two "B" roads skirt Bowland, one leads to Slaidburn, an austere gray village in which there is an excellent inn called Hark To Bounty. An almost feudal grasp on the village by its ancient landlords has forbidden any modern building, with excellent results. Bowland itself is unbelievably wild and remote, so that it comes as no surprise to learn that it was hereabouts that the famous Lancashire witches practised their debaucheries in the reign of James I, happenings that form the basis of Harrison Ainsworth's story, *The Lancashire Witches*.

Southeast from Slaidburn on B6478 is Clitheroe, yet another place with its castle perched on a knoll above the town. It may be regarded as the capital of the Ribble Valley area. A little way to the south are the ruins of Whalley Abbey, once the big religious house of the district and still exhibiting many signs of former wealth and prosperity, but the finest scenery is to the east where, once more, the Pennine hills mold its nature. Like that of the Lune, the Ribble is a vale of pretty villages, with Downham (northeast of Clitheroe) one of its gems.

The great hill of Pendle (to the east of Clitheroe) dominates the southern horizon and, although less in area than Bowland, retains the same wildness and feeling of remoteness.

The Seaside Resorts

West of the Bowland Hills and the road between Lancaster and Preston (A6) are the flatter lands of the Fylde, mainly devoted to farming, but with Blackpool, on the coast, serving as a magnet to those who would enjoy the offerings of one of the brashest holiday centers in the whole of Europe. Each summer, its theaters and homes of entertainment are occupied by the very top personalities of show business, who contrive to play before packed houses from late spring until well into the autumn. Fall is the season for the traditional Blackpool Illuminations, an extravaganza of colored lights along the seafront.

Preston is at the top of the Ribble estuary, a paradise for migratory wading birds.

THE ISLE OF MAN

Set almost in the center of the northern part of the Irish Sea between England and Ireland, and with the coasts of Scotland and Wales also visible from many parts, the Isle of Man combines something of the beauty of all its neighbors in one compact mass of land, covering an area of 227 square miles, with its greatest length only 30 miles and its maximum width little more than ten.

Necromancer's Island, some have called it, as a reminder that legend still speaks of its first ruler as one Manannan-Beg-y-Leir, from whom the name is derived, who was able to cause the mists to descend and so shield it from the eyes of any who coveted its charms.

Today, while linked with Britain in so many ways and, of course, having the Queen as monarch, it has its own Legislative Council, which can be said to correspond to the House of Lords at Westminster, and the House of Keys, which is its equivalent to the House of Commons. They pass the laws of the island, these being proclaimed annually at a fascinating ceremony on Tynwald Hill, in the center of the island, on old Midsummer Day, which falls on July 5 or, if that is a Saturday or Sunday, on the following Monday. In 1979 the island celebrated 1000 years of its Parliament with a re-enactment of the original Tynwald ceremony, the Grand Althing, and many other festivities.

Between the fanciful times of King Manannan and the present, much has happened to mold the story of the Isle of Man, with each successive period making its own contribution to the fabric of one of the most fascinating places within the British Isles.

The island's three-legged symbol represents the arms of Man, and its earliest appearance was on the Manx Sword of State (c. 1300). Its motto— *quocunque jeceris stabit*—means "it will stand wherever you throw it."

The center of the island is a mountainous mass of gorse-gold moorland, reaching its highest point at the summit of Snaefell (2,036 feet), and intersected by thirteen deep glens of compelling beauty. At the northern end of the island, however, the land flattens out as it reaches towards the Point of Ayre, which, in clear weather, seems a mere stone's throw from the hills of Scotland. To the south there is a similar flat expanse near Castletown, which houses Ronaldsway, the airport for the island.

Apart from these two sandy stretches, the coastline is mainly given over to high cliffs that rise majestically from the Irish Sea to encompass the rocky coves, fishing harbors, broad bays and bathing beaches.

Douglas

Daily sea services from Heysham near Lancaster, and summer sailings from Liverpool and Fleetwood, near Blackpool, serve Douglas, the largest town on the island and the best center for the visitor. A thriving holiday resort which captures something of the gaiety of Blackpool, its easy access from Lancashire makes it a favorite haunt of people from the mainland towns, many of whom find it hard to tear themselves away from its amusements to explore the mountainous interior of the island.

No one can deny the grandeur of Douglas Bay, which makes a majestic sweep from Onchan Head to the north to Douglas Head at the south. The promenade follows the same curve, although at the southern end it stops at the harbor, where the River Dhoo and the River Glass converge and flow between the town and the headland. Here are the larger boarding houses and hotels, one of which, the Castle Mona, is interesting as it was the residence of the last of the Dukes of Atholl to be connected with Man. Also along the Central and Harris promenades are the various places of entertainment, including the lovely Gaiety Theater and nearby Villa Marina, both with lively summer shows—and, for younger people, the Palace Lido Laser Disco, reckoned to the largest in the world. There's also the Palace Casino and Whisper's Nightclub, open until 5 A.M. The horse-drawn tramcars which ply along the promenade are a distinct feature of the town in summer. And if you want to see the island's famous tailless cats, Nobles Park is the place to visit.

Among the most important events of the Isle of Man calendar are the famous Tourist Trophy races each June and the amateur Manx Grand Prix in September. The circuit, on closed public roads around the island, is certainly demanding and dangerous—many professional riders now refuse to compete here. But the challenge of the Isle of Man is deep-rooted among motorcycling aficionados, and thousands of enthusiasts flock here each year for the world-famous races.

On the opposite coast to Douglas is the small cathedral city of Peel, frequently referred to as "Sunset City" because of the magnificent colorings that come to sky and sea when the sun goes down beyond the western horizon, bringing a fairy glow to the warm red sandstone walls of its ancient buildings.

The road from Douglas to Peel passes through a broad valley which separates the northern and southern uplands. On the outskirts of Douglas, this passes the church at Kirk Braddan, and then goes on to St. John's, where the Tynwald ceremony already referred to takes place.

The Tynwald

Tynwald "hill" itself is an artificial mound, 12 feet high and 240 feet in circumference. There, after a service in the nearby church and a colorful procession, the Lieutenant-Governor, the Bishop of Sodor and Man and members of the Legislative Council and House of Keys gather to hear a recital of the various acts that have received the Queen's signature during the past twelve months and which now become law.

This is the oldest outdoor continuous "parliament" in the world and has its origin in the old form of administration carried out by the Vikings, who held sway in the Isle of Man for a lengthy period and who have also left many interesting monuments in the form of carved crosses and the like in different parts of the island.

Peel, a fascinating place of old alleyways, red sandstone buildings, and sandy shore, is the traditional home of the Manx kipper, and one can see the sheds where the herrings are cured or "kippered."

Most visitors, however, will make for the group of red sandstone buildings on the detached St. Patrick's Isle, which form Peel Castle and Cathedral. The ancient Celts are believed to have had the first church on this spot, where St. Patrick preached in A.D. 444 but this was destroyed in a Viking raid in the 8th century. Later, the Norsemen themselves had a fortification of sorts on the little isle, kings Godred and Olaf both dying there.

For several centuries afterwards, the place housed both church and fortress. The cathedral, dedicated to St. German and the cathedral church of the diocese, was rebuilt originally on the site of the older church by one Simon of Iona in 1126, although the diocese itself is said to have been founded by "King" Olaf nearly a century before. Later bishops added to the structure, but it was always one of the smaller cathedrals in the British Isles and even in the mid-17th century was in a somewhat dilapidated condition. Although efforts towards restoration have been made, these seem to have been of little avail.

As a fortress, the castellated sections of the buildings have housed prisoners, including the Earl of Warwick, who was confined to one of the towers of Richard II after plotting against the crown in the late 14th century.

Peel is also the home of the replica Viking longship, Odin's *Raven,* which was sailed from Norway to the Isle of Man in 1979 to commemorate the Millennium of Tynwald. Peel Castle is currently the center of one of the most exciting archeological digs in Britain. Finds so far have included the richest Viking pagan grave yet discovered in the British Isles, as well as a hoard of Viking silver, the ring of an English knight and a beautiful necklace of amber and glass beads.

Ramsey, 16 miles north of Douglas and the chief town of the northern part, is a pleasant coastal resort from where one can visit the Point of Ayre, at the northern extremity of the island, as well as the interesting zoological gardens recently established at The Curraghs, close to the entrance to Sulby Glen, a magic place of woods and waterfalls.

Snaefell and Its Railway

There are two principal routes between Douglas and Ramsey. One climbs across the eastern slopes of Snaefell and commands fine views over the island and across the Irish Sea; the other keeps nearer the coast, going through Laxey and passing the entrances to some delightful little glens leading down to the shore on the way to Maughold, where the cliff scenery is magnificent, before dropping into Ramsey.

From Laxey, a valley goes inland towards Snaefell. This was once the center of a prosperous mining industry, and a feature is the pump wheel, built in 1854 to drain water from the underground workings, which in places extend to a depth of 2,000 feet. It is maintained in working order by the Isle of Man Government as a showpiece of 19th-century engineering.

Laxey, too, is the terminus of the electric Snaefell Mountain Railway, which carries visitors to the very summit of the mountain. Here, on clear days, you can have wonderful views across the sea to the four countries of England, Scotland, Wales and Ireland, not to mention the whole of the island itself, set like a panoramic map below. Train enthusiasts will also enjoy the Manx Electric Railway, which runs from Douglas to Ramsey, and the Isle of Man Narrow Gauge Steam Railway, which runs between Douglas and Port Erin, as well as the Groudle Glen Railway near Douglas—all dating from the late 19th century.

In the southern half of the island is Castletown, once the Manx capital, but now simply a pleasant holiday resort whose sheltered harbor is guarded by Castle Rushen, one of the best-preserved medieval fortresses in Britain. The road to Castletown from Douglas passes the delightful gardens at Rushden Abbey, once a Cistercian Monastery.

It is in this southern section of the island that the coastal scenery rises to its full grandeur. Port St. Mary and Port Erin, both picturesque in themselves, are close to the magnificent cliffs, which show their real majesty at Spanish Head, opposite which the isolated rocky isle of the Calf of Man, now a bird sanctuary maintained by the Manx National Trust, rises in abrupt loneliness from the deep sea. And between Port Erin and Peel, Niarbyl Bay is a place for the connoisseur of all that is best in British coastal scenery.

PRACTICAL INFORMATION FOR
THE NORTHWEST

HOW TO GET TO THE ISLE OF MAN. It is very easy to combine a visit to the Lake District with one to the Isle of Man. The *Isle of Man Steam Packet Seaways* car-carrying ferries operate out of Heysham, backed up in summer by sailings from Liverpool. Heysham is only a few miles south of the Lake District and is easily accessible from London and the south on the M6 motorway. The crossing from Heysham takes about 3¾ hours, and operates throughout the year, with one afternoon sailing daily. At peak periods, for example during the TT races, many extra sailings are laid on. A connecting train service links Heysham Ferry Terminal and Lancaster Station on the London-Glasgow rail route. In summer there are through boat trains to Heysham Harbour from Manchester and Preston.

The Isle of Man Airport is at Ronaldsway, near Castletown (in Summer, an airport coach service runs to and from Douglas). Air services are operated throughout the year by *Manx Airlines* from London (Heathrow), Blackpool, Liverpool, Manchester, Glasgow, Belfast and Dublin; also by *Jersey European Airways* from Blackpool and Belfast, with connections from Exeter and Jersey. *Manx Airlines* also operate additional Summer flights from Birmingham, Leeds, Newcastle and Edinburgh. *Euroair* have recently introduced a summer-only service linking the Isle of Man with Carlisle and Dundee.

HOTELS AND RESTAURANTS. The Northwest can boast of many old inns scattered through the Lake District, some of them with incredible names. All are well worth a visit. Although the Lake District has plenty of comfortable hotels, there are few of the modern, luxury ones. There are also some notable regional food specialties—try Cumberland butter, made with rum, Grasmere gingerbread and Westmorland "tatie pot." Visitors to the Isle of Man should try "Queenies," tiny scallops fried with bacon—or the renowned Manx kippers (traditionally smoked herrings).

The Isle of Man is seasonal and most of the hotels and guest houses close by the last week of September though the larger hotels in each resort stay open with limited accommodation during the winter. Best to book well ahead for the summer season.

Details about our grading system, plus other relevant information about hotels and restaurants, will be found at the beginning of the book in the *Facts at Your Fingertips* section.

Ambleside (Cumbria). *Rothay Manor* (E-M), tel. (053 94) 33605; 18 rooms, all with bath. Thoughtful care, delightful bedrooms. Renowned restaurant has regional specialties and flawless service. Wonderful hospitality—but be sure to take plenty of exercise to preserve your waistline. Must book. Also good for buffet lunches and marvelous afternoon teas. *Kirkstone Foot Country House* (M), Kirkstone Pass Rd., tel. (053 94) 32232; 14 rooms with bath. Beautiful 17th-century building with excellent restaurant. *Nanny Brow* (M), Clappersgate, tel. (053 94) 32036; 19 rooms, 16 with bath or shower. Friendly and well-run. *Wateredge* (M), Borrans Rd., tel. (053 94) 32332; 23 rooms with bath or shower. Overlooking Lake Windermere, homely cottage atmosphere with good food. Lawns extend to lakeside.

Bassenthwaite (Cumbria). 130 acres of grounds run smoothly down to the lake from *Armathwaite Hall* (M), tel. (059 681) 551; 39 rooms with bath or shower. The situation, service and hospitality of this beautiful country house add up to a memorable stay. *Castle Inn* (M), tel. (059 681) 401; 22 rooms with bath or shower. Mountain views and enjoyable homely food. *Pheasant Inn* (M), tel. (059 681) 234; 20 rooms with bath or shower. A characteristic Elizabethan inn, coaching style.

Borrowdale (Cumbria). *Lodore Swiss* (E), tel. (059 684) 285; 72 rooms with bath. Lakeland hotel beside Derwent Water. Exceptionally well-equipped with sporting facilities. Good restaurant. Ideal for families. *Borrowdale* (M), tel. (059 684) 234; 35 rooms with bath or shower. A friendly place to stay in glorious surroundings.

Brampton (Cumbria). *Farlam Hall* (E–M), tel. Hallbankgate (069 76) 234; 13 rooms with bath or shower. Converted 17th-century farmhouse with beautiful grounds. Excellent local cooking, log fires, highly recommended. *Tarn End* (M), Talkin Tarn, tel. (069 77) 2340, 6 rooms, 4 with bath. French restaurant overlooking lake.

Buttermere (Cumbria). *Bridge* (M), tel. (059 685) 252; 22 rooms with bath. Views over the hills.

Carlisle (Cumbria). *Crest* (M), Kingstown, tel. (0228) 31201. 94 rooms with bath. Modern hotel at junction A7/M6.
At **Faugh.** *String of Horses Inn* (M), Heads Nook. Tel. Hayton (022 870) 297. 17th-century inn, now luxurious hotel, with 13 rooms with bath or shower.

Charnock Richard (Lancs.). *TraveLodge* (M), M6 Motorway Service Area, tel. Coppull (0257) 791746; 103 rooms with bath in reliable motel-style accommodation midway between London and Scotland.

Cockermouth (Cumbria). *Trout* (M), Crown St., tel. (0900) 823591; 23 rooms, 22 with bath or shower. Comfortable rooms and good food. *Wordsworth* (M), Main St., tel. (0900) 822757; 18 rooms, 4 with bath, 6 with shower. An old inn beside the River Cocker.

Coniston (Cumbria). Beautifully situated *Sun* (M), tel. (053 94) 41248; 11 rooms, all with bath or shower. Wonderful view of mountain scenery in all directions. *Black Bull* (I), Yewdale Rd., tel. (053 94) 41335; 7 rooms, 4 with shower. Ancient village inn with home comforts and friendly welcome.

Crooklands (Cumbria). *Crooklands Inn* (M), tel. (044 87) 432; 15 rooms with bath. Country inn well recommended for both accommodation and kitchen. Good restaurant in converted barn.

Eskdale (Cumbria). *Bower House Inn* (M), Eskdale Green, tel. (09403) 244; 21 rooms with bath. Modest and enjoyable.

Glenridding (Cumbria). *Glenridding* (M), tel. (085 32) 228; 45 rooms, 40 with bath or shower. Views of the lakes and hills.

Grasmere (Cumbria). *Michael's Nook* (L–E), tel. (09665) 496; 11 rooms with bath. A highly individualistic establishment of great charm; a superb restaurant with excellent wines. *Gold Rill* (E), Langdale Rd., tel. (096 65) 486. 16 rooms with bath. Stands close to the lake. *Wordsworth* (E), tel. (096 65) 592; 35 rooms with bath. Comfortable hotel with reliable *Prelude* restaurant. *Swan* (M), tel. (096 65) 551; 36 rooms with bath or shower, was visited by Sir Walter Scott and Wordsworth. *White Moss House* (M), Rydal Water, tel. (096 65) 295; 7 rooms with bath. Quiet stone house overlooking Rydal Water. Excellent English cooking in restaurant.

Isle of Man. Ballasalla. Restaurant. *La Rosette* (M), tel. (0624) 822940. Charming restaurant 8 miles from Douglas. French food of very high quality. Must book.

Castletown. *Golf Links* Fort Island (E–M), tel. (0624) 822201; 65 rooms with bath or shower. Surrounded by the sea—and the links course. Refurbished accommodation to high standard is complemented by well-cooked food and friendly service; tennis, seawater pool.

Douglas. Largest resort on the island. Plenty of entertainment and good center for exploring. *Admiral House* (E), Loch Promenade, tel. (0624) 29551. Sumptuously refurbished with comfortable *Captain's Table* restaurant. Modern *Palace* (M), tel. (0624) 74521. 138 rooms with bath, pool, and the only public casino in Britain. On the central promenade. *Sefton* (M), tel. (0624) 26011. 80 rooms with bath or shower; also good indoor pool and health club. There are many good restaurants.

Onchan. *Boncompte's* (E), tel. (0624) 75626. International cuisine. Overlooks Douglas Bay.

Peel. *Lively Lobster and Rampant Bull* (M), tel. (0624 84) 2789. Specializes in fish and makes good use of local sea food.

Kendal (Cumbria). *Woolpack Inn* (M), Stricklandgate, tel. (0539) 23852; 57 rooms with bath or shower. So called because its bar was once a wool trade auction room.

Keswick (Cumbria). *Underscar* (E–M), Applethwaite, tel. (076 87) 72469; 18 rooms with bath or shower. Italianate country house in own grounds. *Derwentwater* (M), Portinscale, tel. (076 87) 72538. 46 rooms with bath. Extensively refurbished. *Red House* (M), Skiddaw, tel. (076 87) 72211. 23 rooms, 18 with bath. Lovely mountain views. *Royal Oak* (M), Station St., tel. (076 87) 72965; 43 rooms, 22 with bath, 2 with shower. In town.

Newby Bridge (Cumbria). *Swan* (M), tel. (053 95) 31681; 36 rooms with bath. Good touring center at the foot of Lake Windermere.

Penrith (Cumbria). *George* (M), Devonshire St., tel. (0768) 62696; 31 rooms with bath or shower. One-time coaching inn in town center.

Pooley Bridge (Cumbria). *Sharrow Bay* (L), tel. (085 36) 301; 30 rooms, 24 with bath. Beautiful location 2 miles south of Pooley Bridge on scenic Howtown road. Excellent cuisine; well-appointed bedrooms. Room charges include dinner. *Leeming on Ullswater* (E), Watermillock, tel. (085 36) 622. 24 rooms, all with bath. Immaculate Georgian manor house with gardens leading down to Ullswater. *Old Church* (M), Watermillock, tel. (085 36) 204; 12 rooms, 7 with bath. 18th-century house on site of medieval church. Good hospitality and food.

Rosthwaite (Cumbria). *Scafell* (M), tel. Borrowdale (059 684) 208; 20 rooms with bath. A lovely country house with good food.

Troutbeck (Cumbria). *Mortal Man* (M), tel. Ambleside (053 94) 33193; 13 rooms, 7 with bath, 1 with shower. Stone inn; good home-made food.

Underbarrow (Cumbria). **Restaurant.** *Greenriggs* (M), tel. Crosthwaite (044 88) 387. 18th-century house in lovely countryside with enterprising restaurant. Also has 12 rooms.

Windermere (Cumbria). *Langdale Chase* (E), tel. Ambleside (053 94) 32201; 35 rooms, 33 with bath, beautifully furnished country house with glorious views. John Tovey's *Miller Howe* (E), Rayrigg Rd., tel. (096 62) 2536. Beautiful location. 13 rooms with bath. Closed Jan. and Feb. Expertly combines comfort and superbly original cooking. Staying here is an experience in how it should be done—and so seldom is. *Old England* (E), tel. (096 62) 2444; 84 rooms with bath. Comfortable and right by the waterside.
Beech Hill (M), Newby Bridge Rd., Bowness, tel. (096 62) 2137; 45 rooms with bath. Modern with good views and cuisine, indoor pool, sauna. *Lindeth Fell* (M), Upper Storrs Park Rd., Bowness, tel. (096 62) 3286; 15 rooms, all with bath or shower. Pleasantly refurbished; country house ambience. *Craig Foot* (M), Lake Rd., Bowness, tel. (096 62) 3902; 10 rooms in comfortable country house with lake views. *Wild Boar* (M), Crook, tel. (096 62) 5225; 38 rooms with bath. Said to be where last wild boar of Cumberland met its death. 2½ miles south of Windermere. Good restaurant. *Linthwaite* (M–I), Bowness, tel. (096 62) 3688; 11 rooms with bath. Great views. Closed Nov.–Easter.
Restaurant. *Porthole Eating House* (M), Bowness, tel. (09662) 2793. Cosy, reputable restaurant serving Italian dishes. Closed Tues. and Dec.–mid-Feb.

PLACES OF INTEREST. The Northwest does not have a massive pile such as Castle Howard among its stately homes, but it does have a plethora of smaller—some indeed intimate—places, many connected with such literary figures as Wordsworth. It is generally a softer, greener area, and the buildings reflect that fact.
For more details about visiting the places mentioned below, see the relevant section in *Facts at Your Fingertips* or our chapter on *Historic Houses*.

Cumbria. Brantwood, Coniston (tel. 0966 41396). John Ruskin's home, 1872–1900, full of his possessions and art; lovely setting with nature trail. Open all year. Mid-Mar.–mid-Nov., daily, 11–5.30; winter, Wed.–Sun., 11–4.
Dalemain House, between Penrith and Pooley Bridge (tel. 085 36 450). Medieval, Tudor and Georgian house, art treasures, Westmorland Yeomanry Museum. Open Easter–mid-Oct., daily (except Fri. and Sat.), 11.15–5.15.
Dove Cottage, and **Wordsworth Museum,** Grasmere (tel. 096 65 544). The early home of Wordsworth (1799–1808). Reopened in early 1979 after major restoration work. Open Mar. and Oct., Mon.–Sat., 10–4.30, Sun. 11–4.30; Apr.–Sept., Mon.–Sat. 9.30–5.30, Sun. 11–5.30; also late-Dec. and early-Jan., daily 11–4.30.
Holker Hall, Cark-in-Cartmel (tel. 044 853 328). 16th-century house with deer park and hot-air balloon displays. Lakeland Motor Museum. Open Easter–late-Oct., daily (except Sat.), 10.30–4.30. Park open until 6.

Laurel and Hardy Museum, Ulverston (tel. 0229 52292). Posters, letters, film shows and much, much more from the two comedians. Opening arrangements unconfirmed at presstime. Please check.

Levens Hall, near Kendal (tel. 053 95 60321). Elizabethan house with lovely gardens full of topiary work. Open Easter Sun.–Sept., Sun.–Thurs., 11–5.

Muncaster Castle, Ravenglass (tel. 065 77 614). Famous for its rhododendrons and azaleas. Both castle and grounds open Good Fri.–Sept., daily (except Mon. but open Bank Holiday Mon.). Castle 1.30–4.30; grounds 12–5.

Rydal Mount, Ambleside (tel. 0966 33002). Wordsworth's home from 1813 till his death in 1850. Much memorabilia; interesting small garden designed by the poet. Open Mar.–Oct., daily, 9.30–5; Nov.–Feb., daily, 10–4.

Sizergh Castle, near Kendal (tel. 05295 60070). Home of the Strickland family for 700 years. Open April–Oct., Sun., Mon., Wed. and Thurs., 2–5.45; gardens from 12.30. (NT).

Townend, Troutbeck, near Windermere (tel. 05394 32628). A rare example of a 17th-century farmhouse; much original oak furniture. Open Apr.–Oct., daily (except Mon.—unless Bank Holiday—and Sat.), 2–6 (or sunset if earlier). (NT).

Wordsworth House, Cockermouth (tel. 0900 824805). The birthplace of the poet. Mentioned in *The Prelude.* Audio-visual display. Open Apr.–Oct., daily (except Thurs.), 11–5, Sun. 2–5. Closed Good Fri. (NT).

Isle of Man. Castle Rushen, Castletown. On the site of the Viking capital of the island. 14th-century towers and stronghold with state apartment. Open daily all year, Sun. morning only. Across harbor, *Nautical Museum* (tel. 0624 5522). Open weekdays 10–1, 2–4, Sun. 2–5.

Peel Castle, Peel. Situated on St. Patrick's Isle. Existing ruins date from 8th to 14th centuries and have associations with Sir Walter Scott. Open mid-May–Sept., daily, Sun. afternoons only.

Lancashire. Gawthorpe Hall, Padiham (tel. 0282 78511). 17th-century manor house restored in Victorian times. Hall open Apr.–end Oct., Tues.–Thurs., Sat. and Sun. 2–6. Garden open daily all year 10–6. (NT)

Hoghton Tower, near Preston (tel. 025 485 2986). Striking fortified house in dramatic position. Dolls and walled gardens. Open Easter Sat.–Mon., then every Sun to end Oct. (also Sat. and Sun. in Jul., Aug.), and Bank Holidays: all 2–5.

Leighton Hall, Carnforth (tel. 0524 734474). 12th-century house, rebuilt 18th century. Beautifully sited. Home of Gillow family, with their interesting furniture. Extensive grounds. Flying displays of eagles and falcons (weather permitting), at 3.30. Open May–Sept., Tues.–Fri., Sun. and Bank Holiday Mon., 2–5.

Wigan Pier Heritage Centre, Wigan (tel. 0942 323666). Local life and industry c. 1900; recreates a Northern town at the turn of the century; also has world's largest working mill steam engine. Winner of 1986 "Come to Britain" Award. Open daily 10–5.

Rufford Old Hall, Rufford (tel. 0704 821254). Medieval building with remarkable ornate roof, furniture, arms and armor. Museum of Lancashire life. Open Apr.–early Nov., daily except Fri., 1–5; garden from 11. (NT)

WALES

Land of Poetry and Song

> The Land of my Fathers so dear to my soul,
> The land which the poet and minstrel extol.
> Her valiant defenders, her patriots so brave
> For freedom their life blood they gave.

It is indeed rare in this modern world to find a national anthem that stresses the artistic, as opposed to the political, aspect of the country; but it is necessary to understand fully this attitude before one can appreciate the subtle change that takes place as we pass the borderline between England and Wales. For no one can cross this frontier without realizing that he is no longer in England. This is due not only to the frequent duplication of place names in two languages on the signposts, but to an immediately apparent difference in the buildings, the villages, the shape of fields and the attitude of the people. All these will vary according to which of the main entrances to Wales you use—the north or the south—because never were the geographical differences more marked than they are in this tiny country. And make no mistake, it *is* a country, not a spare-part county for England.

For the people of Wales represent the remnants of those pugnacious Celtic people who were subjected to centuries of Roman rule, underwent the invasions of the Saxons who drove them to their mountain fastnesses, and endured the phenomenal organizing efficiency of the Norman conquerors without ceding one iota of their cultural independence. It is possibly not without significance that when the Romans landed in A.D. 43 they swept up through England without any great trouble, but it took them another thirty years to subdue Wales. It took the Saxons a hundred years to do something of the same sort, although in their case they pushed the Welsh into what they must have regarded as non-viable mountains and left them there. They didn't know the Welsh.

And here, perhaps, is the secret of the essential difference of the Welsh. An old Welsh proverb says, "The Celt always fights and always loses." Militarily and politically this has been true of the Welsh, but, during those centuries of ceaseless strife, the Welshman came to realize that there was something deeper, more important than political or military triumph, something he had always been unconsciously struggling to preserve, an indefinable passion for music and poetry and in this last battle, the Welshman has belied the proverb and emerged victorious.

Thus, very briefly, we have an explanation of the extraordinary tenacity with which this people has clung to its traditions, its customs, its language, and its own way of life, although politically it has been merged long since and has accepted the supremacy of Westminster with less difficulty than the Irish or the Scots.

Revival and Radicalism

This same fierce individualism explains two striking characteristics of the Welsh people—their non-conformity in religion; and radicalism (or zeal for reform) in the political and social spheres.

At the time of the Civil War, the religious and social upheaval which was tearing England apart spread to Wales. Here the non-conformists, or protesting faction, rapidly gained ground in a country where the people had been neglected for so long. Neither the English nor their language were understood, and here was a new doctrine being preached to them in Welsh. The oldest non-conformist place of worship in Wales, Maesyronnen Congregational Chapel at Glasbury, was built soon afterwards, in 1696. Then, not many years later, in 1743, John Wesley and his followers came to preach. Their faith and fervor, and spontaneous hymn-singing were just what the people needed, and soon the Methodist movement became a spearhead for a great religious revival. Little chapels sprang up in every village, but it was a hundred years later, in the middle of last century, that most of those to be seen today were built—at the time of the industrial revolution, when a second religious revival was under way.

Misery from the Mines

This was after the huge South Wales coalfield was discovered; it was to change the face of Wales. Until then, Wales had been almost entirely an agricultural country—bitterly poor, certainly, and often oppressed. A series of catastrophic harvests caused a constant stream of emigrants to the United States, and at the same time a fierce struggle was developing between landlords (who often spoke only English and who frequently lived in England), and the peasants. Side by side with this rural unrest was a greater menace—the discontent caused by the industrial explosion. That had not only laid waste the green valleys, but it made living and working conditions intolerable. People were herded together into houses, which, because of the steepness of the valleys, had to be built in terraces one above the other, till half the population of Wales was concentrated there, and opportunities for oppression were unlimited. There were riots at Merthyr, and a Chartist march on Newport, where the Westbury Hotel was besieged.

The anguish of the valleys was the catalyst that in Wales (England had her own problems) brought about early corporate moves towards trade, or labor, unions. Another pioneering influence was that of Robert Owen, born in Newtown, Mid Wales, who applied his Utopian socialist ideals to factory reform in Scotland. There is a small museum dedicated to him in Newtown, where he was buried. But nothing effective was possible until there was parliamentary reform, and an extension of the franchise. This came in 1867, and a year later, a general election gave the vote to industrial workers. For the first time the valleys had a voice, right inside the British Parliament. It began as Liberal, but they soon returned their own member, which eventually led to the birth of a new party, Labour. This naturally became synonymous with the labor unions.

Many Welshmen made their mark in British political life: Lloyd George as World War I statesman and Prime Minister, Aneurin Bevan as the passionate social reformer and voice of the valleys; more recently, George Thomas (now Lord Tonypandy) as a gifted Speaker of the House of Commons, and Neil Kinnock, present leader of the Labour Party. However for many Welshmen today politics means the defense of their language, customs and way of life. The Welsh genius flowers most often in the artistic and creative worlds, in music, theater and poetry. Witness the poet Dylan Thomas, a memorable and controversial character; another poet, R. S. Thomas, who is still weaving his magic from an obscure country parish; actor Richard Burton who died in 1984; Emlyn Williams, playwright and actor; Clough Williams-Ellis, brilliant architect and landscape artist, who created the dream village of Portmeirion and died, in his 90s, in 1978; and Mary Quant and the late Laura Ashley, fashion designers and trendsetters.

DISCOVERING WALES

Wales measures 200 miles from north to south. The south is where coal was mined (most pits have now closed), and the site of the only two big cities in the whole country, Cardiff and Swansea, with a combined population of less than half that of Birmingham. Modern Cardiff was built on a combination of docks and coal, though the city is now a thriving administrative and commercial center. The south also now has steel and general industrial activities. The north, on the other hand, has Snowdonia and could be said to have agriculture, tourism and forestry as its chief industries, slate mining now playing a very minor part. This could well have something to do with the attitude of the north and south Welsh to one another. North Walians sometimes call those in the south *Hwntws*, meaning the "people far beyond"—and one imagines that it is the pale that they are beyond. They are regarded as spendthrift, drinkers, strikers, anything you like that is uncomplimentary. In the south they call those in the north

Gogs, a nasty shortened version of *gogledd* meaning "north," and regard them as mean, fanatical, Welsh-speaking soccer players. In the south they speak English and play rugby.

New regional names are hard to accept if, in fact, local people ever do accept them. The Welsh (as do the English) tend to stick firmly to their old county names. Four of the new county names, introduced in 1974, are based on ancient Welsh kingdoms (Gwynedd, Powys, Gwent and Dyfed); the other counties are Clwyd, South, West and Mid Glamorgan.

It is not necessary for the traveler to get up-tight about the Welsh language. Those who do speak Welsh as a first language (now only one-fifth of the population) will also converse in English. Place names may look a bit daunting, especially those which seem to have no vowels, but have a go. Welsh is not as hard to pronounce as it looks at first sight. In fact its pronunciation is almost entirely phonetic.

Each of the consonants has only one sound—**b, d, h, l, m, n, p, t** are all as in English; **c** is always hard, as in *cat;* **ch** as in Scottish *loch;* **dd** the same as *th* in *this;* **f** same as v; **ff** same as English f; **g** always hard, as in gate; **ll** is the classic Welsh problem, something like hl; **r** is trilled as in *merry;* **s** is hard as in *essay.*

The dipthongs are—**ng** either as in *long* or **longer,** e.g. Bangor; **ph** as in *phone;* **rh** a trilled r followed by the aspirate; **th** as in *thin.*

The vowels in Welsh are **a, e, i, o, u, w, y,** and they have two values, short and long—**a** as in English ah, or as in French á; **e** with any ay sound, or e as in *pen;* **i** as in *machine,* or as in *pin;* **o** as in *gore,* or as in *not;* **u** rather depends on where in Wales you are, in the north it can be like a French u, in the south like both of the i sounds above; **w** can be like the oo in *pool,* or the oo in *good;* **y** long can be like the Welsh i, short like the u in *gun.*

The vowels are short when followed by two or more consonants, or by c, ng, m, p, t, and long when followed by b, ch, d, f, ff, g, s, th.

As a rule the stress is on the penultimate syllable. In some place names it is thrown forward on to the last syllable, e.g. Caer**dydd,** Ponty**pridd,** Llan**rwst.**

Chepstow to Monmouth

If you enter Wales in the south, it would be a great pity not to stop off at Chepstow to see the Wye Valley and particularly Tintern Abbey. You can get to Chepstow by train from Gloucester, or by road on M4. It is accessible from junction 22, immediately after crossing the Severn Bridge.

Chepstow itself is worth seeing. The medieval walls still encircle its narrow streets, and one of the town gates still stands, where from the 14th century traders had to pay feudal dues. Then there are the remains of its great Norman castle, the first stone-built fortress in Britain, high on the cliffs above the river.

Six miles upstream one comes to Tintern, straggling along the west side of the river with the abbey standing out on the wide bed of the valley. It is a most beautiful building on a most beautiful site, and there is quite enough of it left for one to be able to people it in one's imagination. Stay at one of the small hotels there in order to catch, with any luck, an early morning bonus when the sun slants through the tracery of the abbey's west window.

Having got this far, if time allows, continue along the lovely Wye to Monmouth, where you must turn west to avoid going into England. The town does, in fact, show signs of English influence in, for instance, its black-and-white buildings. It was here also that Henry V was born, in 1387. There is a statue to him in Agincourt Square, as there is also to Charles Rolls, co-creator of the Rolls-Royce car. The town has a fortified bridge over the River Monnow, which joins the Wye just below the town.

Cardiff

Take the A40 southwest from Monmouth and you pass the 15th-century Raglan Castle thought to be an early example of keeping up with the Joneses. It has two drawbridges, one for "occasions" and the other a sort of tradesman's entrance. It is one of the comparatively rare castles built by a Welshman instead of an Englishman, and there is a great deal of it left, with enough embellishment to evoke the grandeur in which the early Welsh gentry lived.

The A449 from Raglan to Newport leads to the meager remains of Usk Castle. The town is a pleasant, small market town. At Newport one can rejoin M4 and be in Cardiff within minutes.

Financially, industrially and commercially Cardiff is the most important city in Wales, but those things are not exactly exciting touristically. Neither is there much point in seeing the once-important docks, which are just the same as docks the world over. Even the evil reputation of Tiger Bay has been diluted if not washed away. But what Cardiff has to offer is a Civic Center of extreme distinction, magnificent parklands and a fascinating city-center castle.

There still persists an idea that Cardiff, because it was once a coal town, is dirty. Nothing could be further from the truth. Its Civic Center is, in fact, constructed of dazzling white Portland stone. Buildings of great architectural style are set on wide, tree-lined avenues. The domed City Hall, Law Courts and not-to-be-missed National Museum of Wales are all here, just a short walk from the main shopping streets. Several Cardiff theaters stage impressive performances. The New Theater, all red velvet and chandeliers, is the home of the Welsh National Opera Company, one of Britain's most imaginative. The Sherman has a wide variety of offerings, from dance to films. St. David's Hall, wonderfully spacious, has theater in the round, concerts and even sports.

The castle, which also stands just on the edge of the shopping center, is an unusual "three-in-one" historic site with Roman, Norman and Victorian associations. It stands on the site of a Roman fort, which had a ditch and an embankment beside the River Taff, enclosing eight acres. The Normans used what was left of the Roman defences and built a motte and bailey. By the 14th century, walls, towers and a second moat had appeared, and gradually the castle was enlarged and demilitarized until, between 1867 and 1875 the current Marquess of Bute, who owned it, caused it to be updated and enlarged by William Burges, who was responsible for the Protestant cathedral in Cork and who had an addiction to the French Gothic style. The result is that both the inside and outside of Cardiff Castle are an utter Victorian ego flight. The wildly decorated rooms can be seen by the public on guided tours, and visitors can also attend medieval banquets there.

Caerphilly to St. Fagan's

Six miles north of Cardiff on A469 is the huge pile of Caerphilly Castle, one of Britain's great surviving medieval fortresses equaled in size only by Dover and perhaps Windsor. The feature which seems to create most excitement in visitors is its leaning tower, which leans further than Pisa's, in Italy. This was possibly the result of an abortive attempt by Cromwell's men to blow it up. They also drained the moat and lakes, but these have been refilled, so that it is now possible to see how this great fortress was designed and operated. (Incidentally, the booklet *Castles and Historic Places in Wales* put out by the Wales Tourist Board is an absolute mine of information.)

From Caerphilly it is easy to cross westward about four miles to see the enchanting little Castell Coch on A470. This, too, was the work of William Burges by order of the third Marquess of Bute, working on it at the same time as they were perpetrating the Cardiff Castle facelift, but this must have been their leisure task. The whole thing is so like a romantic, fairy-tale castle that one can only enjoy it.

From Castel Coch it is possible to reach Llandaff Cathedral without going back into Cardiff, if you should so wish. Llandaff is now counted as part of Cardiff, but it still has an individual, village-like quality, especially about the cathedral green and the River Taff nearby. The Cathedral of St. Teilo—or at least the ecclesiastical site on which it stands—has been there for fourteen centuries. During that time Oliver Cromwell's soldiers used it as an ale house; it has been a post office; it has suffered collapse of a tower and a pinnacle and bombing by the Nazis. But it still stands, and contains Jacob Epstein's magnificent sculpture *Christ in Majesty*.

On west again from Llandaff to St. Fagan's where the Welsh Folk Museum is housed in the castle that stands imposingly at the top of a cliff face in the village. Here we have an Elizabethan mansion built inside the walls of a medieval castle, itself standing in a formal garden. Many of the rooms are furnished in period, a modern museum block contains everyday objects of Welsh life while, outside in the estate, old buildings have been rescued from afar and re-erected. It is a truly fascinating place.

The Gower Peninsula

Swansea marks the end of the industrial region of south Wales. And, as if to make amends for the one-time desecration of so much natural beauty—though the industrial scars are disappearing—the Gower Peninsula, on the neck of which Swansea stands, offers magnificent cliff scenery and unspoilt beaches. Mumbles, a bus ride from Swansea, is a favorite holiday resort and water sports center and an admirable spot from which to explore this beautiful coastline. The southwestern part of the peninsula is English-speaking, with English place names such as Cheriton, Overton, Pilton-Green, Fernhill, and Knelston, and the inhabitants refer to those living in the northeastern districts as those living in the "Welshries."

In the Penclawdd region of the Gower Peninsula you may see another sight to remind you sharply that you are in a land where ancient ways of life remain vigorous in spite of the impact of our mechanized civilization. For here the cockle women set forth at low tide, each on a donkey and with her head enveloped in a shawl fastened in the Arab fashion to protect her against the wind that can at times rage fiercely across the sands. Two, three, or four miles they trot, their donkeys splashing along in the shallow water, and looking exactly like a convoy of Bedouins in a flooded Sahara. The cockles lie hidden just under the surface, and with quick, dexterous fingers the cocklewomen scrape the sand and scoop them into their baskets where they are washed with sea water. With full baskets they make for the shore to prepare the cockles for the market. In Swansea, or in Carmarthen on market day, you will easily find them and you may enjoy cockles and vinegar very cheaply.

Several ruined castles, such as those at Penrice and Oystermouth, prove the importance of Gower in ancient days. At Llanrhidian stands an enormous cromlech known as Arthur's Stone. It is said locally that at night time it comes down to the sea to quench its thirst.

Mountains and Valleys

East of Swansea, beyond Neath, lie the valleys—the Rhondda is the most famous—so well described by Richard Llewellyn in *How Green Was My Valley*. But things have changed, and a new book might be called *How Black Was My Valley*, because the slag heaps are green again, thanks to land reclamation schemes. Their attractions for the tourist include craft centers, riding schools, canal restoration and mining museums. At Blaenafon, a coal mine known as Big Pit has been turned into a unique mining museum with guided underground tours.

As you travel north and west the skyline fills with lordly mountains; Carmarthen Van (meaning peak); the summits of the Brecon Beacons and, to the east, the Black Mountains—not to be confused with the Black Mountain, singular, in the west. These wild, windswept uplands stretch from the fertile Vale of Towy to the Wales/England border, and are now protected as the Brecon Beacons National Park. This is the home of the sturdy wild Welsh mountain pony, and also of vast flocks of sheep. Brecon and Abergavenny, the two principal towns in the area, are places where you may well pick up a bargain in the antique shops and local sales—perhaps a hand-carved wooden Welsh love spoon like those Brecon's museum displays. Both towns are also popular centers for pony-trekking, fishing, and walking in the Beacons.

Six miles west of Brecon, hidden away near the small village of Libanus is the well sited Mountain Centre, which has an information bureau, a buffet serving refreshments, and a marvelous panoramic view of the Beacons. Before leaving this scenic corner of Wales, try to fit in a trip to Craigy-Nos in the Tawe Valley. Here you can go on a conducted 45-minute walk *under* a mountain through the spectacular illuminated Dan-yr-Ogof Caves.

Starting from Pant on the edge of Merthyr Tydfil there is a narrow-gauge railway—the Brecon Mountain Railway—which currently runs to Pontsticill, two miles distant. The views from this line across the lake to the Brecon Beacons are superb.

Through the town of Carmarthen flows the Towy, famed for its salmon and, historically, its coracle-men. The coracle, a tiny craft which has been

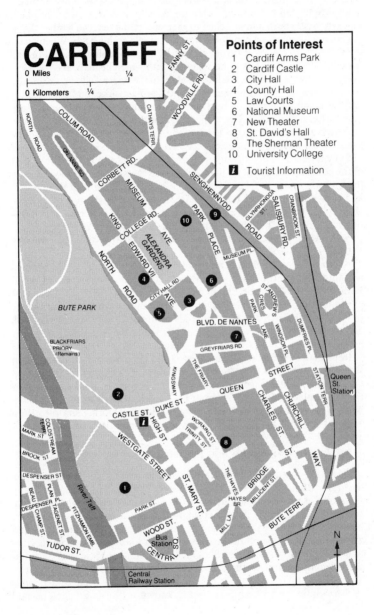

CARDIFF

0 Miles ¼

0 Kilometers ¼

Points of Interest

1   Cardiff Arms Park
2   Cardiff Castle
3   City Hall
4   County Hall
5   Law Courts
6   National Museum
7   New Theater
8   St. David's Hall
9   The Sherman Theater
10 University College

i Tourist Information

used by fishermen in this part of Wales for thousands of years, is a sort of wicker basket over which a leathery skin has been stretched to make it watertight. On the inside, across the middle, is a small wooden plank that serves as a seat, and attached to each end of the seat is a leather thong the coracle-man uses when he carries the coracle on his back. When walking he looks like a giant turtle, and when he places his frail shell on the water it is fascinating to see the dexterity with which he maneuvers it. Coracles are now a rare sight, confined mainly to the River Teifi, on the border of what used to be Carmarthenshire and Cardiganshire, and each year in August a coracle regatta is held there, something which can be seen nowhere else in the world. For a special grandstand view of it try to get to Cilgerran Castle, perched at the top of a precipice forming a bend in the river, along which the coracles race.

Carmarthen is a quiet country town with an ancient castle now a part of the council offices. But on market days the town is full of lively, chattering folk who come in from the surrounding countryside with their wares, and the sing-song lilt of the Carmarthen accent fills the narrow streets. (Nearly every region in Wales has a slight difference in accent which distinguishes it from the others, but it is difficult for a non-Welshman to appreciate this. Between north and south Wales the difference is very marked.)

Around Carmarthen is a soft, undulating, fertile countryside watered by innumerable little trout streams, and stretching northwards as far as Lampeter and Newcastle Emlyn on the Teifi. This river is one of the best game-fishing rivers in Wales, giving prize salmon, sewin and trout. As we progress northwards the scenery tends to become more sharply defined, and the little mountain streams more hurried as they sing their way over pebbly beds.

Immediately south of Carmarthen is the great spread of Carmarthen Bay which stretches from Gower to, at least, Tenby, and on it is Laugharne, an ancient township of great charm. It was the home, and is now the burial place, of Dylan Thomas. He lived in what was once the Boathouse—now a museum devoted to Dylan's life and work—and the neighborhood inspired his most celebrated work, *Under Milk Wood.*

South Pembrokeshire and Preseli

Down the coast to Tenby and we are in what used to be Pembrokeshire, the region that fills the southwestern tip of Wales. This area is in many ways one of the most curious in Wales. You may doubt whether Pembrokeshire is in Wales, for all around are English names like Deeplake, New Hedges, Rudbaxton. Indeed, south of Trefgan it is difficult to find a Welsh name, whilst off the coast near Milford Haven, the two bird sanctuary islands of Skomer and Skokholm add another (Scandinavian) linguistic complication to the scene. And you may wander over much of South Pembrokeshire without finding anyone who even understands Welsh. South Pembrokeshire, in fact, is known as "Little England beyond Wales."

This curious situation came about like this. The southern half of Pembrokeshire was conquered in the 11th century by one of Normandy's aristocratic soldiers with the help of William Rufus. When the Fleming weavers arrived in England during the reign of Henry I, he sent some of them to Pembrokeshire to teach the Norman settlers their trade. They then intermarried with the Normans and became completely anglicized. Traces of the Flemish influence are still to be seen, in the cottages and the lugsail fishing boats in the Milford Haven. Neither will you be disappointed if you look for Norman castles in the area. Tenby itself is an antiquarian's delight with its ancient walled town and historical remains, whilst the practical inhabitants have also utilized to the full its unique position on a cliff overlooking Carmarthen Bay and its firm sandy beaches to turn it into the most sophisticated seaside resort in South Wales.

Caldy Island, a couple of miles south of Tenby, is tiny but enchanting in the profusion of its beaches and coves. The southern part of the island swarms with seabirds whose shrill cries are at times almost deafening. Despite its size Caldy has a monastery where the monks carry on farming and weaving, and also make chocolate and their world-famous perfumes, the latter prepared from a closely guarded formula. It is a pot-pourri of lavender, gorse, ferns and flowers which grow in masses on the island.

Manorbier, on the road to Pembroke, is perhaps best known as the birthplace of Giraldus Cambrensis, a splendidly perceptive scholar of mixed Welsh and Norman blood who became a roving reporter of 12th-century Welsh life. The castle stands hugely on the cliff top overlooking the sea and is still lived in. It is, however, open to the public at regular times in summer.

Pembroke is worth a visit if only to see the great castle, one of the most impressive in Wales and the birthplace of Henry VII in 1457. It is easily accessible by road from Tenby, and the drive permits one also to stop a moment at Lamphey, in ancient times the bishops of St. David's country hide-away. The ruins stand in a most attractive setting just outside the village and at the end of a long avenue. It is clear they did themselves extremely well here. The ruins of the palace are open to the public, and there is a country house hotel close by.

The first people to settle Milford Haven across the water from Pembroke were Quakers who had had to leave Nantucket Island, Massachusetts, in 1793. It is easy to see even now the advantages its magnificent natural harbor with its numerous creeks gave it. Henry II used it in 1172 as the base from which he sailed to conquer Ireland, and until the early 19th century it still retained its importance as a point of departure for more peaceful voyagers to Ireland. It had one of the best fleets of fishing trawlers in Britain, but it has now become a major oil terminus. This is not something that everyone finds attractive, so the local tourist office encourages visitors to learn to love the tankers by taking the two hourly cruise in the *M. V. Tudor Rose* from Pembroke Dock—Hobb's Point pier—up stream to Landshipping and down to Thorn Island. Thorn Island has a strange, 19th-century blockhouse fort, now an hotel. Along the Milford Haven there are also a number of delightful little bays and villages, particularly Angle, which can be visited equally well by land.

Above a curve of the Eastern Cleddau stands Picton Castle, surrounded by stunning woodlands and gardens. The flowering season for the large collection of shrubs, gathered from all over the world, lasts from Christmas till autumn. The 12th-century castle (viewing from the gardens only) also houses the Graham Sutherland Gallery, open to the public, a collection of the works of this famous British painter, donated to the nation by

Lord Goodman. Sutherland spent much time in Pembrokeshire, and many of his works were inspired by the area.

On the way from Pembroke to Picton by road, A4075, look for Carew Castle magically sited on the banks of the river, and make a little diversion to Llawhaden Castle, another hideaway for the bishops of St. David's. They entertained here in guest apartments constructed in pairs, each with a "sittingroom" and bed-chamber with a latrine—a 12th-century suite, in fact.

On the banks of the Western Cleddau, which flows into Milford Haven, is Haverfordwest, English in aspect and sentiment; a town such as you might find in one of the English southern counties, with its picturesque steep streets and its purposeful air of a prosperous little market town. The 13th-century Church of St. Mary is probably one of the finest of its kind in Wales.

At Haverfordwest we have begun to leave behind the comparative lowlands of the extreme south, and the road westwards, A487, climbs round the top of St. Bride's Bay and drops down into St. David's, a very small and very friendly village yet nevertheless a city on account of its cathedral. This is a place that has been described as the "holiest ground in Great Britain," for here, in the midst of a tiny village, is the venerable Cathedral of St. David, and the shrine of the Patron Saint of Wales, where his bones rest in a casket behind the high altar. Unlike any other cathedral it does not seek to dominate the surrounding countryside with its enormous mass, for it is set, quaintly enough, in an enormous hollow, and the visitor must climb down 39 steps (called locally the Thirty-Nine Articles) to enter the cathedral. This may have, either way, something to do with the fact that an early Pope decreed that two pilgrimages to St. David's were equal to one to Rome.

The first view of this cathedral is quite extraordinary for, from a distance, only the square tower can be seen, and it is only by approaching the vast hollow that one can see that there is a cathedral built within it. From the outside, St. David's has a certain simple austerity that harmonizes well with the green, windswept countryside where it is built, but the interior is endowed with a richness that more than recompenses for this external severity. In the hush of this ancient building one can recapture the atmosphere of those days nearly 1,400 years ago when this was almost the sole outpost of Christianity in the southern half of the British Isles.

Not far from St. David's are the ruins of the Chapel of Saint Non, the mother of St. David, and tradition has it that St. David himself was born here. As everywhere in this most westerly point of Wales, the coastal scenery is unsurpassed for rugged grandeur, and as such is preserved as the Pembrokeshire Coast National Park.

The coast road, A487 still, which is not by any means always in sight of the sea, next comes down into Fishguard and Goodwick, the twin towns holding hands on either side of Fishguard Bay. Goodwick is at sand level and has the terminus for the main South Wales railway line from London. It is also the embarkation point for the B & I and Sealink British ferries for Rosslare in Southern Ireland.

Fishguard itself is fiercely perched on a steep hill, while at the bottom of the hill is Lower Fishguard, clustered about its pretty little fishing harbor. In the square at Fishguard the Royal Oak Inn still displays mementoes of the ludicrous attempted invasion in 1797 of around 1,300 French troops under an American commander, one Colonel Tate. The whole thing was a thirty-six hour farce. Landed on the far side of the peninsula from Goodwick, they were without cover or tents and lit themselves huge fires while the good people of Fishguard looked down on them in wonderment. After two nights they surrendered, without firing a shot, to the 600-strong local troops plus some scythe and pitchfork carriers, lining neatly up on the Goodwick sands to lay down their arms. The Fishguard commander was the Earl of Cawdor, of the Macbeth family, who happened to be living in Fishguard at the time.

And that was the last invasion of Britain.

Inland from Fishguard are the Preseli Mountains, noted unfortunately for rain, but also as the place from which the blue stones forming Stonehenge's inner ring were taken. The whole place is thick with standing stones and cromlechs, and there is also a Roman camp. Eastwards you can drive down into the quiet, rolling, typically Welsh farming country until you will come to the River Teifi where the coracle men operate, the salmon jump, and the water bustles over stones and between the pointed bridge piers. It isn't mapped due east of Fishguard, but northeast, but you will notice that everything in Wales seems to lie northwest to southeast, or northeast to southwest, which is what makes driving across Wales such a long, zigzag business. Thus, setting out eastwards from Fishguard one inevitably arrives at the border of the old county of Cardigan, which is now in the region known as Dyfed.

Cardigan and the Pembrokeshire Coast Path

Cardigan—the town as opposed to the county—is the southern starting point of what is known in Tourist Office literature as Mid Wales (they have three such booklets well worth getting: South Wales, Mid Wales, and North Wales). This charming little market town is perched astride the Teifi on an ancient bridge, it was the scene of a never-allowed-to-be-forgotten victory by the Welsh over the Norman army in 1136. It has a castle, private, and just across the bridge into St. Dogmael's is the remains of an abbey. The Welsh name for Cardigan is Aberteifi, meaning Mouth of the Teifi. Its position at the mouth of the river is very important to it, because beyond St. Dogmael's it becomes a wide, sandy shore most excellent for quiet, family holidays.

Two miles northwest of St. Dogmael's is also found one end of the Pembrokeshire Coast Path which stretches 180 miles round the coast of Pembrokeshire to Amroth, which is near Saundersfoot, right back in Carmarthen Bay. You can join or leave the path at several points, mostly where inns are available for overnight stops, and there is also a special bus service linking the particularly interesting stretches. Be prepared for magnificent cliff scenery made up of sandy coves or forbidding cliffs, coastal flowers in great profusion, and a huge, noisy seabird population. Also, on occasions, wind. Walkers are warned not to regard the trek as child's play and to exercise sensible care. Particulars from any Wales Tourist Board office. There is one in Cardigan.

Leaving Cardigan on the east side of the Teifi estuary, the road goes straight out as if intending to hurl itself into the sea, but ends in a scatter of rather prim houses, and an hotel. This is Gwbert, an isolated hamlet which stands on the cliff top above a mixture of giant rocks and clean sand.

After a series of little, almost unused, coves there is ultimately nothing but rocks, humping blackly out of a very clear, extremely deep inshore sea, which quite soon will become part of the much wider Cardigan Bay. At the point where the two waters meet stands Cardigan Island, a great eminence, covered equally in undernourished grass and bird droppings. At nesting time there is standing room only for the gulls, while its cliff caves and those of the mainland are favorite haunts of seals. They can hardly ever resist bobbing up to have a look at people.

The up-market Cliff Hotel at Gwbert must undoubtedly be numbered among the best placed in Britain, and has its own comic nine-hole golf course on which the visitors are free to play. More serious players will find a "proper" 18-hole course farther inland.

The Mid Wales Coast

From this point northwards, the coast displays its particular Mid Wales character. It is a mixture of little coves that hardly anybody has yet noticed, such as Mwnt, with its tiny church; coves which once were little but *have* been noticed, such as Aberporth; to places like New Quay which are somewhat overwhelmingly noticed in summer. All the same, there are not many serious seaside resorts—in the English sense—in Wales, although Barmouth, which actually possesses a promenade, is one of them. Ideally situated on the northern side of the picturesque estuary of the Mawddach, with its two-mile-long promenade, its wide expanse of golden beaches, its facilities for sea, river, and mountain lake fishing, even 100 years ago Barmouth was one of the most popular holiday resorts in Great Britain. Tennyson wrote part of his *In Memoriam* whilst staying there, and was inspired to write *Crossing the Bar* by the spectacle of the Mawddach rushing to meet the sea. Darwin worked on *The Origin of Species* and *The Descent of Man* in a house by the shore; Shelley stayed there with his wife in 1812; Ruskin was a constant visitor and was trustee of the St. George's cottages built there by the Guild of St. George in 1871.

Aberystwyth makes the best of several worlds because, besides being undeniably a holiday resort, it is the oldest university town in Wales; it houses the magnificent National Library of Wales; has a little harbor and quite clearly a life of its own. Beautifully situated on the shores of Cardigan Bay, with a fine wide beach curving from the university buildings at the southern end to Constitution Hill at the northern extremity, Aberystwyth stands almost midway between north and south Wales. There are few towns in Wales that can boast such a wide variety of scenery within their immediate neighborhood. Inland, a magnificent mountain road passes the Rheidol power station, and then climbs along the flanks of Plynlimon to the huge Nant y Moch Dam, near the summit, and winds down the other side. But whether you go to Devil's Bridge along the beautiful Rheidol Valley, or up to Plynlimon through the wild but entrancing Llyfnant Valley, or merely stroll over Constitution Hill to the lovely little beach at Clarach, you will see to the north the beginnings of the rugged mountain scenery so typical of north Wales, whilst to the south the hills and valleys of northern Dyfed slope away more gently.

Devil's Bridge is one of the most extraordinary sights in Great Britain. It is served by the Vale of Rheidol Narrow Gauge Railway, British Rail's last remaining steam-operated line. Clamped between two rocky cliffs through which a torrent of water pours unceasingly into a dark pool far below, this bridge well deserves the name it bears—*Pont y Gwr Drwg*, or Bridge of the Evil One, for legend has it that it was the devil himself who built it. There are really three bridges, and the lowest of all is 800 years old.

To the north of Devil's Bridge, Plynlimon raises its hoary head and bids you take heed that you are now on the threshold of north Wales, for its northern slopes stretch down to the River Dovey, which is the natural boundary between north and south Wales. The Severn and the Wye both spring from the flanks of this giant.

Besides the Vale of Rheidol Railway going up to Devil's Bridge, there are four other narrow-gauge lines nearby to delight the enthusiast: the Talyllyn Railway with its coastal terminus at Tywyn; just a few miles up the coast there is the two-mile Fairbourne Railway to Barmouth Ferry; and the Ffestiniog Railway from Porthmadog which climbs its way for 14 miles through increasingly wild country to Blaenau Ffestiniog. From here bus services run to Llechwedd Slate Caverns which run a conducted tour on the miners' tramway, which can be an interesting if awe-inspiring experience. Finally, at Bala Lake there is a narrow-gauge railway doing a four-and-a-half-mile trip along one side of the lake.

All along the coast there is fishing—from shore or boats—and surfing from various beaches lying between Borth and Harlech. At Ynyslas there are magnificent sands and dunelands, with superb views across the Dovey Estuary to Aberdovey.

An old song with a plaintive melody, *The Bells of Aberdovey*, has made Aberdovey famous. A legend relates that centuries ago the sea burst the protecting wall and submerged a large part of the town including the church, and it is said that if you listen carefully you will still hear the faint sound of the bells as they sway to and fro with the movement of the water. Debussy's *Cathédrale Engloutie* was probably inspired by this same legend, but lacks the simple charm of the old Welsh melody. Aberdovey is a quiet little town, unpretentious but hospitable, with fine sandy beaches and an equable climate that attract great numbers of visitors.

In 1402 the great Welsh hero, Owain Glyndwr, was declared Prince of Wales in Machynlleth (Powys), farther up the Dovey, before he began his brilliant but ill-fated campaign to drive out the English. The place in which he is said to have held his first parliament may still be seen. Machynlleth today, peaceful and law-abiding, is a favorite spot for anglers and a good motor touring center.

A few miles upstream from Barmouth is the ancient mountain town of Dolgellau, beautifully situated at the foot of Cader Idris. A neat, stone-built center with hotels, guest house and farmhouse accommodation available, it also has shops. Finding small places in Wales which have shops of any significance is not always easy, but Dolgellau is the market town for a number of villages round about. It is markedly Welsh in speech and custom.

Looming over the town is Mynydd Moel, one of the peaks of the famous Cader Idris. This mountain, whose Welsh name means the Chair of Idris, is connected by ancient legend with Idris, the heroic warrior-bard. It is said that anyone sleeping for a night in that part of the mountain reputed to be the actual chair of the bard will awaken either a poet or a madman. The Talyllyn narrow-gauge railway runs from Tywyn on the coast to the foothills of Cader Idris. There are five recognized routes on which to walk up to Cader Idris, or for those strong of foot and head there is the famous Precipice Walk above the winding Mawddach estuary.

Harlech

From the south side of the Mawddach, all the way up to the Glaslyn estuary, the coast is sand—real, usable sand beaches. Almost on the coast, reached from A496, is Harlech Castle, probably the most evocative building in Wales—strangely enough, for both the Welsh and English. Built in 1283, it then stood on its promontory overlooking an inlet of the sea, which has since receded. It still, however, provides absolutely breathtaking views of Snowdon; of the Lleyn Peninsula; of a great expanse of Cardigan Bay, as well as to the Cader Idris range and on, forty miles, to Plynlimon.

The story of the great defence of the castle by Dafydd ab Einion in the 15th-century War of the Roses is told in that well-known and stirring march *The Men of Harlech* which Welshmen, even today, are liable to sing in moments of great stress.

About two miles south of Harlech there is a favourite yachting creek called Llanbedr, from which 2,000 stone steps are built into the mountainside. Popularly called the Roman Steps and thought to have been built for the use of Roman soldiers guarding the pass, they nevertheless remain an archeological mystery. Llanbedr church bears a Bronze Age sign on one of its stones.

The Glaslyn Estuary just north of Harlech marks the end of the Mid-Wales district according to the Tourist Office, and there, on a wooded peninsula stands the strange, Italianate creation of the late Sir Clough Williams-Ellis, a little pale-washed village which looks as though it has escaped from the Mediterranean. It is called Portmeirion. Its pottery is famous. The village is private, but people may visit it on payment of a toll. The one, good, hotel was badly damaged by fire early in 1981, and accommodation is mainly in cottages, though the restaurant has remained open.

The Snowdonia National Park

Portmeirion is within the Snowdonia National Park, which means that it is lapped in scenic luxury. The Park consists of 840 square miles of countryside containing mountains, lakes, forests, and twenty-five miles of coast all with one thing in common—beauty; and, to a lesser extent, solitude. It is not a park in the usually accepted meaning of that word, but an area of ordinary, working country designated "park" for its own preservation and the enjoyment of the public. Several main roads slant across it, and there are a number of lesser, unclassified, wild roads. Or, if you prefer, you can hop on and off the Snowdon Sherpa, which is a circular bus service with pick-up points all round the park. (More detailed information from the local tourist offices.) There are also various nature trails to follow on foot, and eight information centers.

The lead in Snowdonia is, of course, played by Snowdon itself, the highest mountain in England and Wales (3,560 feet), which can be ascended by foot or by mountain railway from Llanberis. It is the central point of interest in Snowdonia National Park, one of three such parks in Wales. It is impossible to describe the magnificence of the view on a clear day. To the northwest the Straits of Menai, Anglesey, and beyond to the Irish Sea, to the south the mountains of South Gwynedd, Harlech Castle, and Cader Idris, and all around great towering masses of rock, wild and barren of vegetation. If you take the railway from Llanberis, telephone from the terminus to ascertain whether the peak is free from mist, for you will lose much if you arrive when clouds, as often happens, encircle the monster's brow. Always also take with you a sweater or anorak however hot it may be in the valley when you set out, because you will need it up the top, where there is a restaurant and bar selling hot drinks as well as the more usual beverages. It is, naturally, possible to walk up Snowdon, but it is not something which should be undertaken on impulse. Snowdon demands its toll of lives every year.

The lower terminus of the Snowdon railway is at Llanberis, which is the heart of the famed Llanberis Pass, and just across the road, so to speak, is the Gilfach Ddu terminus of the Llanberis Lake Railway. Laid on the track of a disused slate-quarry railway, it runs along the eastern shore of Llyn Padarn, providing splendid views of both the lake and Snowdon, behind it.

At its southern end, Llanberis Pass runs into the valley of Nant Gwynant which leads to Beddgelert, a popular mountain village surrounded by marvelous scenery and enhanced by the rivers Glaslyn and Colwyn. With three hotels, a number of guest houses and farmhouses offering accommodation, plus a well-run caravan site, it is a good center from which to tour or walk.

Betws-y-coed, in the Gwydyr Forest, is at the meeting place of two valleys and is another excellent center for viewing Snowdonia. Slightly larger than Beddgelert, it has a summer theater, and the nearby Swallow Falls. If you follow the Vale of Conwy down through Llanrwst, of which the three-arched bridge was designed in 1636 by Inigo Jones, you come to Bodnant Garden (off A470). Laid out in 1875, the 87 acres are particularly famed for their rhododendrons, camellias and azaleas. But its reputation as the finest garden in Wales does not rest solely on those; it has also terraces, rock and rose gardens and pinetum—it is, in fact, magnificent.

Continue northwards and you arrive on Wales's greatest leisure coast, stretching in almost unbroken sands from Penmaenmawr in the west, to Prestatyn in the east. Just round the corner from there the sand ends and one is facing the Dee Estuary, with one of the less appealing parts of England on the other side. As would be expected, this north coast stretch of sand has been transformed more or less from end to end into one continuous seaside resort incorporating Rhyl, Pensarn, Abergele—a little away from the sea but a great caravan place—Colwyn Bay, Rhos on Sea and Llandudno, the greatest.

Cradled in Orme's Bay, between the rocky precipices of Great Orme's Head and Little Orme's Head, Llandudno pursues its successful career as one of the most frequented of all Welsh seaside resorts. It is a favourite spot for visitors from the north of England and the Midlands, for it provides practically everything that a holiday-maker can desire. Superb sandy beaches, a magnificent situation in the shelter of Orme's Bay, safe, first-class bathing facilities, theaters, cinemas, and all the amenities of an up-to-date seaside resort, and yet down the valley of the Conwy River, within easy distance by road or rail, lie the mountains and ancient towns, supremely indifferent to the encroachment of modern civilization.

Let us follow suit, and return down the valley through Betws-y-coed and the Vale of Ffestiniog to the Lleyn Peninsula, but stopping off first to have a look at Conwy. Do not be deterred by the spread of the 12,000 population—the old town, encircled by a three-quarter mile wall with 22 semicircular towers, embraces an old world. The castle, with eight towers and massive curtain walls, was built by Edward I of England, as a headquarters for the final stages of his battle against the Welsh. He was himself besieged there at one point. He later perpetrated a historic con trick (see following page) on the Welsh at Caernarfon Castle, 24 miles down the coast. Conwy was built in a little over five years and, astonishingly, the walls were limewashed. It must have looked stunning against its backdrop of mountains. Today, three bridges span the river in front of it: Telford's chunky yet elegant chain suspension bridge; Robert Stephenson's rather less attractive tubular rail bridge; and the modern road bridge, which is said to be perfectly arched. See also two ancient houses still in use, though not as residences—Plas Mawr and Aberconwy—and, if you like mussels, don't forget to try them at Conwy where for centuries they have been gathered at the harbor bar, for despatch in sealed bags all over England.

The Lleyn Peninsula

The Lleyn Peninsula is that piece of land which forms the north coast of Cardigan Bay and points like an accusing finger down St. George's Channel at the Atlantic. Entrance to it on the south side is through Porthmadog, leading on to Criccieth, Pwllheli, Abersoch and Aberdaron. The railway goes only as far as Pwllheli, but frequent bus services permit the visitor to explore further.

Lleyn has been described as the Land's End of Wales. It is certainly remote, Welsh speaking and very ancient. Pwllheli is proud of its sands, which it claims to be the finest in Wales. But the view across Tremadog Bay with its towering background of mountains would be enough to justify its reputation as one of the leading resorts of the Lleyn Peninsula. A fascinating tradition surrounds Porthmadog. Long before Columbus sailed on his great journey of discovery, a Welshman named Madog ab Owain Gwynedd set sail for the new world from Ynys Fadog. Though he never returned, many centuries later it was discovered that a remote North American Indian tribe showed inexplicable traces in their language of Welsh phonetics. Whether the two have any connection we shall never know, but it opens up intriguing possibilities.

Criccieth, with its 13th-century castle ruins, is a pleasant little resort and again, the panorama of sea and mountain across Tremadog Bay is breathtaking in its loveliness. Not far away is the village of Llanystumdwy, where the Welsh statesman, Lloyd George, went to school (the village has a small museum dedicated to him), and where he is buried. "Y Gegin," the little theater, in Criccieth, presents Welsh and English plays, folk dances and singing from time to time though it is mainly used for art exhibitions in the summer.

Abersoch is a small village with a big beach, a harbor, a number of hotels and increasing popularity among sailing enthusiasts. Car parking is sometimes difficult in high summer. Aberdaron, on the other hand, retains its picturesque fishing-village character. Don't miss Y Gegin Fawr, café and souvenir shop in what was once a rest house for pilgrims to Bardsey Island the "sacred island," where legend tells that 20,000 saints lie buried. Known in ancient time as the Gate of Paradise, three pilgrimages to Bardsey Island were counted by the Church as equivalent to one pilgrimage to Rome. (It may be recalled that two pilgrimages to St. David's were considered sufficient.) On the northern shores of Lleyn is the small summer resort of Nefyn, set on a cliff overlooking the Bay of Nefyn. It is a quiet resort with safe bathing and a golf course nearby. A bus service connects it with Caernarfon.

Caernarfon

Caernarfon lies at the southern end of the Menai Straits, the grim majestic mass of its castle reflected in the now peaceful waters of the Seiont River. Tragedies and bloody encounters were witnessed by these silent, sullen walls, erected by Edward I in the 13th century as a symbol of his determination to reduce the Welsh to complete subjection.

But in 1284, it is said, the crafty monarch thought of an amazing scheme. Knowing that the proud Welsh chieftains would accept no foreign prince, he promised to designate a ruler who could speak no word of English. He sent his Queen, Eleanor of Castile, who was expecting a child, post-haste to Caernarfon that she might be delivered there, and in this cold stone fortress the Queen gave birth to a son. Triumphantly, Edward presented the infant to the assembled chieftains as their prince "who spoke no English, had been born on Welsh soil, and whose first words would be spoken in Welsh." The ruse worked, and on that historic day was created the first Prince of Wales of English lineage. Since then the eldest son of the ruler of England has usually been designated Prince of Wales.

In July, 1969, Caernarfon glowed again with pageantry when Queen Elizabeth II presented her eldest son, Prince Charles, to the people of Wales as their prince. This was the first time the ceremony had been held for 58 years, since 1911, in fact, when Prince Edward, the late Duke of Windsor, was presented by his father, George V. Today this Royal town is a market center for farmers and growers on both the Lleyn and Anglesey. A market is held each Saturday on the square before the castle.

Isle of Anglesey

The Isle of Anglesey, known in early days as Mona, the Mother of Wales, is joined to the mainland by the Menai suspension bridge, one of the most extraordinary engineering feats ever achieved, especially when one considers that it was constructed in 1820. The main railway line from London passes over the Britannia tubular bridge which, although not as graceful as the suspension bridge, is a technical masterpiece, designed by Stephenson and finished in 1850. Damaged by fire in 1970, it was reopened in January 1972. The new Britannia Road Bridge also eases traffic flows on the narrow Menai Bridge.

Among the many villages on Anglesey is one famous as having the longest bona fide name of any place in the world:

LLANFAIRPWLLGWYNGYLLGOGERYCHWYRN-
DROBWLLLLANTYSILIOGOGOGOCH

However, you will no doubt be relieved to know that everyone refers to it simply as Llanfair PG. This famous tongue-twisting place name has recently been beaten in length by the name of a halt on the Fairbourne Railway (see *The Little Trains of Wales* in the "Practical Information" section), though Fairbourne's efforts are inspired more by publicity seeking than linguistic authenticity.

Anglesey used to be notable for its rich cornfields, reputedly sufficiently extensive to feed all of Wales—hence the name Mona, Mother of Wales. It has now settled for gentle, mixed agriculture. Charming, unpretentious seaside resorts are dotted about the northwest tip of Anglesey. From Holyhead a regular ferry service runs daily to Ireland. Holyhead is also a notable holiday resort, and from the granite rock of Mynydd y Twr, called in English, Holyhead Mountain, there is a superb view of Snowdonia, the Isle of Man and, on a clear day, even of Ireland.

Beaumaris is the assize town of the island, and a quiet, dignified, seaside place, with facilities for yachting, bathing, and golf; it is much more like an English southcoast town than a Welsh one, with elegant houses and a lot of turfed space. Its castle, a huge fortress brooding close to the sea and of singular interest to military experts, was the last to be built by Edward I, in 1293, to guard northwestern Gwynedd.

There is a secondary road all the way round the edge of Anglesey—very convenient for touring the various resorts—while A5 cuts straight across from Holyhead to the mainland via the new Britannia Road Bridge (take the old A5 route if you want to drive across the picturesque Menai Suspension Bridge). But pause on the way, at Llanfair PG, to visit Plas Newydd, an 18th-century house by James Wyatt, which, besides being charming in itself, is magnificently placed for viewing the Straits and Snowdon. It contains Rex Whistler's largest wall painting, and a military museum with Waterloo relics.

Eastwards to Llangollen

Immediately over the Straits the railway slips into Bangor (the A5 now bypasses it), a cathedral and university city which derives its name from *Banchor* or "chief choir," a religious institution founded in the 6th century by St. Deiniol, who also built the original church, destroyed by the Normans and rebuilt by them in the 12th century. Today it is a very active township and sailing center with, just one mile to the east, Penrhyn Castle containing a collection of over a thousand dolls. It is fully furnished and is an outstanding example of neo-Norman architecture, dating from 1827. It is sumptuous inside and outside, and stands in extensive gardens and parklands.

It is easy to get back to the A5 from the castle, to thread one's way among the magnificent Snowdonia peaks to Capel Curig—ideal for anybody's mountain holiday; then on to the Vale of Llangollen and Llangollen itself (it is also possible to get there by train, but not so simply).

North of Llangollen are moors, mountains and the gentle Vale of Clwyd, where one finds Rhuddlan Castle; the pocket-size cathedral of St. Asaph; Denbigh Castle and the little town of Ruthin. At Ruthin, in the shadow of the Clwydian hills, the old red sandstone castle has been converted into a comfortable country hotel, renowned throughout Wales for the medieval banquets that take place nightly during most of the year. In Ruthin is also preserved an ancient stone block on which, so legend has it, King Arthur ordered the beheading of Gildas, the historian.

Llangollen is cradled among tree-covered hills in a hollow beside the River Dee. Spanning the river is a medieval bridge that is one of the traditional Seven Wonders of Wales, but this charming little town is best known for the International Musical Eisteddfod, held here each year in July, with singers and folk dancers from many lands competing with their Welsh hosts. Here, too, is the black-and-white half-timbered home of the eccentric "Ladies of Llangollen," who lived there for 50 years with their servant known as "Molly the Basher." The inside of their house, Plas Newydd, is thick with carved oak, and they made a tourist attraction of it even during their lifetime. The River Dee, which laps the northern edge of the town, is full of salmon. Another waterway, the Llangollen Canal, also runs beside the town, and at the Wharf there is an excellent Canal Museum. It is possible to go cruising on this 46-mile long canal, a branch of the even longer Shropshire Union Canal. A few miles to the east, near Chirk, the Pontcysyllte Aqueduct, 121-ft. high and 1,007-ft. long, takes the canal out of Wales into Shropshire.

Erddig, Chirk and Southwards

Ten miles from Llangollen and one south of Wrexham is one of the most fascinating National Trust properties in Wales, if not in Britain. Erddig is a typical, 17th-century Welsh squire's house with much of the original furniture and a collection of early 18th-century gilt and silver furniture. There is a range of domestic outbuildings including a laundry, bakehouse, sawmill and smithy, all in working order, and the gardens have been restored to their original perfection. But beyond all that there is something else. The Yorke family who owned the house for 240 years, until 1973, were uniquely enlightened in their treatment of staff. They even commissioned portraits of their staff and displayed them on the walls, symbolizing what, today, Erddig rewards its visitors with—an insight into the now-vanished "upstairs, downstairs" life of a country house.

Chirk Castle, which stands south of Wrexham and close to the Llangollen Canal, is a 14th-century Marcher fortress, with examples of four centuries of decorations. The gardens are formal with clipped yews, the driveway is one-and-a-half miles long and the iron entrance gates are truly magnificent. They are the work of the Davies Brothers of Bersham, 18th-century iron artists whose work is to be found all over Clwyd and Cheshire.

Chirk is on the very border of England and Wales, but further into Wales, on the same level, there is a wide area of very Welsh country, embracing the wild Ceiriog Forest; the Penllyn Forest, south of Bala Lake; the Dyfnant Forest with Lake Vynwy; and the region continues south down through the mountains to Rhayader, Llandrindod Wells, Builth Wells, Llanwrtyd Wells and so to Llandovery which is on a level with Brecon.

This great north/south expanse of mountains and little valleys appears on the Wales Tourist Board map as almost entirely an area of outstanding beauty—and who should say them nay? Anything above Aberystwyth can be counted as Welsh speaking, a land of hill farmers, of little fields neatly outlined with farm buildings and suspicious sheepdogs; a land over which the Welsh drovers trudged with their sheep, cattle and geese on the way to markets as far away as London; and life even today is certainly not soft. Aberystwyth is also the unofficial capital of Mid Wales, the most peaceful and unexplored region of Wales. They make the most of the natural environment in this part of the world by staging a wide-ranging "Festival of the Countryside" here each year. The festival consists of a programme of over 600 events—everything from farm open days to a "Mid Wales Stampede"—which runs throughout the summer (details from Mid Wales Development, Ladywell House, Newtown, Powys; tel. 0686 26965).

Mid Wales's once-famous spa towns are an incongruous feature, lending a little Edwardian glitter to a pastoral scene. Llandrindod Wells, (the only one where spa waters still flow), Llanwrtyd Wells, Builth Wells, and Llangammarch Wells, all on or near the road from Shrewsbury to Swansea. Llandrindod Wells, with its sulphurous, saline, and chalybeate waters, is famed throughout Great Britain, whilst Llangammarch Wells once had the distinction of possessing the only springs in Great Britain containing barium chloride, so useful for the treatment of diseases of the heart. All of them have a legacy of good hotels and that indefinable something that attaches to spas, wherever they may be. But the Welsh ones can no longer be considered as spas, but as inland resorts which are, rather amusingly, now devoted to the pursuit of physical exercise. This is an area in which riding schools abound, and pony trekking probably first saw the light of day. If, however, you are a spa person rather than a pony trekker, you can still have a very comfortable, restful holiday in a region where you hardly ever hear an aeroplane and the countryside is unbelievably beautiful.

PRACTICAL INFORMATION FOR WALES

HOW TO GET AROUND. North and Central Wales are reached by rail from London, Euston station. South Wales' trains depart from Paddington. The high-speed InterCity 125 has cut the rail time between London and Cardiff to as little as 1¾ hours, traveling at speeds of up to 125 mph. By air from Manchester and elsewhere to Cardiff/Wales Airport, at Rhoose, near Barry (apply to Information Desk, Cardiff/Wales Airport, South Glamorgan. Tel. Rhoose (0446) 711211.

The transport system in Wales is well developed for east-west travel by public transport, but north-south journeys are often slow and tortuous, though there is the convenient north-south Traws Cambria bus service. However, it is still easy to get about, provided you plan your journeys carefully as public transport services are relatively infrequent away from the main centers. Initial informa-tion on traveling to Wales by express bus is available from *National Express,* Victoria Coach Station, London SWI. Also worth checking out are two of British Rail's most scenic branch lines—the Cambrian Coast, running from Aberystwyth to Pwllheli, and the Heart of Wales between Swansea and Shrewsbury.

The best road approach to South Wales is by M4 motorway straight through to Cardiff over the Severn Bridge. 149 miles, easily covered in 2½ hours and the road continues now to beyond Swansea. For mid-Wales, take M40 to Oxford, then A44 which eventually ends at Aberystwyth, a fast route as far as Worcester, then fairly slow. A5 goes all the way from London to Holyhead in North Wales, 260 miles, but the distance might be covered more quickly by taking M1 and M6 to north of Birmingham, then joining A5 at junction 12.

However good the public transport may be, there is nothing to touch the freedom, enchantment and inspiration of motoring in the grass-banked, secret lanes of Wales—where the buses can't go—or near its wild and rocky coast. Apart from one's feet or a horse, it is the only real way to see Wales.

HOTELS AND RESTAURANTS. The places mentioned below are all in or near some of the loveliest parts of Wales. Some hotels in the small spots may be simple, but any inconveniences will be amply compensated for by the scenery.

Drinking laws differ slightly from those in England, and in one or two parts of the Principality you cannot drink on a Sunday, except as a resident of your hotel. Welsh food is simple. Fresh local produce, like poultry, lamb and fish, is best. Wayside inns and farms provide delicious home cooking. Near the coast, try crabs, shrimps, lobsters, sewin (seatrout) and salmon. A growing number of hotels and pubs provide first-class imaginative cooking.

If you plan to visit Wales during either the National Welsh, or International Musical Eisteddfodau and want to stay somewhere near the venues for these events, book your hotel well ahead. The Wales Tourist Board, P.O. Box 1, Cardiff CF1 2XN, produce useful guides.

Details about our grading system, plus other relevant information about hotels and restaurants, will be found at the beginning of the book in the *Facts at Your Fingertips* section.

Aberdyfi (Aberdovey), (Gwynedd). *Trefeddian* (M), tel. (065 472) 213; 44 rooms, all with bath or shower, next to golf links and unrivaled views. Modernized, with heated pool, tennis, solarium, putting green. Closed early Jan. to mid-Mar.

Abersoch (Gwynedd). *Porth Tocyn* (M), tel. (075 881) 2966; 18 rooms, all with bath and shower (closed mid-Nov.–mid-Mar.), splendidly sited among gardens; Welsh mountains to the rear. Hotel Restaurant (M) with good international cuisine and excellent wine list.

Aberystwyth (Dyfed). *Conrah Country House* (M), Chancery, tel. (0970) 617941; 22 rooms, 19 with bath; extensive grounds with fine views. No children under 5. *Four Seasons* (M), 50–54 Portland St., tel. (0970) 612120; 33 rooms, most with bath. Relaxed, family-run hotel situated downtown. *Groves* (M), 42–46 North Parade, tel. (0970) 617623; 12 rooms, 5 with bath. Central, comfortable hotel with restaurant.

Restaurants. *Rummers* (M), Treschan Bridge, tel. (0970) 5177. Harbor wine bar/bistro boasting 30 different lagers. *Gannets* (I), 7 St. James

Square, tel. (0970) 617164. Small bistro with wholesome home-style cooking and vegetarian meals. Closed Sun.

Babell (Clwyd). **Restaurant.** *Black Lion Inn* (M), tel. (0352) 720239; 16th-century inn with splendid home-cooked food. Must book. Closed Sun., first week of Nov. and first week of Feb.

Bala (Gwynedd), center for Snowdonia National Park. *Pale Hall* (E–M) Llandderfel, tel. (06783) 285; 19 rooms, all with bath. Opulently restored country mansion near Bala, in parkland setting. Gymnasium, pool, sauna, shooting and fishing. *White Lion Royal* (M), High St., tel. (0678) 520 314; 22 rooms, all with bath.

Beaumaris (Anglesey, Gwynedd). *Bulkeley Arms* (M), tel. (0248) 810415; 42 rooms with bath or shower. Modest and traditional hotel overlooking Menai Straits with view of Snowdonia. *Henllys Hall* (M), tel. (0248) 810412; 25 rooms with bath or shower. One-time monastery on peaceful grounds, with pool, sauna and tennis. *Liverpool Arms* (M), tel. (0248) 810362; 10 rooms, 8 with bath, 2 with shower. Refurbished old inn with nautical associations.
Restaurants. *Bottles* (I), tel. (0248) 810623. Cheerful, stone-flagged bistro. *Ye Olde Bull's Head* (M), tel. (0248) 810329. 17th-century, with oak-beamed dining room. Closed Sun. evenings.

Beddgelert (Gwynedd). *Bryn Eglwys* (M), Railbridge, tel. (076 686) 210; 16 rooms, 12 with bath, deep in Snowdonia National Park beside the river Glaslyn. Spectacular views, good home-cooked fare. *Royal Goat* (M), tel. (076 686) 224. 31 rooms with bath. Superb mountain views.

Betws-Y-Coed (Gwynedd). *Park Hill* (M), tel. (069 02) 540; 11 rooms, 8 with bath or shower. Smart and friendly, with good home cooking. *Plas Hall* (M), tel. Dolwyddelan (06906) 206; 16 rooms, all with bath or shower. Peaceful hotel near Betws-y-Coed. The only place in England and Wales with year-round salmon fishing.
Restaurant. *Ty Gwyn* (M), tel. (06902) 383. Charming 17th-century coaching inn.

Bontddu (Gwynedd). *Bontddu Hall* (M), tel. (034 149) 661; 23 rooms, 19 with bath; splendid views of Cader Idris and the Mawddach estuary. Closed Jan. to Easter.

Brechfa (Dyfed). *Ty Mawr Country House Hotel and Restaurant* (M), tel. (026 789) 332; 5 rooms, all with bath. Homespun hostelry in peaceful, off-the-beaten-track location.

Brecon (Powys). *Castle of Brecon* (M), The Avenue, tel. (0874) 4616; 44 rooms with bath or shower. Built into the fabric of Brecon's medieval castle. *Wellington* (M), The Bulwark, tel. (0874) 5225. 21 rooms with bath. Modernized hotel, right in the middle of town.

Caernarfon (Gwynedd). *Stables* (M), Llanwnda, tel. (0286) 830711. 3 miles out on A499. 14 rooms, most with bath. Comfortable hotel and good restaurant offering Welsh and international cuisine.

Caersws (Powys). On the river Severn *Maesmawr Hall* (M), tel. (068 684) 255; 17 rooms, 12 with bath or shower; surrounded by extremely attractive grounds.

Cardiff (S. Glamorgan). *Angel* (E), Castle St., tel. (0222) 32633; 98 rooms, 83 with bath. Has stylish public rooms. *Holiday Inn* (E), Mill Lane, tel. (0222) 399944; 182 rooms with bath. Brand new and impressively designed. *Park* (E), Park Place, tel. (0222) 383471; 108 rooms with bath. Still has a friendly set of staff. *Inn on the Avenue* (M), Circle Way East, Llanedeyrn, tel. (0222) 732520; 150 rooms with bath. Striking, modern hotel on fringes of city.
Restaurants. *Gibsons* (M), Romilly Crescent, Canton, tel. (0222) 41264. Pleasant bistro near city center with imaginative cuisine. Closed Sun. evenings. *Harvesters* (M), Pontcanna St., tel. (0222) 32616; recommended; dinner only Sat. Closed Sun.

Cardigan (Dyfed). *Penbontbren Farm Hotel* (M), Glynarthen, tel. (0239) 810248; 10 rooms with bath or shower in tastefully converted farmhouse. Very unusual, very Welsh.
Restaurant. *Rhyd-Garn-Wen* (M), Croft, tel. (0239) 612742. Country restaurant worth seeking out; dinner only. Also provides first-class guesthouse accommodations.

Carmarthen (Dyfed). *Ivy Bush Royal* (M), Spilman St., tel. (0267) 235111; 80 rooms with bath or shower. Modernized, central location.

Colwyn Bay (Clwyd). *Seventy Degrees* (M), Penmaenhead, tel. (0492) 516555; 41 rooms with bath. Beautiful location. Modern modular architecture with sweeping views out to sea. Elegant decor.

Criccieth (Gwynedd). Beautifully situated *Bron Eifion* (M), tel. (076 671) 2385; 19 rooms, 14 with bath, 5 with shower, is well recommended. *Parciau Mawr* (M), tel. (076 671) 2368; 13 rooms, 9 with bath or shower. Beautiful location, in own grounds. Closed Nov.–Feb.

Crickhowell (Powys). *Bear* (M), tel. (0873) 810408; 12 rooms, 2 with bath, 6 with shower. Lovely old inn with antiques and home cooking. *Gliffaes* (M), tel. Bwlch (0874) 730371; 19 rooms, 18 with bath or shower. Closed Jan.–March. 2½ miles west, off A40. Overlooking River Usk, between Brecon Beacons and Black Mountains.

Denbigh (Clwyd). *Llanrhaeadr Hall* (M), Llanrhaeadr, tel. (074578) 313. Mansion in the verdant Vale of Clwyd. Its drawing room is truly magnificent. Suite also available (E).

Eglwysfach (Dyfed). *Ynshir Hall* (M), tel. (065 474) 209; 11 rooms, 6 with bath. Beautiful location. Surrounded by rhododendrons and magnolias in grounds covering many acres; nearby bird sanctuary. Closed mid-Nov.–Feb. (except Xmas and New Year).

Glyn Ceiriog (Clwyd). *Golden Pheasant* (M), tel. (069172) 281; 18 rooms with bath or shower. Comfortable, 200-year-old hotel furnished with antiques and Victorian fabrics. Restaurant serving local specialties.

Gwbert-On-Sea (Dyfed). *Cliff* (E–M), tel. (0239) 613241; 70 rooms, 58 rooms with bath, 12 with shower. Stands in 30 acres; heated outdoor pool, magnificent situation overlooking Cardigan Bay. Closed Jan.

Harlech (Gwynedd). *Maes-y-Neuadd* (M), Talsarnau, tel. (0766) 780200; 14 rooms, 11 with bath. 14th-century manor house in secluded setting with breathtaking views of Snowdonia. Restaurant noted for imaginative cooking.
Restaurant. *Cemlyn* (M), High St., tel. (0766) 780425. Small, intimate spot specializing in local lobster.

Haverfordwest (Dyfed). *Wolfscastle* (M), tel. (043787) 225; 15 rooms with bath or shower. Centrally located for touring Pembrokeshire. Reputable restaurant.
Restaurants. *Hungry Caterpillar* (M), Solva, Nr. Haverfordwest, tel. (0437) 721323. Well-known restaurant set in huge barn with extensive menu.

Lake Vyrnwy (Powys). *Lake Vyrnwy* (M), Llanddwyn, tel. (069173) 244; 30 rooms with bath or shower. Rambling, old-fashioned hotel in spectacular, remote setting.

Lamphey (Dyfed). *Court* (M), tel. (0646) 672273; 22 rooms with bath. Georgian house near ancient Bishops' Palace.

Llanarmon Dyffryn Ceiriog (Clwyd). *Hand* (M), tel. (069 176) 666; 14 rooms with bath. Old inn in attractive remote village near Llangollen. In the same village square and under same ownership is the *West* (M), tel. (069176) 665; 14 rooms, 8 with bath. Restaurant's specialties include lobster croquettes.

Llanberis (Gwynedd). **Restaurant.** *Y Bistro* (M), tel. (0286) 871278. Award-winning place to eat, with Welsh specialties. Closed Sun. (except Bank Holidays) and most of Jan.

Llanddewi Skirrid (Gwent). *Walnut Tree Inn* (E), tel. (0873) 2797. Highly recommended restaurant. Excellent Italian and continental cuisine served in informal, intimate atmosphere. Imaginative menu changes daily. Best to book; ask directions when doing so. Closed Sun.

Llandrillo (Clwyd). *Tyddyn Llan* (M), tel. (049084) 264; 9 rooms with bath or shower. Small, immaculate hotel near Corwen; worth seeking out.

Llandrindod Wells (Powys). *Metropole* (E–M), Temple St., tel. (0597) 2881/2; 121 rooms with bath. Grand, stylish hotel with excellent cuisine.

Llanerch (I), Waterloo Rd., tel. (0597) 2086; 13 rooms, 7 with bath. 16th-century coaching inn with comfortable rooms, home cooking.

Restaurants. *Emporium* (M), Temple St., tel. (0597) 4574. Spacious, airy, pine-furnished restaurant. *Ffaldau* (M), Llandegley, tel. (059787) 421. Oak-beamed, with some rooms, dating from 16th-century, noted for its homemade desserts.

Llandudno (Gwynedd). *Bodysgallen Hall* (E), tel. (0492) 84466; 28 rooms most with bath. Recently-renovated historic house, now an hotel of great style. Off B5115, in own garden. *Empire* (M), Church Walks, tel. (0492) 79955; 64 rooms, all with bath. *Gogarth Abbey* (M), West Shore, tel. (0492) 76211; 41 rooms, 35 with bath, 6 with shower; where Lewis Carroll wrote *Alice in Wonderland. Imperial* (M), The Promenade, tel. (0492) 77466; 111 rooms, 109 with bath. *St. George's* (M), St. George's Place, tel. (0492) 77544; 90 rooms with bath, for seaside grandeur. *St. Tudno* (M), North Parade, tel. (0492) 74411; 21 rooms, 19 with bath, 2 with shower. Enchanting, well-run hotel, right on seafront; highly recommended.

All (M) hotels offer good standards of food and accommodations.

Llangammarch Wells (Powys). *Lake* (M), tel. (05912) 202; 26 rooms with bath or shower. Gracious, old-world, Scottish-style country lodge.

Llangollen (Clwyd). *Bryn Howel* (M), tel. (0978) 860331; 38 rooms with bath. Beautiful location, 2¾ miles E on A539, overlooking the River Dee and Llangollen canal. *Hand* (M), Bridge St., tel. (0978) 860303; 59 rooms with bath or shower. A coaching inn beside the meandering river.

Restaurant. *Gales* (I), 18 Bridge St., tel. (0978) 860089. Winebar/bistro, with accommodation, dating from 1775.

Llanrwst (Gwynedd). *Meadowsweet* (M), Station Rd., tel. (0492) 640732; only 10 rooms with shower, but excellent food. If you stay elsewhere, you can still eat here. *Plas Maenan* (M), tel. (049 269) 232. 15 rooms with bath. Views of Snowdonia, comfortable "Welsh" hotel.

Llanwrda (Dyfed). *Glanrannell Park* (M), Crugybar, tel. (05583) 230; 8 rooms, 5 with bath. A real away-from-it-all hotel, with gregarious host. Closed Nov.–Mar.

Monmouth (Gwent). *King's Head* (M), Agincourt Sq., tel. (0600) 2177; 28 rooms, 22 with bath, 6 with shower. Attractively modernized 17th-century coaching inn.

Newport (Dyfed). **Restaurant.** *Pantry* (M), Market St., tel. (0239) 820420. Best restaurant in West Wales. Super, unfussy cooking and excellent sweets. Not to be missed. Closed Mon. lunchtime, except Bank Holiday Mon.

Newport (Gwent). *Celtic Manor* (E), The Coldra, tel. (0633) 413000; 17 rooms with bath. Spacious modernized Victorian mansion. *Ladbroke* (M), The Coldra, tel. (0633) 412777. 119 rooms with bath. Comfortable; good food.

Pembroke (Dyfed). *Old King's Arms* (I), Main St., tel. (0646) 683611; 21 rooms all with bath. Their restaurant is well recommended. Standard cuisine.

Penarth (S. Glamorgan). The *Caprice Restaurant* (E–M), Esplanade, tel. (0222) 702424. Good international cuisine with ambitious wine list. Overlooks sea.

Penmaenpool (Gwynedd). *George III* (M), tel. (0341) 422525; 14 rooms, 7 with bath. Charming old hotel on edge of lovely Mawddach estuary. Delicious seafood.

Penrhyndeudraeth (Gwynedd). *Portmeirion* (E), tel. (0766) 770228. 14 rooms with bath in main hotel, 20 rooms with bath in village. Elegant hotel set in Italianate fantasy village has been restored to its original Victorian splendor after a disastrous fire some years back. Accommodation is increased by 20 fully serviced rooms in cottages around the village. Those who value one-of-a-kind hotel will love it.
Restaurant. *Golden Fleece* (I), Tremadog, tel. (0766). Oak-beamed pub-bistro with homemade specialties.

Pwllheli (Gwynedd). *Plas Bodegroes* (M), tel. (0758) 612363; 7 rooms 3 with bath. Fine old house with the emphasis on creative cuisine. Closed Jan.

Ruthin (Clwyd). *Ruthin Castle* (M), Castle St., tel. (082 42) 2664; 60 rooms with bath. Beautiful location. 13th-century castle with substantial 19th-century renovations. Medieval banquets also held here.

St. David's (Dyfed). *Old Cross* (M), Cross Sq., tel. (0437) 720 387; 17 rooms with bath. The restaurant is excellent value; reasonable wine list. Closed Nov.–Feb. *St. Non's* (M), tel. (0437) 720239; 20 rooms with bath. Friendly hotel with good restaurant. *Warpool Court* (M), tel. (0437) 720 300; 25 rooms, 16 with bath, 9 with shower. Splendidly situated with sea fishing and indoor swimming pool. Excellent restaurant with first-class wines. Closed early Jan.–mid-Feb.
Restaurant. A few miles up the coast, at tiny Porthgain harbor, is the *Harbour Lights* (M–I), tel. (03483) 549. Charming restaurant, superb salads and main meals.

Swansea (W. Glamorgan). *Dragon* (E), The Kingsway, tel. (0792) 51074; 118 rooms with bath. *Windsor Lodge* (M), Mount Pleasant, tel. (0792) 42158; 18 rooms, 14 with bath or shower. Tastefully converted Georgian house.
Restaurant. *Welsh Heritage* (M), Prospect Place, tel. (0792) 473886. Traditional dishes. Welsh laverbread (made from seaweed) at both restaurants.

Tal-y-llyn (Gwynedd). *Minffordd* (M), tel. (065473) 665; 7 rooms, 3 with bath, 2 with shower. Beautifully located little hotel beneath Cader Idris mountain. Good food. Closed Jan. and Feb.

Tenby (Dyfed). *Fourcroft* (M), Croft Terrace, tel. (0834) 2886. 38 rooms, 36 with bath, 2 with shower. Closed Nov. to Easter. *Heywood Lodge* (I), Heywood Lane, tel. (0834) 2684. 13 rooms, 4 with bath, 1 with shower. Country house atmosphere within walking distance of town and beaches. Open May–Sept.

Tintern Parva (Gwent). *Beaufort* (M), tel. (029 18) 777; 25 rooms, 15 with bath, 10 with shower. Faces ancient Tintern Abbey.

Trecastle (Powys). *Castle* (M), tel. (087482) 354. Old coaching inn with 6 tastefully appointed bedrooms.

Usk (Gwent). *Three Salmons* (M), Bridge St., tel. (029 13) 2133; 28 rooms, 25 with bath, 3 with shower. Splendidly comfortable ancient inn—well recommended. At nearby **Llangybi,** *Cwrt Bleddyn* (M), tel. (063349) 521; 31 rooms with bath. New, luxurious hotel with high standards of decor, in 17-acre grounds.

Whitland (Dyfed). *Waungron Farm* (M), tel. (0994) 240682; 14 rooms with bath. Friendly, unusual little hotel on working farm; good value.

Whitebrook (Gwent). **Restaurant.** *Crown* (M), tel. (0600) 860254. Village pub transformed into first-class restaurant with excellent wines. Also has 12 small rooms with bath.

PLACES OF INTEREST. Wales, a land of myth and mystery, has an abundance of castles and great houses, all set in landscape which enhances their effect on the visitor. Many of the buildings are in the guardianship of the National Trust (NT). The list below is only a selection of the sights to see; further details from local tourist information centers.

Clwyd. Chirk Castle, near Wrexham (tel. 0691 777701). Built 1310 and exterior unaltered, inhabited continuously for 650 years. Open mid-Apr.–end Sept., daily (except Mon. and Sat. but open Bank Holiday Mon.); also Sat. and Sun. in Oct.; all 12–5. (NT)

Erddig, near Wrexham (tel. 0978 355314). Fascinating country house-with-a-difference that gives a unique insight into "upstairs, downstairs" life. Open Apr.–mid-Oct., daily except Fri., 12–5. (NT)

Plas Newydd Museum, Llangollen. (tel. 08242 2201). The picturesque black-and-white home of the "Ladies of Llangollen," full of carvings and curios from 18th- and 19th-century celebrities. Superb gardens. Open May–Sept., weekdays 10–7, Sun. 11–4. Oct.–Apr. by arrangement.

Dyfed. Cilgerran Castle, Cilgerran (tel. 0239 614829). Dramatic 13th-century ruins set above deeply wooded gorge; favorite subject for painters since 18th-century. Open Apr.–end Sept., Mon.–Sat. 9.20–6.30, Sun. 2–4; winter (when key must be collected from The Old Post House in village) Mon.–Sat. 8–7, Sun. 9–6.

Dolaucothi Roman Gold Mines, Pumsaint (tel. 05585 359). The only place in Britain where Romans mined for gold. Exhibition center, guided underground tours in summer. Open mid-Apr.–Oct., daily 10–5. (NT)

Dylan Thomas Boathouse, Laugharne (tel. 099421 420). Waterside home of the poet, on his beloved "heron-priested shore." Now a museum dedicated to his life and work. Open Easter–Oct., daily, 10–6.

Pembroke Castle, Pembroke (tel. 0646 684585). Magnificent, well-preserved 12th-century castle, birthplace of Henry VII. Open Apr.–end Sept. daily 9.30–6; Mar. and Oct. daily 10–5; Nov.–Feb. Mon.–Sat. 10–4.

Picton Castle, Haverfordwest (tel. 043786 296). Famed collection of Graham Sutherland paintings. Castle open Easter Sun. and Mon. and following Bank Holidays; mid-July–mid-Sept., Sun. and Thurs. 2–5. Gallery open Apr.–Sept., daily exc. Mon (unless Bank Holiday), 10.30–12.30, 1.30–5. Grounds open Apr.–Sept. daily 10.30–5. Not easy to get to without car.

Solva Nectarium, Solva (tel. 0437 721323). Wander through large collection of butterflies and other insects preserved in their natural habitat. Open Easter–end Oct., weekdays 10–6, Sun. 2–6.

St. David's Cathedral, St. David's. Beautifully-located cathedral on the site of St. David's 6th-century monastic community. Fine medieval church architecture. Open at all reasonable hours.

Museum of the Woollen Industry, near Llandysul (tel. 0559 370453/370929). Collection of textile machinery and displays relating to Wales's historic woollen industry. Open Apr.–Sept., Mon.–Sat.; Oct.–Mar., Mon.–Fri.; all 10–5.

Gwent. Big Pit Mining Museum, Blaenavon (tel. 0495 790311). Authentic coal mine, now open to visitors. Underground tours of old workings. Open Mar.–Dec, daily, from 10.

Caerleon Amphitheater and Legionary Museum, Caerleon (tel. 0633 421462/423134). Objects found on the Roman Legionary fortress of Isca. Huge Roman bathhouse complex recently unearthed and also on view. Museum open Tues.–Sat. 10–5, Sun. 2.30–5. Fortress Baths open mid-Mar.–mid-Oct., daily, 9.30–6.30; remainder of year weekdays 9.30–4, Sun. 2–4.

Penhow Castle, near Newport (tel. 0633 400800). A fortified farmhouse dating from the 13th and 14th centuries. Imaginatively restored, it is the oldest inhabited castle in Wales. "Soundalive" stereo tours available. Open Good Fri.–Sept., Wed.–Sun., Holidays 10–6; winter Wed. only 10–5. Evening candelit tours for parties by appointment.

Tintern Abbey, Tintern (tel. 02918 251). Ruined medieval abbey, in sylvan Wye Valley setting. Open mid-Mar.–mid-Oct., daily, 9.30–6.30; mid-Oct.–mid-Mar., Mon.–Sat., 9.30–4, Sun. 2–4.

Tredegar House and Country Park, Newport (tel. 0633 62275). Handsome, brick-built 17th-century country house; one of the finest in Wales. On spacious parklands. House open Apr.–Sept., Wed.–Sun. and Bank Holidays, 12.30–4.30. Country Park open all year until dusk.

Gwynedd. Beaumaris Castle, Anglesey (tel. 0248 810361). Guarding the entrance to the Menai Strait, this is acknowledged as the finest example of medieval defence planning in Britain. Open mid-Mar.–mid-Oct. daily 9.30–6.30; winter Mon.–Sat. 9.30–4, Sun. 2–4.

Bodnant Garden, near Conwy (tel. 049 267 460). Beautiful terraced gardens. Open mid-March–Oct., daily, 10–5. (NT).

Caernarfon Castle, 13th-century, and **Conwy Castle** are two of Edward I's fortresses for subduing the Welsh. Both are open mid-Mar.–mid-Oct., daily, 9.30–6.30; and mid-Oct.–mid-Mar., weekdays 9.30–4, Sun. 2–4.

Gloddfa Ganol Slate Mine (tel. 0766 831493) and **Llechwedd Slate Caverns** (tel. 0766 830306). Both located at Blaenau Ffestiniog, once the slate capital of N. Wales. Tours of old caverns, slate-splitting demonstrations, etc. Both open daily, Apr.–Oct. The former is open Easter–Sept. daily 10–5.30 and the latter are open Apr.–Oct. daily 10–5.15.

Harlech Castle, Harlech (tel. 0766 780552). 13th-century, famous in song (*Men of Harlech*). Open mid-Mar.–mid.Oct., daily, 9.30–6.30; mid-Oct.–mid-Mar., weekdays 9.30–4, Sun. 2–4.

Museum of Childhood, Anglesey (tel. 0248 810448). An Aladdin's cave of music boxes, magic lanterns, trains, cars, toy soldiers and rocking horses. Open daily 10–5.30, Sun. 12–5.

Penrhyn Castle, Bangor (tel. 0248 353084). Built of Mona marble. Castle and garden open Apr.–Oct., daily (except Tues.), 12–5; from 11 in July and Aug.

Plas Mawr, Conwy. Finest example of an Elizabethan town house in Wales. Almost completely original. Open Apr.–Sept., daily, 10–6; daily in Oct., 10–4; Nov., Feb. and Mar., Wed.–Sun., 10–4.

Plas Newydd, Isle of Anglesey (tel. 0248 714795). Fabulous views of the Snowdonia range. Military museum; Rex Whistler wall-painting. Open Apr.–Sept., daily exc. Sat., 12–5; July and Aug. 11–5. Fri. and Sun only in Oct., 12–5. (NT).

Powys. Brecknock Museum, Brecon. Local and natural history of this part of mid-Wales. Agricultural and domestic bygones, porcelain and pottery. Open all year, Mon–Sat., 10–5 (but closed Good Fri.).

Dan-yr-Ogof Show Caves, Abercrave (tel. 0639 730284). Spectacular show cave complex with three separate underground tours. Open Easter–Oct., daily, 10–5.

Powis Castle, Welshpool (tel. 0938 4336). Dates from 13th century; beautiful gardens. Open mid-Apr.–end June, daily (except Mon. and Tues. but open Bank Holiday Mon.) 12–5; July and Aug., daily (except Mon. but open Bank Holiday Mon.) 11–6; Sept. and Oct., daily (except Mon. and Tues.) 12–5. (NT)

Rock Park Spa, Llandrindod Wells (tel. 0597 4307). Reopened spa, on 18-acre wooded parkland. Authentic Edwardian pump room and small exhibition. Open daily Apr.–Oct., 10–6.

Tretower Court, Crickhowell. Fine medieval house. Open mid-Mar.–mid-Oct., daily, 9.30–6.30 (Sun. 2–6.30); winter 9.30–4 (Sun. 2–4).

South, Mid and West Glamorgan. Caerphilly Castle, Caerphilly. Massive castle, right in the middle of the town, with well-preserved water defenses. Medieval military architecture at its most powerful. Open mid-Mar.–mid-Oct., daily, 9.30–6.30; mid-Oct.–mid-Mar., Mon.–Sat., 9.30–4, Sun. 2–4.

Cardiff Castle, Cardiff (tel. 0222 31033, ext. 716). Begun in the 11th century, richly-decorated interior. Open Mar., Apr., Oct., daily, 10–5; May–Sept., daily, 10–6; Nov.–Feb., daily, 10–4.30. Conducted tours. Roman excavations on view.

Cyfarthfa Castle, Merthyr Tydfil. Built as the home of a 19th-century ironmaster. Contains a delightful museum with reminders of Merthyr's industrial past. Open Apr.–Sept., Mon.–Sat., 10–1, 2–6, Sun. 2–5; Oct.–Mar., Mon.–Sat., 10–1, 2–5, Sun. 2–4; closes 1 hr. early every Fri.

National Museum of Wales, Cathays Park, Cardiff (tel. 0222 397951). The history of Wales, with collections and exhibitions covering archeology, art, botany, geology, industry and zoology. Also modern European painting and sculpture. Open Tues.–Sat., 10–5; Sun. 2.30–5. Closed Good Fri.; also Mon.

Welsh Folk Museum, St. Fagans (tel. 0222 569441). Grounds of St. Fagans Castle contain buildings from all parts of Wales, re-erected to form an unusual folk-park. Open weekdays 10–5, Sun. 2.30–5, (closed Good Fri.).

Welsh Miners Museum, Afan Argoed Country Park, Port Talbot (tel. 0639 850975/850564). Life of early Welsh miners (who included children); traditional miner's cottage and equipment. Eye-opener to those bad old days. Open Apr.–Oct., daily, 10.30–6; winter, Sat. and Sun. only, 10.30–5.

THE LITTLE TRAINS OF WALES. There is a greater concentration of narrow-gauge railways in Wales than anywhere else in the country. No less than 10 such lines operate here, carrying around one million passengers a year. Eight of the railway systems are promoted jointly as *The Great Little Trains of Wales,* and most are accessible by British Rail. A Narrow Gauge "Wanderer" tourist ticket is available, which gives unlimited travel on most of the railways (not Snowdon Mountain or Fairbourne).

Ffestiniog Railway. 13 miles from Porthmadog to Blaenau Ffestiniog. Gauge 1 foot 11½ inches. Magnificent views of Snowdonia. Open Mar.–Nov. and Xmas.

Talyllyn Railway. 7¼ miles from Tywyn to Nant Gwernol. Gauge 2 feet 3 inches. Great views.

Vale of Rheidol Railway. 11¾ miles from Aberystwyth up to Devil's Bridge. Gauge 1 foot 11½ inches. Only narrow gauge and sole remaining steam service operated by British Rail. Beautiful views of the Vale as the train climbs towards Devil's Bridge.

Llanberis Lake Railway. Laid on the route of a closed branch railway. Commences in the center of Padarn Country Park, adjacent to the North Wales Quarrying Museum.

Welshpool & Llanfair Light Railway. Runs for 8 miles, from Welshpool (Raven Square) to Llanfair Caereinion, through beautiful pastoral scenery. Gauge 2 foot 6 inches.

Snowdon Mountain Railway (tel. 0286 870223). Britain's only rack-and-pinion line, runs to Snowdon summit, 3,560 feet. Gauge 2 foot 7½ inches. Finest views by rail in Britain. Expensive. Open mid-Mar.–end Oct. weekdays and most weekends, June–Sept. daily (weather permitting) 9–5.

Fairbourne Railway. Runs for 2 miles alongside one of the most attractive Cardigan Bay beaches from Fairbourne to Barmouth Ferry. Gauge 12¼ inches. Boasts the longest place name, so it claims, in the world, by recently creating this impossibly long name for a halt on the line: *Gorsafawddacha'idraigodanheddogleddolonpenrhynareurdraethceredigion*

("Mawddach Station with its dragon's teeth on North Penrhyn Drive by the golden sands of Cardigan Bay"!).

Bala Lake Railway. 4½ miles from Llanuwchllyn, alongside the largest natural lake in Wales. There is a picnic site with toilet facilities at the intermediate station of Llangower.

Brecon Mountain Railway. 2 miles, gauge 1 foot 11¾ inches. Runs mostly within the Brecon Beacon's National Park. Superb views towards Pen y Fan, 2,906 feet.

Welsh Highland Railway. Runs for only a short distance, at present, from Porthmadog, though there are plans to extend it. Limited opening.

SCOTLAND

Land of Mountain and Flood

Scotland is a small country, no bigger than the state of Maine, U.S.A., containing barely a tenth of the United Kingdom's population. Yet the idea of Scotland is world-embracing. She has produced some of the world's stormiest history, most romantic heroes and heroines, most admired literature and most important inventions. Her local products, customs, music and traditional dress—whisky, haggis, tartan, tweed, bagpipes—are local all over the globe. Scots throughout history, especially those who emigrated to the U.S.A., Canada, Australia and New Zealand, have been superb propagandists for the land of their ancestors, the land they love.

Despite assurances to the contrary you may receive from any red-blooded Scot, this land is not a nation-state. But she is much more than a region of the United Kingdom. Less than three centuries ago she was an ancient and independent kingdom and she entered into union with England and Wales of her own free will. Distinctive institutions survive: she has her own church, her own law and lawcourts, her own banks and banknotes, her own burghs (pronounced "burras" and quite different from England's boroughs) with their own provosts (equivalent to English mayors). It rouses the Scots to fury when their southern partners trample on Scotland's identity—as when the radio announcer, for example, refers to the Queen of England. She is the Queen of Great Britain.

Scotland's countryside, from the rolling Border hills to the distant misty islands, is 90% scenic, often spectacularly so. You may agree with the

Scots, after your tour, that they inhabit the most beautiful country on earth.

There are really two Scotlands, the Lowlands (not low at all, but chains of hills along river valleys) where the populous towns are found and the Highlands, which include the highest mountains in the British Isles, the wildest lochs (lakes), and most of the islands. It is often assumed that as you travel north you proceed from Lowlands to Highlands. In fact it is more of an east-west divide. The Lowland character is maintained, with a few interruptions, to Caithness in the far northeast, and if you travel due west from any point on Scotland's east coast you will eventually arrive in the Highlands. Edinburgh, a hilly city, is Lowland. Places near Glasgow, at sea-level in the same latitude, are Highland. Scotland's highest villages, Leadhills and Wanlockhead, are in the Lowlands, not the Highlands!

In the Highlands the kilt is still everyday wear for a minority. In the Lowlands you will see it worn only by members of pipe bands or Highland regiments—or the occasional foreign visitor. Lowland speech is the familiar *braw bricht munelicht nicht* Scots accent. Highlanders speak a pure, soft English. But naturally the distinctions have become blurred; there are more Highlanders nowadays in the Lowlands (particularly Glasgow) than the Highlands. In some Highland places you may see roadsigns in both English and the old native language, Gaelic.

Sunshine and Showers

Considering that Scotland overlaps the latitude of Greenland, her climate is reasonably temperate and equable. In the west the mountains and promontories claw down the clouds from the Atlantic and bring rain, more often in the form of persistent drizzle than of violent downpours. July is rather wetter than January. But the sea, penetrating far inland up the sea lochs, moderates winter cold. Palm trees flourish in several western districts. It is this unpredictable mix of sunshine and showers which has produced the wonderful color harmonies of forest and loch, the variegated foliage of park and seaboard, and the magical effects of rainbows and mists which Scotland's makers of legends and poetry have exploited.

Eastern Scotland is drier and cooler, both winter and summer. Edinburgh's annual rainfall is no higher than Rome's. For the summer visitor the great bonus is the long day—only three or four hours of darkness in May and June. Round the isles of Orkney and Shetland even the lighthouses are switched off in summer.

Macbeth and Company

At first glance Scotland's landscape looks fresh and green and youthful . . . then your eye falls on a crumbling Dark-Age ruin or a megalithic standing stone and you realize you are in an ancient land. The countryside looks peaceful. Sheep crop the hill pastures, traffic moves at a leisurely pace, villagers wander about aimlessly, putting you in mind of fish in an aquarium . . . but this is deceptive too. Scotland is proud of her turbulent history. You quickly discover that for many Scots the past is as real as the present. They love to rake through history's trash-can and turn up dubious relics.

Prominent among many prehistoric stone circles and tombs are those at Daviot near Inverness, Callernish on the island of Lewis and Maeshowe in Orkney; there are Bronze-Age villages at Jarlshof in Shetland; traces of the Antonine Wall, an earthen mound built by the Romans from sea to sea across the narrow neck of the central Lowlands, are visible at numerous places between Falkirk and Glasgow. Those are genuine historical sites. Examples of the legendary ones are the tree at Fortingall where Pontius Pilate was born, the grave of Queen Guinevere at Meigle and the tomb of the magician Merlin near Peebles.

After the Romans went home, Scotland was plunged again into a morass of myth and legend. If you visit the long gallery of the Palace of Holyroodhouse in Edinburgh you will see the portraits of 111 kings of Scotland, all the way back to Fergus I in 330 B.C. King Charles II had them painted to reinforce his belief in the divine right of kingship, but more than half of them are quite fictitious.

Scotland before A.D. 1000 was a nest of warring tribes, each with its "king" who exercised brief authority over a small area before being slain by his successor. In the Dark Ages, after Roman times, there were Picts in the north, Scots (from Ireland) in the west, Britons in the southwest and Angles or Anglo-Saxons in the southeast. Viking raiders and Christian monks helped unite them under King Malcolm Canmore who secured the throne of all Scotland in 1057, soon after the events which Shakespeare dramatized in *Macbeth*.

Subsequent kings fell increasingly under English influence until in 1328 Robert the Bruce achieved Scotland's independence. That did not put an end to bitter struggles against the English, nor to the equally bloody religious conflicts which divided Scot from Scot.

Robert the Bruce's daughter launched the tragic but tenacious Stuart dynasty of monarchs with whose misfortunes much of Scotland's later history is associated. You will see their palaces and battlegrounds all over the country, and will often cross the trails of Mary, Queen of Scots and Bonnie Prince Charlie, most heavily romanticized of all British historical characters.

In 1603 the crowns of the two nations, England and Scotland, were united and in 1707 full political union was accomplished. The nation called Great Britain was born. The obvious benefits to Scotland did not immediately become apparent, and discontent north of the border was expressed in the Jacobite (followers of Jacobus, the Latin for James, Stuart) rebellions of 1715 and 1745.

Bonnie Prince Charlie's defeat at Culloden in 1746 marked the end of Stuart hopes but not of the Stuart line. Through the ramifications of royal genealogies the present Queen of Great Britain (not to mention most of Europe's royalty, enthroned or in exile) stands in direct descent from the first of the Stuarts.

Scotland and England

Since 1707, Scotland's history has largely been that of Great Britain of which she forms a part. Her economy and politics were inevitably assimilated to those of England, but she preserved her own religion (Presbyterianism), her own social organization and customs and her own legal and financial systems.

Scotland's institutions are under constant threat from her more populous and powerful southern neighbor. She still issues her own colorful banknotes—best spend them in Scotland, since some English shopkeepers may not recognize them—but Scottish banks in practice are virtually subsidiaries of English banks. Half the major industrial and commercial concerns in Scotland have their headquarters in England (and a further 15% in the U.S.A.). Scotland's famous old railroad companies have all been merged into the British Rail network, with head offices in London.

Scots who decided that if you can't beat 'em you should join 'em have done rather well, playing a notable part in British affairs, particularly in politics, medicine, journalism and the diplomatic service. In the very highest offices of church and state, three out of five Archbishops of Canterbury earlier this century were Scots (not bad for a country whose own church rejects bishops!), and six out of ten successive British prime ministers were Scots. In the development of the British Empire and Commonwealth, Scottish merchants and administrators generally outnumbered English, Welsh and Irish. Relative to the population, Scotland today has more than her share of members of the British parliament at Westminster, as well as quite a few top British civil servants.

Most of Scotland's internal affairs are conducted from St Andrew's House in Edinburgh. Patriots clamor for a Scottish Assembly which will sit in Edinburgh and administer all Scottish affairs under the crown. But periodical polls and referenda and national election results have hitherto shown a disinclination to take drastic steps towards self-government.

Scotland's post-Union politics have oscillated between social-democratic and radical and have thrown up the occasional noteworthy reformer. Some Scots, including Robert Burns, supported the French Revolution of 1789. Keir Hardie founded the Labor Party in 1888 (but had to go to England to find a seat in Parliament). A Communist party, dedicated to making Scotland a People's Republic, was formed in 1920, and up to World War II several Scottish towns elected Communists to represent them at Westminster. Since 1945 none have done so. The more recent phenomenon has been the rise and uneven progress of a Scottish National party which campaigns for total separation from England. The two main British parties—Conservative and Labor—have wooed and appeased the nationalists at various times, but Home Rule for Scotland is no nearer realization than it has ever been.

The Kirk

Religion in Scotland was for centuries, and to some extent still is, a part of daily life to a degree unknown in England. The minister (clergyman) is prominent in his community, as in Ireland. Old-fashioned interdenominational bigotry has not been entirely eradicated.

About 20 denominations flourish in Scotland but the majority of Scots, about 65%, are members of the Kirk, the Presbyterian Church of Scotland. Next come the Roman Catholics, about 25%, many of Irish origin and settled in and around Glasgow; then the Episcopalian Church of Scotland, organized under seven bishops and sometimes regarded (incorrectly) as the Church of England in Scotland; then a few dissenters from the Kirk, notably the Free Presbyterians and "Wee Frees" whose outspoken criticisms of Sunday sport and the like gain them headlines from time to time in the national media.

No ecclesiastical buildings in Scotland can compare with the magnificent cathedrals of England. All her medieval church architecture has suffered from English invaders, 16th-century reformers and 19th-century restorers, and her great abbeys stand in picturesque decay. But every village has its kirk and larger places have churches for all denominations, to which visitors are always welcome.

In the western Highlands and islands, where the dissenting Presbyterians hold sway, Sunday is a very quiet day with no shops open and no public transport running.

Food and Leisure

Most hotels in Scotland are medium to small, often family owned. The majority are comfortable and friendly. Food is usually wholesome but remember that Scotland is traditionally the "Land o' Cakes" and don't be surprised at the quantities of buns, pancakes, scones and biscuits. More imaginative fare is served in places which carry the *Taste of Scotland* plaque and offer dishes with outlandish names like Cullen Skink (fish soup), Partan Bree (crab with rice and cream) and Edinburgh Fog (syllabub). Worth investigating are Loch Fyne herring, Arbroath "smokies" (smoked haddock), Aberdeen-Angus steak and the spicy haggis, usually served with "neaps and tatties" (mashed turnip and potato).

Whisky goes with everything. Try the "single malts"—the pale, unblended spirits, now growing fashionable and expensive. Purists drink their "malts" neat, though water, ice and even mineral water may be added to blended whiskies. Beer comes "light" or "heavy" and real ales—notably Pentland, Belhaven and Greenmantle—are gaining in popularity. The old time "spit-and-sawdust" Scottish pub (an exclusively male preserve) survives in provincial places but has gone upmarket in city centers.

For the sportsman, Scotland has it made. Golf first, as the home of golf is St. Andrews. You can play on the famous Old Course, which belongs to the town, and there are dozens of other superb courses around the country, Gleneagles, Troon, and Carnoustie among them.

You can fish for salmon and trout on river and loch, and sea angling is also immensely popular. August 12 opens the grouse shooting season; and other game include pheasant, partridge, snipe and duck, plus red and roe deer. Curling, on frozen loch or artificial rink, is practised winter and summer.

The Scots are notable gardeners, and in summer many private gardens are open to the public. Some belong to the National Trust for Scotland, which also owns many historic houses to which the public is admitted. Scotland is rich, too, in ancient castles, abbeys and churches.

For the walker and the pony-trekker there are miles of trails through the glens and over the high pastures. Scotland is a paradise for the birdwatcher (ospreys, eagles, whooper swans and rare seabirds) and for the yachtsman or small-boat sailor. Three districts—Cairngorm, Glencoe and Glenshee—are busy winter sports centers, and others are developing.

In spring and summer many towns hold cultural festivals. The big one is Edinburgh's, mid-August to early September. Summer is also the season for the Highland Gatherings in the romantic settings of Cowal and Glenfinnan (Strathclyde region), Aboyne and Braemar (Grampian) and other venues of the clans and their brawny caber-tossing and hammer-throwing champions.

PRACTICAL INFORMATION FOR SCOTLAND

Much of the practical information for Great Britain generally (see *Facts at Your Fingertips* at the beginning of this book) applies to Scotland. The details given below, together with the data which you will find in Practical Information for Edinburgh, will help you plan the Scottish portion of your trip. But if you are spending more than a day or two in Scotland, you should really obtain our separate publication, *Fodor's Scotland.*

GETTING TO SCOTLAND BY AIR. Scotland is linked with most parts of the world, either directly or through London. The main airport for transatlantic flights is Prestwick, south of Glasgow. There are also summer services between Glasgow, Edinburgh and/or Aberdeen and the near Continent of Europe. Most air travelers to Scotland arrive from London (Heathrow) on the *British Airways* shuttle services—hourly to Glasgow, two-hourly to Edinburgh, flying time one hour. Your seat is guaranteed, whether you pay on the flight or buy a ticket (which may be used for any flight) beforehand. *British Midland* (from London Heathrow) and *British Caledonian* (from London Gatwick) also operate frequent services to Glasgow and Edinburgh. On their "stand-by" options the standard fares of around £76 oneway are much reduced. *British Airways* (from Heathrow) and *Dan Air* (from Gatwick) have between them six flights a day to Aberdeen.

The airport buses from Prestwick (Glasgow) charge £7 for the trip into Glasgow. The Citylink buses, however, make the same trip for £3 and are just as fast.

GETTING TO SCOTLAND BY TRAIN. Britain's fastest trains run very frequently from London (King's Cross) to Edinburgh and Aberdeen and from London (Euston) to Glasgow. The 393-mile London-Edinburgh run is accomplished in 277 minutes. Most major cities of England have frequent express services to Scotland and there are overnight trains, with sleepers both first and second class, between London, Bristol and Plymouth in the south and Glasgow, Edinburgh, Perth, Dundee, Aberdeen and Inverness in the north.

Connections between Glasgow and Edinburgh and other parts of Scotland are well co-ordinated, but don't forget that in the puritanical western Highland regions very few trains run on Sundays.

GETTING TO SCOTLAND BY COACH. Coaches, or long-distance buses, are the cheapest means of transport to Scotland from other parts of Britain. *Scottish Bus Group* run daily and nightly between London (Victoria Coach Station) and Glasgow, journey time 8 to 8½ hours including stops for meals. There is also one express service a day taking 1½ hour less. *Cotters Tours* do the trip from London to Glasgow and Edinburgh in 8 hours and have catering facilities and videos on board. They start from Gloucester Road, near the underground station of that name, not far from the Penta Hotel.

Several other coach operators, notably *Eastern Scottish, National Express, Alexanders* and *Stagecoach* have regular services into Scotland from London, Liverpool, Birmingham, Coventry, Leeds, Middlesbrough, Newcastle and other towns and holiday resorts in England.

GETTING TO SCOTLAND BY CAR. From London or from your port or airport of arrival you can reach Scotland on an excellent system of motorways and highways. Edinburgh and Glasgow are both within 400 miles of London, a trip for which regular road-users allow 7 hours. (If you are heading for the far north of Scotland, another 300 miles, you should allow a further 8 to 9 hours.)

If you arrive with an automobile from the Continent of Europe the first stage of your journey will be by car-ferry to one of the Channel ports or East Coast ports of England. The only direct car-ferry link that Scotland has with foreign places is a boat which calls at Scrabster (Caithness) in the course of its summer-only once-a-week voyage between Denmark, Norway, the Faroe Islands and Iceland.

TRAVELING IN SCOTLAND BY AIR. There is a good network of air routes across the mainland and islands of Scotland. Many inhabited islands of the Shetland, Orkney and Hebrides groups have their own airports or landing strips. By international standards single fares over short distances are quite expensive, but *British Airways* has fly/drive packages to Orkney and Shetland of four to 14 days from all main U.K. airports. You make arrangements through *British Airways* travel shops or any *Pickfords Travel* office.

TRAVELING IN SCOTLAND BY RAIL. The principal cities of Edinburgh, Glasgow, Perth, Dundee and Aberdeen are linked with each other and with the border towns of Carlisle and Berwick-upon-Tweed by fast frequent services. North of Glasgow and Aberdeen the trains are fewer and they tend to stop at every little station; at least there is usually some spectacular scenery to admire.

It is hard to keep up with the bewildering variety of special offers which *British Rail* announce, but here are a few steady favorites of keen rail travelers:

BritRail Pass. Applies to all Britain, but must be bought outside Britain (see *Facts at Your Fingertips*). Permits unlimited travel over the whole network for one, two, three or four weeks. Substantial reductions for under-25s.

Freedom of Scotland Rover. Seven-day or 14-day tickets, 2nd class only, valid also for *Caledonian MacBrayne* sailings in Firth of Clyde. Available from most Scottish stations and certain English ones, or from any *British Rail* travel agent. Adult ticket £42 (seven days), £66 (14 days).

Highlands and Islands Travelpass. Unlimited travel on trains, buses and boats in the Highlands and islands. It also covers your journey between the Highlands and Edinburgh, Glasgow or Aberdeen. Valid 7 or 14 days; £33 or £50 in low season, £50 or £75 in high season (June–September). A comprehensive guide and timetable is supplied. Apply in person to *Brit-

ish Rail at Glasgow, Edinburgh, Aberdeen, Paisley, Stirling or Inverness stations; at main bus stations in Glasgow or Edinburgh, or to *Caledonian MacBrayne,* The Ferry Terminal, Gourock PA19 1QP. Postal or telephone applications to Hi-Line, Dingwall, Ross-shire IV15 9SL, tel. (0349) 63434.

TRAVELING IN SCOTLAND BY CAR. Motorways in Scotland have not progressed much farther than Stirling and Perth but main highways everywhere are well-engineered and fast and, on account of the relative scarcity of traffic, a joy to drive on. North of Inverness and Fort William roads are often tortuous, sometimes single-track with passing places, sometimes ending in a cul-de-sac.

The well-known car-rental firms are represented in all cities and at major airports. Under their one-way plan you may return the automobile to a place different from that at which you hired it. Caravans, motor-caravans and bicycles may also be hired in various localities: contact a local *Tourist Information Centre.* The *Scottish Tourist Board,* PO Box 8, Wishaw ML2 7BN, produces a touring map, price £3.20 by post, and a useful *Enjoy Scotland* pack (including the map) for £6.90 by post.

Caledonian MacBrayne, Ferry Terminal, Gourock PA19 1QP, offer interesting inclusive deals for motorists island-hopping on the ferries. You can make on-the-spot arrangements at their offices, or at the Tourist Information Centers, at the piers of the western ferry ports.

TRAVELING IN SCOTLAND BY BUS. From Easter to October processions of coaches leave Scotland's main bus stations on half-day, whole-day and longer tours. Scots themselves are greatly addicted, so they must be good value! But try the local buses too, for an insight into regional life, character and history. Local *Tourist Information Centres* and bus stations can often provide details of runabout tickets which, for around £15, entitle you to unlimited bus travel within a specified area for seven days.

HOTELS AND RESTAURANTS. Most regular visitors to Scotland agree that in recent years there has been a tremendous improvement in the standards of accommodations, food and services. More hotel-keepers nowadays are professionally trained, more Swiss, French and Italian chefs are brought in and the Scottish Tourist Board pursues a wise policy of encouraging the upgrading of existing establishments rather than the construction of new ones. There *are* important new developments, of course— since 1980 the notoriously ill-served city of Glasgow, for example, has gone swiftly upmarket with the four newest and biggest hotels in Scotland.

The dignified old railway and hydropathic hotels of Scotland, enormous brooding baronial piles for the most part, have today passed into the hands of giant hotel chains. Their original upper and middle class clientele has been replaced by conference delegates and tour bus parties. Yet though often relentlessly modern, and accordingly lacking in personality and charm, a certain grandeur is still in evidence.

For a more personal touch, there are a good many small country house hotels, among them some of the best in the country. Often run by dedicated professionals, they offer high standards of comfort, cleanliness and service. We list a number of the best of these establishments in our hotel listings.

Bars in Scotland may open from 11 A.M. to 11 P.M., subject to local regulations and the one-man business's need for an hour to relax after lunch, although hotel residents can be served alcohol at any time. Some hotel bars and pubs open all day on Sundays. Civilizing factors are the growth and popularity of "real" ale and the provision of beer gardens.

It is easier than it formerly was for the traveler in Scotland to sample a genuine Scottish cuisine. Some dishes are undeniably stodgy, but many are well worth trying.Venison, grouse and river trout, for instance, can all be cooked in various exciting ways.

National foods more likely to be tasted in hotels nowadays, especially since the *Taste of Scotland* campaign was launched, however, are finnan haddies and Arbroath smokies (fish). Haggis is a succulent, spicy mixture of chopped offal (heart, liver, lungs, etc) and oatmeal cooked in a sheep's stomach. Scottish baking—cakes, bread, pies, etc.—is extremely good and very filling.

In some hotels other than the topflight "high tea" is served as the evening meal. This usually consists of a savory course—often with french fries—followed by tea, toast and cakes. Normal time for this meal is about 5.30 or 6.

Tipping is not normally expected if a service charge has been added to the check. If no service charge has been made then 10–12% is sufficient.

Light lunches and evening meals are served in most pubs and hotel bars every day. Quality varies, but you'll normally get good value for money, with a three-course meal often around £3.

Details about our grading system, plus other relevant information about hotels and restaurants, will be found at the beginning of the book in the *Facts at Your Fingertips* section. We should, however, point out that prices, both in hotels and restaurants, will be in the lower end of each grade.

MUSEUMS, HOUSES AND GARDENS. In the Practical Information section you will find details of museums, galleries, houses, castles and gardens. Check opening times if possible: they do occasionally vary.

Full details on all museums and galleries in Scotland are given in the excellent guide published by the Scottish Tourist Board, *Scotland: 1001 Things to See*.

Many historic Scottish castles and houses—not to mention islands, stretches of coastline, gardens, cottages and waterfalls—are in the care of the National Trust for Scotland. An annual membership fee of £13.50 (£22 for a family), with reductions for the young or the elderly, entitles you to visit most properties free. Application forms from the NTS at 5, Charlotte Square, Edinburgh EH2 4DU. But entrance charges to houses and museums in Scotland are so small, and often non-existent, that the membership is of value only to the most dedicated stately-homes buffs.

A most agreeable organization called Scotland's Gardens Scheme operates from 26 Castle Terrace, Edinburgh EH1 2EL. Through its activities several hundred gardens, from the most elaborate and formal to the most quaint and wild, are periodically open to the public. A nominal admission charge covers owners' expenses and leaves a little over for charity. Teas are usually provided and tours of the house or some village-fête-like entertainment offered. The booklet *Scotland's Gardens* is available from the above address, for £1 or £1.30 including postage in the U.K., with details of openings for the current year. Opening times are also published week by week in the following Scottish newspapers: *Glasgow Herald, Scotsman, Edinburgh Evening News, Dundee Courier* and *Aberdeen Press & Journal.* They normally appear on Fridays, since most gardens open on Saturdays or Sundays. Where gardens are open in the locality you happen to be in, you will see yellow posters in shop windows, advertising the fact.

SHOPPING. Shops are usually open 9–5 or 9–5.30; in country districts from 8.30; in Highland villages whenever the shopkeeper feels like it. Most shops close one afternoon per week, either Tuesday, Wednesday or Thursday. Nowadays many shops open all day on Sundays, but certain large stores remain closed on Mondays. Every Scottish town has a "local" holiday on Monday two or three times a year and a "trades holiday" (which affects some shops) for two weeks in midsummer; the dates vary from place to place. On January 1 and 2 the Scots recuperate from Hogmanay (New Year's Eve) and these are blank days in the calendar for virtually everyone.

In Scotland, many visitors go for tweeds, designer knitwear, Shetland and Fair Isle woollens, tartan rugs and materials, Edinburgh crystal, Caithness glass, Celtic silver and pebble jewelry. The Scottish Highlands bristle with old "bothies" (farm buildings) which have been turned into small craft workshops where visitors are welcome—but not pressured—to buy attractive hand-made items of bone, silver, wood, pottery, leather and glass. Hand-made chocolates, often with whisky or Drambuie fillings, and the traditional "petticoat tail" shortbread in tin boxes are popular; so too, at a more mundane level, are boiled sweets in jars from particular localities—Berwick cockles, Jethart snails, Edinburgh rock and suchlike crunchy items. Dundee cake, a rich fruit mixture with almonds on top, and Dundee marmalades and heather honeys are among the other eatables which visitors take home from Scotland.

On most purchases VAT (Value Added Tax) at 15% is charged. Under retail export schemes, this charge may be refunded. Unfortunately, not all Scottish shops operate the scheme, but those which specialize in souvenir and peculiarly Scottish goods—kiltmakers, bagpipe makers and so on—will be familiar with the routine. If you have difficulty, and if the saving on the concession is worth your while, contact the VAT Office, H.M. Customs & Excise, 44 York Place, Edinburgh EH1 3JG, tel. (031) 556 2433.

EDINBURGH

The Festival City

We will be covering the approaches to Edinburgh from the south in the next chapter, here we are going to take a look at the city itself, one of the richest in Britain for its combination of legend and beauty.

Edinburgh—pronounced, by the way, Edin-burra, *not* Edin-burg—is crowned by its deservedly famous Castle, which is certainly *the* tourist attraction of the Scottish capital city. Perched on its cragged rock, above the shops and gardens of the equally famous Princes Street, it just begs to be visited.

Once there you will get your first taste of the chronicle of Scottish history which will engulf you from now till the time you leave the country. You will hear the story of how Randolph, Earl of Moray, nephew of freedom fighter Robert Bruce, scaled the heights one dark night in 1313, surprised the English guard and recaptured the Castle for the Scots. At the same time he wiped out every building there except St. Margaret's Chapel, dating from around 1076, so that successive Stuart Kings had to rebuild the place bit by bit. This accounts for the Castle's relatively modern appearance.

From the castle battlements there is a superb view over the city and the River Forth, with the Forth bridges in the distance, reaching across to the "Kingdom" of Fife. On a clear day the vista is one of breathtaking loveliness. Clear days are frequent now: Edinburgh is officially smokeless and the nickname "Auld Reekie" no longer applies. If it is *really* "misty," you can recall that it was in just such a *haar* (or Scotch mist) that Queen Margaret and Mary Queen of Scots first came to their capital.

One of the prime things to see in the castle are the "Honours of Scotland" which survived a variety of vicissitudes until they were eventually "rediscovered" in 1818. They consist of the scepter, sword-in-state and crown, remodeled in 1540 by order of King James V, made of Scottish gold, 94 pearls, 10 diamonds and 33 other jewels.

Near St. Margaret's Chapel you will find Mons Meg, a famous 15th-century cannon which used to be dragged at great expense round the Borders in attempts to frighten the English invaders. Royal salutes still crash out from other, more modern, guns and the "one o'clock gun" is still a daily occurrence, except on Sundays.

The great palace buildings of the Castle are ranged around three sides of a square, the fourth side being taken up by the Scottish National War Memorial. The Royal Apartments are on the eastern side. It was in one of the rooms here that the future James VI of Scotland and I of England was born—a small room hanging over the steeply falling rockface of the Castle. The early Scottish parliaments met in the Great Hall on the south side of the Palace Yard.

A modern camera obscura—a sort of projecting telescope—on Castle Hill, near the Esplanade, gives surprising close-ups of distant corners of the city and suburbs.

If you're fortunate enough to be in the city during mid-August/early September, be sure to get tickets for the Military Tattoo which takes place on the Castle Esplanade, with the floodlit Castle as a dramatic backcloth, twice nightly during the three-week run of the Edinburgh International Festival of Music and Drama.

The Royal Mile

If you're keen on the historical aspect of the city, then a saunter down the so-called Royal Mile puts you in touch with Edinburgh life from its earliest times. The Royal Mile is made up of a continuous row of streets leading from the Castle down to the Palace of Holyroodhouse, which took over in importance from the Castle as the home of the Royal Stuarts. In sequence, the streets that make up the Royal Mile are the Esplanade, Castle Hill, Lawnmarket, Parliament Square, High Street and Canongate. These streets, with their gaunt tenements—some reaching five, seven, or even nine stories in height—and their passages and closes leading off into even more tenements or "lands," are crammed on to the ridgeback of "the Mile." This really *was* Edinburgh until the 18th century saw expansions to south and north.

Everybody lived here, the richer folk on the lower floors, with families getting poorer the higher in the buildings they were—and a teeming, jostling throng they must have made. Imagine how the cry of *gardy-loo* must have sent many an 18th-century citizen scurrying for cover to avoid being hit with the contents of his neighbor's slop-bucket being hurled into the street from far above! The old cry also is a reminder of the close ties with France that Scotland maintained for centuries; it is a corruption of *gardez l'eau.*

There are guided walking tours of the Royal Mile which concentrate on its historical, and more sinister aspects. For besides being the haunt

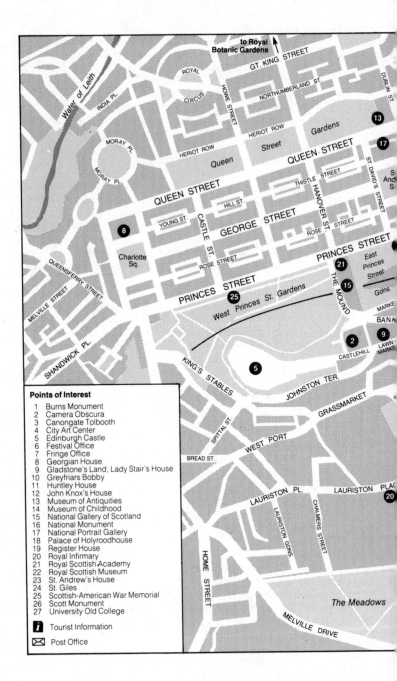

Points of Interest

1 Burns Monument
2 Camera Obscura
3 Canongate Tolbooth
4 City Art Center
5 Edinburgh Castle
6 Festival Office
7 Fringe Office
8 Georgian House
9 Gladstone's Land; Lady Stair's House
10 Greyfriars Bobby
11 Huntley House
12 John Knox's House
13 Museum of Antiquities
14 Museum of Childhood
15 National Gallery of Scotland
16 National Monument
17 National Portrait Gallery
18 Palace of Holyroodhouse
19 Register House
20 Royal Infirmary
21 Royal Scottish Academy
22 Royal Scottish Museum
23 St. Andrew's House
24 St. Giles
25 Scottish-American War Memorial
26 Scott Monument
27 University Old College

i Tourist Information

✉ Post Office

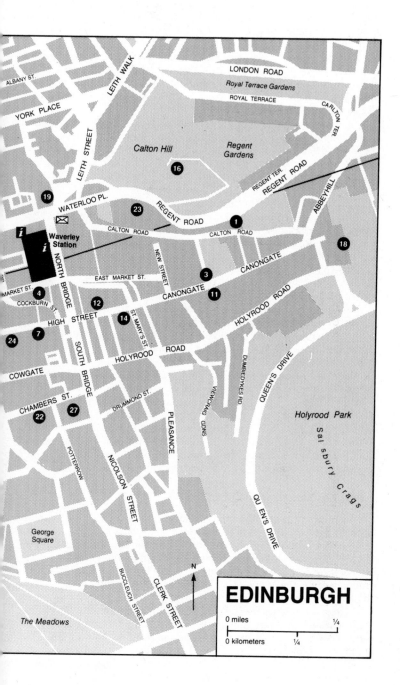

EDINBURGH

| 0 miles | 1/4 |
| 0 kilometers | 1/4 |

of Kings, its alleys hid body snatchers, murderers, robbers, witches and warlocks. It has its share of ghosts too, including a piper who vanished trying to find a secret passage from the Castle to Holyroodhouse. It is said you can still hear his pipes.

Sir Walter Scott, Robert Louis Stevenson, David Hume, James Boswell, Allan Ramsay, Christopher North—these and many other well-known names are associated with Edinburgh's Old Town. But perhaps three are more famous than any others—John Knox, Mary, Queen of Scots, and Prince Charles Edward Stuart.

St. Giles' cathedral (not really a cathedral but a "High Kirk") dates from Norman times. It is an interesting church to visit, especially to see the small, lovely Chapel of the Most Noble Order of the Thistle, Scotland's highest order of chivalry and the counterpart to England's Order of the Garter. The Queen holds a ceremony for the Order here when she visits Edinburgh, and the rich dark-green velvet robes make a striking pageant against the grey stones. The chapel itself is not so old, as it was only designed in 1911, but parts of the Cathedral may date from around 1120.

Near to the east door of the Cathedral is the Mercat Cross. This was a focal point for many events in Edinburgh life. As its name suggests it was a mercantile center, in early days, it also saw executions and was the spot where royal proclamations were—and still are—made. The present cross is comparatively modern, dating from the time of Gladstone, the great Victorian prime minister and rival of Disraeli.

The Palace is still the official royal residence in Scotland, and the Queen stays there when visiting the city. She uses the throne room for investitures and other ceremonies and usually holds a garden party in the grounds.

The Palace is open to the public when the Queen is not there, and is well worth going round. Apart from the charged memories of Mary, there are those 111 royal portraits—all looking startlingly alike and most of them of kings who never existed—as well as tapestries and some beautifully-kept furniture. As the Palace is a royal residence it can also be closed without warning at times other than during a royal visit.

From the park behind the Palace you can make your way up the 800 feet to Arthur's Seat. It is a steep walk, but well worth it for the views from here and from its neighboring eminence, Salisbury Crags. They are a kind of twin of the Castle Rock, and, like it, volcanic in origin.

Princes Street and the New Town

Princes Street is the humming center of 20th-century Edinburgh; a ceaseless promenade of natives and visitors alike along its mile or so of shops on one side and gardens opposite. Citizens lament the disappearance of the dignified old shops which lined this street; multiple stores have replaced them all. The street is still a grand viewpoint for the dramatic grouping of the Castle complex on its rocky outcrop, and the long tail of Royal Mile tenements descending from it.

There is a lot to see in Princes Street besides the shops. Outstanding in every sense is the Scott Monument, a Gothic spire 200 feet high. Anyone with sufficient energy to climb its 287 inside steps will be rewarded with a tremendous all-round view of the city. A little farther along is the neo-classical home of the Royal Scottish Academy and the famous Mound, the embankment connection between Old Town and New. Behind the

Academy stands the Scottish National Gallery. Hereabouts, at the foot
of the Mound, you can listen on Sunday evenings to soap-box orators of
all persuasions, both amateur and professional.

In the eastern end of the gardens you can see the memorial to David
Livingstone, the famous Scots missionary whose African meeting with
H.M. Stanley is part of Scots-American history. At the western end is the
American memorial to Scottish soldiers of World War I. Its beauty, and
the simplicity of the inscription, make it one of the treasures of the capital.

American visitors may wish to walk through Waterloo Place and climb
Calton Hill, with its classical unfinished monument to the dead of the Pen-
insular Wars, for in Old Calton Burying Ground is a monument to the
combined memories of Abraham Lincoln and the Scottish-American soldiers who fell in the American Civil War.

To the north of Princes Street lies the New Town—not really new now,
for it dates mostly from around late 18th and early 19th centuries. Apart
from the sheer pleasure of walking around admiring the buildings, there
are several to be visited. In Charlotte Square is the National Trust for Scotland's Georgian House; and in Queen Street the National Portrait Gallery
and the National Museum of Antiquities. George Street is a fine, wide
thoroughfare with some interesting shops and buildings; while parallel,
on either side, run Rose Street and Thistle Street, narrow lanes crammed
with pubs, coffee bars and boutiques.

What else of Edinburgh? The Royal Botanic Garden, especially noted
for its rock garden; the zoo at Corstorphine; the Royal Scottish Museum,
so absorbing that one could well spend several days in it alone.

There are the Commonwealth Pool and the Meadowbank Sports Stadium, both important athletics venues, and the dry ski-slopes on the Pentland Hills (still within the city's boundaries) where novices can prepare
for the Highland winter sports season.

The multifarious sights and amenities of Edinburgh suit all ages and
all tastes. A good introduction to them is one of the guided City Bus Tours,
starting and finishing at Waverley Bridge, off Princes Street. On them you
establish your bearings in this unique city which, while building itself into
an important administrative, banking, insurance, printing and brewing
center, still breathes the atmosphere of the past. You can always feel the
past in Edinburgh, because you're hardly ever out of sight of the grim old
Castle on its rock, "Dun-Edin," the throne of the Pictish kings.

On Edinburgh's Doorstep

Dramatic views of Edinburgh's skyline frame the rear window of your
automobile or bus as you head for her pastoral or seagirt surroundings.
Forty minutes from town you can be on a lonely beach, or among the
grouse and the heather.

North of the Firth of Forth, which is swiftly crossed by massive old
railroad bridge or graceful new road bridge, you enter the "Kingdom"
of Fife. The district nearest to Edinburgh includes mining villages and rolling hills, fringed with sandstone cliffs and ribbons of silver sand. Try a
half-day excursion to Aberdour, a tiny holiday resort patronised by the
discerning few. It's immortalized in the ballads of Sir Patrick Spens and
the Bonnie Earl of Moray and its small boats will take you out to the islands of the Forth: Inchcolm, Inchmickery and Inchkeith.

At nearby Dunfermline, in the abbey, seven kings of Scotland, including Robert the Bruce, are buried. This town has been enriched by the generosity of its native son, Andrew Carnegie. One of his bequests was a fine public park, Pittencrieff Glen, complete with peacocks and floral extravaganzas.

On the south side of the Forth, in Lothian region, you can strike out from Edinburgh in any direction and arrive at stately homes and ruined fortresses, many of them open to the public in summer. Blackness Castle on the west of Edinburgh and Tantallon and Dunbar Castles on the east are worth visiting. East Lothian is a district of old-world villages and prosperous market towns, notably Haddington, 17 miles from the capital, a Georgian town once decayed and now sympathetically restored. Its large parish church, a beacon of faith in the irreligious past, earned itself the name of "Lamp of Lothian."

Nine miles west of Edinburgh, the feudal village of Dalmeny stands guard over the southern end of the Forth Rail Bridge. Cottages are arranged round a village green, the squat greystone church is said to be Scotland's best Norman example and you can walk or drive through Dalmeny Park (Earl of Rosebery), inspecting the commemorative trees which visiting statesmen and royalty have planted.

Rosslyn Chapel's ecclesiastical splendor, at Roslin nine miles south of Edinburgh, is embedded in a sombre industrialized glen, the heart of the Midlothian coalfield. The Chapel's florid Prentice Pillar was carved by an enthusiastic novice during his master's absence abroad. On return, the stonemason struck the presumptuous apprentice dead. Roslin has a castle on a 600-foot crag. Its inn was once a staging-post for travelers between England and Scotland, and the names of numerous celebrities—Dr. Johnson, Robert Burns, Queen Victoria, King Edward VII and others—are carved on its facade.

The above are just a few scenic and historic examples from the environs of Edinburgh. Notes on some other places worth seeing will be found in the final chapter.

PRACTICAL INFORMATION FOR EDINBURGH

HOTELS. Only a few of Edinburgh's 300-odd hotels and guest-houses can be mentioned here. You may book accommodations at the *Tourist Information and Accommodation Center,* Waverley Market, 3 Princes Street, EH1 1BQ, tel. (031) 557 2727, or pick up an *Accommodation Book* from the Department of Public Relations and Tourism, 9 Cockburn Street, Edinburgh EH1 1BR, tel. (031) 226 6591. If you arrive by air, contact the Information/Accommodations desk at Edinburgh airport, tel. 333 2167.

Note: dial the Edinburgh code 031 if you are calling from outside the city. Code numbers for other places are found in the code book provided in public call boxes. In case of difficulty, call the operator by dialing 100.

Details about our grading system for hotels and restaurants, plus other relevant information, are given in the *Facts at Your Fingertips* section at the beginning of this book.

Caledonian (L), west end of Princes Street (tel. 225 2433). 254 rooms with bath. Handsome and modernized railway hotel maintaining its original dignity and elegance.

George (L), 19 George St. (tel. 225 1251). 195 rooms with bath. Imposing 18th-century building in the heart of the New Town. Comfortable and well run, with fine restaurant and two bars.

Royal Scot (L), 111 Glasgow Rd. (tel. 334 9191). 252 rooms with bath. To the west of the city near the M8 highway. Somewhat bleak modern exterior and stark decor are compensated for by young enthusiastic staff and excellent service.

Roxburghe (L), Charlotte Sq. (tel. 225 3921). 76 rooms with bath. Staid and well-run, with some delightful rooms overlooking Charlotte Square. Its *Consort* restaurant (E) adds a modern touch.

Sheraton (L), Festival Square Rd. (tel. 229 9131). 263 rooms, all with bath. Opened in 1985. Maintains high Sheraton standards and aims at the top of the market.

Howard (E), Great King St. (tel. 556 1393). 25 rooms with bath. Like many of the newer hotels in Edinburgh, this is a conversion from Georgian townhouses with some attractive features. Handily central in Great King Street.

North British (E), east end of Princes Street (tel. 556 2414). 201 rooms, 175 with bath. The *Caledonian's* twin, at the other end of Princes St. A somewhat faded grandeur is succumbing to slow but ambitious improvements.

Murrayfield (M), 18 Corstorphine Rd. (tel. 337 1844). 22 rooms, 9 with bath. 12 minutes from center. Useful for a quiet stay at reasonable cost.

Redholme House (M), 20 Colinton Rd. (tel. 447 2286). 17 rooms, 1 with bath. Country-house style within the city boundaries. Comfortable with log fires. Big saving on weekly rates.

Royal British (M), 20 Princes St. (tel. 556 4901). 77 rooms, 76 with bath. Rather restricted for space, but has long held its own while flashier establishments have come and gone.

GETTING ABOUT. By Bus. The maroon-coloured city buses operate a frequent service all over the city and suburbs from early A.M. to late P.M. Fares are reasonable: pay as you enter, so carry 10p and 5p pieces with you. To see Edinburgh, take a City Tour from Waverley Bridge. There are frequent departures, various options, an instructive commentary and all quite inexpensive. From the Sales Office, Waverley Bridge (tel. 226 5087) you can buy concession tickets for unlimited city bus travel by the day or longer periods, with a free-half-day conducted tour.

By Train. The principal railroad station in Edinburgh is Waverley. Fast trains run regularly to Glasgow, Dundee, Perth, Aberdeen etc., and to all English main-line stations.

By Plane. From Edinburgh Airport (British Airways, British Caledonian and British Midland) there are air services to Aberdeen, Orkney, Shetland, Glasgow, London Heathrow, London Gatwick, Manchester and Ireland. An airport bus connects Edinburgh Airport with the Edinburgh City Terminal at Waverley Bridge. There is also a daily bus service between Edinburgh (Waverley Bridge) and Prestwick Airport.

Car Hire. *Avis Rent-a-Car,* 100 Dalry Rd., (tel. 337 6363); *Godfrey Davis Ltd.,* 24 East London St., (tel. 661 1252); *Hertz,* 10 Picardy Place (tel. 556 8311); and many more. *Avis* and *Hertz* have desks at the Airport.

A three-hour sightseeing trip in a chauffeured automobile, arranged through city-center travel agencies, costs around £50, including admission charges to historic buildings etc., tips and parking fees.

USEFUL ADDRESSES. *Tourist Information and Accommodation Center,* Waverley Market (tel. 557 2727); *Scottish Travel Center,* 14 South St. Andrew Street, EH2 2AZ; *Citizens' Advice Bureau,* 58 Dundas Street, EH3 6QZ (tel. 557 1500); *American Consul* 3 Regent Terrace, EH7 5BN (tel. 556 8315); *Automobile Association,* 18 Melville St (tel. 225 3301); *Royal Automobile Club,* 17 Rutland Sq. (tel. 229 3555); *British Airways,* 32 Frederick Street, EH2 2JR (tel. 225 2525); *British Rail,* Waverley Station, EH1 1BB (tel. 556 2451).

Tele-tourist Information Service for daily events in Edinburgh (May–Sept.), dial 246 8031.

Boots the Chemist (Drugstore) is open till 9 at night (4.30 Sun.), at 48 Shandwick Pl.

Taxi ranks: Waverley (228 1211); Leith Walk; Tollcross (229 5221).

THE EDINBURGH FESTIVAL. Just after World War II, Edinburgh inaugurated a three-week season that has become world-famous as the Edinburgh International Festival of Music, Drama, and Art. The title gives only a slight idea of the immense range of attractions—exhibitions of painting and handcrafts, ballet, instrumental recitals, a festival of documentary and other films—these are only a few of the items on the varied program.

Orchestras, opera companies, theatrical groups, dance troupes, singers and instrumentalists, conductors, artists, writers and film directors from all over the world and, of course, from Scotland itself, take part.

Alongside the prestigious Festival, a largely irreverent Festival Fringe has developed and is now big business: several hundred small troupes and individuals—professional and amateur—offering experimental, avant-garde and satirical entertainments. Some are frankly terrible, but a few big names in the theater today got their chance at the Edinburgh Fringe of past years; and a Fringe performance—where seats are cheap and surroundings often makeshift—is always an experience.

One of the greatest of all attractions at Festival time is the spectacular Military Tattoo, with massed pipe bands parading regimental tartans under the floodlit battlements of the Castle.

Booking details. The Festival takes place each year during the last two weeks in August and the first week in September. For detailed program write to the Festival Office, 21 Market St., EH1 1DF (tel. 226 4001). Telephone bookings may also be made on 225 5756. Details regarding the *Film Festival* can be had from the Director, Edinburgh International Film Festival, Filmhouse, 88 Lothian Road, Edinburgh EH3 9BZ (tel. 228 6382). *Tattoo* bookings and enquiries should be addressed to the Tattoo Office, 1 Cockburn St., Edinburgh EH1 1QB.

The Festival Fringe program is obtainable from the *Festival Fringe Society,* Royal Mile Center, 170 High St., Edinburgh EH1 1QS (tel. 226 5257).

MUSEUMS, GALLERIES AND GARDENS. You don't need reminding, as you explore Edinburgh, that this is a capital city with all the capital amenities and national institutions. The streets and squares are a living museum; but some gloomy-looking building may also hold much of the rough glamor of Scotland's history and traditions.

Note: some of the opening hours listed below may be extended during the Edinburgh Festival.

Canongate Tolbooth, 163 Canongate. Highland dress, tartans. Open Mon.–Sat. 10–5 (10–6, June–Sept). During Festival, Sun. 2–5.

City Art Centre, 2 Market St. A Scottish Arts Council museum and gallery with high-class contemporary paintings, sculpture and photography. Mon.–Sat. 10–5 (10–6, June–Sept.). During Festival, Sun. 2–5.

Edinburgh Zoo, Corstorphine Rd. Daily, 9–6, in winter 9–sunset.

Huntly House (City Museum), 142 Canongate. Principal museum of city history; old-fashioned Scots kitchen; Edinburgh glass and silverware. Mon.–Sat. 10–5, Oct.–May (10–6 June–Sept). During Festival, Sun. 2–5.

John Knox's House, 45 High St. Sole survivor of 16th-century domestic architecture in town. Open Mon.–Sat 10–5, Apr.–Oct.; 10–4, Nov.–Mar.

Lady Stair's House, Lawnmarket. Relics of Burns, Scott (including his rocking horse) and R. L. Stevenson. Mon.–Sat., 10–5 (10–6, June–Sept.).

Museum of Childhood, 42 High St. Games, toys and dress. Open Mon.–Sat. 10–5; (10–6, June–Sept.). During Festival, Sun. 2–5.

National Gallery of Scotland, The Mound. European and British artists 1300–1900. Mon.–Sat. 10–5, Sun. 2–5.

National Library of Scotland, George IV Bridge. Mon.–Fri. 9.30–8.30, Sat. 9.30–1.

National Museum of Antiquities, 1 Queen St. (east end). Celtic and Roman finds. Mon.–Sat. 10–5, Sun. 2–5.

Palace of Holyroodhouse. Canongate. Official residence of royal family in Scotland. Relics of Mary, Queen of Scots. Mon.–Sat. 9.30–5.15, Sun. 10.30–5.15; Mon.–Sat. 9.30–3.45, Nov.–Mar. Closed during royal visits, usually in mid-May and late June.

Royal Botanic Garden, Inverleith Row. During British Summer Time open 9–one hour before sunset, Sun. 11–one hour before sunset; rest of year Mon.–Sat. 9–sunset, Sun. 11–sunset.

Royal Scottish Academy, The Mound, Contemporary Scottish artists. Annual Exhibition, late April to July and Festival exhibitions. Open Mon.–Sat. 10–6, Sun. 2–5.

Royal Scottish Museum, Chambers St. Largest overall collection in the United Kingdom. Outstanding scale models in Technology Department. Startling display of Chinese attire, worn by dummies with waxwork heads. Mon.–Sat., 10–5, Sun. 2–5.

Scottish National Gallery of Modern Art, John Watson's College, Belford Rd. 20th-century paintings and sculpture. Open Mon.–Sat. 10–5, Sun. 2–5. During Festival, Mon.–Sat. 10–6, Sun. 11–6.

Scottish National Portrait Gallery, Queen St. (east end). Prominent Scots from 16th century to present day. Open Mon.–Sat. 10–5, Sun. 2–5. During Festival, Mon.–Sat. 10–6, Sun. 11–6.

Wax Museum, 142 High St. Includes a Chamber of Horrors. Mon.–Sat., 10–7 (Mon.–Sat. 10–5, Oct.–Mar.).

ENTERTAINMENT. Theaters. The *Royal Lyceum,* Grindlay St., with resident company, does serious plays and some variety. The *King's Theatre,* Leven St., offers plays, opera, ballet and revues. The small *avant-garde Traverse.* West Bow, specializes in modern drama as—in a more

472   EXPLORING BRITAIN

experimental way—do the *Netherbow Arts Centre,* 43 High St., and *Theatre Workshop,* 34 Hamilton Place.

Music. The *Usher Hall,* Lothian Road, is Edinburgh's principal concert hall, where the *Scottish National Orchestra* and visiting virtuosi and choral groups frequently appear. The *Playhouse,* Greenside Place, has occasional opera but mostly folk and rock concerts.

Nightlife. There is a total absence of smart nightclubs in Edinburgh. For live music and jazz try: *Platform Once,* next door to the Caledonian Hotel in Princes Street; the *Kangaroo Club* in Easter Road; the *Venue,* in Calten Road; the *Gilded Balloon,* at 209 Cowgate (and with restaurant); and the *Amphitheater* in Lothian Road. The biggest disco is *Outer Limits,* West Tollcross. Along with the best light show in Edinburgh, it has three separate features: the only roller disco in Edinburgh (*Coasters*); the *Bermuda Triangle* for reggae; and the *Hoochie-Coochie Club,* strongly alternative. Centrally situated, at the west and east ends of Princes Street respectively, are the popular *Rumours* (also known as *Pipers*), in Lothian Road, and *Buster Browns* in Market Street. *Annabels* on Semple St., a favorite with off-duty waiters and Oriental students, is roomy and quite respectable and tourists have free membership. *Oscars,* Shandwick Place, is likewise respectable and does not admit under-23s. *Millionaires,* Frederick St., is noted for its sensible decor and ingenious range of cocktails (do not confuse it with the tacky disco next door). *Cinderellas Rockerfellas,* St. Stephen St., is relatively plush and expensive; you may eat there at a price. *Mistys,* Portobello, is lively and cheap. The gay club called *Fire Island,* Princes St., does not encourage the merely curious. *Sinatras,* a jungle of tropical foliage in the St. James Center (east end of Princes Street), has a twice-weekly (currently Mondays and Wednesdays) singles club.

Movies. The *ABC,* Lothian Rd., the *Dominion,* Church Hill, and the *Odeon,* Clerk St., are three-in-one movie houses showing latest releases. *Filmhouse,* Lothian Rd., shows classic and art movies. *La Scala,* Clerk St., offers non-stop porn.

Casinos. Gambling opportunities in Edinburgh are strictly limited. Try the *Regency,* Great King St. (tel. 556 2828) or the *Martell,* 7 Newington Rd. (tel. 667 7763) for blackjack or American roulette. Membership is free but it takes 48 hours to process the card.

RESTAURANTS. Edinburgh is splendidly served with restaurants of wide and cosmopolitan variety, notably Italian and more recently Oriental. Innumerable pubs offer bar lunches at agreeable prices, and department store restaurants (especially those with a window on Princes Street) are very popular. A good number of old castles, country houses and coaching inns all round Edinburgh have become successful restaurants. Much patronized by Edinburghers are *Johnstounburn House* at Humbie, winner of a Scottish Tourist Board award, 30 minutes; the old but expertly renovated *Horseshoe Inn* at Eddleston, 35 minutes; *La Potinière* at Gullane, intimate, French cuisine, advance booking essential, 25 minutes.

Listed below are some typical city restaurants.

Prestonfield House (L), Priestfield Rd. (tel. 667 8000). Stately home and secluded garden, elegantly restrained; highly recommended for that special evening out. Also has a few rooms. 1 mile from city center. Open Sun. with limited menu.

Le Chambertin (E), 19 George St. (tel. 225 1251). Successful restaurant in the George Hotel offering good and fairly original food in attractive setting. Closed Sat. lunch and Sun.

Handsel's (E), 22 Stafford St. (tel. 225 5521). Interesting menus, often with a base of local produce (Scots beef, Orkney oysters); worth trying.

Howtowdie (E), 27a Stafford St. (tel. 225 6291). Interesting decor, food combines Scottish and French culinary traditions—a traditional mix for which Edinburgh is famous.

Caledonian (M), Princes St. (tel. 225 2433). Part of refurbished *Caledonian Hotel,* this first-floor restaurant has become the daily rendezvous of moderately well-heeled business people. Friendly and generous service at lunchtime buffet counter.

Cramond Inn (M), Cramond village, 5 miles from city center (tel. 336 2035). High-class seafood in intimate atmosphere at this one-time longshoreman's "howff" above the estuary where the Romans collected oysters. Must book. Closed Sun.

Kalpna (M), St. Patrick's Sq. (tel. 667 9890). The city's only Indian vegetarian restaurant. Wide choice of curries, plus marvelous homemade ice creams. Immaculate friendly service. Open for after-theater suppers.

Lancers (M), 5 Hamilton Pl. (tel. 332 3444). Classic Bengali and north Indian dishes. All in all, an essential stopping-off point for anyone with a taste for Indian food.

Le Marché Noir (M), Eyre Place (tel. 558 1608). A pleasant little place, making its mark; can be claustrophobic when all tables are occupied. Helpful, good-humored Anglo-French staff, a mainly French cuisine with excellent ragouts and original seafood/fish concoctions. Essential to book.

Martin's (M), 72 Rose Street North Lane (tel. 225 3106). In a quiet backwater off Princes Street. The layout is modest but food is delicate and varied, with oysters, snails, game, salmon and traditional Scottish dishes all featured. Reservations essential.

Skippers (M), 1a Dock Pl., Leith (tel. 554 1018). Down by the docks, two miles from center, in a developing complex of bistros and craft galleries. Well-ordered though often congested; imaginative seafood.

Tinelli's (M), 139 Easter Rd. (tel. 652 1932). Among the best Italian restaurants. One or two home-cooked specialties; good cheeses. Located in a rather insalubrious area.

Cornerstone Cafe (I), St. John's Church, west end of Princes Street (tel. 229 4541). Developed out of a Festival-season snack bar. It's unlicensed, clean, friendly, and deals mainly in wholefoods. Very reasonably priced. Open daytime only.

Dragon Pearl (I), 20 Union Pl. (tel. 556 4547). Not much to look at, but generally acknowledged as the best of Edinburgh's Chinese restaurants.

Fat Sam's (I), 56 Fountainbridge (tel. 228 3111). Not the place for a quiet tête-a-tête, but it's good for generous and inexpensive Italo-American cuisine. Stays open all hours. Crowded most evenings, and best to reserve a table.

L'Auberge (I), 56 St. Mary Street (tel. 556 5888). French restaurant. Tourist menu (lunchtime) and gastronomic menu.

New York Steam Packet (I), 31 North Rose Street Lane (tel. 225 4663). Cheerful, lively at night; convivial atmosphere, more than a hamburger joint.

Rake's (I), South St. David Street (tel. 556 6375). Regency-style wine bar with cheap and generous food. Hot dishes really hot. A mixed clientele.

Viva Mexico (I), 10 Anchor Close (tel. 226 5145). Authentic Mexican food and beers in the heart of the Old Town.

Waterfront Wine Bar (I), 1c Dock Pl. (tel. 554 7427). If you can't get into *Skippers,* this place is right next door. Blackboard menu, mostly seafood, has been praised for enterprise; service may be less good.

FLORA MACDONALD

DISCOVERING SCOTLAND

Where Grandeur Springs

From the border at Carter Bar, at the summit of the Cheviot Hills, there are extensive views over the Scottish Lowlands to the Eildon Hills. And it is from here that the traveler coming north by road from Newcastle and avoiding the main A1 coast road gets his first feel of Scotland (A68).

Bonchester Bridge is the first place to make for, on A6088, passing through the Border National Forest Park. Bonchester has the remains of a hill fort said to have been built in the second century.

A slight variation to the east will take you to Jedburgh, on A68. This is an ancient town, the first of many that you will meet in Scotland, famous for its Border Abbey, and a great one, though now only a beautiful ruin. Following A68 will bring you to St. Boswell's and, slightly beyond, Dryburgh Abbey, once more a ruin, but this time with a wonderful situation by the River Tweed, and some ornate and historic tombs. Farther on, again, comes Melrose, a charming town and the site of yet another abbey, once great, and this time heavily restored. This trio of magnificent abbey buildings and another at Kelso on A698 show how rich and prosperous these border lands once were—and how much fought over.

Just off the A7, before the junction with the A72, lies Abbotsford House, the home of Sir Walter Scott. The novels of Scott are not read much nowadays, in fact some of them frankly are difficult to wade through, but the mystique that he created, the aura of historical romance, has outlasted his books. It is worth visiting Abbotsford, just to feel the atmosphere that the most successful writer of his day created and to see the conditions in which he wrote, driving himself to pay off his endless debts. The building, a simple farmhouse called Clartyhole when he bought it, is an incongruous pseudo-baronial, pseudo-monastic pile which reflects Scott's gentlemanly aspirations. It now has a gently seedy atmosphere.

If you have headed north from Carter Bar to Bonchester Bridge, then you will be able to join the A7 at Hawick. Here lie the ancient border towns of Hawick, Selkirk, Galashiels and (on A72) Peebles, where the countryside is lush and green, with its rolling hills deep cleft by gorges and waterfalls. Border sheep graze in thousands. Scotland exports their coarse wool and imports merino and angora for her own tweed and knit-wear industry.

Making steadily for Edinburgh, the capital, the visitor will come upon Howgate, on A6094, an attractive little village. Four miles southeast of Howgate is Gladsmuir Reservoir, in winter a favorite roosting place for enormous flocks of greylag and pink-footed geese. On the road into Edinburgh try, too, to see Rosslyn Chapel (off A6094, to the left), which has some really fine carving and sculpture (see the end of the *Edinburgh* chapter).

North from Edinburgh

From Edinburgh (described in a separate chapter) follow the A9 to South Queensferry. This ferry was named after Queen Margaret, who found refuge in Scotland after the Norman conquest and subsequently married the Scottish king, Malcolm Canmore. It was when she traveled between Edinburgh and their other home in Dunfermline, Fife, that the name Queensferry came into being. Fife, lying north of the Forth from Edinburgh, proudly styles itself as a "kingdom," and its long history lends some substance to the boast. From earliest times, its earls were first among Scottish nobility, and crowned her kings. Within its confines many great monasteries were founded, and nearly every village has some remnant of history. Nowadays the Forth can be crossed only by rail or the awe-inspiring road bridge. Once over the water into the Kingdom of Fife—a mixture of lovely countryside and awful mining towns—take the M90 road north.

You can detour for a few minutes to Dunfermline (east off the motorway at Junction 3), with the ruins of the church and abbey built by King David to the memory of his mother, Saint Margaret. It was a place of pilgrimage for centuries. Bruce lay buried there, as did Saint Margaret herself. But the relics of Margaret were hidden for safety during the Reformation, and only a fragment of her tomb remains. The bones of Bruce were found again in 1818 and now lie beneath his memorial statue in the New Abbey Church. Dunfermline's modern prosperity was greatly advanced by the munificence of Andrew Carnegie, who was born here. His birth-place, memorial, and the Carnegie Library are features of the town.

Just beyond Dunfermline is Culross, an attractive palace complex, belonging to the National Trust for Scotland. The restoration of this tiny town into a living example of 16th and 17th century "burgh life," is still going on, and the results so far make fascinating viewing.

To the west of Culross, and poised to the north of both Edinburgh and Glasgow, is the admirable touring center of Stirling, with excellent rail links and a dramatic castle perched on a 250-foot rock. From the ramparts you can see Loch Lomond's mountains and, at your feet, seven battlefields. The dearest to Scottish hearts, Bannockburn, lies under a nexus of motorways two miles from Stirling. It has a large Visitor Center and a fine equestrian statue of Robert the Bruce, who defeated the English here in 1314. Another monument, to his unlucky predecessor William Wallace, towers over the A997 road. The new university is nearby and has some good-value self-catering accommodation for summer visitors.

On M90, north of Dunfermline, lie Kinross and Loch Leven, where Mary, Queen of Scots was forced to sign the deed of abdication in her island prison in the Loch; she later escaped under romantic circumstances and made her last bid for her throne at the Battle of Langside, near Glasgow, in 1568. The modern fame of Loch Leven stems from the international angling matches that take place there and after hard frost the grand curling matches on the ice. Here you are within easy distance of Falkland Palace, romantic seat and garden of the Stuart monarchs, and Largo, where Alexander Selkirk, the original Robinson Crusoe, was born. The castaway's statue and the house he built on his return stand near the seafront.

The Golfer's Heaven

St. Andrews, on the east coast, is known the world over as the home of golf. To get a starting time for a round of golf on the hallowed "Old Course," ask your hall porter to put your name on the ballot on the day before play. For the other three courses the rule is first-come first-served, but they are seldom crowded.

Even if you're not a golf addict, there's much to do and see. Here Scots kings were crowned, John Knox preached, and earlier reformers were burned at the stake. Pilgrims came in pre-Reformation times to visit the shrine that traditionally housed relics of St. Andrew the Apostle. Try to see the university and the ruined cathedral and castle. Early in August, there is all the excitement of the Lammas Fair, which dates back to medieval times and was later a hiring fair for farm servants. Nowadays, it completely fills one main street to the exclusion of all traffic. The fishing villages of Crail and Anstruther—pronounced *Anster*—are worth visiting.

Head west and north across the Tay Road Bridge. This fine piece of engineering was opened in the autumn of 1966, just months after its builder, Willie Logan, crashed to death in an aeroplane near his Highland home. Logan had taken over the debts of a small business not many years before, and gradually attained his reputation as Scotland's most reliable contractor. A staunch church-man, he refused to allow work on the sabbath—but unlike many firms uncaring of such principle, he always honored completion dates.

Dundee and Perth

Dundee is a fine shopping place with a long history. Rail travelers approach Dundee by the famous Tay bridge, a spectacle almost as famous as that over the Forth. The first Tay Bridge was the scene of the great railway disaster of 1879, when its high girders fell during an exceptional December gale. Famed for jute, jam and journalism, Dundee is the fourth city of Scotland, attractive, well situated, industrious. From it you can visit

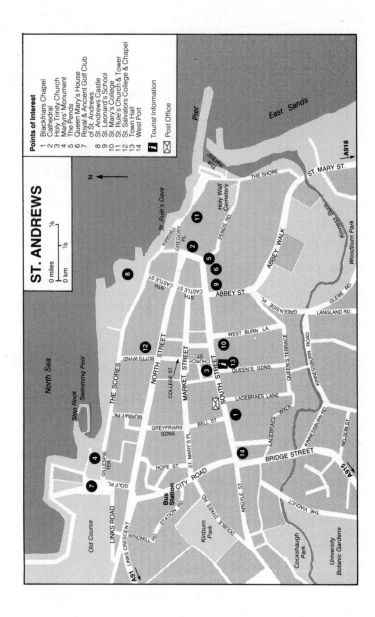

ST. ANDREWS

0 miles   ⅛
0 km   ⅛

N ←

Points of Interest

1   Blackfriars Chapel
2   Cathedral
3   Holy Trinity Church
4   Martyrs' Monument
5   The Pends
6   Queen Mary's House
7   Royal & Ancient Golf Club
    of St. Andrews
8   St. Andrews Castle
9   St. Leonard's School
10 St. Mary's College
11 St. Rule's Church & Tower
12 St. Salvators College & Chapel
13 Town Hall
14 West Port

i   Tourist Information
⊠   Post Office

places like Arbroath, whose ruined abbey was the scene of the great Declaration of Independence of 1320; Glamis Castle, with its royal connections; Kirriemuir, where J. M. Barrie was born; and Carnoustie and Montrose for golf.

Next, go along the fast road (A85) to Perth, a pleasant market town in rich, gentle farmland. Perth is a pretty, clean, thriving place, whose most famous and vivid literary connection is with Scott's *The Fair Maid of Perth.* Other historical memories concern James I (of Scotland) who was murdered here, and John Knox, who preached one of his earliest sermons here and began the iconoclastic revolution which swept Scotland. Many small hotels offer bed-and-breakfast accommodations.

A few miles away is Scone, where many of the Scottish kings were crowned on the Stone of Destiny, which was taken to England by Edward I, the "hammer of the Scots," and ever since has performed the same function in Westminster Abbey. Like so many places in Scotland, Scone is bubbling over with history, and lies at the country's heart in more ways than one. Although little is left above ground of the buildings which were here when those ancient kings came to be crowned, Moot Hill still stands. Here, tradition says that handfuls of earth from all over Scotland were brought, so that the chieftains could swear allegiance, standing on their own land. History goes back even further, to the Picts, those strange blue-painted tribes who lived here and whose defiance forced the Romans to build Hadrian's Wall. This was the site of the palace of the High King of the Picts. Scone Palace was rebuilt in 1803, the seat of the Earls of Mansfield. It has some lovely collections of French furniture, china and ivories.

From Dunkeld to Culloden

The greatly improved A9 road from Perth crosses the Grampians to the Spey Valley and Inverness.

Dunkeld (15 miles from Perth) has a 15th-century cathedral, shattered now, but with part used as a parish church. The site is particularly lovely, sitting as it does on the banks of the Tay in well-tended grounds. The group of small buildings—the Little Houses (18th century)—near the cathedral, have been attractively restored, and include an excellent small crafts shop for gifts.

Pitlochry (28 miles), set in the wooded valley of the Tummel, is a popular tourist center offering a variety of attractions not the least of which is the summer festival of theater. After living in a tent since 1949, the Festival graduated to a full-scale, properly built theater in 1981. Sited on a slope above the new road by-passing the town, it has—as well as enjoyable performances—a restaurant and other amenities, plus it commands a beautiful view.

Loch Faskally has a hydro station at its southern end, with a fish pass complete with observation chamber; a little to the north is the famous Queen's View across Loch Tummel. To the east, Glenshee is one of Scotland's three main skiing centers in winter.

The road then threads the Pass of Killiecrankie (31 miles) where "Bonnie Dundee" defeated King William III's troops in 1689 but was himself killed. The National Trust for Scotland's information center close by includes a display of the battle.

At Blair Atholl (35 miles) is the white-turreted Blair Castle, seat of the Duke of Atholl, with its fine collection of furniture, portraits and china. The Atholl Highlanders form the Duke's private army, the only one in Britain.

Those travelers from around the world who are named Robertson, Duncan, McInroy or MacConnochie, should visit the Clan Donnochaidh Museum at Calvine (40 miles), which is full of reminders of their clan's long history.

The next stretch of road is bleak, climbing to the Pass of Drumochter (1,484 feet) and crossing from Atholl into Badenoch. The first place of interest is Newtonmore (70 miles) on the river Spey, where there is a clan museum for the MacPhersons. Kingussie, the capital of Badenoch, has also a museum, "Am Fasgadh" (the Shelter), portraying Highland life over the centuries. Newtonmore is also a Cairngorms ski resort and makes a fair center for touring the area. Not far away are the ruined Ruthven Barracks, where Bonnie Prince Charlie's Highlanders assembled after Culloden, hoping that he would take the field again. The Prince's message, however, was terse: "Let every man seek his safety the best way he can."

A few miles to the north, at Kincraig, the Highland Wildlife Park has a fine collection of native animals, including some, like bison, wolves and bears, now nationally extinct but which used to range this part of Scotland.

Aviemore (85 miles) is now the main tourist center for Speyside, with a modern complex of hotels, cinema, ice rinks, swimming pool and sports center, set in wonderful countryside. To the east are the Cairngorm mountains, a major skiing ground, and the 12,000-acre Glenmore Forest Park. The chairlift rises to 3,600 feet and the highest restaurant in Britain, *The Ptarmigan*. The views are superb.

At Carrbridge (92 miles) don't miss the Landmark Visitor Center, the first of its kind in Europe, where 10,000 years of Highland history are shown in an audio-visual theater. As a skiing resort, Carrbridge is Aviemore's little brother.

Over another summit, Slochd (1,332 feet) and the A9 reaches Inverness (116 miles), "capital of the Highlands" and a bustling little town attractively set on the river Ness. There is a picturesque castle and a good museum with Jacobite relics; while a few miles away is the battlefield that in 1746 ended Jacobite hopes—Culloden.

In and Around Aberdeen

Before reaching Inverness, it is possible to turn east on A938, to Grantown-on-Spey, and the road leads straight into a famous whisky area. Distilleries with world-famous names are to be seen every few miles on the long journey to Aberdeen.

Aberdeen itself, headquarters of Britain's North Sea oil industry, holiday center and busy fishing port, is a fine shopping place, with much of interest historically. It is a brisk city, built largely of granite, which gives it a new look. It stands between the mouths of two rivers, the Don and the Dee, and has a university, which managed to save some of its pre-Reformation treasures, so that its library is well worth a visit by historians. St. Machar's Cathedral (1530) is the only granite cathedral in Britain. The post-Reformation part of the university, the Marischal College, is also magnificent, dominated by the 260-ft.-high Mitchell Tower. Worth seeing, too, is the Brig o' Balgownie, an early 14th-century bridge, with some interesting buildings nearby. Provost Skene's House, an ancient building, has been converted into a museum of the city's past domestic life.

Within easy reach of Aberdeen are the Castles of Mar, a dramatic group of historical buildings unsurpassed anywhere in the country, and open to the public. Closest to the city are Drum, near Peterculter, with its great 13th-century square keep; and pretty Castle Fraser, set in rolling parkland, where there is an exhibition devoted to the castles. Crathes, near Banchory, is a fine tower house, built in 1553, and boasting magnificent painted ceilings and splendid gardens. Finally there is Craigievar, a fairy tale tower house. Some of the most romantic castles are in the hands of the National Trust for Scotland and these and others are open to viewing. You could visit them all in a day, by car or excursion bus, for they are all sited on or near the Deeside roads which trace the River Dee westward from Aberdeen almost to its source.

As you approach the headwaters of the Dee, in increasingly delightful scenery, you will pass Balmoral Castle, the royal family's summer residence. The castle's gardens and ballroom are open to visitors between May and July. Farther on is Braemar, scene of the most famous Highland Gathering, held in September under royal patronage; in fact, the Queen usually times her visits to Balmoral to coincide with the Braemar Gathering. Here, too, is the house where Robert Louis Stevenson wrote *Treasure Island.*

Returning to Aberdeen after this excursion down the Dee, head northward to Peterhead (A92 and 952). Westward along the coast road (A950 and 98) you next go through Macduff, Banff and Cullen to Fochabers. This is a section of the country that is often missed by visitors, and it is rather off the beaten track. But there are some attractive harbors, awe-inspiring cliffs and the ruins of many coastal fortresses.

The next stop is Elgin, one of the most pleasant towns in all Scotland. Its chief monuments are its ruined cathedral and the restored Greyfriars Abbey Church. The town is a center of the Jacobite cult, and its historical society collection includes the only surviving copy of the Proclamation offering £30,000 for the betrayal of Prince Charles Edward Stuart, when he was on the run after the Battle of Culloden in 1746. There were no takers in the Highlands.

Hard by Elgin is Lossiemouth, birthplace of Ramsay MacDonald, one of the Scots prime ministers of Britain, and not far away is Gordonstoun, where the Queen's husband, Prince Philip, and their three sons went to school.

Inverness

One of the most pleasant features of Inverness is the spectacle of the three suspension bridges. In the Town Hall is a portrait of Flora Macdonald, who guided Prince Charlie in his flight of safety and final exile. Her memorial can be seen on the Castle Hill.

Interesting buildings in this fine town include the castle and the high court; Abertarff House (17th-century), now a Gaelic museum; the Town House, containing interesting historical relics, and the Clock Tower, all that remains of Cromwell's Fort. At the foot of the town cross on the Exchange is the Clach-na-Cudainn stone, dating back perhaps 1,000 years. Old washerwomen were supposed to have used it as a resting place on their way down to the river with their tubs. Men from Inverness are still called "Clach-na-Cudainn boys" the world over.

Just outside Inverness is Tomnahurich Cemetery, or "hill of the fairies," which is renowned for its beautiful layout and serene atmosphere. The farming land around Inverness and the Moray Firth is the richest in Scotland.

Also just outside the town (4 miles) is the site of the Battle of Culloden, when Bonnie Prince Charlie and his forces were crushingly defeated on 16 April, 1746. It was after this battle that Flora Macdonald's aid came in so handy. There is an excellent Visitors Center on the ground where the battle was fought, and a memorial stone. The defeat was indeed crushing. Of Charlie's 5,000 men, exhausted after an all-night march, some 1,000 were killed in the battle and subsequent pursuit, and about the same number taken prisoner. The British force, under Cumberland, nicknamed "Butcher," numbered around 9,000 strong, and lost only 50, with 200 wounded. It was effectively the end of Highland revolt against the Hanover crown, and was followed by repressive measures—just to make sure.

During July, August and September there are many Highland Gatherings and Games held within easy reach of Inverness, culminating with the Northern Meeting Piping Competitions, held in Inverness in September.

Life in the Wild

Northwest of Inverness are the wild, picturesque glens, forests and moorlands which are the last untouched corner of the British Isles. Here, in the ancient Caledonian forests north of Loch Ness, it is still possible to see the country's remaining indigenous wild animals: ranging from the mild-mannered red deer, a mere four-and-a-half-ft. tall and weighing only about 280 lbs. when fully-grown but still the country's largest wild animal, down to the shy wild cat. You can see herds of red deer from the car or train, but you have to walk to find the quieter, rare beasts—and you have to be prepared to get up early or stay up late as well.

In the gray light of dawn, it is possible to catch a glimpse of the tiny roe deer or the bushy-tailed wild cat out on the forest track, and in the woodland itself you may find the fat capercaillie, Scotland's largest game bird. Walk farther, up on to the moors, and you may well see the king of the Scottish skies, the magnificent golden eagle.

Scotland's wildlife is slowly recovering from the depredations wrought by man and nature during the past few centuries. The golden eagle and the peregrine falcon are on the increase; the goshawk is returning; snowy owls are back in the Shetland Isles and the golden-eye duck is now breeding on the mainland. Perhaps most publicity has been given to the osprey, which has returned to nest in several parts of Scotland, and is on view near Dunkeld and Boat of Garten. The wild cat and the pine marten are holding their own, whooper swans are common on Scottish lochs in winter, and otters (almost extinct in England) still inhabit the banks of Highland and Lowland streams.

The Road to John o' Groats

North of Inverness the only "towns" are mere villages, set on the edge of peaty, windswept moorland.

If you want to reach the very tip of Scotland at John o' Groats you have two choices, both scenic. You can take the marine drive round the shores of interlocking firths, through Bonar Bridge, Golspie, Brora, Wick and Thurso, with a detour between Wick and Thurso taking you to John o' Groats.

North of Golspie is Dunrobin Castle, a Victorian enlargement of a 13th-century building that is about to be transformed into a leisure complex, in a fine setting by the sea. Indeed, all the way up this coast there are points of interest, none startling, but all adding to an understanding of life and history in these parts. Brora is famous for a particularly good malt whisky called Clynelish. At Kintradwell the killing of the last wolf in Britain is reported on a carved stone. Kildonan is known as the site of at least two gold rushes. Prehistoric remains have been found in the region around Latheron, while the Grey Cairns of Camster, near Lybster, are neolithic chambers that can be visited. The village of John o' Groats is said to be named after a Dutchman, Jan de Groot, who settled in the region in the 16th century with two brothers. You should be warned not to expect a simple, rocky, natural landscape, undisturbed by the excesses of commercialism—it has stretched its greedy paw even to this remote spot.

Halfway between John o' Groats and Dunnet lies the Castle of Mey which belongs to Elizabeth, the Queen Mother.

Alternatively, you can take the longer route up northwards from Lairg, through Altnaharra, a fine spot for trout and salmon fishing (on A836), to the coast at Tongue, where you will find some fine views along the rugged shore. Then eastward to Dounreay, where lies the Experimental Nuclear Reactor Establishment—if you feel like contemplating the shape of things to come—and so on to John o' Groats via Thurso.

The Orkney and Shetland Islands

Across the Pentland Firth from John o' Groats lie the Orkney and Shetland groups of islands. Here we are in the ancient sea-kingdom of the Norsemen, for the islands look towards Scandinavia. The ancient Norse festival of Up Helly Aa' is celebrated in Lerwick at the end of January with the burning of a Viking ship after it has been dragged through the town in a torchlight procession.

This ancient kingdom of Zetland, together with Orcadia, was not handed to Scotland until the 15th century, when they formed part of the dowry of a Scandinavian princess about to marry James III, King of Scotland. The islands are virtually bare of trees, due to heavy winter gales, but have a relatively mild climate since the Gulf Stream swirls around them. Seascapes and voes (fiord-like inlets) are unique. Sullom Voe, formerly bleak and lonely, now contains one of Britain's biggest and busiest oil terminals.

Kirkwall, capital of Orkney, is another fascinating town, with a harbor, narrow paved streets, old stone houses and splendid cathedral of St. Magnus which was founded in 1137, by which time Orkney had been civilized for centuries. The cathedral has been in the news of recent years as the focal point of a Festival based on the work of the modern composer, Peter Maxwell Davies, who lived here. His music often reflects the sea and legends of this part of Scotland.

Nearby is Scapa Flow, once a great naval base and scene of the scuttling of the German fleet in 1919. During the last war, when Churchill was in

charge of the Admiralty, he ordered Scapa Flow to be shut in from the
east by the erection of barriers linking four islands. These Churchill Barriers, built at a cost of two million pounds, are an engineering wonder of
the north.

If you decide to stay awhile in the Orkneys there are plenty of other
interesting places to see, notably the Stone Age village of Skara Brae, Maes
Howe burial mound, the prehistoric Standing Stones of Stenness, and the
1,000-ft cliffs of Hoy.

A half-way house between the Orkneys and Shetlands is Fair Isle. There
is an air service as well as a mail boat (from Grutness on Shetland), so
the island is not cut off. It belongs to the National Trust for Scotland, and
you should get in touch with them first if you are thinking of visiting. Perhaps the most remarkable thing about Fair Isle is the bird observatory,
with a huge number of species. There is a hostel for bird watchers, simple
but adequate for the dedicated ornithologist.

Shetland is the *Ultima Thule* of the Romans, the northernmost limits
of Britain, where it never really becomes dark during midsummer and the
Aurora Borealis flickers in the northern sky.

Lerwick, capital of the 100 islands that make up the 70-mile-long Shetland chain, not only provides shelter for fishing trawlers from many nations, and direct ferry connections with Aberdeen, but it is also a vital link
in the chain of servicing for the oil rigs. The international flavor is carried,
too, by the airport at Sumburgh, on the southern tip of the island. Nearby
is Jarlshof, where the homes of Bronze Age Shetlanders, three villages'
worth, have been excavated. The site was inhabited, too, by people of the
Iron Age and by the Vikings, who gave it its name.

Halfway up the west coast from Sumburgh to Lerwick lies St. Ninian's
Isle, not really an island, rather a small peninsula connected to the mainland by a narrow neck of sand. Here was found, in 1958, St. Ninian's Treasure, a hoard of wonderful silver bowls and jewelry, now on show in the
National Museum of Antiquities in Edinburgh. Higher up this stretch of
coast is Scalloway, with its ruined castle and the mess left behind by the
oil bandwagon. Shetland's coastal scenery is truly awe-inspiring, with sea-
bird-haunted cliffs soaring in places to 1,300 feet.

The Northwest Coast

To pick up the coverage of the mainland once more we will return to
Lairg. Running northwest from Lairg is Loch Shin, Sutherland's largest
loch. A838 follows its northern edge, through scenery which is sometimes
stark. But once the coast is reached the change is clear. Turning west and
then south after Laxford Bridge on A894, this miraculous coast reveals
its sheer beauty, with all sorts of unusual wild flowers coloring the grasses.
(You may wish to make a slight detour before starting, to reach hidden
Tarbet—one of four or five places in Scotland with the same name. In summer, you can get to the bird sanctuary of Handa Island from here.)

On the way south there is a car ferry at Kylesku (five minutes, free)
to reach Unapool. Join the A835 and cross the edge of the Inverpolly Nature Reserve, a staggeringly lovely area. Off to the right is an unnumbered
road that leads to Achnahaird and Achiltibuie. From the latter you can
cross to the Summer Isles, which lie offshore, seaward of Loch Broom.

These are remote, almost uninhabited islands now, though they were once significant to the fishing industry. They can also be reached from Ullapool.

Ullapool is still an important fishing port, but is also a center from which you can take the car ferry to Stornoway on the Isle of Lewis in the Outer Hebrides.

All down the west coast, and especially between Lochinver and Kyle of Lochalsh, sea lochs thrust salty fingers into the loneliest landscapes in Scotland, carrying the Atlantic's salty tang among the moors and deer forests and reminding one that in Scotland you can never be more than 40 miles away from the sea or a sea loch. The only penalty, but one infinitely worth paying, is to have to make constant winding detours as the road follows the convolutions of seashore and mountain.

Lochinver, Ullapool, Plockton and Gairloch are all beautiful little towns, and wonderful stopping places. A friendly reception is guaranteed by the courteous western Highlanders, but don't expect anything to happen in a hurry. Time means nothing in this part of Scotland—so many other things are of greater importance. After Gairloch, continue south to Achnasheen on A832, where you turn west on A890, for Shieldaig, another pretty village, Strome Ferry and Kyle of Lochalsh.

Over the Sea to Skye

Kyle of Lochalsh has one of the car ferries over to Skye (it takes only five minutes). In the height of summer, there may appear to be endless queues of cars, but they soon disappear. Anyway, it's good entertainment watching the traffic getting on and off. The ferrymen with their knitted navy-blue caps, skins tanned to the color of strong tea, are equally good to see and hear—and will give you some very useful holiday information too.

Of all the Scottish islands perhaps Skye has most to offer the visitor. It is fey, mysterious and mountainous, an island of sunsets which linger brilliantly till late at night, and beautiful, soft mists. Much-photographed are the really old crofts, still inhabited, with their thick stone walls, earth floors and thatched roofs.

From Kyleakin, the attractive little port with its ruined castle, the road (A850) goes through Broadford and Portree, both pleasant towns. Uig (on A856) in the north of the island is worth a visit, as is Dunvegan in the west (A850, A863). Dunvegan Castle, a massive stronghold, ancestral seat of the Macleod chiefs, claims to be the oldest inhabited dwelling in Scotland.

Down the western side, the road leads through spectacular scenery to Elgol in the south. This tiny village looks across to the Cuillin Hills and to Soay, from which shark fishing was organized by writer Gavin Maxwell shortly after the war. Maxwell wrote his best-seller, *Ring of Bright Water,* from his home near Glenelg on the mainland, which also has a summer ferry to Skye. For a quick tour of the Inner Hebrides or western isles, however, the best port is Mallaig (A830). In summer you can embark at noon, call at Skye, Eigg, Rhum and Canna and be back in Mallaig by dusk.

The Western Isles

Beyond Skye, in a protective arc, lie the Outer Hebrides—Lewis and Harris, North and South Uist, with the intervening Benbecula and Barra and Eriskay tagged on at the southern tip. Lewis and Harris is in fact one island, arbitrarily divided by an unmarked border. Its capital is Stornoway, with its huge fishing harbor. There you can see explorer Alexander Mackenzie's birthplace and visit the lovely grounds of Lews Castle, which dominates the town. A short drive from Stornoway is Scotland's Stonehenge, a 40-ft. prehistoric circle of stones known as the Standing Stones of Callanish. Thirteen monoliths encircle one large cairn, and other stones which may have formed concentric circles are dotted about.

Lewis and Harris is a mountainous island, famous for its rugged fishermen and its tweed. This can be bought at roadside cottages for less than you would pay elsewhere, if you're lucky. The southern port of Tarbert—no more than a collection of cottages and shops, a motel and fjord-like harbor—has ferry services to Skye and Lochmaddy in North Uist.

North Uist, Benbecula and South Uist are a trio of islands linked by bridges and causeways, allowing you to motor their length from Lochmaddy to Lochboisdale—a half-day drive of endless fascination. Southward, like a fluttering tail to the kite-shaped group, lie Eriskay, where Bonnie Prince Charlie first landed; Barra, with gaunt Castle Kishmul islanded in the bay; and tiny Berneray, whose lighthouse on a 583-foot cliff has the largest arc of visibility in the world.

Farther south along the west coast lie other groups of islands that are more accessible from Glasgow—Coll, Tiree, Iona, Staffa, Colonsay, Mull, Jura, Islay, Bute and Arran. The first six may be fairly easily seen by traveling by road or rail from Glasgow to Oban, and thence by boat. (Mull, Coll, Tiree and Islay also have air links with Glasgow.) On Mull lies Tobermory Bay, which through the centuries has been the scene of treasure hunts for the Spanish galleon that was wrecked there after the defeat of the Spanish Armada in 1588. Almost every summer a hopeful search is carried on in the bay.

Iona is famed as the cradle of Christianity in western Scotland. It is the island of St. Columba but his bones were transferred to Dunkeld during the 9th century. Of recent years the Church of Scotland has authorized the establishment of the "Iona Community" scheme here. Fifty-two of the ancient kings of Scotland were buried on Iona, not to mention princes, bishops, and chieftains. The original monastery has completely disappeared, but a cathedral was rebuilt at the beginning of this century, and the island attracts pilgrims from all over the world, who find a sanctuary sacred long before Christianity came to the North.

Islay, Bute and Arran are best known as holiday resorts, and Arran is particularly well worth visiting. A complete miniature version of Scotland, it has its own mountains, lochs and glens, as well as a castle at Brodick and a delightful bay at Lamlash. Brodick Castle is the creation of the Hamilton family, frequently powerful in the nation's affairs. Now run by the National Trust, the castle contains, among other treasures, the remnants of the collection of William Beckford, the eccentric millionaire who created Fonthill. His works of art came to the Hamiltons by the marriage of the tenth Duke to his daughter. The island is best reached by steamer from Ardrossan, on the Firth of Clyde.

On Islay, near the town of Port Charlotte, stands a memorial to a number of American soldiers who lost their lives when the *Tuscania* was torpedoed near the island in 1918. Many of the victims are buried in the local cemetery. Islay is famous for its whisky—the tiny island has no less than four distilleries.

Jura is a wild island with only a scattering of people living on it. Triple peaks, called the "Paps of Jura," attract climbers and hardy walkers who visit the island in summer.

The Highlands

If you have followed our route down the west coast, described above, you will have skirted the Highlands and glimpsed the wildest and most majestic Scottish scenery. Now you turn inland, but still hugging the shores of those penetrating sea lochs, and come to Fort William, which is the West Highland crossroads. Behind the town the highest mountain in the British Isles, Ben Nevis (4,406 ft.) dominates the vista.

At this point you have a choice of roads. You can pass through the Great Glen (A82), north-east to Inverness, along the 60-mile Caledonian Canal which links three riverine lochs, Lochy, Oich and Ness. The engineer Thomas Telford started improving this natural waterway with locks and sluices in 1803 and it was opened to shipping 44 years later. For cruising boats and small fishing craft it provides a safe and picturesque alternative to the long and often stormy passage round the north of Scotland. On a point of land near Drumnadrochit, Loch Ness, you may see people gazing hopefully lochwards, and even some with sonar equipment. This is where most alleged sightings of the notorious monster "Nessie" have occurred.

The other road from Fort William (A82 southbound) disentangles itself from the sea lochs and climbs through Glencoe ("Glen of Weeping"), scene of the most violent massacre in Scottish history. On February 13th, 1692, the MacDonald clansmen and their wives and children were treacherously slain by their guests the Campbells in pursuit of a political vendetta. Survivors were mercilessly hunted down, or died of exposure. To this day the MacDonalds and Campbells are hostile to one another.

Turn east on A85 and you enter the lakeland of the central Highlands. From its "lochans" (small inland lochs) come the streams which feed the Tay, Scotland's longest river (119 miles). This is great trout and salmon fishing country. The hills and forests are alive with tales of Rob Roy the Highland freebooter, romanticized in the novels of Sir Walter Scott.

Strathclyde

The A82 road, heading for Glasgow (described later in this chapter) passes into Strathclyde region, which contains more inhabitants than the other eight regions of Scotland put together. Glasgow's urban sprawl accounts for most of them; but Strathclyde elsewhere is a country of green and flowery sea lochs and savage hills. (The most rugged parts of the National Forest Park north of the Clyde are facetiously known as "the Duke of Argyll's Bowling Green.")

Within an hour of Glasgow you are traveling the full length (28 miles) of Loch Lomond, with splendid views of its multifarious wooded islets. A short detour takes you through the Trossachs ("bristly country"), rich in memories of R.L. Stevenson's *Kidnapped,* of clan feuds and of Scott's *Lady of the Lake.* This land of "darksome glens and gleaming lochs" is

Scotland's most popular touring area. Along with the grandeur of the landscapes goes an extraordinary botany, innumerable species of wild flowers at all seasons and some magnificent gardens of azaleas and rhododendrons, of which perhaps Crarae Lodge on Loch Fyne is the most beautiful.

If you want to hurry on to the scenic and historic southwest country of Strathclyde, go through the Clyde tunnel or cross the city of Glasgow on its modern flyovers. The A8 and A78 roads lead seawards along the banks of the Clyde—an astonishingly narrow river, considering the enormous ships which have been launched there, but one which broadens rapidly to its firth, to a kaleidoscope of isles and shipping. Paddle-steamer excursions "doon the watter" to Rothesay on the Isle of Bute have been popular with Glaswegians ever since 1812, the year Henry Bell started the world's first regular steamboat service. On the mainland, Gourock, Wemyss Bay and Largs are ferry ports for the islands and the opposite shore: the routes of Neil Munro's comic coasting skipper in his *Para Handy Tales.*

Going south, Troon and Turnberry are known to golfers everywhere and between those seaside championship courses stands Culzean (pronounced *Cullane*) Castle on a dramatic clifftop. This is one of Robert Adam's finest castellated mansions, inside and out. With its surrounding "country park" and model farm-buildings Culzean is the most-visited of all the National Trust for Scotland properties. The penthouse apartment reserved for President Eisenhower in his lifetime is now a V.I.P. hospitality suite. Another apartment, full of World War Two mementoes with an audio-visual presentation, designed to explain exactly who this man Eisenhower was, is rather out of key with the classical harmonies of the environment.

On the route between Culzean and the airport at Prestwick (25 miles) you pass through the pleasant town of Ayr, notable as a family seaside resort and the homeland of Robert Burns. It's not easy to appreciate the intensity of affection which Scots, somewhat irrationally, have for their national poet. Don't mock him or you will make enemies in Scotland! To them he is more than a poet; he is champion of the underdog, exposer of cant and hypocrisy and (like so many Scots) a sucker for a noble cause. Burns idolatry is rife, especially around his native Alloway, now a suburb of Ayr. There is a formidable Burns Interpretation Center there, the starting-point for a Burns Heritage Trail which takes you on a circuit of about 90 miles through the villages whose belles inspired his love-poems, the farms whose unmanageable bogs broke his spirit and the pubs and rustic clubs where he tried to drown his sorrows.

Dumfries and Galloway

The Burns Trail touches at the "howffs" (taverns) of Dumfries, where the poet dissipated his last energies and, also in Dumfries, the house where he died in 1796, as well as the elaborate mausoleum in which he is buried.

Westward from this important market center and its riverside walks lies the land of Galloway, rather neglected by travelers to Scotland, sparsely populated but by no means desolate. There are lakes and noble pine forests. The gardens of the great houses—Castle Kennedy, Ardwell, Logan and others—are a generous tribute to the warmth and moisture of the climate. From Arbigland on the Solway Firth came John Paul Jones ("I have not yet begun to fight"), sometimes described as the father of the U.S. Navy. The font in the neighboring parish church of Kirkbean, dedicated to John Paul Jones, was presented in 1945 by the U.S. Navy Department. By coincidence, George Washington's personal physician, Dr. Craik, also came from this hamlet of minuscule population.

Fragmentary castles and tottering abbeys, evidence of centuries of turmoil, litter the maritime districts. Try to see Dundrennan, where Mary, Queen of Scots passed her last night in her native country (1568) before embarking on weary years of imprisonment in England; also Sweetheart Abbey (13th century), which was designed as a repository for the heart of John Balliol, after whom the well-known Oxford College was named.

Going into England from Dumfries by the A75 road you say farewell to "Caledonia, stern and wild" at the village of Gretna Green. Up to 1856, and unofficially afterwards, runaway couples were married here according to old Scots law, before witnesses and without ceremony. The village blacksmith usually performed the office of priest and his forge and anvil remain as relics of some tragic and romantic elopements.

Glasgow

Glasgow and Edinburgh, equally venerable cities and only 45 miles apart, offer startling contrasts in many respects. Edinburgh is proud, reserved, age-of-elegance. Glasgow is aggressive, exuberant, industrial-revolution. Each city professes a jokey contempt for the other. (Sample: an Edinburgh newspaper sets up a competition for its readers. First prize, a week's holiday in Glasgow. Second prize, *two* weeks' holiday in Glasgow.)

Glasgow at first glance is nothing much to look at. The city and its immediate surroundings support two million people, nearly half Scotland's population: a logical starting point for your "MacRoots" pilgrimage. There are large Jewish, Irish and Italian communities and the descendants of many poor peasants from the once-poverty-stricken north. (The railway bridge across Argyle Street is still known to Glaswegians as "The Hielandman's Umbrella.") Fifty years ago the slums of dockland and the Clyde banks were notorious for violence, disease and desperate overcrowding. The Gorbals district was a household name all over Britain for urban deprivation. The Communist activists in the shipyards ("Red Clydeside") were thorns in the Government's flesh throughout the 1920s and 1930s.

The old slum quarters are wastelands now. Their inhabitants have moved into tower-block apartment houses on the city perimeter or have taken up residence in the "new towns" of Cumbernauld, East Kilbride and Irvine. These satellite communities are not exactly tourist attractions, but they interest sociologists. They are growing to fixed limits and about a quarter of their houses are occupier-owned—a high proportion by Scottish standards. They have taken pressure off the congested city and have provided a healthier social mix.

The great shipyards of the Clyde are much cleaner and quieter now than in the days when the transatlantic liners and the battleships of the Royal Navy were constructed here. These days, their business is high-tech rig, platform and module development for the oil rigs of the North Sea. Much of Clydeside is now a wasteland and surviving businesses are in corporate

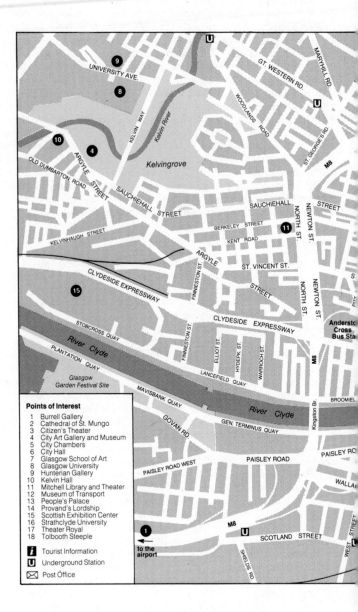

Points of Interest

1 Burrell Gallery
2 Cathedral of St. Mungo
3 Citizen's Theater
4 City Art Gallery and Museum
5 City Chambers
6 City Hall
7 Glasgow School of Art
8 Glasgow University
9 Hunterian Gallery
10 Kelvin Hall
11 Mitchell Library and Theater
12 Museum of Transport
13 People's Palace
14 Provand's Lordship
15 Scottish Exhibition Center
16 Strathclyde University
17 Theater Royal
18 Tolbooth Steeple

i Tourist Information
U Underground Station
✉ Post Office

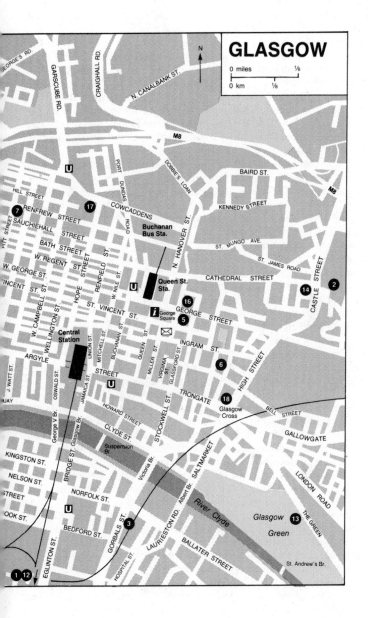

GLASGOW

N

0 miles   ⅛

0 km   ⅛

GEORGE'S RD.

GARSCUBE RD.

CRAIGHALL RD.

N. CANALBANK ST.

M8

U

HILL STREET

RENFREW STREET   7

PITT STREET

SAUCHIEHALL   STREET

BATH STREET

W. REGENT STREET

W. GEORGE ST.

'INCENT ST.

W. CAMPBELL ST.

WELLINGTON ST.

Central Station

ARGYLE STREET

J. WATT ST.

OSWALD ST.

QUAY

17

COWCADDENS

PORT DUNDAS ROAD

DOBBIE'S LOAN

Buchanan Bus Sta.

N. HANOVER ST.

Queen St. Sta.   U

HOPE ST.

RENFIELD ST.

WINE ST.

ST. VINCENT ST.

i   George Square

✉   5   16

GEORGE   STREET

BAIRD ST.

M8

KENNEDY STREET

ST. MUNGO AVE.

ST. JAMES ROAD

CATHEDRAL   STREET

CASTLE STREET

14   2

MITCHELL ST.

JAMACA ST.

UNION ST.

BUCHANAN ST.

MILLER ST.

QUEEN ST.

VIRGINIA ST.

GLASSFORD ST.

INGRAM   ST.

6

TRONGATE

HIGH STREET

18
Glasgow Cross

BELL   STREET

GALLOWGATE

U

KINGSTON ST.

NELSON ST.

STREET

OOK ST.

1 12

EGLINTON ST.

George V Br.

BRIDGE ST.

Glasgow Br.

HOWARD STREET

CLYDE ST.

Suspension Br.

NORFOLK ST.

U

BEDFORD ST.

GORBALS ST.

3

HOSPITAL ST.

LAURIESTON RD.

STOCKWELL ST.

Victoria Br.

Albert Br.

SALTMARKET

BALLATER STREET

River Clyde

Glasgow Green

LONDON ROAD

THE GREEN

13

St. Andrew's Br.

or foreign ownership. Even more dramatic changes have taken place on the sites of the Queens and the Prince's Docks. They have become the Scottish Exhibition and Conference Center and the 1988 Garden Festival respectively.

Around the black, sluggish Clyde you can easily lose yourself in a labyrinth of docks, basins and slipways. This was where much of Britain's history of war and commerce and of the expansion of the British Empire began, starting with the day in 1765 when James Watt, walking on Glasgow Green, solved the problem of steam propulsion. Before that date Glasgow's merchant adventurers had established the tobacco trade with the southern states of the U.S.A. The galleried auction rooms and warehouses of significantly-named Virginia Street recall a transatlantic connection which first brought fame and wealth to Glasgow.

The city coat-of-arms portrays the legend of St. Mungo, sometimes called St. Kentigern, a 6th-century missionary who founded a chapel on the Clyde banks. The site is now occupied by Glasgow cathedral (13th century), the most complete of Scotland's cathedrals. (It would be completer still if 19th-century architectural vandals had not pulled down its two graceful towers.) The crypt where St. Mungo lies buried has the finest Norman vaulting in Europe.

The cathedral makes a good starting-point for a walk round the sights of central Glasgow. On one side of Cathedral Square is the Necropolis (graveyard) with a conspicuous monument to John Knox. On the other side, don't miss Provand's Lordship, a typical 15th-century town house well furnished with tapestries, stained glass and portraits. Tradition holds that three Scottish monarchs—James II, James IV and Mary—lodged here at various times.

On the south side of the Square, George Street leads back to George Square in the busy shopping district of the city center—a district which is enclosed in the triangle formed by Sauchiehall Street, Buchanan Street and Argyle Street. Where traffic once moved at a crawl, some thoroughfares are now all-pedestrian, with trees, shrubs and flower-beds in the shopping precincts, and the solid Victorian buildings are seen to good advantage. Note the Mitchell Library, the largest public reference library in Europe, and the handsome neoclassical Stirling Library. Mitchell and Stirling were tobacco barons of the 18th century.

It is almost 300 years since Daniel Defoe, author of *Robinson Crusoe,* described Glasgow as the "cleanest and beautifullest and best-built of cities"—you will not recognise it from that description today. But efforts have been made to clean up Glasgow. There are now more than 70 parks and recreation grounds, specially-built walkways along the Clyde and even a nature trail within the city.

Glasgow's largest area of peaceful and secluded greenery is Pollok Park, only three miles from the city center, and just off Paisley Road. Here you will find Haggs Castle, a 16th-century building which houses a delightful children's museum. Pollok House, a graceful mansion with fine silver, glass and Spanish art collections, is here too, as is the St Mungo herd of wild (though not savage) Highland cattle. Finally, you'll also find the celebrated Burrell Gallery here. This opened its doors in November 1983 to display the world-famous Burrell Collection of 8,000 art works from ancient Mesopotamia to contemporary France, including tapestries, stained glass, paintings, sculptures, porcelain, and stone and wood carvings. The Burrell Gallery was chosen as Britain's "Museum of the Year" in 1985.

In other green places of Glasgow such as Bellahouston, Glasgow Green and above all Kelvingrove, you will find rustic seclusion and cultural assets rivalling those of any city in Britain.

Kelvingrove Park is a short bus-ride from George Square. The best Renaissance and modern painters are represented in its Art Gallery. Facing it, across the river, stands Glasgow University, a formidable Scottish-baronial pile barely 100 years old, although the University itself was founded in 1451. The Royal Botanic Gardens are in this district too, on Great Western Road, and from them it is another short trip back to George Square.

Scotland's only Opera House is Glasgow's Theatre Royal, home of Scottish Opera and Scottish Ballet. Glasgow is the headquarters of the Scottish National Orchestra and the prestigious Citizens' Theatre. The Glasgow School of Art has the important Mackintosh Library, a memorial to Charles Rennie Mackintosh, innovative artist-designer who died in 1928, and whose renown increases as time goes by. Glasgow's cultural renaissance continues, and the city has been chosen as European Cultural Capital for 1990.

Try to take a ride on the Glasgow Underground, 100 years old but brilliantly modernized. Or board the diesel-electric commuter train which whisks you in minutes to the sea lochs and kyles (straits) of the Firth of Clyde. As a nexus of rail routes and motorways which can deliver you in less than an hour to Edinburgh, Stirling, Loch Lomond, the Burns country and the golfing resorts of the Clyde coast, Glasgow is an excellent place to get out of!—but a good place to get into also, if you have time to wander around and meet warm-hearted people. A best-selling 1930s novel about Glasgow was called *No Mean City*—and that sums it up.

PRACTICAL INFORMATION FOR
THE REST OF SCOTLAND

HOTELS AND RESTAURANTS. Throughout the Regions you will find considerable variations in the distribution and types of accommodations and restaurants. On some routes in season it seems that every other cottage is offering bed and breakfast, and certain small towns and villages, in Central Region for instance, offer a spread of tourist accommodations out of all proportion to their size. Grampian has some splendid country hotels with log fires and rich furnishings and where you will eat well. Other areas have inexpensive accommodations and food, but standards are only adequate, and luxurious hotels are few. Many hotels open in the summer only. The Highlands and Islands may have self-catering cottages for rent, but much of the Region has never known supermarkets, delicatessens or wine bars.

Glasgow was historically a poor oasis for the traveler, but there are now some big city-center hotels, both expensive and moderate, with some good and reasonable small hotels and guest houses in the suburbs, with easy transportation into town. A feature of Glasgow's hotels is the excellent breakfasts, usually included in the price of the room. All the larger hotels have restaurants that are open to non-residents.

The area code preceeds each telephone number.

Abbotsinch (Strathclyde). *Excelsior* (E), tel. (041) 887 1212. 290 rooms with bath. One of the best British airport hotels and right next to the check-in desk. Discreet bars, average restaurant.

Aberdeen (Grampian). *Caledonian Thistle* (M–E), Union Terrace, tel. (0224) 640233. 77 rooms, 70 with bath. Old city-center hotel handsomely refurbished. *Holiday Inn* (E), tel. 770011; 154 rooms, all with bath. Close to the airport on A96. *Royal* (M), Bath St., tel. (0224) 585152; 43 rooms with bath. Old-established, face-lifted, central with a good restaurant. *Furain Guest House* (I), 92 North Deeside Road, Peterculter, tel. (0224) 732189. 8 rooms, 4 with bath. Cheerful red granite house, family-run, on river 5 miles from city.

Restaurant. *Gershwins* (E), tel. (0224) 313377. In *Tree Tops,* Springfield Rd. Split level, period decor, pianist. Fashionable rendezvous.

Aberfoyle (Central). *Bailie Nicol Jarvie* (M), tel. (087 72) 202. 37 rooms with bath. The wild men of Rob Roy's "clachan" (tavern) would not recognize their old drinking den on the fringe of the Trossachs, now enlarged and attractively modernized.

Restaurant. *Old Coachhouse* (M), tel. (087 72) 535. Fishing net hangs on wall, but menu is cosmopolitan.

Arran, Isle of (Strathclyde). *Douglas* (M), in Brodick, tel. (0770) 2155; 26 rooms, 12 with bath. Modern, comfortable, with food of good standard; sauna. *The Lagg* (M), at Kilmory, tel. (077 087) 255; 18 rooms, 9 with bath. 300-year old building with old-fashioned charm and good food.

Auchterarder (Tayside). *Gleneagles* (L), tel. (076 46) 2231; 254 rooms, all with bath. One of the most famous hotels in the land, stands among endless golf courses and gardens, heated pool, tennis, squash, sauna, but ordinary cusine. Now owned by Guinness the brewers, it is scheduled for more refinements, including a luxury health farm.

Aviemore (Highland). *Coylumbridge* (L), tel. (0479) 810661; 175 rooms with bath; on A951. Tennis, close to Loch Morlich for yachting and skiing on slopes above; English and French food. *Post House* (E), tel. (0479) 810771; 103 rooms with bath. In the Aviemore Sports Center, lively and modern, with high-quality bedrooms, sauna. *Badenoch* (M), tel. (0479) 810261; 81 rooms, 60 with bath. Modern hotel in Sports Center.

High Range (M), tel. (0479) 810636; 8 rooms with bath. Central building with surrounding chalets on outskirts of town in lovely wood with extensive mountain views; tavern bar and bistro.

Ayr (Strathclyde). *Belleisle House* (E), tel. (0292) 42331; 7 rooms, 14 with bath. On outskirts of town by golf course.

Restaurant. *Bobby Jones* (I), tel. (0292) 284268. Much praised for food and value.

Ballater (Grampian). *Tullich Lodge* (L), tel. (0338) 55406. 10 rooms, 8 with bath. Lovely baronial house; restaurant has fine cuisine based on local produce.

Bridge of Allan (Central). *Royal* (M), tel. (0786) 832284; 33 rooms, 24 with bath. Associations with Dickens and Robert Louis Stevenson.

Callander (Central). *Roman Camp* (E), tel. (0877) 30003; 14 rooms with bath. An old hunting lodge with fabulous gardens bordering river; food consistently good. There is also a chapel and a library. *Glenorchy* (M), Leny Rd., tel. (0877) 30329; 14 rooms, 7 with bath. Large, cozy guesthouse with superior amenities.
Restaurant. *Pip's Coffee House* (I), Ancaster Square, tel. (0877) 30407. Good lunch stop. Wide choice of dishes, despite name.

Castle Douglas (Dumfries & Galloway). *King's Arms* (M), tel. (0556) 2097; 14 rooms, 8 with bath. Welcoming and comfortable, with excellent food.

Dirleton (Lothian). *Open Arms* (E), tel. (062 085) 241. 7 rooms, all with bath. Light, airy atmosphere, enterprising cooking with traditional Scots dishes. Handy for golf and sightseeing on East Lothian coast.

Dryburgh (Borders). *Dryburgh Abbey* (M), tel. (0835) 22261. 27 rooms, 19 with bath, 3 with four-poster beds. Right next to the Abbey ruins, and handy for lunch when visiting the site.

Dumfries (Dumfries & Galloway). *Cairndale* (M), English Street, tel. (0387) 54111. 44 rooms with bath. Central. Pleasant atmosphere, excellent meals.

Dundee (Tayside). *Angus* (E), tel. (0382) 26874; 58 rooms with bath; modern, comfortable, and well-run. *Invercarse* (M), tel. (0382) 69231; 39 rooms with bath. Excellent restaurant. In grounds overlooking the River Tay, fishing.
Restaurant. *Raffles* (I), Perth Road, tel. (0382) 26344. Deservedly popular pull-up on main road.

Dunfermline (Fife). *King Malcolm* (E), Wester Pitcorthie, tel. (0383) 722611. 48 rooms with bath. Spacious hotel, popular with conference organizers. *Keavil House* (M), Crossford, tel. (0383) 736258; 32 rooms with bath, some (E). Old-fashioned, intimate, country-style hotel, triumphing over drab surroundings.

Dunkeld (Tayside). *Dunkeld House* (L), tel. (035 02) 771. 31 rooms with bath. Delightful setting by the river, with 100 acres of grounds. Fine base for the area. Good-value restaurant with solid fare.

Elgin (Grampian). *Eight Acres* (E), Sheriffmill tel. (0343) 3077. 57 rooms, 54 with bath. Admirably furnished with modern taste. Indoor/outdoor sports.

Forres (Grampian). *Parkmount House* (I), St. Leonard's Road, tel. (0309) 73312. 7 rooms, 2 with bath. Pleasant location between town center and golf course. Neat rooms, sensible cuisine based on Scottish recipes. *Relais Routiers* recommended.

Fort William (Highland). Just north of Fort William at Torlundy is *Inverlochy Castle* (L), tel. (0397) 2177. 16 rooms, all with bath. Regal welcome in a Highland castle where Queen Victoria once slept. Gastronomic cuisine, every reasonable whim satisfied.

Gairloch (Highland). *The Old Inn* (M), tel. (0445) 2006. 7 rooms with bath, plus 8 rooms, none with bath, in the adjacent lodge. Cheerful oasis in wilderness of the west.

Gatehouse of Fleet (Dumfries & Galloway). *Murray Arms* (E), tel. (055 74) 207. 17 rooms with bath. Typical main-street coaching inn, expensively restored. Here, it is said, Robert Burns wrote *Scots Wha He'e*. Old-fashioned rooms but first-class service and imaginative cuisine.

Glamis (Tayside). *Strathmore Arms* (M), (030 784) tel. 248. Village pub right beside castle, converted into a smart restaurant. Excellent food.

Glasgow (Strathclyde). Telephone area code 041. *Holiday Inn* (L), Argyle Street (tel. 226 5577). 296 rooms, all with bath. Another city-center innovation of the most up-to-date kind. Has French restaurant, coffee shop and terrace buffet.
Burnside (E), East Kilbride Road (tel. 634 1276). 16 rooms. Some distance from center, but highly rated for all-round quality. *Crest* (E), 377 Argyle Street (tel. 248 2355). 121 rooms with bath. New hotel on main shopping street. Traditional Scottish and vegetarian food in restaurant. *Hospitality Inn* (E), 36 Cambridge Street (tel. 332 2311). 316 rooms with bath. A new and, for the moment, successful competitor of the Holiday Inn. Huge and barracks-like, but centrally located. *Tinto Firs* (E), 470 Kilmarnock Rd. (tel. 637 2353). 27 rooms with bath. More country-house than city style, on park-like south side but handy for center.
Beacons (M), 7 Park Terrace (tel. 332 9438). 36 rooms with bath. Quiet and dignified hotel overlooking rustic Kelvingrove Park yet close to main downtown area. *Central* (M), Gordon Street (tel. 221 9680). 211 rooms, 170 with bath. Typical Victorian railroad hotel with thick carpets, mob-capped chambermaids and ample rooms from another era. *Stakis Ingram* (M), Ingram Street (tel. 248 4401). 90 rooms with bath. In a tight web of city-center streets. Art-nouveau restaurant has ample cuisine and sound wines.
Apsley, (I), 903 Sauchiehall Street (tel. 334 3510). 17 rooms, 2 with bath. Comfort and cuisine well above its price level. *Crookston* (I), 90 Crookston Road (tel. 882 6142). 23 rooms, 10 with bath. Quiet atmosphere. Food writers have praised generous cuisine. *Duncans* (I), 59 Union Street (tel. 221 4580). 60 rooms, 10 with bath. Smallish rooms but otherwise well-equipped. Fairly ordinary cuisine. Extremely reasonable rates.
Pond (I), Great Western Road (tel. 334 8161). 137 rooms with bath. The pond it overlooks is no Loch Lomond, but the hotel is well sited if you are heading that way. *Queen's Park* (I), 10 Balvicar Drive (tel. 423

1123). 30 rooms, 11 with bath. Good all-around standard, flexible meal hours.

Restaurants. *Ambassador* (L), 19 Blythswood Square (tel. 221 3530). International cuisine. Pre-theater meals. Dancing every evening except Mon. *Four Seasons* (L), Albany Hotel, Bothwell Street (tel. 248 2656). Continental and Scottish cuisine. Impressive layout and discreet atmosphere. Dancing.

La Bonne Auberge (E), 7a Park Terrace (tel. 332 3520). Quiet surroundings and discriminating French menu. *Buttery* (E), 652 Argyle Street (tel. 221 8188). Good plain cooking in a civilized atmosphere. Vegetarians catered for. *Fountain* (E), Charing Cross (tel. 332 6396). Used by Glaswegians for special occasions. Cheaper *Pub Bistro* downstairs. *Rogano* (E), 11 Exchange Place (tel. 248 4055). An old favorite of Glasgow's diners-out. Specializes in French dishes and elaborate seafood. *Boston Pizza* (M), 18 Gibson Street (tel. 339 7195). Vivacious Italian ambiance, Neopoloitan and international cuisine, original cocktails, good cheap house wine. *La Costeria* (M), 51 West Regent Street (tel. 331 1980). Continental and predominantly Italian. Good place for a civilized meal late Sun. evening. Open till midnight. *Fouquet's* (M), 7 Renfield Street (tel. 226 4958). Imaginative Franco-Scottish cuisine, big wine list. Cellar atmosphere, brickwork and mosaics. Incorporates reputable wine bar. *Rotunda North* (M), 28 Tunnel Street (tel. 204 1238). On Clyde bank, near Exhibition Center. Own parking lot. Imaginative restoration of old fort. Four levels comprise wine bar, pizzeria, French restaurant (expensive at night), and roof cocktail bar with panoramic views of river and Festival site. *Peking Inn* (M), 191 Hope Street (tel. 332 8971). Pastel decor, Peking and Cantonese cooking. Over 100 dishes. *Sloan's* (M), Argyll Arcade (tel. 221 8917). Sturdy British cuisine among unique decor of etched glass and Victorian mahogany paneling.

Cul-de-Sac Creperie (I), Ashton Lane (tel. 334 4749). Candlelight, accordionist, nimble French waiters, snails. *Arnott's* (I), Sauchiehall Street Centre (tel. 332 6833). Department store offering elegant service for morning coffee, lunch, tea and scones, and high tea. *Auld Highland Farmhouse* (I), 32 Queen Street (tel. 226 4183). Home baking and cooking, salad counter. No alcohol. *Change at Jamaica* (I), Clyde Place (tel. 429 4422). Just south of the river, under railway bridge. Clean, modern decor, big menu featuring a little of everything. A late-night haven, usually closes around 5 A.M. *Lucky Star* (I), 92 Sauchiehall Street (tel. 332 6265). Big and unpretentious with good Chinese food from extensive menu. Open late; closed Sun.

Gullane (Lothian). *Greywalls* (L), tel. (0620) 842144; 24 rooms with bath. A striking building by the great Edwardian architect, Lutyens. Handy center for golfers; fine restaurant. *Mallard* (M), tel. (0620) 843288; 20 rooms with bath. Efficiently run. Largely golfing and sporting clientele.

Restaurants. *La Potinière* (I), tel. (0620) 843214. Extremely good, French-style table d'hôte and wine. Very small dining room. Early booking essential. *Tartufo* (I), tel. (0620) 842233. Enterprising Continental cuisine, truffles with everything.

Inverness (Highland). *Kingsmills* (L), Culcabock Road, tel. (0463) 237166; 54 rooms with bath. Country-house elegance in pleasant gardens.

Squash courts. *Queensgate* (M), Queensgate, tel. (0463) 237211. 60 rooms, all with bath. Modern town-center hotel of all-round excellence.

Kinclaven (Tayside). *Ballathie House* (E), tel. (025 083) 268; 30 rooms, all with bath. Fantastic pseudo-French-baronial chateau, but nothing bogus about comforts and amenities. Own kitchen-garden produce. Trout fishing.

Kyle of Lochalsh (Highland). *Lochalsh* (M–E), tel. (0599) 4202; 45 rooms, 42 with bath. Offers beautiful views of the Isle of Skye across the Loch from the front rooms; beware the bagpipes. An ideal touring center.

Langbank (Strathclyde). *Gleddoch House* (L), (047 554) tel. 711. 20 rooms, all with bath. House of dignity and exclusive character on south Clyde shore, 18 miles from Glasgow. Fine views across Clyde; large lawns and gardens, and probably the best hotel restaurant in Scotland. Country club adjacent.

Letham (Fife). *Fernie Castle* (M), tel. (033 781) 381; 15 rooms, all with bath. Dates back to 1653 and has been converted into a hotel; cuisine and service of high standard.

Lewis, Isle of. *Caberfeidh* (E), Stornoway, tel. (0851) 2604. 40 rooms with bath. The most expensive hotel in Outer Hebrides.

Melrose (Borders). *Burt's* (M), Market Square, tel. (089 682) 2285. 21 rooms, 18 with bath. Cozy 18th-century inn with fine home cooking.

Nairn (Highland). *Golf View* (E), tel. (0667) 52301. 55 rooms with bath. Famous seaside and sporting hotel, spacious location. Imaginative Highland cuisine. Gourmet nights and weekly Grand Buffet in paneled restaurant.

Newton Stewart (Dumfries & Galloway). *Kirroughtree House* (L), tel. (0671) 2141. 24 rooms with bath. Stately country house hotel. Richly furnished; with highly disciplined staff and superior food. Children, pets and exuberance frowned on.

Old Meldrum (Grampian). *Meldrum House* (E), tel. (065 12) 2294. 11 rooms, 8 with bath. Best type of country-house hotel with much-praised cuisine, especially game pie and venison.

Peat Inn (Fife), about 6½ miles southwest of St. Andrews at the junction of B940/B941. Much praised is the *Peat Inn* (E), tel. (0334 84) 206. Boasts traditionally fine wines and menu, changing with the availability of seasonal ingredients, but shows signs of resting on earlier laurels. Open Tues.–Sun. for bar lunches and restaurant dinners.

Peebles (Borders). *Peebles Hydro* (M), tel. (0721) 20602. 139 rooms, all with bath. Two miles from town near Tweed bank. Heated pool, sauna, sports facilities. Popular conference center.

Perth (Tayside). *Sunbank House* (I), 50 Dundee Road, tel. (0738) 24882. 6 rooms, 3 with bath. Fine graystone mansion in best residential area near Branklyn Gardens. Views over Tay estuary. Unpretentious, solid comforts.
Restaurant. *Hunting Tower* (M), Crieff Road, tel. (0738) 83771. Superior country restaurant in historic center close to city.

Pitlochry (Tayside). *Green Park* (M), tel. (0796) 2537; 39 rooms, 34 with bath. Overlooking Loch Faskally, good touring base.

Prestwick (Strathclyde). *Carlton Hotel* (M), Ayr Road, tel. (0292) 76811. 39 rooms, all with bath. Superior modern stopover but you might get bored on a long stay.

St. Andrews (Fife). *Old Course* (L), tel. (0334) 74371. 150 rooms, 146 with bath. Biggest and newest hotel in St. Andrews with balcony views over Old Course. Behind the stark exterior, an atmosphere of luxury. *Argyle Private Hotel* (I), North Street, tel. (0334) 77007. 21 rooms, 13 with bath. Good amenities, reasonable rates. Bar.
Restaurant. *Grange* (I), tel. (0334) 72670. Old farmhouse-type building; excellent bar lunches individually prepared. Candlelit dinners; good selection of malt whiskies.

Skye, Isle of (Highland). At Isle Ornsay, *Kinloch Lodge* (E), tel. (047 13) 214; 10 rooms, 8 with bath. Small, comfortable, personally run by Lord and Lady Macdonald in courteous style, excellent food.
At Skeabost Bridge, near Portree, *Skeabost House* (E), tel. (047 032); 202; 27 rooms, 18 with bath. Well-decorated bedrooms, largest log fire imaginable in lounge; excellent. Closed Oct.–Apr.
At Uig, the *Uig Hotel* (M), tel. (047 042) 205, 25 rooms with bath; welcoming and praised by readers for comfort and cuisine. Closed Oct. to Easter.

South Queensferry (Lothian). *Hawes Inn* (M), tel. (031) 331 1990. 6 rooms, no private baths. Creaking old-world inn near disused ferry slip on Forth. Features in R.L. Stevenson's *Kidnapped.* 30 minutes from Edinburgh.

Stewarton (Strathclyde). *Chapeltoun House* (L), tel. (0560) 82696. 6 rooms, all with bath. Luxurious country house run with flair and friendliness. Painstakingly prepared food, and especially noteworthy baking. Many antiques.

Stirling (Central). *Golden Lion* (M), King Street, tel. (0786) 75351. 84 rooms, 50 with bath. Venerable staging post with much coming and going, but efficiently run. First-class cuisine.
Restaurant. *Heritage* (M), 16 Allan Park, tel. (0786) 3660. Elegant, French-owned 18th-century establishment; fanlights and candles. Not surprisingly, there's a Gallic flavor to its cuisine.

Stranraer (Dumfries & Galloway). *North West Castle* (M), tel. (0776) 4413. 77 rooms with bath. Historic house with Arctic exploration connections, hence the name. High standard of comfort and amenities. Curling holidays offered.

Tarbert (Strathclyde). *Stonefield Castle* (E), tel. (088 02) 836; 33 rooms with bath. Lovely castle in miraculous surroundings; with fishing, boating; comfort and food are worth rather high prices.

Thornhill (Central). **Restaurant.** *Lion and Unicorn* (M), tel. (0786 85) 204. A place of real character. Try the fillet steak on a cast-iron platter.

Tongue (Highland). *Tongue* (M), tel. (080 05) 206. 21 rooms, 17 with bath. Country house in splendid setting; rooms average—some are (I)—but grills and baking good, and service beyond reproach.

Turnberry (Strathclyde). *Turnberry* (L), Maidens Rd., tel. (065 53) 202. 128 rooms with bath. An historic golfing hotel, "absolutely sensational in every respect," says a reader—a golfer, naturally.

Whithorn, Isle of (Dumfries and Galloway). **Restaurant.** *Queen's Arms* (I), tel. (098 85) 369. An old inn on remote but scenic harbor. Fish, lobster, Galloway beef and regional cheeses.

SELF-CATERING. This type of holiday has become so popular in Scotland that it is essential in high season to book well in advance of your arrival. The booklet *Scotland: Self-Catering Accommodation,* published annually, costs £4.50 by post from the *Scottish Tourist Board,* P.O. Box 15, Edinburgh EH1 1UY. The annual holiday brochure, available free from the same address or from any *Tourist Information Centre,* contains several pages about the chief self-catering operations and also a list of addresses of *Area Tourist Boards,* from which more detailed information is freely available.

Several castles and country houses offer self-catering apartments and in most areas there is a broad choice of custom-built holiday chalets, Highland cottages, shooting lodges and the like. Rentals can be as much as £600 a week and as little as £10 a week.

Many caravan parks have static caravans for hire for around £75 a week. In their advertisements the "Thistle" emblem denotes inspection and approval by the *Scottish Tourist Board.* Self-contained apartments are also available for rent in summer at university halls of residence in Glasgow, Edinburgh, Stirling, Dundee and Aberdeen. If you prefer a city center you will find flats (apartments) to rent in the heart of Glasgow or Edinburgh. If you seek real solitude, there are *Forestry Commission* cabins locked away in lonely pinewoods. But try to book early or avoid July and August and remember that one week is usually the minimum rental period.

PLACES OF INTEREST. Castles, great houses, museums, monuments and gardens listed below are a representative selection of the many hundreds which are described in such publications as *Scotland: 1001 Things to See* (Scottish Tourist Board) and *Scotland's Gardens* (Scotland's Gardens Scheme, Castle Terrace, Edinburgh EH1 2EL). Where no telephone

is given in our listing below, ring (031) 226 2570, the Ancient Monuments
Division of the Scottish Development Department in Edinburgh.

Borders. Abbotsford House, Melrose, tel. (089 62) 043, was the home
of Sir Walter Scott. Open mid-Mar.–Oct., Mon.–Sat., 10–5, Sun., 2–5.

Bowhill, near Selkirk, tel. (0750) 20732. Home of the Dukes of Buc-
cleuch, attractively sited and with plenty of fine pictures to see (including
Gainsborough, Canaletto and a da Vinci). Open: house, July–Aug.,
Mon.–Sat. 1–4.30, Sun. 2–6; park and playground, Apr.–Aug., Mon.–Sat.
(Fri. only when house open) 12–5, Sun. 2–6.

Manderston, near Duns, tel. (0361) 83450. Apotheosis of Edwardian
house and garden design. A must for those interested in domestic history.
Mid-May to late Sept., Thurs. and Sun., 2–5.30. Also Bank Holiday Mon.
late May and Aug.

Mellerstain House, near Gordon, tel. (057 381) 225. Outstanding Adam
house; lovely interior and views. Open Easter, then May–Sept., daily (except Sat.), 12.30–5 (last adm. 4.30).

Traquair House, Innerleithen, tel. (0896) 830323. Reputed to be the oldest inhabited house in Scotland, unaltered from 1664. Associated with
Mary, Queen of Scots and the Jacobite risings. *Objets d'art,* embroideries
and manuscripts date from 12th century. Brews and sells own ale. Open
Easter Sat.–early Oct., daily, 1.30–5.30 (July–mid-Sept., 10.30–5.30).

Central. Bannockburn Heritage Center, off M80, 2 miles from Stirling,
tel. (0786) 812664. Audiovisual display and battle site. Site is open all year
round, Visitor and Information Center Apr.–Oct., daily 10–6.

Doune Motor Museum, Doune village, tel. (0786) 841203. Earl of
Moray's collection of vintage cars, including second-oldest Rolls Royce
in the world. Open Apr.–Oct., daily 10–5, June–Aug., daily 10–6.

Linlithgow Palace, Linlithgow. Birthplace of Mary, Queen of Scots.
Open Apr.–Sept., 9.30–7, Sun. 2–7; Oct.–Mar., 9.30–4, Sun. 2–4.

Dumfries and Galloway. Burns' House, Burns Street, Dumfries. The
house where Robert Burns died in 1796. Period furnishings and relics of
the poet. Open Apr.–Sept., Mon.–Sat. 10–1 and 2–7, Sun. 2–7; Oct.–Mar.,
Tues.–Sat 10–12 and 2–5.

Castle Kennedy Gardens, Stranraer, tel. (0776) 2024. Lovely gardens
on peninsula between two lochs; superb flowering shrubs. April to Sept.,
daily 10–5.

Drumlanrig Castle, near Thornhill tel. (0848) 30248. Another castle of
the Duke of Buccleuch. A striking pale pink, and filled with art and other
treasures, including Bonnie Prince Charlie relics. Open May–Aug.,
Mon.–Sat. (closed Fri. in May and June) except Fri. 1.30–4.15 (11–5 in
Aug.), Sun. 2–6.

Fife. Culross Palace, Culross. Well-restored 17th-century buildings,
fine painted ceilings. Adjoins historic Town House, Abbey and Nunnery.
Open Apr.–Sept., Mon.–Sat. 9.30–7, Sun. 2–7; Oct.–Mar., Mon.–Sat.
9.30–4, Sun. 2–4.

Falkland Palace, Falkland, tel. (033 757) 397. French Renais-
sance/Scottish baronial hunting stronghold of Stuart monarchs. Lovely

garden. Open Apr.–Sept., Mon.–Sat. 10–6, Sun. 2–6; Oct., Sat. 10–6, Sun. 2–6.

Kellie Castle, Fife, near Pittenweem, tel. (033 38) 271. Historic Lowland house. Open May–Sept., daily except Fri. 2–6; Apr. and Oct., Sat. and Sun. 2–6; gardens all year, daily 10–sunset.

Grampian. Balmoral Castle, near Ballater, tel. (0338) 4334. The Queen's Highland home. Gardens and a ballroom exhibition portraying royal life in the 19th century, including Landseer paintings. Open May–July, Mon.–Sat only, 10–5.

Craigievar Castle, near Alford, tel. (033 983) 635. Built 1612–1626. Most romantic of Scottish baronial castles. Open May–Sept., daily 2–6; grounds all year, daily 9.30–sunset.

Crathes Castle, Banchory, tel. (033 044) 525. 16th-century Jacobean castle with painted ceilings. Open Apr. and Oct., Sat. and Sun. 11–6; May–Sept. daily 11–6; gardens all year 9.30–sunset (NTS)

Drum Castle, near Aberdeen, tel. (033 08) 204. Ancient pile (part dating from 13th century), shows the passage of history in Scottish houses. May to Sept., daily, 2–6; gardens all year, daily 9.30–sunset. (NTS).

Leith Hall, Kennethmont, tel. (046 43) 216. A good place to see how Scottish life was lived over the centuries; also has many Jacobite relics. May–Sept., daily 11–6; garden all year, daily 9.30–sunset.

Highland. Carrbridge Landmark Visitor Centre, Carrbridge, near Grantown-on-Spey. Audio-visual display and exhibition of Highland history. Open June–Sept., daily 9.30–9.30; Oct.–May 9.30–5.

Cawdor Castle, Nairn, tel. (066 77) 615. A draw for any student of Shakespeare, and still owned by the Thane (Earl) of Cawdor. Very impressive, with parts from the 14th century. Open May–Sept., daily 10–5.30.

Dunrobin Castle, Golspie, tel. (040 83) 3177. Opulent Victorian castle on 13th-century seashore foundations. Estate exhibits, including steam fire engine. Open June–mid-Sept., Mon.–Sat. 10.30–5.30, Sun. 2–5.30.

Dunvegan Castle, Isle of Skye, tel. (047 022) 206. Dates from 13th century and continuously inhabited by chiefs of Clan MacLeod. Open Easter–mid-May, early–late Oct., daily, 2–5; mid-May–Sept., daily, 10.30–5. Closed Sun.

Lothian. Dalmeny House, South Queensferry, tel. (031) 331 1888. Collection of paintings and Napoleonic material of the Earl of Rosebery, in mock-Tudor (early 19th-century) house. Open May–Sept., Sun.–Thurs., 2–5.30.

Dirleton Castle and Gardens, Dirleton, tel. (062 085) 330. 13th-century castle with lovely gardens. April to Sept., Mon.–Sat. 9.30–7, Sun. 2–7; Oct. to Mar., weekdays 9.30–4, Sun. 2–4.

Edinburgh Castle etc.—see separate chapter.

Hopetoun House, South Queensferry, tel. (031) 331 2451. Fine example of 18th-century Adam architecture. Deer parks and grounds laid out on Versailles pattern. Open Easter, then May–Sept. daily 11–5.

The House of the Binns, near Linlithgow, tel. (0506) 831255. Historic house with fine 17th-century plaster ceilings. Open Easter, May–Sept., daily (except Fri.), 2–5 (park, 10–7). (NTS).

Palace of Holyroodhouse—see separate chapter.

Tyninghame House, near Dunbar, tel. (062 086) 330. Extensive walled gardens, apple walks, roses, pets' cemetery, ancient trees and abbey ruins. Open June–Sept., Mon.–Fri., 10.30–4.30.

Strathclyde. Brodick Castle, Isle of Arran, tel. (0770) 2202. Fortress site since Viking times, then seat of Dukes of Hamilton. Magnificent gardens, furniture, art. Castle open 1–3 Apr. and May–Sept., daily 1–5; rest of Apr. and 1–15 Oct., Mon., Wed., and Sat. 1–5; gardens all year, daily 9.30–sunset.

Burns' Cottage, Alloway, near Ayr, tel. (029 241) 215. Burns' birthplace and adjoining museum. Open June–Aug., Mon.–Sat. 9–7, Sun. 10–7; Apr.–May and Sept.–Oct., Mon.–Sat. 10–5 (Sun. 2–5); Nov.–Mar., Mon.–Sat. 10–4.

Burrell Collection, Pollok Park, Glasgow, tel. (041) 649 7151. A gallery in a woodland setting built especially to display one of the great art collections of all time. Tapestries, stained glass, paintings, carpets, china, bronzes, stone and wood carvings of every nation and all ages. Open Mon.–Sat. 10–5, Sun. 2–5.

Culzean Castle, Maybole, tel. (065 56) 269. One of the finest Adam designs in Scotland, built in late 18th century. Beautiful gardens laid out in 1783. Open 1–10 Apr. and May–Aug., daily 10–6; rest of Apr. and Sept.–Oct., daily 12–5. Country park all year, daily 9–sunset. (NTS).

Glasgow City Art Gallery and Museum, Kelvingrove Park, tel. (041) 357 3929. Huge spacious hall, attracts 1 million visitors a year. Fine collection of paintings, sculpture, ceramics, arms and armor, silver, jewelry, costumes, etc. Open daily 10–5, Sun. 2–5.

Glasgow Botanic Gardens, Great Western Rd. tel. (041) 334 2422. 42 acres of gardens, glasshouses, plus Kibble Palace collection of tree ferns and temperate flora. Open daily 7–dusk; Kibble Palace 10–4.45.

Haggs Castle, 100 St. Andrew's Drive, tel. (041) 427 2725. Museum of social history, emphasis on children at work and play through the centuries. Activities for young visitors. Open Mon.–Sat. 10–5, Sun. 2–5.

Hill House, Upper Colquhoun Street, Helensburgh, tel. (0436) 3900. Outstanding architectural achievement of Glasgow's art nouveau celebrity, Charles Rennie Mackintosh. Open daily 1–5. (NTS).

Hunterian Museum, Glasgow University, 82 Hillhead Street, tel. (041) 330 4221. Geology and archeology. Incorporates an art gallery (Rembrandt, Chardin and Whistler) and Charles Rennie Mackintosh House (interiors and art works from the designer's Glasgow home). Open Mon.–Fri. 9.30–5, Sat. 9.30–1. Mackintosh House closed lunchtime.

Inveraray Castle, Inveraray, tel. (0499) 2203. Center for the Clan Campbell since the 15th century. Combined Operations military museum in park commemorates U.S. and Canadian forces. Open July and Aug., Mon.–Sat. 10–6, Sun. 1–6; Apr.–June and Sept., Mon.–Sat. (except Fri.) 10–1 and 2–6, Sun. 1–6.

David Livingstone Center, Blantyre, near Hamilton, tel. (0698) 823140. Birthplace of explorer/missionary David Livingstone, with memorial, museum. Open Mon.–Sat. 10–6, Sun. 2–6.

Museum of Transport, Kelvin Hall, Dumbarton Road, tel. (041) 357 3929. Trains, buses, bicycles, streetcars, horse-drawn vehicles and model ships. Old subway station. History of Scottish automobile industry. Open Mon.–Sat. 10–5, Sun. 2–5.

People's Palace, Glasgow Green, tel. (041) 554 0223. A 100-year-old city museum illustrating textiles and shipbuilding, the feminist movement, landmarks of Glasgow's political and cultural history. Open Mon.–Sat. 10–5, Sun. 2–5.

Pollok House, 2060 Pollokshaws Road, Glasgow, tel. (041) 632 0274. Adam mansion in parkland and pasture, housing important fine arts. House open weekdays 10–5, Sun. 2–5.

Springburn Museum, Ayr Street. New railway museum built around four famous old locomotive works. Open Mon.–Fri. 10.30–5, Sat. 10–1, Sun. 2–5.

Third Eye Center, 350 Sauchiehall Street. Continuous exhibitions and music recitals, concerts, etc. Open Tues.–Sat. 10–5.30, Sun. 2–5.30.

Weaver's Cottage, Kilbarchan, tel. (050 57) 5588. A refreshing change from the round of stately homes. A typical 18th-century weaver's home, with his loom, and domestic utensils. Open Easter–May, Sept., and Oct., Tues., Thurs., Sat., and Sun., 2–5; June to Aug., daily 2–5. (NTS).

Tayside. Blair Castle, Blair Atholl, tel. (079 681) 207. Built c. 1269, home of the Duke of Atholl. Jacobite relics, splendid selection of antique toys, firearms, tapestries, etc. Open Easter–mid-Oct., Mon.–Sat. 10–5, Sun. 2–5.

Frigate Unicorn, Victoria Dock, Dundee, tel. (0382) 21555. The oldest warship afloat; the *Unicorn* served the Royal Navy for 140 years and now exhibits shipboard life of yesteryear. Open Mon. and Wed.–Sat. 11–1 and 2–5, Sun. 2–5.

Glamis Castle, near Kirriemuir tel. (030 784) 242. Partly 14th-century, seat of Earls of Strathmore and present Queen Mother's childhood home. Grounds laid out by Capability Brown. May–Sept., daily (except Sat) 1–5. In nearby Glamis village, picturesque Kirkwynd Cottages house the noteworthy *Angus Folk Museum* of feudal, domestic and farming relics.

"Little Houses", Dunkeld (A9). An important restoration of 20 picturesque cottages lining avenue between town center and cathedral. Several "lads o' pairts" born there, including a Canadian prime minister. National Trust shop and information center. Open Apr.–May and Sept.–Dec., Mon.–Sat. 10–1 and 2–4.30; June–Aug., Mon.–Sat. 10–6, Sun. 2–5.

Museum of Scottish Tartans, Drummond St., Comrie, tel. (0764) 70779. Open Apr.–Oct., Mon.–Sat. 10–5, Sun. 2–5; Nov.–Mar., Mon.–Fri. 11–3, Sat. 10–1.

Scone Palace, near Perth, tel. (0738) 52300. Home of the Earl of Mansfield. Many treasures to be seen in state rooms. Built in 1803, incorporating parts of old palace originally built on site. Open Easter–mid-Oct., Mon.–Sat., 9.30–5, Sun. 1.30–5; July and Aug., daily 10–5.

Scottish Horse Museum, Dunkeld, tel. (035 02) 296. Memorabilia—modest but evocative—of Tullibardine's Horse, a cavalry regiment raised in the district. Open May–mid-Oct., Mon.–Sat. 10.30–1.30 and 2–5, Sun. 2–5.

Index

General Information
The letter H indicates Hotels and other accommodations.
The letter R indicates Restaurants.

Transportation to major cities and towns from London will be found in the Practical Information section at the end of each chapter.

Air travel
    from N. America, 10–11
    from the Continent & Ireland, 11–12
    in Great Britain, 31–32
Auto travel
    in Great Britain, 20–23
    rentals, 21–22

Background & customs, 37–47
Bed & breakfast accommodations, 15
Bus travel, 29–30

Climate, 2–3
Costs, 1
Credit cards, 2
Currency & exchange, 1–2
Customs
    American & Canadian, 32–33
    British, 13

Drinking laws, 18–19
Duty free, 33

Electricity, 19

Food & drink, 79–86

Handicapped travelers, 17–18
Historic buildings & gardens, 9–10, 52–66
History, 48–51
Hotels & other accommodations,
    13–17

Hours of business, 18–19

Information sources, 5–7
Inland waterways, 31

Mail & telegrams, 19–20

Packing & clothing, 3
Passports & visas, 3–4
Performing arts, 67–78
    ballet, 75–76
    festivals, 77–78
    music, 76–77
    opera, 72–75
    theater, 68–72

Rail travel, 23–27
    historic & scenic steam railways, 28–29
Restaurants, 17

Ship travel
    from N. America, 11
    from the Continent & Ireland, 12
Shopping, 19
Special events, 7–9

Tipping, 17
Telephones, 20
Travel agents, 4–5
Travelers' checks, 1

Youth hostels, 16–17

Geographical

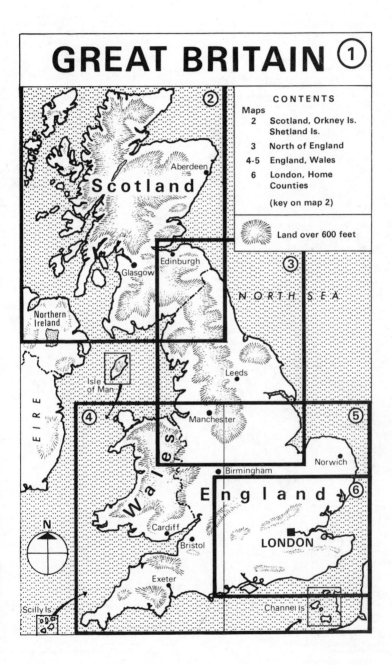

GREAT BRITAIN ①

Land over 600 feet

②

Scotland

Aberdeen

Edinburgh

Glasgow

③

NORTH SEA

Northern Ireland

EIRE

Isle of Man

Leeds

④

Manchester

Wales

⑤

Norwich

Birmingham

England

⑥

Cardiff

LONDON

Bristol

N

Exeter

Scilly Is

Channel Is

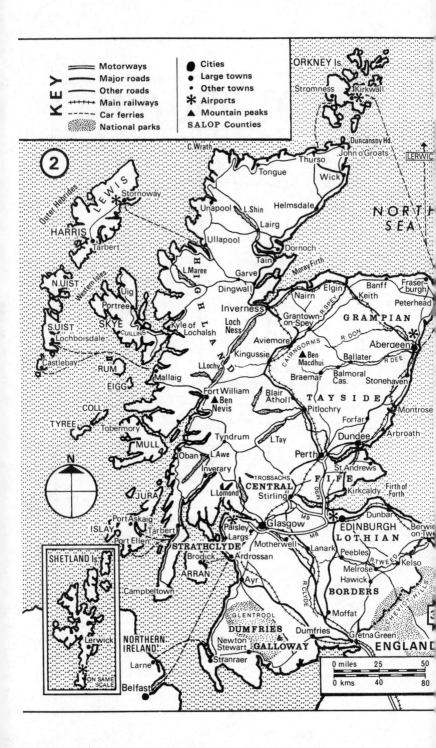

KEY

- —— Motorways
- —— Major roads
- —— Other roads
- ++++ Main railways
- ---- Car ferries
- National parks

- ● Cities
- ● Large towns
- • Other towns
- ✳ Airports
- ▲ Mountain peaks
- **SALOP** Counties

②

LERWIC

ORKNEY Is.
Stromness Kirkwall
Duncansby Hd.
John o'Groats

C.Wrath
Tongue Thurso Wick
Helmsdale

NORTH SEA

Outer Hebrides
LEWIS Stornoway
HARRIS
Tarbert

Unapool L.Shin
Lairg
Ullapool
Tain Dornoch
Garve Moray Firth
L.Maree
Dingwall Elgin Banff Fraserburgh
Nairn Keith Peterhead

N.UIST
Uig Portree
S.UIST SKYE
Lochboisdale CUILLINS Kyle of Lochalsh
Castlebay
RUM
EIGG

Inverness
Loch Ness
Aviemore
Kingussie CAIRNGORMS R.DON Aberdeen
▲Ben Macdhui R.DEE
L.Lochy Ballater
Mallaig Braemar Balmoral Cas. Stonehaven
Fort William Blair Atholl
▲Ben Nevis Pitlochry TAYSIDE
Forfar Montrose
Tyndrum Arbroath
L.Tay
Dundee
L.Awe Perth
Oban St.Andrews
Inverary TROSSACHS FIFE
L.Lomond CENTRAL Kirkcaldy Firth of Forth
Stirling M90
Dunbar

GRAMPIAN
R.SPEY
Grantown-on-Spey

HIGHLAND

Western Isles
COLL
TYREE Tobermory
MULL
JURA

ISLAY
Port Askaig Tarbert
Port Ellen

N
(compass)

Paisley Glasgow Mg EDINBURGH
Largs M8 LOTHIAN
STRATHCLYDE Motherwell Berwick-on-Tw
Brodick Ardrossan Lanark Peebles
ARRAN Melrose Kelso
Ayr R.TWEED
Campbeltown Hawick
BORDERS
CHEVIOT HILLS

③

SHETLAND Is.

Lerwick

ON SAME SCALE

NORTHERN IRELAND
Larne
Belfast

GLENTROOL
DUMFRIES &
Newton Stewart GALLOWAY
Stranraer Dumfries Gretna Green
R.CLYDE Moffat ENGLAND

| 0 miles | 25 | 50 |
| 0 kms | 40 | 80 |

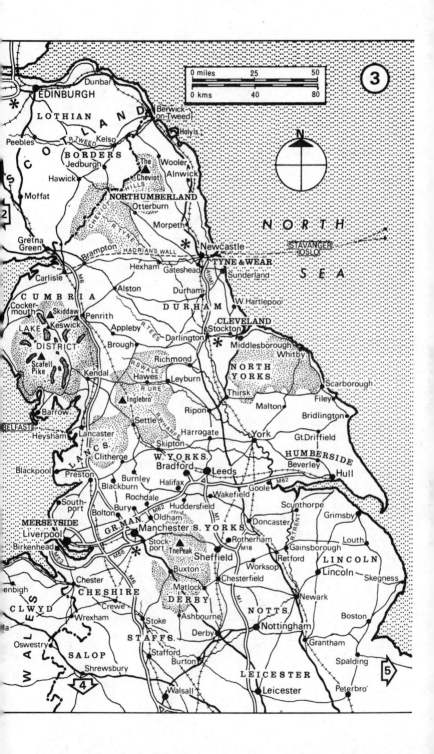

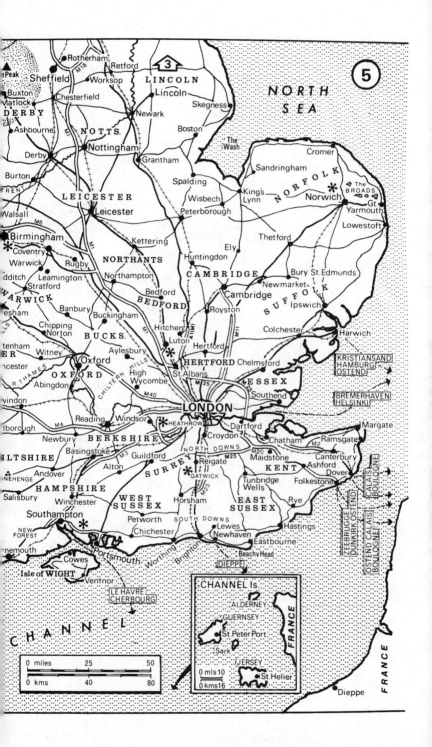

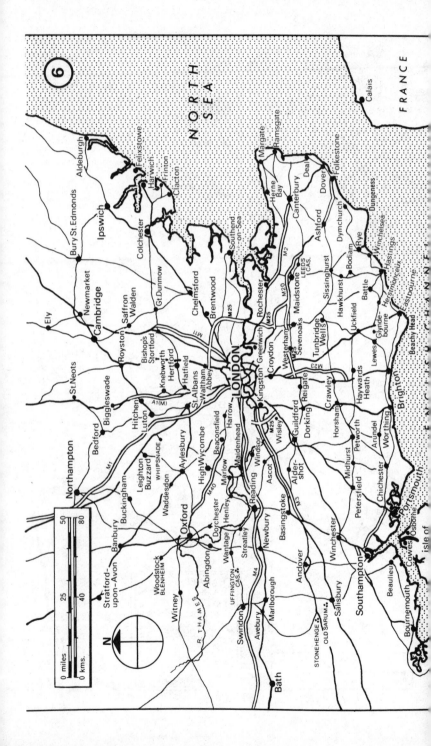

Fodor's Travel Guides

U.S. Guides

Alaska
American Cities
The American South
Arizona
Atlantic City & the
  New Jersey Shore
Boston
California
Cape Cod
Carolinas & the
  Georgia Coast
Chesapeake
Chicago
Colorado
Dallas & Fort Worth
Disney World & the
  Orlando Area

The Far West
Florida
Greater Miami,
  Fort Lauderdale,
  Palm Beach
Hawaii
Hawaii *(Great Travel
  Values)*
Houston & Galveston
I-10: California to
  Florida
I-55: Chicago to New
  Orleans
I-75: Michigan to
  Florida
I-80: San Francisco to
  New York

I-95: Maine to Miami
Las Vegas
Los Angeles, Orange
  County, Palm Springs
Maui
New England
New Mexico
New Orleans
New Orleans *(Pocket
  Guide)*
New York City
New York City *(Pocket
  Guide)*
New York State
Pacific North Coast
Philadelphia
Puerto Rico *(Fun in)*

Rockies
San Diego
San Francisco
San Francisco *(Pocket
  Guide)*
Texas
United States of
  America
Virgin Islands
  (U.S. & British)
Virginia
Waikiki
Washington, DC
Williamsburg,
  Jamestown &
  Yorktown

Foreign Guides

Acapulco
Amsterdam
Australia, New Zealand
  & the South Pacific
Austria
The Bahamas
The Bahamas *(Pocket
  Guide)*
Barbados *(Fun in)*
Beijing, Guangzhou &
  Shanghai
Belgium & Luxembourg
Bermuda
Brazil
Britain *(Great Travel
  Values)*
Canada
Canada *(Great Travel
  Values)*
Canada's Maritime
  Provinces
Cancún, Cozumel,
  Mérida, The
  Yucatán
Caribbean
Caribbean *(Great
  Travel Values)*

Central America
Copenhagen,
  Stockholm, Oslo,
  Helsinki, Reykjavik
Eastern Europe
Egypt
Europe
Europe *(Budget)*
Florence & Venice
France
France *(Great Travel
  Values)*
Germany
Germany *(Great Travel
  Values)*
Great Britain
Greece
Holland
Hong Kong & Macau
Hungary
India
Ireland
Israel
Italy
Italy *(Great Travel
  Values)*
Jamaica *(Fun in)*

Japan
Japan *(Great Travel
  Values)*
Jordan & the Holy Land
Kenya
Korea
Lisbon
Loire Valley
London
London *(Pocket Guide)*
London *(Great Travel
  Values)*
Madrid
Mexico
Mexico *(Great Travel
  Values)*
Mexico City & Acapulco
Mexico's Baja & Puerto
  Vallarta, Mazatlán,
  Manzanillo, Copper
  Canyon
Montreal
Munich
New Zealand
North Africa
Paris
Paris *(Pocket Guide)*

People's Republic of
  China
Portugal
Province of Quebec
Rio de Janeiro
The Riviera *(Fun on)*
Rome
St. Martin/St. Maarten
Scandinavia
Scotland
Singapore
South America
South Pacific
Southeast Asia
Soviet Union
Spain
Spain *(Great Travel
  Values)*
Sweden
Switzerland
Sydney
Tokyo
Toronto
Turkey
Vienna
Yugoslavia

Special-Interest Guides

Bed & Breakfast
  Guide: North America
1936...On the
  Continent

Royalty Watching
Selected Hotels of
  Europe

Selected Resorts
  and Hotels of the U.S.
Ski Resorts of North
  America

Views to Dine by
  around the World